MW00352243

Mastering the AS/400

Second Edition

A PRACTICAL, HANDS-ON GUIDE

BY JERRY FOTTRAL

Library of Congress Cataloging-in-Publication Data

Fottral, Jerry, 1947-
    Mastering the AS/400 / by Jerry Fottral. -- 2nd ed.
    p. cm.
    Includes index.
    ISBN 1-882419-77-4 (pbk.)
    1. IBM AS/400 (Computer) I. Title. II. Title: Mastering the AS
four hundred
    QA76.8.I25919 F68 1999
    005.4'445--ddc21

                          98-25502
                          CIP

Published by **29th Street Press**
DUKE COMMUNICATIONS INTERNATIONAL
Loveland, Colorado

Copyright © 1998 by Jerry Fottral

All rights reserved. No part of this book may be reproduced in any form by any electronic or mechanical means (including photocopying, recording, or information storage and retrieval) without permission in writing from the publisher.

It is the reader's responsibility to ensure procedures and techniques used from this book are accurate and appropriate for the user's installation. No warranty is implied or expressed.

This book was printed and bound in Canada.

ISBN 1-882419-77-4

2 3 4 5 6 WL 1 0 9 8

This book is lovingly dedicated to my family,
who tolerated with good cheer a substantial amount of neglect;
and to my friend, Jane,
who gave me more than inspiration,
nagged me the whole time,
and wouldn't let me quit when I really felt like it.

Acknowledgments

Many people contributed to the creation of this book. Those who I would especially like to thank include my friend and colleague from the University of Iowa, John Marmet, without whose help and eagerness to share his expertise this work may never have started.

Friend and former student, Becky Menke, who not only served as sounding board for many of the ideas presented in the labs, but whose tireless efforts and word processing skills contributed greatly to the compilation of the original materials.

My son, Mayo Fottral, who gave up many hours to type revisions to the first edition, and my daughter, Masumi Fottral, who worked tirelessly typing revisions and new material for the second edition.

My colleagues Christine Keith, David Nelson, and Bill Finley, who helped proofread the second edition.

My best friend and colleague, Jane Montgomery, who offered much valuable criticism of the first edition and gave me support and encouragement while working on the second edition.

The 29th Street Press (formerly Duke Press) publisher Dave Bernard and assistant acquisitions editor Trish McConnell for prodding me to finally get moving on the second edition and for their kindness and understanding along the way.

The 29th Street Press editorial staff, particularly managing editor Trish Faubion, whose patience, professionalism, and good humor have seen us through to the end. Also, copy editor Dawn Cyr, assistant editor Rob Carson, senior editor Barb Gibbens, and editorial assistant Stephanie Stephens for their assistance entering my text and figure revisions for the second edition; art director John Morris-Reihl for the cover redesign; and Angie Anderson, Martha Nichols, Janice Paris, and Lynn Riggs for their production work.

The students of many classes of Intro to AS/400 at Kirkwood Community College deserve a special note of thanks. Your comments, criticisms, and suggestions were a major influence as the early materials evolved into this book. My purpose was to provide useful information and exercises to encourage your own desire to learn, but without your efforts and the feedback you gave me, I could not have the confidence I do that this book really works.

Marie Fox

Table of Contents At a Glance

Table of Contents

Preface

THE PURPOSE OF THIS BOOK

IBM's AS/400 is still a relatively new technology, different in many important ways from other computers — large and small — that have gone before it. But there should be no doubt by now that the AS/400 is here to stay and that the demand will continue to grow for trained programmers and operators who can use the AS/400 to its best advantage.

Having accepted the responsibility several years ago for training students to meet this need, I was immediately overwhelmed by the lack of affordable, suitable materials for this purpose, especially in a structured, hands-on lab environment.

Driven by panic, I immediately set out to put together lab materials that would impress upon students the unique character of the AS/400 while teaching them the introductory skills they would need to go on to higher-level AS/400 courses.

Those lab materials have evolved into this textbook, which I hope will provide serious students of the AS/400 with a guidebook that opens to them the horizons of this remarkable machine. If this book succeeds, students who complete it should have a solid foundation in AS/400 library-object structure, utilities and database management capabilities, application development tools, and OS/400 Control Language.

Currently, the course that this book was designed for is a prerequisite to all AS/400 programming and database courses at Kirkwood Community College. As such, it eliminates the need to cover introductory topics such as SEU, PDM, and DDS in programming and database courses.

INTENDED AUDIENCE

This book was originally intended for students of a 2-year technical curriculum at a community college, probably as a second-semester course following a general introduction to computers. I hope, however, that computer professionals from other platforms who need to work on the AS/400 — as well as university students trying to program on the AS/400 without benefit of an introductory course — will find this book useful as a self-study guide for getting up to speed in the shortest possible time.

SPECIAL FEATURES

The primary teaching methodology of this book is structured, hands-on lab exercises. It is essential that all students have access to an AS/400 and, if not to a formal instructor, to an experienced programmer who can serve as mentor. I firmly believe that the best way to become familiar with the terrain of a new environment is to work your way through it on the ground — and that is exactly the orientation of this book.

I expect that students will spend at least as much time working through the extensive lab exercises at the end of each lesson as in reading and studying the text itself. I am convinced that students who diligently work through the labs — not just to finish them, but with a sense of exploration and a dedication to understanding — will come away with a sense of accomplishment and the confidence to journey on.

SUMMARY OF CONTENTS

This book is divided into twelve lessons. Each lesson consists of a text, which presents and explains the concepts that are the lesson's focus; and a lab, which allows the immediate transmission of concept into application. The text of each lesson begins with a lesson overview and a list of objectives and ends with a list of key terms that must be mastered to explain and communicate the concepts.

Each lab consists of an ordered number of activities, or steps, that guide the student through the lab's objective. A number of questions in each lab serve to document the student's observations as (s)he progresses through the lab. At the end of each lesson is a short summary that highlights the important concepts.

Lesson 1 provides an overview of the AS/400 environment from a programmer's or operator's perspective. It provides initial exposure to menus, entry screens, list screens, and information screens. And it emphasizes the availability of interactive help on the system and, in this second edition, provides an introduction to InfoSeeker, new with V3R1/V3R6.

Lesson 2 examines Control Language (CL) syntax and uses CL examples to help students create a library, examine their library list, and change their user profile.

Lesson 3 provides an introduction to object-based systems and, more specifically, to objects on the AS/400. It explains in detail the concept of library lists and how objects are stored and retrieved on the system. It also introduces printer spooling and the use of output queues.

Lesson 4 covers in detail the entire operation of printing output from printer device files through the spooling subsystem to output queues and printer writers. Students learn how to manage spooled files and how to print them when needed.

Lesson 5 provides an introduction to Data Description Specifications (DDS) as the primary means of describing database files. The chapter also provides a brief introduction to Source Entry Utility (SEU) and Programming Development Manager (PDM). Using SEU, students describe a database physical file in DDS.

Lesson 6 builds on the use of PDM and SEU and describes the process of compiling a database source physical file member to create a file object. In this second edition, students create a physical file and add records using the Data File Utility (DFU).

Lesson 7 introduces Query/400 and covers many of its more useful features, including join queries. Students create several queries and learn to change query output from display to a printed report.

Lesson 8 provides an introduction to logical files. The lesson explains simple, multiple-format, and join logical files and presents examples of each. Students also are introduced to projection, selection, and access paths. Students create new physical files and then base several new logical files on them.

Lesson 9 covers the procedures for making changes to an existing database file, explaining and contrasting the CRTDUPOBJ (Create Duplicate Objects) and CPYF (Copy File) commands. In addition, this second edition introduces the powerful new parameters of the CHGPF (Change Physical File) command that let you change the record format of a file while keeping the data intact. This lesson also introduces object and library authorization and the different levels of authority, including authorization lists and group profiles.

Lesson 10 covers the creation of permanent Data File Utility (DFU) programs. The lesson explains various features and options of permanent DFUs and presents examples of DFUs for keyed files and multiple-format logical files. Students create their own DFU programs. In addition, in this second edition, this lesson provides a brief introduction to Structured Query Language (SQL), which provides students with another tool to query and update their files. Students use command-line SQL to query the database and add, change, and delete database records.

Lesson 11 provides an overview of Screen Design Aid (SDA). The lesson covers many features of SDA and explains how to create menus and display files.

Lesson 12 introduces CL programming. The lesson explains many of the important commands that provide structure and flexibility to CL programs. Students create several working CL programs.

NOTE TO STUDENTS

The basic premise of this book is that craftsmanship comes from the practical application of concepts, and it follows that the greatest potential benefit of this book is in the lab exercises. Please approach each lab exercise in the spirit of discovery and challenge. If your goal is truly to learn, then insist on not merely observing, but understanding what you are doing in the labs. Do not work mechanically through them — you will end up learning little. If questions arise that are not answered in the materials, remember that the AS/400 itself contains a great deal of interactive help.

NOTE TO INSTRUCTORS

In the lab exercises, students create their own libraries, output queues, and other objects as needed. Initially, all that is required to get them started is a *PGMR class user profile with *NONE special authority. (This is not the default for programmer class, but no special authority is required and allowing students job control can cause problems.) I do not use group profiles for Intro students. Nor do I restrict any commands beyond the implicit restrictions of their class authority. I have found this arrangement to work very well with no serious problems for several years and several hundred students.

Lesson 1

Communicating with the System

Lesson Overview

The AS/400 is not a simple machine; its operating system, OS/400, is one of the most sophisticated on the market today. To a new user, the apparent complexity may seem like a huge jigsaw puzzle waiting to be solved. What we hope to provide with this first lesson is simply a place to start collecting critical pieces of the puzzle.

This lesson provides initial exposure to a number of topics necessary for a basic understanding of the AS/400 user interface, as well as introduces concepts related to system organization. This lesson also introduces some basic work management concepts (e.g., how jobs enter, run, and leave the system).

You should be aware from the beginning that a thorough grasp of the concepts and a diligent attitude toward learning and retaining the associated vocabulary is essential for success. Although the AS/400 itself will provide much help in your learning, you are strongly encouraged to ask questions of your instructor or mentor.

Objectives

Students will be able to

- ✓ Sign on to the AS/400, properly entering user name and password
- ✓ Explain the difference between system and subsystem
- ✓ Describe the two most common types of jobs
- ✓ List several attributes of a user profile
- ✓ List several features of the AS/400 operating system
- ✓ Explain the function of AS/400 Control Language (CL) and enter a CL command on a command line with proper syntax
- ✓ Explain the purpose of system values and how to check them
- ✓ Describe four types of displays, their use, and their components
- ✓ Explain the relationship between CL commands and AS/400 menu paths

THE SYSTEM

The AS/400 is a **multiuser**, **multitasking** system (a system on which two or more people can perform two or more tasks concurrently) optimized for the efficient execution of business applications. The basic unit of work on the AS/400 is a **job**. On the AS/400, the term job refers generally to a unit of work, including all programs, files, and instructions necessary to perform that work. Examples of jobs running on an AS/400 would be an interactive user session for updating a customer master file or a program compilation running unobtrusively in the background.

All jobs on the AS/400 are run in **subsystems**. A subsystem, defined by a **subsystem description**, is where the system brings together the resources needed to process work. The components of the subsystem description determine how the system uses resources to process jobs within the subsystem. When the base operating system is installed, the AS/400 has several different subsystems already defined and active, each one having a separate subsystem description.

Some attributes of subsystems whose actual values are defined in the subsystem description include the subsystem name (e.g., QINTER for the interactive subsystem, QBATCH for the batch subsystem), how many jobs can run in the subsystem at one time, which storage pools the subsystem will use (main storage on the AS/400 is divided into a number of different storage pools), and which job queues the subsystem will work from. It is necessary to have different subsystems because there are many different types of jobs with different characteristics and often conflicting needs. If all of these various jobs were thrown together and treated equally, the overall performance of the system would suffer. The system administrator can change the existing subsystem descriptions and create new subsystems when necessary. In this way, (s)he can tailor subsystems to efficiently handle the needs of different jobs; for example, to ensure that long-running jobs requiring no user interaction but significant CPU time do not interfere with high-priority interactive jobs needing fast response time. Within subsystems, individual jobs can be prioritized to begin execution sooner or later, and after they begin execution can be given a higher or lower run-time priority.

TYPES OF JOBS

Jobs can originate from several sources and are classified by how they originate on the system. In this course, and in general, you will deal mostly with two types of jobs: interactive and batch.

An **interactive job** begins when a user signs on to an AS/400 and terminates when the user signs off the AS/400 or the job is ended. Interactive jobs run in conversational mode, which means there is a dialogue of sorts between the user and the program, utility, or operating system function. Because of this conversational back-and-forth nature of interactive jobs, any CPU- or I/O-intensive request a user makes could lock up the workstation keyboard until the request is completed. Therefore, it is often advisable to direct such requests to a subsystem designed to handle them — that is, to submit them as batch jobs.

Batch jobs can execute without user intervention; they do not require data or controlling values to be input through the workstation once they have started. Batch jobs are sent to a **job queue** until they can begin execution. A job queue is a staging area, managed by the subsystem in which the job will run, where batch jobs wait in line for their turn at processing. Each batch subsystem can execute only a limited number of batch jobs concurrently. If no other higher priority jobs are waiting, a batch job can start right away; otherwise, it must wait its turn.

Typically, you would submit as a batch job a report program that reads many records from a database file and performs standard calculations written into the logic of the program. Once such a program started, it would require no input from the operator or requester of the report. If such a program were run interactively, the DASD (Direct Access Storage Device, or hard disk) access time required for the large file could be substantial, and the workstation could be tied up for a long time.

Also, to minimize disruption of work flow, certain tasks encountered during a normal interactive session can be packed up and sent off as batch jobs. Consider a programmer in the midst of an interactive session who needs to compile a large program for testing. If (s)he runs the compile as part of an interactive job, (s)he will be locked out of the system during the several minutes it may take to complete the compilation. If other tasks on the computer need attention, (s)he could submit the compilation as a batch job from within the interactive job. Then, while the compilation runs in a batch subsystem, (s)he could go on to other tasks.

OS/400

OS/400, the AS/400's operating system, is a very complex and rich set of programs that not only controls traditional functions such as data access, storage, and task management, but also incorporates features that would normally require separate software components on other systems — features such as communications support, database management, security, and interactive support.

All AS/400s are shipped with basic OS/400 support, which includes predefined system settings for work-management functions that allow interactive and batch jobs to run without need for a customized installation. Later, subsystems can be created and system resources allocated to optimize work-load distribution and throughput according to the special needs of a particular business.

OS/400 is an object-based operating system. An **object** is anything on the system that has a name and takes up space in storage. A large number of objects are supplied by IBM through OS/400 and the licensed program products and typically have names beginning with Q. Programmers and operators create other objects and name them, usually according to the shop's naming convention.

The system can locate an object by its name, and once located, the object can further identify itself to the system by functional attributes that are a part of the object. Objects are grouped into types. An **object type** determines how the object is used on the system (i.e., the actions that can be taken when using the object). Common object types include programs, files, and commands. Object types also include user profile objects, which contain information about a user, and subsystem description objects, which contain the characteristics of a subsystem. Object type is always assigned by the system and is determined by the command used to create the object. We continue to explore this concept of objects throughout the course.

For all its complexity, one of the more remarkable things about OS/400 is that it provides a single, consistent user interface to its various functions through **Control Language** (CL) commands.

CONTROL LANGUAGE

OS/400 CL is flexible and powerful and allows direct access to OS/400 functions. More than 1,500 individual CL commands are available. Each individual command is an object on the AS/400. Most CL commands consist of a command name and one or more **command parameters**. A command parameter is a value, specified along with a command, that controls and limits the operation of the command and names the files, programs, or other objects it will work on. Individual commands can be entered on a **command line** (a line beginning with the symbol ===> that appears near the bottom of certain types of display screens), or they can be grouped together into a **CL program** to perform a specific task. Such a program can then be compiled and run from a command line or from within a high-level language (HLL) program (e.g., RPG, Cobol, or C).

You don't need to memorize a large number of CL commands because you can access most OS/400 functions available to interactive jobs through the **menu interface** of the AS/400. As you choose a series of menu selections, the system determines the CL commands to be run to satisfy your request.

SYSTEM VALUES

System values are control and configuration attributes that let you customize certain operating system functions. They define critical aspects of the environment and the general rules that all jobs on the system must follow. System values are not objects, but they describe characteristics of the system that can be displayed or, in many cases, changed with CL commands. Many system values come preset with the operating system; others need to be set when the system software is installed. The categories of system values include

- *Date and time* — these values let you set and change the date and time kept by the system and made available to application programs and utilities.

- *Editing values* — these values control how dates, decimal values, and numbers involving currency symbols are formatted.

- *System control* — these values let you define or obtain certain controlling values of your system, such as operator console name, user assistance level, and date and time to automatically **IPL** (Initial Program Load) the system (an IPL is the AS/400 version of a "boot" process, which loads the operating system when the power is turned on).

- *Library list values* — These values define the system library list and initial user library list. A **library list** is an ordered group of libraries used by a job to search for objects it needs for processing.

- *Allocation values* — these values let you control the number of active jobs and how much main storage will be used for different functions needed to run jobs.

- *Message and logging values* — these values control how the system handles and records certain types of messages.

- *Storage system values* — these values define the minimum size and activity level (number of active jobs) of the base storage pool.

- *Security values* — these values control certain aspects of security on the AS/400, for example the maximum number of invalid sign-on attempts allowed.

Most users can display current system values and, when necessary, authorized users can change these values. This capability to customize system values for a particular job environment can lead to a more efficiently running system. In the lab for this lesson you learn how to examine system values.

LICENSED PROGRAMS

Besides the operating system, which must be present on all AS/400s, there are a number of software components available from IBM that extend the functions and capabilities of the system and allow installations to tailor it to the type of work and the communications environment they need. These are **licensed program products**. A few of these are shipped with all AS/400s at no additional cost, but for the most part they are chargeable, the actual cost usually being determined by the size of the system and the number of users having access to that product. Most of the licensed program products fall into one of several categories:

- *Application development tools* — A group of utilities for programmers that greatly expedites the application development process. These tools include an all-purpose smart editor called Source Entry Utility (SEU), Screen Design Aid (SDA), an interactive file update utility called Data File Utility (DFU), and a programmer's workbench suite called Programming Development Manager (PDM).

- *OfficeVision* — An integrated family of utilities that provide daily, weekly, and monthly calendars for both individuals and groups; mail and message handling; creation and updating of documents and folders; and word processing.

- *Communications support* — A large number of Client Access (formerly known as PC Support) programs that let the AS/400 connect programmable workstations (PCs) through various PC operating systems including Windows and OS/2.

- *Programming languages* — Traditionally the AS/400 has supported a number of programming languages by making compilers available as licensed programs. In the past, Pascal, PL/I, Basic and Fortran were supported, but current and future compiler support will be targeted at RPG, C, C++, Cobol, and Java. In addition, Structured Query Language (SQL) is available through the DB2 Query Manager and SQL Development Kit.

There are a number of other licensed program products that are not clearly in any of the above categories and provide services such as automatic routing and database access for incoming customer calls (Call Path/400), mainframe-style interactive screen support (CICS/400), and double-byte character support for ideographic languages such as Chinese, Japanese, and Korean. In fact, there are many more such products designed to extend the versatility and usefulness of the AS/400.

You can see which licensed programs are installed on your AS/400 by going through the LICPGM (Work with Licensed Programs) menu. You learn how to get there in the lab.

USER PROFILE

When we refer to a **user**, we mean any person who is signed on to the system. This may include students, programmers, data entry personnel, operators, or administrators. To perform work on the AS/400, a user needs to be known to the system. A user becomes known to the system when a security officer or administrator creates a **user profile** object for that user. A user profile not only identifies a user, but also describes the user's authority and is the source of several operational characteristics of his/her job. (At the lowest level of system security, it is possible to sign on without having a predefined user profile, but most installations operate at a security level requiring user profiles for each user.)

Later, we examine user profiles in more detail and see that they contain information defining, for example, a user's

- *class*, such as casual user, programmer, operator, security officer
- *special authorities*, such as job control, capability to save system software, capability to create or change user profiles
- *initial program*, the program to be run when sign-on is completed
- *group profile*, which assigns a user to a group of users with similar authorities and restrictions

At this time, you need only be aware of the two user profile values necessary to sign on: *User* name or ID and *Password*.

Sign-On

Figure 1.1 shows a normal AS/400 **sign-on screen**. In the upper right corner is information that identifies the system, subsystem, and **display device** (or display station). A display device is the workstation hardware (monitor and keyboard) you use to communicate with the system.

(As will be the case with many of the figures used throughout this text, certain values shown in Figure 1.1 — such as the System value and display device name — will be different for your AS/400. Although more than half a million AS/400s are now installed worldwide, it is a safe bet that no two are exactly the same, so certainly figures dealing with configuration values or individual users could have wide variations from place to place.)

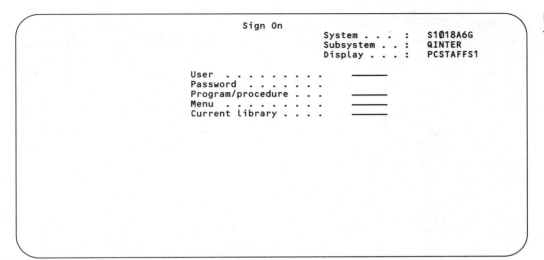

Figure 1.1
Typical Sign-On Screen

To sign on and start an interactive job, a user must type his/her user name and password. A user name is one to 10 characters long; the security administrator determines its value according to the standards of the installation. The user name may be a simple first initial, last name combination such as JSMITH. Or it may be a more symbolic code, perhaps indicating the user's location or department; for example, JMS05DM could mean a user with the initials JMS of department 05 in Des Moines.

For a sign-on attempt to succeed, the user name entered must match the name of the user profile object created by the system security officer or administrator. If a nonexistent user profile name is entered, the system displays an appropriate error message. An error also occurs if the user name is valid but the password entered at the sign-on screen does not match the current password stored in the corresponding user profile. In both cases, the sign-on attempt fails.

When proper values are entered on the sign-on screen for User and Password, the system proceeds to collect attributes to define the interactive job. Most attributes are taken from a special or default **job description**, but some attributes come from the user profile or from system values.

When sign-on is completed, the interactive job is directed to the subsystem shown on the display (e.g., QINTER in Figure 1.1). Jobs from all physical display devices may run in the same subsystem, or different display devices may direct their jobs to different subsystems. A system administrator knowledgeable in **work management** and performance tuning makes these decisions.

User Interface

Unless system defaults are changed, most AS/400 interactive jobs begin by displaying the AS/400 Main menu shown in Figure 1.2.

Figure 1.2
AS/400 Main Menu

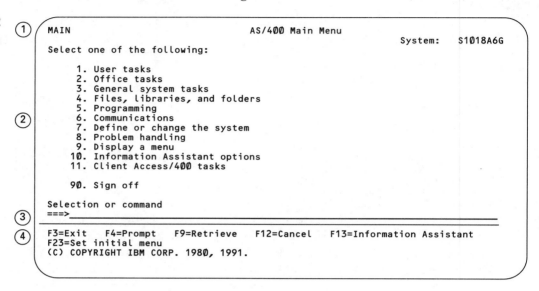

```
MAIN                          AS/400 Main Menu
                                                        System:    S1018A6G
   Select one of the following:

          1. User tasks
          2. Office tasks
          3. General system tasks
          4. Files, libraries, and folders
          5. Programming
          6. Communications
          7. Define or change the system
          8. Problem handling
          9. Display a menu
         10. Information Assistant options
         11. Client Access/400 tasks

         90. Sign off

   Selection or command
   ===>

   F3=Exit    F4=Prompt    F9=Retrieve    F12=Cancel    F13=Information Assistant
   F23=Set initial menu
   (C) COPYRIGHT IBM CORP. 1980, 1991.
```

In a hierarchy of menus, the Main menu is the highest-level menu on the AS/400, and it can be the starting point to define a menu path to accomplish a specific task. Menus are connected in such a way that a menu choice at a higher level can take you to a lower-level menu. You move through the menu hierarchy until the task is defined to the system. For example, if you wanted to create a **library** (a directory of related objects) on an AS/400, you would follow the menu

Figure 1.3
AS/400 Menu Path for
Creating a Library

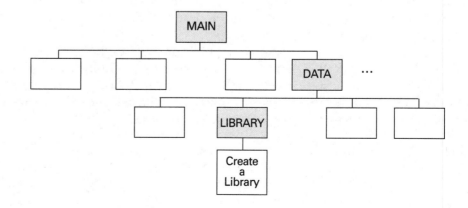

path shown in Figure 1.3, starting with the Main menu. We step through this process in the next section.

MENU SCREENS

Let's begin our discussion of AS/400 display screens by examining the **menu screen** format. A menu screen has four primary sections, as indicated in Figure 1.2.

1. The **screen header**, including

   the menu ID in the upper left corner,

   the menu description, centered on the first line,

   the system name in the upper right corner.

2. The numbered list of **menu options**.

3. The selection or **command line**, indicated by ===>.

   On this line you can type the number of a menu selection, or you can enter a CL command to be executed.

4. The list of active **function keys**.

Below the two-line list of active function keys is a message line (in Figure 1.2, the line showing the IBM copyright notice) and a status line showing cursor coordinates, whether a message is waiting to be displayed, and the status of the keyboard. (The status line is not shown in the figures.)

All menu screens have this general appearance. The header information and list of menu options, of course, change, depending on the menu. The list of enabled function keys also changes slightly from menu to menu.

Now that you are familiar with the format of a menu screen, let's look again at the Main menu in Figure 1.2. You can take several possible actions from a menu display:

- You can type and enter a menu choice and go on to the next screen.

- You can ask for Help.

- You can type a CL command and either prompt for parameters or run the command.

- You can use a function key.

Although most system functions can be invoked directly by using CL commands, many novice users prefer to use menu paths to describe the task to perform and then let the system choose the appropriate command. For example, let's use the menu path to create a library — a task you will be performing soon. If you entered a 4 (Files, libraries, and folders) on the command line of the Main menu, you would see the Data menu shown in Figure 1.4. (Although the description of the menu is "Files, Libraries, and Folders," to the operating system, its proper name is "DATA").

Figure 1.4
Files, Libraries, and
Folders Menu

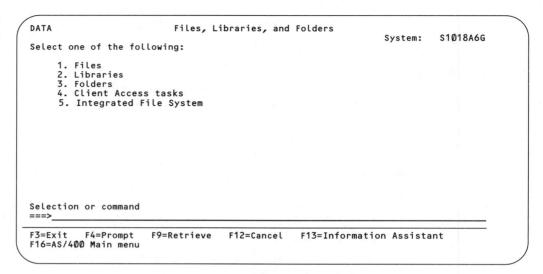

```
DATA                      Files, Libraries, and Folders
                                                        System:    S1018A6G
Select one of the following:

     1. Files
     2. Libraries
     3. Folders
     4. Client Access tasks
     5. Integrated File System




Selection or command
===>_____

 F3=Exit    F4=Prompt    F9=Retrieve    F12=Cancel    F13=Information Assistant
 F16=AS/400 Main menu
```

Notice the similarity in format between the Main menu and the Data menu. From the Data menu you can take choice 2 (Libraries) by typing a 2 on the command line, then pressing the Enter key. This takes you to the Library menu shown in Figure 1.5.

Figure 1.5
Libraries Menu

```
LIBRARY                          Libraries
                                                        System:    S1018A6G
Select one of the following:

     1. Work with libraries
     2. Create a library
     3. Save a library
     4. Restore a library

    50. Save library members in System/36 format
    51. Restore library members from System/36 format

    70. Related commands




Selection or command
===>_____

 F3=Exit    F4=Prompt    F9=Retrieve    F12=Cancel    F13=Information Assistant
 F16=AS/400 Main menu
```

Option 2 (Create a library) on the Library menu suggests that, after three menus, you have just about pinned down what it is you want to do. When you select option 2 from the Library menu, the system displays the screen shown in Figure 1.6. The system uses this type of screen, generically referred to as an **entry screen**, to request information from a user.

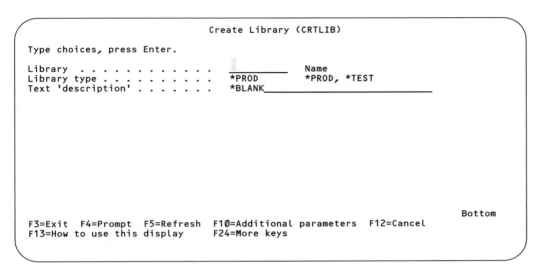

Figure 1.6
Create Library (CRTLIB)
Command Prompt
Screen

ENTRY/COMMAND PROMPT SCREENS

Let's take a moment to study the screen shown in Figure 1.6. You can see clearly that it is different from a menu screen. First, notice that the heading is different. Rather than the name of a menu, the heading, "Create Library," is the name of a CL command in English followed by its AS/400 abbreviation, "CRTLIB," in parentheses. Also in contrast to a menu screen, this screen does not identify the system, and instead of a numbered list of menu choices, you see a list of command parameters. The screen does display a list of active function keys but no selection or command line.

This type of screen is considered an entry screen because the system is waiting for you to enter the value or values it needs to process your request. In this case, you would be entering parameter values for the CRTLIB (Create Library) CL command, which the system must execute to create a library. The cursor, as indicated in Figure 1.6, would be positioned at the first character of the Library parameter entry field. Because the system is prompting you for a parameter value it needs to run a command, we refer to such a screen as a **command prompt screen**. A command prompt screen is one kind of entry screen. Although we reached this particular CRTLIB command prompt screen via a menu path, if you already knew the command name, you could reach the same screen by typing CRTLIB on any command line and pressing the prompt key, F4.

Look at Figure 1.6 again. Note that you can request additional parameters by pressing function key F10. When you press F10, the screen shown in Figure 1.7 appears.

So that you can see more easily the elements that comprise a command prompt screen, Figure 1.8 shows the CRTLIB command prompt screen divided into three columns.

Figure 1.7

Create Library
Command Prompt
Screen (with Additional
Parameters)

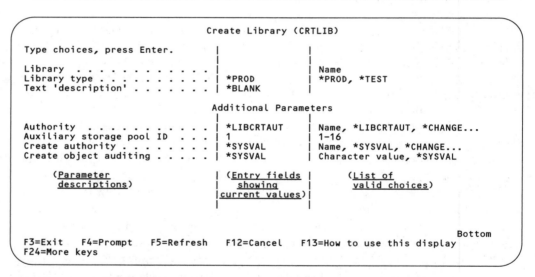

```
                             Create Library (CRTLIB)

 Type choices, press Enter.

 Library . . . . . . . . . . . .    _____     Name
 Library type . . . . . . . . . .   *PROD          *PROD, *TEST
 Text 'description' . . . . . . .   *BLANK_____

 Additional Parameters

 Authority  . . . . . . . . . .     *LIBCRTAUT     Name, *LIBCRTAUT, *CHANGE...
 Auxiliary storage pool ID  . . .   1              1-16
 Create authority . . . . . . .     *SYSVAL        Name, *SYSVAL, *CHANGE...
 Create object auditing . . . . .   *SYSVAL        Character value, *SYSVAL




                                                                   Bottom
 F3=Exit   F4=Prompt   F5=Refresh   F12=Cancel   F13=How to use this display
 F24=More keys
```

Figure 1.8

Create Library
Command Prompt
Screen (Divided into
Three Columns)

```
                             Create Library (CRTLIB)

 Type choices, press Enter.        |            |

 Library . . . . . . . . . . .  |            |  Name
 Library type . . . . . . . . .  | *PROD      |  *PROD, *TEST
 Text 'description' . . . . . .  | *BLANK     |

                              Additional Parameters
                                |            |
 Authority  . . . . . . . . . .  | *LIBCRTAUT |  Name, *LIBCRTAUT, *CHANGE...
 Auxiliary storage pool ID  . .  | 1          |  1-16
 Create authority . . . . . . .  | *SYSVAL    |  Name, *SYSVAL, *CHANGE...
 Create object auditing . . . .  | *SYSVAL    |  Character value, *SYSVAL

      (Parameter            | (Entry fields |    (List of
       descriptions)        |   showing     |     valid choices)
                            |current values)|
                            |            |

                                                                   Bottom
 F3=Exit   F4=Prompt   F5=Refresh   F12=Cancel   F13=How to use this display
 F24=More keys
```

Notice that for each parameter the prompt screen provides a description, an entry field showing the parameter's current value (if any), and (for most parameters) a list of valid values. If the full list of valid values cannot be displayed, ellipses (…) indicate additional choices. You can view the entire list of valid values by positioning the cursor anywhere on the line containing the parameter in question and pressing function key F4.

To run a command, you must provide a value for any **required parameter** (i.e., one whose value must be specified for the AS/400 to execute the command). In the case of the CRTLIB command, the Library parameter is a required parameter. An attempt to run the command without a value for the Library parameter would result in an error. For other parameters in this example, you can use the **default values** provided, or you can type over any default values you need to change. Later lessons cover command prompting in more detail; but for now it is important only that you can identify a command prompt screen, that you know how to access such a screen, and that you know the reason for using it.

USING HELP

Let's now consider a third type of screen, an **information screen**. Information screens do not give you menu choices to select from or prompt fields to fill in. They simply provide information you request and give you a way back to where you were when you asked for the information.

A common type of information screen is the Help screen. You can get Help information on the AS/400 from almost any kind of display. Suppose you were creating a library and weren't sure what the parameter, "Library type," meant. You could place the cursor anywhere on the line for that parameter (the cursor doesn't have to be on the input field), and then press the **Help key**, F1.

Field or Context-Sensitive Help

When you request information about a particular area on a screen, such as the Library type parameter, you are requesting what is referred to as **field** or **context-sensitive Help**. To continue with our example, if you place the cursor on the Library type field of the CRTLIB command prompt screen and press the F1 Help key, a window appears on the screen (Figure 1.9) that contains information about the parameter.

```
                         Create Library (CRTLIB)

 Type choices, press Enter.
 Library  . . . . . . . . . . . . .               Name
 Library type . . . . . . . . . .    *PROD        *PROD, *TEST
 Text 'descrip ................................................................
                  :            Library type (TYPE) - Help             :
                  :                                                    :
                  :  Specifies the type of library being created.      :
                  :                                                    :
 Authority  .  :  *PROD                                               :
 Auxiliary sto :      This is a production library.  Database files in :
 Create author :      production libraries cannot be opened for updating if :
                  :      a user is in debug mode and he requested that  :
                  :      production libraries be protected.            :
                  :                                                    :
                  :  *TEST                                             :
                  :      This is a test library.  All objects in a test library :
                  :                                                    :
                  :                                              More... :
                  :  F2=Extended help   F10=Move to top   F11=InfoSeeker :
 F3=Exit    F4= :  F12=Cancel           F20=Enlarge       F24=More keys  :
 F24=More keys  :...................................................... :
```

Figure 1.9
Field Help Text for
Library Type Parameter

Notice that the window appears just below (or sometimes just above) the field for which you requested help and that it has its own list of active function keys. You can enlarge the window, so that it fills up the entire screen, by pressing function key F20. To cancel the help request and return to the previous screen, you would press function key F12.

Extended Help

If you were looking at a field Help window and wanted more information about the screen in general, you would press function key F2 for **extended Help**. In our continuing example, pressing function key F2 from "Library type" Help would give you general information about the CRTLIB command. This extended Help would then list and describe all of the command's parameters, as well as their possible values. For a screen other than a command prompt screen, extended Help describes the parts of the screen and any entry fields or options that are available on the screen.

If you press function key F2 (for extended Help) from the field Help screen shown in Figure 1.9, the system displays the screen shown in Figure 1.10.

Figure 1.10

Extended Help for the Create Library Command

```
                          Create Library (CRTLIB)
 ..............................................................................
 :                       Create Library - Help                                :
 :                                                                            :
 :    The Create Library (CRTLIB) command adds a new library to the           :
 :    system.  Before any objects are placed into a library, the library      :
 :    must have been created.                                                 :
 :                                                                            :
 :    Restriction:  You must have *AUDIT special authority to specify a        :
 :    value other than *SYSVAL on the CRTOBJAUD parameter.                    :
 :                                                                            :
 :        Note:  Do not precede an entry with an asterisk unless that          :
 :        entry is a "special value" that is shown (on the display or in       :
 :        the help information) with an asterisk.                             :
 :                                                                            :
 : Library (LIB)                                                              :
 :                                                                            :
 :    Specifies the name of the library that is created.  You should not       :
 :    use a name that begins with the character Q.  The system assumes         :
 :                                                              More...        :
 : F3=Exit help      F10=Move to top    F11=InfoSeeker    F12=Cancel           :
 : F13=Information Assistant    F14=Print help                                 :
 :                                                                            :
 ..............................................................................
```

Notice that extended Help begins by explaining what the command (CRTLIB, in this case) does, then lists and explains the command's parameters. "More..." at the bottom right side of the screen tells you that more screens of information are available. To see these additional screens, you would press the Page Down (Shift + Roll up) key.

You can get extended Help by pressing function key F2 from a field Help screen, as we did just now, or you can get it directly by pressing the Help key when the cursor is not in a context-sensitive area of a screen. On a command prompt screen, if the cursor is anywhere on the several lines above the first parameter line — including the screen header — or on a blank line below, pressing function key F1 should take you directly to extended Help.

The AS/400 has thousands of Help screens, and you should not hesitate to use them when you have a question about how a certain screen can be used or about what the possibilities are for responding to a prompt. We rely heavily on Help screens in the lab for this chapter and in subsequent labs.

InfoSeeker

Before we leave our discussion of AS/400 Help, we should examine briefly some additional information retrieval features of Help. On versions of OS/400 earlier than V3R1/V3R6, pressing F11 from an extended help screen started a function called **search index**. (From help screens within some licensed programs (e.g., Application Development Tools), F11 still invokes the search index function.) Basically, search index lets you enter a search word that the system tries to find in its internal index of topics. If the system finds topics in the index related to the search word, it returns a list of those topics. For each of the topics listed, you can choose to display or print the related text. We examine the function of search index later in this lesson.

For most help screens from V3R1/V3R6 on, the search index feature has been replaced by **InfoSeeker**. InfoSeeker is the access to the AS/400 Soft Copy Library, all the manuals related to the operating system and licensed program products, on-line. This information is available through a hierarchy of "book shelves" that contain "books." Bookshelves are essentially collections of technical manuals related to a specific topic. InfoSeeker comes with a large number of bookshelves already built and loaded with books, but the system administrator can change the content of these bookshelves or eliminate them entirely if desired. Also new bookshelves can be built and populated with the appropriate books.

This soft copy library can be installed on PCs or a PC network and accessed through IBM's Book Manager Library Reader program. But if InfoSeeker is installed on the AS/400, it may require substantial disk storage, especially if the manuals themselves are stored on the system's hard drive, so not all installations may choose to use InfoSeeker. Furthermore, even if your installation has InfoSeeker running on the AS/400, individual users must have a system directory entry to access the InfoSeeker data.

You can find out whether you have InfoSeeker access by pressing F11 from a help screen showing F11=InfoSeeker as enabled. Alternatively, you can enter the CL command STRINFSKR (Start InfoSeeker) from any command line. If a screen labeled "InfoSeeker" appears but a message saying "There are no bookshelves or books to display" is shown, it is likely you are not enrolled in the system directory. (The exact reason can be determined by examining the job log, a topic covered later.)

However, if a screen similar to Figure 1.11 appears, you probably have access to the bookshelves displayed there.

Figure 1.11
InfoSeeker Bookshelf
Display

```
                              InfoSeeker
Type options, press Enter.
  1=Open    2=Search    4=Remove from view    8=Display description
  9=Put in shelf

Opt     Description
  _        (S) Online Library Reference Bookshelp
  _        (S) Office Vision
  _        (S) work place for noriaki.I
  _        (S) AS/400 Operations Management
  _        (S) OS/400 V3R6 Commonly Used Books Bookshelf
  _        (S) Office and Decision Support
  _        (S) General System and Publications Information Bookshelf
  _        (S) AS/400 V3R6 Client/Server Bookshelf
  _        (S) AS/400 V3R6 System Management and Operation Bookshelf
  _        (S) AS/400 V3R6 Communications and Networking Bookshelf
  _        (S) AS/400 V3R6 AD Programming Lang and Tools Bookshelf
  _        (S) AS/400 V3R6 Database and Files Bookshelf
  _        (S) AS/400 V3R6 Application and System Support Bookshelf
                                                               More...
F3=Exit     F5=Refresh    F6=Change list    F11=Display data    F12=Cancel
F13=Sort    F14=Clear markers
(C) COPYRIGHT IBM CORP. 1980, 1995.
```

You can "open" a bookshelf (get to the list of books contained in the bookshelf) by selecting option 1. From the entry to InfoSeeker, most — if not all — list items will be prefixed by letter S in parentheses. This means the entry is a bookshelf. (It is possible that the entry screen could show individual books as well; these would be prefixed by a B in parentheses.)

When you select the Open option on a bookshelf, InfoSeeker expands the bookshelf for you, displaying all the books in the bookshelf and letting you open or search an individual book. Opening a book is much like opening a hard-copy manual — you start with the table of contents and from there you link to the text portion of the manual for a certain topic.

InfoSeeker Tour

For a quick tour of InfoSeeker, let's say you wanted more information about subsystems on the AS/400, how they are used, subsystem descriptions, and so on. On the InfoSeeker bookshelf list shown in Figure 1.11, you would look for a bookshelf description that might include information about subsystems. There are at least a couple of possibilities here, but concepts that are related to the overall system as opposed to programming languages, utilities, and other licensed program products are quite likely to be found in the Commonly Used Books bookshelf, so you might start looking there.

Entering a 1 in the option field for that bookshelf lists all the manuals contained in the bookshelf, as shown in Figure 1.12. As you can see, one of the manuals is *OS/400 Work Management.* Remembering that subsystem is a work management concept, you can try searching that manual.

Entering a 2 in the option field for a book brings you to the search screen as shown in Figure 1.13.

```
            Bookshelf-OS/400 V3R6 Commonly Used Books Bookshelf

Type options, press Enter.
  1=Open    2=Search    4=Remove from shelf    8=Display description
  9=Put in shelf

Opt      Description
 _       AS/400 Softcopy Library V3R6
 _       AS/400 System Operation Quick Reference V3R6
 _       AS/400 System Operation V3R6
 _       Getting Started with AS/400 V3R6
 _       AS/400 System Startup and Problem Handling V3R6
 _       OS/400 InfoSeeker - Getting Started V3R6
 _       OS/400 InfoSeeker Use V3R6
 _       AS/400 Publications Reference V3R6
 _       OS/400 Security - Reference V3R6
 _       OS/400 Backup and Recovery - Basic V3R6
 _       OS/400 Backup and Recovery - Advanced V3R6
 2       OS/400 Work Management V3R6
 _       AS/400 Programming Reference Summary V3R6
                                                                 More...
F3=Exit    F5=Refresh    F6=Search all    F11=Display data    F12=Cancel
F13=Sort   F14=Clear markers
```

Figure 1.12
List of Manuals in Commonly Used Books Bookshelf

```
                                Search
Type search request, press Enter.

Match type . . . . . . . . .  3        1=Fuzzy
                                       2=Exact, any case
                                       3=Exact, case sensitive


Search for:
  Subsystems_____
_____




Phrase separator . . . . . .  ,
Wildcard . . . . . . . . . .  *



F3=Exit     F6=List searches    F9=Retrieve    F10=Change search options
F11=View search results        F12=Cancel     F13=Word check
(C) COPYRIGHT IBM CORP. 1980, 1995.
```

Figure 1.13
InfoSeeker Search Prompt Screen

Because "subsystem" is a commonly used term in work management, we try to avoid a large number of search hits by entering the term as "Subsystems" and requesting an exact, case-sensitive match, as illustrated. Even so we might get a warning that a large number of search matches were found, but if we forge ahead, a screen similar to the one shown in Figure 1.14 should next appear.

Figure 1.14
Search Results of Work
Management Manual
for Search Word
"Subsystems"

```
                       Search Results - Subsystems
                                                           Lines 1 to 7 of 7
To view topic, tab to topic heading, press Enter
To expand or compress lines, tab to + or -, press Enter.

  + 4.0   Chapter 4.   Subsystems
  + 4.9   Active and Inactive Subsystems
  + 4.17.1 Relationship between Job Queues and Subsystems
  + 4.11.8 Pool Numbering Schemes
  + 4.11.9 How to Number Pools
  + 14.5.4 Using the WRKSYSSTS Display to Observe System Status
  + E.0   Appendix E.   Work Management APIs and Exit Programs




                                         Bottom of List of search matches
 F3=Exit     F5=Show topics only   F6=Show first matches    F11=Go to
 F12=Cancel  F13=Show all matches for a topic    F24=More keys
```

Judging from the list of search matches, a whole chapter of the Work Management manual is devoted to subsystems. To get to the beginning of that chapter, use the tab key to move the cursor to the chapter heading, then press Enter to jump into the manual at that location. Doing so from Figure 1.14 takes you right into the text at as shown in Figure 1.15.

Figure 1.15
Beginning Text of
OS/400 Work
Management Manual,
Chapter 4, Subsystems

```
               Book-OS/400 Work Management V3R6
               4.0   Chapter 4.   Subsystems
                                          Topic lines 1 to 17 of 45

 4.0  Chapter 4.  Subsystems
  A subsystem is a single, predefined operating environment through which
  the system coordinates the work flow and resource use.  The system can
  contain several subsystems, all operating independently of each other.
  Subsystems manage resources.  The run-time characteristics of a subsystem
  are defined in an object called a subsystem description.

  Each subsystem can run unique operations.  For instance, you can set up
  one subsystem to handle only interactive jobs, while another subsystem
  handles only batch jobs.  Subsystems can also be designed to handle many
  types of work.  The system allows you to decide the number of subsystems
  and what types work each subsystem will handle.

  The system relies on subsystem descriptions when starting subsystems.
                                                         More...
 F2=Set       F3=Exit book   F6=Search   F10=Move to top   F11=Go to
 F12=Cancel   F13=Services   F14=Go to next match          F24=More keys
```

From there you can page down to read through the topic, page up to see what precedes this topic or use **hypertext links** (displayed in yellow on color monitors or in high intensity and underlined on monochrome monitors) to jump to other topics. These links work by letting you tab to one of the linking words or phrases and then press Enter to display more information about that topic. All of the entries in the search results list shown in Figure 1.14 are hypertext links.

In summary, InfoSeeker lets you search a book (or bookshelf) for a certain word or phrase, display related information, and print topics from the text when required. Overall, InfoSeeker provides a fast, efficient way of looking up information in manuals and is most useful to programmers, operators, and technical users. We don't require InfoSeeker access in this text because many beginning students probably do not have it, but you should be aware of InfoSeeker, and if you need it, you should talk to your system administrator about enrollment in the system directory.

Information Assistant

Another function key found on help screens from V3R1 of the operating system is F13=Information Assistant. Pressing F13 takes you to a menu named Info whose description is "**Information Assistant** Options." (Because this is a menu, you can also access it from any command line by using the CL GO command — i.e., GO INFO.)

The menu has several options, as shown in Figure 1.16. Although all users should be able to get to this menu, the usefulness of some of the options depends on how individual systems are configured and the level of authority the individual user has.

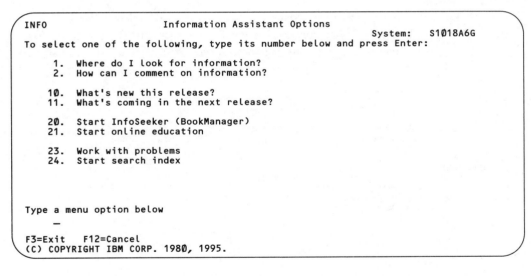

```
  INFO                  Information Assistant Options
                                                  System:   S1018A6G
  To select one of the following, type its number below and press Enter:

       1.  Where do I look for information?
       2.  How can I comment on information?

      10.  What's new this release?
      11.  What's coming in the next release?

      20.  Start InfoSeeker (BookManager)
      21.  Start online education

      23.  Work with problems
      24.  Start search index



  Type a menu option below
      _

  F3=Exit    F12=Cancel
  (C) COPYRIGHT IBM CORP. 1980, 1995.
```

Figure 1.16

Information Assistant Options — F13 from the AS/400 Help Screen

Choices 1 and 2 provide a little insight about finding information and providing feedback about the quality of information to IBM.

Choice 10 lists the improvements in the current installed release of the operating system over the previous release. It provides hypertext links to a number of different topics, but the information provided is brief, at best. For many of the topics, however, references to more in-depth coverage are provided. Choice 11 previews the upcoming operating system release but only if the pertinent information has been made available to the current release.

Choice 20 is another way to start InfoSeeker, in addition to the Help screen's F11 key or the STRINFSKR command. The same restrictions apply: InfoSeeker must be installed, and you must be enrolled in the system directory.

IBM makes a number of online education courses available for a cost, and if your installation has purchased and installed these, Choice 21 lets you see the courses you are enrolled in and start or continue working on a course. If Choice 21 comes up empty, either there are no courses on your system or you have not been authorized to use them. See your system administrator for more information.

System operators or administrators use Choice 23 to document problems encountered on the system and their resolution. Without special authority, you probably cannot use the WRKPRB (Work with Problems) command this menu choice invokes. Choice 24 lets you start the search index function mentioned earlier. If no indexes are currently attached to your profile, this option gives you a way to add a search index or indexes. If one or more indexes are already available, you can search those indexes for a search word and display or print whatever information is found. In a later lab we add an index and use it to search for certain topics.

Search Index

Just to show how the search index works, let's assume option 24 was taken from the INFO menu. If this user had already selected the Application Development Tools (ADT) index to use for the search index, a screen similar to the one shown in Figure 1.17 would appear.

Figure 1.17

Search Index Starting
Screen with Application
Development Tools
Index

```
                               Search Index

  Type options, press Enter.  (+ indicates an expandable topic)
    5=Display topic    6=Print topic    7=Expand topic    8=Compress topic

  Opt    Topic
         AS/400 System Information
         Application Development Tools Information
           About ADT Information (ADT)
    _    + Application Development Tools (ADT)
    _    + Application Development Manager/400 (App)




                                                                   Bottom
  Or type search words and press Enter.  (*indicates a topic match)
  _____
  F3=Exit help    F5=All topics    F6=Main topics    F11=Hide structure
  F12=Cancel         F13=Information Assistant    F18=More indexes    F24=More keys
```

If you tab the cursor to the command line and enter the search word "object type" (a search "word" doesn't have to be a single word), a list of related topics like that shown in Figure 1.18 should display.

```
                           Search Index

Type options, press Enter.  (+ indicates an expandable topic)
   5=Display topic    6=Print topic    7=Expand topic    8=Compress topic

Opt    Topic
       Application Development Tools Information
 _       + Application Development Tools (ADT)
 _         + Programming Development Manager (PDM)
 _           + Using Objects (PDM)
 _         *     Changing an Object Using DFU (PDM)
 _         *     How Objects are Organized (PDM)
 _       + Application Development Manager/400 (App)
 _         *   User-Defined Types (App)



                                                           Bottom
Or type search words and press Enter.  (*indicates a topic match)

object type_____
F3=Exit help    F5=All topics    F6=Main topics    F11=Hide structure
F12=Cancel      F13=Information Assistant    F18=More indexes    F24=More keys
```

Figure 1.18

Sample Search Index
Related Topics List

Note that this screen is different from other screens we have discussed so far. The screen is not a menu or an information screen, and it's not a command prompt screen, yet its general format is very common on the AS/400.

LIST OR WORK WITH SCREENS

The type of screen shown in Figure 1.18 is called a **list screen**, list processing screen, or often a "Work with" list screen because it so commonly results from running a "Work with" CL command. We use these list screens extensively in our labs and explain more about their power and flexibility in later lessons.

On the list screen in Figure 1.18, note that under the screen heading it says, "Type options, press Enter." Four options are provided:

5=Display topic   6=Print topic   7=Expand topic   8=Compress topic

Other list screens may have a larger number of options; some only one. Beneath the options is the item list — in this case, a list of topics returned by the search. You may type an appropriate option in front of any topic, and the system will process your request. In fact, you can type the same or different options for several items before pressing Enter. When you press Enter, the system processes them all from top to bottom, one after another.

To find out about "How Objects are Organized (PDM)," you would type 5 on the option field for that topic. The system would then display Figure 1.19, which provides some basic information and defines some terms related to object organization. Notice that more pages of information are available (as indicated by "More…" at the bottom right corner of the screen).

Figure 1.19

Help Screen that
Provides Information
about Object
Organization in PDM

```
Help                        How Objects are Organized (PDM)

  Objects are the basic unit on which commands perform operations on
  the AS/400 system.  For more information about how objects are
  organized on the AS/400 system and how they relate to PDM, refer to
  the Programming Development Manager User's Guide and Reference.

  An object is a named unit that consists of a set of features that
  describe the object.

  There are many types of objects.  For example, the object type for a
  library is *LIB, the object type for a file is *FILE, and the object
  type for a program is *PGM.

  Objects also have subtypes know as attributes.  For example, the
  attribute of an object of type *PGM could be RPG to describe the
  type of program.

  A library is a special type of object of type *LIB that is used to
  group related objects.  Therefore, a library is a directory to a
                                                              More...
F3=Exit help    F10=Move to top    F12=Cancel    F13=Information Assistant
F14=Print help
```

We now have briefly discussed four different types of screens the AS/400 uses to communicate with interactive users. They are

1. **Menu** screens

2. **Entry** screens

   Command prompt screens are a common entry screen.

3. **Information** screens

   Help screens are often-used types of information screens. Help screens include extended Help and field or context-sensitive Help.

4. **List** screens, also known as list processing or work with list screens

Being familiar with these screen types and knowing how each is used can help you overcome that sense of being lost in a foreign environment users so often have as they learn about a new system. As you work through the lab exercises, try to identify each screen you encounter — it will help maintain your orientation. Think about how you got to each new screen, and if you do get lost, remember that function key F12 backs you out one screen at a time. When you successfully complete a task, use F3 to return to a common starting point, such as the Main menu.

Key Terms

batch job

CL program

command line

command parameters

command prompt screen

context-sensitive Help

Control Language (CL)

default values

display device

entry screen

extended Help

field Help

function keys

Help key

hypertext link

Information Assistant

information screen

InfoSeeker

interactive job

IPL (Initial Program Load)

job

job description

job queue

library

library list

licensed program product

list screen

menu interface

menu options

menu screen

multitasking

multiuser

object

object type

OS/400

required parameter

search index

sign-on screen

subsystem

subsystem description

system values

user

user profile

work management

Lab 1

INTRODUCTION

This lab is intended to provide experience with the main topics covered in Lesson 1 text: system values, licensed program products, and basic CL command use. We examine these topics through use of the four types of screen displays: menus, information screens, entry screens, and lists. Rather than building objects or generating some output, the goal of this lab is to become accustomed to navigating the user interface by exploring some critical system components.

Part 1

Goals	Recognize the AS/400 sign-on screen
	Sign on successfully
Start at	AS/400 sign-on screen
Procedure	Enter a valid user ID and password

1.1. Make sure the power is turned on at your workstation. If the screen shows no display, try pressing the space bar and turning up the brightness control on your terminal. You should see the AS/400 sign-on screen, similar to Figure 1.1, page 7.

If you are not yet at this screen, you are probably working at a nondedicated terminal that requires you to switch sessions or "boot" to a local area network. Because there are many different possibilities for connecting workstations to AS/400s, your instructor/mentor should provide you with specific instructions. If you need help, ask your instructor/mentor for assistance.

1.2. The Sign-on screen is a special type of entry screen. You are expected to key in and enter certain information to identify yourself to the system, but function keys and Help information are not available.

Look at the identification information in the upper right corner of the screen.

1.2a. What values are shown for the System, Subsystem, and Display attributes of your workstation?

The Display name is the name by which your workstation is known to the system. It will also be the name of your interactive job.

Begin the sign-on procedure by typing your first initial plus (without spacing) last name as User. A space character is not a valid character within a name. A user name, like most system level names on the AS/400, has a maximum of 10 characters. So if your whole last name won't fit, just key as many characters after your first initial as space allows and truncate the rest. If this is not how the system administrator entered the user ID of your user profile, your instructor/mentor will provide other information.

FLastname

Your user name will appear in capitals, even if your keyboard is not shifted to uppercase.

Keyboard mapping is another area where there are differences from one installation to another (or even for different types of keyboards or connections within installations). Generally the Tab key on a PC keyboard equates to the 5250 (older, nonprogrammable workstation) keyboard's Field Advance key. The 5250 Field exit key, which erases everything in the current field from the cursor location and then jumps to the next input field, may be mapped on PC keyboards to either the right Control (Ctrl) key or the Enter key, depending on which 5250 emulation product was used (or whether remapping was done). If you are working through a Windows client, you should see a toolbar with a keyboard button at the top of your screen. Clicking on that button lets you find out how various system functions are mapped on your keyboard.

Do not press Enter yet, but use the Tab, New line, or Field exit key to move to the password input field.

`tab/new-line/field exit`

Initially, all student profiles are created using the same password as your user ID, your first initial, and up to nine characters of your last name. Remember as you key in your password that for security purposes the characters are not displayed on the screen, so type carefully!

FLastname

If you think you made a mistake and haven't pressed Enter yet, backspace and type over. If you typed too many characters the first time, press the Field exit key (after you have typed your password) to erase the rest of the input field above and to the right of the cursor.

When you have keyed in your password, press the Enter key. Remember the Enter function may be mapped to the right Control key on your keyboard.

Enter

If an error code and the message "Password not correct for user profile" appear near the bottom of the screen, try rekeying your password, then pressing the Field exit key and Enter. If the same message persists, ask your instructor/mentor for assistance.

If you see a different message — "User (user name) does not exist" — your user profile cannot be found and you need to have your instructor/mentor check it out before you can go any farther.

Part 2

Goals	Recognize menu screen Follow menu path to licensed programs Find out which licensed programs are installed on your system
Start at	MAIN menu (GO MAIN)
Procedure	Enter choice 7 from MAIN Enter choice 2 from DEFINE Enter choice 10 from LICPGM

2.1. Once you have successfully signed on, you should be looking at the AS/400 Main Menu, similar to Figure 1.2, page 8. Notice the cursor located on the Selection or command line. You may either select a menu choice by typing its number or enter a command on this line.

Let's follow a menu path to examine the installed IBM licensed programs on your system. The sub-menu descriptions are not always very clear and sometimes you may guess wrong, but licensed programs are part of the definition of the system, so choice 7, "Define or change the system" might be a good guess. Type 7 on the command line, then press Enter.

7
Enter

2.1a. What is the "proper" name (as it is known to the system) of the "Define or Change the System" menu?

2.2. From here, option 2 is the obvious candidate for our purpose. Type 2 on the command line, then press Enter.

2
Enter

2.2a. Which of the four screen types discussed in the text are you now looking at? (Be careful: despite its name, it has neither an options list nor input fields to select options.)

2.3. Let's take choice 10 to display installed licensed programs. Type 10, then press Enter.

10
Enter

The screen you are looking at now should be similar to the one shown in Figure 1.20, but the actual list of programs will differ, depending on what is installed on your system.

Figure 1.20
Display Installed
Licensed Programs
Screen

```
                    Display Installed Licensed Programs
                                                      System:    S1018A6G
     Licensed    Installed
     Program     Status        Description
     5716SS1     *COMPATIBLE   OS/400 - Library QGPL
     5716SS1     *COMPATIBLE   OS/400 - Library QUSRSYS
     5716SS1     *COMPATIBLE   Operating System/400
     5716SS1     *COMPATIBLE   OS/400 - Extended Base Support
     5716SS1     *COMPATIBLE   OS/400 - Online Information
     5716SS1     *COMPATIBLE   OS/400 - Example Tools Library
     5716SS1     *COMPATIBLE   OS/400 - *PRV CL Compiler Support
     5716SS1     *COMPATIBLE   OS/400 - Host Servers
     5716CB1     *COMPATIBLE   Integrated Language Environment COBOL/400
     5716CB1     *COMPATIBLE   ILE COBOL/400 - COBOL/400
     5716CL1     *COMPATIBLE   Application Dev ToolSet Client Server/400
     5716CM1     *COMPATIBLE   Communications Utilities/400
     5716CX1     *COMPATIBLE   ILE C/400
     5716DCT     *COMPATIBLE   Language Dictionaries for OS/400
                                                            More...
     Press Enter to continue.

     F3=Exit   F11=Display release    F12=Cancel
     (C) COPYRIGHT IBM CORP. 1980, 1995.
```

Like many displays on the AS/400, this screen has more than one format. The function key F11 is used to change the display from one format to another.

2.3a Press F11 to cycle through the screens. How many formats does this display have?

Display the screen that shows "Installed Release."
All program components have a Licensed Program number, a Description, and an Installed Release, which gives the Version, Release, and Modification for each component. Because IBM has upgraded the operating system and most of the licensed programs approximately yearly, the installed release values tell you which "edition" of the software you have.

2.3b. Of the four types of screens we discussed in the text, which type is this? 1~8

2.3c. Which "edition" of operating system software is your system using?

2.3d. What is the licensed program number of Application Development ToolSet/400?

2.3e. What is the licensed program number of Query/400?

We use Application Development ToolSet/400 and Query/400 extensively in later labs.

Programming languages most commonly used on the AS/400 include RPG, Cobol, and C. For now, the AS/400 also supports Pascal, Fortran, Basic, and PL/I. C++ and Java are relative newcomers to the AS/400, and you may not yet find these languages among the installed licensed programs of some traditional RPG or Cobol shops. The relational database language, SQL, is another powerful tool available for accessing and manipulating database files.

2.3f. List the languages installed on your system.

Part 3

Goals	Use Help to get more information about displays

Start at	Command line: GO LICPGM
	Enter choice 10 from LICPGM

Procedure	Press Help key/F1 from Display Installed Licensed Programs screen

3.1. The cursor should still be in the upper left corner of the screen. If your display does not show the Installed Release column, press F11 to change formats until that column appears. Notice again the layout of the screen — a title, system identifier, three columns of information and enter/function key information toward the bottom. Extended Help explains the purpose of the screen as well as the type of information provided. Now press the Help key (F1) to get more information about this display.

F1

You should now be looking at the extended Help for Display Installed Licensed Programs, Figure 1.21.

Figure 1.21
Display Installed
Licensed Programs
Help Screen

```
                    Display Installed Licensed Programs
..............................................................................
                           Display - Help
:                                                                          :
: The Display Installed Licensed Programs display shows a list of          :
: licensed programs, optional parts of the licensed programs, and          :
: IBM-supplied user libraries installed on your system.                    :
:                                                                          :
:      Note:  New licensed programs or new optional parts of licensed      :
:      programs that are shipped independently of an operating system      :
:      release will not appear on this display until the next release      :
:      of the operating system is installed.  Use the Display Software      :
:      Resources (DSPSFWRSC) command to see a list of the new licensed      :
:      programs or optional parts of licensed programs that were           :
:      shipped independently of an operating system release.                :
:                                                                          :
:      Use F11 to see alternate views of this display.  Alternate views     :
:      display the installed status, the installed release level, and the   :
:      number associated with each part of the licensed program.            :
:                                                             More...       :
: F3=Exit help   F10-Move to top    F11=Search Index    F12=Cancel          :
: F13=Information Assistant          F14=Print help                         :
..............................................................................
```

Extended Help explains the display in general, then gives information about specific parts of the display — in this case, the columns of information. Whenever "More…" appears at the bottom right corner of the screen, you can use the Page down or Shift + Roll up keys to see the next screen of information. Page down now and read the explanation of "Installed Release."

Page down

3.1a. How can you tell whether a licensed program has not been installed successfully? Now press F12 to exit extended Help and press F11 to change to the screen format showing "Product Part."

F12

F11

Context-sensitive Help provides information about the field or column upon which the cursor is positioned. Move the cursor to the column header itself or anywhere below it within the Product Part column of data, then press F1 for help.

F1

A window should appear describing the meaning of "Product Part." Instead of "More…", the word "Bottom" should be displayed in the lower right corner of the screen, indicating that there is no additional information about this topic. Context-sensitive Help gives you information only on the cursor-selected field, but you can learn about other areas of the screen by asking for Extended Help (F2) from a Context-sensitive Help screen.

3.1b From the "Product Part" Help display, what do all licensed programs have in common?

Part 4

Goals	Use the Position to field to change the displayed part of a list
	Locate and display information about specified system values

Start at	MAIN menu — use F3 to back up or GO MAIN

Procedure	Enter choice 7 from MAIN
	Enter choice 8 from DEFINE
	Use Page Up/Down and the Position to field to locate specified
	system values

If you have just finished Part 3, press F3 from the Licensed Program list until you have returned to Main menu. You should always try to use F3 to back out to a starting screen when you have finished the current task.

4.1. We've mentioned system values as being control and configuration values critical to system operation. Let's use the menu path to examine some system values.

We will start with the same second-level menu because "system values" would seem to have something to do with the "Define or change the system" selection.

7

Enter

4.2. From the DEFINE menu, take choice 8, Work with system values.

8

Enter

You should now be looking at the screen in Figure 1.22.

```
                     Work with System Values
                                             System:    S1018A6G
    Position to  . . . . . ._____    Starting characters of system value
    Subset by Type . . . . .*ALL___     F4 for list

    Type options, press Enter.
      5=Display

            System
    Option  Value       Type     Description
      _     QABNORMSW   *SYSCTL   Previous end of system indicator
      _     QACGLVL     *MSG      Accounting level
      _     QACTJOB     *ALC      Initial number of active jobs
      _     QADLACTJ    *ALC      Additional number of active jobs
      _     QADLSPLA    *ALC      Spooling control block additional  storage
      _     QADLTOTJ    *ALC      Additional number of total jobs
      _     QALWOBJRST  *SEC      Allow object restore option
      _     QALWUSRDMN  *SEC      Allow user domain objects in libraries
                                                               More...
    Command
    ===>
    F3=Exit   F4=Prompt   F5=Refresh   F9=Retrieve   F11=Display names only
    F12=Cancel
```

Figure 1.22
Work with System
Values Screen

This is a list screen, also called work with list or list processing screen. The list consists of a number of similar items that the user can perform processing options on. In this case the items are all system values, and the only option provided with a user's or programmer's authority is Display. The system security officer or another user with sufficient authority would also have a change option. Notice that all system values begin with Q.

4.3. With the cursor in the first option field, press Help (F1).

F1

Because Option is a designated area of the screen, you get field (or context-sensitive) Help, which tells you only how to use that field. Now press function key F2 for extended Help.

F2

Read the general description of the Work with System Values display.

4.3a. Where can you find a listing of the shipped (as they come from IBM) system values? *Work management*

Read the help information about using the Position to field.

4.3b. What predefined value positions you to the bottom of the list?

For most list screens it is possible to show only a subset of the list (i.e., a part of the entire list) by specifying some subset selection criterion. In the case of the Work with System Values list, the criterion would be the type of system value.

4.3c. How many different system value types does the Help text show? Note that *ALL is not a system value type but a keyword or special value that means "include all values."

4.4. Press F3 to return to the Work with System Values list.

F3

4.4a. What is the current value of Subset by Type?
4.4b. Can you find among the list items all of the different types mentioned in the Help text in this list? (You may need to page down.)
4.4c. Which system value would you display to find out to the level of user assistance set for your system?

Move the cursor to the option field next to that system value name. Type 5 to display the value, then press Enter.

5
Enter

4.4d. To what level is your system user assistance set?

Notice that this time an option (5) taken from a list screen has brought you to an information screen. Other options from other list screens may take you to an entry screen, a command prompt, or another list screen. Still other options may run a command, leaving you at the same screen.

Also notice that there are three ways to get out of this screen: Enter, F3, and F12; they all take you to the same place — back to the list screen. Press Enter (or F3 or F12) to return to the work screen.

Enter (F3 or F12)

4.5 You know from the previous Help information that on List screens with a Position to field, typing *TOP or *BOT positions the list to the very first or very last item in the list.

Back tab the cursor to the beginning of the Position to field. Type *BOT, then press Enter.

Back tab
*BOT
Enter

4.5a. What is the last system value name in the list?

4.6. Move the cursor back to the beginning of the Position to field.

To find out how many times you can make a mistake while trying to sign on, locate the maximum sign-on attempts value. Perhaps you are fairly sure that the system value name starts with "QMAX..." If you key the beginning characters of a list item you are searching for, the system displays that part of the list starting with the first item matching the characters you entered. Let's try it!

Type QM on the Position to field and press Enter.

QM
Enter

Move the cursor to the option for Maximum sign-on attempts allowed, take the display option, and press Enter.

(Display option)
Enter

4.6a. How many attempts are allowed on your system?

Now return to the list screen. The cursor should still be on the option field for QMAXSIGN.

Let's see what happens if you type a value in the Position to field less than the lowest (first) value on the list. (Relative values are determined by the computer's collating sequence; as in a telephone directory, anything beginning with A through P would be less than something beginning with Q.)

Move the cursor to the Position to field (use back tab) and type a single letter less than Q, then press Enter.

4.6b. Where in the list has the cursor been repositioned?
4.6c. What predefined value could you have used to accomplish the same thing?

4.7. Using the information displayed for the appropriate system value, answer the following questions:

4.7a. Is your system set to AUTOmatically configure newly installed local (not virtual) devices?

Use Help for the system value discovered in Step 4.7a to answer the next two questions:

4.7b. Autoconfiguration names each device according to a naming convention. What other system value controls which naming convention will be used?
4.7c. Does a change to the system value found in Step 4.7a take effect when the system is re-IPLd or right away?
4.7d. Display the system value discovered in Step 4.7b that controls the naming convention. Which naming convention does your system use?
4.7e. According to the naming convention, what kind of device would the device name PRT01 be used for?
4.7f. From the system value list, find the device name your system identifies as the system console.
4.7g. How many system values are there having to do with passwords? (Hint: OS/400 spells password PWD.)

You examine other system values in later labs, but now you need to look at another frequently used type of entry screen to complete your tour of common user displays.

First, return to the AS/400 Main Menu by pressing F3 two or three times.

F3 F3 (F3)

Part 5

Goals	Become familiar with the command prompt screen
	Recognize required parameters of command prompt
	Use Help to get information about specific parameters
Start at	Any command line (press F3 to back out to a command line if necessary)
Procedure	Enter CPYF on the command line
	Request Help from the CPYF command prompt screen

5.1. In the text of Lesson 1, we briefly discussed CL and examined the syntax of CL commands. We said that most commands have parameters, but the system doesn't expect us to remember all the parameters and their order for each command. Of course, when you type a command, you may include the required parameters if you know them; but if you don't know how to enter them, or which ones you need, you can use the command prompting facility by simply pressing F4 after typing the command. Then the system displays a command prompt entry screen for you. Or, if you type only a command name and press Enter, the operating system displays a prompt screen if the command requires parameter values.

Let's see how command prompting works.

Type CPYF, for the CL Copy File command, on the command line and press Enter.

CPYF
Enter

You should now see an entry or command prompt display with a message appearing at the bottom of the screen.

5.1a. What does the message say?

Notice the plus sign (+) at the right side of the message line. If an action causes more than one message, or if a message won't fit on the single line provided, the + appears to let you know more of the message exists. To get to the additional message text, move the cursor down to the message line and press Page down.

5.1b. What does the rest of the message say?

The input fields for missing required parameter values are highlighted in reverse image blocks on the screen. This happens whenever you run a command (by pressing the Enter key) without providing necessary parameter values. Normally, if you realize that parameter values are required, you would use the prompt function (F4) instead of pressing Enter.

5.2. The command prompt screen shows you information that the system needs to execute the command. For many parameters the system provides default values. Those values are already entered on the line when the command is initially prompted. The default value for the From member parameter, for example, is *FIRST, meaning the first member (subset of records) in the file. Default parameter values are most often predefined "special values" that begin with an asterisk (*).

Notice the indentation of Library under From file and To file. All objects are logically part of a library; the Library value qualifies the file object name, telling the system which library to search for the file object. So Library is not a separate parameter, but part of the From file or To file object name. The default library value is *LIBL, another special value that tells the system to search the list of libraries assigned to this job. We explore the important concept of a library list in more detail in the next lesson.

Also notice that the only valid choice listed for From file is Name (i.e., no special values are allowed for this parameter). This means that you must identify the From file, specifying the user-defined name given to the object when it was created. This is not an unreasonable request — after all, even an intelligent operating system such as OS/400 can't read your mind to find out which file you want to copy!

5.2a. What is the default for Print format?

Even if a command has several screens of parameters, as the CPYF command does, those parameters that you must provide a value for are shown on the first screen. The entry fields of these required parameters will be blank, with the underlines in high intensity (on color displays, the underlines will be white or a contrasting color). If you tried to run the command without supplying the required values, the entry fields would display in reverse image, along with an error message.

For other parameters, you can simply type over any defaults that need to be changed.

5.3. You can use the AS/400 online Help facility when you need to know what a certain display is for, what a particular command does, or what value a certain parameter requires. On many displays, specific information about a given entry can be obtained from context-sensitive help by moving the cursor to that area or line and then pressing the Help key.

For example, let's see what Help tells you about the From file parameter. Position the cursor anywhere on the From file line of the CPYF command prompt screen. Now press the Help key (F1) to get information from the system about the meaning of the From file parameter.

F1

5.3a. The file you name must be one of four types of files — what are they?

General Help that explains the purpose of the screen, the command, entry fields, and perhaps function keys is called extended Help. You can get extended Help in one of two ways:
• Press F2 from a field Help screen like the one you are looking at now. Go ahead, try it.

F2

• The second way is to press F1 or Help from a non-field-sensitive area on the screen.

From the extended Help for the CPYF command that you should be looking at now, press F3 to return to the CPYF command prompt screen.

F3

Place the cursor in a part of the screen that is not sensitive to an entry or zone. For example, move the cursor up so it is on a line anywhere above the first input field line.
Now press F1 or the Help key.

F1

You should see the same Copy File Help screen you saw when you pressed F2 for extended Help previously.

Let's review the organization of extended Help. First, there is an explanation of the general topic — in this case, the CPYF command. Now Page down and you begin to see field Help — in this case, explaining the parameters of the CPYF command and their possible values.

Page down

Many screens of Help information are available for the CPYF command because it has a large number of parameters and therefore many fields.

Now use F3 to exit Help and F3 again to return to the AS/400 Main Menu.

F3 F3

From the Main Menu you can take choice 90 to Sign off, and this will return you to the AS/400 Sign-on screen.

Whenever you are finished using the workstation, please remember to follow your installation's lab procedures to protect the equipment and leave the workstation ready for the next user.

Mastering the AS/400, Second Edition

Lab 1 Answer Sheet

Name: _____

Date Due: _____   Class Time: _____

1.2a. System: _____   Subsystem: _____   Display: _____

2.1a. _Define_ _____

2.2a. _____ Menu _____   2.3a. ____ 3 _____

2.3b. _____   2.3c. _____

2.3d. _____   2.3e. _____

2.3f. _____

3.1a. _____

3.1b. _____

4.3a. _Work Management Book_ _____

4.3b. ____ *BOT _____   4.3c ____ 8 _____

4.4a. ____ *ALL _____

4.4b. _____

4.4c. ____ QASTLVL _____   4.4d ____ *BASIC _____

4.5a. ____ QYBAR _____   4.6a ____ 15 _____

4.6b. ____ *TOP _____   4.6c ____ *TOP _____

4.7a. _____   4.7b _____

4.7c. _____   4.7d _____

4.7e. _____

4.7f. _____   4.7g. _____

5.1a. _Parameter FROMFILE required_   _Parameter TOFILE required_

5.1b. _____

5.2a _____

5.3a. _____

IN SUMMARY

In this lesson, we examined some important AS/400 characteristics. We discussed the interactive nature of the system and the idea of how jobs are run in subsystems. We know that an interactive job is started when a user signs on to the system and that, at normal operational security levels, there must be a user profile for a sign-on to be successful.

Once on the system, most users rely on several different types of screens to accomplish their tasks. Most work on the system can be done by traversing a series of menus. As we progress down the menu path, we are clarifying to the system what task we want to accomplish until an appropriate command can be executed. The command may take us to another screen, such as an information or list screen, or it may run a program; or if the command has no required parameters, it may invoke a system function.

We have also examined the AS/400's Help facility, and we realize that for most system displays, Help is available both at the extended and at the field or "context" level.

As you work through subsequent lab exercises, you should always try to maintain your orientation — what kind of display you are at, what the purpose of that display is, and how you got there. And use Help freely when you have questions about a display or are uncertain of the meaning of an input field or use of a function key.

The AS/400 can tell you a lot about itself if you just ask for Help.

Lesson 2

Using CL

Lesson Overview

To help you gain confidence when communicating with the AS/400, in this lesson we examine some additional Help and prompting features of the four screen types we discussed in Lesson 1. We also investigate CL commands in more detail and see how the AS/400 facilitates the preparation of commands for execution. Armed with that knowledge, you will create a user library and then change your user profile so it will recognize your newly created library as the current library. Along the way, you gain knowledge about libraries and library lists, and about how they are used on the AS/400.

Objectives

Students will be able to

✓ Enter a CL command from a command line correctly

✓ Distinguish between keyword and positional notation

✓ Use command prompt screens to provide parameter values

✓ Use the GO command to display menus of related commands

✓ Identify the four parts of the library list

✓ Create a user library

✓ Change their user profile so that the library they create is the current library

✓ Use Help to obtain information about libraries

✓ Display system values

✓ Change their password

CL COMMANDS

As we mentioned in Lesson 1, OS/400 Control Language (CL) is the primary interface to operating system functions. You use CL to interact with and get work done on the system. On the AS/400, you have a choice: You can key in CL commands and execute them directly from a command line, or you can follow a menu path to a command prompt screen, a work-with-list screen, or an information screen. Unlike some systems, the AS/400 does not make you select one mode or the other — the system is not exclusively menu driven or command driven. For example, within an interactive job, you can use a command when it is convenient, or you can use a menu path if you can't determine the appropriate command. As you begin working with CL commands, you need to understand the syntax of the language.

CL SYNTAX

In general, **syntax** refers to the proper arrangement of words to form phrases, clauses, and sentences. A somewhat more rigorous definition would be the selection and ordering of language elements to form meaningful expressions.

Luckily, the syntax of OS/400 CL is simple and straightforward. All CL commands consist of a command name, and most CL commands require one or more parameters. Spaces are used to separate the command name from its parameters and also to separate multiple parameters when a command requires them. A simplified syntax notation for a CL command entered on a command line would look like this:

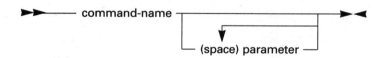

For example, in the command

```
CRTLIB PAYROLL
```

the command name is CRTLIB (Create Library) and the specified parameter is PAYROLL.

Command Names

Let's examine in more detail the structure of command names. Most command names consist of a verb or action part and a noun or receiver of the action (an object, in the grammatical sense). The CRTLIB command used above — where CRT stands for create and LIB stands for library — is an example of this command name form. In addition, some command names use a third segment, which functions as an adjective modifier to the noun. For example, the CL command CRTRPGPGM tells the system to create an RPG program — not a Cobol program (CRTCBLPGM) or a CL program (CRTCLPGM).

Most verb, noun, and modifier abbreviations are three characters long, and many use the first consonants of the English word, skipping the vowels. As you can see, the use of "LIB" to represent "library" is an obvious exception to this (pretty loose) rule.

Listed in Table 2.1 are a number of more commonly used verb abbreviations, the words they represent, and an example of their use.

Table 2.1

Commonly Used CL Verbs

CL Verb	English	Example	Description
CALL	Call	CALL	Executes a program
CLR	Clear	CLROUTQ	Clear Output Queue
CPY	Copy	CPYF	Copy File
CRT	Create	CRTCBLPGM	Create Cobol Program
DLT	Delete	DLTUSRPRF	Delete User Profile
DSP	Display	DSPMSG	Display Message
EDT	Edit	EDTOBJAUT	Edit Object Authority
GRT	Grant	GRTUSRAUT	Grant User Authority
INZ	Initialize	INZTAP	Initialize Tape
OPN	Open	OPNQRYF	Open Query File
RCL	Reclaim	RCLSPLSTG	Reclaim Spool Storage
RCV	Receive	RCVNETF	Receive Network File
RLS	Release	RLSSPLF	Release Spooled File
RMV	Remove	RMVLIBLE	Remove Library List Entry
RST	Restore	RSTLICPGM	Restore Licensed Program
RTV	Retrieve	RTVSYSVAL	Retrieve System Value
SAV	Save	SAVCHGOBJ	Save Changed Object
SBM	Submit	SBMJOB	Submit Job
SND	Send	SNDMSG	Send Message
STR	Start	STRSEU	Start Source Entry Utility
WRK	Work with	WRKSYSSTS	Work with System Status

Most of the verb examples listed in Table 2.1 are consistent in that they use three letters; and unless the English word begins with a vowel (e.g., Edit, Open, Initialize), or doesn't contain three consonants (e.g., Save), they use only consonants in the abbreviation.

However, two commonly used command verbs are exceptions to this rule:

- CALL — used to execute a program
- GO — used to display a menu

Neither command is used in combination with a noun or modifier abbreviation. We discuss these two CL commands in more detail later. For now, as we look at the command names in the Example column of the CL verb list, we can make some observations about the use of the noun and modifier parts of a command name:

1. Not all nouns and modifiers use three letters. For example,
   D stands for Description
   E stands for Entry
   F stands for File of Field
   L stands for List
   Q stands for Queue

2. Some nouns always need a modifier. For example, although you can Copy a File (CPYF), you cannot Work with a Queue; you must Work with a Message Queue (WRKMSGQ), an Output Queue (WRKOUTQ), or a Job Queue (WRKJOBQ). Neither can you Display a Description; you must Display a File Description (DSPFD), an Object Description (DSPOBJD), a File Field Description (DSPFFD), and so on. List (L) also always seems to be attached to a modifier: Library List (LIBL), Authorization List (AUTL), Distribution List (DSTL), and so on.

3. Some nouns/modifiers are the names of utilities or language compilers:
   C   C (a programming language)
   CBL   Cobol (a programming language)
   CL   Control Language
   DFU   Data File Utility
   RPG   Report Program Generator (a programming language)
   SDA   Screen Design Aid utility
   SEU   Source Entry Utility

The two CL verb forms used most commonly with these noun forms are

- STR — used to start (begin execution of) a utility (e.g., STRSEU)
- CRT — used to create (compile from source code) a program using the named language product (e.g., CRTRPGPGM)

Keyword Notation

An important part of CL command syntax is the use of a **parameter keyword**, a significant word that names a command parameter. CL commands use **keyword notation** to explicitly identify a command's parameter. When you use parameter keywords, the parameter value must follow the keyword immediately and the value must be enclosed in parentheses, as the following syntax statement illustrates:

command-name keyword1(value1) keyword2(value2) ...

Each keyword(value) set is a single parameter. One or more spaces must separate the command name from the first parameter and each parameter from the next parameter. When you use keyword notation, the order of parameters is not essential. Consider again the CRTLIB command. When you type CRTLIB on a command line and prompt for the command (F4), the CRTLIB command prompt screen appears (Figure 2.1).

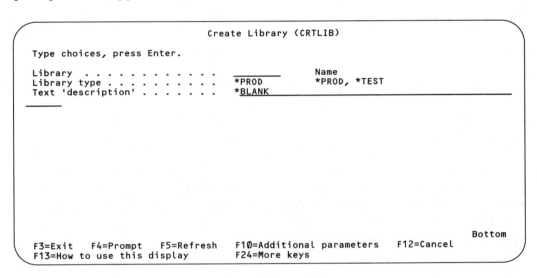

Figure 2.1
Create Library
Command Prompt
Screen

    From this screen you can see that the normal order of parameters is Library, Library type, and Text. Yet if you use keyword notation, either of the commands shown below, or any of the several other possible permutations, entered on a command line or in a CL program, would work:

```
CRTLIB LIB(PAYROLL) TYPE(*TEST) TEXT('Payroll Development')

CRTLIB TYPE(*TEST) TEXT('Payroll Development') LIB(PAYROLL)
```

Both commands work because the system properly interprets a specified parameter value as belonging to the named keyword immediately preceding the value.

    You can determine the parameter keywords for any CL command by observing the command's prompt screen in an alternate, or keyword, format. For example, to get to the CRTLIB command prompt keyword display from the initial command prompt screen shown in Figure 2.1, you might first want to press function key F24 to view additional function keys. After you press function key F24, the screen shown in Figure 2.2 appears.

Figure 2.2
Create Library
Command Prompt
Screen Showing
Additional Function
Keys

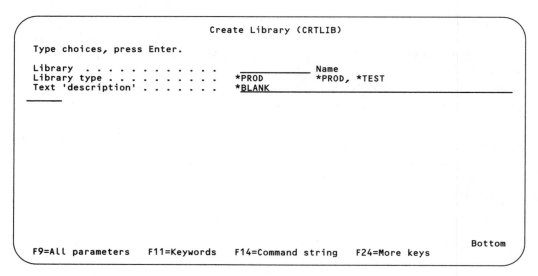

```
                                Create Library (CRTLIB)
         Type choices, press Enter.

         Library  . . . . . . . . . . . .                      Name
         Library type . . . . . . . . . .   *PROD       *PROD, *TEST
         Text 'description' . . . . . . .   *BLANK
         _____



                                                                           Bottom
           F9=All parameters    F11=Keywords    F14=Command string    F24=More keys
```

The active function key list now includes F11=Keywords. Recall how we used F11 to change the screen format of the "Display Installed Licensed Programs" display in Lab 1. In the Command Prompt context, the F11 key acts as a toggle between the initial (Choices) command prompt screen (Figures 2.1 and 2.2) and the prompt screen's keyword format, shown in Figure 2.3.

Figure 2.3
Create Library
Command Prompt
Screen in Keyword
Format

```
                                Create Library (CRTLIB)
         Type choices, press Enter.

         Library  . . . . . . . . . . . LIB         _____
         Library type . . . . . . . . . TYPE        *PROD
         Text 'description' . . . . . . TEXT        *BLANK
         _____



                                                                           Bottom
           F9=All parameters   F11=Choices   F14=Command string   F24=More keys
```

All screens have a certain number of active function keys, depending on the type of screen. When many function keys are active and they cannot all be displayed on the two lines allowed, F24=More keys is displayed. But if you know that a function key is active for a certain screen, you can use it even if it isn't displayed in the two-line function key list. For example, function key F11 works from any command prompt screen; knowing that, you don't have to press F24 first just to see that F11 is active.

By looking at Figure 2.3, you can see that the keywords (LIB, TYPE, and TEXT) we used earlier for the CRTLIB command were correct. If you enter values for the parameters, the command prompt screen looks like the one shown in Figure 2.4.

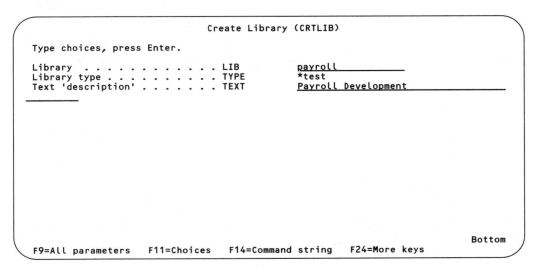

Figure 2.4
Create Library Command Prompt Screen with Parameter Values Entered

Notice that even though the value for TEXT is a character string constant, and as such must be enclosed in single quotes (apostrophes), you don't need to enter the quote marks — the command prompter syntax checker inserts them for you automatically.

After you type in the necessary parameter values, you can press Enter to execute the command. If the values you enter are valid and the command executes successfully, a message indicating a successful result is displayed, as shown at the bottom of the screen in Figure 2.5.

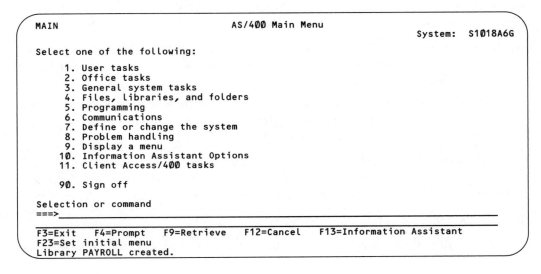

Figure 2.5
Message Indicates CRTLIB Command Executed Successfully

To recall the command, you can press function key F9 on a screen with a command line. All commands entered or prompted from a command line during an interactive session are maintained in a stack. You can recall an earlier command (one lower in the stack) by repeatedly pressing F9. If you press F9 from the screen shown in Figure 2.5, the previous command (CRTLIB), and as many parameters as will fit on the command line, displays in keyword notation (depending on the system value). Even if all the parameters don't fit, the values are not lost and are shown on the entry fields if you ask for command prompting (F4) again. Figure 2.6 shows the result of pressing F9 after having successfully executed the CRTLIB command.

Figure 2.6
Results of Successfully
Executed CRTLIB
Command Retrieved
by F9

```
Main                            AS/400 Main Menu
                                                      System:   S1018A6G
  Select one of the following:

      1. User tasks
      2. Office tasks
      3. General system tasks
      4. Files, libraries, and folders
      5. Programming
      6. Communications
      7. Define or change the system
      8. Problem handling
      9. Display a menu
     10. User support and education
     11. PC Support tasks

     90. Sign off

  Selection or command
  ===> CRTLIB LIB(PAYROLL) TYPE(*TEST) TEXT('Payroll Development')

  F3=Exit     F4=Prompt     F9=Retrieve    F12=Cancel     F13=User support
  F23=Set initial menu
  Library PAYROLL created.
```

Positional Notation

You can execute a command without using keywords, and this is referred to as **positional notation**. When you use positional notation, the order in which parameters are specified is very important. Positional notation works as long as

- the values you enter for a particular parameter correspond exactly by position to the sequence of parameters as shown on the command prompt (or in the IBM *CL Reference* manual).

- you do not exceed the limit of positional parameters allowed for a particular command. (Each command has a maximum positional parameter attribute, which sets the limit for that command.)

To illustrate, if you want to create a test library named PAYROLL, you would need to supply the library name and the value *TEST for the Type parameter because *PROD is the default. Using positional notation, you would enter the command:

```
CRTLIB PAYROLL *TEST
```

But if you changed the order of parameter values without specifying keywords,

```
CRTLIB *TEST PAYROLL
```

the system would reject the command and issue an error message saying "Value '*TEST' for parameter LIB not a valid name." In other words, without the keywords, the system assumed that the value *TEST was for the first parameter, which is Library, not Type.

Likewise, if you try to create a production library named payroll with a text of "Production Lib" by entering the command

```
CRTLIB PAYROLL 'Production Lib'
```

the system would issue an error message saying "'Production Lib' not valid for parameter TYPE." If you add the default value for the Type parameter, thinking you could then get the values in the correct relative positions, you might enter

```
CRTLIB PAYROLL *PROD 'Production Lib'
```

but the system again would issue an error message saying "Number of positional parameters exceeds limit of 2" (see rule 2 above).

As you can see, using positional notation can be tricky. So what's the conclusion? In general, and especially until you get used to the commands and parameters you use frequently, you should rely on command prompting and just enter or change the parameter values you need on the entry field of the command prompt screen. Before long you will find it more convenient to simply type commands directly on a command line without prompting — particularly for those commands that use the defaults or require you to enter only a single parameter.

A *cautionary note*: Don't worry too much about all these abbreviations and commands — there's no need to try to memorize a long list of them. We cover specific commands in more detail when we need to introduce them in the text and labs. The most productive time to study them is when you will be using them. You will be able to recall commands you use often without much effort. But in case you're not convinced, the AS/400 has menus to help you find the commands you're looking for; and once you've found a command, you can easily get to a command prompt screen.

MENUS OF COMMANDS

AS/400 command menus are also organized hierarchically. The easiest way to get to the highest level of the command-menu hierarchy is simply by pressing the prompt key (F4) from any empty command line. Let's say you just signed on to the system and your cursor is sitting on the Main menu command line waiting for action. If you press function key F4, without typing in anything else, the screen shown in Figure 2.7 will appear.

Figure 2.7
Major Command
Groups Menu (MAJOR)

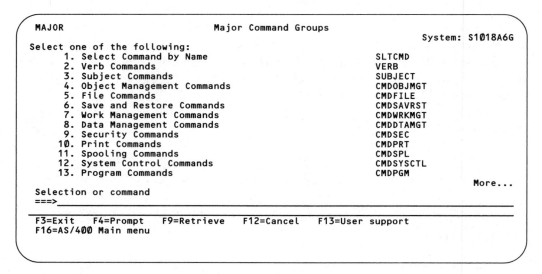

```
 MAJOR                      Major Command Groups
                                                             System: S1018A6G
 Select one of the following:
       1. Select Command by Name                 SLTCMD
       2. Verb Commands                          VERB
       3. Subject Commands                       SUBJECT
       4. Object Management Commands             CMDOBJMGT
       5. File Commands                          CMDFILE
       6. Save and Restore Commands             CMDSAVRST
       7. Work Management Commands               CMDWRKMGT
       8. Data Management Commands               CMDDTAMGT
       9. Security Commands                      CMDSEC
      10. Print Commands                         CMDPRT
      11. Spooling Commands                      CMDSPL
      12. System Control Commands                CMDSYSCTL
      13. Program Commands                       CMDPGM
                                                           More...
 Selection or command
 ===>_____

 F3=Exit   F4=Prompt    F9=Retrieve    F12=Cancel   F13=User support
 F16=AS/400 Main menu
```

This is a menu of major command groups whose proper name, as you can see, is MAJOR. This menu arranges its choices by broad categories so that if you wanted, for example, to peruse a list of all the verb or action commands, you could select option 2, Verb commands. Entering 2 on the command line of the MAJOR menu displays the first page of the Verb Commands menu (Figure 2.8).

Figure 2.8
Verb Commands
Menu (VERB)

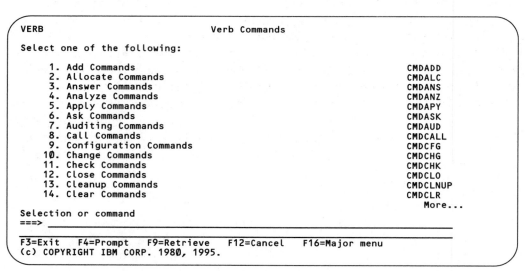

```
 VERB                          Verb Commands
 Select one of the following:

       1. Add Commands                           CMDADD
       2. Allocate Commands                      CMDALC
       3. Answer Commands                        CMDANS
       4. Analyze Commands                       CMDANZ
       5. Apply Commands                         CMDAPY
       6. Ask Commands                           CMDASK
       7. Auditing Commands                      CMDAUD
       8. Call Commands                          CMDCALL
       9. Configuration Commands                 CMDCFG
      10. Change Commands                        CMDCHG
      11. Check Commands                         CMDCHK
      12. Close Commands                         CMDCLO
      13. Cleanup Commands                       CMDCLNUP
      14. Clear Commands                         CMDCLR
                                                           More...
 Selection or command
 ===> _____
 F3=Exit   F4=Prompt   F9=Retrieve   F12=Cancel   F16=Major menu
 (c) COPYRIGHT IBM CORP. 1980, 1995.
```

The options displayed on the Verb Commands menu all lead to lower-level menus that contain all the possible commands (all the valid verb-modifier-noun combinations) for the selected verb.

As you can see by looking again at the options available from the Major Command Groups menu (Figure 2.7), there are also menus of commands grouped by Subject (noun), as well as by functional category (e.g., Work Management, Security, Print). The menu names of these latter categories, as well as of the lower-level menu choices from the VERB and SUBJECT menus, all begin with CMD; what follows is the verb, noun, or functional category abbreviation.

For example, if you want to see the different Clear commands available on the system, selecting option 14 from the VERB menu would take you to the Clear Commands (CMDCLR) menu shown in Figure 2.9.

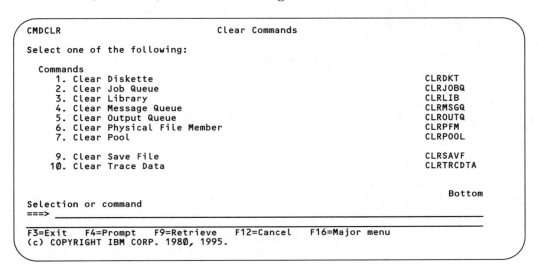

Figure 2.9
Clear Commands
Menu (CMDCLR)

From this menu, selecting the option for a specific command (e.g., 5 for Clear Output Queue) usually takes you to the command prompt screen for that command. So if you type 5 on the command line of the CMDCLR menu and press Enter, the Clear Output Queue (CLROUTQ) command prompt screen (Figure 2.10) appears.

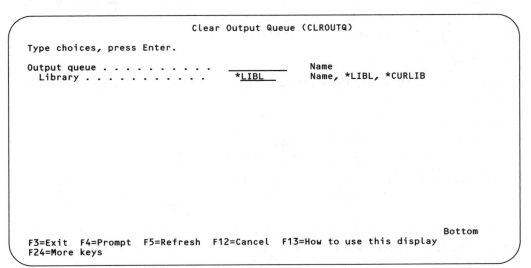

Figure 2.10
Clear Output Queue
(CLROUTQ) Command
Prompt Screen

This is a typical command-prompt entry screen. It shows the actual command name, CLROUTQ, at the top and has entry fields for parameter values. As you can see, the Output queue parameter requires you to name a value for the output queue object, and the Library parameter defaults to the predefined value *LIBL. Both contextual and extended Help are available from this screen.

Here are a few more examples showing how all commands related to a specified verb or noun (subject) can be displayed by a named menu:

Command Group	Menu name
Copy commands	CMDCPY
Display commands	CMDDSP
Work with commands	CMDWRK
Library commands	CMDLIB
Message commands	CMDMSG
Output queue commands	CMDOUTQ
User Profile commands	CMDUSRPRF

Menus of command groups are especially useful when you know an action (verb) you need to take but are not sure how to specify the noun to take it on, or, on the other hand, if you know the noun but are not sure how to specify the verb, or whether the intended verb is permitted for that noun.

THE GO COMMAND

You can get directly to any menu, including menus of command groups, by using the **GO command**. This command always has one required parameter, a menu name. For example, as the diagram in Figure 2.11 illustrates, if you want to go directly to the menu of Clear commands, without having to go through the menus MAJOR and VERB, you would enter the command

```
GO CMDCLR
```

on any command line and the CMDCLR menu would be displayed.

Figure 2.11
Getting to the Clear
Commands Menu

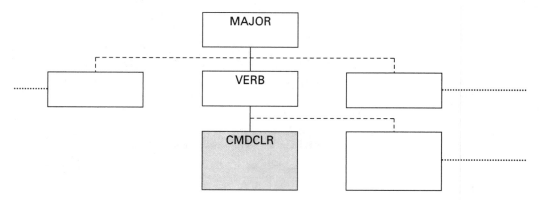

Instead of traversing the entire path, the GO command lets you take a shortcut to a known point along the path.

To see how this process works, let's suppose you want to check the current values of your user profile, but you are not sure which command to use. You can deduce from what we've already covered that the abbreviation for profile is likely to be PRF. So in this case, the shortest route would be to use the GO command to have the system list all commands related to profiles. On any command line you would simply type

GO CMDPRF

and press Enter. This action would result in display of the Profile Commands (CMDPRF) menu shown in Figure 2.12.

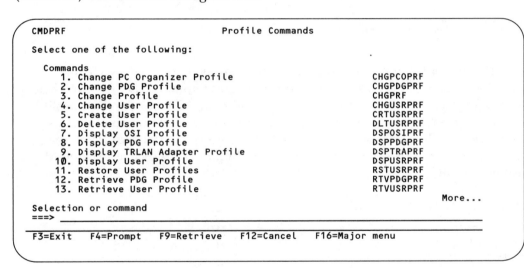

Figure 2.12

Profile commands Menu (CMDPRF)

From this menu, you can find the command you need, Display User Profile, which is option 10. Selecting option 10 takes you to the command prompt screen for the Display User Profile (DSPUSRPRF) command, as shown in Figure 2.13.

Figure 2.13
Display User Profile
Command Prompt
Screen

```
                        Display User Profile (DSPUSRPRF)

 Type choices, press Enter.

 User profile . . . . . . . . . .    _____    Name, generic*, *ALL
 Type of information . . . . . .    *BASIC__     *BASIC, *ALL, *CMDAUT...
 Output . . . . . . . . . . . . .   *_____     *, *PRINT, *OUTFILE




                                                                  Bottom
 F3=Exit  F4=Prompt  F5=Refresh  F12=Cancel  F13=How to use this display
 F24=More keys
```

This screen requires that you enter a user profile name and shows default values for two parameters — Type (*BASIC) and Output (*). Let's assume that you would take the default values for Type and Output. As for the User profile name, unless you have security administrator authority, the only valid value is your own user profile name. So if user JSMITH were to type in her own ID on the entry field and press Enter, the Display User Profile — Basic screen (Figure 2.14) would appear.

Figure 2.14
Display User Profile –
Basic Screen

```
                        Display User Profile - Basic
 User profile . . . . . . . . . . . . . . . . . :   JSMITH

 Previous sign-on . . . . . . . . . . . . . . :   01/17/98   12:58:40
 Sign-on attempts not valid . . . . . . . . . :   0
 Status . . . . . . . . . . . . . . . . . . . :   *ENABLED
 Date password last changed . . . . . . . . . :   01/11/98
 Password expiration interval . . . . . . . . :   *SYSVAL
 Set password to expired . . . . . . . . . . :   *NO
 User class . . . . . . . . . . . . . . . . . :   *PGMR
 Special authority . . . . . . . . . . . . . :   *NONE
 Group profile . . . . . . . . . . . . . . . :   *NONE
 Owner  . . . . . . . . . . . . . . . . . . . :   *USRPRF
 Group authority . . . . . . . . . . . . . . :   *NONE
 Group authority type . . . . . . . . . . . . :   *PRIVATE
 Supplemental groups . . . . . . . . . . . . :   *NONE
 Assistance level . . . . . . . . . . . . . . :   *SYSVAL
 Current library  . . . . . . . . . . . . . . :   *CRTDFT
                                                                  More...
 Press Enter to continue.

 F3=Exit   F12=Cancel
 (c) COPYRIGHT IBM CORP. 1980, 1995.
```

This screen shows a user the current values of his/her user profile; the password never appears, not even when the security officer executes the command. For any display such as this, even though it's an information display, you can get field Help about the meaning of parameters or extended Help about the command or display.

LIBRARY LISTS

When you need to use any system object or some object you have created (e.g., to read data from a data file), the system searches for that object in your **library list**. A library list is the definition of the path of libraries a job searches when trying to find programs, files, or other AS/400 objects named in a command. You have seen a reference to the library list in several commands you have already examined. In the common case of an object name being required as a parameter (e.g., for the CPYF command's From file parameter) the library part of the object name typically defaults to *LIBL, which means the library list of that job.

A library list is created for each job, usually from system values, and also from the user profile's Current library value when the user profile is activated at sign-on. An interactive job's library list contains the names of a limited number of libraries to which a user needs access, and the library list can be modified by various CL commands. A library list consists of four parts (Table 2.2):

Table 2.2

The Library List

Part of Library List	Examples of Content
System (up to 15)	QSYS
	QHLPSYS
	QUSRSYS
Product (none, 1, or 2)	QPDA
	QRPG
Current (1 only)	JSMITH (created by programmer J. Smith)
User (up to 25)	QGPL
	QTEMP
	PAYLIB (a user library for payroll programs)

System Library List

The **system library list** contains up to 15 libraries the system needs to operate; you usually won't modify the system library list. You can determine which libraries will be placed in the system portion of your library list by looking at the system value QSYSLIBL. Previously, you used menus to get to a Work with System Values screen, but let's try a shortcut. Because you know the name of the system value you're looking for, you can use the DSPSYSVAL (Display System Value) command.

If you prompt for DSPSYSVAL command parameters, you see that the only two are System value and Output. System value is required, and Output has a default value of *. To check the possibilities for the Output parameter, you would move the cursor to the Output field line and press the Help key. The screen shown in Figure 2.15 would appear.

Figure 2.15
Field Help for Output
Parameter of
DSPSYSVAL Command

```
                           Display System Value (DSPSYSVAL)
   Type choices, press Enter.

   System value . . . . . . . . . .                QABNORMSW, QACGLVL...
   Output . . . . . . . . . . . . .      *         *, *PRINT
                      .................................................
                      :                Output (OUTPUT) - Help                 :
                      :  Specifies where the output from the command is sent.  :
                      :                                                        :
                      :  The possible values are:                             :
                      :                                                        :
                      :  *                                                     :
                      :      The output is displayed (if requested by an       :
                      :      interactive job) or printed with the job's spooled :
                      :      output (if requested by a batch job).             :
                      :  *PRINT                                                :
                      :                                                  More... :
                      :  F2=Extended help   F10=Move to top   F11=InfoSeeker  :
     F3=Exit    F4=  :  F12=Cancel          F20=Enlarge       F24=More keys   :
   F24=More keys    :.................................................:
```

As the Help text indicates, the * means that the output of the display command would go to your workstation screen. Now, if you enter the system value QSYSLIBL on the DSPSYSVAL command prompt screen, an information screen like that shown in Figure 2.16 appears.

Figure 2.16
Display System Value
Information Screen

```
                           Display System Value
   System value . . . . . :   QSYSLIBL
   Description  . . . . . :   System part of the library list

   Sequence                              Sequence
   number    Library                     number    Library
       0
      10      QSYS
      20      QSYS2
      30      QHLPSYS
      40      QUSRSYS




                                                              Bottom
   Press Enter to continue.

   F3=Exit    F12=Cancel
```

If your computer's system value for QSYSLIBL has been changed from the shipped values, the display might have some additional libraries in the list. But the shipped system libraries should include

- QSYS — Contains essential system objects, such as system programs and commands, as well as pointers to all other libraries
- QHLPSYS — Contains all the Help information for different screens, including the Search Index information
- QUSRSYS — Contains other IBM-supplied objects needed for various system functions

Product Library

The the operating system inserts the **product library** when it is needed for some task the user has requested. For example, if a user requests compilation of an RPG program, the library containing the necessary translator programs, QRPG, is inserted as a product library during the compile process and then removed when it is finished. The operating system handles this adding and removing of the appropriate product libraries automatically, and no operator intervention is needed.

Current Library

The **current library** is the default library into which newly created objects are placed. When a current library is specified, it follows the product library in the list. The current library is significant because it is searched before other user libraries when an object is requested.

It is helpful for each user to have his/her own library to keep track of test files, programs, screen layouts, query reports, and so on. Having individual libraries prevents conflicts with other users about object names because every object of the same type must have a unique name within a single library. In the lab for this lesson, you create a library and then assign that library as your current library by changing the value of the user profile's Current library parameter. Once this is done, all objects you create will go into your library automatically, unless you specify otherwise.

User Library List

The **user library list** names the libraries that organize the programs, screens, data files, and applications users need to do business on the system; the user library list can contain up to 25 library names. Because different users perform different types of work and have different requirements, the user library list can be customized for each user or for several users with similar needs. You can customize the user library list by running an initial startup program at sign-on or by executing CL commands when needed as the job, either batch or interactive, runs. Normally, many different users need to share objects in user libraries; objects in the current library tend to belong to and are used by an individual.

For most jobs, several IBM-supplied libraries, which begin with the letter Q, are also included in the user list. These libraries are specified in the QUSRLIBL system value and normally include at least QTEMP and QGPL.

Objects within Libraries

You should now understand the following about the relationship among objects, libraries, and library lists:

1. When objects are created, they must be placed "in" (associated with) a library. This association is logical — object storage locations are assigned by the system; objects are not physically stored within a library area on disk.

2. Unless you specify otherwise, most new objects are placed in the current library, if one is designated for the job. (There are a few object types that are always created in QSYS.)

3. If no current library is designated, a default IBM-supplied user library is used.

4. Unless you specify otherwise, the library list is searched for requested objects. This is the meaning of *LIBL as the Library value for an object name in a CL command.

5. The library list is searched in the following order: system library list, product library, current library, and user library list. Individual libraries are searched in the order specified on the library list, from top to bottom.

6. The needs of the individual user determine the libraries included in the user library list.

7. Every individual user on the system may have a unique, personally tailored library list; but more commonly, groups of users with similar work requirements have the same or similar library list with, perhaps, only the current library being unique.

We examine these library list concepts again, and in more detail, in the following lessons, and you apply them in lab exercises from this lesson on.

Key Terms

current library

GO command

keyword notation

library list

parameter keyword

positional notation

product library

syntax

system library list

user library list

INTRODUCTION

This lab concentrates on some basic skills that every programmer, operator, or technical user often needs. As you work through the lab you become more familiar with online Help for getting information about a display or input field. You use the GO command to get to a command menu and to shortcut a menu path. You create a library and modify your user profile using the CHGPRF (Change Profile) command. You display and change your library list. You also change the password of your user profile.

Lab 2

Part 1

Goals	Use Help to get information about a display
Start at	MAIN menu
Procedure	Press the Help key from an empty command line or other non-sensitive area of the Main menu

1.1   If you are not already signed on, sign on as before using your first initial plus last name (up to 10 characters total) as User. Remember that the Field exit key jumps you down to the beginning of the next entry field when you are finished entering characters on the current line. For Password, type your user ID again. Ignore the last three entries and press Enter. At this time you should see the Main menu display.

When the cursor is not on a particular item in a menu list, general (extended) Help about the screen itself is available just by pressing the Help key. Because the cursor is now on the command line, press the Help key from there to get extended Help.

1.2.   You should now see the first of the AS/400 Main Menu — Help screens, as shown in Figure 2.17. This series of screens contains useful information about function keys and the GO command discussed in the text. It also describes the range of operations available with each Main menu choice. Hypertext links are provided for additional information about the high-lighted topics.

Lab 2

Read through the Main menu Help screens and answer the following questions on the answer sheet:

1.2a. Which command key (function key) pulls up the last command run from the command line?

1.2b. Which menu option would you use to change your password?

1.2c. Which main menu option(s) would you use to display the status of a device?

1.2d. Which option(s) would you use to display the history log?

1.2e. Which option would let you work with the hardware resources of the system?

1.2f. What would you enter to show a list of menus related to both programming and problem handling? (Read carefully "How to use a Menu.")

Figure 2.17
AS/400 Main Menu –
Help

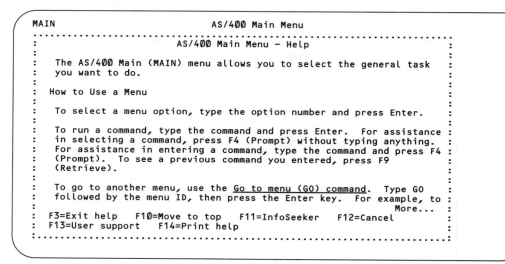

```
MAIN                        AS/400 Main Menu
...............................................................
:                     AS/400 Main Menu – Help                  :
:                                                              :
:  The AS/400 Main (MAIN) menu allows you to select the general task  :
:  you want to do.                                             :
:                                                              :
:  How to Use a Menu                                           :
:                                                              :
:   To select a menu option, type the option number and press Enter.  :
:                                                              :
:   To run a command, type the command and press Enter.  For assistance  :
:   in selecting a command, press F4 (Prompt) without typing anything.  :
:   For assistance in entering a command, type the command and press F4  :
:   (Prompt).  To see a previous command you entered, press F9  :
:   (Retrieve).                                                :
:                                                              :
:   To go to another menu, use the Go to menu (GO) command.  Type GO  :
:   followed by the menu ID, then press the Enter key.  For example, to  :
:                                                    More...   :
:  F3=Exit help    F10=Move to top    F11=InfoSeeker    F12=Cancel  :
:  F13=User support    F14=Print help                         :
:..............................................................:
```

When you are finished, return to the Main menu.

1.3. If you have questions about a certain menu selection, you could move the cursor to that area on the screen before pressing Help, as you did on entry fields of a command prompt screen. This would give you contextual, or field-sensitive, Help. Now move the cursor up to the line for option 6 (Communications) and press Help to see how this option is used. Return to the Main menu.

1.4. Move the cursor back to the command line. You could use the new line key on this screen, or F9 will move the cursor there directly, recalling the previous command if there was one.

Lab 2

Part 2

Goals	Access a menu using the GO command; display your user profile
Start at	MAIN menu
Procedure	Enter GO CMDPRF
	Select the option for CHGPRF
	Use context-sensitive Help

2.1   As you have learned, the GO command can be used to get directly to a menu. To get additional information about using this command, type GO on the command line, then press Help.

Use the GO command Help to answer the following question, then return to the Main menu.

2.1a. What is the difference between a "special value" and a "generic name"?

2.2.   We can also use the GO command to take us to a menu of related commands. From this menu we can select the specific command we need and then prompt for parameters.

The format of this command requires GO CMDxxx where xxx is the verb portion of the command or the noun subject on which the command will perform its action. To see a menu of the various profile commands, for example, type GO CMDPRF on the command line, then press Enter. Please do that now.

2.2a. How many different user profile commands are there?

2.3   If we want a description of any of these commands, we could move the cursor to the selection and press Help or just type the selection number on the command line, then press Help. Using this technique, study the command descriptions of the CHGPRF (Change Profile) and CHGUSRPRF (Change User Profile) commands.

2.3a. What are two essential differences between the CHGPRF and CHG-USRPRF commands?

2.4.   You can run (execute) any of the commands from the menu either by typing the command itself or by entering its option number on the command line. For example, select the Change Profile command (not Change User Profile) by entering its option number on the command line, then pressing Enter.

2.5. You should now be looking at the prompt screen for the CHGPRF command (Figure 2.18).

Figure 2.18

Change Profile
Command Prompt
Screen

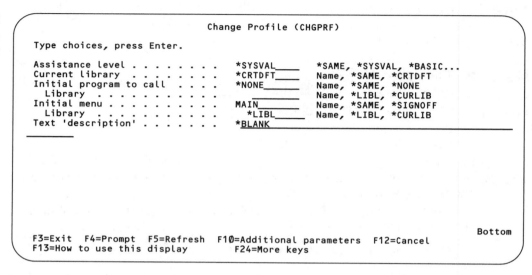

```
                            Change Profile (CHGPRF)

 Type choices, press Enter.

 Assistance level . . . . . . . .   *SYSVAL____    *SAME, *SYSVAL, *BASIC...
 Current library  . . . . . . . .   *CRTDFT____    Name, *SAME, *CRTDFT
 Initial program to call  . . . .   *NONE_____    Name, *SAME, *NONE
   Library  . . . . . . . . . .    _____    Name, *LIBL, *CURLIB
 Initial menu . . . . . . . . . .   MAIN_____    Name, *SAME, *SIGNOFF
   Library  . . . . . . . . . .     *LIBL_____    Name, *LIBL, *CURLIB
 Text 'description' . . . . . . .   *BLANK_____

 _____




                                                                     Bottom
 F3=Exit  F4=Prompt  F5=Refresh  F10=Additional parameters  F12=Cancel
 F13=How to use this display       F24=More keys
```

Although you reached this screen by going to a menu of related commands, you could also have gotten here by entering the command itself, CHGPRF, and then requesting prompting (F4) from any command line.

2.5a. What is listed as your current library?

2.5b. With the Current library parameter value as it is, what actual library will be used as your default current library?

2.6. Exit Help, returning to the Change Profile screen. Study the entries on this screen.

2.6a. According to the screen, which menu will you first see after signing on?

2.6b. If you wanted to go directly to the Programming menu (option 5 on the Main menu) after signing on, what would you change this parameter value to? (Remember how a menu is identified?)

Part 3

Goals	Change your user profile Obtain additional message text Create a user library
Start at	CHGPRF command prompt
Procedure	Change the CURLIB parameter Press Help on the message line Create your library (CRTLIB)
Caution	Complete Part 3 entirely before signing off. If you change your profile and don't create the new library with the same name as the CURLIB parameter value, your normal sign-on procedure will fail. You will need to enter QGPL for the Current Library field of the sign-on screen.

3.1. If you have just signed back on at this time, type CHGPRF on the command line and press F4 to prompt. This should bring you to the Change Profile command prompt screen shown in Figure 2.18.

We would like each student to have his/her own library in which to store objects created during the course, so let's try to change the value of Current library to a library with the same name as your user name (sign-on User ID). Normally you would create the library before changing the user profile, but we have chosen this sequence to examine the system's response and practice getting additional text of a system message.

With the cursor on the Current library entry field, type your user name (first initial and last name) over the default value. Remember the asterisk (*) in *CRTDFT is part of the default special value and must be typed over when you change the value. Press the Field exit key if your name is shorter. Notice that if your first initial plus last name exceeds 10 characters, the cursor jumps down to the next entry field; if so, be careful not to erase anything by over typing. Now press Enter.

3.1a. What does the message at the bottom of the screen say?

3.2. When a message is not clear, or you aren't sure how to respond, the AS/400 Help feature will once again prove useful. Move the cursor to the message line and press the Help key. The Additional Message Information display (Figure 2.19) should appear on your screen.

This type of information screen identifies a message by an ID, a type, date and time sent, and severity code. Severity level 00 is the lowest level, an informational or warning message. The message type means it does not require a response. Also some explanation is given about the cause, and steps to take for recovery are provided.

Figure 2.19
Additional Message Information for CPI2243

```
                        Additional Message Information

Message ID . . . . . . :    CPI2243       Severity . . . . . . . :    00
Message type . . . . . :    Information
Date sent  . . . . . . :    01/11/98      Time sent  . . . . . . :    20:23:39

Message . . . . :    Object JSMITH in library QSYS not found.
Cause . . . . . :    Object JSMITH in library QSYS type *LIB was not found.
  The object is referenced in user profile JSMITH.  The object name or library
  name may be incorrect.  If the library name is not specified, the object may
  be in a library that is not contained in the library list.
Recovery  . . . :    Change the object name or library name using the Change
  User Profile (CHGUSRPRF) or Change Profile (CHGPRF command), or create the
  object in the specified library.




                                                                       Bottom
Press Enter to continue.

F3=Exit    F6=Print   F9=Display message details
F10=Display messages in job log   F12=Cancel   F21=Select assistance level
```

In this case, the system is trying to tell you that your change-profile request, although granted, does not really make sense because the library you would like to make current cannot be found (i.e., the library name is misspelled or the library does not exist as an object in QSYS, the system library).

The Recovery information indicates that you should check the spelling of the library name you used for the Current library value. But, in this case, it is not that the library name was misspelled; the library simply hasn't been created yet. So you need to take the second piece of advice from Recovery, and create it.

3.3. Exit Help, then press F3 if necessary to return to the Main menu. Select option 4 and press Enter. This will take you to the Files, Libraries, and Folders menu.

From the Files, Libraries, and Folders menu (DATA), select option 2, Libraries, and press Enter. From the Library menu, select the option to create a library and press Enter.

You have just used the menu selection path to arrive at a command prompt screen.

3.3a. What is the actual command name?

It is important to realize that instead of reaching this screen through the menu path, you could have typed the command itself (assuming you knew it) on any command line, then pressed F4 for prompting.

3.4. When keying the following parameter values, remember not to press Enter until you have completed the command prompt screen and are ready to run the command.

Type your user name (as for sign-on) as the value for Library name. When you enter a parameter shorter than the maximum length of the input field, the Field exit key moves the cursor ahead to the next field. Then change Library type to *TEST by over typing the default value. For Text description, type in your full name and the course name (e.g., "Jane M. Smith, Intro AS/400"). Remember, you don't need to type the quotation marks. Now press Enter.

3.4a. To which screen have you returned?

3.4b. What is displayed on the message line at the bottom?

Part 4

Goals	Display your library list Change your library list's current library
Start at	LIBRARY menu
Procedure	Execute the DSPLIBL command Execute the CHGLIBL command

4.1. Now you have changed your user profile and created a library. Let's see whether that library has been activated yet. You should be looking at the Libraries menu now (Figure 2.20).

```
  LIBRARY                      Libraries
                                               System:    S1018A6G
    Select one of the following:

        1. Work with libraries
        2. Create a library
        3. Save a library
        4. Restore a library

       50. Save library members in System/36 format
       51. Restore library members from System/36 format

       70. Related commands




    Selection or command
    ===> _____

    F3=Exit    F4=Prompt    F9=Retrieve    F12=Cancel    F13=Information Assistant
    F16=AS/400 Main menu
```

Figure 2.20

Libraries Menu (LIBRARY)

Lab 2

4.1a. If you were not at the screen shown in Figure 2.20, what action would you take from any command line to get there?

4.2. The Library menu doesn't really include library list commands, although you could get to them by selecting option 70, Related commands. Instead, let's try going directly to a menu of library list commands by entering GO CMDLIBL on the command line.

You should now be looking at a screen similar to the one shown in Figure 2.21.

Figure 2.21
Library List
Commands Menu
(CMDLIBL)

```
CMDLIBL                    Library List Commands

Select one of the following:

   Commands
      1. Add Library List Entry                              ADDLIBLE
      2. Add Project Library List                            ADDPRJLIBL
      3. Change Library List                                 CHGLIBL
      4. Change System Library List                          CHGSYSLIBL
      5. Display Library List                                DSPLIBL
      6. Edit Library List                                   EDTLIBL
      7. Remove Library List Entry                           RMVLIBLE
      8. Remove Project Library List                         RMVPRJLIBL

   Related Command Menus
      9. Library Commands                                    CMDLIB

                                                             Bottom

Selection or command
===> _____

F3=Exit   F4=Prompt   F9=Retrieve   F12=Cancel   F16=Major menu
(c) COPYRIGHT IBM CORP. 1980, 1995.
```

4.3. The library list (*LIBL) contains the names of a limited subset of libraries the system will check one after another to find an object you wish to work with. This feature saves having to specify the particular library in which the object is stored whenever you need to reference it, letting you use only the object's simple name.

First, let's display your library list by taking the option to Display Library List from the CMDLIBL menu. Let the Output parameter default to display (*), and run the command (press Enter).

4.3a. How many libraries are currently in your library list?
4.3b. Is the library you just created on the list?

Unless you have signed off and back on again since Step 3.4, you should not find your new library on the library list. When you change the Current library parameter of your user profile, it doesn't immediately change the library list of the current job; the change takes effect the next time you sign on.

To get your newly created test library into the library list, you can use one of several commands to change the library list during your interactive job.

4.4. Return to the CMDLIBL menu. Now find the command to change your library list and enter its option number on the command line.

You should now be looking at a CHGLIBL (Change Library List) command prompt screen similar to the one shown in Figure 2.22.

```
                    Change Library List (CHGLIBL)

 Type choices, press Enter.

 Libraries for current job  . . .   ALLUSER___   Name, *SAME, *NONE
                                    QGPL_____
              + for more values    QTEMP_____
 Current library . . . . . . . .   *CRTDFT      Name, *SAME, *CRTDFT








                                                               Bottom
 F3=Exit  F4=Prompt  F5=Refresh  F12=Cancel  F13=How to use this display
 F24=More keys
```

Figure 2.22
Change Library List
Command Prompt
Screen

4.5. From this screen, you can add or remove libraries from the Libraries for current job parameter.

4.5a. Use Help to find out which part of the library list is affected by changes to this parameter value.

An additional parameter lets us change the current library.

4.5b. What is the keyword for this parameter? (Can you remember the function key that toggles between choices and keywords?)

Tab or new line down (don't use the Field exit key) to the Current library parameter and type your new library name, erasing the default value, then press Enter.

Unless you misspelled your library name, you should be back at the CMDLIBL menu with the message "Current library changed to ..." displayed on the message line.

4.6. Now press F9 twice to retrieve the DSPLIBL (Display Library List) command, then run the command (press Enter). You should see your library, designated current library (list type is CUR). If this is not so, review Part 3 to create your library and/or Step 4.5 to change your library list.

Before going on, you must be sure that your test library has been added to your library list.

4.7. Recall from the text that a library list can comprise four list types: system, product, current, and user. But not all library list types are always present in a particular library list.

4.7a. Record on the answer sheet all libraries in your library list that belong to each library list type.

4.7b. Which type is not represented in your list, and why do you suppose that is so?

When you have finished recording your library list information, press F3 until you have returned to the Main menu.

Part 5

Goals	Change your user profile's password
Start at	USER menu
Procedure	Select the option to Change Password from the USER menu
	Type your old password
	Type your new password twice; press Enter

5.1. Now that you have created a library and made it your current library, it may be time to establish a little security over your work environment. Because most installations standardize on some form of a user's name as the user profile identification, the User part of the sign-on requirement (the user-profile name) would not be hard to figure out, so you don't want to leave your password at the same value for very long.

The password, like other AS/400 names, can be from one to 10 alpha characters — including the special characters @, #, and $ — or numbers (but it cannot begin with a number). For security purposes it is better to use a moderately long password — not just one or two characters — and to avoid easily discovered personal names such as those of your spouse, children, or pets.

Because the security of a user profile is in many cases extremely important, the AS/400 has a number of security system values that limit password format and use. For example, the same password may be limited to a certain minimum or maximum length, may not use repeating characters, and may not be able to be used twice within a set number of changes.

A good candidate for a password would be some personal or technical term, perhaps in a foreign language. Being a potter who studied in Japan, I, for example, use the Japanese names of some of my favorite stoneware and porcelain glazes. These are not passwords the average hacker would be likely to hit upon.

It is easy to change your password, and some installations require that you do so regularly. In fact, this policy can be enforced by setting the system value QPWDEXPITV, or password expiration interval, to the number of days for which passwords are valid.

But one thing you should remember about passwords is that if you change yours and then forget it, nobody can find it for you. Passwords are not made available to anyone on the system, regardless of special authority. Not even the system security officer can find out your password, should you forget it. But if you do get in a jam, (s)he can change your user profile to recognize a different password so you can get back on the system.

5.2. To change your password, first select User tasks from the Main menu. Then, from the USER menu, select option 8 to change your password.

This takes you to the Change Password screen, Figure 2.23.

```
                          Change Password
Password last changed . . . . . . . . . . :    01/22/98

Type choices, press Enter.

  Current password  . . . . . . . . . . . .

  New password  . . . . . . . . . . . . .

  New password (to verify)  . . . . . . . .




F3=Exit                    F12=Cancel
```

Figure 2.23

Change Password Screen with Cursor on Current Password

The cursor will be positioned on the Current password entry field, but you can't see the field entry area and nothing you key on this screen will be displayed. Don't press the Enter key until you are finished. Type in your current password and press the Field exit key.

The system asks for your current password so that someone else can't change your password if you happen to leave your workstation for a short time without signing off.

The cursor should now be on the entry field for New password. Carefully type your new password, then press the Field exit key. Now repeat your new password on the New password (to verify) line, then press Enter.

If all goes well, you should be back at the USER menu and the message "Password changed successfully" should be displayed. If not, you may get a message on the Change Password screen saying "New password and verify password not the same." If this happens, try again, and be sure to key in the new password accurately on both lines. When you have changed your password, return to the Main menu and sign off.

Mastering the AS/400, Second Edition

Lab 2 Answer Sheet

Name: _____

Date Due: _____   Class Time: _____

1.2a. _____F9_____   1.2b. _____Option 1 user post (8)_____   1.2c. _____3_____

1.2d. _____8_____   1.2e. _____7_____   1.2f. _____GO PR* PRO*_____

2.1a. _____Specific value is preceded by an * a generic value is followed by an *_____

2.2a. _____21_____

2.3a. _____CHGPRF only allows you to chg some of the values_____

_____

2.5a. _____   2.5b. _____

2.6a. _____main_____   2.6b. _____Program_____

3.1a. _____

3.3a. _____

3.4a. _____

3.4b. _____

4.1a. _____

4.3a. _____   4.3b. _____

4.5a. _____   4.5b. _____

4.7a. Libraries   List type

_____   _____

_____   _____

_____   _____

_____   _____

4.7b. _____

_____

IN SUMMARY

In this lab, you have used both extended Help and field Help to answer questions about menu choices and command parameters. You should not hesitate to use Help in the future whenever a question arises or you need more information than the lab exercise provides.

You have also found out how to change your user profile, display additional message information, create a library, display your library list, and change your library list. The library list is an important concept on the AS/400. It is used to efficiently locate requested objects and can be changed to accommodate the needs of a job. For user applications, the current library is most important, not only because it is searched before other libraries in the user library list, but also because it is used for newly created objects unless we specify otherwise. You will be expected to identify and describe the following commands: GO, CHGPRF, CRTLIB, DSPLIBL, and CHGLIBL.

Lesson 3

Objects

Lesson Overview

One of the most important architectural concepts of the AS/400 is that of objects. Objects are the internal structures on which the instruction set of the AS/400 operates. Almost every named entity on the AS/400 is an object: these objects include libraries, source files, commands, programs, database files, user profiles, authorization lists, device descriptions, and many more. Hardware devices are not objects, but all hardware devices that can be used by applications and OS/400, such as display devices, printers, tape drives, and diskettes, are described to the system by device-description type objects that define their operational characteristics.

In this lesson we see how objects are identified on the AS/400 (e.g., library, name, and type) and we examine where objects are stored when they are created and how they are located when requested. We also introduce a few library list commands that can help ensure that the system can find an object. And finally, we introduce the concept of spooling and examine how output queues work with spoolers to manage printed reports created by users.

Objectives

Students will be able to

✓ List several advantages of object-based computer systems

✓ Explain the purpose of object types and list several common ones

✓ Describe how the system uses a library list to locate a requested object

✓ Demonstrate the use of a qualified name to reference an object

✓ Use the CHGLIBL (Change Library List) and EDTLIBL (Edit Library List) commands to change the order of user libraries in a library list

✓ Explain the importance of spooling

✓ Describe the function of an output queue

✓ Determine where spooled output goes by examining user profile, device description, and job description entries

THE AS/400 OBJECT-BASED ARCHITECTURE

On the AS/400, all **objects** are encapsulated. That is, objects are protected by an outer layer, or interface, that identifies the object and specifies the operations that can be performed on the object. Applications and OS/400 relate to an object through this interface and never deal with hardware-specific details.

Such details are handled by low-level **licensed internal code** instructions, which are translated across the machine interface (MI) from the application programs and OS/400 instructions above (Figure 3.1). This licensed internal code is created by IBM and is specific to the AS/400. The internal code translates object-based instructions of the "**logical machine**" (i.e., application programs and OS/400) into low-level machine instructions that drive the system processor and other hardware of the "**physical machine.**"

Figure 3.1

AS/400 Layered Machine Architecture (IMPI Model)

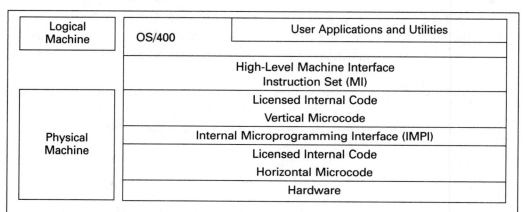

MI is object oriented. Vertical microcode provides OS functions such as I/O support and storage management; also translates MI instructions into IMPI. IMPI instructions handle security, database integrity, task management and other functions as well as traditional computation and branching operations. They are translated by Horizontal microcode into Control words that drive the system processor and hardware.

As you can see from Figure 3.1, an action requested on an object (e.g., by a CL command) is passed through the machine interface and converted into licensed internal code before it is effected in the hardware. This **high-level machine interface** layer serves the very useful purpose of insulating the logical machine from the physical machine so that programs are not dependent on the hardware.

This translation of the high-level machine instruction set by licensed internal code to carry out hardware operations is called **Layered Machine Architecture**.

The lower levels of microcode "know" the details of the hardware, and the microcode must be updated whenever new hardware is added to the system. Operating system upgrades from one version and release to another accomplish this task. But existing applications and OS/400 deal with hardware only through the MI and so are not directly affected by changes in the hardware. The high-level machine interface makes the AS/400 a hardware-independent platform, able to take advantage of new technology without causing problems for existing applications. This independence also protects the knowledge investment of programmers and users because the screens they use to do their work at the level of the logical machine may change only slightly even though massively significant changes may occur at the hardware level. The change to 64-bit Power PC RISC processors in the new AS/400s is a case in point. Software written for the older 48-bit CISC processors is quickly converted without recompilation (in most cases) and runs as true 64-bit software on the new RISC boxes — with no need for slowed-down emulation or costly rewrites — even though, at the processor hardware level (as well as many other hardware components), the AS/400 is an entirely different machine!

The vertical and horizontal microcode layers of the CISC processors have been rewritten as System Licensed Internal Code (SLIC) with an object-based kernel on the new RISC-powered AS/400s. New code (more than 1 million lines of the total, which exceeds 2.5 million lines of code below the MI) was written in C++, providing all the benefits of object-oriented programming such as code reuse, error reduction, and efficiency. The old HLMI has been renamed TIMI, Technology Independent Machine Interface.

The new Advanced Series and Advanced Server RISC-power AS/400s are the first computer systems to have completed the transition to true 64-bit computing. The ability of the AS/400 to adapt so quickly to take advantage of new technology makes the AS/400 virtually obsolescence proof! Certainly the AS/400 of today is a far cry from the first AS/400s, with modern hardware components dramatically smaller, faster, denser, less expensive and consuming less electrical power than their predecessors. And the AS/400 of tomorrow will be a very different machine from that of today. And yet software written 10 years ago for the earliest B and C series machines still runs on the most current RISC boxes, only a whole lot faster! What a great return on software development costs, not to mention the investment made by programmers to master their skills.

Besides program-hardware independence, the AS/400's object-based design has other advantages over conventional architecture: it provides a consistent approach to object management and security, protection against inadvertent misuse of an object, and the ability to reference an object by its simple name.

Because programs do not deal directly with hardware and are therefore not concerned with physical storage addresses, all storage on the AS/400, both main and secondary, is treated as a single homogenous mass called single-level storage. When objects are created, they are written to this **single-level storage** and are assigned a permanent virtual address that is placed in a pointer managed by the library in which the object "resides." This virtual storage address will not be reused during the life of the system, even after the object itself has been deleted. An address translation algorithm at the microcode level provides efficient, direct addressing of the object in real memory. Real memory management (both main and secondary) become functions of the internal code and not of the applications. Among other advantages, this allows the same object to be shared by different jobs concurrently.

TYPES OF AS/400 OBJECTS

All objects are categorized by **type**. An object's type defines its purpose and how it can be used on the system (e.g., the operations that can be performed on the object). OS/400 provides more than 40 object types that encompass all applications and system resources including programs, data, and hardware. IBM can add new object types as required.

Table 3.1 lists a few common types of objects and the object-type special values (beginning with *) that identify them. When you create an object you give it a name, but the object type is assigned by the system. The command you use to create the object indicates the object's type. For example, the command CRTUSRPRF (Create User Profile) indicates object type *USRPRF; the command CRTLIB (Create Library) indicates object type *LIB.

Table 3.1

Common AS/400 Object Types

Object Type	Object Description	Attribute (Subtype)
*AUTL	Authorization List	
*CMD	Command	
*DEVD	Device Description	
*FILE	File	PF Physical File
		LF Logical File
		DSPF Display File
		PRTF Printer File
*JOBD	Job Description	
*LIB	Library	
*OUTQ	Output Queue	
*PGM	Program (executable)	Tells source language (e.g., CBL, RPG, CLP)
*QRYDFN	Query Definition	
*USRPRF	User Profile	

Some CL commands work with any type of object, but each type of object has certain CL commands that can be used only for that type. For example, DSPOBJD (Display Object Description) works for objects of any type, but DSPUSRPRF (Display User Profile) works only for a *USRPRF type object.

When an object is created, it "goes into" a **library**. It is important to realize that a library is not a physical collection of objects, but a directory to a group of related objects. Libraries can be used to organize objects by owner, by application category (i.e., all HR files and programs), or for security purposes. A library provides a logical reference to objects using address pointers. In addition to address pointers, the type and authorization of each object is associated with the library entry for that object. In this way, when you request an object by name, the system — when it finds a matching object name in a library — can determine whether the object type is appropriate for the request and whether you are authorized to use the object.

REQUESTING AN OBJECT

When you request an object, either by selecting a menu option or by entering a command, it usually is not necessary to specify the name of the library in which the object resides because when you specify a **simple object name** (i.e., up to a 10-character name without a library reference), the system searches the job's current library list from top to bottom to locate an object matching the name and with a type appropriate for the request.

For example, let's say you want to use the CALL command to execute a program. The CALL command's only required parameter is the name of the program; so if you want to run a program named ACTCUS (to list all active accounts in a customer file), you would enter the command

```
CALL ACTCUS
```

on a command line.

If your library list looks like the one shown in Table 3.2, the system will find program ACTCUS in library ARLIB and execute it (assuming you have the authority).

Notice that although an object named ACTCUS exists in library MYLIB, which is higher in the library list, the system ignores it because its object type is *FILE, the wrong type for the command. The only valid object type for a CALL command is *PGM. By including the object type in the library entry the system

Table 3.2

Example of a Library Search

Direction of Search	Part of Library List	Library	Contains Object	Object Type
↓	System	QSYS QHLPSYS QUSRSYS	... ...	
	Current	MYLIB	ACTCUS PROGA FILEB ...	*FILE *PGM *FILE
	User	ARLIB	FILEM ACTCUS ...	*FILE *PGM <
		TSTLIB1	FILEX ACTCUS ...	*FILE *PGM

can determine immediately, without ever having to locate and load the actual object, whether its type is appropriate for the operation requested (in this case, a program CALL).

Notice also that another program of the same name, ACTCUS, exists in library TSTLIB1. Because the system searches library ARLIB first, given its higher position in the list, the search ends when the system finds program ACTCUS in library ARLIB. The program found in library ARLIB is the one executed, not the program of the same name in library TSTLIB1. When adding new libraries to the library list, it is very important to keep this top-to-bottom search order in mind.

QUALIFIED NAMES

If you want to run program ACTCUS in library TSTLIB1, you can proceed in two ways: You can use a **qualified name** for the object, or you can modify the library list. The most direct approach would be to use a qualified name to explicitly identify the object. A qualified name includes a reference to a library as well as the 10-character object name. It takes the form

```
libref/objname
```

where *libref* is either an explicit library object name (e.g., TSTLIB1) or a reference to part of a library list (e.g., *CURLIB or *USRLIBL).

Thus, to execute program ACTCUS in library TSTLIB1, you would specify the following CALL command:

```
CALL TSTLIB1/ACTCUS
```

In this case, because you have specified a library name, the system searches only library TSTLIB1 for program ACTCUS. The system does not search any part of the library list, whether or not it successfully locates a suitable object in the named library.

You should remember the following about the use of qualified names:

- The library specified in an explicit qualified name does *not* need to be on your library list, but you (the requester) must be authorized not only to use that library but also to use the object within the library. So the first thing the system does is determine whether you have proper authority to the library you named. On the other hand, when you use a simple unqualified name, the search for an object is limited to your library list. The system already determined that you are authorized to use the library list libraries when your job began. Processing your user profile, among other things, validates your authorization to the libraries in your library list.
- If you are authorized to the library specified in an explicit qualified name but the system cannot find a matching object name of appropriate type, or if you are not authorized to use the object, the system does not search beyond the specified library. Instead, the system returns a message such as "Object (OBJNAME) in library (LIBNAME) not found," or "Not authorized to object (OBJNAME) in library (LIBNAME)."

In summary, most object references use a simple name, which is always syntactically correct in a CL command. It may be necessary to use a qualified name if

- objects with the same name and type exist in more than one library in your library list
- you need an object that is not in any library in your library list

In any case, to use a qualified name, you need authority adequate for the intended use, both to the object and to the library.

LIBRARY LIST COMMANDS

Often during an interactive job it may be necessary to add or remove libraries from the library list or change the order of libraries already on the list. A library that has been removed from the library list still exists on the system, of course, but simple name references cannot be used by that job to access its objects.

The AS/400 supports a number of CL commands that let you work with a library list. We introduce several of these commands in this section.

The DSPLIBL Command

Remember that every job uses a library list to locate objects. An initial library list is created for each job from job description and user profile attributes and from system values. In the lab for this lesson you explore those attributes to understand the source of your own initial library list. But any time you need to check the current contents of the library list, the DSPLIBL (Display Library List) command is most useful.

This command requires no parameters; it simply displays your job's current library list on the workstation screen. Figure 3.2 shows the output of the DSPLIBL command entered (with no parameters) on the command line.

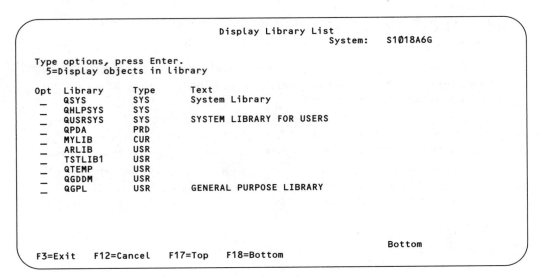

```
                          Display Library List
                                       System:    S1018A6G

   Type options, press Enter.
     5=Display objects in library

   Opt  Library      Type     Text
    _   QSYS         SYS      System Library
    _   QHLPSYS      SYS
    _   QUSRSYS      SYS      SYSTEM LIBRARY FOR USERS
    _   QPDA         PRD
    _   MYLIB        CUR
    _   ARLIB        USR
    _   TSTLIB1      USR
    _   QTEMP        USR
    _   QGDDM        USR
    _   QGPL         USR      GENERAL PURPOSE LIBRARY



                                                            Bottom
    F3=Exit    F12=Cancel    F17=Top    F18=Bottom
```

Figure 3.2
Sample Library List

The library list shown in Figure 3.2 is similar to the one illustrated in the previous table, but with a few more libraries added to make it more realistic.

The CHGCURLIB Command

A library list is not a static, unchanging entity, and often you may need to add new libraries or change the order of libraries currently in the list. You can use several different commands to change the current library or the user part of your library list.

One of these commands, the CHGCURLIB (Change Current Library) command, lets you specify a different library to occupy the spot of current library in your library list. As you can see from the CHGCURLIB command prompt screen (Figure 3.3), the only required parameter value is the name of the library that will become the new current library. The prompt screen shows the library ALLUSER already typed in as the new current library.

Figure 3.3

Change Current Library
Command Prompt
Screen

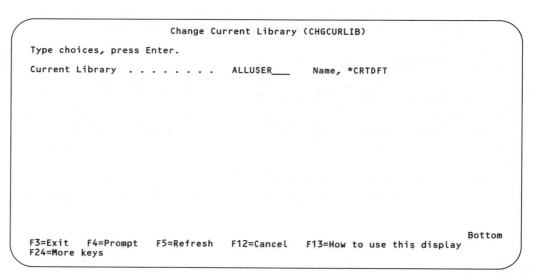

```
                         Change Current Library (CHGCURLIB)

 Type choices, press Enter.

 Current Library  . . . . . . . .   ALLUSER___    Name, *CRTDFT




















                                                                         Bottom
 F3=Exit    F4=Prompt    F5=Refresh    F12=Cancel   F13=How to use this display
 F24=More keys
```

After running the CHGCURLIB command with library ALLUSER specified, the library list would look like the one shown in Figure 3.4 (the library list is displayed by using the DSPLIBL command).

Notice that library ALLUSER is now the current library and that the previous current library, MYLIB, has vanished from the list. This is an important point to keep in mind when using the CHGCURLIB command: The old current library is not added to the user part of the list; it is removed from the list altogether. For this reason, the CHGCURLIB command would not be the best choice when you only want to change the relative order of libraries already in the user part of the library list.

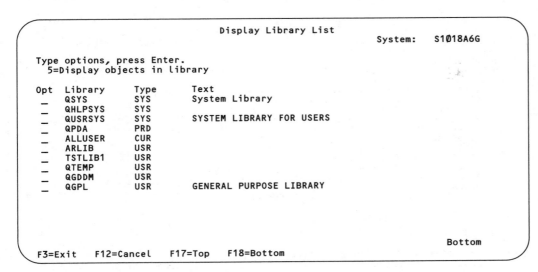

Figure 3.4
Changed Library List Showing a New Current Library

```
                        Display Library List
                                              System:    S1018A6G

Type options, press Enter.
  5=Display objects in library

Opt  Library     Type     Text
  _  QSYS        SYS      System Library
  _  QHLPSYS     SYS
  _  QUSRSYS     SYS      SYSTEM LIBRARY FOR USERS
  _  QPDA        PRD
  _  ALLUSER     CUR
  _  ARLIB       USR
  _  TSTLIB1     USR
  _  QTEMP       USR
  _  QGDDM       USR
  _  QGPL        USR      GENERAL PURPOSE LIBRARY




                                                            Bottom
 F3=Exit    F12=Cancel    F17=Top    F18=Bottom
```

The ADDLIBLE Command

The ADDLIBLE (Add Library List Entry) command lets you add a new library to the user library portion of the library list. The ADDLIBLE command prompt (Figure 3.5) shows library MYLIB being added to the library list. Remember that this command only affects the user part of the library list. The default of *FIRST for list position causes the added library to be placed at the top of the user library list.

Figure 3.5
Add Library List Entry, with MYLIB Specified

```
                   Add Library List Entry (ADDLIBLE)

 Type choices, press Enter.

 Library  . . . . . . . . . . .   MYLIB_____    Name, *CRTDFT
 Library list position:
   List position  . . . . . . .   *FIRST__     *FIRST, *LAST, *AFTER...
   Reference Library  . . . . .   _____     Name











                                                         Bottom
 F3=Exit    F4=Prompt    F5=Refresh    F12=Cancel    F13=How to use this display
 F24=More keys
```

The DSPLIBL command output (Figure 3.6) shows the results of executing our example ADDLIBLE command.

Figure 3.6
Changed Library List,
with MYLIB Added

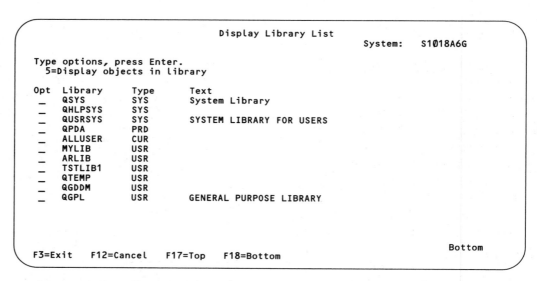

```
                              Display Library List
                                                 System:    S1Ø18A6G

  Type options, press Enter.
    5=Display objects in library

  Opt   Library      Type       Text
   _    QSYS         SYS        System Library
   _    QHLPSYS      SYS
   _    QUSRSYS      SYS        SYSTEM LIBRARY FOR USERS
   _    QPDA         PRD
   _    ALLUSER      CUR
   _    MYLIB        USR
   _    ARLIB        USR
   _    TSTLIB1      USR
   _    QTEMP        USR
   _    QGDDM        USR
   _    QGPL         USR        GENERAL PURPOSE LIBRARY


                                                              Bottom
  F3=Exit    F12=Cancel    F17=Top    F18=Bottom
```

Notice that MYLIB has been inserted at the top of the user library list. If you wanted to remove a single library from the user library list, you would use the RMVLIBLE (Remove Library List Entry) command.

The CHGCURLIB, ADDLIBLE, and RMVLIBLE commands each work on a single library. But sometimes you need to change the relative order of libraries already on the list or add (or remove) several libraries at a time. Two commands — the CHGLIBL and EDTLIBL commands — let you perform those functions.

The CHGLIBL Command

The CHGLIBL (Change Library List) command lets you add, remove, or change the order of libraries in your user library list. You can also use the CHGLIBL command to change the current library. Let's look at how you can use this command to modify the library list to run program ACTCUS in library TSTLIB1. Because

Figure 3.7
Change Library List
Command Prompt
Screen

```
                        Change Library List (CHGLIBL)
  Type choices, press Enter.

  Libraries for current job  . . .     ARLIB_____    Name, *SAME, *NONE
                                       TSTLIB1___
                                       QTEMP_____
                                       QGDDM_____
                 + for more values     QGPL_____
  Current library . . . . . . . .      MYLIB_____    Name, *SAME, *CRTDFT




                                                              Bottom
  F3=Exit    F4=Prompt    F5=Refresh    F12=Cancel    F13=How to use this display
  F24=More keys
```

the library list is searched from top to bottom, you can accomplish this goal by moving library TSTLIB1 higher in the library list than library ARLIB.

Figure 3.7 shows a command prompt screen for the Change Library List command, using a library list just like the one shown in Figure 3.2. Each library name is an entry field and you can type over an existing name (to replace it with a different library name), or add new libraries by entering a plus sign on the + for more values field.

Also, the current library can be changed by typing over the Current library value displayed on the screen and replacing it with the desired library name. This command requires that you retype names to change the order of libraries, but the command can be used from within a CL program as well as interactively.

In Figure 3.8, the positions of libraries ARLIB and TESTLIB1 have been reversed. Now, after executing the CHGLIBL command, the original CALL command

CALL ACTCUS

runs the program from library TSTLIB1 because it is higher in the list and will be searched before library ARLIB.

```
                        Change Library List (CHGLIBL)

   Type choices, press Enter.

   Libraries for current job  . . .    TSTLIB1___    Name, *SAME, *NONE
                                        ARLIB_____
                                        QTEMP_____
                                        QGDDM_____
                  + for more values     QGPL_____
   Current library  . . . . . . . .     MYLIB_____   Name, *SAME, *CRTDFT




                                                                  Bottom
   F3=Exit   F4=Prompt   F5=Refresh   F12=Cancel   F13=How to use this display
   F24=More keys
```

Figure 3.8
Change Library List, Placing TSTLIB1 before ARLIB

The EDTLIBL Command

Another command that lets you work on multiple libraries is the EDTLIBL (Edit Library List) command. This command permits adding libraries to your library list and/or changing the relative order of the libraries simply by renumbering the list. For the purpose of changing the order of user libraries in an interactive job, the EDTLIBL command is the easiest of these commands to use. When using the EDTLIBL command, you don't need to retype library names — all you need to do to reorder them in the list is to change their sequence numbers.

To see how the EDTLIBL command works, let's again assume that your library list is similar to the one shown by the DSPLIBL command in Figure 3.2. Figure 3.9 shows the EDTLIBL command prompt screen before any changes are made.

Figure 3.9

Edit Library List
Prompt Screen

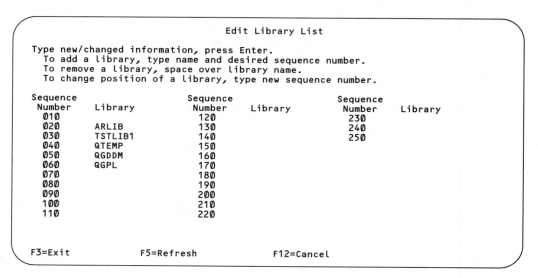

```
                              Edit Library List
       Type new/changed information, press Enter.
         To add a library, type name and desired sequence number.
         To remove a library, space over library name.
         To change position of a library, type new sequence number.

       Sequence                      Sequence                     Sequence
        Number    Library             Number   Library             Number   Library
         010                           120                          230
         020      ARLIB                130                          240
         030      TSTLIB1              140                          250
         040      QTEMP                150
         050      QGDDM                160
         060      QGPL                 170
         070                           180
         080                           190
         090                           200
         100                           210
         110                           220



       F3=Exit              F5=Refresh              F12=Cancel
```

As you can see, the screen reflects the user library portion of the library list shown with the DSPLIBL command in Figure 3.2.

To change the relative positions of libraries ARLIB and TSTLIB1, you would type over the sequence numbers, as shown in Figure 3.10.

Figure 3.10

Edit Library List
(Changed)

```
                              Edit Library List
       Type new/changed information, press Enter.
         To add a library, type name and desired sequence number.
         To remove a library, space over library name.
         To change position of a library, type new sequence number.

       Sequence                      Sequence                     Sequence
        Number    Library             Number   Library             Number   Library
         010                           120                          230
    >    030      ARLIB                130                          240
    >    020      TSTLIB1              140                          250
         040      QTEMP                150
         050      QGDDM                160
         060      QGPL                 170
         070                           180
         080                           190
         090                           200
         100                           210
         110                           220



       F3=Exit              F5=Refresh              F12=Cancel
```

When you press Enter, the command executes, changing the order of the libraries. If you use F9 to recall the DSPLIBL command and run it again, the modified library list appears as shown in Figure 3.11. Notice that library TESTLIB1 is now ahead of library ARLIB in the library list.

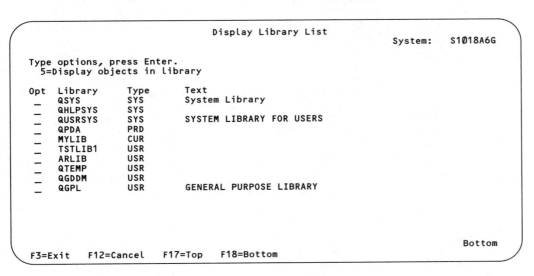

Figure 3.11

Sample Library List after Editing

```
                        Display Library List
                                              System:    S1018A6G

Type options, press Enter.
  5=Display objects in library

Opt  Library      Type     Text
 _   QSYS         SYS      System Library
 _   QHLPSYS      SYS
 _   QUSRSYS      SYS      SYSTEM LIBRARY FOR USERS
 _   QPDA         PRD
 _   MYLIB        CUR
 _   TSTLIB1      USR
 _   ARLIB        USR
 _   QTEMP        USR
 _   QGDDM        USR
 _   QGPL         USR      GENERAL PURPOSE LIBRARY


                                                          Bottom
  F3=Exit    F12=Cancel    F17=Top    F18=Bottom
```

Once again, if you use the command

`CALL ACTCUS`

the version of program ACTCUS in library TSTLIB1 executes, not the version of the program in library ARLIB.

LOCATING AN OBJECT

As we have demonstrated, the system searches the library list from top (system libraries) to bottom (user libraries) when a request is made using a simple object name. On the other hand, referencing an object with an explicit qualified name causes the system to search only the named library, if you are authorized to use it. Figure 3.12 illustrates the steps the system takes when it searches for a requested object.

Figure 3.12
Locating a Requested
Object

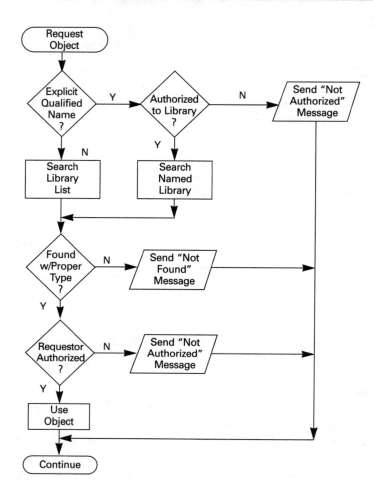

STORING OBJECTS

You have learned how the system finds an object. Now let's examine how the system determines in which library an object should be stored. Where an object is stored depends on its type and whether you specify a particular library in which to store the object.

Objects are created using a create — CRT*xxx* — command. For most create commands, the *xxx* specifies the type of object you are creating. For example, when you created a library in Lab 2, the command

```
CRTLIB JFOTTRAL
```

told the system you were creating a library, so the system assigned object type *LIB to the new object. Likewise, if you were creating a Cobol program, the command CRTCBLPGM, if successful, results in a new object of type *PGM, not *FILE or *USRPRF.

Some object types are associated only with the system library QSYS and you can't put them anyplace else. Libraries (*LIB), user profiles (*USRPRF), and device descriptions (*DEVD) are examples of these object types.

Most types of objects, however, can go in any library, including user libraries; and for these objects, a Library entry field will be included on the CRT*xxx* command. For example, look at the command prompt for the CRTOUTQ (Create Output Queue) command (Figure 3.13).

Figure 3.13
Create Output Queue
Command Prompt
Screen

```
                        Create Output Queue (CRTOUTQ)

 Type choices, press Enter.

 Output queue . . . . . . . . . .               Name
   Library . . . . . . . . . . .     *CURLIB    Name, *CURLIB
 Order of files on queue  . . . .    *FIFO      *FIFO, *JOBNBR
 Text 'description' . . . . . . .    *BLANK


                          Additional Parameters
 Display any file . . . . . . . .    *NO        *NO, *YES
 Job separators . . . . . . . . .    0          0-9, *MSG
 Operator controlled  . . . . . .    *YES       *YES, *NO
 Authority to check . . . . . . .    *OWNER     *OWNER, *DTAAUT
 Authority  . . . . . . . . . . .    *USE       Name, *USE, *ALL, *CHANGE...




                                                               Bottom
 F3=Exit   F4=Prompt   F5=Refresh   F12=Cancel   F13=How to use this display
 F24=More keys
```

(An output queue is an object containing a list of spooled files that you can display on a workstation or write to a **printer device**. We talk more about output queues under "Printer Spooling.")

Notice that the Output queue parameter includes an entry field for Library (its default value is *CURLIB). This Library field is important because it determines in which library the output queue will be placed. If you remember our earlier discussion, you will notice that the library field is the *libref* part of a qualified name (libref/objname). If you have designated a current library in your library list — for example, by having previously changed your user profile Current library to your own library, or by running a CHGCURLIB command within your interactive job — the create command using the default of *CURLIB will send the new output queue to your current library. If, however, you have not created or designated a current library, the new object will go to the library acting as the "create default" (*CRTDFT) in your user profile. And we all know which library that is, right? (If you need to refresh your memory, please refer to Step 2.5 in Lab 2.)

Of course, you could specify the receiving library by keying in a library name for the parameter value of a create command. This would be similar to using an explicit qualified name to locate an object, and the same warning would apply: If you name a library on a create command, you must have the proper authority to add new objects to the named library; otherwise, the create command fails.

Figure 3.14 shows the sequence the system follows when storing an object. Exceptions to Figure 3.14 are those object types always placed in library QSYS (e.g., *USRPRF, *LIB, *DEVD).

Figure 3.14

Storing a New Object

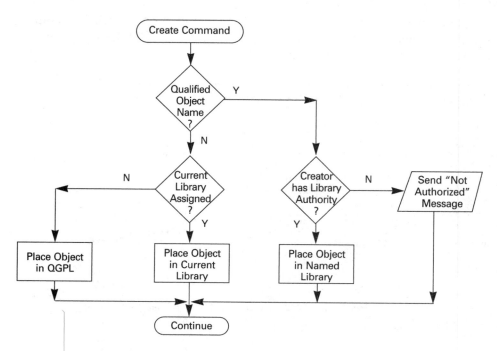

OBJECTS THAT HELP MANAGE WORK FLOW, OR THE CONCEPT OF SPOOLING

The system spooler is a specialized part of the operating system with its own dedicated subsystem, QSPL. It stages and controls batch jobs before they begin execution, and it manages each printed report (called a **spooled file**) created by a job before it goes to an actual printer device.

You can think of the spooler as the air traffic control facility at a major airport. Air traffic controllers avoid potentially dangerous competition for limited resources (e.g., air space, runways) by instructing planes to remain on the runway or in a holding pattern, until cleared to take off or land.

As the diagram in Figure 3.15 illustrates, the spooler controls incoming batch jobs — placing them in a job queue until they can land (begin execution) — and printed output — placing it in output queues like planes lined up at a runway until the runway (writer) is available and they can take off (print).

Figure 3.15

The Spooler at Work

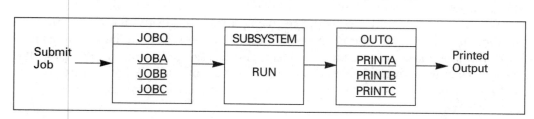

Without job **spooling**, the processor and limited main storage would be overwhelmed by too many unruly batch jobs all demanding to run at once. Likewise, without print spooling, printer buffers would be constantly overflowing and the processor would slow to a crawl waiting for printers to catch up. Operators would have no option to place huge print jobs on hold until later or give important jobs a higher priority to make them print sooner. And if users had no option to look at screen displays of print output (still in electronic form in an output queue) before deciding whether to go ahead and print, just think of all the paper wasted from printing unnecessary output, such as nonessential program compile and error listings, useless job logs, and reports run with bad data.

You should understand that job spooling pertains to batch jobs — interactive jobs do not go into a job queue but start at a workstation. In this lesson's lab you examine output queues, so for now we concentrate on the output side of spooling.

Printer Spooling

To create printed output, a program, OS/400 utility, or print-key function must write the output data to a **printer file**. A printer file is a type of device file that determines the attributes that printed output will have. It defines the formatting, page size, and special printing features, and may specify an **output queue**. Numerous IBM-supplied printer files are available for use by general-purpose printing and system utilities. Also, users can use the CRTPRTF (Create Printer File) command to create new print files for special reports or printing conditions. If the printer file does not specify another output queue, the output queue currently assigned to the job will be used. The sequence of operations will appear as follows:

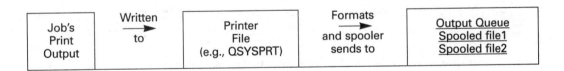

Spoolers use queues to temporarily hold printed output from various programs. Each item of printed output in an output queue represents a single report, program compile, print screen operation, and so on, and each of these is called a **spooled file**. Spooled files are "printed output" in the sense that they are formatted and ready to print; but until they are written to a physical printer device, they exist only as a collection of bits on magnetic storage media. You can think of output queues as areas of secondary storage managed by the spooler that can grow or shrink in size as more spooled files pile up in the queue or are sent off to a physical printer device.

Output queues are created automatically by describing a new printer device to the system using the CRTDEVPRT (Create Device Description (Printer)) command. Likewise, if the device description is deleted, the output queue goes away, too. Every printer on the system should have an output queue created in this way that takes the same name as the printer device. For example, if there is a physical printer device PRT01, there should also be an output queue PRT01.

However, there can be problems when many different users' printed output is directed to the same queue. If the output queue is attached to a printer that is working, inevitably a lot of wasted printed output will be generated unless all spooled files are held (kept in the queue) from the outset. But then the number of spooled files held in the queue may become quite high, and determining what belongs to whom and managing its disposition (i.e., whether a spooled file should be printed, kept on hold, sent to a different queue/printer, or deleted) becomes difficult.

Figure 3.16 shows a Work with Output Queue screen that lists one page of the spooled files from several users.

Figure 3.16
Work with Output Queue Screen

```
                            Work with Output Queue

    Queue:    PRTXX          Library:    QUSRSYS         Status:   HLD

    Type options, press Enter.
      1=Send  2=Change  3=Hold  4=Delete  5=Display  6=Release  7=Messages
      8=Attributes      9=Work with printing status

    Opt  File        User       User Data   Sts   Pages  Copies  Form Type   Pty
    _    QSYSPRT     JMCKINSTRY              RDY     1      1     *STD        5
    _    QSYSPRT     BHARRIS                 RDY     1      1     *STD        5
    _    QSYSPRT     EMCCARTHY               RDY     1      1     *STD        5
    _    QSYSPRT     MSHEDENHEL              RDY     1      1     *STD        5
    _    QSYSPRT     EMCCARTHY               RDY     1      1     *STD        5
    _    QSYSPRT     EMCCARTHY               RDY     1      1     *STD        5
    _    QSYSPRT     DWRIGHT                 RDY     1      1     *STD        5
    _    QSYSPRT     BWHITLATCH              RDY     1      1     *STD        5
    _    QSYSPRT     BWHITLATCH              RDY     1      1     *STD        5
    _    QSYSPRT     DWRIGHT                 RDY     1      1     *STD        5
                                                                       More...
    Parameters for options 1, 2, 3 or command
    ===>
     F3=Exit    F11=View 2    F12=Cancel    F22=Printers    F24=More keys
```

The output queue status is HLD to prevent the indiscriminate printing of those files, each of which shows that it is ready to print (status RDY).

Luckily, the existence of an output queue is not dependent on a printer because you can use the CRTOUTQ command to create a new output queue in any user library. This is not normally a restricted command and generally it is a good idea for users, at least trained users, to create and manage their own output queues and dispose properly of their own spooled files.

In the lab for this lesson, after investigating where your printed output currently goes, you create your own output queue to hold future printed output.

In the next lab you deal with handling spooled files once they have arrived in a designated output queue.

Key Terms

attributes

high-level machine interface (MI)

licensed internal code (LIC)

library

logical machine

object

object type

output queue

physical machine

printer device

printer file

qualified name

simple object name

single-level storage

spooled file

spooling

Lab **3**

INTRODUCTION

Every job has a set of attributes that describes its environment, resources, and capabilities. These attributes come from several sources, including the job description, the user profile, system values and — for interactive jobs — the workstation device description.

In this lab you examine some attributes of your interactive job. You also look at information about the job description, user profile, and workstation device description. All of these are objects and, as such, have commands for each object type, including commands to display the values they contain. You use these commands to answer such questions as "What happens to the output of a print operation?" "Why does the print output go to a certain output queue and not somewhere else?"

By learning the answers to these questions, you will find out what is necessary to control your own printed output. To gain control, you create a new object and an output queue, and change your user profile so that your future interactive jobs will use the output queue you created.

In this and subsequent labs, the instruction to "print screen" refers to the AS/400 system print screen function and not to a workstation's printer's screen print. System print screen always creates a spooled file and displays the message "Print operation complete to the default printer device file." You must then press Reset (left Ctrl on the micros) to go on.

Part 1

Goals	Use the Print Screen function of the AS/400 system printer
	Use Work with User Jobs to find your own active job
	Examine your job status attributes
	Locate spooled files created by your job

Start at	Sign-on screen

Procedure	Sign on
	Follow menu path to Work with User Jobs
	Work with your job's status attributes
	Work with spooled files

1.1. Sign on as usual.

Printed output can originate from several different sources. For example, the AS/400 Data File Utility, an interactive file update utility, creates a listing of adds, changes, and deletes — called an Audit Log — whenever it is used. Also, when programs or data file specifications are created, a compile listing showing source code and error messages is generated. In addition, many user applications produce various printed reports. What all types of printed output on the AS/400 have in common is that they go into an output queue as spooled files before they are printed. To find out where your printed output goes, you use another convenient way to create printed output: the print system screen. To send a screen image to the default output queue, just press the Print key if you are using a nonprogrammable workstation. For PCs ask your instructor for the system print-screen key.

1.2. Use print screen to print the Main menu. Do not expect to see anything printing right away — remember that printed output is first spooled to an output queue, where it may remain indefinitely.

1.2a. What message is returned?

When the keyboard locks because of a returned system message, press Reset (left Ctrl) to clear and unlock the keyboard.

1.3. Select the General system tasks option from the Main menu, then print the screen from the System menu when it appears.

1.4. Select the Jobs option from the System menu. Print the screen from the Job menu, and then from that menu select the Work with jobs option.

1.4a. Which of the four basic screen types is this? *Cmd entry*

1.4b. To get to this screen directly, without taking the menu path, what would you do?

1.5. Use extended Help to read about working with user jobs.

1.5a. What does "*" mean for the USER parameter?

Every job has a particular status at any time, depending on whether it's waiting to run, it's in process, or it's finished.

1.5b. Use contextual Help to examine the STATUS parameter. As a job runs, what are the different statuses it could pass through? (*ALL means all possible statuses; it is not a type of status.)

Change the STATUS parameter value to *ACTIVE, but don't run the command yet!

1.6. Press F10 to see additional parameters. Use Help to find an explanation of the valid values for the ASTLVL parameter. It may be useful to enlarge the Help window. Select the system user interface value and type that value over the current ASTLVL parameter value. Using the default values for the other parameters, run the command.

You should now see a Work with User Jobs screen similar to the one shown in Figure 3.17. The screen layout should be the same. However, the items listed will be different and there may be several pages. (If you have arrived at a screen with quite a different appearance, back up and review the Help information and check your ASTLVL value from the WRKUSRJOB command prompt. Make sure you have chosen the system user interface value.)

```
                          Work with User Jobs                    S1018A6G
                                                    01/22/98   09:06:16
     Type options, press Enter.

       2=Change   3=Hold   4=End   5=Work with   6=Release   7=Display message
       8=Work with spooled files   13=Disconnect

     Opt   Job       User      Type     -----Status------   Function
       _   PCSTAFF   ASUSER    CMNEVK   ACTIVE
       _   PCSTAFF   ASUSER    CMNEVK   ACTIVE              *  -PASSTHRU
       _   PCSTAFFS1 BMENKE    INTER    ACTIVE              CMD-WRKUSRJOB
       _   PCSTAFFS1 JFOTTRAL  INTER    SYSREQ              PGM-QMNSYSRQ
       _   PU30411   QSECOFR   CMNEVK   ACTIVE              *  -PASSTHRU
       _   PU30411E  QSECOFR   INTER    ACTIVE              PGM-QPGMMENU

                                                                 Bottom
     Parameters or command
     ===>
     F3=Exit   F4=Prompt   F5=Refresh   F9=Retrieve   F11=Display schedule data
     F12=Cancel   F21=Select assistance level
```

Figure 3.17
Work with User Jobs Screen

1.7. From the Work with User Jobs list processing screen, find your own active job. (Look under the User column for your user ID.) Select the option that lets you work with your job.

1.8. From the Work with Job screen, select the option to display job status attributes of your job.

You should now see a screen similar to the one shown in Figure 3.18, but with different values for the parameters Job, User, and Number. These three variables are used to identify interactive and batch jobs on the system.

Figure 3.18
Display Job Status
Attributes Screen

```
                          Display Job Status Attributes
                                                         System:    S1018A6G

   Job:   PCSTAFFS1      User:    JSMITH        Number:   095555

   Status of job . . . . . . . . . . . . . . . :    ACTIVE
   Entered system:
      Date  . . . . . . . . . . . . . . . . . . :    01/22/98
      Time  . . . . . . . . . . . . . . . . . . :    09:03:30
   Started:
      Date  . . . . . . . . . . . . . . . . . . :    01/22/98
      Time  . . . . . . . . . . . . . . . . . . :    09:03:31
   Subsystem . . . . . . . . . . . . . . . . . :    QINTER
      Subsystem pool ID . . . . . . . . . . . . :    2
   Type of job . . . . . . . . . . . . . . . . :    INTER
   Special environment . . . . . . . . . . . . :    *NONE
   Program return code . . . . . . . . . . . . :    0
   Controlled end requested  . . . . . . . . . :    NO
   System  . . . . . . . . . . . . . . . . . . :    S1018A6G


                                                                  Bottom
   Press Enter to continue.
   F3=Exit    F5=Refresh    F12=Cancel    F16=Job menu
```

1.8a. Generally speaking, what are job status attributes? (Use Help.)

1.8b. The system assigns a unique serial number to every job as it starts. What number has been assigned to your job?

1.8c. How is the job name assigned to an interactive job? (Use Help.)

Note your job name here for future reference: ___Q PADEVOOIO___

Remember that the values for job name, the system assigned job number, and the user profile name that started the job are the three pieces of information used to identify every job to the system.

1.8d. What date and time did your job start?

1.8e. Which subsystem is your job running in?

Press Enter or F12 when you have finished examining your job status attributes.

1.9. From the Work with Job screen, select the Work with spooled files option. This selection takes you to a list screen showing spooled files created during your current job. Other spooled files you created during other jobs, and that are still on the system, don't display here. So if you sign off after printing the screen, and then the next day take the same menu path back to this screen, you won't see the spooled files created in the earlier session. There is, of course, a command to work with all spooled files by user. We use that command soon.

If the printer writer of the default output queue was not started, or if there was no writer attached to the output queue when you did the print screen, there should be three spooled files showing with status RDY.

1.9a. What file name do they have?

This file name is the printer device file used by the Print key function.

Now use the Display option to verify that the spooled files are actually your printed screens. You can take an option on more than one list item.

The Display Spooled File display uses the first several lines of each screen for ID information. The actual spooled file starts under the ruler line. If the job requests it, four lines of user and system information are also prefixed to each print file. These lines appear directly under the ruler line.

Press F12 to return to the Work with Job Spooled Files display. Notice that the display tells you to which device or queue each spooled file is currently assigned. If your print files are in an output queue, their status should be RDY or HLD and you should leave them there and not attempt to print them at this time. If a writer was attached and started, and the screens printed, they should show status FIN. In that case, retrieve your output from the printer room and clip it to your answer sheet (but not right now).

Part 2

Goals	Find a command from a menu of related commands
	Examine a printer file's description to find out parameter values

Start at	Any command line

Procedure	Go to the CMDDSP menu
	Display the file description for the system print screen printer file

To answer the question "Why did your print output go to this output queue?" you must remember that OUTQ is a parameter of both the printer file, which specifies the format of the printed output, and also of the job. If the printer file specifies a certain output queue, that is where any printed output using that printer file goes.

In answer to question 1.9a, you should have written down the name of the printer file that was used to create your spooled output. Remember that the printer file is an object and if we examine it we can see where it sent its output. Now let's find a command to display that printer file's description.

Lab 3

2.1 On a command line, enter the command to take you to a menu of Display (DSP) commands.

   You should be looking at a screen like the one shown in Figure 3.19.

Figure 3.19
Display Commands
Menu (CMDDSP)

```
 CMDDSP                          Display Commands

  Select one of the following:

    Commands
      1. Change Device Desc (Display)               CHGDEVDSP
      2. Create Device Desc (Display)               CRTDEVDSP
      3. Display Access Code                        DSPACC
      4. Display Access Code Authority              DSPACCAUT
      5. Display Access Group                       DSPACCGRP
      6. Display Active Prestart Jobs               DSPACTPJ
      7. Display APPN Information                    DSPAPPNINF
      8. Display Authority Holder                   DSPAUTHLR
      9. Display Authorization List                 DSPAUTL
     10. Display Authorization List DLO             DSPAUTLDLO
     11. Display Authorization List Obj             DSPAUTLOBJ
     12. Display Authorized Users                   DSPAUTUSR
     13. Display Breakpoints                        DSPBKP
                                                          More...

  Selection or command
  ===>_____

  F3=Exit    F4=Prompt    F9=Retrieve    F12=Cancel    F16=Major menu
```

2.2 Find the command to display a file description and enter its number on the command line. At this point you should see a command prompt screen like the one shown in Figure 3.20.

Figure 3.20
DSPFD Command
Prompt Screen

```
                          Display File Description (DSPFD)

  Type choices, press Enter.

  File . . . . . . . . . . . . . .              Name, generic*, *ALL
    Library  . . . . . . . . . . .     *LIBL    Name, *LIBL, *CURLIB...
  Type of information  . . . . . .     *ALL     *ALL, *BASATR, *ATR...
                + for more values
  Output . . . . . . . . . . . . .     *        *, *PRINT, *OUTFILE
  File attributes  . . . . . . . .     *ALL     *ALL, *DSPF, *PRTF, *DKTF...
                + for more values




                                                                  Bottom
  F3=Exit    F4=Prompt    F5=Refresh    F10=Additional parameters    F12=Cancel
  F13=How to use this display          F24=More keys
```

2.3. Enter the name of the printer file discovered in question 1.9a for File name, and run the command.

   Now you should see a display of the file description as shown in Figure 3.21.

2.3a. What value is assigned to the Device parameter under Printer Attributes? (You need to page down.)

2.3b. What value is assigned to the Spooled output queue under Spooling Description?

```
                          Display Spooled File
File  . . . . . :     QPDSPFD              Page/Line    1/1
Control . . . . .                          Columns      1 - 78
Find  . . . . . .

*...+....1....+....2....+....3....+....4....+....5....+....6....+....7....+..
   01/22/98              Display File Description

DSPFD Command Input
   File  . . . . . . . . . . . . . . . . . . . . : FILE       QSYSPRT
     Library . . . . . . . . . . . . . . . . . . :            *LIBL
   Type of information . . . . . . . . . . . . . : TYPE       *ALL
   File attributes . . . . . . . . . . . . . . . : FILEATR    *ALL
   System  . . . . . . . . . . . . . . . . . . . : SYSTEM     *LCL
File Description Header
   File  . . . . . . . . . . . . . . . . . . . . : FILE       QSYSPRT
   Library . . . . . . . . . . . . . . . . . . . :            QSYS
   Type of file  . . . . . . . . . . . . . . . . :            Device
   Device type . . . . . . . . . . . . . . . . . :            Printer
   Auxiliary storage pool ID . . . . . . . . . . :            01
Device File Attributes
   Externally described file . . . . . . . . . . :            No
   File level identifier . . . . . . . . . . . . :            0901021215754
                                                                  More...

F3=Exit    F12=Cancel    F19=Left    F20=Right    F24=More keys
```

Figure 3.21
Display Spooled File Description Screen

You should have found that for both parameters, this printer file defers to the job description. You could create a printer file with specific values for these and other parameters, and in most installations there will indeed be customized printer files for special print jobs. But QSYSPRT is a general-purpose print file so it points back to the controlling job for any changes to the device or output queue.

Part 3

Goals	Find the job definition attributes of your job Find the job description used by your job and specified 　by your user profile Examine the job description for certain parameter values Examine the device description of your workstation Find and display the system values defining the system printer
Start at	Work with Job screen for your active job
Procedure	Display job definition attributes Display your user profile Display the job description of your active job Display the device description of your workstation Display system value QPRTDEV

Lab 3

Now let's examine the job attributes of your current interactive job.

3.1 Press F12 until you return to the Work with Job screen for your job. If you are unable to find the screen or have just signed back on, enter WRKUS-RJOB on the command line and then take option 5 on the active job that will be on the Work with User Jobs list.

3.2 From the Work with Job screen, select the Display job definition attributes option. You should now be looking at a screen like the one shown in Figure 3.22.

Figure 3.22
Job Definition
Attributes Screen

```
                        Display Job Definition Attributes

                                                       System:   S1018A6G
   Job:    PCSTAFFS1     User:    JSMITH     Number:    095555

   Job description . . . . . . . . . . . . . . . . . . . . :   QDFTJOBD
     Library . . . . . . . . . . . . . . . . . . . . . . :     QGPL
   Job queue . . . . . . . . . . . . . . . . . . . . . . :
     Library . . . . . . . . . . . . . . . . . . . . . . :
   Job priority (on job queue) . . . . . . . . . . . . . :
   Output priority (on output queue) . . . . . . . . . . :   5
   End severity  . . . . . . . . . . . . . . . . . . . . :   30
   Message logging:
     Level . . . . . . . . . . . . . . . . . . . . . . . :   4
     Severity  . . . . . . . . . . . . . . . . . . . . . :   0
     Text  . . . . . . . . . . . . . . . . . . . . . . . :   *NOLIST
   Log CL program commands . . . . . . . . . . . . . . . :   *NO
   Printer device  . . . . . . . . . . . . . . . . . . . :   PRTXX
   Default output queue  . . . . . . . . . . . . . . . . :   *DEV
     Library . . . . . . . . . . . . . . . . . . . . . . :

                                                              More...
   Press Enter to continue.
   F3=Exit   F5=Refresh   F9=Change job   F12=Cancel   F16=Job menu
```

These are the attributes of the job that came from the job description (and other sources) when the job was started.

3.2a. Which job description was used to define your interactive job?
3.2b. Which printer device was assigned?
3.2c. What is the value for Default output queue parameter?

3.3. Return to the Work with Job screen and on the command line key in the command to DiSPlay your USeR PRoFile. Remember to name the profile you want to display.

Page down and find the Job description value. The value should agree with the value discovered in question 3.2a. Normally, if not overruled by a workstation entry, the user profile determines the job description to use for an interactive job.

Note the job description used by your user profile: _____

3.4. A job description is an object, and like most objects, can be displayed. Return to the Work with Job command line. Using the GO command to reach a menu of related commands, find the command to display a job description.

3.4a. What is the menu number of this command?

3.5. Request the command by entering its menu number. For the Job description name, use the name you found in your user profile, noted in Step 3.3 above, then run the command.

Now you should be looking at a screen similar to the one shown in Figure 3.23.

```
                        Display Job Description

                                             System:   S1018A6G

   Job description:   QDFTJOBD       Library:   QGPL

   User profile . . . . . . . . . . . . . . . . . . . :  *RQD
   CL syntax check . . . . . . . . . . . . . . . . . :  *NOCHK
   Hold on job queue  . . . . . . . . . . . . . . . :  *NO
   End severity . . . . . . . . . . . . . . . . . . . :  30
   Job date . . . . . . . . . . . . . . . . . . . . . :  *SYSVAL
   Job switches . . . . . . . . . . . . . . . . . . . :  00000000
   Inquiry message reply  . . . . . . . . . . . . . :  *RQD
   Job priority (on job queue) . . . . . . . . . . :  5
   Job queue  . . . . . . . . . . . . . . . . . . . . :  QBATCH
     Library . . . . . . . . . . . . . . . . . . . . . :    QGPL
   Output priority (on output queue)  . . . . . . . :  5
   Printer device . . . . . . . . . . . . . . . . . . :  *USRPRF
   Output queue . . . . . . . . . . . . . . . . . . . :  *USRPRF
     Library . . . . . . . . . . . . . . . . . . . . . :

                                                   More...

   Press Enter to continue.
   F3=Exit    F12=Cancel
```

Figure 3.23
Display Job
Description Screen

3.5a. What value is given for Printer device?
3.5b. What value is given for Output queue?

Wow! Are you starting to feel a little dizzy? Let's see if you've got this right:

- Your user profile tells which job description to use when you sign on (start the interactive job).
- If the job description you noted in Step 3.3 is not QDFTJOBD, your school/installation has set up a special job description for student profiles. In that case, it is also likely that installation-specific values have replaced the defaults used by QDFTJOBD for certain parameters such as Printer device and Output queue. And, of course, some of the displays you see will be a little different from the ones illustrated here. Have your instructor/mentor interpret the differences for you, but understand that although specific values can be assigned for different job attributes at different levels, the process of collecting these attributes and defining a job is the same on all systems.
- If your user profile specifies QDFTJOBD, that job description points right back to the user profile for certain values, such as printer and output queue.

This makes sense because you wouldn't want to tie a generic job description (QDFTJOBD) used as a default by many jobs to a specific printer or output queue. This job description is generalized even further by pointing to system values (*SYSVAL) for other attributes. For example, page down to the last page of the job description display.

3.5c. What is the last attribute of the job description listed, and what value is used?

3.5d. How might it be possible to have a tailored library list for any user that would take effect as soon as (s)he signs on? (Hint: The answer requires at least two steps. Keep in mind that QDFTJOBD does not necessarily have to be used by all user profiles.)

3.6. If your job description uses *USRPRF for Printer device and Output queue, then let's see what values it picks up as it points back to the user profile. Press Enter to return to the command line. Then retrieve the DSPUSRPRF command and execute it again.

3.6a. What values are supplied for the output queue and printer device?

If your user profile has not been tailored, the default values for Output queue and Printer device point in turn to the workstation. A workstation, being a device, has an ID or name, and also a description associated with it. This description is an object of type *DEVD (device description) and has a display command you can use on it.

3.7. Press Enter and F12 as needed to return to the Work with Jobs screen. Remember where the interactive job name comes from? If you're not sure, move the cursor to the area on the screen where the job is identified and ask for Help.

Now let's use a command to examine the device description values. Type **DSPDEVD** on the command line and prompt for the command. Enter your workstation device name on the input field. (If you aren't sure about your device name, review question 1.8c of this lab.)

Figure 3.24
Display Device
Description Screen

```
                         Display Device Description              S1018A6G
                                                        02/25/98 18:55:53
   Device description . . . . . . . . :   PCSTAFFS1
   Option . . . . . . . . . . . . . . :   *BASIC
   Category of device . . . . . . . . :   *DSP

   Device class . . . . . . . . . . . :   *VRT
   Device type  . . . . . . . . . . . :   3197
   Device model . . . . . . . . . . . :   C1
   Online at IPL  . . . . . . . . . . :   *YES
   Attached controller  . . . . . . . :   QVIRCD0001
   Keyboard language type . . . . . . :   USB
   Character identifier . . . . . . . :   697   37
   Allow blinking cursor  . . . . . . :   *YES
   Print device . . . . . . . . . . . :   *SYSVAL
   Output queue . . . . . . . . . . . :   *DEV
   Printer file . . . . . . . . . . . :   QSYSPRT
    Library  . . . . . . . . . . . . . :      *LIB

   Press Enter to continue
                                                            More...

   F3=Exit   F11=Display keywords   F12=Cancel F15=Display associated device
```

You should be looking at a screen like the one in Figure 3.24, except your workstation name should be entered for the Device description value. Notice that the value for Print device is *SYSVAL, and that the value for Output queue is *DEV.

3.7a. Use field Help to learn what *DEV means for Output queue. What does it indicate?

3.7b. Use field Help again to find out about the Print device value. Which system value specifies the default system printer?

3.8. Return to the command line and run the command to display the system value discovered in item 3.7b. If you are not sure which command to use, execute the GO command to get to the menu of DSP commands.

3.8a. Which printer device is currently assigned to the system value?

Because the Help information told you about value *DEV for the Output queue parameter, you realize that the value used for Output queue will be the same as the name of the printer device. Every printer device has an output queue of the same name, so by default printed output is sent to the output queue of the printer device designated as the system printer (QPRTDEV). Now you understand why your print screen files ended up where they did, right?

Let's review (for students whose user profiles have not been tailored and are therefore still using job description QDFTJOBD):

a. When you sign on, your user profile specifies a job description to be used, QDFTJOBD.
b. In the process of assembling job attributes, QDFTJOBD points back to the user profile for Printer and Output queue attributes.
c. The user profile default values for Printer and Output queue point to the workstation where the job starts.
d. If the Print device and Output queue values for the workstation device description have not been changed, they both, in effect, point to the system value QPRTDEV.
e. Finally, the value assigned to QPRTDEV is what is used to define the Printer and Output queue attributes for the job.

Suppose we decided that every user should have his/her own output queue. Then if you wanted to have all your printed output sent to your own output queue, where would be the best place to effect this change?

You could set up a separate job description for each individual user, with the user's own output queue specified in the job description. This technique would interrupt the chain of pointers at Point b in the review list above. But that would require a potentially large number of job descriptions, which would result in considerable system overhead and system maintenance.

Or you could change the workstation device description at Point d, if you knew that every user used only a single workstation and, conversely, each workstation was used by no other user. But that is an unlikely scenario, and you would prefer to have a user's output go to his/her own output queue, regardless which device (s)he may be working at.

So Point c looks like the best bet. If you change the user profile Output queue value to the name of an output queue created just for that user, the current reference to the workstation will no longer apply. The job description will look at the user profile, the user profile will name a specific output queue, and that will be the output queue used by the job. Wherever that user signs on, his or her printed output will go to the same output queue — unless, of course, the printer file names a specific output queue instead of the default, *JOB.

We will use this method for managing output created in this class. Before you make the change to your user profile, however, you need to create your new output queue.

Part 4

Goals	Verify your current library
	Create an output queue
	Change your user profile to use the new output queue

Start at	Any system command line

Procedure	Display your library list
	Create an output queue
	Change the user profile

We would like to use the default current library when creating an output queue, but it would be prudent to check first to make sure your library is indeed the current library for your job.

4.1. First, run the DSPLIBL (Display Library List) command to make sure your own library is the current library in your library list. If it is not, stop right now and go back to Lab 2. Repeat the steps to create your own library (the system will tell you if it already exists) and to change the Current library parameter of your user profile. Then use the CHGCURLIB (Change Current Library) command to assign your library as the current library.

4.2 Now type the command to CReaTe an OUTput Queue on the command line, and prompt for parameters. Use your user name, the same name as the library you created in Lab 2, as the name of the output queue. (My output queue will be Jfottral in library Jfottral.)

4.2a. What value is supplied for the Library parameter?

With the exception of the few object types that always go into library QSYS, the system defaults to the current library when you create an object.

Type your full name and the class name in the Text field, then press Enter.

4.2b. What message is displayed on the screen?

If the message did *not* indicate successful creation of the output queue, you need to ask your instructor/mentor for help.

4.3. Now change the user profile value by prompting for the CHGPRF (Change Profile) command. You need to display additional parameters and page down to the Output queue parameter. Be sure to change only the Output queue, not the Print device.

Type in your output queue name and press Enter.

Remember: Many user profile changes, including this one, do not take effect until the next sign-on, so even if you printed more screens now without signing off, they would still end up in the same place as before.

In the next lab you make sure your new output queue is functioning properly and you take care of those Print screen spooled files still hanging out in the default output queue. But for now you may return to a menu with a sign-off selection, or just enter the SIGNOFF command from any command line.

Mastering the AS/400, Second Edition

Lab 3 Answer Sheet

Name: _____

Date Due: _____   Class Time: _____

1.2a. _Print operations complete to the default printer device file_

1.4a. _Entry list_   1.4b. _WRKUSRJOB from any cmd line F4_

1.5a. _Current user profile_

1.5b. _____

1.8a. _Active, ID characteristics & thresholds of job_ _DSC OUTQ JOBQ TFRJOB TFRBCA EOJ_

1.8b. _____

1.8c. _____

_____

1.8d. _____   1.8e. _____

1.9a. _____   2.3a. _____   2.3b. _____

3.2a. _____   3.2b. _____   3.2c. _____

3.4a. _____   3.5a. _____   3.5b. _____

3.5c. _____

3.5d. _____

_____

3.6a. _____

3.7a. _____

_____

3.7b. _____

3.8a. _____   4.2a. _____

4.2b. _____

IN SUMMARY

In this lesson we examined some of the important attributes of objects. We learned that objects are identified by library, name, and type. We saw that an object name is usually determined by the creator of the object, but object type is assigned by the system, depending on the command used to create it. Usually an object is placed in a job's current library, but if an explicit library name is used when it is created, the object goes in that library if appropriate authority exists. We know that there are a few types of objects that always go into the system library, QSYS.

We also examined some useful library list commands that let us change our current library or change and resequence our user library list. And we explored the mysteries of printing — from print files to output queues to printer writers to physical printer devices — and how those components work with spoolers to manage printed reports.

In the lab we explored job attributes and saw how they can be assigned by different sources such as the workstation device, user profile, job description, and system values. Most interesting jobs will include values from each of these sources.

Lesson 4

Handling Spooled Files

Lesson Overview

In this lesson we discuss how to handle spooled files once they reach output queues. We look at how you can use the WRKOUTQ (Work with Output Queue) and WRKSPLF (Work with Spooled File) commands to manage spooled files. We explain how to use several options frequently taken from WRKOUTQ and WRKSPLF list screens, and we examine how your choice of assistance level affects the appearance of these screens. We also discuss printer functions and look at options available for controlling printers and responding to messages.

Objectives

Students will be able to

✓ Explain the components of printer spooling
✓ Describe the differences between the WRKOUTQ (Work with Output Queue) and WRKSPLF (Work with Spooled File) commands
✓ Examine the contents of an output queue, and release, hold, or reroute spooled files to output queues with attached writers
✓ Work with a list of printers
✓ Display printer messages and print selected files
✓ Recognize the difference between screen formats when Basic or Intermediate assistance level is selected for certain display screens

PRINTER FILES

In the last lesson we discussed printer device files and output queues. A short review of these AS/400 objects might be useful here.

A printer device file is an object that specifies format and other print attributes of printed output produced by an application program, utility, or system operation. You can create or change printer device files by using the CRTPRTF (Create Printer File) and CHGPRTF (Change Printer File) commands, respectively.

For example, let's look at what you can do with the CHGPRTF command. In the last lab, you learned that printer file QSYSPRT is used to control the format of output generated by the Print key. The first screen of the CHGPRTF display for QSYSPRT is shown in Figure 4.1.

Figure 4.1

Change Printer File Command Display for Printer File QSYSPRT

```
                         Change Printer File (CHGPRTF)

 Type choices, press Enter.

 File . . . . . . . . . . . . . > QSYSPRT        Name, generic*, *ALL
   Library  . . . . . . . . . .     *LIBL        Name, *LIBL, *ALL, *ALLUSR...
 Device:
   Printer  . . . . . . . . . .     *JOB         Name, *SAME, *JOB, *SYSVAL
 Printer Device Type  . . . . . .   *SCS         *SAME, *SCE, *IPDS...
 Page size:
   Length--lines per page . . . .   66           .001-255.000, *SAME
   Width--positions per line  . .   132          .001-378.000, *SAME
   Measurement method . . . . . .   *ROWCOL      *SAME, *ROWCOL, *UOM
 Lines per inch . . . . . . . . .   6            *SAME, 6, 3, 4, 7.5, 7,5...
 Characters per inch  . . . . . .   10           *SAME, 10, 5, 12, 13.3, 13...
 Overflow line number . . . . . .   60           1-255, *SAME
 Record format level check  . . .   *NO          *SAME, *YES, *NO
 Text 'description'   . . . . . .   'System non-described printer file'_____
 ____
                                                                      Bottom
 F3=Exit    F4=Prompt    F5=Refresh  F10=Additional parameters  F12=Cancel
 F13=How to use this display         F24=More keys
```

On this first screen you can see some of the formatting parameters common to printer files: lines per page (66), print positions per line (132), lines per inch (6), and characters per inch (10). Subsequent screens show parameters that control attributes such as print quality, font, duplexing, overlay, output queue, form type, and number of copies.

The physical layout of lines and pages of printed output is determined when data from an application or utility is sent to a particular printer file. (The application itself determines which data is sent and how fields will be formatted on each printed line.) The formatted output, a spooled file still in electronic form (i.e., not yet printed), is then sent, under control of the **system spooler**, to an output queue. The following diagram illustrates this process:

The system spooler is a part of the operating system dedicated to the control and management of printed output. From the time printed output is formatted by a printer file until it leaves the system, it is monitored by the system spooler. The spooler, or "spool job," runs in its own subsystem and functions independently within control parameters established at the system and job levels. Users and operators can interact with the spooler via a number of CL commands.

PRINTER WRITER

After a spooled file has arrived at an output queue, the next step in creating printed output deals with transferring it to a physical printer device. A spooler component known as a printer writer is the means by which this is accomplished. A **printer writer** is the software connection between an output queue and a physical printer. A printer writer is generated automatically when a printer device (a physical printer) is described to the system. The creation of this device description generates not only a printer writer but also an output queue, both of which have the same name as the printer device.

To illustrate, let's look at the device description for a printer named PRT01 (Figure 4.2).

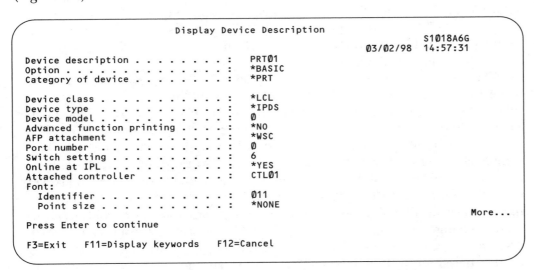

```
                    Display Device Description
                                                       S1018A6G
                                            03/02/98  14:57:31
Device description . . . . . . . . :    PRT01
Option . . . . . . . . . . . . . . :    *BASIC
Category of device . . . . . . . . :    *PRT

Device class . . . . . . . . . . . :    *LCL
Device type  . . . . . . . . . . . :    *IPDS
Device model . . . . . . . . . . . :    0
Advanced function printing . . . . :    *NO
AFP attachment . . . . . . . . . . :    *WSC
Port number  . . . . . . . . . . . :    0
Switch setting . . . . . . . . . . :    6
Online at IPL  . . . . . . . . . . :    *YES
Attached controller  . . . . . . . :    CTL01
Font:
   Identifier . . . . . . . . . . . :    011
   Point size . . . . . . . . . . . :    *NONE
                                                       More...
Press Enter to continue

F3=Exit    F11=Display keywords    F12=Cancel
```

Figure 4.2
Display Device Description for Printer PRT01

This description (only the first screen of the Display Device Description command's output for printer PRT01 is shown) could have been created automatically when the printer was attached (cabled) to the system; or, if the system were not set to autoconfigure newly attached devices, the description could have been created using the CRTDEVPRT (Create Device Description — Printer) command.

Regardless of how the device description was created, both a printer writer and an output queue with the same name came into existence at that time. The printer writer will always be "connected" to the physical printer device that generated it. Normally, on the other side, the writer will be "attached" to the output queue created along with the printer device description (i.e., the output queue with the same name as the printer). However, as the following illustration indicates, with the CHGWTR (Change Writer) command, the printer writer can be attached to a different output queue:

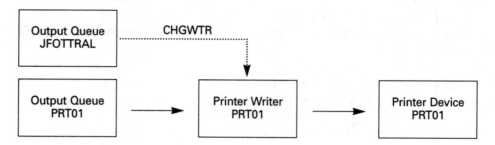

CHANGING WRITERS

As you know, output queues can be created that have no relationship to a physical printer and, therefore, have no printer writer attached to them. You created such an output queue in your last lab.

Using the CHGWTR command, you can attach the printer writer for printer PRT01 to output queue JFOTTRAL or any other output queue. If you attach output queue JFOTTRAL to printer writer PRT01, for instance, the writer begins sending spooled files that are ready to print from the newly attached queue (JFOTTRAL) to printer PRT01.

This technique can be useful in certain cases. For example, suppose that the writer for printer device PRT01 is currently attached to printer output queue PRT01. Now suppose that a number of spooled files needing a nonstandard paper stock are in output queue NITEQ. Perhaps they were created by a night batch process. When the operator is ready to print them, (s)he could simply turn off the printer, change forms, and then change the writer to the output queue holding the reports (NITEQ). Because the writer is now attached to output queue NITEQ, when the printer is started, it will print only the reports in the NITEQ output queue, those needing the special forms. In this way, the operator avoids having to hold or change the priority of other spooled files in printer output queue PRT01. Also, no new spooled files will enter the printer output queue and start printing on the special forms. When the NITEQ reports have been printed, the operator can return to the standard stock and change the writer from NITEQ back to printer output queue PRT01.

As you can see from this example, changing writers involves some responsibility. Once spooled files have printed, the writer must be changed, typically back to the printer output queue to which it was attached originally. This process could lead to problems of priority control and authorization. If, for example, someone changed the writer to his/her own output queue before it had finished printing the spooled files in the originally attached printer output queue, users waiting for their printed reports would be upset. To prevent such problems from occurring, many installations let only a system operator start, stop, or change printer writers.

So if you (or other individual users) are not authorized to change writers, how do you print a spooled file when your own output queue has no writer attached to it? Instead of changing the writer, you change the spooled file's output queue. Using the CHGSPLFA (Change Spooled File Attributes) command, you can cause a spooled file to be sent to an output queue with an attached, active writer. Normally, this would be the output queue of a printer device, as the following illustration indicates:

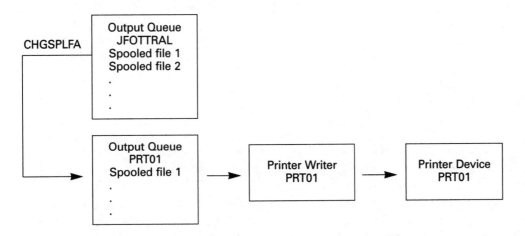

In the illustration, spooled files in output queue JFOTTRAL can be changed (sent) to output queue PRT01. This printer output queue has an active writer and will allow the spooled files to print on printer PRT01 when their turn comes.

CHANGING SPOOLED FILES

The AS/400 supports several important commands that let you change or invoke spooler operations and make changes to spooled print files. The Work with commands let you perform most of these operations from list-processing screens, offering a convenient and fast way to redirect spooled files; change the attributes of spooled files; or hold, release, or display spooled files.

Two commands similar in function but different in how they select spooled files to include in their lists are

- WRKOUTQ — The Work with Output Queue command lists all spooled files in a named output queue regardless of which user's job created them.

- WRKSPLF — The Work with Spooled File command lists all spooled files created by a user regardless of which output queues they are in.

WORKING WITH OUTPUT QUEUES

The WRKOUTQ (Work with Output Queue) command prompt screen is shown in Figure 4.3.

Figure 4.3

Work with Output
Queue Command
Prompt Screen

```
                        Work with Output Queue (WRKOUTQ)

 Type choices, press Enter.

 Output queue . . . . . . . . . .   *ALL_____   Name, generic*, *ALL
   Library  . . . . . . . . . . .   _____     Name, *LIBL, *CRULIB, *ALL
 Output . . . . . . . . . . . . .   *_____        *, *PRINT









                                                                    Bottom
 F3=Exit  F4=Prompt  F5=Refresh  F12=Cancel  F13=How to use this display
 F24=More keys
```

Notice that the Output queue parameter defaults to *ALL. If you ran the command as is, it would gather information about all the output queues on the system and list them in alphabetical order by queue. Depending on the number of queues on your system, this command could take a little while to process. And you may not be authorized to use any output queue other than your own anyway.

Therefore, when using the WRKOUTQ command, always be sure to specify which output queue you want to work with by providing an Output queue parameter value rather than taking the default (*ALL). For example, if you want to list all print files in output queue PRTXX, you can enter the command in positional

Figure 4.4

Work with Output
Queue List Screen for
Output Queue PRTXX

```
                              Work with Output Queue

   Queue:    PRTXX            Library:    QUSRSYS          Status:    HLD

   Type options, press Enter.
     1=Send    2=Change    3=Hold    4=Delete    5=Display   6=Release    7=Messages
     8=Attributes          9=Work with printing status

   Opt   File        User        User Data     Sts    Pages    Copies   Form Type   Pty
     _    QSYSPRT     CPAN                      RDY      1        1       *STD         5
     _    QSYSPRT     CPAN                      RDY      1        1       *STD         5
     _    SCHOOLFRF   JFOTTRAL                  RDY      8        1       *STD         5
     _    DBCULTPF    JFOTTRAL                  RDY      6        1       *STD         5
     _    INITDSP     JFOTTRAL                  RDY      3        1       *STD         5
     _    INITPGM     JFOTTRAL                  RDY      4        1       *STD         5
     _    QSYSPRT     ASOPR                     RDY      2        1       *STD         5
     _    QSYSPRT     ASOPR                     RDY      1        1       *STD         5
     _    QPDZDTALOG  SPHILLIPS                 RDY      1        1       *STD         5
     _    QPQUPRFIL   SPHILLIPS                 HLD      1        1       *STD         5

                                                                              Bottom
   Parameters for options 1, 2, 3 or command
   ===> _____
   F3=Exit    F11=View 2    F12=Cancel    F20=Writers    F22=Printers
   F24=More keys
```

notation on the command line as

`WRKOUTQ  PRTXX`

The output would first display in a format similar to that shown in Figure 4.4. You can see that several different file names from several different users are in the PRTXX output queue.

Figure 4.5 is another view of the list, obtained by pressing F11, that shows the job name, user name, and job number (in the middle three columns) of the job that created the spooled file.

```
                          Work with Output Queue

  Queue:    PRTXX           Library:    QUSRSYS         Status:   HLD

  Type options, press Enter.
    1=Send    2=Change    3=Hold    4=Delete   5=Display   6=Release   7=Messages
    8=Attributes          9=Work with printing status

  Opt   File        File Nbr   Job         User       Number  Date      Time
    _   QSYSPRT          1      PC309S1     CPAN       095593  07/22/98  18:34:24
    _   QSYSPRT          2      PC309S1     CPAN       095593  07/22/98  18:34:28
    _   DBCULTPF         1      DBCULTPF    JFOTTRAL   095845  07/26/98  19:13:36
    _   INITDSP          1      INITDSP     JFOTTRAL   096034  07/28/98  16:41:27
    _   INITPGM          1      INITPGM     JFOTTRAL   096035  07/28/98  16:42:32
    _   QSYSPRT          1      DSP00       ASOPR      096249  08/02/98  19:50:16
    _   QSYSPRT          1      DSP00       ASOPR      096333  08/03/98  19:12:46
    _   QPDZDTALOG       1      PCSTAFFS1   SPHILLIPS  097783  08/26/98  17:22:20
    _   QPQUPRFIL        2      PCSTAFFS1   SPHILLIPS  097783  08/26/98  17:22:56

                                                                          Bottom
  Parameters for options 1, 2, 3 or command
  ===>
  F3=Exit    F11=View 2    F12=Cancel    F20=Writers    F22=Printers
  F24=More keys
```

Figure 4.5
Work with Output Queue, View 2 of Output Queue PRTXX

You might recall that these three values are used to identify a job on the system. You can see that when a job creates several different spooled files — all with the same job name, user name, and job number — they can be identified within the job by the spooled file number, which is assigned to each spooled file consecutively as it is placed in a queue. The spooled file number is shown under the File Nbr column in Figure 4.5. Regardless of which output queue a spooled file is written to — and a job can write spooled files to several different output queues — each spooled file is assigned a unique file number within the job. This file number, along with its job name, user name, and job number, distinguishes any spooled file from all other spooled files on the system.

For example, file numbers 1 and 2 in Figure 4.5 identify the different print files created by user CPAN during job number 095593. These spooled files are both in output queue PRTXX, but CPAN may have other spooled files (numbered 3, 4, 5, and so on) in other output queues.

The options available from the screen shown in Figure 4.5 let you perform several useful operations on individual — or groups of — spooled files. A brief description of the options follows (you can use Help to get more detailed information):

1=Send	Used to route a copy of a file across a network.
2=Change	Used to change attributes of a spooled file, such as number of copies, whether the file should be kept on the queue after printing, which queue to move it to, and so on.
3=Hold	Used to prevent printing of a file; for example, to wait until special forms can be mounted on a printer.
4=Delete	Used to get rid of unnecessary spooled files — you will be asked to confirm, and if you do, specified spooled files will be erased from the system.
5=Display	Used to view a spooled file. With this option, you can make sure that the file you are planning to hold, delete, or send is the right one.
6=Release	Used to let a held file (option 3) go ahead and print.
7=Messages	Used to view messages that may be generated if a problem arises in the printing of a file.
8=Attributes	Used to check details of formatting and printer requirements for a spooled file.
9= Printing Status	Used to find out where a file is in the printing process. For example, a file may be waiting on a message or waiting for files ahead of it to print.

Although the WRKOUTQ command lists spooled files in the specified queue that belong to other users, you may not be authorized to take options on these files. For example, if user CPAN, having no special authority, tried to display user JFOTTRAL's spooled file SCHOOLFRF (listed in Figure 4.6), the message "Not authorized to spooled file" would appear.

Figure 4.6
Work with Output
Queue with "Not
Authorized" Message

```
                            Work with Output Queue

        Queue:    PRTXX        Library:    QUSRSYS        Status:    HLD
        Type options, press Enter.
          1=Send   2=Change   3=Hold   4=Delete   5=Display   6=Release   7=Messages
          8=Attributes        9=Work with printing status

        Opt    File        User        User Data    Sts    Pages    Copies    Form Type    Pty
          _    QSYSPRT     CPAN                      RDY       1        1       *STD          5
          _    QSYSPRT     CPAN                      RDY       1        1       *STD          5
          5    SCHOOLFRF   JFOTTRAL                  RDY       8        1       *STD          5
          _    DBCULTPF    JFOTTRAL                  RDY       6        1       *STD          5
          _    INITDSP     JFOTTRAL                  RDY       3        1       *STD          5
          _    INITPGM     JFOTTRAL                  RDY       4        1       *STD          5
          _    QSYSPRT     ASOPR                     RDY       2        1       *STD          5
          _    QSYSPRT     ASOPR                     RDY       1        1       *STD          5
          _    QPDZDTALOG  SPHILLIPS                 RDY       1        1       *STD          5
          _    QPQUPRFIL   SPHILLIPS                 HLD       1        1       *STD          5

                                                                                    Bottom
        Parameters for options 1, 2, 3 or command
        ===>
        F3=Exit    F11=View 2    F12=Cancel    F20=Writers    F22=Printers
        F24=More keys
        Not authorized to spooled file.
```

Normally, this would not cause a problem because users would only work with their own spooled files and would not need to perform list options on other users' spooled files. The system operator, however, may need to hold or change priorities of spooled files to schedule printing efficiently. (S)he would therefore have spool control special authority over files spooled to a printer output queue. This special authority, granted through the user profile, lets the operator take necessary actions (e.g., hold, change, release, delete) on spooled files in the output queue.

When using the WRKOUTQ command, it is important to be familiar with the available function keys. You have seen already that F11 provides an alternate view of the list, and you can see that F3=Exit and F12=Cancel work as usual. You can use F20 to examine the status of all printer writers on the system, if they are active or on a job queue. If you need to check the status of printers on the system, function key F22 takes you to such a list, shown either as Figure 4.7 for Basic assistance level or Figure 4.8 for Intermediate assistance level. (We talk more about assistance levels later in this lesson.)

The items in the two lists are the same, but both the format and the options vary, depending on the assistance level. You can change the assistance level by using function key F21.

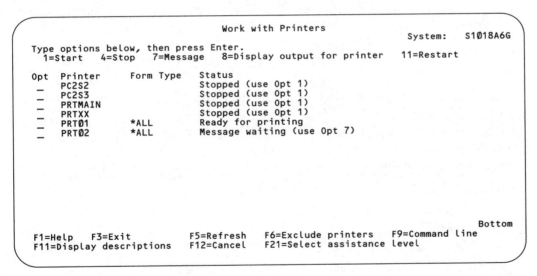

```
                          Work with Printers
                                                   System:    S1018A6G
      Type options below, then press Enter.
        1=Start    4=Stop    7=Message    8=Display output for printer    11=Restart

      Opt   Printer      Form Type    Status
        _    PC2S2                     Stopped (use Opt 1)
        _    PC2S3                     Stopped (use Opt 1)
        _    PRTMAIN                   Stopped (use Opt 1)
        _    PRTXX                     Stopped (use Opt 1)
        _    PRT01        *ALL         Ready for printing
        _    PRT02        *ALL         Message waiting (use Opt 7)






                                                                    Bottom
      F1=Help    F3=Exit         F5=Refresh    F6=Exclude printers   F9=Command line
      F11=Display descriptions   F12=Cancel    F21=Select assistance level
```

Figure 4.7
Work with Printers, Basic Assistance Level

Figure 4.8
Work with All Printers,
Intermediate Assistance
Level

```
                           Work with All Printers

 Type options, press Enter.
   1=Start   2=Change   3=Hold   4=End   5=Work with   6=Release
   7=Display messages   8=Work with output queue

 Opt  Device    Sts   Sep  Form Type   File        User        User Data
  _   PC2S2     END
  _   PC2S3     END
  _   PRTMAIN   END
  _   PRTXX     END
  _   PRT01     STR  *FILE  *ALL
  _   PRT02     MSGW *FILE  *ALL

                                                              Bottom
 Parameters for options 1, 2, 3, 4, 6 or command
 ===> _____
 F3=Exit   F11=View 2   F12=Cancel   F17=Top   F18=Bottom   F24=More keys
```

When a printer has a status of MSGW or Message waiting, as printer PRT02 does, choosing option 7 from either screen lets you view the message — and respond to it if you are authorized. Selecting option 7 — in this case, for printer PRT02 — results in the Additional Message Information screen shown in Figure 4.9.

Figure 4.9
Additional Message
Information for Printer
PRT02

```
                      Additional Message Information
 Message ID . . . . . . . :   CPA3387        Severity . . . . . . :   99
 Message type . . . . . . :   INQUIRY
 Date sent . . . . . . . :   08/15/98        Time sent . . . . . :   02:34:45
 From program . . . . . . :   QSPWTRM1        Instruction . . . . :   0000

 Message . . . . :   Device PRT02 not available. (C R)
 Cause . . . . . :   Writer PRT02 cannot use device PRT02 because the device is
   not powered on or varied on or is in use by another job.
 Recovery . . . :   Before entering a response, use the Work with
   Configuration Status (WRKCFGSTS) command to identify the status of the
   device. Vary on or power on the device if necessary.  Type C to cancel the
   request or type R to try the request again.
 Possible choices for replying to message . . . . . . . . . . . . . . . :
   C -- Enter C to cancel the writer.
   R -- Enter R to retry using the device.

                                                              Bottom
 Type reply below, then press Enter.
   Reply . . . . _____
 F3=Exit   F6=Print   F9=Display message details   F12=Cancel
 F21=Select assistanct level
```

The message tells you that the printer is not powered on, and it gives you two options for reply: C for cancel and R for retry. If you were the system operator, you could respond by turning on the printer and then typing R for Retry on the reply line.

As you can see, using function key F22 gives you an easy way to check the status of printers from your own output queue.

WORKING WITH SPOOLED FILES

The other Work with command, WRKSPLF (Work with Spooled Files), has a format similar to the WRKOUTQ command, but with one major difference: It lists all spooled files belonging to a single user regardless of which output queues they are in. The command prompt for the WRKSPLF command looks like the one shown in Figure 4.10.

```
                      Work with Spooled Files (WRKSPLF)

 Type choices, press Enter.

 Select files for:
   User  . . . . . . . . . . . . .   *CURRENT__    Name, *CURRENT, *ALL
   Print device . . . . . . . . .   *ALL_____    Name, *ALL, *OUTQ
   Form type  . . . . . . . . . .   *ALL_____    Form type, *ALL, *STD
   User data  . . . . . . . . . .   *ALL_____    User data, *ALL
 Output . . . . . . . . . . . . .   *_____        *, *PRINT




                                                               Bottom
 F3=Exit   F4=Prompt   F5=Refresh   F10=Additional parameters   F12=Cancel
 F13=How to use this display        F24=More keys
```

Figure 4.10
Work with Spooled Files Command Prompt Screen

Notice that the value of the first parameter, User, defaults to *CURRENT. AS/400 Help text will tell you that *CURRENT means "only files created by the user running this command are selected." The default values of *ALL for the other parameters mean that the list will not be restricted by printer device, form type, or user data. So when you enter the command on the command line with no parameters (i.e., you take the defaults), you get a list of all your own spooled files. Such a display would be similar to the one shown in Figure 4.11.

As you can see in this partial list, spooled files belonging to user JFOTTRAL are on four different output queues. The spooled files are listed in the order created: older files at the top of the list, within priority, within status. This command, therefore, is especially useful when you need to locate print files you may have created under different jobs, using different output queues.

The available options are the same as for the WRKOUTQ command, and they work the same way.

Figure 4.11

Work with All Spooled
Files List Screen for
User JFOTTRAL

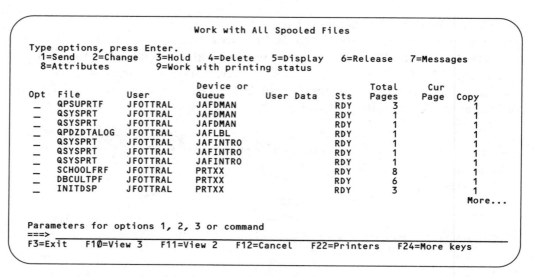

```
                           Work with All Spooled Files

 Type options, press Enter.
   1=Send    2=Change    3=Hold    4=Delete    5=Display    6=Release    7=Messages
   8=Attributes          9=Work with printing status

                              Device or                   Total    Cur
 Opt   File        User      Queue     User Data    Sts   Pages    Page   Copy
  _    QPSUPRTF    JFOTTRAL  JAFDMAN                 RDY      3             1
  _    QSYSPRT     JFOTTRAL  JAFDMAN                 RDY      1             1
  _    QSYSPRT     JFOTTRAL  JAFDMAN                 RDY      1             1
  _    QPDZDTALOG  JFOTTRAL  JAFLBL                  RDY      1             1
  _    QSYSPRT     JFOTTRAL  JAFINTRO                RDY      1             1
  _    QSYSPRT     JFOTTRAL  JAFINTRO                RDY      1             1
  _    QSYSPRT     JFOTTRAL  JAFINTRO                RDY      1             1
  _    SCHOOLFRF   JFOTTRAL  PRTXX                   RDY      8             1
  _    DBCULTPF    JFOTTRAL  PRTXX                   RDY      6             1
  _    INITDSP     JFOTTRAL  PRTXX                   RDY      3             1
                                                                        More...

 Parameters for options 1, 2, 3 or command
 ===>
 F3=Exit    F10=View 3    F11=View 2    F12=Cancel    F22=Printers    F24=More keys
```

CHANGING SPOOLED FILE ATTRIBUTES

Earlier, we talked about changing a spooled file to an output queue with an active
writer. Let's see how that works. Let's say you want to print spooled file
SCHOOLFRF, which (according to the Work with All Spooled Files screen shown
in Figure 4.11) is in output queue PRTXX. First you would select option 2
(change) on the Work with All Spooled Files screen. This would bring you to the
Change Spooled File Attributes screen shown in Figure 4.12.

Figure 4.12

Change Spooled File
Attributes on Spooled
File SCHOOLFRF

```
                    Change Spooled File Attributes (CHGSPLFA)

 Type choices, press Enter.

 Spooled file . . . . . . . . . . > SCHOOLFRF      Name, *SELECT
 Job name . . . . . . . . . . . . > SCHOOLFRF      Name, *
   User . . . . . . . . . . . .  >   JFOTTRAL      Name
   Number . . . . . . . . . . .  >   095843        000000-999999
 Spooled file number . . . . . . > 1               1-9999, *ONLY, *LAST
 Printer  . . . . . . . . . . .     PRTXX          Name, *SAME, *OUTQ
 Print sequence . . . . . . . . .   *SAME          *SAME, *NEXT
 Form type  . . . . . . . . . . .   *STD           Form type, *SAME, *STD
 Copies . . . . . . . . . . . . .   1              1-255, *SAME
 Restart printing . . . . . . . .   *STRPAGE       Number, *SAME, *STRPAGE...



                                                                      Bottom
 F3=Exit    F4=Prompt    F5=Refresh    F10=Additional parameters    F12=Cancel
 F13=How to use this display        F24=More keys
```

The cursor would be positioned on the first input-allowed field, the Printer parameter value, which is now set to PRTXX. Because you want to print this file, you would type over PRTXX and specify the name of a printer with an active writer (e.g., PRT01). When you press Enter, the command is executed and you are returned to the Work with All Spooled Files list screen. Now the screen, shown in Figure 4.13, indicates that file SCHOOLFRF has a status of *CHG (changed) and that the Device or Queue is PRT01.

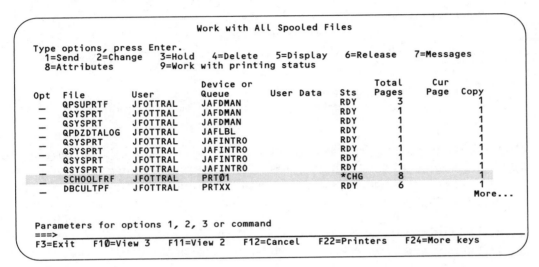

Figure 4.13

Work with All Spooled Files, with SCHOOLFRF Changed

You should understand that although you changed the Printer parameter value, file SCHOOLFRF will actually be sent to the output queue of the printer specified. If other large print jobs of an equal or higher priority are already on the queue, or if the queue itself is on hold, or if the printer device is out of paper or not turned on, your spooled file — although ready — might not print right away.

If you refresh your screen by pressing F5 and the printer is ready to go with no backlog of print files, your spooled file would probably show a status of PRT for printing.

You can perform several other useful functions with the Change option. This time, let's look at the attributes for spooled file DBCULTPF, and let's request additional parameters by pressing F10. The resulting screen is shown in Figure 4.14.

Figure 4.14

Change Spooled File
Attributes for File
DBCULTPF

```
              Change Spooled File Attributes (CHGSPLFA)

  Type choices, press Enter.

  Spooled file . . . . . . . . . . > DBCULTPF     Name, *SELECT
  Job name . . . . . . . . . . . . > DBCULTPF     Name, *
    User . . . . . . . . . . . . . >   JFOTTRAL   Name
    Number . . . . . . . . . . . . >   095845     000000-999999
  Spooled file number  . . . . . . > 1            1-9999, *ONLY, *LAST
  Printer  . . . . . . . . . . . .   PRTXX        Name, *SAME, *OUTQ
  Print sequence . . . . . . . . .   *SAME        *SAME, *NEXT
  Form type  . . . . . . . . . . .   *STD         Form type, *SAME, *STD
  Copies . . . . . . . . . . . . .   1            1-255, *SAME
  Restart printing . . . . . . . .   *STRPAGE     Number, *SAME, *STRPAGE...

                     Additional Parameters

  Output queue . . . . . . . . . .   *DEV         Name, *SAME, *DEV
    Library  . . . . . . . . . . .                Name, *LIBL, *CURLIB
  File separators  . . . . . . . .   0            0-9, *SAME

  More...

  F3=Exit   F4=Prompt   F5=Refresh   F12=Cancel   F13=How to use this display
  F24=More keys
```

From this screen, you can specify a different type of form to print on, change the
number of copies, or specify where to restart in case printing is interrupted.

The Output queue parameter, the first one listed under Additional
Parameters, lets you send this print file to another output queue not attached to a
writer in case, for example, you want to send a report to a co-worker's output
queue for her to review before printing.

The next screen (Figure 4.15) provides even more parameters.

Figure 4.15

Change Spooled File
Attributes, Second
Screen

```
              Change Spooled File Attributes (CHGSPLFA)

  Type choices, press Enter.

  Page range to print:
    Starting page  . . . . . . . .   1            Number, *SAME, *ENDPAGE
    Ending page  . . . . . . . . .   *END         Number, *SAME, *END
  File becomes available . . . . .   *FILEEND     *SAME, *JOBEND, *FILEEND...
  Save file  . . . . . . . . . . .   *NO          *SAME, *NO, *YES
  Output priority  . . . . . . . .   5            1-9, *SAME, *JOB
  User data  . . . . . . . . . . .   '         '  User data, *SAME
  Align page . . . . . . . . . . .   *NO          *SAME, *NO, *YES
  Print quality  . . . . . . . . .   *STD         *SAME, *STD, *DEVD, *DRAFT...
  Form feed  . . . . . . . . . . .   *DEVD        *SAME, *DEVD, *CONT, *CUT...
  Print fidelity . . . . . . . . .   *CONTENT     *SAME, *ABSOLUTE, *CONTENT
  Print on both sides  . . . . . .   *NO          *SAME, *NO, *YES, *TUMBLE...
  Pages per side . . . . . . . . .   1            *SAME, 1, 2, 4

                                                                  More...

  F3=Exit   F4=Prompt   F5=Refresh   F12=Cancel   F13=How to use this display
  F24=More keys
```

Two of the more useful parameters let you specify a range of pages to be printed (Page range to print) and retain a spooled file in an output queue after printing (Save file). If Save file is set to *NO, the normal default, the spooled file will no longer be available after printing.

The operator can use the output priority parameter to schedule when certain files should print in relation to other files. For example, if several files are waiting to print, the operator can give an important file a higher priority, moving it ahead of others in the queue.

Another useful parameter is User data. This parameter lets you add up to 10 characters of identifying information to a spooled file. You can then use this identifying information to organize spooled files by function or application and to select specific spooled files to be listed by specifying a value for the User data parameter on the WRKSPLF command.

ASSISTANCE LEVELS

As we noted earlier, the system supports two assistance levels — **Basic assistance level** and **Intermediate assistance level** — for certain types of AS/400 displays. The assistance level determines the amount of information displayed and how the information is formatted. The assistance level is set by a system value, but it can be changed for individual users by a user profile parameter. Also, you can change it as you view those screens having alternate assistance levels by using function key F21.

Let's look again at the Work with All Spooled Files display in Figure 4.13. Like the Work with All Printers screen, the WRKSPLF command display can appear in two different formats, depending on the assistance level. The difference in formats for the WRKSPLF command is quite pronounced. If you press function key F21 and select Basic, you see a screen like the one shown in Figure 4.16.

```
                    Work with Printer Output
                                              System:    S1018A6G
  User . . . . . .    JFOTTRAL

  Type options below, then press Enter.  To work with printers, press F22.
     2=Change    3=Hold   4=Delete   5=Display        6=Release   7=Message
     9=Work with printing status    10=Start printing   11=Restart printing

        Printer/
  Opt    Output      Status
        PRTXX
    _     DBCULTPF    Printer stopped (use Opt 10)
    _     INITDSP     Printer stopped (use Opt 10)
    _     INITPGM     Printer stopped (use Opt 10)
        PRT01
    _     SCHOOLFRF   Printer message (use Opt 7)
    _     QPQUPRFIL   Printed and kept (use Opt 6 to reprint)
        Not Assigned
    _     QPSUPRTF    Not assigned to printer (use Opt 10)
    _     QSYSPRT     Not assigned to printer (use Opt 10)
                                                            More...

  F1=Help   F3=Exit      F5=Refresh   F6=Completed printer output
  F11=Dates/pages/forms   F12=Cancel   F22=Work with printers   F24=More keys
```

Figure 4.16
Work with Printer Output, Basic Assistance Level

This screen organizes its list by printer. If a spooled file is not in a printer output queue, you are told only that it is "Not assigned." You can't tell which output queue it's in. The alternate display (F11) shows date and time, but still doesn't specify the output queue.

Also, if you select the Change option for a file listed on the Work with Printer Output screen in Basic assistance level, you can change only a limited number of attributes. Figure 4.17 shows the screen that results when you specify the Change option for file DBCULTPF (listed in Figure 4.14).

Figure 4.17

Change Printer Output
for File DBCULTPF,
Basic Assistance Level

```
                            Change Printer Output
 User . . . . . . . . :    JFOTTRAL     Date . . . . . . . . :   07/26/98
 Printer output . . . :    DBCULTPF     Time . . . . . . . . :   19:13:36
 Pages . . . . . . . :     6
 Status . . . . . . . :    Printer stopped

 Type choices below, then press Enter.

     Printer to use . . . . . .    PRTXX          Name, F4 for list

     Copies and pages:
        Number of copies . . . .   1              1-255
        First page to print  . .   1              Number
        Last page to print . . .   *LAST          Number, *LAST

     Type of forms  . . . . . .    *STD           Form type, *STD

     Print this output next . .    N              Y=Yes, N=No

     Save printer output  . . .    N              Y=Yes, N=No


  F1=Help    F3=Exit    F5=Refresh    F12=Cancel
```

Notice the differences between this screen and the one you saw in Figure 4.14. The name of the screen is Change Printer Output — rather than Change Spooled File Attributes, as you saw at the Intermediate assistance level — and it displays fewer parameters. For example, no option is available to send this spooled file to another nonprinter output queue; nor can you change priority or add identifying user data as you can on the CHGSPLFA prompt screen.

For most requirements, the Basic assistance level Work with Printer Output interface would be adequate; but for certain options, you may need to be sure your assistance level is set to Intermediate when working with spooled files.

In the lab that follows you have a chance to practice controlling some print output of your own. So now that you have a basic understanding of how spooling works, let's give it a try!

Key Terms

Basic assistance level

Intermediate assistance level

printer writer

spool control special authority

spooled files

system spooler

INTRODUCTION

In this lab you should become familiar with finding spooled files and taking appropriate actions to display, print, or send them to other output queues. In the lab, instructions to print a screen refer to the system print facility, not to a network or workstation print screen. If you are not sure of the difference, be sure to ask your instructor/mentor.

Before starting this lab, you should be sure that you have successfully completed Lab 3. That is, you should have created an output queue in your own user library and changed your user profile to use that output queue.

Lab 4

Part 1

Goals	Display your spooled files using the Work with Printer Output screen
	Use the information displayed on this screen to identify spooled files
	Use the Change Printer Output display to send a spooled file to a printer

Start at	Any command line

Procedure	Go to USER menu
	Select the option to Work with your spooled output files

1.1. Sign on as usual. You want to work with the spooled files you created in the previous lab, so select 1, User tasks, starting from the Main menu. (We're following a menu path in this lab to increase your familiarity with the commands.) From the USER menu, read through the initial list of tasks that can be performed and choose the appropriate one. This choice should take you to the Work with Printer Output screen (Figure 4.18).

If the screen you see at this time doesn't look like Figure 4.18, and instead is titled Work with All Spooled Files, use function key F21 to change the assistance level to Basic.

Figure 4.18

Work with Printer Output Screen

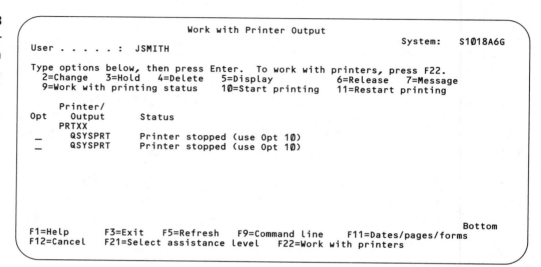

```
                          Work with Printer Output
                                                      System:   S1018A6G
User . . . . . :  JSMITH

Type options below, then press Enter.  To work with printers, press F22.
  2=Change   3=Hold   4=Delete   5=Display          6=Release   7=Message
  9=Work with printing status    10=Start printing  11=Restart printing

      Printer/
Opt    Output      Status
      PRTXX
  _     QSYSPRT    Printer stopped (use Opt 10)
  _     QSYSPRT    Printer stopped (use Opt 10)




                                                                 Bottom
F1=Help       F3=Exit    F5=Refresh    F9=Command line   F11=Dates/pages/forms
F12=Cancel    F21=Select assistance level    F22=Work with printers
```

1.2. On this screen, printer files are listed under the printer device whose output queue currently contains them.

    1.2a. Move the cursor to the Printer/Output column and use Help to find out the value that would display for the printer if the spooled file were in an output queue not belonging to a printer.

1.3. Return to the Work with Printer Output screen. A different view of this display is available by pressing the F11 key. Please do that now.

    With this view, the date and time of creation, number of pages, number of copies, and form type are displayed. F11 typically presents an alternate view of a list or command prompt screen. Now switch back to the Status display by pressing F11 again. Move the cursor over to the Status column and press Help. Use the appropriate function key to enlarge the Help window.

    1.3a. What status will be displayed if a spooled file is currently printing?

1.4. Exit Help and look again at the Work with Printer Output screen. Notice how the list items are formatted under the Printer/Output column; the output file names are grouped within a printer device name and indented two positions.

    1.4a. On your display, what name is used for the Output file? List all the different names if there are more than one.

    1.4b. How are the Output file names assigned? (Where do they come from?)

Lab 4

1.5. From this screen, you can take various options for spooled files. One of them is the Change option that lets you change certain attributes of a spooled file. Select that option now for the first file in your list by typing 2 in the option input field, and then pressing Enter.

1.6. You should now be looking at the Change Printer Output screen (Figure 4.19). Use extended Help to read about the meaning of these attributes and the possible values they can take.

```
                          Change Printer Output

  User . . . . . . . . . :  JSMITH       Date . . . . . . . . :  08/02/98
  Printer output . . . :  QSYSPRT        Time . . . . . . . . :  11:01:19
  Pages . . . . . . . :  1
  Status . . . . . . . :  Printer stopped

  Type choices below, then press Enter.

      Printer to use . . . . . .   PRTXX___     Name, F4 for list

      Copies and pages:
        Number of copies . . . .   1__          1-255
        First page to print  . .   1__          Number
        Last page to print . . .   *LAST        Number, *LAST

      Type of forms  . . . . . .   *STD____     Form type, *STD

      Print this output next . .   N            Y=Yes, N=No

      Save printer output  . . .   N            Y=Yes, N=No


  F1=Help    F3=Exit    F5=Refresh    F12=Cancel
```

Figure 4.19
Change Printer Option Screen, Basic Assistance

1.6a. Can any user change any printed output to print next?

Exit Help and look again at the Change Printer Output screen.

1.7. Notice that although you can redirect a spooled file to a defined printer, no option is available to send a spooled file to another (nonprinter) output queue.

On some entry screens a list of valid parameter values can be generated by pressing F4 on an input field. When this is true, the values themselves often vary from one system to another, such as printer names, which depend on the naming convention and number of printers in a particular installation. This capability is identified by showing F4 for list as a choice.

For the spooled file we are currently changing, let's use this feature to select a different printer to use by pressing the prompt key with the cursor on the entry field.

1.7a. List all printers whose status is not Stopped that can be selected at this time.

Now change the parameter value by selecting PRT01 from the prompt list. Press Enter to place the selected printer name in the entry field. Press Enter again to execute the command and return to the Work with Printer Output screen.

1.7b. What message is displayed on the message line?

Notice the changed status of your spooled file.

Part 2

Goals	Change the assistance level for Work with Spooled Files Test system print screen to ensure that output is going to your output queue Change your existing system printer spooled files to your own output queue

Start at	Work with Printer Output (WRKSPLF, Basic assistance level)

Procedure	Press F21 to change the assistance level Print the screen, then press F5 to find the new spooled file Select option 2 on the PRTXX spooled files to change to your own output queue

2.1 Now print the Work with Printer Output screen itself. If you are using the AS/400 System print function, the message "Print operation complete to the default printer device file" should appear at the bottom of your screen. Remember to press the Reset key after the message appears.

2.1a. Does the new print file appear on the screen?

This type of screen is not automatically updated when, for example, a new spooled file enters an output queue. To update the screen, press function key F5.

2.1b. To which printer is the new spooled file assigned?

The spooled file you just created should have gone to your own output queue, but the problem here is that you can't tell which output queue the spooled file is in; you can tell only that it is not in a printer output queue.

The current Work with Printer Output screen displays as it does because Basic assistance level is in effect. Although this display is useful in showing which spooled files are in a given printer's output queue, it does not show which output queue a spooled file is in if that queue is not a printer queue. Also, some spooled files of different status don't show up at all. The change option that you just looked at also lacks certain functions when taken from a Basic assistance level. But you can see a different display of spooled files by using a different assistance level.

2.2. Find the function key to select the assistance level and press it. Select Intermediate for the assistance level, then press Enter.

Notice the different title and format of this screen.

2.2a. How many spooled files are there?

2.2b. Which output queues are they in?

2.3. If you have no spooled files, or if there are none in your own (user-name) queue, create one by printing the current screen. Reset to clear the message, then press F5 to refresh.

At this point, all system print screens should be going to your own output queue. You should now have at least one spooled file in your user-name output queue. If the file you just created went to PRTXX (the default output queue) instead, you need to review Lab 3, making sure that

a. your user-name *OUTQ actually exists in your library

b. your user profile output queue parameter was changed to the user-name output queue that you created (CHGPRF, prompt, check OUTQ parameter)

If both a and b above are true but your output is still going to the default output queue, you may just need to sign off and back on again. *If that doesn't do it, you need to seek help from your instructor/mentor before going on.*

2.4. Under the Device or Queue column, you should also see one or more files listed in the PRTXX (default) queue. If so, select option 2 for each of those files so that you can change them to your own queue. When you press Enter (after typing 2 in the Opt field for each file to be changed) you should see a Change Spooled File Attributes command prompt screen (Figure 4.20). The cursor will be on the Printer parameter.

```
                    Change Spooled File Attributes (CHGSPLFA)

 Type choices, press Enter.

 Spooled file . . . . . . . . . . > QSYSPRT      Name, *SELECT
 Job name . . . . . . . . . . . . > PCSTAFFS1    Name, *
   User . . . . . . . . . . . . . >   JSMITH     Name
   Number . . . . . . . . . . . . >   096221     000000-999999
 Spooled file number  . . . . . . > 2            1-9999, *ONLY, *LAST
 Printer  . . . . . . . . . . . .   PRTXX____    Name, *SAME, *OUTQ
 Print sequence . . . . . . . . .   *SAME        *SAME, *NEXT
 Form type  . . . . . . . . . . .   *STD_____   Form type, *SAME, *STD
 Copies . . . . . . . . . . . . .   1____        1-255, *SAME
 Restart printing . . . . . . . .   *STRPAGE__   Number, *SAME, *STRPAGE...




                                                                  Bottom
 F3=Exit   F4=Prompt   F5=Refresh   F10=Additional parameters   F12=Cancel
 F13=How to use this display        F24=More keys
```

Figure 4.20

Change Spooled File Attribute Screen, Intermediate Assistance

You could send the spooled file to another printer from this field, just as you could from the Change Printer Output screen of Basic assistance. But you really want to send these files to a different output queue, your own, not a printer.

2.5. First, you need to find the Output queue parameter. (If it's not on the initial screen, try looking at Additional parameters.) Use Field advance (Tab) or New line to move down to the Output queue parameter. Type in your output queue name. Remember, your output queue name does not begin with an asterisk (*).

    2.5a. Why is it not necessary to specify your library name for the Output queue Library field?

Now press Enter. Do the same for any other files that were sent to PRTXX.

If the spooled file you sent to PRT01 earlier hasn't printed yet, it will still show device or queue PRT01. In that case, leave it there — it should print later, after the printer is turned on, messages are responded to, earlier print jobs are finished, or other problems are resolved. At this point, the Work with All Spooled Files screen should show that all other spooled files are in your own user-name output queue. *Do not proceed until you are certain of this.*

Part 3

Goals	Use the Work with Output Queue command to find and hold a spooled file
	Send a spooled file to a printer; delete other spooled files
	Check the printer output queue and release a spooled file
	Check for messages pending for a printer
Start at	WRKSPLF at the Intermediate assistance level
Procedure	Go to the command to work with your output queue
	Select option 2 to change to a printer output queue
	Select option 4 to delete
	Use F22 to work with printers
	Select option 8 to work with printer output queue
	Select option 6 to release a spooled file

3.1. Without leaving the Work with All Spooled Files screen, print the screen and then reset. From the command line, type the command to work with output queues, and request parameter prompting. (Not sure of the command? Try GO CMDOUTQ.)

Specify your own output queue (do not use *ALL), and run the command.

The Work with Output Queue command is concerned only with the files in the specified queue. This differs from the Work with Spooled Files command, which lists all output files for a given user regardless of queue.

3.1a. How many files are in your output queue now?

To find a particular spooled file in a list, you could use option 5 to display each one until you found the one you were looking for. Or, keeping in mind that more recently created spooled files appear at the bottom of the list, within priorities, you could use F11 on the Work with Output Queue screen to display an alternate view showing date and time of creation; that information should help you locate the spooled file more quickly.

3.2.   Find the print screen file created in Step 3.1 and select the appropriate option to hold it. You should notice the change in its status. Delete the other files.

3.2a. What happens when you select the delete option?

Go ahead and confirm to delete your other spooled files.

3.3.   Use F9 to retrieve the previous WRKOUTQ command and change the OUTQ parameter value to PRTXX. (Be sure to delete excess characters within the parentheses.) Run the command and page through the files in the queue. Do you find any files with your user name? If so, delete them. At this point, there should be no files in the PRTXX output queue with your name. *Be sure that this is true before going on.*

3.4.   To print the file held in Step 3.2, you need to send it to a printer with an active writer, such as PRT01. First return to your own output queue by pressing F3 from the WRKOUTQ PRTXX display screen. (If this does not take you to the Work with Output Queue display for your own queue, either recall or enter the WRKOUTQ command that names your output queue.) Now there should be only the single held spooled file in your output queue. Using the change option, change the printer parameter value to PRT01. Press Enter to make the changes.

3.5.   Back at the Work with Output Queue screen, find the function key for Printers and press it. You should now see a list of printers similar to that shown in Figure 4.21.

If your display is titled Work with all Printers and formatted differently, you are probably using Intermediate assistance level. To make your display appear similar to Figure 4.21, change to Basic assistance level.

Figure 4.21
Work with Printers
Screen, Basic
Assistance

```
                              Work with Printers
                                                    System:    S1018A6G
   Type options below, then press Enter.
     1=Start   4=Stop    7=Message    8=Display output for printer    11=Restart

   Opt   Printer      Form Type    Status
    __    PC2S2                     Stopped (use Opt 1)
    __    PC2S3                     Stopped (use Opt 1)
    __    PRTMAIN                   Stopped (use Opt 1)
    __    PRTXX                     Stopped (use Opt 1)
    __    PRT01        *ALL         Message waiting (use Opt 7)
    __    PRT02        *ALL         Message waiting (use Opt 7)




                                                                    Bottom
   F1=Help    F3=Exit        F5=Refresh  F6=Exclude printers   F9=Command line
   F11=Display descriptions  F12=Cancel  F21=Select assistance level
```

3.5a. What is the current status of PRTXX? of PRT01? of PRT02?

From the list of printers, choose PRT01 and select the option to display output for the printer.

3.5b. Is your spooled file in the list?

Return to the Work with Printers display and change the assistance level to Intermediate. Select option 8 on device PRT01, but notice that this time the option is defined as Work with Output Queue.

3.5c. Now how many files display? Is your file (the print screen of Work with All Spooled Files) there?

Select the option to display your file to make sure it's the one you redirected. What is its status? If its status is hold, as it should be, release it.

3.6. Once you have released your print file, the change in status should register and the file should print. If you refresh the screen at this point, the file should be gone or the status should show it is printing. If it has not printed, check the status of the queue itself to make sure it is not on hold. (The output queue status is displayed in the upper right corner of the screen.) If the queue is on hold, notify the system operator.

Another possibility is that the printer could be "ended" (status END). If so, starting the printer may do the trick; but again, this is the system operator's job, so ask the operator to start the printer, if necessary.

If the printer is not on hold and not ended, there may be messages that require a reply. From the Work with All Printers screen, select option 7, Display Messages. If messages such as "Verify alignment on device PRT01" are pending, they need to be replied to before printing can continue. This is also the operator's responsibility; please alert the AS/400 operator to the need for a reply to the message.

3.7.   By this time your file should have printed, as well as the earlier spooled file you printed from the PRTXX output queue in Step 1.7. Be sure to collect the printed output (get it from the operations room) and clip or staple it to your answer sheet. When you return to the Work with Output Queue screen for the printer and refresh, your print file should be gone. If you have carefully followed the above instructions and still can't get your file to print, see your instructor/mentor.

3.8.   You should now have hard-copy printout of two display screens to hand in with your answer sheet. Also, you should have deleted any other of your print files on output queue PRTXX, and your own output queue should now be empty. Files on output queues take up disk space. Disk space costs money and is limited. Everyone should perform necessary housekeeping on spooled files they create to keep clutter to a minimum. Whenever you are about to end a session, use the WRKSPLF command to clean up any spooled files you have. Print out those that need printing and delete anything else not required for future reference.

Part 4

Goals	Change the Assistance level parameter of your user profile
Start at	Any command line
Procedure	Type CHGPRF and prompt; find and change the Assistance level parameter value

4.1.   To avoid confusion caused by different assistance levels, it would be beneficial for everyone to be on the same assistance level from this point on. From a command line, prompt for the CHGPRF (Change Profile) command.

The default value of the Assistance level parameter is *SYSVAL, but each user can specify his/her own assistance level regardless of what the system is set to. Change the value to *INTERMED, for intermediate level, then press Enter. (Of course, if QASTLVL on your system is already set to *INTERMED, this change will have no effect.)

This change causes commands whose display output varies depending on assistance level to use the intermediate display the first time that command is executed. It does not automatically change levels for commands run previously and whose assistance level has been selected (F21). So if you just selected *BASIC for the WRKSPLF command, this change to your user profile does not cause the WRKSPLF display to come up as *INTERMED the next time you use it. And of course, you can still select a different assistance level for any command having a variable display (e.g. WRKSPLF, WRKOUTQ, WRKWTR, DSPMSG). And if you do so, that display will remain at the level you selected until you change it back, even if you sign off and back on again. So the user profile change affects only command displays that have not been selected yet. Eventually you will find that the intermediate level is more useful to work with because it provides more complete information and allows greater flexibility.

Mastering the AS/400, Second Edition

Lab 4 Answer Sheet

Name: _____

Date Due: _____   Class Time: _____

1.2a. _____ Not assigned _____

1.3a. _____ Printing page X of y (currently printing) _____

1.4a. _____

1.4b. _____

1.6a. _____ No you have to have spool control   * SPLCTL _____

1.7a. _____

1.7b. _____

2.1a. _____   2.1b. _____

2.2a. _____   2.2b. _____

2.5a. _____

_____

3.1a. _____

3.2a. _____

3.5a. _____   _____   _____

3.5b. _____   3.5c. _____

In Summary

In this lesson you have extended your knowledge of printer spooling. You have seen how the spooler component called the printer writer, which sends spooled files to a printer file device, can be "attached" to different output queues. You have also seen how a spooled file can be changed, sending it to an output queue with a writer already functioning. You have learned about two important Work with commands: WRKOUTQ (Work with Output Queue), which lists all spooled files in a specified output queue, and WRKSPLF (Work with Spooled Files), which lists all spooled files on the system that belong to a user. You have examined options common to both commands, and you have seen the difference in display format and functions available depending on user assistance level, *BASIC or *INTERMED.

In the lab you have used options to delete or change the status of spooled files, and you have moved spooled files to a queue with a printer attached. You have looked at the printer's output queue, held print files, and released a print file to be printed. It is important that you understand these tasks. For all future occasions when you must generate printed output, you need to manage the spooled files in your own output queue. For example, you need to dispose of unnecessary files and direct good files to a printer queue, so that you can print them when required.

Lesson 5

Describing a Database File

Lesson Overview

In this lesson we introduce the concept of externally described files and explain how to use the Data Description Specifications (DDS) language to describe a physical database file. We also introduce the Programming Development Manager (PDM) and the Source Entry Utility (SEU), two AS/400 tools important not only for creating database files, but also for developing programs.

In the lab, you create a source physical file and then use PDM to create a source member. You also use SEU to enter DDS source code for a database physical file into the source member, which you save for use in a subsequent lab.

Objectives

Students will be able to

- ✓ Tell the difference between externally described and program described files
- ✓ Demonstrate the basic operations of SEU
- ✓ Use PDM to move from a list of libraries to a list of objects to a list of members
- ✓ Use DDS to describe a simple physical file
- ✓ Create a source physical file and enter specifications for a data file member using SEU

FILE VARIETIES

On the AS/400, all files are classified as object type *FILE. Within that classification, the AS/400 recognizes 12 varieties of *FILE type objects. A particular *FILE type is identified by a subtype, or attribute. The system assigns the attribute, which describes how the file is to be used within the system, when a file is created; the attribute assigned is determined by the CL command used to create the file. It is beyond the scope of this text to explain all file attributes, but programmers and operators commonly use several of them, and those bear mentioning here. These common file attributes include

PRTF   Printer files, which we discussed in Labs 3 and 4, format output from programs or utilities to create spooled print files in output queues.

DSPF   Display files are similar to printer files in function, but they format data going to or coming from display screens rather than printers. Display files let you format data on screen displays and control color, high intensity, reverse image, and other display attributes. You can also control placement of constants, such as screen identification information and field identifiers. Application programs and utilities can write data to and read data from display files. You create your own display files in a later lesson.

PF   Physical files have two distinct functions: to hold and organize user data, such as a customer master file or sales transaction file, and to organize source programs and source data file descriptions written by programmers in languages such as Cobol, RPG, and DDS. In the latter capacity, physical files are similar to source program libraries or source file subdirectories used by other operating systems. Under OS/400, these two functions are distinguished by an attribute identifier: PF-DTA for data physical files and PF-SRC for source physical files.

LF   Logical files are created over physical database files and cannot be created before the physical file. A logical file is always based on one or more physical files. Logical files do not contain data; rather, they store access paths, or pointers, to records in physical files. You can think of logical files as "filters" or limiting "views" of data stored in physical files. You can use logical files to secure data (for example, to restrict the type or amount of data presented to an application) or for efficiency (for example, to present data records in an order different from the order in which they are stored in the physical file).

Now let's look at how to describe physical files to the system (you learn more about logical and display files — and how to create them — in later lessons). You can describe physical files to OS/400 two ways: as program-described files or as externally described files.

PROGRAM-DESCRIBED FILES

Physical files described at the record level contain only a record name and record length. Any program that uses a file described in this manner must supply field-level attributes (e.g., field name, data type, field length) for every field in the record. Because files described at the record level require the programs that use them to provide additional specifications, they are referred to as **program-described files**.

Program-described files can be useful when you need to convert older, nonrelational files to the AS/400 relational database format or when you need to move files from another system to the AS/400. But the permanent use of program-described files is not recommended because having to describe a record's fields in every program that uses the file is tedious and prone to errors.

EXTERNALLY DESCRIBED FILES

Physical files that contain detailed field-level descriptions of their records, as well as information about how the file is to be accessed, are referred to as **externally described files**. That is, the detailed description of the file exists outside of, or external to, the programs that use the file.

Because an externally described file contains field-level descriptions within the file object itself, the file carries its own record "blueprint" with it wherever it goes. Consequently, any user program or system utility that accesses the file can determine the details of its record layout and all field-level attributes just by knowing the object's name (assuming the program is authorized to use the file).

Externally described files offer several major advantages:

- *Standardized record formats* — Because field attributes (including field names) are stored in the file object itself, the use of externally described files eliminates the confusion caused when programmers use different names for the same field. Also, with externally described files it is almost impossible to incorrectly specify field length, data type, or number of decimal positions because these critical attributes are contained in the file object. You can easily check or compare an externally described file's record format by executing a DSPFFD (Display File Field Description) command on the file object.

- *Utilities that are easier to use* — Because the file objects describe themselves and name all their fields and attributes, system utilities (e.g., Query/400, Data File Utility, Screen Design Aid) can obtain this critical information directly from the file. Consequently, less work is required on the programmer's part when using these utilities to update data files, create queries and reports, and code display files.

- *Less-tedious programming* — When programmers use externally described files in programs written in high-level languages (HLLs) such as Cobol and RPG, they no longer need to code the record structures and field-level specifications in each program that uses the file. Instead, they simply name the file and indicate to the compiler that it is externally described; when the program is compiled, the information in the file is pulled into the program and converted into the proper syntax for the HLL. Because the file object itself is the source of the record format information, and not a source library member or a copy book (a source code description separate from the physical data structure), you eliminate the possibility of pulling in a wrong version of the record format when the program is compiled.

Externally described files contain information at three levels of data hierarchy: the file level, the record format level, and the field level. This hierarchy can best be illustrated by looking at a file field description display for an existing database physical file. You can access such a display through a menu path, but getting there is somewhat indirect. A more direct approach is to use the DSPFFD command; the only required parameter is the file name. If you ran the command on a database physical file named STUPF in library JSMITH, the display shown in Figure 5.1 would appear.

Figure 5.1

Display File Field Description Screen for File STUPF

```
                          Display Spooled File
 File  . . . . . :   QPDSPFFD                    Page/Line   1/1
 Control . . . . .                               Columns     1 - 78
 Find  . . . . . .
 *...+....1....+....2....+....3....+....4....+....5....+....6....+....7....+...
                      Display File Field Description
  Input parameters
    File  . . . . . . . . . . . . . . . . . . . :   STUPF
      Library . . . . . . . . . . . . . . . . . :   JSMITH
  File Information
    File  . . . . . . . . . . . . . . . . . . . :   STUPF
      Library . . . . . . . . . . . . . . . . . :   JSMITH
    File location . . . . . . . . . . . . . . . :   *LCL
    Externally described  . . . . . . . . . . . :   Yes
    Number of record formats  . . . . . . . . . :     1
    Type of file  . . . . . . . . . . . . . . . :   Physical
    File creation date  . . . . . . . . . . . . :   08/07/98
    Text 'description'. . . . . . . . . . . . . :   Jane Smith, Intro AS/400
  Record Format Information
    Record format . . . . . . . . . . . . . . . :   STUPFR
    Format level identifier . . . . . . . . . . :   4248C5858BD3E
                                                                      More...

  F3=Exit    F12=Cancel    F19=Left    F20=Right    F24=More keys
```

The file information tells you the file name (STUPF), the library name (JSMITH), the file location (*LCL, which means the file is on the local system — it is not a distributed database file or located on a remote system), that the file is externally described, the number of record formats (1), and the file type (physical).

The record format information lists the **record format** name (a physical file contains a single record format, which must be named); in this case, the record format name is STUPFR. The system also uses a format level identifier to ensure that programs and files agree on version.

On the second screen of the display (Figure 5.2), you can see two additional record format attributes: number of fields and record length.

```
                        Display Spooled File
 File  . . . . . :  QPDSPFFD                Page/Line   1/22
 Control . . . . .                          Columns     1 - 78
 Find  . . . . . .
 *...+....1....+....2....+....3....+....4....+....5....+....6....+....7....+...
      Number of fields  . . . . . . . . . . . . :       8
      Record length . . . . . . . . . . . . . . :     116
 Field Level Information
                 Data      Field   Buffer    Buffer      Field
       Field     Type     Length   Length   Position     Usage    Column Heading
       SOCSEC    ZONED      9  0       9          1       Both     SOCSEC
       FNAME     CHAR      15         15         10       Both     FNAME
       ACTBAL    ZONED      7  2       7         25       Both     ACTBAL
       LNAME     CHAR      20         20         32       Both     LNAME
       WPHONE    ZONED     10  0      10         52       Both     WPHONE
       ADDR1     CHAR      25         25         62       Both     ADDR1
       ADDR2     CHAR      25         25         87       Both     ADDR2
       ZIP       ZONED      5  0       5        112       Both     ZIP



                                                              Bottom
 F3=Exit    F12=Cancel    F19=Left    F20=Right    F24=More keys
```

Figure 5.2

Display File Field
Description Screen,
Page 2

The essence of an externally described file is in the field level information. All the critical information is already there, in the file object. For each field, the system records a name, data type, length (characters and digits), length in bytes, position in the record buffer, field usage (input, output, or both), and a column heading for use by utilities. This may seem like a lot of information for each file to carry around with it — and overhead is involved in creating and maintaining it. But remember, once recorded, this information never needs to be repeated, and it is always available for programs and utilities to use and for you to see should questions about the file's record format arise.

Record format is an important concept for externally described files. OS/400 examines record formats to determine whether two files share the same record structure (e.g., in a CPYF (Copy File) command). Figure 5.2 shows all the defining characteristics of record format, which include the number of fields and total record length, the relative order of fields, and each field's name, data type, and length.

Creating an Externally Described Database File

The process of creating an externally described database physical file involves three distinct steps:

1. *Describe*: You must first describe the file's record format and field-level attributes at the source language level, much as you would first write a computer program in a source language (e.g., C, RPG, Cobol, Basic).

2. *Create*: After you describe the file, you can create the file object by compiling the source language file description. This step is analogous to creating an executable machine-level object program by compiling Cobol or RPG source.

3. *Insert data*: When you've successfully compiled the source description into a *FILE type object, you can insert, or load, data into the file.

In this lesson, you learn in more detail how to describe a database file. In Lesson 6, you learn more about creating the database file and inserting data into it.

METHODS OF DESCRIBING DATABASE FILES AT THE FIELD LEVEL

There are three approaches to describing files at the field level. You can use the Interactive Data Definition Utility (IDDU), Structured Query Language (SQL), or Data Description Specifications (DDS).

IDDU

IDDU is a menu-driven, interactive approach to describing database files that originated with one of the AS/400's ancestors, the System/36. For that reason, IDDU might be the preferred method for programmers experienced on that system, but this approach does have some limitations. The primary limitation is that IDDU can be used only for physical database files; you cannot use it to describe logical or display files.

IDDU stores its file descriptions in a data dictionary format (a dictionary-like listing of field names and their attributes) under the control of OS/400. Although easy to learn and use, IDDU's lack of power and flexibility, and the fact that you must use another method for describing other file types, prevents it from becoming the method of choice for programmers and operators new to the IBM midrange platform.

SQL

SQL is a powerful relational database language that lets you describe and create physical or logical files. You can also use SQL to limit access to, maintain, and retrieve information from files, regardless whether they were created with SQL.

SQL is a standardized database language used not only on the AS/400, IBM mainframes, and PCs, but also on many other vendors' platforms. SQL's wide support means SQL-based applications are highly portable, which provides a significant incentive for learning SQL.

However, using SQL exclusively to define, control, and manipulate database files does have certain drawbacks. First, the SQL/400 licensed program product is not part of the base operating system support; you must purchase it separately, just as you would a Cobol, C, or RPG compiler. Second, SQL is a powerful tool capable of wasting huge numbers of DASD I/O operations and CPU machine cycles if misused, and mastering it requires a fairly steep learning curve. Third, the object overhead created by SQL collections, catalogs, indexes, data dictionaries, views, journals, and journal receivers is significant compared to DDS-described physical and logical files. And finally, you cannot use SQL alone to describe and create a display file with any degree of sophistication for screen interactive I/O. Regardless of your proficiency with SQL, you need another tool for display files.

DDS

DDS is a language used to code source descriptions for several types of files, including physical and logical database files, display files, and printer files. For the most part, DDS offers a wider range of function and greater flexibility than either IDDU or SQL.

The Screen Design Aid (SDA), a powerful generator of display file screens for interactive jobs, converts user-supplied screen layout specifications into DDS source. Likewise, the Report Layout Utility (RLU) facilitates report design and modification and converts user specifications into DDS source. For physical and logical files, SEU, a general-purpose editor, lets you enter and syntax-check DDS source statements. The availability of these utilities, along with the convenience and flexibility they provide for describing physical and logical files, makes learning DDS a worthwhile if not necessary endeavor for AS/400 professionals.

In this book, we focus on DDS because it is the most commonly used method for describing files on the AS/400. Although the complexity of DDS precludes anything more than a brief introduction here, you will have at least some initial exposure to the language and an indication of its capability.

Before we begin the discussion of DDS, however, we need to introduce two important software tools, both of which are part of Application Development Tools (ADT). Although not included in the base operating system, ADT is such a valuable aid for creating and maintaining programs and files of all kinds that it would be inconceivable to attempt such work without it.

The first tool is the **Programming Development Manager** (PDM). PDM provides a convenient way to create source members and access SEU and many other useful tools for programmers. With the possible exception of smaller shops that do no programming, PDM is installed on all systems.

The second tool is the **Source Entry Utility** (SEU), which is used to enter all kinds of source code on the AS/400. SEU is a "smart editor" that not only knows the line formats of different languages' source statements, but also can check for syntax errors in the source statements of various languages, including RPG, Cobol, CL, and DDS. SEU is indispensable for programming as well as for describing physical and logical database files using DDS.

INTRODUCTION TO PDM

PDM is a workbench environment that lets programmers and system operators navigate the three levels of the AS/400's object-based architecture: the library level, the object level, and the member level. PDM, which provides access to AS/400 functions through a standard list interface, lets you move easily from one level to the next. For instance, you can start at the library level, then drop down to the object level. From the object level, you can either go back up to the library level or drop down to the member level.

Through PDM, you can work with libraries, objects, or members by selecting from predefined options; alternatively, you can define your own options, similar to creating macros in other software products. You can start PDM by following a menu path: From the MAIN menu, select choice 5 to reach the PROGRAM menu, and then choice 2 to reach the PDM menu. Alternatively, you can simply type the STRPDM (Start PDM) command on any command line to go directly to the PDM menu. You can also use the appropriate Work with command (e.g., the

WRKOBJPDM — Work with Objects Using PDM — command) to go immediately to PDM lists of libraries, objects, or members.

The STRPDM Command

The PDM menu you reach when you follow the menu path or execute the STRPDM command is similar to the one shown in Figure 5.3.

Figure 5.3
PDM Menu Screen

```
                    AS/400 Programming Development Manager (PDM)
  Select one of the following:

       1. Work with libraries
       2. Work with objects
       3. Work with members

       9. Work with user-defined options




  Selection or command
  ===> _____

  F3=Exit       F4=Prompt      F9=Retrieve      F10=Command entry
  F12=Cancel    F18=Change defaults
```

As you can see, the three levels of the AS/400 object-oriented architecture (libraries, objects, and members) are listed as menu choices. A fourth choice (Work with user-defined options) lets you define or change your own PDM options. We examine user-defined PDM options later, but for now let's see how the PDM library, object, and member levels are connected.

Selecting choice 1, Work with libraries, results in an entry screen that asks for the name of the library or libraries you wish to work with. At this screen, you can request a list of user libraries, a list of libraries whose names all begin with certain characters (e.g., entering a generic name such as JAF* lists all libraries beginning with JAF), or a list of all libraries in your library list (by taking the default, *LIBL).

When you take the default, the system displays a Work with Libraries Using PDM screen similar to the one shown in Figure 5.4 (the composition of the library list will vary from user to user).

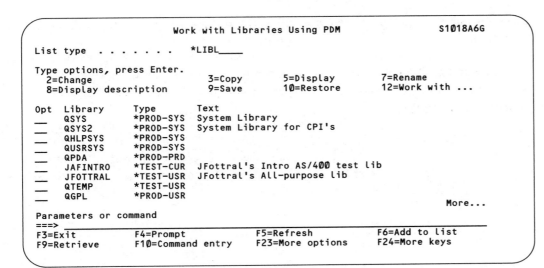

Figure 5.4
Work with Libraries
Using PDM Screen

Work with Libraries Using PDM

The Work with Libraries Using PDM screen displays text (if any) for each library, and each list item occupies an entire line of the display. Because of this, the entire library list for some users' jobs won't fit on a single screen (that's why you see "More..." at the bottom of the screen in Figure 5.4). If you press function key F11 (which does not appear on the initial function key list; to see it, press F24), the list is formatted to show library names and types only. When the text field is not displayed, as many as three columns of listed items can appear at once, as in Figure 5.5 (although the display has room for three columns, the library list shown here needs only two columns).

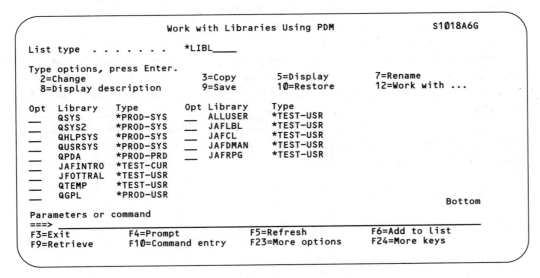

Figure 5.5
Work with Libraries
Using PDM Screen
(Alternate Format)

Notice that you can take various actions on the listed libraries by entering the appropriate option number on the input field for a particular list item. More options are available than those displayed above the list; to view them, press F23. You can also display IBM-supplied user-defined PDM options (which use letters instead of numbers) by pressing F16. When you select an option, PDM invokes the appropriate CL command. PDM supplies required command parameters based on a list item's name and type and on the name of the library or file the PDM list item came from.

Because PDM draws from information contained in its list, you are spared considerable keying effort. In addition, you can select the same option for multiple objects in the list, and PDM will repeat the necessary command automatically. For example, you can specify option 7 — to rename an object — for several different libraries, as illustrated in Figure 5.6 for libraries JAFINTRO, JAFLBL, JAFDMAN, and JAFRPG.

Figure 5.6
Example of Selecting the Same Option for Multiple Libraries

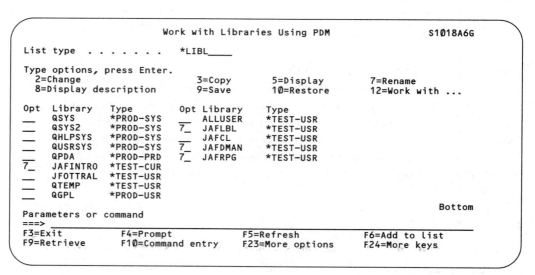

```
                         Work with Libraries Using PDM              S1018A6G

    List type . . . . . . .    *LIBL____

    Type options, press Enter.
      2=Change                 3=Copy          5=Display        7=Rename
      8=Display description    9=Save          10=Restore       12=Work with ...

    Opt  Library   Type       Opt  Library   Type
    __   QSYS      *PROD-SYS   __   ALLUSER   *TEST-USR
    __   QSYS2     *PROD-SYS   7_   JAFLBL    *TEST-USR
    __   QHLPSYS   *PROD-SYS   __   JAFCL     *TEST-USR
    __   QUSRSYS   *PROD-SYS   7_   JAFDMAN   *TEST-USR
    __   QPDA      *PROD-PRD   7_   JAFRPG    *TEST-USR
    7_   JAFINTRO  *TEST-CUR
    __   JFOTTRAL  *TEST-USR
    __   QTEMP     *TEST-USR
    __   QGPL      *PROD-USR
                                                                       Bottom
    Parameters or command
    ===> _
    F3=Exit          F4=Prompt          F5=Refresh         F6=Add to list
    F9=Retrieve      F10=Command entry  F23=More options   F24=More keys
```

Before pressing Enter, you might want to see the actual command the specified option invokes. You can do so by pressing function key F4. You will then see the command prompt screen — in this case, for the RNMOBJ (Rename Object) CL command — as shown in Figure 5.7.

You can see that all parameters have been given values. The object (name) and object type values came from the PDM list item for which the option was taken. The new object value is the same as the current library name. Executing the command like that would make no sense and would result in an error (you can't rename an object to the same name), but PDM still assigns the value to facilitate the change. The point is that all PDM options invoke commands, and when you type in an option and request prompting, you see the prompt screen for the command PDM is prepared to execute. You can also see how list item values have been substituted for the command as parameter values.

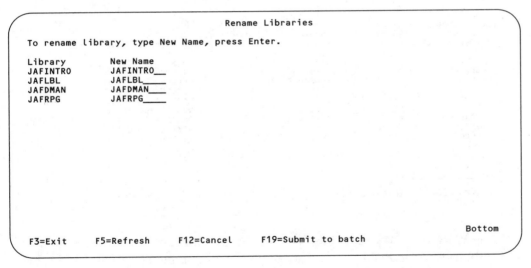

```
                         Rename Object (RNMOBJ)

 Type choices, press Enter.

 Object . . . . . . . . . . . . . > JAFINTRO      Name
   Library . . . . . . . . . . . > QSYS          Name, *LIBL, *CURLIB
 Object type . . . . . . . . . . > *LIB          *ALRTBL, *AUTL, *CFGL...
 New object . . . . . . . . . . > JAFINTRO__     Name




                                                              Bottom
 F3=Exit   F4=Prompt   F5=Refresh   F12=Cancel   F13=How to use this display
 F24=More keys
```

Figure 5.7
Rename Object
(RNMOBJ) Command
Prompt Screen

Now let's cancel the prompt (F12) and return to the PDM screen in Figure 5.6. If you press Enter from this screen, the system displays the Rename Libraries input screen (Figure 5.8), where you can supply new names for all the selected libraries at once.

```
                         Rename Libraries

 To rename library, type New Name, press Enter.

 Library        New Name
 JAFINTRO       JAFINTRO__
 JAFLBL         JAFLBL____
 JAFDMAN        JAFDMAN___
 JAFRPG         JAFRPG____




                                                              Bottom
 F3=Exit      F5=Refresh      F12=Cancel      F19=Submit to batch
```

Figure 5.8
Rename Libraries
Input Screen

For example, if you want to change all JAF prefixes to JER, you can do so easily simply by keying over the prefix of the displayed library names, leaving the class designators as they are. Modifying or typing in new library names is the closest you would come in this case to entering parameter values.

As we have shown, when using PDM you can select an option on several list items at the same time, and the options will either be grouped together, as for renaming, or will be processed one after another. You can also select different options on different list items, in which case the options will be processed from top to bottom and grouped (e.g., all the Rename options together) where applicable.

Now that we have seen how PDM handles options selected on list items, let's see how Work with Libraries Using PDM connects to the next level (objects) in the AS/400 object-based hierarchy.

Work with Objects Using PDM

Using defaults, Work with Objects Using PDM displays a list of all objects in a specified library. If you don't specify a library, PDM uses the library name from the preceding PDM session. You can get to the Work with Objects Using PDM screen from the PDM menu (Figure 5.3) by selecting choice 2. If you are already at a Work with Libraries Using PDM screen, you can get to the Work with Objects Using PDM screen by selecting option 12 on one of the libraries in the list. For example, in Figure 5.6, selecting option 12 on library JAFINTRO takes you to the Work with Objects Using PDM screen shown in Figure 5.9. (In PDM, you can return to the library list from the Work with Objects Using PDM screen by pressing F12 when you are finished with the object list.)

Figure 5.9

Work with Objects Using PDM Screen (Three-Column Format, Page 1)

```
                          Work with Objects Using PDM                    S1018A6G
      Library . . . . .    JAFINTRO__        Position to . . . . . . . :_____
                                             Position to type  . . . . :_____

      Type options, press Enter.
        2=Change      3=Copy          4=Delete       5=Display      7=Rename
        8=Display description          9=Save        10=Restore     11=Move ...

      Opt Object      Type    Opt Object      Type    Opt Object      Type
       __ CLPGM01     *PGM     __ DFUF1CHG    *FILE    __ LFILE01     *FILE
       __ CLPGM02     *PGM     __ DFULF1DSP   *FILE    __ QCLSRC      *FILE
       __ CLPGM03     *PGM     __ FILE01      *FILE    __ QCMDSRC     *FILE
       __ DFUF1CHG    *PGM     __ FILE01B     *FILE    __ QDDSSRC     *FILE
       __ DFULF1DSP   *PGM     __ FILE01BK    *FILE    __ QQMFORMSRC  *FILE
       __ GRADEPGM    *PGM     __ FILE01DTA   *FILE    __ QQMQRYSRC   *FILE
       __ JAFINTRO    *OUTQ    __ F1TEST      *FILE    __ QTXTSRC     *FILE
       __ BUCKET1     *FILE    __ GRADEDSP    *FILE    __ TESTLF      *FILE
                                                                        More...
      Parameters or command
      ===>
      F3=Exit         F4=Prompt          F5=Refresh        F6=Create
      F9=Retrieve     F10=Command entry  F23=More options  F24=More keys
```

The Work with Objects Using PDM screen, in a format similar to the Work with Libraries Using PDM screen, lists all objects in a single library and — in the three-column format displayed here — shows their type. If you press F11 to change the screen's format, only a single column of objects is displayed, but attribute and text are shown for each (Figure 5.10).

The attribute information PDM lists for *FILE and *PGM type objects can be useful if you are trying to find the source code used to create the object. The attribute for *PGM type objects indicates the language in which the program was written. For example, at the top of the list shown in Figure 5.10, several programs have the attribute CLP, meaning Control Language Program; their source code can normally be found in source physical file QCLSRC. Two other programs have

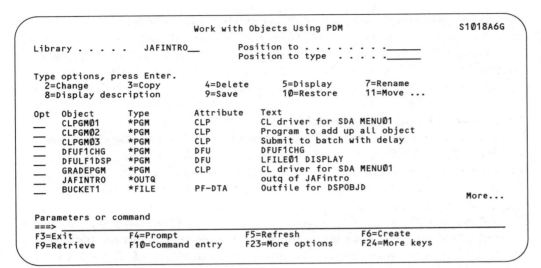

Figure 5.10
Work with Objects
Using PDM Screen
(Single-Column Format,
Page 1)

```
                    Work with Objects Using PDM              S1018A6G

  Library . . . . .   JAFINTRO__     Position to . . . . . . . .:_____
                                     Position to type  . . . . .:_____

  Type options, press Enter.
    2=Change        3=Copy        4=Delete      5=Display     7=Rename
    8=Display description          9=Save       10=Restore    11=Move ...

  Opt  Object      Type     Attribute   Text
  __   CLPGM01     *PGM     CLP         CL driver for SDA MENU01
  __   CLPGM02     *PGM     CLP         Program to add up all object
  __   CLPGM03     *PGM     CLP         Submit to batch with delay
  __   DFUF1CHG    *PGM     DFU         DFUF1CHG
  __   DFULF1DSP   *PGM     DFU         LFILE01 DISPLAY
  __   GRADEPGM    *PGM     CLP         CL driver for SDA MENU01
  __   JAFINTRO    *OUTQ                outq of JAFintro
  __   BUCKET1     *FILE    PF-DTA      Outfile for DSPOBJD
                                                                 More...

  Parameters or command
  ===>
  F3=Exit          F4=Prompt        F5=Refresh       F6=Create
  F9=Retrieve      F10=Command entry  F23=More options  F24=More keys
```

the attribute DFU, indicating they are "permanent" DFU Change or Display programs created by the AS/400 Data File Utility. Notice that the *OUTQ type object has no attribute; in user libraries, generally only *FILE and *PGM type objects show attributes. The last object listed is a file named BUCKET1; the attribute PF-DTA indicates this object is a database physical file.

Another example of the Work with Objects Using PDM display (Figure 5.11) shows a number of files with the attribute PF-SRC, indicating they are source physical files holding source programs, file descriptions, and so on.

Figure 5.11
Work with Objects
Using PDM Screen
(Single-Column Format,
Page 3)

```
                    Work with Objects Using PDM              S1018A6G

  Library . . . . .   JAFINTRO__     Position to . . . . . . . .:_____
                                     Position to type  . . . . .:_____

  Type options, press Enter.
    2=Change        3=Copy        4=Delete      5=Display     7=Rename
    8=Display description          9=Save       10=Restore    11=Move ...

  Opt  Object      Type     Attribute   Text
  __   LFILE01     *FILE    LF          First LF view of FILE01
  __   QCLSRC      *FILE    PF-SRC      CL Source
  __   QCMDSRC     *FILE    PF-SRC      Source PF for new commands
  __   QDDSSRC     *FILE    PF-SRC      DDS source for Intro AS/400
  __   QQMFORMSRC  *FILE    PF-SRC      Query Mgmt Form Source
  __   QQMQRYSRC   *FILE    PF-SRC      Query Mgmt Source Select
  __   QTXTSRC     *FILE    PF-SRC      Text Source
  __   TESTLF      *FILE    LF
                                                                 More...

  Parameters or command
  ===>
  F3=Exit          F4=Prompt        F5=Refresh       F6=Create
  F9=Retrieve      F10=Command entry  F23=More options  F24=More keys
```

The file named QDDSSRC is a source physical file intended to hold source code for database and display files described using DDS. The name itself is symbolic. Although a name beginning with Q is usually an IBM-supplied name, this particular file was created by a user. Programmers commonly use IBM's naming convention as an aid in recognizing source physical files. The names of IBM's default source physical files begin with a Q and include the type of source the file is intended to store. For example, default source physical files in IBM-supplied library QGPL are named QCLSRC (if they contain CL source programs), QRPGSRC (if they hold RPG source programs), and so on. The DDS portion of the name QDDSSRC indicates that the source physical file holds members coded in DDS; the SRC part of the name stands for "source."

Notice that most of the options displayed on the Work with Objects Using PDM screen are similar to those on the Work with Libraries Using PDM screen. Additional options available for working with objects include 4=Delete and 11=Move. Option 12=Work with has been bumped to a second display of options, which you can view by pressing function key F23.

Just as you can use the Work with option on a selected library from the Work with Libraries Using PDM list to get to this list of objects, you can use the "Work with" option on a specified object from the Work with Objects Using PDM screen to get to some kind of a Work with list. The nature of the list screen you see depends on the type and attribute of the list item upon which you took the option. A *FILE object whose attribute is PF, whether a source or database physical file, usually contains one or more data components called **members**. The Work with option taken on such an object takes you to the lowest level of PDM, Work with Members Using PDM.

Work with Members Using PDM

Selecting option 12 on source physical file QDDSSRC results in a Work with Members Using PDM screen like the one shown in Figure 5.12 (the list of members will be different for different users).

Figure 5.12
Work with Members
Using PDM, QDDSSRC

```
                              Work with Members Using PDM                    S1018A6G
     File  . . . . . .     QDDSSRC___
        Library . . . .    JAFINTRO__            Position to  . . . . ._____

     Type options, press Enter.
        2=Edit          3=Copy   4=Delete 5=Display      6=Print      7=Rename
        8=Display description  9=Save  13=Change text  14=Compile  15=Create module...

     Opt  Member       Type        Text
     __   FILE01       PF_____   DDS_of_PF_file01
     __   F01V01       LF_____   1st_LF_desc._for_file01
     __   F1TEST       PF_____   Source_DDS_for_FILE01
     __   GRADEDSP     DSPF_____   Display_file_for_grade_generator
     __   LFILE01      LF_____   First_LF_view_of_FILE01
     __   LFILE01B     LF_____   Modified_LFILE01
     __   MENU01       DSPF_____   menu01_for ADMIN user
     __   RLUTEST1     PRTF_____   Printer_file_from_RLU
                                                                      More...
     Parameters or command
     ===>
     F3=Exit           F4=Prompt          F5=Refresh          F6=Create
     F9=Retrieve       F10=Command entry  F23=More options    F24=More keys
```

When you want to create or change a source member in a source physical file, this Work with Members Using PDM screen provides an efficient work environment.

The File and Library fields at the upper left remind you which member list you are viewing. Because these fields are both input-enabled, you can change to the member list of another file and/or library by keying over the displayed value(s) and pressing Enter.

The options list for working with members is different from the options list for working with objects. Although no save/restore capability is available for individual members, you can use option 9 to save the file of which the member is a part. In addition, an edit option (2) lets you modify existing source file members, and a print option (6) lets you create hard copy of the source code.

Creating a Member Via SEU

To create a new member from the Work with Members Using PDM screen, you use function key F6. Pressing F6 invokes the STRSEU (Start SEU) command and takes you to the command prompt screen for that command (Figure 5.13).

```
                       Start Source Entry Utility (STRSEU)
   Type choices, press Enter.

   Source file  . . . . . . . . . . > QDDSSRC      Name, *PRV
     Library  . . . . . . . . . . . >   JAFINTRO   Name, *LIBL, *CURLIB, *PRV
   Source member  . . . . . . . . .   *PRV_____  Name, *PRV, *SELECT
   Source type  . . . . . . . . . .   *SAME_____  Name, *SAME, BAS, BASP, C...
   Text 'description'  . . . . . . .  *BLANK_____







                                                                        Bottom
   F3=Exit   F4=Prompt   F5=Refresh   F12=Cancel   F13=How to use this display
   F24=More keys
```

Figure 5.13
Start Source Entry
Utility (STRSEU) Screen

As the figure shows, PDM supplies the first two parameter values (source file name and library name) based on the file and library information on the preceding PDM screen. For the source member parameter, you enter the name of the source program or file description you plan to create. Usually, you use the same name you intend to use for the compiled program or file; it is less confusing to use the same name for both the source member and the object created from it. The batch compile option on the Work with Members Using PDM screen assigns the member name to the newly created object by default.

As an example, let's name the new member EMPPF (EMPloyee Physical File). For most parameters, it doesn't matter whether you use uppercase or lowercase; except for quoted strings, SEU changes them to uppercase.

The value supplied for the source type parameter is important. In addition to determining which source language syntax checker and prompter is used, it tells PDM which Create command (CRT*xxx*) to use when the source member is compiled. For file descriptions, the source type can be either PF (for a physical file), LF (logical file), or DSPF (display file). Because we are creating a physical database file, we use type PF. The system stores the value you enter for the Text 'description' parameter as a quoted string; it is the only case-sensitive parameter value. In our example (Figure 5.14), we describe the file as Employee PF Source. Remember, you do not need to enclose the text with apostrophes (single quotes); the command prompter does that for you.

Figure 5.14
Filled Out STRSEU
Screen

```
                        Start Source Entry Utility (STRSEU)
   Type choices, press Enter.

   Source file . . . . . . . . . > QDDSSRC        Name, *PRV
     Library . . . . . . . . . . >   JAFINTRO     Name, *LIBL, *CURLIB, *PRV
   Source member . . . . . . . .   emppf_____     Name, *PRV, *SELECT
   Source type . . . . . . . . .   pf_____     Name, *SAME, BAS, BASP, C...
   Text 'description' . . . . . .   Employee PF Source_____




                                                                        Bottom
   F3=Exit    F4=Prompt    F5=Refresh    F12=Cancel    F13=How to use this display
   F24=More keys
```

When you press Enter from this screen, the SEU Edit work screen (Figure 5.15) appears. A message at the bottom of the screen tells you the new member has been added to file QDDSSRC.

Figure 5.15
SEU Edit Work
Screen

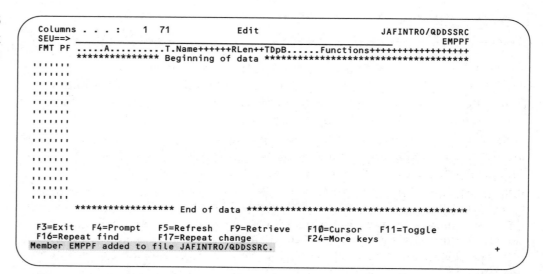

```
   Columns . . . :    1  71          Edit              JAFINTRO/QDDSSRC
   SEU==> _____        EMPPF
   FMT PF  .....A..........T.Name++++++RLen++TDpB......Functions++++++++++++++++++
   *************** Beginning of data *************************************
   '''''''
   '''''''
   '''''''
   '''''''
   '''''''
   '''''''
   '''''''
   '''''''
   '''''''
   '''''''
   '''''''
   '''''''
   '''''''
   '''''''
         **************** End of data *****************************************
   F3=Exit   F4=Prompt    F5=Refresh    F9=Retrieve   F10=Cursor   F11=Toggle
   F16=Repeat find       F17=Repeat change       F24=More keys
   Member EMPPF added to file JAFINTRO/QDDSSRC.                          +
```

The column of apostrophes at the left on the Edit work screen indicates that a screen full of lines has been inserted and that full-screen entry of DDS source code can begin. For fixed-format languages such as DDS, however, it is usually more productive to use prompting to insert one line at a time into the source member work space. When you use prompting, SEU provides a prompt area that identifies each field and indicates its length. When you fill out the prompt and press Enter, the values you entered are correctly formatted in the work area.

Because different programming languages use different formats, you can tell SEU which prompt format to use via a line command (which we discuss shortly), or you can let SEU choose an appropriate format based on the source type value entered on the Start SEU screen. In our example, we used source type PF, and as you can see in the upper left corner of the Edit screen, the format selected is for a physical file (FMT PF). You can also change the prompt format at any time during an edit session, which may be necessary when you are using a language such as RPG, which has several format types.

To use prompting to enter lines of source, first clear the workspace by pressing the Enter key from the Edit work screen (Figure 5.15). The new Edit work screen looks like the one in Figure 5.16.

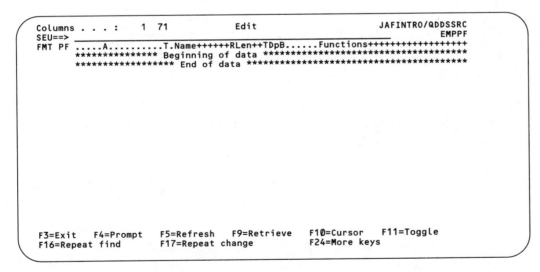

Figure 5.16
Cleared SEU Edit
Work Screen

On the screen's first line, "Columns" identifies the range of columns currently displayed in the work area. Function keys F19 and F20 let you shift the work area window left or right, respectively. The screen title identifies the SEU mode (e.g., Edit or Browse), and JAFINTRO/QDDSSRC identifies the name of the library and source physical file. On the second line is the SEU command line; the source member is identified on the far right. On the third line, you find the current member format (in this case, PF for physical file) and a format ruler indicating the field positions for the format. Because the Beginning of data and End of data markers are on consecutive lines, you can tell that nothing has been entered yet.

SEU Help

A lot of useful Help information is available from SEU. If you press the Help key with the cursor on the SEU command line, for example, the context-sensitive Help shown in Figure 5.17 appears.

Figure 5.17
SEU Command Line
Help Screen

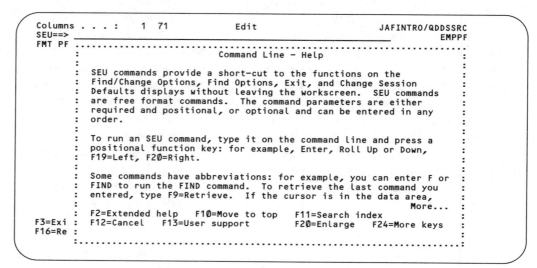

```
Columns . . . :    1  71              Edit               JAFINTRO/QDDSSRC
SEU==>                                                                EMPPF
FMT PF ...............................................................
      :                     Command Line - Help                     :
      :                                                             :
      :  SEU commands provide a short-cut to the functions on the   :
      :  Find/Change Options, Find Options, Exit, and Change Session :
      :  Defaults displays without leaving the workscreen.  SEU commands :
      :  are free format commands.  The command parameters are either :
      :  required and positional, or optional and can be entered in any :
      :  order.                                                     :
      :                                                             :
      :  To run an SEU command, type it on the command line and press a :
      :  positional function key: for example, Enter, Roll Up or Down, :
      :  F19=Left, F20=Right.                                       :
      :                                                             :
      :  Some commands have abbreviations: for example, you can enter F or :
      :  FIND to run the FIND command.  To retrieve the last command you :
      :  entered, type F9=Retrieve.  If the cursor is in the data area, :
      :                                                      More... :
      :  F2=Extended help   F10=Move to top    F11=Search index    :
  F3=Exi :  F12=Cancel    F13=User support         F20=Enlarge  F24=More keys :
  F16=Re :...............................................................
```

This Help text tells you how to use the command line to perform tasks such as saving the source member and finding a certain value in an existing member. (The find option can be useful if you're trying to locate a particular word or phrase in a long program or file description.)

Pressing F2 while displaying context-sensitive Help calls extended Help (Figure 5.18).

Figure 5.18
SEU Edit Help Screen
(Extended Help)

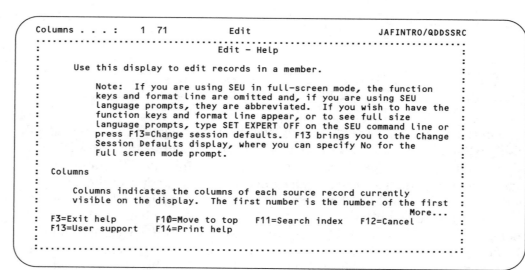

```
Columns . . . :    1  71              Edit               JAFINTRO/QDDSSRC
...............................................................
:                          Edit - Help                          :
:                                                               :
:   Use this display to edit records in a member.               :
:                                                               :
:       Note:  If you are using SEU in full-screen mode, the function :
:       keys and format line are omitted and, if you are using SEU :
:       language prompts, they are abbreviated.  If you wish to have the :
:       function keys and format line appear, or to see full size :
:       language prompts, type SET EXPERT OFF on the SEU command line or :
:       press F13=Change session defaults.  F13 brings you to the Change :
:       Session Defaults display, where you can specify No for the :
:       Full screen mode prompt.                                :
:                                                               :
:   Columns                                                     :
:                                                               :
:       Columns indicates the columns of each source record currently :
:       visible on the display.  The first number is the number of the first :
:                                                      More... :
:   F3=Exit help       F10=Move to top    F11=Search index   F12=Cancel :
:   F13=User support   F14=Print help                         :
:                                                               :
:...............................................................
```

This screen contains several pages of general information about using SEU and about SEU line commands. In the lab, you access the extended Help screen for SEU and read through it.

SEU Line Commands

From the SEU Edit work screen, you can start insert mode simply by typing a line command in the sequence column of the "Beginning of data" line. The sequence column, a seven-position field for each line, is at the far left of the work screen. The sequence column has two purposes: to maintain line sequence numbers for all lines of a source member and to allow entry of SEU line commands. **SEU line commands** let you change the edit work area and manipulate source member lines; for example, you can move, copy, delete, add, or insert lines.

Let's see what happens when you enter an SEU line command. First, you place the cursor one line below and one position to the left of the F in FMT, on the sequence column of the Beginning of data line. The cursor should already be in that position as a result of pressing Enter to clear the Edit work screen, as suggested earlier. If the cursor is not in that position, you can press the Tab or New line key (Shift + Enter on PCs) repeatedly to move it to that position.

If you are editing an existing source member, you can enter a line command over the sequence number of any existing record (line) of the member. In our example, to insert a line with prompting, you would enter the SEU line command IP (I for insert and P for prompting) on the Beginning of data line. The line command (before you press Enter) would look like that shown in Figure 5.19.

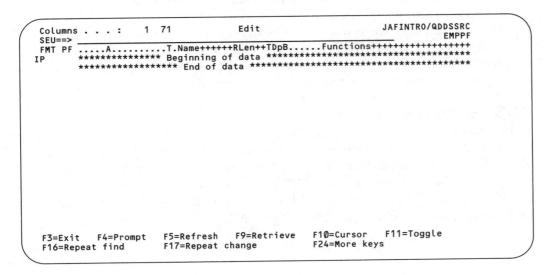

Figure 5.19
IP SEU Line Command to Insert with Prompting

When you press Enter, the screen splits horizontally to show a work area above and prompt lines below, as in Figure 5.20.

Figure 5.20
Prompt for DDS PF
Type with Values
Entered for a Record
Format Line

```
Columns . . . :     1  71            Edit                     JAFINTRO/QDDSSRC
SEU==>                                                                   EMPPF
FMT PF .....A...........T.Name++++++RLen++TDpB......Functions+++++++++++++++++++
       *************** Beginning of data ************************************
'''''''
       ***************** End of data *******************************************



    Prompt type . . .   PF       Sequence number . . .  '''''''

    Name                                   Data      Decimal
    Type      Name        Ref    Length    Type      Positions    Use
    R         EMPPFR____    _     _____     _        _____       _
    Functions
    _____




    F3=Exit    F4=Prompt    F5=Refresh          F11=Previous record
    F12=Cancel              F23=Select prompt   F24=More keys
```

This screen prompts for a DDS source entry for a physical file (PF). Eight entry fields are available, but for now we discuss only those you need to enter a simple physical file description. A more detailed description of DDS will come later.

All entry fields on the SEU prompt screen respond to the Help key, so when you are working in the lab, you can ask for context-sensitive Help on any field about which you have a question.

The minimal database physical file description contains a single record-format entry on the first line. Field-level entries, to describe each field, can follow. For a simple file description, each field-level entry also occupies one line in the editor work space and constitutes one record of the source member when saved.

DDS RECORD FORMAT ENTRY

DDS syntax requires a record-format entry for a physical database file before you can enter a field-level description. To enter a record format (which we've done in Figure 5.20), you need only specify R for the Name Type field and a value for the Name field (the example specifies EMPPFR as the name of the record).

When you press Enter, the record is moved up to the Edit screen work area and a new, empty prompt is provided (Figure 5.21).

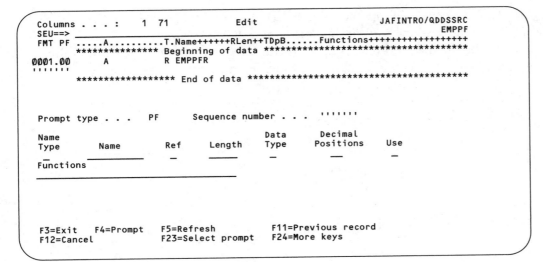

```
  Columns . . . :    1  71          Edit              JAFINTRO/QDDSSRC
  SEU==>                                                          EMPPF
  FMT PF .....A...........T.Name++++++RLen++TDpB......Functions++++++++++++++++++
         *************** Beginning of data *************************************
  0001.00    A        R EMPPFR
  ''''''''
         **************** End of data ******************************************


     Prompt type . . .  PF     Sequence number . . .  ''''''''

     Name                                     Data    Decimal
     Type      Name        Ref     Length     Type    Positions    Use
     _____   _____  _       _____      _       __           _
     Functions
     _____




     F3=Exit   F4=Prompt   F5=Refresh       F11=Previous record
     F12=Cancel            F23=Select prompt F24=More keys
```

Figure 5.21
New, Empty Prompt
Provided after Pressing
Enter

You can see that a sequence number (1.00) has been assigned to the inserted record. The decimal portion of the number lets you insert up to 99 new records between two existing records during the edit session without renumbering.

FIELD-LEVEL ENTRIES

After you insert a record format line, you can enter field-level descriptions. For these, you leave the Name Type field blank. But you must enter values for Name (field name), Length (number of characters or digits), and Data Type (e.g., character, zoned decimal, packed decimal, binary, date, time), and for numeric fields, you must enter the number of decimal positions. For a physical file, then, the four required attributes of a field are name, length, data type, and decimal positions.

Name

For record and field names, use from one to ten characters, the first of which must be uppercase alphabetic (A–Z) or one of the special characters @, $, or #. Subsequent characters can consist of any of these and the numbers 0 to 9 and the underscore character (_). Embedded blanks are not allowed in a name. Within a record format, field names must be unique.

Length

Length is the number of characters or digits in the field. For character, hexadecimal, and zoned decimal fields, the length defines the field size in bytes. The AS/400 uses the Extended Binary Coded Decimal Interchange Code (**EBCDIC**) method of encoding characters and zoned decimal numbers into binary code, and for all code points encompassed by EBCDIC (uppercase and lowercase alphabetic, numbers, special characters), one character equals one byte. So, for example, an address field of length 30 occupies 30 bytes of record buffer space. Languages whose alphabets do not code to EBCDIC (e.g., Japanese, Chinese) use a two-byte-per-character coding scheme called Double Byte Character Set (DBCS). The examples and exercises in this book assume EBCDIC data.

Because length and data type are related, we can't discuss one without the other. Each data type has a valid maximum length, as shown in Table 5.1.

Table 5.1

Data Types and Maximum Lengths

Abbreviation	Data Type	Maximum Length
P	Packed decimal	31 digits
S	Zoned decimal	31 digits
B	Binary	9 digits
F	Floating-point (short)	9 digits
F	Floating-point (long)	17 digits
A	Character	32,766 characters
H	Hexadecimal	32,766 bytes
L	Date	6, 8, or 10 characters
T	Time	8 characters
Z	Timestamp	26 characters

Remember that for numeric data types, the length specification really means the number of **digits** in the field. For date, time, and timestamp types, you do not specify a value for length; it is determined by type. The values shown above for date, time, and timestamp data types are the number of characters needed to display the stored values, not the number of bytes required for disk storage. It is this longer (display) length that is used in the record format. A date field can have three different lengths, depending on which date format is specified by the DATFMT keyword in DDS. If you do not use the DATFMT keyword, the default is *ISO* **format** (International Standards Organization), whose display format is YYYY-MM-DD (ten characters). The default for time format (also *ISO) is displayed as HH.MM.SS (eight characters). You can change this by using either a different time format, such as TIMFMT(*USA), or a different separator, such as TIMSEP(':').

Timestamp includes both the date and time and is formatted as YYYY-MM-DD-HH.MM.SS.UUUUUU (26 characters), where UUUUUU represents millionths of a second. A more detailed discussion of date and time formats and separators is beyond the scope of this text. For more information, see either IBM's *OS/400 DDS Reference V3R2* (SC41-3712) or Paul Conte's excellent book *Database Design & Programming for DB2/400* (Duke Press, 1997).

The obvious advantage to using date type fields is they use four digits to record the year. Although some date formats record only two digits for year, programs written to handle four-digit year fields, using DATFMT *ISO or *USA, for example, should have no Year 2000 problems at all. A less obvious advantage is the ability to perform date duration calculations easily. For example, if the system knows a transaction date (L Type) and the current date, it can calculate the difference in number of days without resorting to complex date-table lookups and without concern about the change of millennium.

Data Type

Data types (except for several DBCS types, which we do not discuss) are listed in Table 5.1. Character, **zoned decimal**, and hexadecimal types all occupy a number of bytes of storage equal to the length of the field. But for other numeric types, the length of the field in bytes is calculated from the number of digits. For example, if a social security number is typed S, the true length of the field is 9 (bytes and digits). But if the same field is typed P, then the value 9 specified for length really means 9 digits, and the true field length is 5 bytes. (Length in bytes of a packed decimal field can be calculated as (total digits / 2) + 1, throw away any decimal part.) This difference in length is due to the way in which numeric data is stored in packed decimal format: two digits per byte except for the rightmost byte, which codes the least significant digit in the high-order four bits and the sign in the low-order four bits. The advantages of storing numeric data in **packed decimal** format are that the field itself is smaller, requiring fewer bytes of storage space, and arithmetic/logic operations are more efficient, requiring fewer intermediate conversion steps. There may be minor disadvantages to storing numbers as packed decimal. For one thing, only a zoned decimal numeric field of a physical file can be redefined as a character field through a logical file. For another, you cannot directly observe the packed decimal field value by using a DSPPFM (Display Physical File Member) command, which does no conversion. (For sensitive data, this may not be a disadvantage at all!) DFU, Query/400, and SQL, on the other hand, convert all numeric representations, including packed decimal, to display format.

Hexadecimal fields can be used to store data whose code is not to be interpreted by the system. You can store any possible binary code in a hexadecimal field. For the most part, hexadecimal fields are treated like character fields. When the binary code corresponds to a printable character in EBCDIC, you can display or print the character, but the system doesn't translate hexadecimal code into other character sets.

The number of bytes of storage occupied by other numeric data types is determined by the number of digits specified for length as shown in Table 5.2.

Table 5.2

Other Numeric Data Types and Storage Bytes

Type	Number of Digits	Bytes of Storage
Binary	1 to 4	2
	5 to 9	4
Floating-point		
Short (single precision)	1 to 9	4
Long (double precision)	1 to 17	8

Floating-point short and long formats are both identified by F for data type, but a long (double-precision) number must be specified with the Float Precision keyword FLTPCN(*DOUBLE). The default is FLTPCN(*SINGLE). Floating-point formats represent values in scientific notation as mantissa and exponent and are generally not used for business applications dealing with integers or dollars and cents values.

Date, time, and timestamp fields all result in a fixed number of storage bytes regardless of the format or separators used (Table 5.3).

Table 5.3

Date, Time, and Timestamp Fields

Type	Display Size	Bytes of Storage (disk)
Date	6, 8, or 10 characters	4
Time	8 characters	3
Timestamp	26 characters	10

The values listed under Bytes of Storage are the field sizes when stored internally on disk. The fields are always expanded to the display size as they are moved to the record format, so both HLL programs and CL commands, such as DSPFFD, deal with these fields according to their display size, with separation characters already inserted. In other words, if you look at a record format containing a timestamp, you see 26 bytes of storage allocated, not 10.

Decimal Positions

You should use a value in the Decimal Positions field for physical file fields that represent numeric data, especially for those fields whose type is packed decimal, zoned decimal, or binary. The value specifies the number of digits to the right of the decimal point, the fractional part of a real number. The value can never be greater than the length. It is important to remember that the Decimal Positions field is a part of the Length field, not an addition to it. For a field defined as BIGNBR   15P 5 the total number of digits is 15, five of which are to the right of the (implied) decimal point.

When you code zero for the **decimal positions**, the field is considered to be an integer (e.g., SOCSEC   9S 0). DDS doesn't insist that you code a value for the decimal positions, and the field is compiled as an integer if you don't. But for documentation and consistency, it is better to code 0 for the Decimal Positions field. For nonintegers, decimal positions are always implied, never explicitly coded in the field; the system keeps track of the implied decimal point for you.

Note that if you don't explicitly provide a data type, the default is A (character) when no decimal positions value is specified. If you provide a decimal positions value and do not specify a data type, DDS defaults to the numeric packed decimal (P) data type.

To illustrate how different types of fields defined in DDS are incorporated into the compiled physical file record format, let's look at an example. Figure 5.22 shows a kind of nonsensical DDS record description, but we can perhaps gain some insight by studying it.

The record has fields of all types except DBCS. The first two fields, SOCSECZ and SOCSECP, are nine-digit integers; because no decimal positions value is coded, the

```
 Columns . . . :    1   71            Edit              JAFINTRO/QDDSSRC
 SEU==>                                                         TESTP
 FMT PF .....A..........T.Name++++++RLen++TDpB......Functions+++++++++++++++++
        *************** Beginning of data *********************************
 0001.00    A          R TESTR
 0002.00    A            SOCSECZ         9S
 0003.00    A            SOCSECP         9P
 0004.00    A            SINGLFLT        9F 5
 0005.00    A            DOUBLFLT       10F 5         FLTPCN(*DOUBLE)
 0006.00    A            SMALLBIN        4B 2
 0007.00    A            LARGEBIN        9B
 0008.00    A            HEXFIELD       33H
 0009.00    A            BIRTHDATE       L
 0010.00    A            BIRTHTIME       T
 0011.00    A            DATETIME        Z
        **************** End of data ****************************************



 F3=Exit   F4=Prompt   F5=Refresh   F9=Retrieve   F10=Cursor   F11=Toggle
 F16=Repeat find       F17=Repeat change           F24=More keys
                                     (C) COPYRIGHT IBM CORP. 1981, 1995.
```

Figure 5.22
A Sample DDS Record Description

default is 0 (we do not recommend this practice, but use it only for illustration). SINGLFLT and DOUBLFLT are single-precision and double-precision floating point numbers. Note that DOUBLFLT requires the FLTPCN(*DOUBLE) keyword to be coded. Next are two **binary** numbers. SMALLBIN has two decimal positions, and LARGEBIN is an integer by default. The hexadecimal field length, 33, should be the actual number of bytes the field occupies. Hexadecimal fields, because they are not numbers, cannot have a decimal positions value coded. At the end are date, time, and timestamp fields, which do not allow coding of either length or decimal positions.

Figure 5.23 shows the compiled file information. The figure itself is the printed output of the DSPFFD command for file TESTP. This command is useful for checking the record format and field definitions of database files.

Figure 5.23
DSPFFD Command
Output Showing
Compiled File
Information for File
TESTP

```
5716SS1 V3R6MØ  950929        Display File Field Description
                3/15/98  21:08:34        Page    1
Input parameters
   File . . . . . . . . . . . . . . . . . . . . . . :  TESTP
     Library . . . . . . . . . . . . . . . . . . . :  JAFINTRO

File Information

   File . . . . . . . . . . . . . . . . . . . . . . :  TESTP
     Library . . . . . . . . . . . . . . . . . . . :  JAFINTRO
   File location . . . . . . . . . . . . . . . . . :  *LCL
   Externally described . . . . . . . . . . . . . :  Yes
   Number of record formats . . . . . . . . . . . :     1
   Type of file . . . . . . . . . . . . . . . . . :  Physical
   File creation date . . . . . . . . . . . . . . :  03/15/98

Record Format Information

   Record format . . . . . . . . . . . . . . . . . :  TESTR
   Format level identifier . . . . . . . . . . . :  4E3E0983A340B
   Number of fields . . . . . . . . . . . . . . . :     10
   Record length . . . . . . . . . . . . . . . . . :    109

Field Level Information

              Data      Field   Buffer   Buffer       Field   Column
   Field      Type      Length  Length   Position     Usage   Heading

   SOCSECZ    ZONED      9  0      9          1        Both    SOCSECZ
   SOCSECP    PACKED     9  0      5         10        Both    SOCSECP
   SINGLFLT   FLTSNG     9  5      4         15        Both    SINGLFLT
   DOUBLFLT   FLTDBL    10  5      8         19        Both    DOUBLFLT
   SMALLBIN   BINARY     4  2      2         27        Both    SMALLBIN
   LARGEBIN   BINARY     9  0      4         29        Both    LARGEBIN
   HEXFIELD   HEX       33        33         33        Both    HEXFIELD
     Coded Character Set Identifier . . . . . :  65535
   BIRTHDATE  DATE      10        10         66        Both    BIRTHDATE
     Date Format . . . . . . . . . . . . . . . :  *ISO
     Coded Character Set Identifier . . . . . :     37
   BIRTHTIME  TIME       8         8         76        Both    BIRTHTIME
     Time Format . . . . . . . . . . . . . . . :  *ISO
     Coded Character Set Identifier . . . . . :     37
   DATETIME   TIMESTAMP 26        26         84        Both    DATETIME
     Coded Character Set Identifier . . . . . :     37
```

Under the Field Level Information heading, you can see that the Field, Data Type, and Field Length information corresponds to the DDS in Figure 5.22. Buffer Length shows the number of bytes each field occupies in the record buffer, and Buffer Position shows where in the buffer each field begins, relative to byte 1. Notice that the packed decimal version of SOCSEC takes five bytes of storage. A single-precision floating point number takes four bytes of storage, whether it is defined as one digit or nine digits. A double-precision number can be from one to seventeen digits but always occupies eight bytes of storage. Notice there is only one data type for the binary numbers; the system determines from the number of digits you specify for length whether to reserve a two- or four-byte field. You can see that the date and time fields default to *ISO format and that their buffer lengths as well as that for the timestamp field are consistent with the information given above. Because BIRTHDATE uses *ISO format (YYYY-MM-DD), it occupies ten bytes in the buffer.

Now let's return to our sample Employee file. If you entered an Employee ID field using prompting in SEU, the completed prompt line would look like that shown in Figure 5.24.

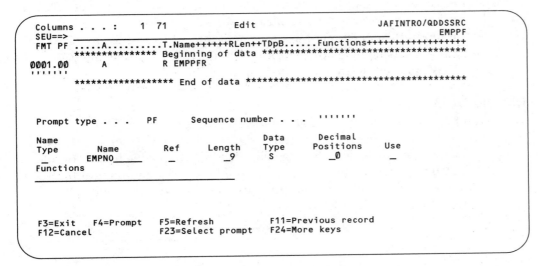

Figure 5.24
Prompt Lines after
Entering an Employee
ID Field

Be careful when entering digits in one of the numeric prompt fields (Length or Decimal Positions); the numbers you type must be right-aligned in the entry field. If you press Field exit after typing the digits, the system properly aligns them in the field and advances the cursor to the next field. After you press Enter, the new line is inserted into the work area following the record format line.

Figure 5.25 shows the work area after several more fields have been inserted and you've pressed F5 to clear the prompt. You can also clear the prompt by pressing F12 or by pressing Enter on an empty prompt.

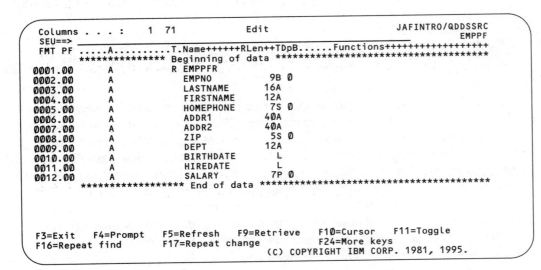

Figure 5.25
SEU Work Area after
Inserting Several More
Fields and Pressing F5

Notice on the SEU display in Figure 5.25 that BIRTHDATE and HIREDATE are coded as date fields, type L. Also note that SALARY is declared as a packed decimal field and EMPNO as a binary field. Normally, the database administrator decides which internal data format to use for different fields. For the example, we chose binary and packed decimal formats partly for illustration, but also because binary is the most efficient format for a nine-digit integer to be used as a key. And the likelihood that calculations will be done with SALARY, as well as the size advantage, make packed decimal ideal for this field.

EXITING SEU

When you have finished entering DDS source, press function key F3 to go to the SEU Exit screen. From there (Figure 5.26), you can decide whether to save the work you have done during your SEU session. If you have made changes or added records, the Change/create member prompt will be set to Y automatically. If you choose not to save your work, just type an N to cause an existing member to be left as it was before the SEU session.

Figure 5.26
SEU Exit Screen

```
                                          Exit
     Type choices, press Enter.

         Change/create member . . . . . . . .   Y            Y=Yes, N=No
           Member  . . . . . . . . . . . . .    EMPMSTPF__   Name, F4 for list
           File  . . . . . . . . . . . . . .    QDDSSRC___   Name, F4 for list
             Library . . . . . . . . . . . .       JAFINTRO__ Name
           Text  . . . . . . . . . . . . . .    Emp_Mast_PF_Source

         Resequence member . . . . . . . . .   Y            Y=Yes, N=No
           Start . . . . . . . . . . . . .      0001.00      0000.01-9999.99
           Increment . . . . . . . . . . .      01.00        00.01-99.99

         Print member  . . . . . . . . . . .   N            Y=Yes, N=No

         Return to editing . . . . . . . . .   N            Y=Yes, N=No

         Go to member list . . . . . . . . .   N            Y=Yes, N=No




     F3=Exit    F4=Prompt    F5=Refresh    F12=Cancel
```

From the Exit screen, you can also change the member name or the file and/or library in which the member will be stored. This capability is useful if you have created a new source member by editing an existing member whose name you do not want changed. As you exit, you can simply assign a new name to the edited (changed) member, thus saving your changes under the new name, leaving the original member intact under the original name.

Options are also available to resequence, print the member, return to editing, or go to a member list. Initial values are displayed for these parameters, but you can change them by keying over them. In most cases, the current values will be the ones you need, and you can just press Enter from the SEU Exit screen and return to the Work with Members Using PDM screen.

In this lesson, you have seen how to use the AS/400 database definition language, DDS, to describe a simple physical file. You have also seen how the general-purpose editor, SEU, facilitates entering DDS language statements through prompting and line commands. And you have seen how PDM, using options or function keys that invoke CL commands, provides a working environment that lets you perform operations on libraries, objects, and members with relative ease.

There is much more to learn about PDM, SEU, and DDS than we can present in this brief introduction, but now you have an idea of how these tools work together to help you create and manage database files, source files, and members. You add more detail to your understanding of these tools in later lessons, but for now, it's time to work through the lab exercise so you can solidify what you've learned so far.

Key Terms

binary

decimal positions

digits

EBCDIC

externally described files

field-level specification

floating point

*ISO format

member

packed decimal

Programming Development
   Manager (PDM)

program-described files

record format

record-format specification

Source Entry Utility (SEU)

SEU line commands

source physical file

zoned decimal

Lab 5

INTRODUCTION

This lab exercise helps you become familiar with PDM and SEU. You create a source physical file, QDDSSRC, in your library. You then use SEU to enter the DDS source code for a data file member named STUPF, which will eventually contain data for a STUdent Physical File.

Part 1

Goals	Create a source physical file
	Examine PDM options
	Use a screen option to move from Work with Objects Using PDM to Work with Members Using PDM

Start at	Any command line

Procedure	Create source physical file QDDSSRC
	Work with Objects Using PDM
	Take option 12 on QDDSSRC to go to Work with Members using PDM

1.1. Sign on to your workstation as usual.

1.2. First, you must create a source physical file. That file will contain file description members; the first member you create will be the DDS for a physical database file. Go to the menu of source commands and select the command to create a source physical file.

    1.2a. What is the command name?

1.3. Name the file QDDSSRC (be sure to spell it correctly), and create it in your own user library (*CURLIB). Ignore the other options, but key in a description consisting of your full name and the class name. Press Enter.

    1.3a. What message is returned?

1.4. Now, get into PDM. Use the GO command to display the PDM-related commands menu.

1.5. On the menu of PDM commands, notice the Start PDM command, which we referred to in the lesson. This command is useful when you need to change defaults or work with PDM options. But when you need to get directly to a list of libraries, objects, or members, the appropriate WRK*xxx*PDM command is more efficient. You want to work with members of the source physical file you just created, but to see how the PDM object and member levels are related, first select the option to Work with Objects using PDM.

1.6. Notice that *PRV is a valid value for the Library parameter and is the normal default. PDM remembers which library you worked with the last time you used Work with Objects Using PDM and returns to it unless you tell it otherwise.

At this time, you are concerned only with objects in your own user (current) library. If the Library parameter value is not your current library name, from the Work with Objects using PDM command prompt screen, either enter your library name or use the default, *CURLIB. You want to look at *ALL objects and *ALL object types and attributes in your library. When you are ready, press Enter to run the command.

1.7. The screen you see now should be similar to the one shown in Figure 5.27.

```
                        Work with Objects Using PDM              S1018A6G

   Library . . . . .   JSMITH____      Position to . . . . . . . . _____
                                       Position to type  . . . . . _____

   Type options, press Enter.
     2=Change       3=Copy         4=Delete      5=Display     7=Rename
     8=Display description          9=Save       10=Restore   11=Move ...

   Opt  Object     Type      Attribute   Text
    _   JSMITH     *OUTQ                 Jane M. Smith, Intro to AS/400
    _   QDDSSRC    *FILE     PF-SRC      Jane M. Smith, Intro to AS/400




                                                                  Bottom
   Parameters or command
   ===>_____
   F3=Exit        F4=Prompt        F5=Refresh        F6=Create
   F9=Retrieve    F10=Command entry   F23=More options   F24=More keys
```

Figure 5.27

Work with Objects Using PDM Screen

1.7a. List the names, types, and attributes of the objects in your library.

1.8. Notice all the object management options and the function keys.

1.8a. How do you display more options?

1.8b. What is the option to find a string?

1.8c. What is the option to Work with the contents of an object?

The Work with Objects level of PDM lets you display objects in a selected library and perform certain management functions on these objects. The "Work with" option lets you examine and perform management functions on the members of certain types of objects. For example, you should have both an output queue created in a previous lab and the source physical file, QDDSSRC, you just created in your Work with Objects Using PDM list. Both of these object types allow the Work with option.

1.9. Take the Work with option on your output queue.

1.9a. What screen have you arrived at?

This screen should look familiar to you from the preceding lab. If you completed that lab correctly, no spooled files are showing, but keep in mind how to get here from PDM. Now press F12 to return to PDM.

1.10. Next, take the Work with option on your newly created source physical file.

1.10a. What screen is displayed now?

1.11. Check the File and Library values at the upper left on the screen. They should tell you that you are in file QDDSSRC of your library. Both fields allow input; you can change lists by typing over either or both values and pressing Enter. This is a quick way to switch between different source physical files in different libraries.

Part 2

Goals	Create a physical file source member using F6 from Work with Members Using PDM Use SEU to enter a simple file description Save the DDS source file description
Start at	WRKMBRPDM your library/QDDSSRC
Procedure	Press F6 to create a member; provide the member name and type PF Use the IP line command in SEU to enter the file description Press F3 to save and exit

2.1. At this time, no member is listed for your source physical file because you just created the file.

2.1a. What action do you take to create a new member? (Examine the screen carefully.)

2.2. Take the action you discovered in Step 2.1. You should see the screen shown in Figure 5.28.

```
                        Start Source Entry Utility (STRSEU)

 Type choices, press Enter.

 Source file  . . . . . . . . . . > QDDSSRC       Name, *PRV
   Library  . . . . . . . . . . . >   JSMITH      Name, *LIBL, *CURLIB, *PRV
 Source member  . . . . . . . . .   *PRV_____     Name, *PRV, *SELECT
 Source type  . . . . . . . . .     *SAME_____    Name, *SAME, BAS, BASP, C...
 Text 'description' . . . . . . .   *BLANK




                                                                       Bottom
 F3=Exit    F4=Prompt    F5=Refresh    F12=Cancel    F13=How to use this display
 F24=More keys
```

Figure 5.28

Start Source Entry
Utility (STRSEU) Screen

2.2a. What kind of screen is this and for what command?

Remember that you arrived at this screen by choosing the Create function from Work with Members Using PDM. This should give you some insight into the workings of PDM. In this case, PDM assumes that because you want to create a member in a source file, you need the editor; so PDM takes you to SEU, the all-purpose editor for AS/400 source files and programs.

Enter STUPF as the source member name. Move the cursor to the source type parameter and press the prompt function key.

2.2b. What is displayed?

Notice the many source types SEU can accommodate. Each different type identifies the PDM attribute of a source file or program member that can be entered using SEU. Each type uses a different language syntax checker for the source code and determines the specific create command to be used to compile the member.

2.3. From the prompted list screen, enter PF as the source type and press Enter to return to the STRSEU command prompt screen. Key in the description using your full name and class name. Press Enter to continue.

2.3a. What message appears at the bottom of the screen?

2.4. Displayed now is the SEU Edit work screen with inserted blank lines indicated by apostrophes on the left (sequence number) margin. You will use SEU's line prompting facility rather than try to key the necessary DDS free-form, so press Enter to get rid of the inserted lines and close up the work space.

The screen should now consist of five lines at the top, a large open area in the middle (the work space for new lines), and the function keys, message line, and status line at the bottom. The cursor should be at the leftmost sequence column position of the Beginning of data line. If it is not, you can press Tab or Field exit to move it there.

Before starting the file description, press Help to view help text for the editor. Carefully read through the information about line commands and function keys. Exit Help when you are finished.

2.5. Key in IPPF on the sequence column of the first line (Beginning of data). The I means insert a line, the first P means prompt for a line, and PF tells the editor what type of prompting to use (insert and prompt for a physical file line). Assuming you properly assigned PF to this member type when you created it, the PF in the line command is redundant, but harmless. IP by itself uses the specified member type to determine the prompt. Press Enter. You should now see the prompt for a physical file line in the lower part of the screen, as in Figure 5.29.

Figure 5.29
SEU Edit Work Screen
with PF Prompt

```
Columns . . . :   1  71           Edit              JSMITH/QDDSSRC
SEU==>                                                        STUPF
FMT PF .....A...........T.Name++++++RLen++TDpB......Functions++++++++++++++++++
        ************** Beginning of data *********************************
''''''''
        ***************** End of data **********************************************


        Prompt type . . .  PF       Sequence number . . .  ''''''''

        Name                                 Data    Decimal
        Type      Name      Ref     Length   Type    Positions     Use
        _                    _       ____     _        __           _
        Functions  ____



        F3=Exit   F4=Prompt   F5=Refresh       F11=Previous record
        F12=Cancel            F23=Select prompt F24=More keys
```

While prompting for DDS, the screen is split between the work area window above and the prompt entry fields for each insertion line below.

2.6. The first line of this file description is the record format line. As mentioned in the text of this lesson, a database physical file has a single record-level entry that names the record format and a number of field-level entries that describe the data fields comprising the file.

Press Help to see the valid values for the Name Type field.

2.6a. What is the value for a record format?

Press Enter or F12 to exit Help. In the Name Type field, key in the value used for a record format.

2.7. In the Name field, enter STUPFR. Recall that the name of the record format is a programmer-supplied value, but a name related to the file name is commonly used. Only the type and name are required for the record format line. Press Enter.

2.7a. What occurs as you enter each inserted line?

Notice that an A is added at column six. DDS source files all have an A in column six, so the editor inserts it for you (but if a line is missing one, nothing bad happens).

2.8. The next lines are for field descriptions. Before you begin keying, let's review some important points regarding prompting with DDS.

- *Point 1*: You can press Enter on an empty prompt line or press the Refresh key (F5) or Cancel to exit prompting. If you get out by mistake, just type IP (or IPPF) over the sequence number of the line after which you want to continue inserting new lines; then press Enter, and you will be back in prompting.
- *Point 2*: Always use the Field exit key to advance to the next prompt field when the characters or numbers entered don't fill the entire field. For numeric values (length and decimal positions), this procedure ensures proper (right) alignment within the field.

Key in the following field descriptions one line at a time. Use Field exit to skip through prompt line input fields not listed below. (If nothing is listed under Decimal Positions, don't key anything in. Zero is valid only for numeric integer fields.) Press Enter to add each new line to the edit file and clear the prompt.

Name	Length	Data Type	Decimal Positions
SOCSEC	9	S	0
LNAME	20	A	
FNAME	15	A	
ADDR1	25	A	
ADDR2	25	A	
ZIP	5	S	0

2.8a. What does Data Type A mean? (Press Help on the Data Type field on the prompt line.)

2.8b. What does Data Type S mean?

You should now see the completed entry screen shown as Figure 5.30.

You might have noticed that the student physical file shown in Figure 5.30, like the employee file described in the text, contains address lines and a Zip code field, but no city or state fields. The reason is that although the files for

Figure 5.30
DDS Source for
Physical File STUPF

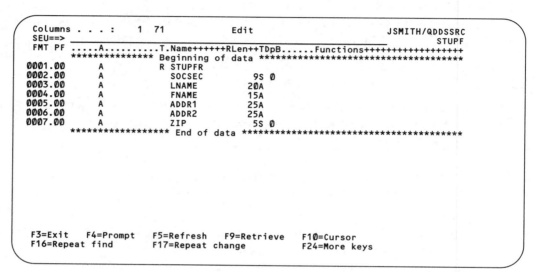

```
Columns . . . :    1  71           Edit                   JSMITH/QDDSSRC
SEU==>                                                                 STUPF
FMT PF .....A..........T.Name++++++RLen++TDpB......Functions+++++++++++++++++++
*************** Beginning of data ************************************
0001.00   A         R STUPFR
0002.00   A           SOCSEC        9S Ø
0003.00   A           LNAME        20A
0004.00   A           FNAME        15A
0005.00   A           ADDR1        25A
0006.00   A           ADDR2        25A
0007.00   A           ZIP           5S Ø
***************** End of data ****************************************



F3=Exit   F4=Prompt   F5=Refresh   F9=Retrieve   F10=Cursor
F16=Repeat find       F17=Repeat change          F24=More keys
```

our lab exercises may be simplified, we would nonetheless like them to conform to important rules for properly designed relational databases. Although an explanation of those rules is beyond the scope of this course, one of them stipulates that the value of a field in a record should not be dependent on the value of another (non-key) field. Because the value for Zip code dictates the valid values for city and state (i.e., city and state are functions of Zip code), including those dependent fields in the same record format with the non-key field ZIP violates that rule and creates a *dependency relationship* within the file. Dependency relationships not only create data redundancy (unnecessary repetition of data), but also open the way for data inconsistency (e.g., records with different city and/or state values for the same Zip code).

We choose to avoid this problem by building a separate file of Zip code records in a later lab, after we have discussed some important concepts dealing with the organization and access of file data.

2.9. Press F3 to get to the SEU Exit screen when you are done.

Notice that should you reach the SEU Exit screen (Figure 5.26) by mistake, the Return to editing option takes you right back.
Press Enter to save your file description, keeping all the default values.

2.9a. What message is displayed when you return to the Work with Members Using PDM screen?

2.10. Exit PDM and sign off.

Mastering the AS/400, Second Edition

Lab 5 Answer Sheet

Name: _____

Date Due: _____   Class Time: _____

1.2a. _____ CRJSRCPF FILE(QDDSSRC) _____

1.3a. _____ File QDDSSRC created in Library INTXO2003L _____

1.7a. _____

_____

_____

1.8a. _____ 1.8b. _____ 1.8c. _____

1.9a. _____

1.10a. _____

2.1a. _____

2.2a. _____ alpha _____

2.2b. _____ Zoned _____

2.3a. _____

2.6a. _____

2.7a. _____

2.8a. _____

2.8b. _____

2.9a. _____ Member STUPF added to File Intro2003/QDDSSRC _____

In Summary

Programmers and operators frequently deal with four kinds of files: physical files, logical files, display files, and printer files. Physical files hold data and may be program-described or externally described. Externally described files can be defined at the field level using IDDU, SQL, or DDS.

To facilitate the definition, creation, and management of files and other objects, PDM provides Work with lists at the library, object, or member level. When files are defined using DDS, a source physical file, QDDSSRC, is created first. QDDSSRC holds descriptions of individual files coded in the DDS language. Each file description is a separate member of the source physical file.

The DDS file description is entered and maintained using the Source Entry Utility (SEU). SEU can be started by a CL command on the command line or through PDM. SEU line commands are used to manipulate individual records of a source member.

With Lesson 5 now complete, you have created objects and members at all three levels of the AS/400 data structure hierarchy. As Figure 5.31 illustrates, the library object contains other objects, including an output queue and a source physical file.

Figure 5.31
Illustration of AS/400
Object Hiearchy

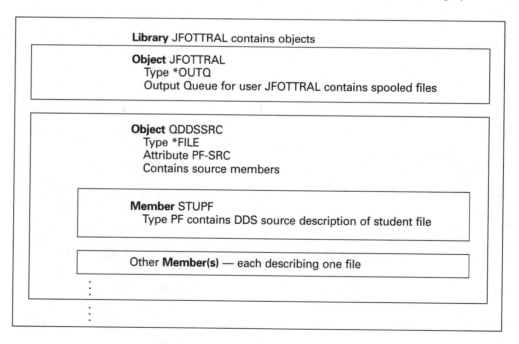

The source physical file, QDDSSRC, contains members. Each member is a description of a file. A source physical file can contain virtually an unlimited number of members.

In the next lesson, you learn how to compile a source file description member, creating a new object of type *FILE in a library.

Lesson 6

Creating and Using an Externally Described Database File

Lesson Overview

In this lesson we extend our knowledge of Source Entry Utility (SEU) so that you can use SEU line commands to modify existing source members easily. We access SEU through the Programming Development Manager (PDM) Work with Members list, as we did in Lesson 5. You also increase your familiarity with PDM as a convenient way to invoke the appropriate Create command when you want to create a file or program from a source member. And finally, you learn enough about Data File Utility (DFU) to be able to enter data records into a database file.

Objectives

Students will be able to

✓ Use SEU line commands to modify an existing source member
✓ Use PDM options to copy and compile source members
✓ Use CL commands or PDM options to display object, file, and file field descriptions
✓ Enter data into a database file using DFU

More About SEU

As we learned in Lesson 5, Source Entry Utility (SEU) is a general-purpose, full-screen editor that lets you enter or modify the source statements that will be used to create an **externally described file**, a CL program, or a high-level language (HLL) program such as RPG, C, or Cobol.

In addition to using SEU to create or edit a source member, you can use SEU to display or print an existing member of a **source physical file**. SEU assumes a source physical file (e.g., QDDSSRC or QRPGSRC) exists (i.e., it must have been created in your library using the CRTSRCPF – Create Source Physical File — command) and requires you to identify that file when you start SEU. In Lab 5 you created a source physical file, QDDSSRC, to contain DDS source members.

Starting SEU

Although it is generally more convenient to invoke SEU by taking a Work with Members Using PDM option on the source physical file member you want to edit, display, or print, you can also call SEU by entering the STRSEU (Start SEU) command from any command line.

If you prompt for the STRSEU command on a command line, a prompt screen similar to the one shown in Figure 6.1 appears.

Figure 6.1
STRSEU Command
Prompt

```
                           Start Source Entry Utility (STRSEU)

  Type choices, press Enter.

  Source file  . . . . . . . . . .     *PRV          Name, *PRV
    Library  . . . . . . . . . . .                   Name, *LIBL, *CURLIB, *PRV
  Source member  . . . . . . . . .     *PRV          Name, *PRV, *SELECT
  Source type  . . . . . . . . . .     *SAME         Name, *SAME, BAS, BASP, C...
  Option . . . . . . . . . . . . .     *BLANK        *BLANK, ' ', 2, 5, 6
  Text 'description' . . . . . . .     *BLANK




                                                                          Bottom
  F3=Exit    F4=Prompt    F5=Refresh    F12=Cancel    F13=How to use this display
  F24=More keys
```

The predefined values (*PRV — previous) displayed for Source file and Source member tell SEU to access the same member from the same source file as the last time the STRSEU command was executed.

The parameter value *SAME for Source type tells SEU to use the source type already specified if you are working with an existing member. If you are creating a new member, *SAME tells SEU to choose a default member type based on the source physical file name. For example, the default for a source physical file named QDDSSRC is PF; but if you choose a non-IBM-supplied name for the source physical file, the Source type would default to TXT. Source type TXT indicates a member whose records contain only 80 characters of text and that cannot be subjected to syntax checking or prompting.

The value specified for the Option parameter of the STRSEU command prompt corresponds to a PDM option (i.e., 2=Edit, 5=Display (Browse), and 6=Print). In our example, the default value (*BLANK) has been specified. Taking the default is the same as typing in the number 2 or taking PDM option 2: The resulting display would be an SEU Edit screen. If you enter the number 5 or 6 as the value of the Option parameter, you can browse or print the source member from the STRSEU command. But just as in starting an Edit session, accessing SEU through the PDM workbench is the more efficient and programmer-friendly way of accomplishing either of these tasks.

The obvious advantage of using PDM is that the other parameter values (Source file, Library, and Source member) are already known to PDM and automatically passed to the STRSEU command. PDM is not an alternative to the STRSEU command — PDM uses the STRSEU command — but PDM automatically fills in the command parameter values for you.

If you press Enter on the STRSEU command prompt screen shown in Figure 6.1 — and the last time you used SEU was to edit a DDS member named EMPPF — the screen shown in Figure 6.2 appears. This is the edit screen for source file member EMPPF as we left it in Lesson 5 (Figure 5.25).

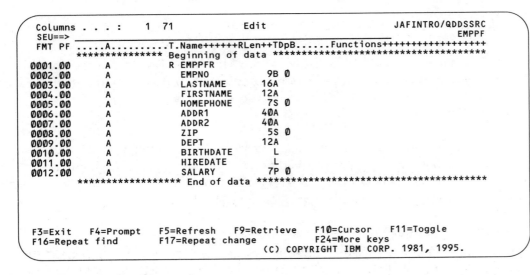

Figure 6.2
SEU Edit Session for Source File EMPPF

ACCESSING SEU VIA PDM

Normally, however, programmers access the SEU Edit screen by choosing the edit option for the source member they want to work with from the Work with Members Using PDM screen.

You can get to the Work with Members Using PDM screen in several ways:

1. Take choice 3 (Work with Members) from the PDM menu that appears when you run the STRPDM command. Then, if necessary, change the values for File and Library name from the Specify Members to Work With screen (Figure 6.3).

Figure 6.3

Specify Members to Work with Screen

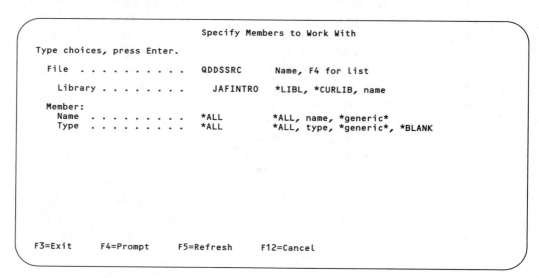

```
                              Specify Members to Work With
      Type choices, press Enter.

        File . . . . . . . . . .   QDDSSRC      Name, F4 for list

          Library . . . . . . . .   JAFINTRO    *LIBL, *CURLIB, name

        Member:
          Name  . . . . . . . . .   *ALL        *ALL, name, *generic*
          Type  . . . . . . . . .   *ALL        *ALL, type, *generic*, *BLANK




      F3=Exit      F4=Prompt      F5=Refresh      F12=Cancel
```

2. Take the "Work with" option on the appropriate source physical file (e.g., QDDSSRC) from the Work with Objects Using PDM screen.

3. Execute the WRKMBRPDM (Work with Members PDM) command from any command line (or from within an initial CL program) and specify the source physical file whose members you want to work with (e.g., QDDSSRC).

Once you get to the Work with Members Using PDM screen, you can start SEU in edit mode by taking the PDM edit option for the appropriate member. The Work with Members Using PDM screen in multicolumn format is shown in Figure 6.4, with the edit option entered for file EMPPF.

SEU LINE COMMANDS

Recall from Lesson 5 that **SEU line commands** are entered on the sequence numbers of the lines to be manipulated. In its simplest form, an SEU line command consists of a single letter (e.g., entering a D on the sequence number of a line you wish to delete).

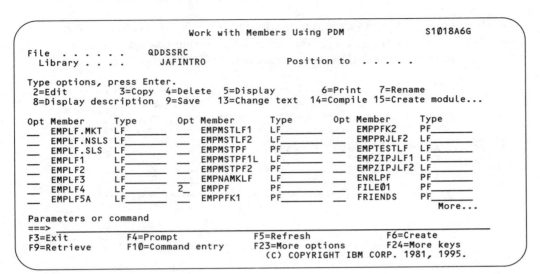

Figure 6.4
Work with Members
Using PDM, Edit Option
Entered for EMPPF

The most commonly used SEU line commands are

C — Used to copy one or more lines to another place in the source member,
retaining the original lines. The copied lines will be properly sequenced at
the new location.

M — Used to move one or more lines to a different place in the source. The
moved lines will be properly resequenced at the new location.

I — Used to insert lines of code. We used the Insert command in Lesson 5.
Because SEU is a full-screen editor, you can Insert a line and then type
directly on it if you wish; or you can use the SEU line command IP, a
variation that inserts and also provides a prompt line, especially useful
for fixed-format or column-oriented languages.

D — Used to delete one or more lines.

Target Designator

The SEU line commands Copy and Move require that you specify the place in the
source code where you want the designated lines of code copied or moved. You
do this by marking the new location with a "target designator": an A for after or a
B for before the line on which the target is entered.

The line commands that manipulate records of source code let you specify a
number of lines to move, copy, or delete. For example, the command to move
three lines would be M3; the command to delete 10 lines would be D10. When the
number of lines to move, copy, or delete becomes too large to count easily (i.e., if it
spans a number of pages), you can mark a block of lines by repeating the command
letter (e.g., MM, CC, DD) on the first and last line of the block. Then the entire
block will be deleted, or moved or copied after or before the target.

In addition, when you designate a target for a Copy or Move command, you
can specify the number of times the copied or moved lines should be repeated. For
example, if you are copying or moving several lines and you want them repeated

four times, you can type A4 on the target line to tell SEU to repeat the designated lines of code four times right after the target line. To demonstrate, observe the SEU line commands entered on source member DEMOPF shown in Figure 6.5.

Figure 6.5
Edit Line Commands

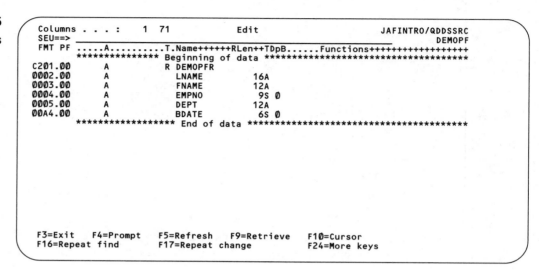

```
Columns . . . :    1  71              Edit                JAFINTRO/QDDSSRC
SEU==>                                                            DEMOPF
FMT PF  .....A..........T.Name++++++RLen++TDpB......Functions++++++++++++++++++
        *************** Beginning of data ***********************************
C201.00     A           R DEMOPFR
0002.00     A             LNAME         16A
0003.00     A             FNAME         12A
0004.00     A             EMPNO          9S 0
0005.00     A             DEPT          12A
00A4.00     A             BDATE          6S 0
        **************** End of data ****************************************




        F3=Exit   F4=Prompt   F5=Refresh   F9=Retrieve   F10=Cursor
        F16=Repeat find       F17=Repeat change          F24=More keys
```

Notice that the first line, the record format line, has a Copy command for two lines (C2); the target, line 6, has been specified as A4. (It doesn't matter that the target designation A4 has been typed over the sequence number 6; you can type a command or target anywhere in the seven-character sequence column.) When the command is executed, the first two lines would be copied four times after line 6, and the newly copied lines would be properly sequenced. The member would look like the one shown in Figure 6.6.

Figure 6.6
Edit Source Member
Showing Lines Copied

```
Columns . . . :    1  71              Edit                JAFINTRO/QDDSSRC
SEU==>                                                            DEMOPF
FMT PF  .....A..........T.Name++++++RLen++TDpB......Functions++++++++++++++++++
        *************** Beginning of data ***********************************
0001.00     A           R DEMOPFR
0002.00     A             LNAME         16A
0003.00     A             FNAME         12A
0004.00     A             EMPNO          9S 0
0005.00     A             DEPT          12A
0006.00     A             BDATE          6S 0
0007.00     A           R DEMOPFR
0008.00     A             LNAME         16A
0009.00     A           R DEMOPFR
0010.00     A             LNAME         16A
0011.00     A           R DEMOPFR
0012.00     A             LNAME         16A
0013.00     A           R DEMOPFR
0014.00     A             LNAME         16A
        **************** End of data ****************************************


        F3=Exit   F4=Prompt   F5=Refresh   F9=Retrieve   F10=Cursor
        F16=Repeat find       F17=Repeat change          F24=More keys
```

COMPILING THE FILE DESCRIPTION

Now that you know how to use a few SEU line commands necessary to edit a source member, let's look at the second step in the three steps (describe, create, load) of file building. In the create step we use the source member that describes the file to compile a file object that the system can use.

Remember that what you have done so far is to *describe* a database file using a DDS source file member (member STUPF created in Lab 5). You can compare the file description to a blueprint of a house (i.e., the blueprint is not the house itself; it is simply a design specification). You described the database file using DDS, a language designed for the convenience of human programmers. But the computer cannot use the DDS file description until it is changed into object code, the "native language" of the computer. The same is true of a source program written in a programming language such as Basic, Cobol, or RPG.

Much as a source program must be translated into executable machine code by a language compiler, so too must a DDS file description be "compiled" into an "executable" file object. As usual, the AS/400 provides more than one way to perform this task: You can enter and execute the appropriate Create command on a command line, or you can use the PDM compile option and let PDM select the proper command and fill in the command parameter values for you.

Create (CRT) Commands

The most direct way to create an object on the AS/400 is to use the proper Create command and prompt for parameters. For example, to create a database physical file object, you would use the CRTPF (Create Physical File) command. On the command prompt you would need to carefully identify by name the source member, the source physical file, and the library. But PDM offers an easier alternative: the Work with Members compile option — option 14.

The PDM Compile Option

Figure 6.7 shows the Work with Members Using PDM screen with the compile option (14) entered for file EMPPF.

Figure 6.7
Work with Members
Using PDM, More
Options

```
                          Work with Members Using PDM

  File . . . . . .    QDDSSRC
    Library . . . .       JAFINTRO          Position to . . . . .

  Type options, press Enter.
    2=Edit           3=Copy   4=Delete   5=Display      6=Print    7=Rename
    8=Display description   9=Save    13=Change text   14=Compile  15=Create module...


  Opt Member     Type       Opt Member     Type
  14  EMPPF      PF_____  __  LFILE01B   LF_____
  __  FILE01     PF_____  __  MENU01     DSPF_____
  __  F01V01     LF_____  __  RLUTEST1   PRTF_____
  __  F1TEST     PF_____  __  SAMP01     PF_____
  __  GRADEDSP   DSPF_____  __  TESTLF     LF_____
  __  INTROMNU   MNUDDS____
  __  INTROMNUQQ MNUCMD____
  __  LFILE01    LF_____

                                                                    Bottom
  Parameters or command
  ===>
  F3=Exit          F4=Prompt         F5=Refresh        F6=Create
  F9=Retrieve      F10=Command entry F23=More options  F24=More keys
```

PDM options that invoke a CL command usually can be prompted, and the compile
option always uses some kind of CRT*xxx* command. In this case, if we used function
key F4 to prompt for the command from the Work with Members Using PDM
screen, we would see the CRTPF command prompt screen shown in Figure 6.8.

Figure 6.8
CRTPF Command
Prompt Screen from
Option 14

```
                       Create Physical File (CRTPF)

  Type choices, press Enter.

  File . . . . . . . . . . . . . > EMPPF         Name
    Library . . . . . . . . . . > JAFINTRO       Name, *CURLIB
  Source file . . . . . . . . . > QDDSSRC        Name
    Library . . . . . . . . . . > JAFINTRO       Name, *LIBL, *CURLIB
  Source member . . . . . . . . > EMPPF          Name, *FILE
  Record length, if no DDS . . . .               Number
  Generation severity level . . .   20           0-30
  Flagging severity level . . . .   0            0-30
  File type . . . . . . . . . . .   *DATA        *DATA, *SRC
  Member, if desired . . . . . . .  *FILE        Name, *FILE, *NONE
  Text 'description' . . . . . . .  *SRCMBRTXT



                                                                    Bottom
  F3=Exit    F4=Prompt    F5=Refresh    F10=Additional parameters   F12=Cancel
  F13=How to use this display        F24=More keys
```

The command itself, CRTPF, was selected from the large list of Create commands.
The member type, PF, of the list member upon which the compile option (14)
was taken told PDM which particular CRT*xxx* command to use. Notice that the
CRTPF command parameter values are either defaults or they have been taken
from the PDM list values.

The File name will be the compiled object name; by default it takes the same
name as the Source member. The Source member name comes from the PDM list
member value that the option was taken on. The Source file and Library values

are substituted from the Work with Members Using PDM File and Library screen headers. Unless you want to give the new file object a name different from the source member or put it in a different library, this command is ready to run.

When you press Enter, PDM submits the CRTPF command to the batch subsystem so that you can continue working while the source member compiles. (Compile in batch is the default PDM option, but it can be changed if you wish.) A message will appear that tells you the compile has been submitted to job queue QBATCH in library QGPL. If no other messages are waiting, your terminal will beep at you when the message indicating the end of the batch job enters your message queue. You can see this message by entering the DSPMSG (Display Message) command on the command line, or by using the IBM-supplied, user-defined PDM option DM (Display Message) on any PDM list member. For Basic assistance level, the messages are grouped by "Messages needing a reply" and "Messages not needing a reply"; the most recent messages will be at the top of the list. An example of a Basic assistance level Work with Messages screen reached by the DSPMSG command is shown in Figure 6.9.

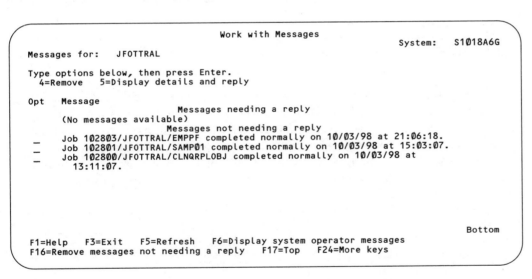

Figure 6.9

Work with Messages — Basic Assistance Level

It shows that the compile of source member EMPPF completed normally. The display message screen lets you change assistance level just like you did earlier for the WRKSPLF screen, using F21.

Because the compile was successful, a new object of type *FILE should have been created in the specified library (usually your current library). To make sure this is the case, you would return to the Work with Objects Using PDM screen by pressing function key F12 from the Work with Members screen, or by typing the WRKOBJPDM (Work with Objects Using PDM) command if you hadn't started from WRKOBJPDM. If you came from the Work with Objects Using PDM screen originally, you would have to refresh the screen (F5) upon returning.

DISPLAYING AN OBJECT'S DESCRIPTION

All objects have descriptions and you can display the description of an object by choosing option 8 from the Work with Objects Using PDM screen. In Figure 6.10 we show that option 8 has been selected for file EMPPF, our newly created database file.

Figure 6.10

Work with Objects Using PDM — Display Description Option Taken on EMPPF

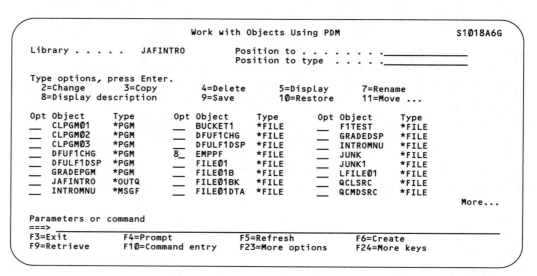

```
                              Work with Objects Using PDM              S1018A6G
   Library . . . . .   JAFINTRO        Position to . . . . . . . .:_____
                                       Position to type . . . . .:_____

   Type options, press Enter.
     2=Change      3=Copy          4=Delete        5=Display      7=Rename
     8=Display description         9=Save          10=Restore     11=Move ...

   Opt Object    Type      Opt Object    Type      Opt Object    Type
   __  CLPGM01   *PGM      __  BUCKET1   *FILE      __  F1TEST    *FILE
   __  CLPGM02   *PGM      __  DFUF1CHG  *FILE      __  GRADEDSP  *FILE
   __  CLPGM03   *PGM      __  DFULF1DSP *FILE      __  INTROMNU  *FILE
   __  DFUF1CHG  *PGM      8_  EMPPF     *FILE      __  JUNK      *FILE
   __  DFULF1DSP *PGM      __  FILE01    *FILE      __  JUNK1     *FILE
   __  GRADEPGM  *PGM      __  FILE01B   *FILE      __  LFILE01   *FILE
   __  JAFINTRO  *OUTQ     __  FILE01BK  *FILE      __  QCLSRC    *FILE
   __  INTROMNU  *MSGF     __  FILE01DTA *FILE      __  QCMDSRC   *FILE
                                                                     More...
   Parameters or command
   ===> _____
   F3=Exit            F4=Prompt          F5=Refresh          F6=Create
   F9=Retrieve        F10=Command entry  F23=More options    F24=More keys
```

When you press Enter after choosing option 8 from the Work with Objects Using PDM screen, the Display Object Description — Full screen appears. This screen displays information the system maintains about all objects: object type; attribute (where applicable); owner; when, where (on what system), and by whom the object was created; and when the object was last modified. The first page of this display, when requested for file EMPPF, would look like the one shown in Figure 6.11.

Figure 6.11

Display Object Description — Full, First Page

```
                      Display Object Description - Full
                                                          Library 1 of 1
   Object . . . . . . . :    EMPPF          Attribute . . . . . :  PF
     Library . . . . . :      JAFINTRO      Owner . . . . . . . :  JFOTTRAL
   Type . . . . . . . . :    *FILE          Primary group . . . :  *NONE

   User-defined information:
     Attribute  . . . . . . . . . . . . :
     Text . . . . . . . . . . . . . . . :   Employee File

   Creation information:
     Creation date/time . . . . . . . . :   09/24/98  19:22:08
     Created by user  . . . . . . . . . :   JFOTTRAL
     System created on  . . . . . . . . :   BUSINESS
     Object domain  . . . . . . . . . . :   *SYSTEM

                                                              More...
   Press Enter to continue.

   F3=Exit    F12=Cancel
   (C) COPYRIGHT IBM CORP. 1980, 1995.
```

Additional pages of this screen would display change/usage information, storage information, and save/retrieve information. The system maintains these attributes for all object types, and they can be displayed by entering the DSPOBJD (Display Object Description) command on any command line. The DSPOBJD command is the command invoked when you select PDM option 8; but when you use PDM, the object name and type (required parameters) are already filled in for you.

DISPLAYING A FILE DESCRIPTION

Another PDM option that lets you display information about an object — 5=Display — is more dependent on object type. Selecting option 5 for file EMPPF results in the screen shown in Figure 6.12. The screen heading, Display Spooled File, indicates that the Display File Description output has been temporarily spooled to an output queue by printer file QPDSPFD.

```
                               Display Spooled File
 File . . . . . :    QPDSPFD                       Page/Line    1/1
 Control . . . . .                                 Columns      1 - 78
 Find . . . . . .
 *...+....1....+....2....+....3....+....4....+....5....+....6....+....7....+...
    10/03/98                 Display File Description
 DSPFD Command Input
   File . . . . . . . . . . . . . . . . . . . . :  FILE      EMPPF
     Library . . . . . . . . . . . . . . . . . :            JAFINTRO
   Type of information . . . . . . . . . . . . :  TYPE      *ALL
   File attributes . . . . . . . . . . . . . . :  FILEATR   *ALL
   System . . . . . . . . . . . . . . . . . . :  SYSTEM    *LCL
 File Description Header
   File . . . . . . . . . . . . . . . . . . . . :  FILE      EMPPF
   Library . . . . . . . . . . . . . . . . . . :            JAFINTRO
   Type of file . . . . . . . . . . . . . . . :            Physical
   File type . . . . . . . . . . . . . . . . . :  FILETYPE  *DATA
   Auxiliary storage pool ID . . . . . . . . . :            01
 Data Base File Attributes
   Externally described file . . . . . . . . . :            Yes
   File level identifier . . . . . . . . . . . :            0941003210614
                                                                   More...

 F3=Exit   F12=Cancel   F19=Left   F20=Right   F24=More keys
```

Figure 6.12

Screen Display from PDM Option 5 for File EMPPF, First Page

Notice that the Display File Description output provides more detail than the Display Object Description — Full screen: it tells not only where the file is stored but also what type it is, and whether it is externally described. Additional pages of the display provide information such as number and size of members, record capacity, how the file can be accessed, record length, and number of fields.

Although the Display File Description output tells you that file EMPPF is externally described, it does not provide much information about the record format of that file. The DSPFD command output shows record length and number of fields, but it doesn't show field-level information. To see the field-level attributes of file EMPPF, you would need to use the DSPFFD (Display File Field Description) command, which we introduced in Lesson 5. You can enter the command on a command line with its single required parameter (file name), or you can invoke the command by entering a user-defined PDM option (FD — Field Description) for file EMPPF from the Work with Objects Using PDM screen.

When you run the DSPFFD command or choose PDM option FD for file
EMPPF, the first page of the output display look likes the one shown in Figure 6.13.

Figure 6.13
DSPFFD Output for File
EMPPF, First Page

```
                                    Display Spooled File
File . . . . . :    QPDSPFFD                       Page/Line   1/1
Control . . . . .                                  Columns     1 - 78
Find . . . . . .
*...+....1....+....2....+....3....+....4....+....5....+....6....+....7....+..

                            Display File Field Description
Input parameters
    File . . . . . . . . . . . . . . . . . . :  EMPPF
      Library . . . . . . . . . . . . . . . . :  JAFINTRO
File Information
    File . . . . . . . . . . . . . . . . . . :  EMPPF
      Library . . . . . . . . . . . . . . . . :  JAFINTRO
    File location . . . . . . . . . . . . . . :  *LCL
    Externally described . . . . . . . . . . :  Yes
    Number of record formats . . . . . . . . :  1
    Type of file . . . . . . . . . . . . . . :  Physical
    File creation date . . . . . . . . . . . :  09/24/98
    Text 'description'. . . . . . . . . . . . :  Emp Mast PF Source
Record Format Information
    Record format . . . . . . . . . . . . . . :  EMPPFR
    Format level identifier . . . . . . . . . :  35231AB4915A0

                                                              More...
F3=Exit    F12=Cancel    F19=Left    F20=Right    F24=More keys
```

Some of the information is the same as that made available by the DSPFD
command. But the second page of the display (Figure 6.14) shows the field-level
descriptions of the record with all field names, data types, sizes, buffer length and
position, field usage, and column-heading information shown.

Figure 6.14
DSPFFD Output for File
EMPPF, Second Page

```
                                    Display Spooled File
File . . . . . :    QPDSPFFD                       Page/Line   1/21
Control . . . . .  +1                              Columns     1 - 78
Find . . . . . .   Number
*...+....1....+....2....+....3....+....4....+....5....+....6....+....7....+...
        Number of fields . . . . . . . . . . . . . :  11
        Record length . . . . . . . . . . . . . . :  160
Field Level Information
             Data       Field   Buffer   Buffer        Field    Column
    Field    Type       Length  Length   Position      Usage    Heading
    EMPNO    ZONED       9  0      4        1           Both     EMPNO
    LASTNAME CHAR        16       16        5           Both     LASTNAME
      Coded Character Set Identifier    . . . . . :  37
    FIRSTNAME CHAR       12       12        21          Both     FIRSTNAME
      Coded Character Set Identifier    . . . . . :  37
    HOMEPHONE ZONED      7  0      7        33          Both     HOMEPHONE
    ADDR1    CHAR        40       40        40          Both     ADDR1
      Coded Character Set Identifier    . . . . . :  37
    ADDR2    CHAR        40       40        80          Both     ADDR2
      Coded Character Set Identifier    . . . . . :  37
    ZIP      ZONED       5  0      5        120         Both     ZIP
                                                              More...
F3=Exit   F12=Cancel   F19=Left   F20=Right     F24=More keys
```

All of this information originally came from the DDS entries coded in source
member EMPPF in source physical file QDDSSRC. In addition, a Coded
Character Set Identifier (CCSID) value is displayed for character fields. This
attribute is added by the CRTPF command and is assigned either by a command

parameter value, by the job, or by a system value. Its value identifies the coding scheme used for character data.

It is important to realize that the information on this display is taken from the compiled file object itself, not from the source. The object contains this information within it, so it can reveal its complete field-level record layout to any application program or utility requesting it. The system does not maintain record description synchronization between the file object and the source member; so if the source member were modified, the modifications would not be adopted by the file object automatically. On the other hand, even if the source member were deleted, the capability of the externally described file to correctly identify its fields would not be compromised.

DFU

We've now covered the first two steps of AS/400 database design: In the previous lesson we described the file (using DDS) and in this lesson we created the file object. Now let's consider the third step: loading or entering data into the file.

When a file is created, it is like a house under construction. The house has gone from the blueprint to a standing framework of studs, rafters, and purlins. The structure is determined, but until the walls and ceilings are finished and furnishings moved in, it is not a functional home. Likewise, the structure of the compiled file has been decided (we just looked at one using the DSPFFD command); but the file is empty, and until it is populated with data records, it is of little use.

There are several possibilities for entering data records into a file. If all or most of the data elements already existed in another file, you could use a CL command or a program to copy that data into your new file. If the data has to be entered from source documents, some kind of interactive data entry program may be required. If there is time and the need warrants, the programming staff may be called upon to create a sophisticated interactive data entry/file maintenance program written in Cobol, RPG, or another HLL.

But for quickly and conveniently populating newly created files with test data — for example, to be used in prototyping new applications — **Data File Utility (DFU)** is a better solution. DFU provides a convenient and easy way to change records in and add records to a physical (or logical) database file — without the need to write a HLL data-entry program. Although DFU's limited validation and formatting capabilities would lessen its potential for end-user applications, it is useful for entering and changing test data, and it is a valuable tool for programmers. DFU is another member of the Application Development team; and along with its partners, PDM and SEU, it would be available on any AS/400 where new program development or program maintenance is done.

You can access DFU by using the STRDFU (Start DFU) command, or by choosing option 18 on a database *FILE type object from the Work with Objects Using PDM screen. If you enter the STRDFU command on any command line, the DFU menu shown in Figure 6.15 appears.

Figure 6.15
STRDFU, DFU Menu

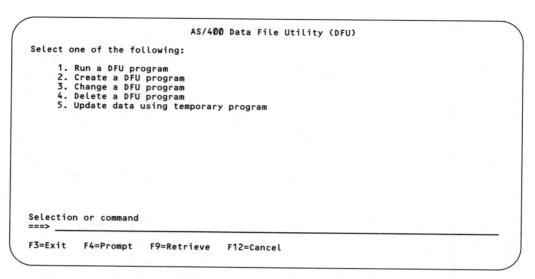

```
                        AS/400 Data File Utility (DFU)
Select one of the following:

    1. Run a DFU program
    2. Create a DFU program
    3. Change a DFU program
    4. Delete a DFU program
    5. Update data using temporary program




Selection or command
===>

F3=Exit    F4=Prompt    F9=Retrieve    F12=Cancel
```

DFU works in two ways: It either creates and executes a temporary entry/update program, or it builds and stores a "permanent" update program that can be called and used again. To update data using a temporary program, you select option 5 from the DFU menu. Providing a temporary update program is also the approach the system takes when you select option 18 on a file from PDM.

The advantage of DFU is that you do not need to specify a screen layout or field headers, or edit and select fields; DFU generates a default update program using the record format field-level attributes and file information stored in the data file object. The disadvantages of DFU are lack of flexibility and, for a temporary DFU, the machine time required to re-create the program each time you need it. We spend more time looking at the process of creating a permanent DFU program in a later lesson; but for now let's see what happens when you select option 5, to update using a temporary program, from the DFU menu.

Using a Temporary DFU Program

Selecting option 5 from the DFU menu takes you to an entry screen that requests the name and member of the file to be updated (Figure 6.16).

Notice, in this case, that the current value of the Data file parameter is not the name of the file we have been using in our example (EMPPF). This is because DFU remembers the last time you used a temporary program and provides that data file name as a default value when you start another temporary DFU from the menu.

You need to type over the old name, replacing it with the name of the file you want to use (in this case, EMPPF). When you press Enter, DFU creates an update program using the field-level attributes from the file description of EMPPF. While this is going on, the message "DFU is creating temporary program QDZTD00001 for you to run" displays on the message line. The screen that appears during this rather short time looks like the one shown in Figure 6.17.

```
                      Update Data Using Temporary Program

 Type choices, press Enter.

     Data file . . . . . . . . .   LFILE01       Name, F4 for list
        Library . . . . . . . . .     JAFINTRO    Name, *LIBL, *CURLIB
     Member  . . . . . . . . . .   *FIRST        Name, *FIRST, F4 for list
```

Figure 6.16
DFU, Update Using a
Temporary Program

```
 F3=Exit     F4=Prompt     F12=Cancel
```

```
                      Update Data Using Temporary Program

 Type choices, press Enter.

     Data file . . . . . . . . .   emppf         Name, F4 for list
        Library . . . . . . . . .     JAFINTRO    Name, *LIBL, *CURLIB
     Member  . . . . . . . . . .   *FIRST        Name, *FIRST, F4 for list
```

Figure 6.17
DFU Prompt Screen
Showing Message

```
 F3=Exit     F4=Prompt     F12=Cancel
 DFU is creating temporary program QDZTD00001 for you to run
```

Starting DFU on an Empty File

The next screen you see is the Work with Data in a File screen (Figure 6.18).
When you start DFU using an empty data file, as EMPPF is currently, Entry mode
is active. The mode displays in the upper right corner of the update screen.

When you're entering data, either the Field advance (Tab) or Field exit key
moves the cursor to the next field. Character data is stored exactly as entered into
the field (if you key leading blanks, the data is stored that way). Numeric data is

Figure 6.18

Filled-In DFU Entry
Screen

```
WORK WITH DATA IN A FILE                   Mode . . . . :   ENTRY
Format . . . . :   EMPPFR                   File . . . . :   EMPPF


EMPNO:        123456789_
LASTNAME:     Slick_____
FIRSTNAME:    Sam_____
HOMEPHONE:    6567890
ADDR1:        123 West Main_____
ADDR2:        Apt. D_____
ZIP:          52040_
DEPT:         Sales_____
BIRTHDATE:    1966-06-06
HIREDATE:     1992-09-01
SALARY:       __22000




F3=Exit                  F5=Refresh          F6=Select format
F9=Insert                F10=Entry           F11=Change
```

treated as right-aligned within the field; 123___ entered in a six-digit integer field would store as 000123. The same value entered for a dollars and cents field with four integers and two decimal positions would also store as 000123, but with an implied decimal point between the 1 and the 2 — interpreted as 0001.23. A temporary DFU doesn't allow entering any editing characters, such as a decimal point or comma for thousands separator, in a numeric field. This also applies to dates and times stored as numbers. For example, you could not enter 6666 or 6/6/66 in a 6-digit field used for a date. To properly enter the date June 6, 1966, in MMDDYY format, you would need to enter 060666, or 60666 (because alignment is on the low-order digit, the leading 0 is not significant), and press the Field exit key. Date and time data (L and T) must be entered with the proper format and separator character. For example, a birth date of August 2, 1956, needs to be entered in an *ISO Date field as 1956-08-02. The fields are shown entered correctly in Figure 6.18. When the last field typed in is numeric, and the maximum number of digits is not entered, you must press Field exit or Tab to exit the field before pressing the Enter key.

When you have inspected the data and you are ready to write the record to the file, you press the Enter key or F10. Pressing either key saves the record, but the Enter key is easier to reach. The system stores the record and then displays an empty entry screen for the next record.

If you realize, after pressing Enter, that there was an error in the data, you must get out of entry mode to correct it because in entry mode you can't back up to retrieve a previously entered record.

Function key F11 takes you to change mode. For the type of files we have created so far, when you first reach change mode, the only input field on the screen will be one named *RECNBR. All physical file records are given a **record number** that indicates their order of entry. For example, the fifth record entered would be record number 5, the hundredth record number 100, and so on. If you know the record number of the erroneous record, you could enter it in this field and DFU would search and retrieve it, if it existed. Otherwise, you can use the Page up key to retrieve the last record entered. From any record currently displayed in change mode, pressing the Page up key takes you to the next lower record number; the Page down key takes you to the next higher record number.

When you have found the bad record and corrected it, you can continue to enter new records by returning to entry mode. This is done simply by pressing function key F10 from change mode.

If you wish to delete the bad record instead of correcting it, you must first display the record under change mode and then press F23. You will be asked to press F23 again to confirm. DFU has the unpleasant habit of enabling other function keys besides those shown at the bottom of the screen, but not showing F24=More Keys. But you can always see the entire list of enabled function keys by using context-sensitive Help (move the cursor to anywhere in the function key area and press F1).

Exiting DFU

When you are finished entering records, function key F3 takes you to the End Data Entry screen (Figure 6.19), which provides a summary of adds, changes, and deletes, and asks whether you really are finished.

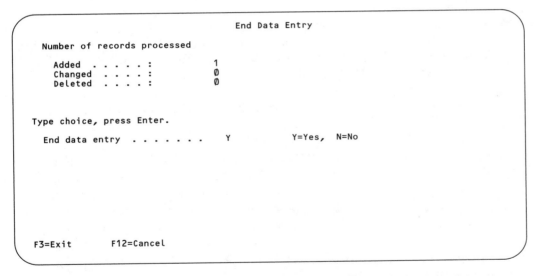

Figure 6.19
DFU End Data Entry
Screen

If you pressed function key F3 by mistake, you could return to the DFU data entry screen by typing N over the default value of Y on the End data entry prompt.

You learn more about DFU in the next lesson; meanwhile, while you use DFU in the lab exercise, don't forget that a considerable amount of online Help is available for DFU if you want to explore the topic further or refresh your memory while using it.

Key Terms

Data File Utility (DFU)   record number   source physical file
externally described file   SEU line commands

Lab 6

INTRODUCTION

In this lab you become more familiar with PDM, using its options to copy source members and create a physical database file. You also use PDM to access SEU and DFU. You practice using SEU line commands to edit a source file member, and you create a temporary DFU program and use it to load data records into a physical file member.

Part 1

Goals	Clear your output queue
	Copy source physical file member STUPF to TESTSEU
	Use SEU to alter TESTSEU, then return it to its original state
Start at	System command line
Procedure	WRKOUTQ youroutq, and print/delete any spooled files
	WRKMBRPDM QDDSSRC
	Copy STUPF to TESTSEU
	Edit the copied member TESTSEU using SEU line commands

1.1. Sign on as usual. From the MAIN menu command line, use the WRKOUTQ (Work with Output Queue) command to examine your output queue. Remember to provide your output queue name as a parameter when you run the command. If your output queue contains spooled files, either delete them or print them now so that you begin this lab with an empty output queue.

1.2. Start PDM, selecting Work with Objects. Specify all objects of all types in your library (these should be the defaults).

1.3. From the objects list in your library, select the option to Work with the source physical file you created in Lab 5.

1.4. At the Work with Members Using PDM list screen, you should see member STUPF. You use this member to practice entering SEU line commands. But to make sure you don't accidentally damage the good member, let's make a copy of it. Take the PDM option to copy member STUPF. You should now see a Copy Members screen similar to the one shown in Figure 6.20.

```
                              Copy Members

 From file . . . . . . . :    QDDSSRC
    From library . . . . :    JSMITH

 Type the file name and library name to receive the copied members.
    To file . . . . . . .    QDDSSRC      Name, F4 for list
       To library . . . . .  JSMITH

 To rename copied member, type New Name, press Enter.

 Member          New Name
 STUPF           STUPF




                                                              Bottom
 F3=Exit     F4=Prompt     F5=Refresh     F12=Cancel
 F19=Submit to batch
```

Figure 6.20
Copy Members, from Work with Members Using PDM Option 3

1.5. At the Copy Members screen, the cursor should be on the To file entry field. You can see that PDM has already provided the file and library names of the member you are copying. You will keep the copy in the same file and library, so Tab or Field advance (not Field exit) the cursor down to the New Name entry field. Name the new member TESTSEU, then press Enter.

    1.5a. After you return to the Work with Members using PDM screen, what message is displayed at the bottom of the screen?

1.6. Now take the option to edit member TESTSEU.

    Let's start editing the member by inserting a new field for middle initial just after the first name field. Remember that SEU line commands such as Insert are typed right over the sequence numbers. Using the New line key, move the cursor to the sequence number for the first name field. Type IP to insert a line with prompting, then press Enter.

    Remember that field entries do not use Name Type. Name the new field MI, give it a length of 1 (remember to Field exit after typing the length), and make it alphanumeric. When you press Enter, notice that the line is inserted following the line on which the Insert command was entered. Also notice that you remain in insert mode, in case you need to insert more than one record.

    To get out of insert mode, as you should do now, press F5 or F12 (you can also press the Enter key on an empty prompt).

1.7. Besides the Insert command, the most useful SEU line commands are Move, Copy, and Delete. The Move and Copy commands require that you specify which lines are to be moved or copied and to what location in the source file they are to be moved or copied. The "location" designator is called the "target." The target is specified by moving the cursor where you want the moved or copied line(s) to go, and then typing either an A for after or a B for before on the sequence number of the target line.

Let's move the last name field by typing M anywhere on the sequence number of the last name field line. To move the last name field after the middle initial field, type A on the middle initial line's sequence number. When you press Enter to execute the line command, the name fields should be in the following order: first, middle initial, last.

To move several lines at a time, you can type the number of lines to be moved immediately after the M (e.g., M5), or you can mark a block of contiguous lines by typing MM on the first line's sequence number and another MM on the sequence number of the last line of the block.

To move all three name fields as a block to a location after the Zip code field, type MM on the sequence number for the first name field and MM on the sequence number for the last name field. Alternatively, because you can easily see that three lines are to be moved, you could type M3 on the sequence number for the first name field. In either case, you need to enter the target designator (A) on the sequence number for the Zip code field. If you haven't already, please do that now; and remember to press Enter to execute the command.

(Note: Target B is allowed on the ** End of data ** line, so you could use that approach instead of entering target A on the Zip code line — the result would be the same.)

1.8. The Copy command is similar to the Move command; the difference, of course, is that the Copy command leaves the copied lines at their original location and clones them at the target location. As with the Move command, you can copy a single line or multiple lines. For example, to copy the two address lines and place them before the first name field, type the Copy command, C2, on the ADDR1 line's sequence number, type target B, on the FNAME field's sequence number, then press Enter.

At this point, your SEU work screen should look like the one shown in Figure 6.21.

Now print the screen showing your changes. At the end of the lab, change the spooled file in your output queue to printer PRT01 (or another printer designated by your instructor/mentor) and hand in the printed output with your answer sheet.

```
 Columns . . . :   1  71            Edit              JSMITH/QDDSSRC
 SEU==>                                                       TESTSEU
 FMT PF .....A...........T.Name++++++RLen++TDpB......Functions++++++++++++++++++
        **************** Beginning of data *********************************
0001.00      A        R STUPFR
0002.00      A          SOCSEC       9S 0
0005.00      A          ADDR1       25A
0006.00      A          ADDR2       25A
0007.00      A          ZIP          5S 0
0007.01      A          ADDR1       25A
0007.02      A          ADDR2       25A
0008.00      A          FNAME       15A
0009.00      A          MI           1A
0010.00      A          LNAME       20A
        **************** End of data *****************************************




 F3=Exit    F4=Prompt    F5=Refresh   F9=Retrieve   F10=Cursor
 F16=Repeat find         F17=Repeat change          F24=More keys
```

Figure 6.21
SEU Showing Changed Member

1.9. The Delete command removes a single line or a block of lines from a source file. To delete a single line, type D on that line's sequence number. To delete a specific number of lines, type D*n* on the first line of the block, where *n* is the number of lines to be deleted. If the block is large, use the block Delete command by typing DD on the first line and DD on the last line of the block to be deleted. As always, the command itself is typed over the sequence number of the line. Unlike the Move and Copy commands, the Delete command does not need a target (i.e., you do not have to specify A or B).

To get more practice, try putting your TESTSEU file back the way it was when you started, in the order SOCSEC, LNAME, FNAME, ADDR1, ADDR2, ZIP. When you are finished, print the screen to hand in with your answer sheet.

1.10. We are done with TESTSEU for now, but we'll keep it in your QDDSSRC file for future use. Exit SEU now. The Exit screen values should specify "Change/create member...Y." Whether or not you successfully returned TESTSEU to its original state, there is no need to save your work, so change that value to N. This will simply keep the original TESTSEU as it was before editing. Leave the other defaulted values alone and press Enter to exit.

Part 2

Goals   Add a field to DDS source member STUPF
Compile the source member creating physical file STUPF
Display a message to find out whether the compile succeeded
Check the record format of the new PF

Start at   Work with Members Using PDM, your library/QDDSSRC

Procedure   Edit STUPF adding the PHONE field
Save and compile STUPF
DSPMSG to check the compile success
DSPFFD to observe the record format

2.1. Make sure you are at Work with Members Using PDM, file QDDSSRC, your library. If not, change the file or library entry fields at the top left of the screen, and enter correct values.

2.2. Take the option to Edit on member STUPF. Make sure you are looking at the SEU work screen for source member STUPF. Insert a field named PHONE right after field FNAME. Make it a 10-digit zoned-decimal (signed) field with no decimal positions. Then reverse the order of the name fields so that field FNAME precedes field LNAME. The source member should now look like the one shown in Figure 6.22.

Figure 6.22
SEU Showing Correct STUPF

```
Columns . . . :    1  71            Edit              JSMITH/QDDSSRC
SEU==>                                                          STUPF
FMT PF .....A..........T.Name+++++RLen++TDpB......Functions++++++++++++++++++++
**************** Beginning of data **********************************
0001.00      A          R STUPFR
0002.00      A            SOCSEC         9S 0
0002.01      A            FNAME         15A
0003.00      A            LNAME         20A
0004.01      A            PHONE         10S 0
0005.00      A            ADDR1         25A
0006.00      A            ADDR2         25A
0007.00      A            ZIP            5S 0
***************** End of data ***************************************




F3=Exit    F4=Prompt    F5=Refresh    F9=Retrieve    F10=Cursor
F16=Repeat find         F17=Repeat change            F24=More keys
```

2.3. Exit SEU, taking the default (Y) for the Change/Create Member option and the defaults for the rest of the options. Be sure to press Enter from the Exit screen.

2.4. From the Work with Members Using PDM screen, type 14 for compile on the option field of the member you just edited (STUPF). Do not press Enter, but prompt for the command. You should now see a screen like the one shown in Figure 6.23.

```
                        Create Physical File (CRTPF)

 Type choices, press Enter.

 File . . . . . . . . . . . . . . > STUPF        Name
   Library  . . . . . . . . . . >   JSMITH      Name, *CURLIB
 Source file  . . . . . . . . . > QDDSSRC       Name
   Library  . . . . . . . . . . >   JSMITH      Name, *LIBL, *CURLIB
 Source member  . . . . . . . . > STUPF         Name, *FILE

 Record length, if no DDS . . . .  _____      Number
 Generation severity level  . . .  20            0-30
 Flagging severity level  . . . .  0             0-30
 File type  . . . . . . . . . . .  *DATA         *DATA, *SRC
 Member, if desired . . . . . . .  *FILE         Name, *FILE, *NONE
 Text 'description' . . . . . . .  *SRCMBRTXT

                                                                 Bottom

 F3=Exit   F4=Prompt   F5=Refresh   F10=Additional parameters   F12=Cancel
 F13=How to use this display       F24=More keys
```

Figure 6.23
Option 14 Prompt on Member STUPF

2.4a. What CL command does PDM option 14 invoke in this context?

The context in which an option is taken is significant, and it is what makes PDM such a powerful tool. The option you select (in this case, option 14) tells PDM which verb form to use as part of the command; the source member type (in this case, PF) tells PDM which noun form to use. So by analyzing the option and member type, PDM can choose the correct command (in this case CRTPF). By default PDM creates an object of the same name as the source member. But, as you can see, you could change the object name on the CRTPF command prompt screen. PDM also places the object in the same library as the source file, unless you specify otherwise on the prompt screen.

2.5. Without making any changes to the default values, press Enter to run the command.

2.5a. What message is displayed at the bottom of the screen?

The message indicates that the compile has been submitted as a batch job (from within your interactive job), and it was sent to the job queue of the batch subsystem, QBATCH. By default, PDM sends option 14 compiles to the batch subsystem so you can continue to work while the compile is running. The programmer or operator can change this, as well as other PDM options, for his/her own PDM environment.

2.6. When the compile finishes, a message is sent to your (user) message queue telling you whether the compile was successful. If no undisplayed message is already waiting in your message queue, the terminal beeps at you and the message waiting indicator (MW on PCs, torn-form symbol on dedicated terminals) lights up on the status line, the bottom-most line of your display device.

You can examine the message by entering the DSPMSG (Display Message) command on the command line, or by entering the IBM-supplied, user-defined PDM option — DM (Display Message) — on any member's option field. If you get to the message queue before the message arrives, you can press function key F10 to display any new messages. If your display is set at the basic assistance level, use function key F5 to refresh instead of F10.

2.6a. What does the message say?

If the message indicates an abnormal end to the compile, you need to return to the source member and compare it very carefully to the member shown in Figure 6.22. Correct any discrepancies in your source code before trying the compile again. If the compile is still unsuccessful, seek help from your instructor/mentor.

2.7. At this point, return to the Work with Objects Using PDM screen by pressing function key F12 twice. After refreshing the screen, you should be able to see the newly created *FILE object in your list (you might need to page up).

2.7a. What is the *FILE object's attribute?   *PF - DTA*

2.8. Because this is an externally described file, detailed information at the file, record, and field level are kept as part of the object itself. You can examine information at the different levels by using appropriate commands.

Move the cursor to the command line (use function key F9) and type the DSPFFD (Display File Field Description) command. This command needs a single parameter value, the name of the file (STUPF), which you can enter as a positional value or by prompting. Run the command.

Examine the file and record format information on the first page of the display, then page down to the field-level descriptions of the record format. You should be looking at a screen similar to the one shown in Figure 6.24.

It is important to realize that although this information originally came from the DDS source member, the information now exists independently as part of the file object itself. Because of this, any program or utility using the file can immediately identify and use the record format, including all fields and their attributes.

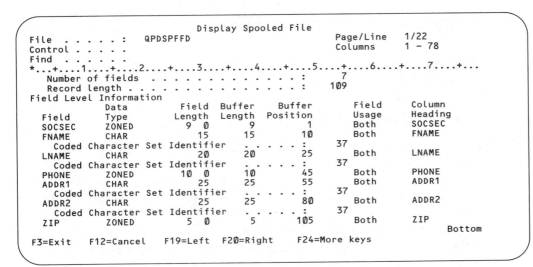

Figure 6.24
STUPF Record Format from DSPFFD

2.8a. How many fields are there in the record and what is the total record length?

Now return to the Work with Objects Using PDM screen.

Part 3

Goals	Start DFU and create a temporary update program
	Add data records to your STUPF file
	Observe the data added to the file
	Locate, identify, and print spooled files created during this lab session

Start at	Work with Objects Using PDM, your library

Procedure	STRDFU
	Take option 5 from the DFU menu
	Add records using DFU
	WRKMBRPDM STUPF, option 5
	WRKOUTQ youroutq

3.1. Now you will use DFU to enter data into your database file member. Enter the STRDFU command on the command line. Choose option 5 from the DFU menu to update using a temporary program; press Enter.

Enter your database file name (STUPF) and take the other defaults. Press Enter.

3.1a. What message is displayed? (Look quickly and write down as much as you can.)

3.2. After a moment or two you should see a screen for interactively entering data and updating your file. This is a temporary DFU that the utility can create on demand for any externally described database file.

3.2a. Which mode are you in?

3.3. Type in the data for the first record. Use your own name, but use Social Security number 111110001. Use fictitious data for the other fields. Do not use any editing characters (e.g., commas or hyphens) in the numeric fields. Use the Field exit key or Field advance (Tab) to jump to the beginning of each field. After typing the Zip code, press Enter.

If you press Enter on an incomplete numeric field, an error code flashes and the keyboard locks up. If this happens, press the Reset key and finish keying the field or press the Field exit key.

Each time you enter a filled-in screen, the current data is stored as a new record and a fresh input screen is provided. If you press Enter too soon (before completing a screen), use function key F11 to switch to Change mode, page up or down until you find the incomplete record, finish it, and then press Enter to save the changes. Function key F10 returns you to entry mode.

3.4. Enter the following data records, pressing Enter after each one:

111110002	111110003	111110004
Bilbo	Karikool	Matilda
Baggins	Clapsaddle	Twiddlebotham
3193778466	3074559999	3193668824
345 Hawthorne Ln.	Sundown Rd.	1812 River Rd.
Apt. Z	Bunkhouse #2	
52302	82301	52404

3.5. Use your own data to add at least 10 more records. Enter Social Security numbers in the range of 111110005 to 111110020. We are using this sequence to help you remember the numbers in later lab exercises. Avoid using the same Social Security number twice, as this will cause problems later on.

Use local Zip codes for at least half the records. After you have entered the last record, press F3 to exit.

3.5a. What screen do you see now? How many records were added?

3.5b. What does the message at the bottom of the screen tell you?

[handwritten: 9 all records added, chgd, or del will be printed]

Press Enter, leaving the defaults as they are. Exit from the next two screens, or until you have returned to the Work with Objects Using PDM screen.

3.6. From the Work with Objects Using PDM screen, enter option 12 on the option field for file STUPF. When you press Enter, you should be at the Work with Members Using PDM screen. Although you took the Work with option on a database physical file, it also has a member and certain limited PDM options are available for the member.

3.6a. What is one of the options you have used on a source file member (your DDS file description) that is not available for a database file member?

Take the option to display the member, and press F4 to prompt.

3.6b. Which CL command is invoked by this option?

Run the command. Shift right. Notice where the last digit of the Zip code lines up on the ruler line.

3.7. Return to the Work with Objects Using PDM screen. Work with your output queue.

3.7a. How many print files has Lab 6 generated?

Two of these files have file names that are not the name of the default printer device file, QSYSPRT, used by the Print Screen key. Display those files. Use the function key to shift your view to the right. Notice that page headers and other information require more than 80 print positions. As you examine these spooled files, keep in mind that they had to have come from actions taken in this lab.

3.7b. What do you think these two files are and where did they come from (what action generated them)?

Reroute your files to printer PRT01 or to the printer designated as your class printer. (The printer writer PRT01 writes to a wide-carriage printer.) Print the files created in this session. Clip the printed output to your answer sheet to hand in.

Mastering the AS/400, Second Edition

Lab 6 Answer Sheet

Name: _____

Date Due: _____

Class Time: _____

1.5a. _____

2.4a. _____

2.5a. _____

2.6a. _____

_____

2.7a. _____

2.8a. _____

3.1a. _____

3.2a. _____

3.5a. _____

3.5b. _____

3.6a. _____

3.6b. _____

3.7a._____

3.7b. _____

_____

_____

In Summary

In this lesson, we covered the creation and data-entry steps of building a database file. Using a slightly modified form of the DDS source file description created in the previous lesson, we employed Work with Members Using PDM option 14 to compile the source member into a file object. The compile option invokes a Create command, the particular flavor of which is determined by the member type. In our example, the CRTPF (Create Physical File) command was invoked. Usually, the PDM compile option eliminates the need to type command parameter values because PDM inserts the values automatically. Also, the compile option normally submits the compile to the batch subsystem, which leaves your workstation available for other work. After the file object has been created successfully, you can display information about the file at the object, file, and record format levels by using the DSPOBJD (Display Object Description), DSPFD (Display File Description), and DSPFFD (Display File Field Description) commands, respectively.

We learned that the DFU utility provides a quick and convenient way to enter and update data in a file. Entry mode allows interactive data entry; change mode retrieves an existing record by record number or via the Page up/Page down keys, letting you make changes to the record.

In the lab exercise, we used SEU line commands to edit a source file. We used the Move, Copy, and Delete SEU line commands to manipulate records in a DDS source member. We then compiled the source file using the PDM compile option and entered data records into the physical file using the temporary entry/update program feature of DFU. In later labs, we build a logical file over the database and use DFU programs to retrieve and update the files.

Introduction to Query/400

Lesson Overview

One of the main components of a database management system is a report generator, or query utility. On the AS/400 this function is provided by Query/400, an IBM licensed program product. Other, more powerful, products are available — both from IBM and from third-party vendors — but Query/400 is widely used, easy to learn, and available on most systems.

In this lesson, we introduce Query/400 and step you through the process of producing a query report based on a single database file. Then we introduce the concept of joined files and create a query to combine data from two files. In the lab, you put into practice what you learn in this lesson by printing a listing of the database file you created in a previous lab.

Objectives

Students will be able to

✓ Describe several features of Query/400, such as record selection, column formatting, summary functions, and report breaks

✓ Create result fields (derived columns) from existing fields

✓ Use Query/400 to generate a display or printed report based on a single file

✓ Change query output from display to a printed report

✓ Determine the need to join two or more files to get the information needed for a report

✓ Use Query/400 to create a report joining data from two files

WHAT QUERY/400 DOES

You can use **Query/400** to obtain information from any externally described database file on the AS/400. The file may have been defined using any of the three methods discussed in Lesson 5: DDS, IDDU, or SQL. Query/400 lets you generate printed reports, screen displays, or new database files using a single file or joining data from up to 32 different files. From one to all fields can be selected and organized into a printed report or display, or written to another file.

You will find that Query/400 is easy to use. It is menu-driven, with entry screens that help you select and format data; no programming skill is required. The majority of query reports take little time to set up once you have gained some experience. For example, the simplest report requires entering only the database file name. Features supported by Query/400 include the following:

- *The selection and arrangement of records* — You can use simple relational expressions to select specific records from files. You then can order these records in ascending or descending sequence by using any field or combination of fields as sort keys. For example, all records in an employee file could be sorted by employee name within department.

- *The selection and placement of fields* — You can choose specific fields to display or print and place them in any desired order. You can edit these fields (e.g., insert slashes in a date field for readability), or you can perform arithmetic operations on them to create new result fields. And you can easily adjust column widths and modify column headings.

- *The specification of report breaks* — You can print or display groups of records sorted by the values of designated sort control fields. Also called control break logic, this Query/400 feature lets you select control fields to be used on up to six levels of report breaks (e.g., department within section within division). You can also choose column functions for desired fields. These allow automatic calculations, such as total and average, to be printed when the value of a sort control field changes. For example, after listing all employees in the same department, you could print a count of employees and the total salary for each department if the employee file is sorted by department.

- *The ability to examine a report layout and preview a report* — At any time during the specification of a query, you can use function key F13 to display a layout of the query output as it might appear on a printer spacing chart. You can also test the query to see what the report will look like with actual data by using function key F5. You then can make any necessary modifications to your query without having to exit Query/400.

- *The execution of query programs* — Although a complete, saved query specification is not a program in the sense of object type (a query is object type *QRYDFN, not *PGM), you can run a query just as you would a program by using option 16 on a *QRYDFN type object from the Work with Objects Using PDM screen, or by entering the RUNQRY (Run Query) command on any command line. When a query runs, it uses the current data from the selected file(s) in the same way a high-level language program (e.g., RPG or Cobol) would when the program executes.

GETTING INTO QUERY/400

The STRQRY (Start Query) command takes you to the Query Utilities menu (Figure 7.1), which provides a list of query functions. Because this screen is a menu, you can also get to it by using the GO command (GO QUERY).

```
 QUERY                       Query Utilities
                                                    System:   S1018A6G
   Select one of the following:

 Query/400
     1. Work with queries
     2. Run an existing query
     3. Delete a query

 DB2/400
    10. Start DB2/400 Query Manager

 Query management
    20. Work with query management forms
    21. Work with query management queries
    22. Start a query
    23. Analyze a Query/400 definition
                                                          More...
   Selection or command
   ===> _____

   _____

   F3=Exit   F4=Prompt   F9=Retrieve   F12=Cancel   F13=Information Assistant
   F16=AS/400 Main menu
   (C) COPYRIGHT IBM CORP. 1980, 1995.
```

Figure 7.1

Query Utilities Menu (QUERY)

For this lesson you will be concerned only with the options listed under the heading Query/400 on the Query Utilities menu. Two of these — Run an existing query and Delete a query — can be performed more conveniently from the PDM environment by taking options 16 or 4 on the appropriate *QRYDFN type list item. The function we're most concerned with in this lesson — Work with queries — takes you to the Work with Queries screen (Figure 7.2).

Figure 7.2
Work with Queries
Screen

```
                                 Work with Queries
   Type choices, press Enter.

      Option  . . . . . .       _           1=Create, 2=Change, 3=Copy, 4=Delete
                                            5=Display, 6=Print definition
                                            8=Run in batch, 9=Run
      Query . . . . . . .       _____  Name, F4 for list
        Library . . . . .       JAFINTRO__  Name, *LIBL, F4 for list




   F3=Exit        F4=Prompt        F5=Refresh        F12=Cancel
```

WORKING WITH QUERIES

You can also reach the Work with Queries screen — and avoid the Query Utilities screen entirely — by running the WRKQRY (Work with Queries) command or by selecting the PDM Work with option (12) for any *QRYDFN type object. From the Work with Queries screen you can create a query; modify, copy, delete, or display an existing query; print a query definition; or run a query either as a batch job or interactively.

To create a new query, you take option 1; you can name the query at that time or wait until the query definition is completed. Other options listed (e.g., 2=Change, 3=Copy) work only with an existing query. If you can't remember the name of an existing query, you can place the cursor on the Query name input field and press function key F4 to prompt for a list of all existing query definitions in the selected library (Figure 7.3 shows such a list).

Figure 7.3
Work with Queries
Prompt List

```
                                 Work with Queries
   Library . . . . . . . .    JAFINTRO__    Name, *LIBL, F4 for list
   Subset  . . . . . . . .    _____    Name, generic*
   Position to . . . . . .    _____    Starting characters

   Type options (and Query), press Enter.
     1=Create   2=Change   3=Copy   4=Delete   5=Display   6=Print
     8=Run in batch   9=Run
   Opt  Query

    _    FILE01QX_
    _    FILE01Q1
    _    FILE01Q1B
    _    FILE01Q2
    _    FILE01Q3
    _    LFILE01Q1
    _    QRYF1AR
    _    SECTQRY1
    _    XYZ

                                                                    Bottom
   F3=Exit        F4=Prompt              F5=Refresh         F11=Display text
   F12=Cancel     F19=Next group
```

The first time you use Query/400, the library displayed is your current library. After that, WRKQRY returns you to the library you were using on the previous occasion.

As with any other Work with list, you can move the cursor down the list and type the option you want next to the query to be used. If the query you are looking for is not in the list, you can change the Library field at the top of the screen to a different value and press Enter to see a new list.

DEFINING THE QUERY

Now let's step through the process of creating a query. When you type a 1 in the option field of the Work with Queries screen and press Enter, the main query specification screen, Define the Query (Figure 7.4), appears.

```
                          Define the Query

Query . . . . . . :                    Option  . . . . . :   CREATE
    Library . . . . :    JAFINTRO       CCSID  . . . . . :   65535

Type options, press Enter.  Press F21 to select all.
   1=Select

Opt     Query Definition Option
 1      Specify file selections
 _      Define result fields
 _      Select and sequence fields
 _      Select records
 _      Select sort fields
 _      Select collating sequence
 _      Specify report column formatting
 _      Select report summary functions
 _      Define report breaks
 _      Select output type and output form
 _      Specify processing options


F3=Exit          F5=Report         F12=Cancel
F13=Layout       F18=Files         F21=Select all
```

Figure 7.4

Define the Query Screen

This screen presents all the available query features you can use to create a customized query. After you select one of these features, Query/400 prompts you through a series of related lower-level screens to define exactly how you want the feature to work for this report. Most of this process is menu-driven — you simply select option numbers or respond to prompts — but parts of some features require you to reorder list items or enter expressions or functions. When you finish the definition of one feature, you return to this Define the Query screen. Then you can select the next feature or Exit and save if you are finished.

SELECTING FILES

When the Define the Query screen first appears, the Specify file selections option is selected automatically (i.e., a 1 is entered for that option). Query/400 automatically selects this option because, at the very least, you must tell Query/400 which file to use.

When you press Enter from the Define the Query screen, you see the Specify File Selections screen shown in Figure 7.5.

Figure 7.5
Specify File Selections
Screen

```
                           Specify File Selections
Type choices, press Enter.  Press F9 to specify an additional
  file selection.

    File . . . . . . . . .   _____   Name, F4 for list
      Library  . . . . . .   JAFINTRO__   Name, *LIBL, F4 for list
    Member . . . . . . . .   *FIRST____   Name, *FIRST, F4 for list
    Format . . . . . . . .   *FIRST____   Name, *FIRST, F4 for list




    F3=Exit               F4=Prompt         F5=Report          F9=Add file
    F12=Cancel            F13=Layout        F24=More keys
```

From this screen you can prompt for physical and logical database files in your current library (the initial default) or another library to which you are authorized.

Pressing function key F4 on the File name input field takes you to the Select File screen shown in Figure 7.6.

Figure 7.6
Select File List Screen
Displayed after
Prompting (F4) on File
Name

```
                              Select File

    Library  . . . . . . .   JAFINTRO__   Name, *LIBL, F4 for list
    Subset . . . . . . . .   _____   Name, generic*
    Position to  . . . . .   _____   Starting character(s)

    Type option (and File), press Enter.
      1=Select

    Opt  File          Opt  File          Opt  File
     _   BUCKET1        _    MOJUNK         _   SAMP01
     1   EMPPF          _    LFILE01        _   TESTLF
     _   FILE01         _    QCLSRC
     _   FILE01B        _    QCMDSRC
     _   FILE01BK       _    QDDSSRC
     _   FILE01DTA      _    QQMFORMSRC
     _   F1TEST         _    QQMQRYSRC
     _   JUNK           _    QTXTSRC

                                                              Bottom
    F4=Prompt         F11=Display text      F12=Cancel       F24=More keys
```

In Figure 7.6, file EMPPF has already been selected for use in this query. If you realized, after looking at the list of files, that this was not the library your file was in, you could simply type over the Library value (JAFINTRO in this example), replacing it with the name of the library of the file you needed. Pressing Enter would then change the display to list files from the new library, assuming, as always, that you are authorized to use that library.

When you press Enter from the Select File screen, Query/400 fills in the File name field (in this case, using file name EMPPF), asks you to confirm that the file name is correct, then returns you to the Define the Query screen. The Define the Query screen should now look like the one in Figure 7.7.

```
                              Define the Query
 Query  . . . . . . :                 Option  . . . . . :   CREATE
   Library . . . . :      JAFINTRO     CCSID  . . . . . . :   65535

 Type options, press Enter.  Press F21 to select all.
   1=Select

 Opt    Query Definition Option
   _  > Specify file selections
   _    Define result fields
   _    Select and sequence fields
   _    Select records
   _    Select sort fields
   _    Select collating sequence
   _    Specify report column formatting
   _    Select report summary functions
   _    Define report breaks
   _    Select output type and output form
   _    Specify processing options

 F3=Exit          F5=Report        F12=Cancel
 F13=Layout       F18=Files        F21=Select all
 Select options, or press F3 to save or run the query
```

Figure 7.7

Define the Query Screen with > Indicating an Option Has Been Used

Notice that a greater-than symbol (>) displayed to the right of the option field has replaced the 1 on the Specify file selections option field; this is to remind you that this feature has been used. (But if you need to, you can always go back and change the values you specified for any feature by taking option 1 on it again.)

PREVIEWING A QUERY LAYOUT

That's all you would need to do to generate a "bare bones" query of a single database file. To see how the query is formatted at this point, you would press function key F13 from the Define the Query screen. The first 72 print/display positions of the query layout for our example are shown in Figure 7.8. (You could see the additional columns of the report by pressing function key F20 to shift the view to the right.)

Figure 7.8

Display Report Layout Screen

```
                          Display Report Layout
                                    Report width . . . . . :        199
Position to line . . . . .          Shift to column  . . . . .
Line    ....+....1....+....2....+....3....+....4....+....5....+....6....+....7..
            EMPNO    LASTNAME          FIRSTNAME    HOMEPHONE    ADDR1
000001 999,999,999  XXXXXXXXXXXXXX    XXXXXXXXXXX   9,999,999    XXXXXXXXXXXXXX
****** ******** End of report layout ********


                                                              Bottom
F3=Exit        F12=Cancel       F19=Left     F20=Right     F21=Split
```

Notice that field names are used as column headers, spaces are inserted between columns, and numeric fields (EMPNO and HOMEPHONE) are edited with commas to separate thousands. Let's say that after viewing the report layout, you decide to change the way the numeric fields EMPNO and HOMEPHONE are edited.

Before you can edit the numeric fields, you must first press Enter or F12 to return to the Define the Query screen. Then you select Specify report column formatting, as shown in Figure 7.9.

Figure 7.9

Define the Query Screen with Specify Report Column Formatting Selected

```
                              Define the Query
Query . . . . . . :                 Option  . . . . . :    CREATE
   Library . . . . :     JAFINTRO    CCSID  . . . . . . :    65535

Type options, press Enter.  Press F21 to select all.
   1=Select

Opt    Query Definition Option
 _   > Specify file selections
 _     Define result fields
 _     Select and sequence fields
 _     Select records
 _     Select sort fields
 _     Select collating sequence
 1     Specify report column formatting
 _     Select report summary functions
 _     Define report breaks
 _     Select output type and output form
 _     Specify processing options

F3=Exit          F5=Report
F13=Layout       F18=Files        F21=Select all
Select options, or press F3 to save or run the query
```

FORMATTING REPORT COLUMNS

The Specify Report Column Formatting screen (Figure 7.10) displays three fields at a time and lets you change column spacing, column headings (which can be up to three lines long), and field length (but if you make the field length shorter than the actual database field, you could lose data in the report).

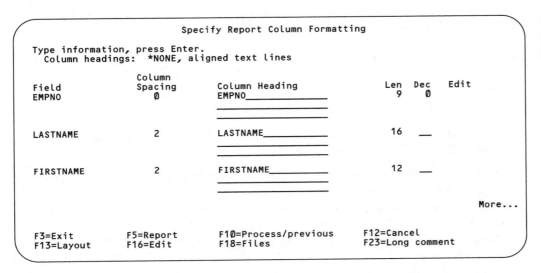

```
                    Specify Report Column Formatting

 Type information, press Enter.
    Column headings:  *NONE, aligned text lines

                    Column
 Field              Spacing    Column Heading          Len  Dec   Edit
 EMPNO                 0        EMPNO_____     9    0
                               _____
                               _____

 LASTNAME              2        LASTNAME_____    16   __
                               _____
                               _____

 FIRSTNAME             2        FIRSTNAME_____    12   __
                               _____
                               _____

                                                              More...

 F3=Exit          F5=Report       F10=Process/previous    F12=Cancel
 F13=Layout       F16=Edit        F18=Files               F23=Long comment
```

Figure 7.10
Specify Report Column Formatting Screen

Here you need to edit numeric field EMPNO, and the function you need is listed among the function keys at the bottom of the screen.

You would move the cursor anywhere in the horizontal zone for field EMPNO (i.e., the line starting with the field name, EMPNO, and the two lines following) and press function key F16, which would take you to the Define Numeric Field Editing screen shown in Figure 7.11.

```
                    Define Numeric Field Editing

    Field . . . . . . . . :  EMPNO
    Text  . . . . . . . . :
    Heading 1 . . . . . . :  EMPNO
    Heading 2 . . . . . . :
    Heading 3 . . . . . . :
    Length  . . . . . . . :  9
    Decimal . . . . . . . :  0
    Sample  . . . . . . . :  999,999,999


    Type choice, press Enter.
       Edit option . . . . .  1      1=Numeric editing choices
                                     2=Date or time editing choice
                                     3=Edit code
                                     4=Edit word




    F3=Exit         F5=Report        F10=Process/previous   F11=Change sample
    F12=Cancel      F13=Layout       F16=Remove edit        F18=Files
```

Figure 7.11
Define Numeric Field Editing Screen for EMPNO

This screen identifies field EMPNO and displays its column headings, length, and a sample of how the field would appear when printed. As you can see, the sample for field EMPNO shows that commas are used as separators.

EDITING OPTIONS

To get rid of the commas, you would use the default Edit option 1, Numeric editing choices. Selecting this option takes you to the Describe Numeric Field Editing screen (Figure 7.12).

Figure 7.12

Describe Numeric Field Editing Screen for EMPNO

```
                              Describe Numeric Field Editing

        Field . . . . . . :    EMPNO

        Type choices, press Enter.

            Decimal point . . . . . . . .   1      1=.   2=,   3=:   4=$      5=None
            Thousands separator . . . . .   2      1=.   2=,   3='   4=Blank  5=None
            Show negative sign  . . . . .   Y      Y=Yes, N=No
              Left negative sign  . . . .
              Right negative sign . . . .   -
            Show currency symbol  . . . .   N      Y=Yes, N=No
              Left currency symbol  . . .   $
              Right currency symbol . . .
            Print zero value  . . . . . .   Y      Y=Yes, N=No
            Replace leading zeros . . . .   Y      Y=Yes, N=No
              Replace with  . . . . . . .   1      1=Blanks
                                                   2=Asterisks
                                                   3=Floating currency symbol
              Single leading zero . . . .   N      Y=Yes, N=No


        F3=Exit        F5=Report           F10=Process/previous      F12=Cancel
        F13=Layout     F16=Remove edit      F18=Files
```

On this screen, you can change the Thousands separator value from comma to None by typing a 5 over the 2, which is the default. Although we won't work with them here, you can see that other options have to do with the display of the negative sign, currency symbol, and leading zeros.

When you change a value on an entry screen such as the Describe Numeric Field Editing screen, it's important that you press the Enter key to save changes and not function key F12; F12 does not save your changes. Although function key F3 saves your changes, it takes you to the query exit screen; don't use F3 unless you are finished specifying the query.

Pressing Enter on the Describe Numeric Field Editing screen returns you to the Specify Report Column Formatting screen (Figure 7.13).

```
                    Specify Report Column Formatting

Type information, press Enter.
   Column headings:  *NONE, aligned text lines

                    Column
Field               Spacing      Column Heading            Len  Dec  Edit
EMPNO                  0         EMPNO_____      9    0    *
                                 _____

LASTNAME               2         LASTNAME_____      16
                                 _____

FIRSTNAME              2         FIRSTNAME_____      12
                                 _____

                                                          More...
F3=Exit          F5=Report      F10=Process/previous    F12=Cancel
F13=Layout       F16=Edit       F18=Files               F23=Long comment
```

Figure 7.13
Specify Report Column
Formatting with *
Indicating Field EMPNO
Has Been Edited

Notice that now an * appears under the Edit column for field EMPNO; this is to remind you that the field has been edited.

Now let's say that after viewing the layout of file EMPPF again you still are not satisfied with the appearance of field EMPNO. The field contains a Social Security number and you would like to separate the parts of the number with blanks (spaces), so it would appear as 999 99 9999. You would use function key F16 again, with the cursor in the EMPNO field horizontal zone and return to the Define Numeric Field Editing screen (Figure 7.14).

```
                    Define Numeric Field Editing

Field . . . . . . . . :  EMPNO
Text  . . . . . . . . :
Heading 1 . . . . . . :  EMPNO
Heading 2 . . . . . . :
Heading 3 . . . . . . :
Length  . . . . . . . :  9
Decimal . . . . . . . :  0
Sample  . . . . . . . :  999999999


Type choice, press Enter.

   Edit option . . . . .  4      1=Numeric editing choices
                                 2=Date or time editing choice
                                 3=Edit code
                                 4=Edit word



F3=Exit          F5=Report      F10=Process/previous    F11=Change sample
F12=Cancel       F13=Layout     F16=Remove edit         F18=Files
```

Figure 7.14
Define Numeric Field
Editing

To use blanks as separators, you need to create an edit word by using option 4. (Option 4 has already been entered in Figure 7.14.) The next screen that appears, Specify Edit Word (Figure 7.15), works like this:

a. The apostrophes delimit the edit word, and initially the number of blanks (spaces) within the apostrophes is equal to the number of digits in the field.

b. As the display indicates, each digit is represented by a blank. To insert an actual blank (spacebar) into the edited field, you would use the ampersand (&) character.

c. If you wanted to use other edit characters (e.g., hyphens or slashes), you would insert them where you needed them to appear within the edit word.

Figure 7.15

Specify Edit Word
Screen

```
                                        Specify Edit Word
    Field . . . . . :    EMPNO          Heading 1 . . . . :    EMPNO
    Length  . . . . :    9              Heading 2 . . . . :
    Decimal . . . . :    0              Heading 3 . . . . :

    Type information, press Enter. (Put quotes around edit words.)
      (Each blank replaced by a digit, each '&' with a blank.)

        Edit word . . . . .    '_____'  _____

    _____
    _____
    _____

        Edit word for
          summary total  . .  _____

    _____
    _____
    _____



    F3=Exit          F5=Report        F10=Process/previous      F12=Cancel
    F13=Layout       F16=Remove edit  F18=Files
```

Following these guidelines, your edit word for the EMPNO field would be specified as shown in Figure 7.16.

```
                         Specify Edit Word

  Field . . . . . :    EMPNO        Heading 1 . . . . :    EMPNO
  Length . . . . :     9            Heading 2 . . . . :
  Decimal . . . . :    0            Heading 3 . . . . :

  Type information, press Enter. (Put quotes around edit words.)
    (Each blank replaced by a digit, each '&' with a blank.)

    Edit word . . . . .    '  &  &   '  _____
  _____
  _____
  _____

    Edit word for
      summary total . .  _____
  _____
  _____



  F3=Exit        F5=Report         F10=Process/previous      F12=Cancel
  F13=Layout     F16=Remove edit   F18=Files
```

Figure 7.16

Specify Edit Word with Edit Characters Entered

Notice that the two ampersands were inserted inside the apostrophes so that the number of spaces (digits) is still nine, the same as the length specified above. If the number of digit place holders within the apostrophes is different from the length value, Query/400 considers it an error and puts the entire quoted string in reverse image until you fix it. It also displays the error message "Edit word does not match field length" at the bottom of the screen.

When you press Enter and return to the Specify Report Column Formatting screen, you can try the Layout function again to see the effect your edit word will have. The Display Report Layout screen for our example query now looks like the one shown in Figure 7.17, and you can see that the blank insertion was successful.

```
                    Display Report Layout
                                    Report width . . . . . :    198
  Position to line . . . . .        Shift to column . . . . . .
  Line    ....+....1....+....2....+....3....+....4....+....5....+....6....+....7..
            EMPNO  LASTNAME           FIRSTNAME      HOMEPHONE   ADDR1
  000001  999 99 9999  XXXXXXXXXXXXXXX  XXXXXXXXXXX  9,999,999   XXXXXXXXXXXXXXX
  ****** ********  End of report layout  ********




                                                          Bottom
  F3=Exit       F12=Cancel      F19=Left      F20=Right      F21=Split
```

Figure 7.17

Display Report Layout Screen – Field EMPNO Edited with Blank Insertion

Using another edit word (Figure 7.18), you could easily format the HOME-PHONE field to eliminate the comma thousands separator and insert a hyphen between the prefix and subscriber code, the standard way of displaying a 7-digit phone number.

Figure 7.18
Specify Edit Word
Screen to Edit Field
HOMEPHONE

```
                              Specify Edit Word
  Field . . . . . :   HOMEPHONE        Heading 1 . . . . :    HOMEPHONE
  Length  . . . . :   7                Heading 2 . . . . :
  Decimal . . . . :   0                Heading 3 . . . . :

  Type information, press Enter.  (Put quotes around edit words.)
    (Each blank replaced by a digit, each '&' with a blank.)

    Edit word . . . . .      '    -     '
  _____
  _____


  Edit word for
    summary total . .      _____
  _____



  F3=Exit          F5=Report          F10=Process/previous     F12=Cancel
  F13=Layout       F16=Remove Edit     F18=Files
```

In Figure 7.18, the hyphen is inserted, but the number of spaces (digit place-holders) remains seven. Also note that when you use an edit word, it isn't necessary to first change numeric editing choices (code 5 to eliminate thousands separators) because all default editing options are turned off automatically if you select an edit code or edit word.

Editing Numeric Date and Time Fields

Although fields whose type is defined as Date or Time are automatically edited according to their format and separators, many older database files store date or time data as numeric zoned or packed decimal fields, and Query/400 edits them as numbers by using the comma thousands separator. You could always create an edit word as we did above, but an easier way to insert slashes, dashes, or colons for date/time fields is to use option 2, Date or Time editing choice, from the Define Numeric Field Editing screen (Figure 7.11).

Selecting option 2 takes you to the Describe Date/Time Editing screen shown in Figure 7.19.

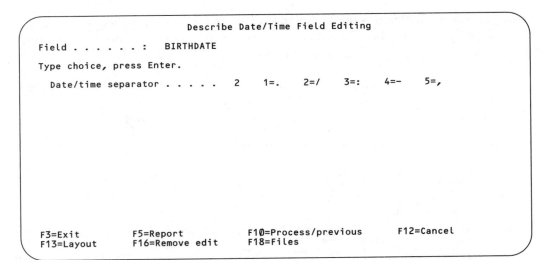

```
/                                                                    \
|                    Describe Date/Time Field Editing                |
|  Field . . . . . . :   BIRTHDATE                                   |
|  Type choice, press Enter.                                         |
|     Date/time separator . . . . .  2    1=.    2=/    3=:    4=-    5=, |
|                                                                    |
|                                                                    |
|                                                                    |
|                                                                    |
|                                                                    |
|                                                                    |
|                                                                    |
|                                                                    |
|                                                                    |
|  F3=Exit         F5=Report        F10=Process/previous    F12=Cancel  |
|  F13=Layout      F16=Remove edit  F18=Files                         |
\                                                                    /
```

Figure 7.19
Selecting Slash (/)
Separators for Field
BIRTHDATE

From this screen, you can choose which separator to use. Choosing option 2, for example, causes a six-digit birth date in MMDDYY format to appear as 6/21/73 for a person born on June 21, 1973.

When a date field is defined as data type L, insertion characters determined by the date format (*ISO uses hyphens) are already part of the field so no further editing is needed. In fact, Query/400 does not permit editing of L type fields.

You have now seen how the Specify report column formatting feature is used to select editing on two numeric fields. The default query uses all fields in the database record; so before going on let's decide which fields you want to include in this report, how you want them arranged, and any other report specifications.

1. You want to select all records but group them by department. Within department you want them sorted in ascending sequence on last name.

2. You want to include the following fields, in the order indicated: DEPT, LASTNAME, FIRSTNAME, HOMEPHONE, EMPNO, BIRTHDATE, HIRE-DATE, SALARY. You don't want to include fields ADDR1, ADDR2, or ZIP.

3. You want more meaningful column headers displayed (e.g., Employee Number instead of EMPNO).

4. You would like a count of employees in each department and a final count of all employees.

5. You would like a subtotal and the average salary for each department and a final total salary for the whole company.

6. You would like to calculate the years employed for each employee and find the average years employed per department.

To accomplish the first specification, you need to sort the records coming into the query by last name within department. Then you can define a report break that lets you print subcounts, subtotals, and averages when the department changes. Figure 7.20 shows the Define the Query screen, where Select sort fields and Define report breaks have already been selected. As in PDM, multiple options can be selected and then processed in order.

Figure 7.20

Define the Query Screen with Two Options Selected

```
                              Define the Query
Query . . . . . . :                    Option . . . . . :   CREATE
   Library . . . . :    JAFINTRO        CCSID  . . . . . :   65535
Type options, press Enter.  Press F21 to select all.
   1=Select

Opt    Query Definition Option
 _   > Specify file selections
 _     Define result fields
 _     Select and sequence fields
 _     Select records
 1     Select sort fields
 _     Select collating sequence
 _   > Specify report column formatting
 _     Select report summary functions
 1     Define report breaks
 _     Select output type and output form
 _     Specify processing options

F3=Exit           F5=Report
F13=Layout        F18=Files           F21=Select all
Select options, or press F3 to save or run the query.
```

SELECTING SORT FIELDS

The first screen that would appear after you press Enter from Figure 7.20, Select Sort Fields, is shown in Figure 7.21.

Figure 7.21

Select Sort Fields Screen with Two Sort Keys Selected

```
                              Select Sort Fields
Type sort priority (0-999) and A (Ascending) or D (Descending) for
   the names of up to 32 fields, press Enter.

Sort
Prty A/D  Field            Text                            Len  Dec
 __   _   EMPNO                                              9   0
 2__  _   LASTNAME                                          16
 __   _   FIRSTNAME                                         12
 __   _   HOMEPHONE                                          7   0
 __   _   ADDR1                                             40
 __   _   ADDR2                                             40
 __   _   ZIP                                                5   0
 _1_  _   DEPT                                              12
 __   _   BIRTHDATE                                         10   L
 __   _   HIREDATE                                          10   L
 __   _   SALARY                                             7   0

                                                     Bottom
F3=Exit           F5=Report       F11=Display names only  F12=Cancel
F13=Layout        F18=Files       F20=Renumber            F24=More keys
```

Query/400 lets you select up to 32 different sort key fields, although in practice more than three or four key fields are seldom used. To specify a sort key, you simply assign a number to the field under the sort priority (Sort Prty) column. Lower numbers have a higher priority, so to produce a report sorted like a telephone book, you might give LASTNAME a priority of 1 and FIRSTNAME a priority of 2. Normal sequence is ascending (A, B, C, …, Z; 1, 2, 3, …, 99) and that is what the A/D (sequence) column defaults to; but if you wanted to list all Zachs before Andersons, you would enter a D in the A/D column for the LASTNAME field.

In this case, we have already given a sort priority of 1 to field DEPT in default ascending sequence and a sort priority of 2 to field LASTNAME, also in ascending sequence. Remember, the lower the number the higher the priority. As they are entered, the values specify to sort the file in ascending sequence by minor sort key LASTNAME, within major sort key DEPT, ascending. This groups all employees alphabetically within their departments. After you press Enter, Query/400 asks you to confirm your choices (Figure 7.22). If you made a mistake or changed your mind, you could make adjustments from this screen.

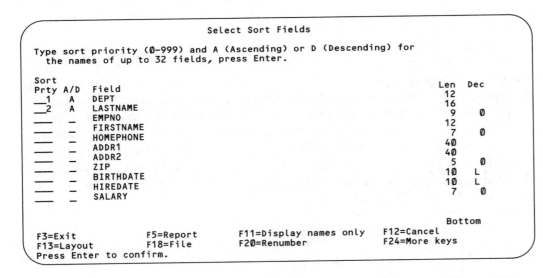

Figure 7.22
Confirm Request for Select Sort Fields

Defining Report Breaks

Because we also selected Define report breaks in Figure 7.20, Query/400 takes us directly to that screen (Figure 7.23).

Figure 7.23
Define Report Breaks
Screen

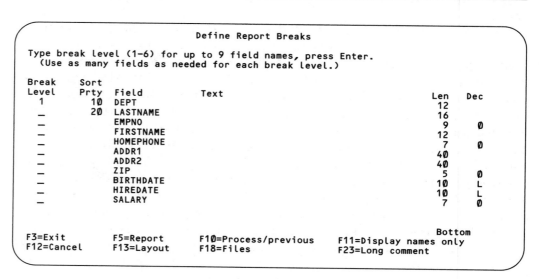

```
                        Define Report Breaks
Type break level (1-6) for up to 9 field names, press Enter.
   (Use as many fields as needed for each break level.)

Break    Sort
Level    Prty   Field      Text                              Len   Dec
 1        10    DEPT                                          12
 _        20    LASTNAME                                      16
 _              EMPNO                                          9    0
 _              FIRSTNAME                                     12
 _              HOMEPHONE                                      7    0
 _              ADDR1                                         40
 _              ADDR2                                         40
 _              ZIP                                            5    0
 _              BIRTHDATE                                     10    L
 _              HIREDATE                                      10    L
 _              SALARY                                         7    0

                                                          Bottom
F3=Exit         F5=Report      F10=Process/previous   F11=Display names only
F12=Cancel      F13=Layout     F18=Files              F23=Long comment
```

Sort fields and control breaks are directly related, so the Define Report Breaks screen already shows that DEPT and LASTNAME have been selected as the sort key fields by displaying their sort priorities.

Now you need to assign a break level to the DEPT field. Query/400 automatically assigns break level 0 to final totals, so you could assign up to six more break levels: the lower the number, the more inclusive the break level. For example, if population records were sorted by city within county within state, you would assign break level 1 to state (most inclusive), 2 to county, and 3 to city (least inclusive) to do subcounts or subtotals on all levels. In this example, you only want a subtotal on DEPT, so Figure 7.23 shows break level 1 typed in for DEPT. Note that sort priority is provided for information only — it is not an input-enabled field on the Define Report Breaks screen. Now when you press Enter, the Format Report Break screen, Figure 7.24, appears.

Figure 7.24
Format Report Break –
Level 0 (Last Record)

```
                        Format Report Break
Break level . . . . . . . :   0

Type choices, press Enter.
   (Type &field in text to have break values inserted.)


   Suppress summaries . . . .   N          Y=Yes, N=No

   Break text . . . . . . . .   FINAL TOTALS_____

Level  Field
 1     DEPT




F3=Exit         F5=Report      F10=Process/previous     F12=Cancel
F13=Layout      F18=Files      F23=Long comment
```

A screen similar to this one will be displayed for each break level requested. The screen shown in Figure 7.24 is for Break level 0; Query/400 automatically generates a level 0 control break that prints final totals after the last record.

As shown on this screen, the Break text for this level defaults to FINAL TOTALS. You could change the Break text by typing over it, but for this example FINAL TOTALS will do just fine. The default of N for Suppress summaries tells you that any summary functions you request, such as count or total, will be printed for break level 0, final totals. (We haven't selected report summary functions yet, but when we do they will be printed/displayed with level 0 control breaks when the query is run.) The display-only information above the function keys reminds you of the other break levels you have chosen and which fields they were selected on.

After pressing Enter, you would see the Format Report Break screen for Break level 1 on field DEPT (Figure 7.25).

Figure 7.25
Format Report Break –
Level 1

```
                        Format Report Break

  Break level  . . . . . . . :   1

  Type choices, press Enter.
    (Type &field in text to have break values inserted.)

    Skip to new page . . . . .   N          Y=Yes, N=No

    Suppress summaries . . . .   N          Y=Yes, N=No

    Break text . . . . . . . .   &DEPT Department Subtotals _____


  Level   Field
    1     DEPT




  F3=Exit          F5=Report        F10=Process/previous    F12=Cancel
  F13=Layout       F18=Files        F23=Long comment
```

You don't want to start on a new page every time the department changes, nor do you want to suppress summaries; so the first two input fields, Skip to new page and Suppress summaries, can be left with their default values of N.

To include the break control field value on the subtotal line, you can ask Query/400 to substitute the actual field value by using the field name, prefixed with an ampersand, as part of the Break text. For example, when the Accounting department subtotals are printed, the value "Accounting" would be substituted for &DEPT on the subtotal line of the printed report. Figure 7.25 shows the Break text entered so that the department name will print before the constant part of the text.

Pressing Enter now returns you to the Define the Query screen. We have now accomplished report specification number 1. You will test it shortly; but first, let's select and sequence the report fields according to specification number 2.

SELECTING AND SEQUENCING FIELDS

From the Define the Query screen, take the option to select and sequence fields and you will see the screen shown in Figure 7.26.

Figure 7.26

Select and Sequence Fields Screen

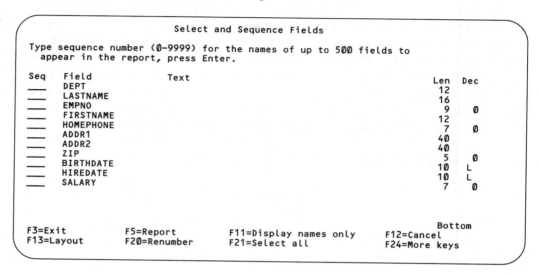

Notice that even though they did not start out in that order, the department and last name fields have moved to the top of the list as a result of being selected as the primary and secondary sort key fields.

On this screen you select fields by giving them a number. The left-to-right order of the fields across the report depends on the relative magnitude of the number, the leftmost field having the lowest number. In Figure 7.27, the fields have been assigned numbers placing them in the order requested in specification number 2.

Figure 7.27

Ordering Fields for a Query Report

```
                           Select and Sequence Fields

  Type sequence number (0-9999) for the names of up to 500 fields to
     appear in the report, press Enter.

  Seq   Field            Text                                Len  Dec
  1__   DEPT                                                 12
  2__   LASTNAME                                             16
  5__   EMPNO                                                 9   0
  3__   FIRSTNAME                                            12
  4__   HOMEPHONE                                             7   0
  ___   ADDR1                                                40
  ___   ADDR2                                                40
  ___   ZIP                                                   5   0
  6__   BIRTHDATE                                            10   L
  7__   HIREDATE                                             10   L
  8__   SALARY                                                7   0



                                                            Bottom
  F3=Exit          F5=Report        F11=Display names only  F12=Cancel
  F13=Layout       F20=Renumber     F21=Select all          F24=More keys
```

You can assign the numbers in any increments as long as they are in the relative order corresponding to their position. For Figure 7.27 they have simply been numbered 1, 2, 3, ... but Query/400 will renumber them in increments of 10.

Notice that the fields not needed in this report are simply left without numbers. If you decide to include one of those fields later, you could return to this screen and give that field a number within an appropriate range to position it before, after, or between any fields currently selected.

When you press Enter, you will be asked to confirm the resequenced list of fields. Pressing Enter again does that and returns you to the Define the Query screen, but you may first want to verify the accuracy of the report as it is defined so far.

From the Select and Sequence Fields screen (or the Define the Query screen), you can press F5 to run the query and show how the report will look at this point. Figure 7.28 shows how the report will be displayed.

```
                            Display Report
                                      Report width . . . . . :      104
      Position to line . . . . .          Shift to column . . . . . .
      Line    ....+....1....+....2....+....3....+....4....+....5....+....6....+....7..
              DEPT          LASTNAME       FIRSTNAME     HOMEPHONE         EMPNO  BI
      000001 Human Res     Hunn           Atilla        857-4211  111 11 0009   19
      000002
      000003      Human Res Department Subtotals
      000004
      000005 Marketing     Disney         Walter        455-2323  111 11 0010   19
      000006 Marketing     Gootch         Martha        848-9799  111 11 0008   19
      000007
      000008      Marketing Department Subtotals
      000009
      000010 MIS           Zanzibar       Tilly         396-3324  111 11 0011   19
      000011
      000012      MIS Department Subtotals
      000013
      000014 Research      Einstein       Albert        363-2550  111 11 0003   19
      000015 Research      Takahashi      Musashi       857-4321  111 11 0004   19
      000016
                                                                  More...
      F3=Exit      F12=Cancel     F19=Left     F20=Right    F21=Split
```

Figure 7.28
Preview of Query Report Format

You can see that the records are properly grouped and sorted by last name within department, and the home phone and employee number fields appear properly edited. A report line is too wide for all fields to display at once, so you can press F20 to shift the view to the right side of the report. You would then see that all fields selected are present and in the correct order.

You have now satisfied the first and second specifications. Now let's work on the third specification and use the Report column formatting feature to change the column headers.

More Report Column Formatting

You have already used the Report column formatting option to edit employee number and home phone, but you can return to any feature as many times as necessary simply by typing 1 on its option field and pressing Enter.

After you do this, you will see the Specify Report Column Formatting screen again (Figure 7.29).

Figure 7.29
Report Column
Formatting

```
                      Specify Report Column Formatting

Type information, press Enter.
  Column headings:   *NONE, aligned text lines

                  Column
 Field           Spacing       Column Heading             Len  Dec   Edit
 DEPT               0          DEPT_____         12   __
                              _____
                              _____
 LASTNAME           2          LASTNAME_____         16   __
                              _____
                              _____
 FIRSTNAME          2          FIRSTNAME_____         12   __
                              _____
                              _____

                                                                  More...

 F3=Exit          F5=Report        F10=Process/previous    F12=Cancel
 F13=Layout       F16=Edit         F18=Files               F23=Long comment
```

Notice that the sequence (and presence) of fields on this screen is different from before (Figure 7.10) and is now determined by our previous select and sequence fields activity.

On this screen you can change column headings by typing over or blanking out the default field name column heading that is currently displayed. Also, you can change column spacing (the number of blank spaces to precede each column) from the defaults of 0 for the first field and 2 for each subsequent field. We will rekey the column headings to mixed case and expand them using two or three lines when necessary. If a column heading is wider than the data field, Query/400 automatically adjusts the column width to avoid truncating any part of the column heading. So when you try to scrunch a lot of data into a narrow report or display, you may want to stack headings on the three lines provided rather than use all 20 print positions allowed per column.

The first display of the modified Report Column Formatting screen is shown in Figure 7.30.

Because the DEPT field is 12 characters wide, the heading has been spelled out. The last and first name column headings have also been expanded, but the data field lengths have been reduced to 14 and 10 for last name and first name, respectively. Character fields are often defined to a larger size than is needed to hold all but the most extreme case of data, and cutting such fields down to a more reasonable size is commonly done to get more columns on a page without having to condense the type beyond readability. If a name had more characters stored in the record than allowed for in the report column, the excess rightmost characters would be truncated; but the query would still run. Also, in the modified report, column spacing for last name and first name has been changed to 1. When you change numeric specifications like column spacing and field length, it

```
                    Specify Report Column Formatting

  Type information, press Enter.
    Column headings:   *NONE, aligned text lines

                      Column
  Field               Spacing      Column Heading            Len  Dec    Edit
  DEPT                   0         Department_____  12
                                   _____
                                   _____

  LASTNAME               1         Last Name_____  14____
                                   _____

  FIRSTNAME              1         First Name_____  10____
                                   _____
                                   _____


                                                             More...

  F3=Exit          F5=Report       F10=Process/previous     F12=Cancel
  F13=Layout       F16=Edit        F18=Files                F23=Long comment
```

Figure 7.30

Specify Report Column Formatting Screen, with Changes

is convenient to tab or field-advance to the desired field, type in the new value, and then use the Field exit key to erase the old value.

Figure 7.31 shows the second screen of Specify Report Column Formatting with changes made to the column headings to improve readability.

```
                    Specify Report Column Formatting

  Type information, press Enter.
    Column headings:   *NONE, aligned text lines

                      Column
  Field               Spacing      Column Heading            Len  Dec    Edit
  HOMEPHONE              2         Home_____            7    0      *
                                   Phone_____
                                   _____

  EMPNO                 2         Employee_____         9    0      *
                                   Number_____
                                   _____

  BIRTHDATE             2         Birthdate_____        10    L
                                   _____
                                   _____


                                                             More...

  F3=Exit          F5=Report       F10=Process/previous     F12=Cancel
  F13=Layout       F16=Edit        F18=Files                F23=Long comment
```

Figure 7.31

Specify Report Column Formatting Screen Showing Changed Column Headings

You can check the layout or run the report from this screen to see immediately what effect your modifications have by pressing F13 or F5. But remember to press Enter to save the changes when you are finished specifying report column formatting.

REPORT SUMMARY FUNCTIONS

Now we need to select report summary functions to satisfy the fourth and fifth specifications. If you select that option from the Define the Query screen, you see a screen like Figure 7.32, but of course without the options entered.

Selecting up to five different functions for a single field, you can add summary information to the control break total lines. You can use options 1 and 2, total and average, only with numeric fields. You can use option 5, count (used to determine the number of records in a control group); option 3, minimum (the algebraically least value or lowest sequence value alphanumeric item in a control group); and option 4, maximum (the algebraically highest value or highest sequence value) for either numeric or character (alphanumeric) fields.

Figure 7.32 shows summary functions selected so far for our sample report.

Figure 7.32

Report Summary Functions to Count Employees and Provide Average and Total Salary

```
                    Select Report Summary Functions
Type options, press Enter.
   1=Total    2=Average    3=Minimum    4=Maximum    5=Count

---Options---   Field           Text                              Len  Dec
_ _ _ _ _       DEPT                                               12
5 _ _ _ _       LASTNAME                                           14
_ _ _ _ _       FIRSTNAME                                          10
_ _ _ _ _       HOMEPHONE                                           7   0
_ _ _ _ _       EMPNO                                               9   0
_ _ _ _ _       BIRTHDATE                                          10   L
_ 1 2 _ _       HIREDATE                                           10   L
_ 1 2 _ _       SALARY                                              7   0




                                                              Bottom
F3=Exit        F5=Report      F10=Process/previous   F11=Display names only
F12=Cancel     F13=Layout     F18=Files              F23=Long comment
```

We are doing a count on last name and a total and average on the salary field. You can also use the layout and report functions from within this feature to check the formatting of the report or to see how it will look with data.

We have met the first five specification requirements and are now ready to tackle the sixth.

DEFINING RESULT FIELDS

Result fields, also called derived columns, are created by performing certain operations on data already contained in one or more fields of each record. The type of operation allowed depends on the data type of the field(s) to be operated on. String operations (concatenate and substring) can be performed on alphanumeric (character) fields. Concatenate puts two character fields (or subfields) together to form a new field with a new name—e.g. FIRSTNAME || LASTNAME becomes FULLNAME (|| is the symbol for concatenate). Substring creates a new field from part of an existing field (e.g., the first byte of FIRSTNAME becomes FIRSTINIT, first initial). We return to character result fields later.

For numeric fields, an almost infinite combination of numeric expressions can be used to create new columns. These expressions consist of numeric field names and/or constants combined with arithmetic operators +, -, /, *. For example, to create a new field, RAISE, defined as 6.2 percent of salary, you would code the expression SALARY * .062, assuming SALARY is a field of the record format.

Query/400 also provides a number of functions for converting between alphanumeric and numeric types and for performing date and time duration calculations on date and time fields. We will use a couple of these functions to calculate the years of employment requested in the report specifications.

When you take the option to define result fields, you are presented with a screen like that in Figure 7.33.

```
                        Define Result Fields

Type definitions using field names or constants and operators, press Enter.
   Operators:  +, -, *, /, SUBSTR, ||, DATE...

Field       Expression                        Column Heading      Len  Dec
_____      _____      _____    ___  ___
            _____      _____
            _____      _____
            _____      _____
_____      _____      _____    ___  ___
            _____      _____
            _____      _____
                                                                  Bottom

Field       Text                                                  Len  Dec
DEPT                                                                12
LASTNAME                                                            16
FIRSTNAME                                                           12
HOMEPHONE                                                            7   0

                                             More...
F3=Exit        F5=Report       F9=Insert       F11=Display names only
F12=Cancel     F13=Layout      F20=Reorganize  F24=More keys
```

Figure 7.33
Define Result Fields Screen

Under Field, you name the new field being defined. Then you key the expression used to derive the new field's value. You may provide a column heading if you don't want the field name used. Length and Decimal positions are often used to shorten the size of a calculated numeric result, including date and time duration, but Query/400 determines the length of any string expression.

For our purposes, a new field named YRSEMPLD (years employed) will be created by converting the duration between current date and HIREDATE to an integer year. The expression is shown in Figure 7.34.

Figure 7.34

Define Result Fields
Screen

```
                          Define Result Fields
Type definitions using field names or constants and operators, press Enter.
   Operators:  +, -, *, /, SUBSTR, ||, DATE...

Field        Expression                        Column Heading      Len  Dec
YRSEMPLD     year(current(date) - hiredate)___ Years_____      ___  ___
             _____   Employed_____

_____  _____  _____    ___  ___
              _____   _____
              _____   _____    Bottom

Field        Text                                                 Len  Dec
DEPT                                                               12
LASTNAME                                                          16
FIRSTNAME                                                         12
HOMEPHONE                                                          7    0

                                                          More...
F3=Exit         F5=Report        F9=Insert       F11=Display names only
F12=Cancel      F13=Layout       F20=Reorganize  F24=More keys
```

The function "current" with argument "date" takes the current date from the system. Other possibilities for the argument include "time" and "time stamp." The date of hire in the date field HIREDATE is then subtracted from current date and the result converted to years. To understand how the arithmetic works, think of the numeric value of any date field as the number of days since the beginning of the calendar, January 1 of 1 AD, or 0001-01-01 in *ISO format. So current date would be the count of all the days since then — a large number. HIREDATE, being closer to the beginning of the calendar, should be a somewhat smaller number, unless the employee had just been hired today. So when HIREDATE is subtracted from the current date, we have the duration of employment in days, and the year function converts that to years. No rounding is done in this conversion and no fraction of a year is calculated. If the current date is August 1, 1998, and date of hire is August 1, 1997, a value of 1 will be returned by the year function, but if hire date is August 2, 1997, then 0 would be returned.

A good overview of the available functions and some examples of their use is available by requesting extended Help from the Define Results Fields screen.

FINISHING THE REPORT

When you create a result field after report fields have already been selected, you need to return to the Select and sequence fields screen to get the new field into the report. Figure 7.35 shows the new field given a sequence number to position it between the HIREDATE and SALARY fields.

```
                    Select and Sequence Fields
Type sequence number (0-9999) for the names of up to 500 fields to
  appear in the report, press Enter.

Seq    Field         Text                                  Len  Dec
 10    DEPT                                                  12
 20    LASTNAME                                              16
 30    FIRSTNAME                                             12
 40    HOMEPHONE                                              7   0
 50    EMPNO                                                  9   0
 60    BIRTHDATE                                             10   L
 70    HIREDATE                                              10   L
 80    SALARY                                                 7   0
 75__  YRSEMPLD      year(current(date) - hiredate)          9   0
 ____  ADDR1                                                 40
 ____  ADDR2                                                 40
 ____  ZIP                                                    5   0

                                                      Bottom
F3=Exit        F5=Report       F11=Display names only  F12=Cancel
F13=Layout     F20=Renumber    F21=Select all          F24=More keys
Press Enter to confirm.
```

Figure 7.35
Select and Sequence Fields Screen with New Field Sequenced

You might notice that Query/400 calculated the field size as nine digits which seems a bit much for the extent of a human life by today's standards. Even Methuselah didn't last that long, and if he had would surely have retired long before reaching the ninth digit. You could change the size of the field to two digits either on the Define result fields screen or from the Specify report column formatting screen.

Finally, to calculate the average years of employment for each department, you need to return to the Select Report Summary Functions screen and take the Average function (2) for the new field YRSEMPLD. This is shown in Figure 7.36. Notice that the date expression is shown; Query/400 automatically shows the expression for a calculated field.

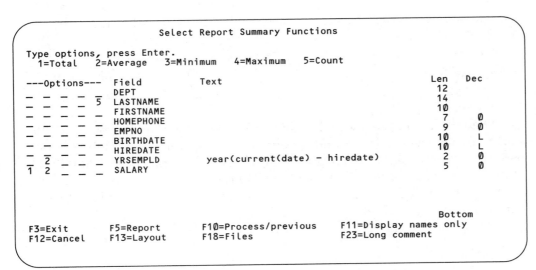

```
                    Select Report Summary Functions
Type options, press Enter.
  1=Total   2=Average   3=Minimum   4=Maximum   5=Count

---Options---   Field        Text                          Len  Dec
_ _ _ _ _       DEPT                                        12
_ _ _ _ 5       LASTNAME                                    14
_ _ _ _ _       FIRSTNAME                                   10
_ _ _ _ _       HOMEPHONE                                    7   0
_ _ _ _ _       EMPNO                                        9   0
_ _ _ _ _       BIRTHDATE                                   10   L
_ _ _ _ _       HIREDATE                                    10   L
_ 2 _ _ _       YRSEMPLD     year(current(date) - hiredate)  2   0
1 2 _ _ _       SALARY                                        5   0

                                                      Bottom
F3=Exit        F5=Report       F10=Process/previous   F11=Display names only
F12=Cancel     F13=Layout      F18=Files              F23=Long comment
```

Figure 7.36
Select Report Summary Functions Screen with YRSEMPLD Field

The output of the completed Query/400 is shown in Figure 7.37. You could see the same information by using the Report function, F5, but would have to shift right as the report is too wide for one screen. The output shown in Figure 7.37 is from printing the query, a technique we cover a little later.

Figure 7.37
Output of the Query
(Without Line
Numbers)

Department	Last Name	First Name	Home Phone	Employee Number	Birthdate	Date of Hire	Years Employed	Salary
Human Res	Hunn	Atilla	857-4211	111 11 0009	1940-06-17	1979-06-01	18	135,000

Human Res Department Subtotals
TOTAL   135,000
AVG   18   135,000
COUNT 1

| Marketing | Disney | Walter | 455-2323 | 111 11 0010 | 1912-10-10 | 1982-10-01 | 15 | 165,000 |
| | Gootch | Martha | 848-9799 | 111 11 0008 | 1935-02-21 | 1993-11-01 | 4 | 55,000 |

Marketing Department Subtotals
TOTAL   220,000
AVG   10   110,000
COUNT 2

| Research | Einstein | Albert | 363-2550 | 111 11 0003 | 1909-04-25 | 1937-03-28 | 61 | 299,950 |
| | Takahashi | Musashi | 857-4321 | 111 11 0004 | 1954-12-01 | 1992-03-30 | 5 | 75,000 |

Research Department Subtotals
TOTAL   374,950
AVG   33   187,475
COUNT 2

Sales	Badman	Billy	355-6789	111 11 0007	1969-07-18	1997-04-15	0	22,500
	Fendor	Denton	656-9876	111 11 0002	1972-11-19	1997-03-29	1	32,500
	Kartblanch	Emil	377-7040	111 11 0006	1947-05-15	1986-05-15	11	48,250
	Rachanoffski	Natasha	377-7383	111 11 0005	1960-04-16	1994-07-01	3	32,000
	Slick	Sam	723-5665	111 11 0001	1966-06-06	1992-10-01	5	28,000

Sales Department Subtotals
TOTAL   163,250
AVG   4   32,650
COUNT 5

FINAL TOTALS
TOTAL   893,200
AVG   12   89,320
COUNT 10

* * * END OF REPORT * * *

When you are finished working with a query, you need to save your work and exit. Normally, when a query sends its output to a display device, it adds line numbers as a leftmost column (see Figure 7.28). These line numbers are not included in printed or database file output, and they do not appear in Figure 7.37.

From the Define the Query screen, pressing F3 takes you to the Exit this Query screen (Figure 7.38).

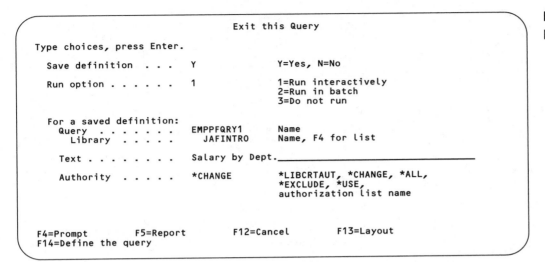

```
                        Exit this Query

Type choices, press Enter.

    Save definition  . . .   Y            Y=Yes, N=No

    Run option . . . . . .   1            1=Run interactively
                                          2=Run in batch
                                          3=Do not run

    For a saved definition:
       Query  . . . . . . .  EMPPFQRY1    Name
          Library  . . . .      JAFINTRO  Name, F4 for list

       Text . . . . . . .   Salary by Dept._____

       Authority  . . . . .  *CHANGE      *LIBCRTAUT, *CHANGE, *ALL,
                                          *EXCLUDE, *USE,
                                          authorization list name


  F4=Prompt        F5=Report        F12=Cancel        F13=Layout
  F14=Define the query
```

Figure 7.38
Exit this Query Screen

EXITING QUERY

The Exit this Query screen shows the defaults that, if taken, would save the query definition and run the query interactively.

For a new query, the Save definition is set to Y and the Run option is set to 1. We'll keep those values for this query. When you save a query definition, you must give it a name if it has not been given one already. And it is usually a good idea to add some descriptive text to help you remember what the query does. When you have completed the screen, pressing Enter saves the definition and runs the query, returning you to the Work with Queries screen.

A CONCEPTUAL FOUNDATION FOR JOINING FILES

In this first query example you have seen how to create a control break report that required the selection of sort fields. You also defined a result field, selected and sequenced fields, and used some report summary functions in the report. This is a very common type of report created over a single file. Query/400 also allows data from more than one file to be combined by specifying a join operation. Simply stated, a join operation allows data elements from records of two or more files to be included in a single result record. Suppose, for example, you needed a listing of all employees in the company sorted by last name and including address, city, state, and Zip code. Two of those data elements, city and state, are not included in the record format of employee file EMPPF. At the end of the last lesson, we talked about the need for a separate Zip code file that could be maintained independently. Figure 7.39 shows the record format information of the DSPFFD (Display File Field Description) command output for such a file.

Figure 7.39

Record Format of File ZIPPF

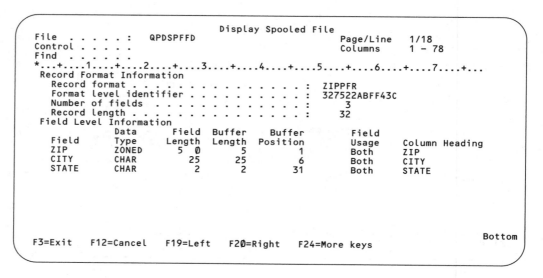

```
                                    Display Spooled File
File  . . . . . :    QPDSPFFD                           Page/Line   1/18
Control . . . . .                                       Columns     1 - 78
Find  . . . . . .
*...+....1....+....2....+....3....+....4....+....5....+....6....+....7....+...
  Record Format Information
    Record format . . . . . . . . . . . . . . . . :   ZIPPFR
    Format level identifier . . . . . . . . . . :     327522ABFF43C
    Number of fields  . . . . . . . . . . . . . :             3
    Record length . . . . . . . . . . . . . . . :            32
  Field Level Information
                  Data     Field   Buffer    Buffer          Field
    Field         Type    Length   Length   Position         Usage    Column Heading
    ZIP           ZONED     5  0       5          1           Both     ZIP
    CITY          CHAR       25       25          6           Both     CITY
    STATE         CHAR        2        2         31           Both     STATE




                                                                            Bottom
 F3=Exit     F12=Cancel     F19=Left     F20=Right     F24=More keys
```

This physical file has been created using DDS, and test data for the Zip codes found in the employee file have been added using DFU. The Zip code file and employee file are related to each other based on what is assumed to be a common value of the ZIP field in each file. A **Bachman diagram** expressing this relationship could be drawn as follows:

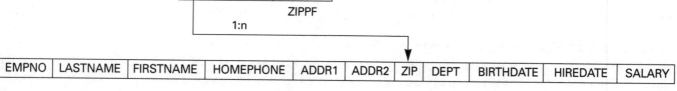

Field ZIP in file ZIPPF is underlined to show that it is the primary key field. A primary key is a field or set of fields whose value or values when taken together are unique for every record in the file. It is the field or set of fields used to identify the record and therefore through which individual records will most often be accessed. In our example, no two records in file ZIPPF will have the same Zip code. This is a reasonable assumption — the postal service would not want to assign the same Zip code to two different physical locations. Of course, large cities might have several different Zip codes, but that would not be a problem. For example, if St. Paul, Minnesota, had 10 different Zip codes, file ZIPPF would have 10 St. Paul records. Each record would have the same city and state values, but a different, unique Zip code value.

Employee file records, on the other hand, might very likely share the same value for Zip code (e.g., when two or more employees live in the same Zip code area). But this is not a problem either because the ZIP field is not the identifying field or primary key of an employee record; it is only an attribute that describes where an employee lives. Because many employees could live in the same area, many records in the employee file could have the same Zip code. In other words, one record in the Zip code file with a unique Zip code value could be related to many records in the employee file (i.e., those employees with the same Zip code). But any one record of the employee file, which has a single Zip code, will always be related only to a single Zip code file record. This common type of relationship, called a one-to-many relationship (abbreviated 1:n), is the foundation of relational database systems, including the AS/400's database manager. Another name for this type of relationship is **parent-child relationship**. A record in a parent file (in our case, ZIPPF) can have many children (i.e., records in file EMPPF), but a record in a child file can have only one parent.

Query/400 lets you easily extract data from two or more files that have a common field such as the ZIP field. The files do not necessarily have to be in a one-to-many relationship, but because this type of relationship is most common, they often are. As we mentioned earlier, up to 32 related files can be joined in a single report, although the number is usually much smaller. When files are joined in a query, it is necessary to specify a **primary file** first. The primary file is not necessarily the parent file of a 1:n relationship (ZIPPF in our example), and you should not confuse the two. Rather, the primary file is the one that contains the critical data we want to report on (i.e., the main topic or focus of the query). In our case, if you want to create a list of employees, the main topic is "employee" and the primary file must be the one containing data primarily describing employees: namely, the EMPPF file. For this query, the child file in the 1:n relationship becomes the primary file because it describes the entity (employee) you are reporting on.

CREATING A JOIN QUERY

When you create a join query, the first option listed on the Define the Query screen, Specify file selections, is most critical. Figure 7.40 shows the Specify File Selections screen with EMPPF typed in as the primary file name. In addition, you have already pressed Enter, and the message at the bottom tells you to "Select file(s) or press Enter to confirm."

Figure 7.40
Specify File Selections
Screen with Primary
File Name Entered

```
                          Specify File Selections
Type choices, press Enter.   Press F9 to specify an additional
   file selection.

   File . . . . . . . .    EMPPF           Name, F4 for list
     Library  . . . . . .      JAFINTRO    Name, *LIBL, F4 for list
   Member . . . . . . . .   *FIRST         Name, *FIRST, F4 for list
   Format . . . . . . . .   EMPPFR         Name, *FIRST, F4 for list










 F3=Exit          F4=Prompt        F5=Report        F9=Add file
 F12=Cancel       F13=Layout       F24=More keys
 Select file(s), or press Enter to confirm.
```

At this point you need to select another file, the Zip code file, and you do so by using function key F9. After you press F9, the Specify File Selections screen displays another set of entry fields for identifying a secondary file (Figure 7.41).

Figure 7.41
Specify File Selections
Screen Showing Fields
for Second File, Default
File ID

```
                          Specify File Selections
Type choices, press Enter.   Press F9 to specify an additional
   file selection.

   File . . . . . . . .    EMPPF           Name, F4 for list
     Library  . . . . . .      JAFINTRO    Name, *LIBL, F4 for list
   Member . . . . . . . .   *FIRST         Name, *FIRST, F4 for list
   Format . . . . . . . .   EMPPFR         Name, *FIRST, F4 for list
   File ID  . . . . . . .   T01            A-Z99, *ID

   File . . . . . . . .    _____        Name, F4 for list
     Library  . . . . . .      JAFINTRO    Name, *LIBL, F4 for list
   Member . . . . . . . .   *FIRST         Name, *FIRST, F4 for list
   Format . . . . . . . .   *FIRST         Name, *FIRST, F4 for list
   File ID  . . . . . . .   *ID            A-Z99, *ID



                                                              Bottom
 F3=Exit          F4=Prompt        F5=Report        F9=Add file
 F12=Cancel       F13=Layout       F24=More keys
```

Notice the File ID entry field, which did not appear on the select screen for only one file. You use this field to define up to a 3-character prefix for field names so Query/400 can distinguish fields with the same name in different files. In this example, ZIP is the only field name common to both files (ZIPPF and EMPPF); but once the File ID is decided, Query/400 qualifies all field names on subsequent screens using the File ID prefix. Query/400 supplies the default File ID of T01, and it would assign IDs of T02, T03, . . ., to any other secondary files we included. You can change these ID names if you wish; it is often more desirable to use a 1- or 2-character abbreviation of the file name. Figure 7.42 shows the completed Specify

File Selection screen: We have named file ZIPPF as the secondary file and given it a File ID of Z; we have given the primary file (EMPPF) a File ID of E.

```
                        Specify File Selections
Type choices, press Enter.  Press F9 to specify an additional
   file selection.

    File . . . . . . . . .   EMPPF        Name, F4 for list
       Library  . . . . . .     JAFINTRO  Name, *LIBL, F4 for list
    Member . . . . . . . .   *FIRST       Name, *FIRST, F4 for list
    Format . . . . . . . .   EMPPFR       Name, *FIRST, F4 for list
    File ID  . . . . . . .   E            A-Z99, *ID

    File . . . . . . . . .   zippf        Name, F4 for list
       Library  . . . . . .     JAFINTRO  Name, *LIBL, F4 for list
    Member . . . . . . . .   *FIRST       Name, *FIRST, F4 for list
    Format . . . . . . . .   *FIRST       Name, *FIRST, F4 for list
    File ID  . . . . . . .   Z            A-Z99, *ID


                                                        Bottom
F3=Exit          F4=Prompt         F5=Report            F9=Add file
F12=Cancel       F13=Layout        F24=More keys
```

Figure 7.42
Completed Specify File Selections Screen with EMPPF as the Primary File and ZIPPF as the Secondary File

Now that you have told Query/400 you are using more than one file, it needs to know the type of join to use. The next display you see will be the Specify Type of Join screen (Figure 7.43). As the screen indicates, Query/400 can select records from the primary and secondary file(s) in three different ways to create the report.

```
                        Specify Type of Join
Type choice, press Enter.

    Type of join . . . . . . . .  1      1=Matched records
                                         2=Matched records with primary file
                                         3=Unmatched records with primary file









F3=Exit          F5=Report         F10=Process/previous
F12=Cancel       F13=Layout        F18=Files
```

Figure 7.43
Specify Type of Join Screen

Before you decide how you want the records selected, let's step through an example of the joining process. If you were joining matching records and could assume the employee and Zip code files included the following records,

EMPPF

111110006 Kartblanch	Emil	...	52338
111110007 Badman	Billy	...	52345
.			
.			
.			

ZIPPF

52233 Hiawatha		IA
52338 Swisher		IA
52402 Cedar Rapids		IA
.		
.		

then the following output could result, depending on the type of join selected:

Joined Query records

Kartblanch Emil	Swisher	IA 52338	
.			
.			
.			

In this example, which ignores other fields in the employee file, a record has been selected for the query because the join field in the primary file record with a value of 52338 matches a join field value of a record in the secondary file. The desired fields from the matching records of both files can then be included in the joined query record.

Which type of join needs to be specified for our example? To answer that question let's describe each of the three types of join operations and, using the limited data from the example above, show what the different output is.

1=Matched Records

The Matched Records type uses what is known in relational database terminology as an **inner join**. An inner join in which one of the matching fields is eliminated from the result record is commonly called **natural join**. With an inner join, a result record is selected when at least one matching record is found in every file. In other words, every primary file record must have at least one matching record in each of the secondary files. But if a record in the primary file has no match in one or more of the secondary files, that primary file record is ignored and nothing is added to the query output.

Using the sample data above, a result record would be added to the query report for Emil Kartblanch because a record with matching Zip code would be found in the Zip code file. But Billy Badman would not be included in the query output because there is no Zip code record that matches his ZIP field value of 52345.

In many cases, you would not want output created for unmatched primary file records, so this type of join would be okay. Consider, for example, a report listing students enrolled in summer classes. There may be 5,000 students in the student master file, but only 1,000 of them are enrolled for summer classes and they would have a record matching their student ID in the summer enrollment file. If a student ID field of a student file record has no match in the file of summer enrollments, you would not want that student listed, so a type 1 inner join would be fine.

2=Matched Records with Primary File

In our example, you want to list all employees, even those who do not have a valid Zip code (i.e., one matching a ZIPPF record). When you need to include all records in the primary file regardless whether there are matching records in the secondary file(s), you need to use the type 2 join, Matched records with primary file, also called an **outer join** (or more correctly, a **left outer join**). With an outer join, all records in the primary file are selected for the query. If no matching record is found in one or more of the secondary files, the selected data fields from those unmatched files are set to default values in the query output record (i.e., zeros for numeric fields, spaces for alphanumeric fields — unless specified otherwise in the source DDS). This is the type of join to select when it is important to include all primary file records in the query, even if some of them may not have matching secondary file records. If you use an outer join, an employee who has an invalid Zip code, or a Zip code that is correct for his/her domicile but that had not been entered into file ZIPPF, would still be listed in the query — only city and state would have values of blanks (spaces). In this way, you would notice the problem easily, and the cause could be corrected. Using our illustration, both Emil and Billy would be listed, but the city and state values for Billy would be set to spaces because they were not retrieved from a matching record of the Zip code file:

Joined Query records from type 2

Kartblanch Emil	Swisher		IA	52338
Badman Billy				52345
.				
.				
.				

3=Unmatched Records with Primary File

Sometimes it is useful to list or display only the records that do not have matches in all files; for example, students not registered in any class, customers not having any outstanding invoices, or in our case, employees not having a valid Zip code. The type 3 query operation accommodates this need. It writes to the query output only those records whose primary file record was not matched to at least one secondary file. This operation is called **difference** in relational database terminology, and you can understand why if you think of it as "subtracting" from the primary file all records matching in the secondary files. What is left, the difference, is the unmatched primary file records. The query record fields from the unmatched secondary file(s) are set to defaults in the output, as in the type 2 outer join. When unmatched primary file records are considered an exception, this is a very useful and powerful tool for identifying and isolating them. Using the illustration, the output would include only the Billy Badman primary file record because Emil's EMPPF record will be "taken away" by the matching ZIPPF record in the difference operation.

Joined Query records from type 3

Badman   Billy   52345

The type 3 join is also referred to as an **exception join**, a term that is a little misleading because result rows are created only when no join occurs.

SPECIFYING THE JOIN RELATIONSHIP

We will examine Query/400 reports created from all three types of join operations to help you understand the different ways they work. First you use a type 2 join because this type meets the criteria for listing all employees. You enter a 2 on the Type of join field shown on the screen in Figure 7.43. Pressing Enter takes you to the Specify How to Join Files screen (Figure 7.44) which, in this case, has the proper relational expression, E.ZIP EQ Z.ZIP, already typed in.

Figure 7.44
Join Relationship
Specified

```
                        Specify How to Join Files
    Type comparisons to show how file selections are related, press Enter.
      Tests:  EQ, NE, LE, GE, LT, GT

    Field                Test      Field
    E.ZIP_____       EQ___     Z.ZIP_____

    _____        ____      _____
    _____        ____      _____
    _____        ____      _____

                                                            Bottom
    _____
    Field             Text                             Len  Dec
    E.EMPNO                                              9    0
    E.LASTNAME                                          16
    E.FIRSTNAME                                         12
    E.ADDR1                                             40
    E.ADDR2                                             40
                                                            More...
    F3=Exit          F5=Report       F10=Process/previous    F11=Display names only
    F12=Cancel       F13=Layout      F18=Files               F24=More keys
```

The relational expression tells Query/400 the condition that defines "matched" records. In our case, the Zip code of an employee record must equal the Zip code of a Zip code file record.

When the relationship-supporting fields of two related files are expected to have equal values, the join is generally referred to as an **equijoin** and the relational operator is EQ or an equal sign (=). Inner joins and left outer joins are both equijoins and when using the difference operation (Query/400's type 3 join), an equality relationship is also specified. To use any other relational operation than EQ for a Query/400 join is very unusual.

Notice that the Specify How to Join Files screen is divided horizontally into two parts. The upper part is used to code the relational expression(s) that define the join. There is usually one expression for each pair of related files. The lower part of the screen lists all fields involved in the primary and secondary files, with their file IDs prefixed to the field name. Both parts of the screen respond to Page up/Page down keys, depending on the position of the cursor. If you move the cursor to the lower half of the screen and press Page down, the rest of the fields in the employee file will be displayed, followed by the fields in the Zip code file. With all of the field names listed for reference, you can avoid incorrectly naming the fields used in the join relational expression(s).

Pressing F11 with the cursor on the lower half of the screen toggles from single field per row display showing text, length, and data type to a multifield per row display showing file IDs and field names only. This format is very useful when you're joining several files with many fields.

When you press Enter from the Specify How to Join Files screen, you return to the Define the Query screen. From there, to simplify the output for our examples, we could select and sequence fields as shown in Figure 7.45.

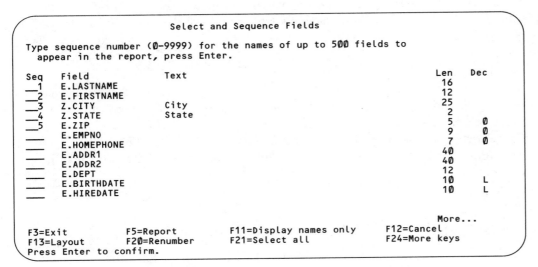

Figure 7.45
Select and Sequence Fields Screen

Please note that any other fields from the employee file could also have been selected for output. Also note that although there is a ZIP field in both the employee file and the Zip code file, it is important to select the one from the primary (employee) file. That way, if no match occurs, at least you can see what value the ZIP field has in the employee file. If you choose the field from the Zip code file, and no match occurs, only zeros would appear in the output.

After selecting and sequencing fields, you can test the query immediately by using function key F5. The output of this query is shown in Figure 7.46.

Figure 7.46

Output of Type 2 Join of EMPPF and ZIPPF

```
                                        Display Report
                                             Report width . . . . . :        73
        Position to line  . . . .            Shift to column . . . . . .
        Line   ....+....1....+....2....+....3....+....4....+....5....+....6....+....7..
                LASTNAME         FIRSTNAME     City                     State       ZIP
        000001 Slick            Sam           Mount Ayr                 IA       50,854
        000002 Fendor           Denton        Guthrie Center            IA       50,115
        000003 Einstein         Albert        Clarinda                  IA       51,632
        000004 Takahashi        Musashi       Cedar Rapids              IA       52,406
        000005 Rachanoffski     Natasha       Cedar Rapids              IA       52,402
        000006 Kartblanch       Emil          Swisher                   IA       52,338
        000007 Badman           Billy                                            52,345
        000008 Gootch           Martha        Pleasantville             IA       50,225
        000009 Hunn             Atilla        Anamosa                   IA       52,205
        000010 Disney           Walter        Amana                     IA       52,203
        ****** ********   End of report   ********

                                                                              Bottom
         F3=Exit        F12=Cancel      F19=Left      F20=Right      F21=Split
```

Besides seeing the need for formatting, notice that no city or state is displayed for the Billy Badman record on line 7. While not explicitly flagging it as such, this is a good indication of an unmatched record condition because you know that the city and state values were supposed to come from the secondary file, ZIPPF. If you checked a listing of all the ZIPPF records, you would see that no record exists for Zip code 52345.

For large files, it would be convenient to have Query/400 search for unmatched records. You can do that simply by returning to the Specify file selections screen and changing the type of join to 3, unmatched records with primary file. Nothing else needs to be changed. After making that change and running the report again, you would see the display shown in Figure 7.47.

This time, the Billy Badman record is listed, verifying that there is no matching zip record.

```
                              Display Report
                                     Report width . . . . . :       73
  Position to line . . . . .          Shift to column . . . . . :
  Line   ....+....1....+....2....+....3....+....4....+....5....+....6....+....7..
          LASTNAME        FIRSTNAME    City                         State     ZIP
  000001 Badman          Billy                                              52,345
  ****** ********   End of report  ********




                                                                      Bottom
    F3=Exit      F12=Cancel     F19=Left     F20=Right     F21=Split
```

Figure 7.47

Display Report of Unmatched Records with Primary File, Type 3 Join

If you again change the type of join — this time to 1, matched records — you would see that the Badman record is missing altogether when the report runs (Figure 7.48). This is how a type 1 inner join works. When a primary record does not have a match in every secondary file, it is not included in the output.

```
                              Display Report
                                     Report width . . . . . :       73
  Position to line . . . . .          Shift to column . . . . . :
  Line   ....+....1....+....2....+....3....+....4....+....5....+....6....+....7..
          LASTNAME        FIRSTNAME    City                         State     ZIP
  000001 Slick           Sam          Mount Ayr                      IA     50,854
  000002 Fendor          Denton       Guthrie Center                 IA     50,115
  000003 Einstein        Albert       Clarinda                       IA     51,632
  000004 Takahashi       Musashi      Cedar Rapids                   IA     52,406
  000005 Rachanoffski    Natasha      Cedar Rapids                   IA     52,402
  000006 Kartblanch      Emil         Swisher                        IA     52,338
  000007 Gootch          Martha       Pleasantville                  IA     50,225
  000008 Hunn            Atilla       Anamosa                        IA     52,205
  000009 Disney          Walter       Amana                          IA     52,203
  ****** ********   End of report  ********




                                                                      Bottom
    F3=Exit      F12=Cancel     F19=Left     F20=Right     F21=Split
```

Figure 7.48

Display of Matching Records for Type 1 Join – No Billy Badman

Although there are still several important query options to be covered, you should be ready to create some queries of your own. We examine additional query options in Lesson 10; meanwhile, don't hesitate to explore — Query/400 provides useful Help information about all of its functions.

Key Terms

Bachman diagram

control break

difference

edit word

equijoin

exception join

join

left outer join

natural join

one-to-many relationship

outer join

parent-child relationship

primary file

primary key

Query/400

report generator

secondary file

Lab 7

INTRODUCTION

In this lab exercise you learn how to use the AS/400 report generator, Query/400, to create a simple printed listing of the physical database file created in the previous labs. An additional lab exercise provides experience in creating join queries.

Part 1

Goals	Examine the data member of your physical file Use STRQRY to create a new query Specify a file for your query Perform report column formatting such as changing headers and editing Run the query and display the report Change the default output to printer Save the query in your library
Start at	Any command line
Procedure	Clear your output queue DSPPFM STUPF STRQRY, work with queries Create a query Define query specifications through Define the Query

1.1. Sign on as usual. As in the previous lab, use the WRKOUTQ (Work with Output Queue) command to ensure that no spooled files are in your output queue. If there are, print or delete them to clear your output queue.

1.2. Now enter the command to Work with Objects Using PDM on a command line. From the Work with Objects Using PDM list screen, take the Work with option on your physical file STUPF.

1.3. This should take you to the Work with Members Using PDM screen, showing member STUPF. Take the option to display the member.

The DSPPFM (Display Physical File Member) command, which this option invokes, shows the data as it is stored within records of the file member, unformatted, with no field separators. The data is not easy to read, but the command is useful if you need to check the contents of fields quickly for data you are using to test applications. (However, if there were numeric data fields whose data type was other than S, for zoned decimal, the DSPPFM command would not convert that data to a display format and you would not be able to read the contents of the field.)

So although the DSPPFM command's output is useful, the lack of formatting and data conversion would make it totally unacceptable for any end-user or permanent report.

Luckily, Query/400 is easy to use, and once you become accustomed to it, you can easily create simple reports.

Exit the DSPPFM command output display and return to the Work with Objects Using PDM screen.

1.4. As you know from the text of this lesson, Query/400 is a menu-driven report generator for the AS/400 that can create screen displays, printed output, or database files. You will use the utility to generate a simple report of your database physical file.

To define a query, begin by typing STRQRY on any command line. Press Enter after keying the command.

1.4a. What type of screen appears? What is its name?

Select 1, Work with Queries, then press Enter.

1.5. You should now be looking at the Work with Queries screen. From this screen you can create a new query or take various options (e.g., Change, Copy, Display) on existing queries. Because you are creating your first query, you need to take option 1. Name the query STUQRY1. Be sure that your library name is entered for the Library part of the Query name parameter, then press Enter.

1.6. The Define the Query screen (Figure 7.49) lets you perform various design and selection options to tailor the query to the application needs.

Figure 7.49

Define the Query Screen

```
                                    Define the Query
Query . . . . . . :      STUQRY1             Option  . . . . . :     CREATE
   Library . . . . :        JSMITH

Type options, press Enter.  Press F21 to select all.
   1=Select

Opt     Query Definition Option
 1        Specify file selections
 _        Define result fields
 _        Select and sequence fields
 _        Select records
 _        Select sort fields
 _        Select collating sequence
 _        Specify report column formatting
 _        Select report summary functions
 _        Define report breaks
 _        Select output type and output form
 _        Specify processing options


F3=Exit           F5=Report          F12=Cancel
F13=Layout        F18=Files          F21=Select all
```

Type 1 to select each option you want to use. Notice that there is already a 1 in front of the Specify file selections option because, at the very least, you must tell Query/400 which file to use.

Because this is a list processing screen, you can type 1 in front of several options and Query/400 will process them one after another. Each option from this screen takes you to one or more lower-level screens where you supply information for that option. When the option is completed, press Enter. Then Query/400 saves your specifications and returns you to the Define the Query screen.

Remember: From within a Define the Query selection (e.g., Define result fields or Select records)

Enter — saves your work and returns you to the Define the Query screen

F3 — saves your work and takes you to the Exit this Query screen

F12 — backs up one screen or returns you to the Define the Query screen *without* saving your work

If you get to the Exit this Query screen by mistake, press F14 to return to the Define the Query screen. Then, with a 1 in front of only the Specify file selections option, press Enter.

1.7. You want to use your physical file, whose name is STUPF. If you couldn't remember the spelling of the name or you wanted to check a list of files, you could prompt from the file entry field. Do that now by pressing F4.

You should see the Select File screen with all files of the specified library listed. Move the cursor to the option field for your student file, STUPF. Type 1 and press Enter.

Notice that the prompt operation has copied the file name into the entry field of the specified file selection screen. The Library and Member defaults should be okay.

1.7a. Use Help to find out what the FORMAT parameter specifies. Is the default all right for your file?

Exit Help and press Enter.

1.7b. What displays now for the FORMAT value?

Read the message on the bottom of the screen and confirm.

1.8. You should have returned to the Define the Query screen. Is the screen any different? The greater-than symbol (>) to the right of the option field indicates an option that has been taken. It is just a reminder; you can go back to that option any time, if necessary, to add information or make changes.

1.9. Notice the function keys below the list. Move the cursor to the function key area and press Help. Read through the descriptions of the function keys.

1.9a. What does F5 do?
1.9b. What does F13 do?
1.9c. What is the main difference between them?

When you use F5 or F13, you can press F12 to return to the previous screen after viewing the display.

1.10. Exit Help. Display the report layout (F13).

1.10a.What is the report width?
1.10b.Notice the column headers. Where do they come from?
1.10c.How are they aligned over the fields?

Notice that fields are separated on the format line, unlike the DSPPFM command output.

1.10d. How are the numeric fields edited?

Use the function key to shift your view to the right so you can see the entire report layout. Exit and return to the Define the Query screen when you are finished.

1.11. You would like to suppress comma insertion editing of the numeric fields and make the column headings easier to understand. To do so, you need to enter the option to Specify report column formatting. Go ahead and do that now.

The Specify Report Column Formatting display divides the screen horizontally into zones for each field named on the left of the display. The first page of the screen should look like the one shown in Figure 7.50. Dotted lines have been added between fields to emphasize the horizontal zones.

Figure 7.50
Specify Report
Column Formatting

```
                         Specify Report Column Formatting
Type information, press Enter.
  Column headings:   *NONE, aligned text lines

                         Column
  Field                 Spacing        Column Heading             Len  Dec   Edit
  SOCSEC                  _0            SOCSEC_____      __9  _0
                                       _____
                                       _____

  FNAME                  _2            FNAME_____      __15  __
                                       _____
                                       _____

  LNAME                  _2            LNAME_____      __20  __
                                       _____
                                       _____

                                                                          More...

  F3=Exit          F5=Report     F10=Process/previous    F12=Cancel
  F13=Layout       F16=Edit      F18=Files               F23=Long comment
```

The column heading values usually come from the COLHDG keyword contained in the physical file object itself. If you do not specify COLHDG values in the source DDS (we did not), the system uses field names as column headings. In the query, if you wish to change or clarify the column heading for the report, you can do that simply by typing over the values that have been taken from the file.

So let's change the column heading for the SOCSEC field to Soc Sec # by typing over the old column heading. Also, change the heading for FNAME and LNAME to First Name and Last Name. You could change any other column headings in the same way — by typing over what is already there. Notice that you can use up to three lines for each column heading, a good idea when the data field is narrow but the column heading is several words.

Do not press Enter yet.

1.12. For each numeric field, you will select the edit function, F16. The function key applies to the field whose horizontal zone the cursor is in. The cursor does not have to be on the field name, but can be anywhere within the (three-line) zone.

Move the cursor back up to the SOCSEC field zone and press F16. You should see a screen like the Define Numeric Field Editing screen shown in Figure 7.51.

```
                     Define Numeric Field Editing

  Field . . . . . . . . . :   SOCSEC
  Text  . . . . . . . . . :
  Heading 1 . . . . . . . :   Soc Sec #
  Heading 2 . . . . . . . :
  Heading 3 . . . . . . . :
  Length  . . . . . . . . :   9
  Decimal . . . . . . . . :   0
  Sample  . . . . . . . . :   999,999,999

  Type choice, press Enter.
     Edit option . . . . .   1      1=Numeric editing choices
                                    2=Date or time editing choice
                                    3=Edit code
                                    4=Edit word




  F3=Exit        F5=Report       F10=Process/previous    F11=Change sample
  F12=Cancel     F13=Layout      F16=Remove edit         F18=Files
```

Figure 7.51
Define Numeric Field Editing Screen

Take a minute to look at this screen. Notice that the name of the field, its heading, length, decimal positions, and a sample showing current formatting displays on the top of the screen. As you make editing changes to the field, the sample changes accordingly.

Notice that there are four choices for the type of editing you need to perform. For normal numeric fields you can select such options as thousands separator and leading zeros through edit option 1. Option 1 is the default, so just press Enter at this time.

You should see the Describe Numeric Field Editing screen shown in Figure 7.52.

Figure 7.52
Describe Numeric Field Editing Screen

```
                     Describe Numeric Field Editing

  Field . . . . . . :   SOCSEC

  Type choices, press Enter.
     Decimal point . . . . . . . .   1      1=.  2=,  3=:  4=$    5=None
     Thousands separator . . . . .   2      1=.  2=,  3='  4=Blank 5=None
     Show negative sign  . . . . .   Y      Y=Yes, N=No
        Left negative sign  . . .    _____
        Right negative sign . . . .  _____
     Show currency symbol  . . . .   N      Y=Yes, N=No
        Left currency symbol  . . .  $ ____
        Right currency symbol . . .  _____
     Print zero value  . . . . . .   Y      Y=Yes, N=No
     Replace leading zeros . . . .   Y      Y=Yes, N=No
        Replace with  . . . . . . .  1      1=Blanks
                                            2=Asterisks
                                            3=Floating currency symbol
        Single leading zero . . . .  N      Y=Yes, N=No



  F3=Exit        F5=Report       F10=Process/previous    F12=Cancel
  F13=Layout     F16=Remove edit  F18=Files
```

Notice some of the options from this screen; for example, how to display decimal point and thousands separator, whether to show negative signs, whether to display a currency symbol, and how to handle leading zeros. For the Social Security number, you would like to eliminate the comma thousands separator, so move the cursor down one line and select option 5, None, for thousands separator. Then press Enter.

1.13. Back at the Specify Report Column Formatting screen, you should notice an asterisk under the edit column (to the far right) for field SOCSEC. This is an indication that the field has been edited.

Press F16 again. This time the sample of the field shown on the Define Numeric Field Editing screen should have changed to reflect your request to eliminate the thousands separator symbol. The sample should display the Social Security number as a nine-digit integer with no comma separators.

Now press F12 to return to the previous screen, Specify Report Column Formatting.

Page down from this screen and make a similar change to the other numeric fields, PHONE and ZIP, eliminating the thousands separator as you did for the Social Security number field. After making these changes, remain at the Specify Report Column Formatting screen.

1.14. Now display the layout again. Do the numeric fields look better?

1.14a. What is the report width now?

When you are finished looking at the layout, press F12 to continue with the Specify report column formatting function.

1.15. It is useful to be able to examine a report with data as you make adjustments to various query definition specifications. Without leaving the Specify Report Column Formatting screen, you can run the report as it is currently defined by pressing F5.

Press F5 at this time.

The display report should now be visible on your screen and it should look something like Figure 7.53.

Notice that lines of the report are numbered serially on the far left side. These line numbers would not appear if the finished query directed its output to a printed report. Also, remember that the default spacing between columns is two character positions. By knowing this, you can see which fields could be shortened on this report without losing data.

```
                                   Display Report
                                          Report width . . . . . :        124
   Position to line  . . . .            Shift to column  . . . . . .
   Line    ....+....1....+....2....+....3....+....4....+....5....+....6....+....7..
           Soc Sec #   First Name      Last Name              PHONE   ADDR1
   000001 111110001   Benny           Badman              3192343456  #1 Nirva
   000002 111110002   Bilbo           Baggins             3199888999  345 Hawt
   000003 111110003   Karikool        Clapsaddle          7076834556  999 Sund
   000004 111110004   Joe             Cool                3193659876  512 Belv
   000005 111110005   Jazmann         Dowhopper           2154567654  12345 Cl
   000006 111110006   Norman          Grubber             5158997890  RR 2
   000007 111110007   Emil            Engobber            5153886543  Clay Wor
   000008 111110008   Harvy           Humpchucker         3194887865  1233 Sha
   000009 111110009   Dingy           Dupekey             3195551212  319 Ditt
   000010 111110010   Ichiro          Tenkaichi           1111111111  111 1st
   000011 111110011   Saigo           Owari               9999999999  9999 99T
   000012 111110012   Chuunan         Mannaka             5555555555  55 Cente
   000013 111110013   Medford         Muggins             5552344321  RR 2
   000014 111110015   Billybob        Goodoboy            7771234567  Nowhere
   000015 111110016   Salamander      Slim                5152334566  10 Main
   ****** ********   End of report   ********
                                                              Bottom

   F3=Exit       F12=Cancel      F19=Left      F20=Right      F21=Split
```

Figure 7.53
Output of Display Report Function

Let's say, for example, that you need to reduce your report to a width of no more than 110 print positions. You can see that both the first name and last name fields of the sample report could be shortened considerably without cutting off any name characters. But if new records with longer names were added to the file later on, the next query report could truncate part of the name. So you might want to shorten a less significant field than name. Shift right and examine the address fields of your report. You can probably shorten them without losing data.

When you have examined your report, press F12 to return to the Specify Report Column Formatting screen. Select one or two fields to shorten — perhaps the address fields. For each field that you wish to shorten, change its length value (Len) accordingly.

Look at the layout again. If necessary, shorten another field until the report lines fit within 110 print positions.

1.16. Use the function key to display the report from the Specify Report Column Formatting screen, and make sure that you have not truncated data in the process of shortening the fields and that the report will look all right when it is printed. If some data has been truncated, readjust print fields accordingly.

When you are satisfied with your report, press Enter (not F3), from the Specify Report Column Formatting screen. Remember, if you go to the Exit this Query screen by mistake, you can press F14 to return to the Define the Query screen.

1.17. The query would run now without any further changes, but you may want to examine the output type to see where the report would be directed. So, on the Define the Query screen move the cursor down to Select output type and output form and take that option.

1.18. The screen you see now should look like the one shown in Figure 7.54.

Figure 7.54

Select Output Type and Output Form Screen

```
                              Select Output Type and Output Form
  Type choices, press Enter.

    Output type  . . . . . . . . . . .   1     1=Display
                                               2=Printer
                                               3=Database file

    Form of output . . . . . . . . . .   1     1=Detail
                                               2=Summary only

    Line wrapping  . . . . . . . . . .   N     Y=Yes, N=No
      Wrapping width . . . . . . . . .   _     Blank, 1-378
      Record on one page . . . . . . .   N     Y=Yes, N=No




  F3=Exit          F5=Report            F10=Process/previous
  F12=Cancel       F13=Layout           F18=Files
```

Three options are available for output type. Use the Help key to find out more about the three output types and to answer the following questions.

1.18a. If you kept the Display option for Output type, what would the output look like?

1.18b. If you took the Printer option, what screen would you see next?

1.18c. If you selected detailed output to a Database file, what would happen to report break and summary function output?

For now, let's leave the default values as they were originally: Display for Output type and Detail for output form. Now press Enter from this screen.

1.19. From the Define the Query screen, press F3 to save the query.

You should now be looking at the Exit this Query screen shown in Figure 7.55.

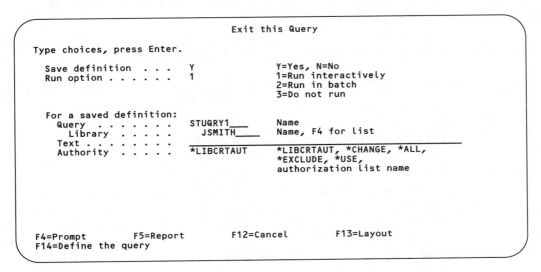

```
                           Exit this Query

Type choices, press Enter.

    Save definition  . . .   Y          Y=Yes, N=No
    Run option . . . . . .   1          1=Run interactively
                                        2=Run in batch
                                        3=Do not run

    For a saved definition:
      Query  . . . . . . .   STUQRY1___   Name
        Library  . . . . .     JSMITH_____  Name, F4 for list
      Text . . . . . . . .   _____
      Authority  . . . . .   *LIBCRTAUT   *LIBCRTAUT, *CHANGE, *ALL,
                                          *EXCLUDE, *USE,
                                          authorization list name




 F4=Prompt       F5=Report       F12=Cancel        F13=Layout
 F14=Define the query
```

Figure 7.55

Exit this Query Screen

The defaults are set to save the definition and to run the query interactively. Also, notice that values you provided when you took the Create a Query option are used for the Query and Library names.

Because you will save the query definition, Field advance the cursor down to the Text field and type in your full name followed by "Query 1 of STUPF." Then press Enter. Because the Run option was set to 1, the query should now be running.

1.20. Use F20 to shift right and examine all the report. It should look just like it looked from the Display the Report function within Query.

When you have examined the report, press F3 to exit the display. This should return you to the Work with Queries screen; pressing F3 again returns you to the Query Utilities menu.

From the Query Utilities menu, pressing F3 one more time should return you to the Work with Objects Using PDM screen.

Part 2

Goals	Find your Query definition on the Work with Objects Using PDM list
	Run the query directly from PDM
	Prompt on the PDM Run option and modify the Output Type and Record Selection parameters of the RUNQRY command
	Find the report and verify record selection
	Change the Query definition to send output to a spooled file
	Add standard page headings to the print Query
Start at	WRKOBJPDM, your library
Procedure	Take option 16 on STUQRY1
	Prompt on option 16 and select only records with Zip codes in your area; send output to printer
	Find the spooled report in your output queue; display and verify WRKQRY; change STUQRY1
	Select output type and form to print
	Exit and run the query
	Print the report

2.1. Page up if you are not already at the top of your Work with Objects Using PDM list.

2.1a. Is there any evidence in your objects list of the query you just created? If you signed off between Parts 1 and 2, you should see your query. If not, Press F5.

The reason you didn't see the query if you are continuing directly from Part 1 is that you entered Query/400 from within Work with Objects Using PDM. Because that screen was not updated while you were in Query/400, you need to refresh the screen after returning to see the new query definition.

2.1b. What is the object type and attribute of the new object?

2.2. Use F23 to display more PDM options. Notice option 16. This option can be used to execute programs, query definitions, and stored DFUs. Enter the Run option on your query definition object. A report should display just as it did previously. Press F3 when you have examined it. PDM options make it very easy to run a query definition or a program from the Work with Objects Using PDM screen.

2.3. Like other PDM options, you can prompt on option 16. Type it again for STUQRY1 and this time prompt. You should see a screen similar to Figure 7.56.

```
                         Run Query (RUNQRY)

 Type choices, press Enter.

 Query . . . . . . . . . . . . . . > STUQRY1      Name, *NONE
   Library . . . . . . . . . . . > JSMITH       Name, *LIBL, *CURLIB
 Query File:
   File . . . . . . . . . . . .  _____     Name, *SAME
   Library . . . . . . . . . .     *LIBL        Name, *RUNOPT, *LIBL, *CURLIB
   Member . . . . . . . . . . .    *FIRST       Name, *RUNOPT, *FIRST, *LAST
               + for more values
 Report output type . . . . . . .  *RUNOPT      *RUNOPT, *DISPLAY...
 Output form . . . . . . . . . .   *RUNOPT      *RUNOPT, *DETAIL, *SUMMARY
 Record selection . . . . . . . .  *NO          *NO, *YES




                                                             Bottom
 F3=Exit    F4=Prompt    F5=Refresh     F12=Cancel   F13=How to use this display
 F24=More keys
```

Figure 7.56
Run Query (RUNQRY)
Command Prompt
Screen

The RUNQRY command will run an existing Query definition object (*QRYDFN) when the name of object is supplied for the Query parameter value; PDM has already filled that in from the list item the option was taken on. Also, certain aspects of the defined Query can be changed at runtime by supplying overriding parameter values from the RUNQRY command. These changes affect only the current run and do not change the Query definition.

2.3a. What does the *RUNOPT value of the output type and output form do?

2.4 Change the value of the Report Output type parameter so that the query output will be sent to a printer (spooled).

Additionally, you can cause the Query to prompt you for record selection when it begins to run by changing the Record selection parameter value to *YES. Do that now.

Even if record selection was not used in the query definition, by typing *YES, you can add record selection at runtime. If record selection was specified in the query definition, you can change the selection criteria or cancel the predefined selection.

At this point, your Report output type parameter value should be *PRINTER, and the Record selection parameter value should be *YES. Press Enter. When you have changed the output to *PRINTER, additional parameters are provided allowing you, for example, to widen a report line from the 132 position default. As that should not be necessary for this report, press Enter again to run the query. After a pause, the Select Records screen should appear. Figure 7.57 shows that screen with a selection expression already entered.

The expression instructs the query to select only those records having ZIP field values in the range of 52000 through 52999 (inclusive). Only records in the input file STUPF having those Zip code values will be included in the query report.

Figure 7.57
Select Records

```
                              Select Records
    Type comparisons, press Enter.  Specify OR to start each new group.
       Tests:  EQ, NE, LE, GE, LT, GT, RANGE, LIST, LIKE, IS, ISNOT...

    AND/OR  Field              Test   Value (Field, Number, 'Characters', or ...)
            ZIP_____       RANGE  52000 52999_____
    _____  _____        ____   _____
    _____  _____        ____   _____
    _____  _____        ____   _____
    _____  _____        ____   _____
    _____  _____        ____   _____
                                                                  Bottom
    Field           Text                                      Len  Dec
    SOCSEC                                                      9    0
    FNAME                                                      15
    LNAME                                                      20
    PHONE                                                      10    0
    ADDR1                                                      25
                                                              More...
    F3=Exit        F9=Insert        F11=Display name only   F12=Cancel
    F18=Files      F19=Next group   F20=Reorganize               F24=More keys
                                      (C) COPYRIGHT IBM CORP. 1988
```

Enter a similar selection expression on your prompt screen, but use a range of Zip code values for your own area, so that you can be sure to select at least a few records from your file. Then press Enter to run the query.

2.5. This time, the output should not have displayed on your workstation screen. Work with your spooled files or output queue and find your report. Query/400 uses a printer file named QPQUPRFIL; if you look under the File column, it should be easy to find.

  2.5a. How many records were selected for your report?
  2.5b. Are the Zip codes of the report records all within the range you selected?

Return to your Work with Objects Using PDM screen and take the Work with option on your Query definition object.

2.6a. At what screen have you arrived?

Take the option to change and on the Query input field press F4 for a list. From the prompt list, move the cursor down to the option field for your query and type 2 to change. It's not necessary to erase the 2 on the line above. Press Enter.

2.7. When a query is saved, all the specifications for it are stored as you last left them. If you take the change option, you can modify an existing query in any way necessary. If you had decided your query should always be printed, you wouldn't want to prompt on the RUNQRY command, like you did in the previous step, every time you ran the report. It would make more sense to change the output type in the query definition itself. Let's change our query so that it uses a spooled printer file as output instead of the display screen. Move the cursor down to the Select output type and form option field and enter 1.

2.8. This time, from the Select Output Type and Output Form screen, take Output type 2 for printer. Leave the other defaults as they are and press Enter. You should be looking at the Define Printer Output screen (Figure 7.58).

```
                         Define Printer Output

  Type choices, press Enter.

     Printer  . . . . . . . .    *PRINT____    *PRINT, name

     Form size:
        Length . . . . . . . .    __          Blank, 1-255
        Width  . . . . . . . .    132         Blank, 1-378

     Start line . . . . . . .     __          Blank, 1-255

     End line . . . . . . . .     __          Blank, 1-255

     Line spacing . . . . . .     1           1, 2, 3

     Print definition . . . . .   N           Y=Yes, N=No



  F3=Exit          F5=Report        F10=Process/previous
  F12=Cancel       F13=Layout       F18=Files
```

Figure 7.58
Define Printer Output
Screen

2.8a. What does *PRINT mean for the printer device?

The form width defaults to 132 print positions, and even though you made your report lines narrower (110 characters), the form size itself can remain at the default of 132. If you got to this point and couldn't remember the exact width of the report, you could use function key F13 to check the width. If your report were wider than 132 positions, you would need to change the Width value to accommodate the report; otherwise, data beyond the 132nd position would be truncated (unless you had changed the previous screen's Line wrapping value to Y).

2.9. It should not be necessary to change any values on this screen, so press Enter to continue. You should now see the Define Spooled Output screen.

2.9a. Based on previous experience, what will happen to your report if you provide no value for the spool the output field?

2.9b. Use Help to find out what happens when you leave Form type blank. Write your answer on the answer sheet.

Unless your instructor/mentor tells you otherwise, leave the form type blank to default to the value specified in the printer device file. Leave the other values as they are and press Enter.

2.10. For now, you will not print a cover page, so type N for the Print cover page option, then press Enter.

You should now be looking at the Specify Page Headings and Footings screen.

2.11. Print the Standard page headings (leave the default at Y) and key in an appropriate page heading such as
`Student File Listing Prepared by: (your name)`.

When you are finished, press Enter to return to the Define the Query screen.

2.12. You have now changed your query definition to direct its output to a spooled print file. From the Define the Query screen, press F3 to save and run the query.

2.13. This time, no changes should be needed from the Exit this Query screen, so simply press Enter to run the query.

You should briefly see a "Query running…" message, then a message indicating successful completion from the Work with Queries screen.

Return to the Work with Objects Using PDM screen. You should still see your query definition listed even though it has been changed. Move the cursor up to the option field for your output queue and work with it.

2.14. Find the new file named QPQUPRFIL and display it. If you aren't sure which spooled file is the more recent, use F11 to display date and time. Is it your query report? (The spacing will look different than when it is printed because the printer form control characters are ignored on the display.)

This report should have more records than the earlier version that used record selection. Also in this report you declined the cover page when you changed your query definition, but the RUNQRY prompted version shows a standard cover page (which would print as the first page). You should also see the page heading with your name that you added to the new report.

2.15. Change this print file to redirect it to printer PRT01 or the printer assigned by your instructor/mentor to print class lab projects. When you retrieve your printed report, hand it in along with your answer sheet.

Additional Lab Exercise

To help you acquire more skill in working with Query/400, this additional lab exercise is recommended. Don't attempt this exercise until you have successfully completed the main lab exercise. The instructions tell you what to do but are less specific about how to do it. The intention is for you to apply what you have learned to new situations. Think about each step and use the abundant Help information available on the system. Rely on your instructor/mentor when you are not sure how to proceed.

1. From the Work with Objects Using PDM screen, take the Work with option on your current query definition, STUQRY1.

2. From the Work with Queries screen, take the option to change STUQRY1.

3. From the Define the Query screen, choose Specify file selections. Use the function key to add a file. Change the File ID of the primary file (STUPF) to S. Now specify a secondary file named ZIPPF in library INTROCLASS. Make its File ID Z.

4. For the Type of join parameter, specify 3, Unmatched records with primary file. This will produce a listing of all student records in your STUPF not having matching Zip codes in the ZIPPF file in the INTROCLASS library.

5. Enter a join relation equating the Zip code of the student file to the Zip code of the ZIPPF file. Remember to use file IDs to qualify the field names. From the Specify How to Join Files screen, run the report.

   If no records are selected for the report, then all Zip codes in your student file must have matched ZIPPF Zip codes. So there would be no unmatched records. We will assume there are at least a few records in your report.

   Because you did not explicitly select fields in the original query, all fields from both files will be included in the report. If you shift right, you will see the column of Zip codes from the student file and next to it the column of default zeros from the unmatched secondary file. City and state will also have default values of spaces.

6. Use the function key to cancel the report and then press Enter to save your file specifications and return to the Define the Query screen.

7. Select and sequence fields, including last name, first name, address 1, city, state, and the student file Zip code field, in that order, for your report.

8. After selecting the fields, use the layout function to make sure the width of the report does not exceed the 132 positions of the standard line width allowed by Select Output Type and Form for printer output.

9. Exit the query. From the Exit screen, save the definition and run the query interactively, but change the query name to STUQRY2. This will save the new query as a separate query definition, keeping the original STUQRY1 intact. Give the new query a text description indicating that it lists student records with unmatched Zip codes.

10. Return to the Work with Objects Using PDM screen and change the library to INTROCLASS. In the INTROCLASS library PDM list, find the physical file named ZIPPF and copy it to your own library.

11. Return to the Work with Objects Using PDM list of your own library. Work with your output queue. Find the report your query just created and display it. On scratch paper, jot down the unmatched Zip codes.

12. Run a temporary DFU on the ZIPPF file you just copied into your library. (Make sure you are running the DFU on your ZIPPF file and not the one in the INTROCLASS library.) Add records for the unmatched Zip codes you jotted down from your student file, using real or fictitious city and state values.

13. Return to the Work with Queries screen and take the change option on your join query, STUQRY2.

14. Using the Specify file selections option, first change the library value of your secondary file (ZIPPF) to your own current library. Then run the query to see whether you added ZIPPF records for all of the previously unmatched student Zip codes. If you were successful, the report should come up empty.

15. Now change the type of join to 2, Matched records with primary file. If you run the report, you should now see all student records listed. Any records still having unmatched Zip codes will show city and state values as blanks.

16. Saving your changes, return to Define the Query and exit. Name the type 2 join query STUQRY3, and give it a text indicating an outer join of ZIPPF on STUPF. Run the query interactively.

17. There should now be two query reports in your output queue. Send them to the class printer and then hand in the hard copy reports to your instructor.

Mastering the AS/400, Second Edition

Lab 7 Answer Sheet   Name: _____

Date Due: _____   Class Time: _____

1.4a. _____

1.7a. _____

_____ 1.7b. _____

1.9a. _____

1.9b. _____

1.9c. _____

1.10a. _____

1.10b. _____

1.10c. _____

1.10d. _____

1.14a. _____

1.18a. _____ 1.18b. _____

1.18c. _____

2.1a. _____ 2.1b. _____

2.3a. _____

2.5a. _____ 2.5b. _____

2.6a. _____

2.8a. _____

_____

2.9a. _____

2.9b. _____

_____

IN SUMMARY

Query/400 creates reports that can be sent to a display device, a printer, or a database file. Using mostly list and entry screens, you can conveniently specify which file(s) to use, which records to select, which fields to include, and how to order them on a report line. You can change column headings and the width of fields; use editing to control the appearance of data; and select summary functions such as total, average, and count on designated fields.

By selecting up to 32 sort fields, you can group records by common field values, and specify control break processing to print subtotals for control groups when needed. Join queries combine data from two or more related files based on matching values of common fields. The one-to-many relationship is the primary relationship between database files, and it usually exists between the primary and secondary files of a join query.

The primary file of a join query is the file whose data best describes the main topic of the report. Query/400 allows three types of operations on the primary and secondary files; these can be referred to as inner or natural join, outer join, and difference. Completed queries are stored as objects of type *QRYDFN and can be run using the RUNQRY command or by taking option 16 from the Work with Objects Using PDM screen.

In this lab, you have created a query report based on one file using several of the options mentioned above and saved it in your user library. In the additional lab exercise, you have used join operations to identify unmatched records, copied and updated a physical file, and created a printed report using an outer join of matched records to the primary file. Many other options are available in Query/400 to tailor reports to users' needs. You explore some of these options, along with reports based on logical files, in subsequent lab exercises.

Lesson 8

Using Logical Files

Lesson Overview

In previous lessons you learned about physical files and how to describe them using DDS. In this lesson we discuss the usefulness of logical files and contrast them with physical files. Specifically, we examine the use of access paths in logical files to retrieve data records in a different order than they are stored in physical files. We also examine several other powerful relational database operations, such as selection, projection, and join, that can be employed through the use of logical files. You step through the process of describing and creating a logical file using several of these operations.

Because any Create command can fail, we want to prepare you for dealing with failed compiles. Thus, in the lab we intentionally cause the initial compile of your logical file to fail. You then learn how to read a job log and a compile listing to determine what caused the compile to fail and how to correct the problem.

Objectives

Students will be able to

✓ Create a simple logical file over an existing physical file

✓ Explain record selection and show how it is coded using DDS

✓ Explain field projection and why it is used

✓ Identify arrival-sequence and keyed-sequence access paths, and show how each is coded in DDS

✓ Locate and use a job log and compile listing to find and correct DDS source code errors

PHYSICAL FILES AND ACCESS PATHS

As you recall from earlier lessons, externally described **physical files** contain data records whose format is defined according to a specific layout. This record format not only specifies the name and relative order of fields, but also identifies each field's data type and length. A physical file has only one record format, which is designated in the DDS source code by an R in the Name Type field, followed by a name for the record format in the Name field.

The record format provides a blueprint of a record's fields, but it does not tell us how records of data can be made available to applications. This information, describing the way in which records can be read or retrieved from files, is called an **access path**.

Access Paths

On the AS/400, there are two kinds of access path: arrival sequence and keyed sequence. Every file uses one access path, and unless otherwise specified, the records in a physical file are both stored and retrieved in **arrival sequence** (i.e., the order in which they were added to the file). Both the EMPPF example file used in the lessons and the STUPF file you created in the lab use arrival-sequenced access paths. No special action was needed to create those files with arrival-sequenced access paths; when no other specific access path information is provided in the DDS source file description, the system defaults to arrival sequence.

Files using arrival-sequenced access paths may have their records read in two ways:

- *Sequentially* — Records are presented one after another in the order in which they entered or "arrived in" the file, first in, first out. This can be illustrated by paging down (or up) from the initial display of a temporary DFU program for an arrival-sequenced file. The tenth record you added to a file would be the tenth record to appear if you paged down from the beginning. Also, the order in which records are listed by a DSPPFM (Display Physical File Member) command is in arrival sequence. To locate the thousandth record in a file being read sequentially, you would need to read through the 999 records preceding it.

- *Directly* — Direct retrieval (random access) implies that you can access a specific record in a file without having to read all the other records preceding it. Any record in an arrival-sequenced file can be directly retrieved if its relative record number is known. These numbers are assigned to records as they are added to a file in a consecutive series of integers, starting from 1. So the thousandth record added to a file would have relative record number 1000. (This may not be true if the DB2/400 is told to reuse deleted record space.) You could randomly read this record without having to page through the preceding 999 records by typing 1000 in the *RECNBR (relative record number) entry field of a DFU in Change mode. In addition, high-level language (HLL) programs can read a file randomly by relative record number.

You should realize that sequential retrieval for a file with an arrival-sequenced access path does not imply the sequencing of records by any field value but only by the order in which records arrived or were entered into the file.

Keyed-Sequence Access Paths

Often it is useful or necessary to be able to read an entire file or access an individual record by the value of a certain field, called the **key field**. For example, it might be useful to retrieve individual records from a large student file by name, regardless of how the records may be physically stored in the file.

You can specify a **keyed-sequence** access path for a physical file when it is created by defining one or more fields in the record format as keys. A program can then process a file's records in key field order, instead of in arrival sequence.

For files containing a large number of records, having the option of processing the file in keyed sequence can be useful. For example, if you needed to find the record for a certain employee in an employee master file, being able to retrieve the record according to a key field such as Social Security number would be much quicker than searching through the file in arrival sequence, and more convenient than trying to remember a meaningless relative record number.

If you know that a file would most often be accessed by the value of a certain field, you could specify a keyed-sequence access path when the file is created. The ZIPPF file introduced in Lesson 7 is a good example. By far the most common access to that file would be through the Zip code field, as in the join relationship for the query, E.ZIP EQ Z.ZIP. So the ZIPPF file could well have been created with a keyed-sequence access path.

SPECIFYING KEY FIELDS

Key fields are specified in the DDS source code of the file description. The key itself can be a single field in the file's record format, or it can consist of several fields used together (a **composite key**). If the value of this field must be unique for every record (a condition we stipulated for the Zip code field of file ZIPPF), the field is a **primary key** and a special file-level keyword, UNIQUE, can be coded in DDS. When the key is treated as a primary key by specifying the UNIQUE keyword, the system does not permit **duplicate keys** (i.e., the insertion of a new record whose key field value is the same as that of an already existing record).

When the UNIQUE keyword is not used, the system allows records having the same key field values to be stored in the file. Although records with duplicate keys are generally made available in first-in, first-out order, you can specify the file-level keyword FIFO to be certain they are. This keyword, used as an alternative to UNIQUE, tells the system to make records with duplicate keys available in first-in, first-out order.

As mentioned, the keyword UNIQUE (or FIFO) is coded in DDS as a file-level entry, before the record-format specification line. The actual declaration of the key follows the field-level DDS specifications. Keys are defined by coding a K in the Name Type field, followed by the name of the field that will serve as the key in the Name field of the DDS specification.

For example, Figure 8.1 shows the DDS specifications for the EMPPF physical file as if it had originally been created with a keyed-sequence access path.

Figure 8.1
DDS for EMPPF Keyed on EMPNO (Social Security Number)

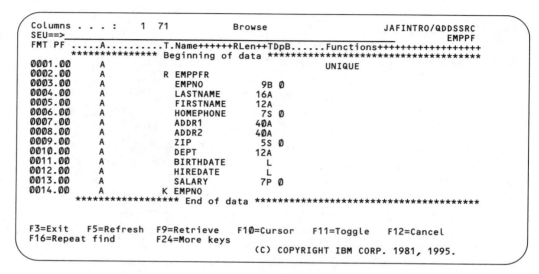

```
Columns . . . :    1  71              Browse              JAFINTRO/QDDSSRC
SEU==>                                                              EMPPF
FMT PF .....A...........T.Name++++++RLen++TDpB......Functions+++++++++++++++++
       *************** Beginning of data **********************************
0001.00   A                                               UNIQUE
0002.00   A          R EMPPFR
0003.00   A            EMPNO          9B 0
0004.00   A            LASTNAME      16A
0005.00   A            FIRSTNAME     12A
0006.00   A            HOMEPHONE      7S 0
0007.00   A            ADDR1         40A
0008.00   A            ADDR2         40A
0009.00   A            ZIP            5S 0
0010.00   A            DEPT          12A
0011.00   A            BIRTHDATE      L
0012.00   A            HIREDATE       L
0013.00   A            SALARY         7P 0
0014.00   A          K EMPNO
       **************** End of data ***************************************


F3=Exit   F5=Refresh  F9=Retrieve  F10=Cursor   F11=Toggle   F12=Cancel
F16=Repeat find       F24=More keys
                                (C) COPYRIGHT IBM CORP. 1981, 1995.
```

The keyword UNIQUE, specified at the file level, tells us that no duplicate keys are permitted. (Remember, when the UNIQUE keyword is specified, DB2/400 does not let you add a record to the file that duplicates an existing key value.) The EMPNO (Social Security) field has been specified as a primary key by using the UNIQUE keyword and by entering a K in the DDS Name Type field and entering the name of the field itself, EMPNO, in the DDS Name field.

Specifying UNIQUE keys makes sense in this example because you would not expect to encounter duplicate Social Security numbers; if you did, it would be an error and the system should alert you. But let's say you need to access records in the file by last name/first name, instead of by Social Security number. In this case, you could not be sure that there would be no duplicate keys. Because there may be a Steven Smith in marketing and a different Steven Smith in sales, using the UNIQUE keyword would be inadvisable. In this example, to be sure that records having duplicate keys were processed in the order entered, you would code the DDS as shown in Figure 8.2.

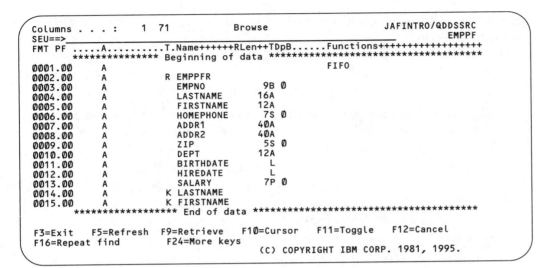

```
Columns . . . :   1  71            Browse              JAFINTRO/QDDSSRC
SEU==>_____ EMPPF
FMT PF .....A...........T.Name++++++RLen++TDpB......Functions+++++++++++++++++++
*************** Beginning of data ***********************************
0001.00   A                                      FIFO
0002.00   A          R EMPPFR
0003.00   A            EMPNO        9B 0
0004.00   A            LASTNAME    16A
0005.00   A            FIRSTNAME   12A
0006.00   A            HOMEPHONE    7S 0
0007.00   A            ADDR1       40A
0008.00   A            ADDR2       40A
0009.00   A            ZIP          5S 0
0010.00   A            DEPT        12A
0011.00   A            BIRTHDATE    L
0012.00   A            HIREDATE     L
0013.00   A            SALARY       7P 0
0014.00   A          K LASTNAME
0015.00   A          K FIRSTNAME
***************** End of data ****************************************

F3=Exit   F5=Refresh  F9=Retrieve   F10=Cursor   F11=Toggle   F12=Cancel
F16=Repeat find       F24=More keys
                         (C) COPYRIGHT IBM CORP. 1981, 1995.
```

Figure 8.2
DDS for EMPPF Keyed on Name

Notice that we have specified a composite key for physical file EMPPF (i.e., two fields are used as the key). The key fields (LASTNAME and FIRSTNAME) are coded in the DDS in order of most significant to least significant. In this way, the access order would be like that of a telephone book, with Smith, Arnold coming before Smith, Betty. Although it may be the primary means of retrieving records, this composite key cannot be a primary key in the strict relational database sense because a primary key requires uniqueness. Because in a large company there could certainly be two or more employees with the same first and last names, the UNIQUE keyword could not be used. Instead, we have coded the keyword FIFO to guarantee first-in, first-out retrieval of records with duplicate keys.

To summarize, physical files can be created with either an arrival-sequenced access path (the default) or with a keyed-sequence access path that lets you retrieve records by the value of a key field. But whether the physical file uses an arrival-sequenced access path or a keyed-sequence access path, a different access path can easily be built over the physical file using a logical file. This capability of a logical file is normally used to provide an alternate keyed-sequence access path over an existing keyed- or arrival-sequenced physical file, but it can also be used to build an arrival-sequenced access path over a physical file created with a keyed-sequence access path. This use of a logical file to build a different access path over an existing physical file is a common and powerful one.

LOGICAL FILES

Perhaps the simplest way to think of **logical files** in general is that they represent different ways to present all or part of the data of one or more physical files. Logical files function as a set of rules that tell DB2/400 how to select, limit, combine, and present the data of the underlying physical file files. Logical files themselves contain no data records, but programs and utilities such as DFU can access and manipulate logical files as if they did. A physical file must exist before any logical file can be based on it and many different logical files can be based on the same physical file.

In any database system, logical files, which for the most part correspond to **views** in a relational database, need to be able to perform several basic functions on physical file data. These include the ability to

- allow the random access of data by the value of a different field than the primary key, or present the logical file in sequence by an alternate key (logical file access path or relational database index)

- select only certain records of the physical file to be included in the logical file and omit the others (selection)

- include only those fields necessary to the user/application from the physical file record format in the logical file, thus ensuring that users have access to data strictly on a need-to-know basis (projection)

- combine data elements (fields) from two or more physical files into a single logical file record format by matching records from the physical files with the value of a common field (join)

There are three distinct types of logical files: simple, multiple-format, and join logical files. We present examples of the latter two later in this lesson, but let's first consider the most commonly used type, the simple logical file. We also use our example of a simple logical file to demonstrate the concepts of access path, selection/omission, and projection.

DESCRIBING A SIMPLE LOGICAL FILE

Simple logical files are created over a single physical file that must already exist as a *FILE type object. When describing a simple logical file, you must name the underlying physical file in the DDS record format statement. For our example, we use physical file EMPPF as the based-on file (the original non-keyed version). In this example, you would use the record-level keyword PFILE, followed by the physical file name in parentheses, to establish the link between the simple logical file and its single based-on physical file. The record format entry would look like this:

```
R EMPPFR                        PFILE(EMPPF)
```

Alternate Access Path

Because physical files can have only one keyed-sequence access path, logical files play an important role by providing the capability to access the data in physical files using a different (alternate) key. As we mentioned above, logical files can serve as indexes that provide another sort sequence (access path) for physical file data — that is, a sort sequence different from the one specified when creating the original physical file.

When a logical file's only purpose is to provide a different access path than the physical file does, as is the case in this example, its description is an easy matter. If you want to access the data records in the underlying physical file

EMPPF in key sequence by last name and first name, the DDS for the simple logical file described in Figure 8.3 would do the job.

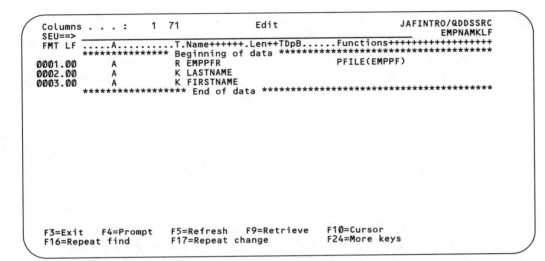

```
 Columns . . . :   1  71          Edit                JAFINTRO/QDDSSRC
 SEU==> _____   EMPNAMKLF
 FMT LF  .....A..........T.Name++++++.Len++TDpB......Functions++++++++++++++++++
 *************** Beginning of data **********************************
 0001.00    A         R EMPPFR                      PFILE(EMPPF)
 0002.00    A         K LASTNAME
 0003.00    A         K FIRSTNAME
 ***************** End of data ****************************************




 F3=Exit   F4=Prompt    F5=Refresh   F9=Retrieve   F10=Cursor
 F16=Repeat find        F17=Repeat change           F24=More keys
```

Figure 8.3
DDS for a Simple Logical File to Access EMPPF by Employee Name

As you can see, the record format name used for the logical file (EMPPFR) is the same as the one used for physical file EMPPF. Regardless whether the physical file is keyed or in arrival sequence, when you use the physical file's record format name for the logical file and do not include any field-level entries, the logical file copies the physical file's record format. All the fields in the original physical file are included in the logical file — with the same attributes. The record format entry must also identify the based-on physical file as the value of the PFILE keyword. The only other entries needed are those to identify the key. By specifying fields LASTNAME and FIRSTNAME as key fields (a K in the DDS Name Type field), we tell the compiler that the new file will have a keyed-sequence access path using the composite key of last name (major) and first name (minor). The compiler expects key field names to be found in the based-on physical file's record format. If you misspell one of the key field names, a compile error results.

To see how this logical file accesses records in physical file EMPPF, let's assume that you have created the logical file EMPNAMKLF and that physical file EMPPF contains data. Let's further assume that you want to create a temporary DFU program to work with the logical file. When you run the temporary DFU program, it displays a prompt for the two key fields (Figure 8.4).

Figure 8.4
DFU for Logical File
EMPNAMKLF in
Change Mode

```
WORK WITH DATA IN A FILE                    Mode . . . . :    CHANGE
Format . . . . : EMPPFR                     File . . . . :    EMPNAMKLF

  LASTNAME:_____
  FIRSTNAME:_____






    F3=Exit              F5=Refresh              F6=Select format
    F9=Insert            F10=Entry               F11=Change
         (C) COPYRIGHT IBM CORP. 1980, 1995.
```

When you type in the name of a known employee and press Enter, DB2/400 searches the logical file access path for matching values. If a match is found, the appropriate record from the physical file is retrieved and displayed on the screen. Figure 8.5 shows the record that would be displayed if you entered "Kartblanch" and "Emil" as the key field values.

Figure 8.5
DFU Showing Record
Retrieved for Key
"Kartblanch," "Emil"

```
WORK WITH DATA IN A FILE                    Mode . . . . :    CHANGE
Format . . . . : EMPPFR____                 File . . . . :    EMPNAMKLF

  LASTNAME:   Kartblanch_____
  FIRSTNAME:  Emil_____
  EMPNO:      111110006
  HOMEPHONE:  3777040
  ADDR1:      RR 1 Box 39_____
  ADDR2:      _____
  ZIP:        52338
  DEPT:       Sales_____
  BIRTHDATE:  1947-05-15
  HIREDATE:   1986-05-15
  SALARY:      48250



    F3=Exit              F5=Refresh              F6=Select format
    F9=Insert            F10=Entry               F11=Change
```

If you were to page up or down from this record, subsequent records would be retrieved in alphabetical sequence by name and displayed. This logical file illustrates the technique of using the same record format name as the physical file's record format. When you do this and supply no field attributes, the logical file includes all the fields from the physical file with their same attributes.

As you have seen, to build a logical file whose only purpose is to provide an alternate access path over the physical file, all you need is DDS source for a record format having the same name as the physical file record format and using the physical file name as the PFILE value. Following the record format entry is a key-level entry (or entries) to identify the key field(s).

Select

Now let's consider the second function of logical files mentioned above: selection. When a logical file uses selection, its population is limited to a certain group of records from the underlying physical file. Selection lets users work only with the data records needed for an application and protects excluded data from users who do not need that data or do not have authorization to it. (This operation was originally called restriction, and that may be a better term because its primary purpose is to restrict access to data that users or applications should not have.)

On the AS/400, you implement selection in DDS by using Select and Omit entries and by specifying keywords that define how the select/omit operation is to be done. Unlike key entries that can be used by both physical and logical files, select/omit entries are used only with logical files.

To illustrate selection, let's assume you want to provide each department manager with information about employees in his/her own department. Creating separate physical files containing employee records for each department is not a good solution for many reasons, and it is not necessary when using a relational database. You can keep all employee data in a single physical file and create different logical files for each department. Figure 8.6 shows the DDS source code for a simple logical file named EMPSLSLF, whose population consists only of Sales department records. We have given this file a keyed-sequence access path, but selection does not require keying and an arrival-sequenced access path would have worked as well.

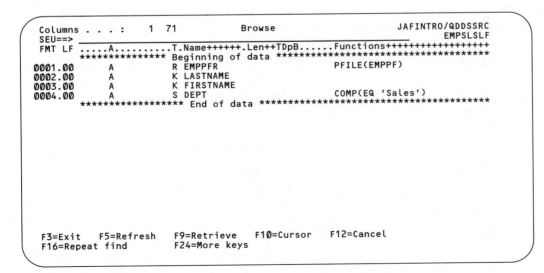

Figure 8.6

Logical File Selecting Only Sales Department Records

Notice that this file is very similar to logical file EMPNAMKLF shown in Figure 8.3. The only difference is the Select entry following the key fields (LASTNAME and FIRSTNAME). The letter S in the Name type field is followed by the name of the field (DEPT) you want to test to determine whether the record should be selected or omitted. Although we are testing the DEPT field in this example, any other field(s) in the logical file could be tested. Remember that because we have coded the logical file with the same record format name as the physical file and with no field-level entries, all physical file fields will be included in the logical file's record format.

The function we have used, COMP(EQ 'Sales'), tells DB2/400 to select physical file records whose DEPT field value is equal to the quoted string constant 'Sales'.

You can use three function keywords with Select and its counterpart, Omit:

- *VALUES*(V1 V2 V3 ...) — selects/omits records where the value of the named field matches one of the values in the list. For alphanumeric and date and time fields, each value must be enclosed by single quotes (apostrophes). Numeric fields code only digits and a decimal point if necessary. For example,

```
S ZIP                           VALUES(52247 52338 52404)
```

selects records for the logical file having a Zip code equal to 52247 or 52338 or 52404.

- *RANGE*(lowval highval) — selects/omits records where the named field contains a value in the range of lowval to highval inclusive. For example,

```
S SALARY                        RANGE(20000 34500)
```

selects records for the logical file having a salary of at least $20,000 and not more than $34,500. For alphanumeric and date and time fields, both values must be enclosed by single quotes.

- *COMP*(op comparand) — selects/omits records where the value of the named field used as the subject of relational operator (op) tests true for the comparand value specified. The valid codes for the relational operator are EQ (equal), NE (not equal), LT (less than), NL (not less than), GT (greater than), NG (not greater than), LE (less than or equal to) and GE (greater than or equal to). If the field is alphanumeric (date or time), the comparand must be a quoted string. For example,

```
S HIREDATE                      COMP(GE '1990-01-01')
```

selects records for the logical file of employees hired since Jauary 1, 1990.

You need to keep a couple rules in mind when coding DDS keywords and their parameters:

- DDS uses uppercase exclusively; all DDS keywords must be entered in uppercase. Only quoted strings can be in mixed case (e.g., 'Sales'). If a quoted string is a constant used to compare an actual database field value, it must be entered exactly as the data is stored. For values stored in database records, DB2/400 is case sensitive (i.e., 'SALES', 'sales', and 'Sales' are not equal). In our example above (Figure 8.6), we used 'Sales' because we know that's how the data is stored in the physical file.

- Keyword parameter values must be enclosed in parentheses. The left parenthesis must immediately follow the keyword. If there are multiple values, at least one space must separate values in the list. This is also true if one of the values is an operator, like EQ in our example; at least one space must separate EQ and the following value 'Sales'.

While following these rules will help you avoid most syntax errors, you can find additional rules and examples of other keywords in IBM's *Data Description Specifications Reference* (SC41-9620).

Omit: The Inverse of Select

The Omit entry, coded with a value O in the Name Type field, functions as the inverse of Select. Sometimes it is easier to state which records we don't want in the logical file than which records we do want. If, for example, the Human Resources department manager asked for a file of all employees except those in Sales, you might find it easiest to code

```
O DEPT                      COMP(EQ  'Sales')
```

Of course, the same logical file could be created by using a Select entry with a NE (not equal) operator:

```
S DEPT                      COMP(NE  'Sales')
```

More than one Select or Omit operation can be performed with a logical file. When the Name Type S or O is repeated for each entry, the series of Selects or Omits is considered connected by logical OR operators; for example,

```
S DEPT                      COMP(EQ  'Research')
S SALARY                    COMP(GE  45000)
```

Taken together, these entries state that records should be included in the logical file if their department is Research *or* if their salary is greater than or equal to $45,000. If either or both conditions are true, the record will be selected for the logical file. As soon as one select or omit condition is satisfied, starting with the first entry coded, the record is selected (or omitted) and not considered again. This fact does have some bearing on the ordering of Select/Omit entries, especially if select and omit are both used. For example, consider employee Jack Sprat of the Marketing department, who has a salary of $38,500. If you coded the DDS in the following order:

```
S DEPT                      COMP(EQ  'Marketing')
O SALARY                    COMP(LT  45000)
```

you are telling DB2/400 to first select any Marketing department records and then, of the records remaining, omit any records where salary is less than $45,000.

This means all records in the Marketing department, regardless of salary, should be selected. That would include Jack, even though his salary is low. Additionally, all remaining records not explicitly omitted (i.e., those having salaries of at least $45,000) will be included in the logical file.

On the other hand, the results achieved by reversing the order of the entries may be quite different. If the DDS were coded

```
O SALARY                        COMP(LT  45000)
S DEPT                          COMP(EQ  'Marketing')
```

you would be telling DB2/400 to first omit all records where salary is less than $45,000 (there goes Jack); and then, of the records remaining, select only those whose department is Marketing. In this case, even though Jack is in Marketing, his record will not be in the logical file because he was first eliminated by the Omit. Once omitted, a record will not be selected.

In effect, the above code says: Select only those records where salary is greater than or equal to $45,000 *and* that are in the Marketing department. This expression using a logical AND may be easier to understand than the Select/Omit combination above; and in fact, you can code multiple selects or omits connected by logical ANDs. When two or more entries are coded and only the first uses the Name Type S or O, the entries are considered logically connected by the AND operator. To code the selection as a logical AND operation, you would simply enter

```
S SALARY                        COMP(GE  45000)
  DEPT                          COMP(EQ  'Marketing')
```

This tells DB2/400 to select records where salary is at least $45,000 *and* that are part of the Marketing department.

It is important to realize the difference in the use of OR and AND with multiple Select/Omit entries. For example, if you coded the following entries:

```
S DEPT                          VALUES('Human Res'  'Sales')
  SALARY                        RANGE(35000  55000)
```

you are specifying that both conditions must be true; the department must be 'Human Res' or 'Sales' *and* salary must be in the range of $35,000 to $55,000 for a record to be selected. Requiring both conditions to be true would select a smaller number of records than using an OR relationship. Simply adding an S Name type to the second line of the above code changes its meaning significantly:

```
S DEPT                          VALUES('Human Res'  'Sales')
S SALARY                        RANGE(35000  55000)
```

This combination connects the two entries using a logical OR. Now we are telling DB2/400 to select any record in the Human Resources or Sales departments and then, of the remaining records, to select all records with Salary in the range of $35,000 to $55,000. This specification would certainly select a much larger number of records for the logical file.

To help you understand this difference, consider the illustration in Figure 8.7.

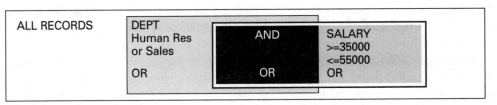

Figure 8.7
Difference in the Use of
OR and AND

The selection using AND would include only the intersection of DEPT and SALARY, shown as the darkest shaded center box, while OR would include all records in any shaded box, including those in the AND box having both conditions true.

Each Select or Omit entry adds a new select "rule" to the file description. Each line that names a field and uses a COMP or VALUES keyword adds one rule, regardless whether that field test was in an AND or OR relationship with a previous select/omit entry. The RANGE keyword is implemented using two limit tests, resulting in two rules although only one field is named. All of the examples we've just covered create two or three rules. Additionally, even a single Select or Omit entry adds one more select or omit rule, inserted automatically, to the logical file. That rule will be the opposite operation of the last one coded and will apply to *all* records not yet selected or omitted. If your logical file includes the following Select/Omit entries:

```
O DEPT                        COMP(EQ  'Human Res')
S SALARY                      COMP(GT  40000)
```

the last rule that DB2/400 adds would be:

```
O                             ALL
```

The Select/Omit Description information of the DSPFD command for a logical file using the Select/Omit entries above is shown in Figure 8.8.

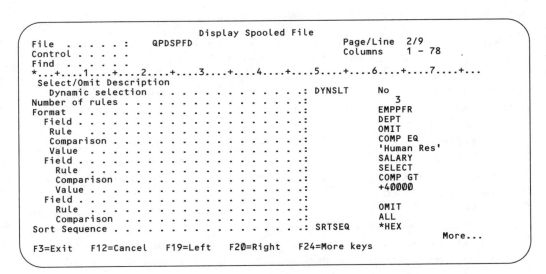

Figure 8.8
Display File Description
for a Logical File with
Select/Omit Entries

(The last O   ALL is not coded in the DDS but added by DB2/400 at compile time.) Notice the number of rules is three; the first two come from the source code and the third is the inverse of the last Select entry.

When any Select/Omit entries are coded for a logical file, this last rule serves the purpose of clarifying what happens to records of the physical file that are neither explicitly selected nor omitted by the coded rules. The keyword ALL takes the place of any COMP, VALUES, or RANGE entry and when it is used, no field name is specified.

It is possible for you to code the last ALL rule yourself, but because you would probably never want to change the default rule of opposites, there would be nothing to gain.

For example, neither

```
S SALARY                        COMP(GT 40000)
S                               ALL
```

nor

```
O SALARY                        COMP(LE 40000)
O                               ALL
```

make much sense. The first example selects everything, and the second omits everything.

A last consideration for using Select/Omit relates to access paths. If a logical file has a keyed-sequence access path, Select/Omit operations are performed on the access path itself. Assume a physical file (EMPPF) had 1,000 records and you compiled a logical file over it with the following description:

```
                                UNIQUE
R EMPPFR                        PFILE(EMPPF)
K EMPNO
S DEPT                          COMP(EQ 'Sales')
```

A new access path would be created for the logical file even if a unique, keyed-sequence access path on EMPNO already existed for the physical file. If exactly half of all employees were sales people, the logical file's access path would have 500 entries, one for each Sales department record in the physical file. When a program opened the logical file, it would read records using the new access path — only those already selected.

This is fine from the standpoint of a program needing only Sales employee records, but now an additional access path exists on the system — one more to take up space and be maintained. For example, if a new employee for the sales department were added to the physical file, then both access paths would have to be updated, and UNIQUE keys require immediate (*IMMED) access path maintenance. You can imagine that if twenty different select/omit logical files, each having a keyed-sequence access path were created, the overhead due to access path maintenance when performing updates, adds, and deletes to the physical file (or through any of the logical files) could be substantial.

In our example, and in many practical situations, the logical file whose code is shown above and its based-on physical file are using the same field (EMPNO) as key. When this is the case, you can instruct DB2/400 not to build a new access path but to share the existing access path and to dynamically select and omit records as they are read through the existing access path. Then only those records that are selected by the logical file's Select/Omit rules are passed on to the application program. There are other factors you must consider before making such a decision, but in many cases using dynamic select/omit can reduce the total number of access paths on the database without negative effects on program performance. To use this technique, simply code the keyword DYNSLT at the file level for the logical file.

Whenever a Select/Omit logical file is being created without a keyed-sequence access path, the DYNSLT keyword (or K   *NONE) must be used. In this case, DYNSLT tells DB2/400 to read the records of the physical file in arrival sequence (even if the physical file itself is keyed) and apply the Select/Omit rules to each record in deciding whether to pass it on to the application program. The term "dynamic" when used with record selection can be a little misleading. As it is used above, dynamic select simply means that the Select/Omit rules have not been used to build a separate index containing only entries for selected records, but instead records are selected "dynamically" as they are read from the based-on physical file. In either case, the Select/Omit rules are hard coded into the logical file and can only be changed by recompiling, so the word "dynamic" really applies to when the rules are being applied, and not to which rules are being used.

Although, for the sake of illustration, the examples above are somewhat frivolous, the Select/Omit operation is in fact a useful and powerful tool for implementing record-level security. It ensures that users have access only to records of a file that they have a demonstrated need to use, and that other records will not be available to them.

In HLL applications, the use of logical files using select/omit can significantly reduce the complexity of program logic, making programs easier to understand and maintain.

Projection

As we mentioned earlier, projection has to do with limiting access to fields of a physical file that are sensitive and need to be secured or are simply unnecessary for a given user or application. Using projection, the logical file record format includes only those fields needed by the applications using the logical file. In other words, a projected logical file's record format is a subset of fields of the based-on physical file. Projection works for field security in much the same way that selection works for record security — the restricted fields are excluded from the logical file's record.

As an example, let's start with the DDS for the original employee file, EMPPF (Figure 8.9).

Figure 8.9
DDS for EMPPF

```
Columns . . . :    1  71              Browse              JAFINTRO/QDDSSRC
SEU==>_____        EMPPF
FMT PF .....A..........T.Name+++++RLen++TDpB......Functions+++++++++++++++++++
         *************** Beginning of data ***********************************
0001.00    A          R EMPPFR
0002.00    A            EMPNO         9B 0
0003.00    A            LASTNAME     16A
0004.00    A            FIRSTNAME    12A
0005.00    A            HOMEPHONE     7S 0
0006.00    A            ADDR1        40A
0007.00    A            ADDR2        40A
0008.00    A            ZIP           5S 0
0009.00    A            DEPT         12A
0010.00    A            BIRTHDATE     L
0011.00    A            HIREDATE      L
0012.00    A            SALARY        7P 0
         **************** End of data *****************************************



F3=Exit   F5=Refresh   F9=Retrieve   F10=Cursor   F11=Toggle   F12=Cancel
F16=Repeat find         F24=More keys
                                     (C) COPYRIGHT IBM CORP. 1981, 1995.
```

Now let's suppose that certain employees in Human Resources need access to records in this file, but you don't want them (or the programmers who write applications for them) to have access to the birth date and salary fields. The best solution would be to create a projected logical file, eliminating those fields from the record format. To do so, you could not simply use the same record format name as the physical file's; you would also need to name the fields you wanted to include. Only the named fields would be projected to the logical file; fields not named would be omitted from the logical file. Figure 8.10 shows the DDS for a logical file using projection to screen out the BIRTHDATE and SALARY fields of the underlying physical file.

Figure 8.10
DDS for EMPPLF1...
BIRTHDATE and
SALARY Not Projected

```
Columns . . . :    1  71               Edit               JAFINTRO/QDDSSRC
SEU==>_____        EMPPLF1
FMT LF .....A..........T.Name++++++.Len++TDpB......Functions+++++++++++++++++++
         *************** Beginning of data ***********************************
0001.00    A          R EMPPFR                    PFILE(EMPPF)
0002.00    A            EMPNO
0003.00    A            LASTNAME
0004.00    A            FIRSTNAME
0005.00    A            HOMEPHONE
0006.00    A            ADDR1
0007.00    A            ADDR2
0008.00    A            ZIP
0009.00    A            DEPT
0010.00    A            HIREDATE
         **************** End of data *****************************************



F3=Exit   F4=Prompt   F5=Refresh   F9=Retrieve   F10=Cursor   F11=Toggle
F16=Repeat find        F17=Repeat change          F24=More keys
                                   ( C) COPYRIGHT IBM CORP. 1981, 1995.
```

In this example, we used the same record format name as the underlying physical file, but this is not a requirement. When you specify field names, as you do with projection, you can use a record format name different from that of the underlying physical file. When only the field name is coded in the DDS, as in Figure 8.10, the other attributes of data type, length, and decimal positions come from the physical file's record format. As with key field names, projection logical file field names must be spelled exactly as they are in the based-on physical file.

Figure 8.11 shows the second page of output from the DSPFFD (Display File Field Description) command for the compiled logical file EMPPLF1.

```
                         Display Spooled File
File  . . . . . :   QPDSPFFD                    Page/Line       1/26
Control . . . . .   +2                          Columns         1 - 78
Find  . . . . . .
*...+....1....+....2....+....3....+....4....+....5....+....6....+....7....+...
             Data       Field  Buffer   Buffer        Field    Column
   Field     Type      Length  Length  Position       Usage    Heading
   EMPNO     BINARY      9  0      4         1         Both     EMPNO
   LASTNAME  CHAR         16     16         5         Both     LASTNAME
     Coded Character Set Identifier   . . . . . :    37
   FIRSTNAME CHAR         12     12        21         Both     FIRSTNAME
     Coded Character Set Identifier   . . . . . :    37
   HOMEPHONE ZONED        7  0      7        33         Both     HOMEPHONE
   ADDR1     CHAR         40     40        40         Both     ADDR1
     Coded Character Set Identifier   . . . . . :    37
   ADDR2     CHAR         40     40        80         Both     ADDR2
     Coded Character Set Identifier   . . . . . :    37
   ZIP       ZONED        5  0      5       120         Both     ZIP
   DEPT      CHAR         12     12       125         Both     DEPT
     Coded Character Set Identifier   . . . . . :    37
   HIREDATE  DATE         10     10       137         Both     HIREDATE
                                                                 More...

   F3=Exit   F12=Cancel   F19=Left   F20=Right   F24=More keys
```

Figure 8.11
DSPFFD on EMPPLF1,
Second Page

It is important to realize that the logical file has a different record format than the underlying physical file (EMPPF). It has a different number of fields and a different record length. A program using this logical file has no access to the BIRTH-DATE and SALARY fields — they aren't there!

You can also combine projection with selection and the use of an alternate access path within a single logical file. Suppose you needed to create a logical file without birth date and salary fields for Human Resources personnel to use, but you did not want them to have access to records of co-workers in the same department. Additionally, suppose you wanted them to be able to access the file randomly by typing in an employee's last name and first name. The DDS for the logical file required to accomplish this (EMPPSKLF1) is shown in Figure 8.12.

Figure 8.12

Logical File
EMPPSKLF1, Using
Selection, Projection,
and Access Path

```
Columns . . . :    1  71          Browse              JAFINTRO/QDDSSRC
SEU==>_____       EMPPSKLF1
FMT LF .....A..........T.Name++++++.Len++TDpB......Functions+++++++++++++++++++
        *************** Beginning of data ****************************************
0001.00     A      R EMPPFR                    PFILE(EMPPF)
0002.00     A        EMPNO
0003.00     A        LASTNAME
0004.00     A        FIRSTNAME
0005.00     A        HOMEPHONE
0006.00     A        ADDR1
0007.00     A        ADDR2
0008.00     A        ZIP
0009.00     A        DEPT
0010.00     A        HIREDATE
0011.00     A      K LASTNAME
0012.00     A      K FIRSTNAME
0013.00     A      O DEPT                       COMP(EQ  'Human Res')
        ***************** End of data *****************************************



F3=Exit    F5=Refresh    F9=Retrieve   F10=Cursor   F11=Toggle   F12=Cancel
F16=Repeat find          F24=More keys
                                   (C) COPYRIGHT IBM CORP. 1981, 1995.
```

CREATING A LOGICAL FILE

When you complete the DDS code for a logical file, you press F3 to go to the SEU Exit screen, as usual. From there you can change the new member name if, for example, it was created by modifying an existing source member that you did not want changed.

When you return to the Work with Members Using PDM screen, a message tells you that the new member has been added to your source physical file. To create the logical file object, you compile the logical file source member by using the same option you use for a physical file: option 14. Figure 8.13 shows the Work with Members Using PDM screen with option 14 taken for source member EMPPSKLF1.

Figure 8.13

Work with Members
Using PDM...Compile
Option on EMPPSKLF1

```
                        Work with Members Using PDM               S1018A6G
   File . . . . . .    QDDSSRC___
   Library . . . .    JAFINTRO__        Position to . . . . ._____

 Type options, press Enter.
   2=Edit       3=Copy   4=Delete 5=Display     6=Print    7=Rename
   8=Display description 9=Save 13=Change text 14=Compile 15=Create module...

 Opt Member     Type       Opt Member    Type       Opt Member   Type
 __  EMPMKTLF   LF_____   __  EMPLF5A   LF_____   __  F01V01    LF_____
 __  EMPNSLSLF  LF_____   __  EMPMSTLF1 LF_____   __  F1TEST    PF_____
 __  EMPSLSLF   LF_____   __  EMPMSTLF1S LF_____   __  GRADEDSP  DSPF____
 __  EMPPLF1    LF_____   __  EMPMSTLF2 LF_____   __  INTROMNU  MNUDDS___
 __  EMPPLF2    LF_____   __  EMPMSTPF  PF_____   __  INTROMNUQQ MNUCMD___
 14  EMPPSKLF1  LF_____   __  EMPMSTPF2 PF_____   __  LFILE01   LF_____
 __  EMPLF4     LF_____   __  EMPPF     PF_____   __  LFILE01B  LF_____
 __  EMPLF5     LF_____   __  FILE01    PF_____   __  MENU01    DSPF____
                                                                 More...
 Parameters or command
 ===>
 F3=Exit        F4=Prompt        F5=Refresh         F6=Create
 F9=Retrieve    F10=Command entry  F23=More options  F24=More keys
 Member EMPPSKLF1 added to file JAFINTRO/QDDSSRC.                      +
```

If you prompt on the compile option, you see the CRTLF (Create Logical File) command prompt screen. In this case, PDM chooses the CRTLF command for the compile option because the source member type is LF. The first screen of the CRTLF command prompt is shown in Figure 8.14.

```
                         Create Logical File (CRTLF)

 Type choices, press Enter.

 File . . . . . . . . . . . . . . . > EMPPSKLF1_   Name
   Library . . . . . . . . . . . . >   JAFINTRO__  Name, *CURLIB
 Source file . . . . . . . . . . > QDDSSRC      Name
   Library . . . . . . . . . . . >   JAFINTRO    Name, *LIBL, *CURLIB
 Source member . . . . . . . . . > EMPPSKLF1    Name, *FILE
 Generation severity level . . .   20____       0-30
 Flagging severity level . . . .   0____        0-30
 File type . . . . . . . . . . .   *DATA        *DATA, *SRC
 Member, if desired . . . . . . .   *FILE_____  Name, *FILE, *NONE
 Physical file data members:
   Physical file . . . . . . . .   *ALL_____   Name, *ALL
     Library . . . . . . . . . .   _____   Name, *CURRENT
   Members . . . . . . . . . . .   _____   Name, *NONE
               + for more values   _____
               + for more values _


                                                                    More...
 F3=Exit   F4=Prompt   F5=Refresh   F10=Additional parameters   F12=Cancel
 F13=How to use this display       F24=More keys
```

Figure 8.14
Create Logical File, First Page

Notice that PDM has filled in the first five parameter values. For File name, PDM uses the name of the source member; but if you wanted the logical file object to have a different name, you could change the File parameter value.

Specifying Access Path Maintenance

When you request additional parameters and page down, you see the second screen of the CRTLF command prompt (Figure 8.15).

```
                         Create Logical File (CRTLF)

 Type choices, press Enter.

 Text 'description' . . . . . . .   Keyed on Name, no BIRTHDATE, SALARY, omit HR
 _____

                      Additional Parameters

 Source listing options . . . . .   _____   *SRC, *NOSRC, *SOURCE...
               + for more values
 System . . . . . . . . . . . . .   *LCL_____     *LCL, *RMT, *FILETYPE
 Maximum members . . . . . . . .   1____          Number, *NOMAX
 Access path size . . . . . . . .   *MAX4GB        *MAXGB, *MAX1TB
 Access path maintenance . . . .   *IMMED         *IMMED, *DLY, *REBLD
 Access path recovery . . . . . .   ____           *NO, *AFTIPL, *IPL
 Force keyed access path . . . .   *NO            *NO, *YES
 Preferred storage unit . . . . .   *ANY           1-255, *ANY
 Rcd format selector program . .   *NONE          Name, *NONE
   Library . . . . . . . . . . .                  Name, *LIBL, *CURLIB
                                                               More...
 F3=Exit   F4=Prompt   F5=Refresh   F12=Cancel   F13=How to use this display
 F24=More keys
```

Figure 8.15
CRTLF Command Prompt Additional Parameters

You can see that a short text description of the logical file has been entered. Notice that the Access path maintenance parameter value defaults to *IMMED. Whether a keyed-sequence access path is being created for the physical file itself, or whether it is defined in a logical file built over the physical file, changes to data record key fields or additions or deletions of data records in the physical file require changes to the access path index entries. When the maintenance parameter value is *IMMED, such changes to the data records affecting index entries cause immediate update of the logical file's access path (and of the access path of the physical file, if it is keyed sequence), regardless whether the changes are made through the logical file or through the physical file.

Immediate maintenance ensures that as soon as a record was added to the physical file it would be available (if selected) to the logical file. This is the desired state of affairs in an environment in which most files are processed interactively. For files whose keyed-sequence access path uses UNIQUE keys, immediate maintenance is not only the default, it is required. But for large physical files with non-unique keys and with high **volatility** (i.e., the population of records changes frequently), as the number of access paths with immediate maintenance increases, the average response time of individual transactions also increases. **Response time** is the time that elapses between a user's request for an action (e.g., pressing a function key to Add a new record to the file) and the system's completion of the action (e.g., the record is written, all *IMMED maintenance access paths are updated, and the system is waiting for the next request). When a large number of access paths require immediate maintenance, the system must take care of those access paths before it can service the next user request. In severe cases, this can contribute to a noticeably slower response time.

To reduce the negative impact on response time, you could limit the number of different access paths built over physical files. For necessary access paths, you could use either delayed (*DLY) or rebuild (*REBLD) maintenance. When you specify delayed maintenance, the system stores the necessary data to update the access path in a temporary file. When the logical file using the access path is needed (e.g., when a query or DFU uses that logical file), its old access path is updated using changes stored in the temporary file. (But even with *DLY maintenance, the access path is constantly updated while the file is in use.) While this approach may require more time when the logical file is opened, it saves much of the ongoing overhead of keeping the access path current throughout the day. Using delayed maintenance is especially useful for non-unique, keyed-sequence logical files that are used infrequently and that are not used by time-critical interactive applications, especially if such files are built over large, active physical files.

When you specify rebuild maintenance, the system neither performs ongoing maintenance nor saves changes — the access path is rebuilt when the logical file using it is opened (i.e., used by a program or utility). If the based-on physical file is very large, this method could be quite time consuming; and it isn't suitable for files used frequently by interactive jobs. But if the logical file is used only by report programs that always run during nonbusiness hours in the batch subsystem, this approach might be ideal. If the based-on physical file is highly volatile, *REBLD maintenance completely eliminates the unnecessary overhead that otherwise results from keeping its access path immediately current.

Although junior programmers will probably not make decisions about access path maintenance, it is important to know that options exist, and that over time choices made have an impact on interactive response time and **throughput** (the amount of work a system can perform within a certain period of time). The database administrator (DBA) will use dynamic Select/Omit, access path maintenance, and other techniques to reduce both the number of access paths and the time required to maintain them.

After you have entered the CRTLF command and the logical file compiles, the system creates a **compile listing** by default. If a message in your message queue indicates that the compile has not been successful, you can display or print the compile listing to determine what errors caused the problem. When the logical file compiles successfully, you should delete the compile listing from your output queue. After the logical file compiles, a new object whose type is *FILE will exist in your library.

Using DFU on Logical Files

Now let's see how a temporary DFU would work with our sample logical file. When you run option 18 (Change using DFU) on logical file EMPPSKLF1 from the Work with Objects Using PDM screen, the screen for the temporary DFU appears in Change mode. This tells you that the logical file contains records; otherwise, the temporary DFU would be in Entry mode. (It is possible, through a logical error in your select/omit specification, to create an "empty" logical file even though abundant data exists in the based-on physical file.)

If you typed the name of a Human Resources employee (e.g., "Hunn" "Atilla") in the key fields and pressed Enter, the key would be displayed in reverse image, indicating an error (Figure 8.16). The error message "Record not found in file EMPPSKLF1 ..." would appear at the bottom of the screen.

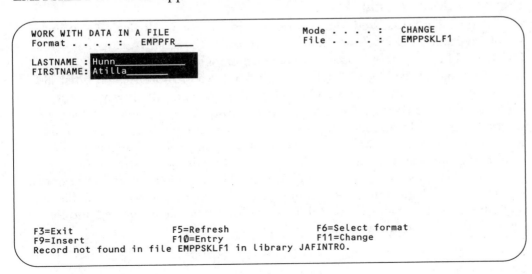

Figure 8.16

Error Message for "Hunn", "Atilla"

As you would expect, Mr. Hunn's record is not included in the logical file because he works in the Human Resources department, and those records have been omitted. When you enter the key of another employee (who is not in Human Resources), the record will be displayed.

Figure 8.17 shows Sam Slick's record and you can see that, as the logical file specified, neither the birth date nor the salary field is displayed.

Figure 8.17
Record Retrieved for
"Slick," "Same"

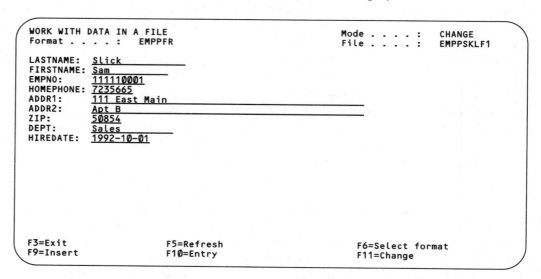

```
WORK WITH DATA IN A FILE                    Mode . . . . :    CHANGE
Format . . . . :    EMPPFR                  File . . . . :    EMPPSKLF1

LASTNAME:   Slick
FIRSTNAME:  Sam
EMPNO:      111110001
HOMEPHONE:  7235665
ADDR1:      111 East Main
ADDR2:      Apt B
ZIP:        50854
DEPT:       Sales
HIREDATE:   1992-10-01




F3=Exit              F5=Refresh             F6=Select format
F9=Insert            F10=Entry              F11=Change
```

If you were to page down from here, the next employee record in alphabetical sequence would appear, as determined by the LASTNAME and FIRSTNAME access path. You could make changes to any of the fields shown in Mr. Slick's record. It is important to understand that such changes, made through the logical file record, affect the data stored in the underlying physical file, EMPPF.

CREATING JOIN LOGICAL FILES

Now that we have discussed some of the basic operations of logical files, using simple logical files as examples, let's broaden our discussion. We talk first about join logical files and then about multiple-format logical files.

A **join logical file** lets you include fields from two or more related physical files in a single record format. This technique gives you a convenient way to pull together data from several files under one file (with a single name) that can be opened and read by application programs. You can use join logical files to display information or print reports, but you cannot use join logical files to update the underlying physical files. Also, you cannot use DFU with join logical files.

Query/400 does support join logical files. When the join operation has been specified in the logical file description, Query/400 treats the join logical file as any other physical or simple logical file — only a single file is selected and no Query/400 join specifications are needed.

As a first example, consider a join logical file that would include data from the EMPPF and ZIPPF physical files as described in Lesson 7. The DDS for such a file is shown in Figure 8.18. The code illustrates several new techniques.

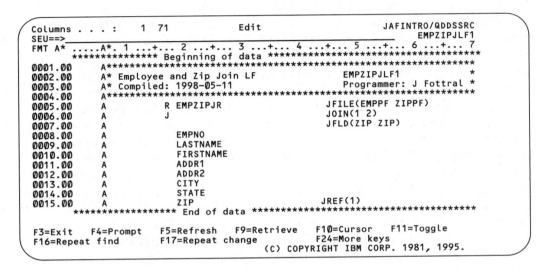

Figure 8.18
Employee and Zip Code Join Logical File

First, some basic identification has been included in the first four lines of code. As the format line indicates, an asterisk in column 7 is a valid character and tells the DDS compiler to treat that line as a comment — and not to syntax check it or try to compile it. It is always a good idea to identify the date compiled, author, and any special techniques employed in the file, and most installations have standards for this type of documentation.

Line 5 names the record format, EMPZIPJR. This record format name can be unique; you gain nothing by using the same name as one of the based-on physical files because all fields included in the join logical file must be named. Also as part of the record format entry (line 5), a JFILE keyword must be coded. This keyword takes the place of the PFILE keyword of a simple logical file and names the physical files that will be participating in the join. Although as many as 32 physical files can be named, three or four are commonly used. As with Query/400, the first file named is the primary file. The primary file is crucial in determining which records will be selected for the join operation, and this file should contain the data that is the primary topic or focus of the report or display. Our report focuses on employees; so the employee file, EMPPF, is the primary file and the Zip code file, ZIPPF, is the secondary file.

Following the record format and JFILE entry are one or more join specifications. These always begin with a J coded in the Name Type field (column 17), followed by the JOIN keyword in the functions field (starting in column 45). There will be one JOIN specification for each pair of files. If you are joining four files, there will be three join entries, each starting with a J Name Type followed by the JOIN keyword; if you are joining two files, as in our example, there is only one entry. The JOIN keyword identifies the two related files, either by name or, as we have done here, by relative number in the JFILE list. Following the JOIN keyword, on a line by itself (line 7 in our example), is the JFLD keyword. Any keyword on a line by itself belongs to the previous file, record, join, field, key, or select/omit entry.

The JFLD keyword identifies the fields from each file that are common (relationship-supporting fields). In our example, both field names are ZIP, but a positional relationship exists between the fields of the JFLD keyword and the files of the JOIN keyword: The first JFLD field name must belong to the first file identified by the JOIN keyword, and the second JFLD field name must belong to the second JOIN file. The implicit relationship is equality of field values (i.e., records from the two files match and are therefore joined when the first JFLD field value equals the second JFLD field value). In Query/400 we explicitly stated this relationship, called equijoin, as E.ZIP EQ Z.ZIP. For a join logical file, the keyword entry JFLD(ZIP ZIP) has the same meaning with the files specified in the order they are. It is important to realize that the relationship-supporting fields of two joined files do not need to have the same name. In our example, both are called ZIP, but one could just as well be EMPZIP and the other ZIPCD. What is important is that what the fields represent be common to both files. Also, for the join to work correctly, their definitions (type and length) must be similar, and they must share the same **domain** (i.e., the entire list of possible values that are valid for the field in any record).

After all JOIN and JFLD specifications (each set starting with J in the Name Type field) are completed, field-level entries are coded. For the most part, the field names are the same as those defined in the underlying physical files. You must name all fields you want included in the join record format. The fields can be from any of the based-on physical files and can be in any order you wish; but if a field name is not unique, as in the case of ZIP in our example, then the JREF keyword must be coded for that field to identify, by name or number, the file from which the field value is to be taken.

PROJECTION, SELECTION, AND ACCESS PATH WITH JOIN LOGICAL FILES

Because DDS-defined join files are always equijoin (e.g. EMPPF.ZIP = ZIPPF.ZIP), usually you want to exclude at least one of the relationship-supporting fields from the join logical file record format. For example, in Figure 8.18 the ZIP field from EMPPF was included while the ZIP field from ZIPPF was not. Because a join logical file is by default an inner join, to include both fields would be redundant — they always have the same value or a join record is not selected. Typically, only certain fields from each of the participating files are projected to the join logical file. You can use any number of fields (but at least one) from the based-on physical files, depending on how the join logical file is to be used. In our example the fields DEPT, BIRTHDATE, HIREDATE, and SALARY have all been excluded.

Select/Omit entries can also be used for join logical files in much the same way as for simple logical files. The field names used for the Select/Omit operation must be part of the join logical file's record format — that is they must be listed in the field entries coded after the JOIN specifications — and can be from any of the based-on physical files. Multiple Select/Omit entries can be coded, and both AND and OR relationships can be used.

Key fields can be used with join logical files, but they must be named in the record format and must come from the primary file only. It is important to emphasize that if no key fields are specified for the join logical file and Select/Omit logic is used, the DYNSLT file-level keyword must be used. (We discussed this keyword earlier in regard to sharing access paths.) Another rule for join logical files is that regardless whether key fields are specified, if the JDFTVAL file-level keyword is used to create a left outer join (Query/400 type 2 join), the DYNSLT keyword is required. Figure 8.19 shows the DDS for a join logical file using Select/Omit to include only employees who live in Cedar Rapids or whose Zip code is in the range of 50000 to 52400.

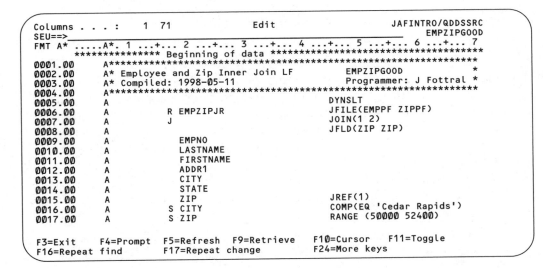

Figure 8.19

Inner Join of Employee and Zip Code files with Field Projection and Record Selection

Both CITY and ZIP are included in the record format, so both can be used for Select/Omit operations. The issue of which ZIP to use is settled by the JREF entry on line 15, so there is no ambiguity about the selection test. Because no key is specified, the DYNSLT keyword is required.

USING QUERY/400 WITH A JOIN LOGICAL FILE

A join logical file is compiled like any other file; and when the compilation is complete, you can use Query/400 to easily create a printed report or display. The Query/400 Specify File Selection screen, filled out for join logical file EMPZIPJLF1 (Figure 8.18), is shown in Figure 8.20.

Figure 8.20

Query/400 Specify File
Selection for Join
Logical File
EMPZIPJLF1

```
                                    Specify File Selection
Type choices, press Enter.  Press F9 to specify an additional
file selection.

   File . . . . . . . . .   EMPZIPJLF1      Name, F4 for list
     Library  . . . . . .       JAFINTRO__  Name, *LIBL, F4 for list
   Member . . . . . . . .   *FIRST____      Name, *FIRST, F4 for list
   Format . . . . . . . .   EMPZIPJR__      Name, *FIRST, F4 for list




F3=Exit            F4=Prompt         F5=Report          F9=Add file
F12=Cancel         F13=Layout        F24=More keys
```

Because all the important join specifications are now a part of the externally described file itself, nothing more than the file name is required here — Query/400 supplies the library and format names. After using the Edit feature of Report Column Formatting to edit the employee number and remove commas from the Zip code, function key F5 was used to examine the output. From the report screen we have used the vertical split feature (F21) of the query report to show how the join worked. In Figure 8.21 you can see the first two fields: employee number and last name to the left of the split screen, and city and state from the ZIPPF file and the Zip code from the employee file to the right.

Figure 8.21

Query Report of
EMPZIPJLF1, with Split
Screen

```
                               Display Report
                                        Report width . . . . . :      169
Position to line . . . .  ____          Shift to column . . . . . .   130_
Line    ....+....1....+....2....+ | 3....+...14....+...15....+...16....+...1
             EMPNO  LASTNAME      | City               State       ZIP
000001 111 11 0001  Slick         | Mount Ayr           IA        50854
000002 111 11 0002  Fendor        | Guthrie Center      IA        50115
000003 111 11 0003  Einstein      | Clarinda            IA        51632
000004 111 11 0004  Takahashi     | Cedar Rapids        IA        52406
000005 111 11 0005  Rachanoffski  | Cedar Rapids        IA        52402
000006 111 11 0006  Kartblanch    | Swisher             IA        52338
000007 111 11 0008  Gootch        | Pleasantville       IA        50225
000008 111 11 0009  Hunn          | Anamosa             IA        52205
000009 111 11 0010  Disney        | Amana               IA        52203
****** ********  End of report  ********
                                                              Bottom
F3=Exit       F12=Cancel       F19=Left     F20=Right     F21=No split
```

There are a couple of important things to observe about this report. First, the records of the report are presented in arrival sequence of the primary physical file. Because neither the primary physical file EMPPF nor the logical file itself uses a keyed-sequence access path, this is what you would expect. Second, not all records of the primary physical file are accounted for — Billy Badman is missing. If you recall, Billy had a Zip code that did not match any ZIPPF record, so his record was also excluded from the Query/400 type 1 (inner) join. The conclusion you might draw (and you would be correct) is that a default join logical file uses what we described in Lesson 7 as an inner join, (i.e., when a primary file record does not match at least one record of every secondary file, it is not included in the join).

You can choose an outer join operation (Query/400 type 2) for a join logical file instead of an inner join simply by including the file-level keyword JDFTVAL in the file description. Figure 8.22 shows a version of our join logical file using the JDFTVAL keyword.

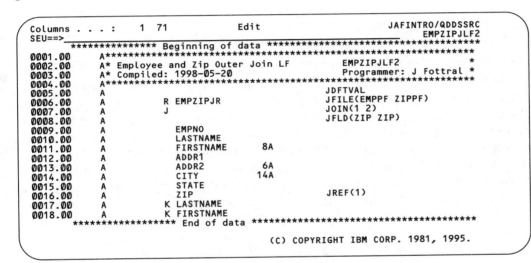

```
Columns . . . :    1  71          Edit              JAFINTRO/QDDSSRC
SEU==>                                                     EMPZIPJLF2
*************** Beginning of data ********************************
0001.00    A****************************************************************
0002.00    A* Employee and Zip Outer Join LF      EMPZIPJLF2          *
0003.00    A* Compiled: 1998-05-20                Programmer: J Fottral *
0004.00    A****************************************************************
0005.00    A                                      JDFTVAL
0006.00    A          R EMPZIPJR                   JFILE(EMPPF ZIPPF)
0007.00    A          J                            JOIN(1 2)
0008.00    A                                       JFLD(ZIP ZIP)
0009.00    A            EMPNO
0010.00    A            LASTNAME
0011.00    A            FIRSTNAME      8A
0012.00    A            ADDR1
0013.00    A            ADDR2          6A
0014.00    A            CITY          14A
0015.00    A            STATE
0016.00    A            ZIP                         JREF(1)
0017.00    A          K LASTNAME
0018.00    A          K FIRSTNAME
*************** End of data ****************************************

                        (C) COPYRIGHT IBM CORP. 1981, 1995.
```

Figure 8.22
DDS for Join Logical File Using JDFTVAL, for Left Outer Join, Keyed Sequence

In addition to the JDFTVAL keyword, some field attributes have been changed — the lengths of the FIRSTNAME, ADDR2, and CITY fields have all been shortened. Because you cannot use join logical files to change underlying physical file data, changes to field attributes made in the logical file are convenient to use to affect presentation format without causing inadvertent modifications of the data. Finally, the new file is keyed on the composite key LASTNAME plus FIRSTNAME. Remember that key fields of a join logical file must come only from the primary file.

To create a query for this new logical file, the previous query was copied and only the file specification was changed, telling it to use the new file EMPZIPJLF2. When the query runs, as you can see in Figure 8.23, the previously missing Billy Badman is included on line 7 and City and State values for that record have defaulted to spaces.

Figure 8.23

Query of EMPZIPJLF2, Outer Join with Split Display

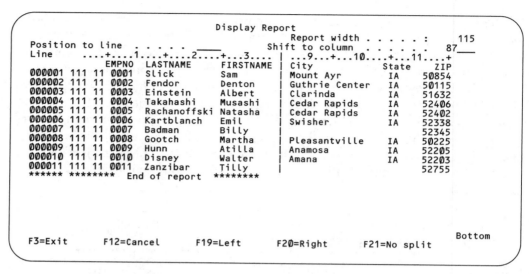

```
                                  Display Report
                                         Report width . . . . . :       115
     Position to line  . . . .    ____   Shift to column  . . . . . .    87__
     Line        ....+....1....+....2....+...3....  | ...9...+...10....+...11....+
                 EMPNO  LASTNAME       FIRSTNAME | City            State   ZIP
     000001 111 11 0001  Slick          Sam       | Mount Ayr         IA   50854
     000002 111 11 0002  Fendor         Denton    | Guthrie Center    IA   50115
     000003 111 11 0003  Einstein       Albert    | Clarinda          IA   51632
     000004 111 11 0004  Takahashi      Musashi   | Cedar Rapids      IA   52406
     000005 111 11 0005  Rachanoffski   Natasha   | Cedar Rapids      IA   52402
     000006 111 11 0006  Kartblanch     Emil      | Swisher           IA   52338
     000007 111 11 0007  Badman         Billy     |                       52345
     000008 111 11 0008  Gootch         Martha    | Pleasantville     IA   50225
     000009 111 11 0009  Hunn           Atilla    | Anamosa           IA   52205
     000010 111 11 0010  Disney         Walter    | Amana             IA   52203
     000011 111 11 0011  Zanzibar       Tilly     |                       52755
     ****** ********  End of report   ********    |

                                                                      Bottom
     F3=Exit       F12=Cancel      F19=Left      F20=Right      F21=No split
```

Billy's Zip code prints because it is taken from the primary file (JREF(1)). Also notice that a new employee, Tilly Zanzibar, has appeared in the report. Apparently her Zip code had not been added to the Zip code file and so with the natural join (no JDFTVAL keyword), her EMPPF record was not included.

Also notice that the report still appears in arrival sequence of the primary file despite the fact that the logical file was keyed. If a programmer wrote an RPG or Cobol program to randomly read records from the logical file when a user typed a last and first name on a display, the access path would function as we expect, and the proper join logical file record would be returned. Also, if the Cobol or RPG program read the entire file sequentially, the keyed-sequence access path would present the records in the order FIRSTNAME within LASTNAME. But neither Query/400 nor SQL displays records in order of a keyed-sequence access path unless sorting is selected. So to display the data as it would be presented through the access path, we have modified the new query to select sorting on our key fields. The output from that modification is shown as Figure 8.24.

If an application program sequentially accessed the join logical file with a keyed-sequence access path, this is the order in which the records would be read.

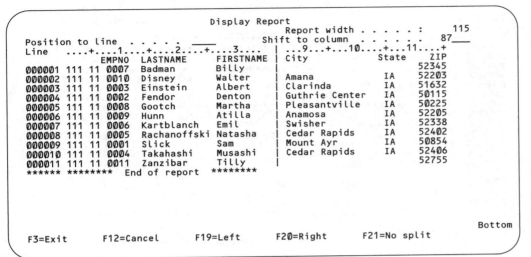

```
                        Display Report
                                    Report width . . . . . :      115
   Position to line  . . . . .   ___      Shift to column . . . . . .   87___
   Line    ....+....1....+....2....+....3....  |  ...9....+...10....+...11....+
            EMPNO   LASTNAME    FIRSTNAME  | City              State   ZIP
   000001 111 11 0007  Badman      Billy      |                           52345
   000002 111 11 0010  Disney      Walter     | Amana              IA     52203
   000003 111 11 0003  Einstein    Albert     | Clarinda           IA     51632
   000004 111 11 0002  Fendor      Denton     | Guthrie Center     IA     50115
   000005 111 11 0008  Gootch      Martha     | Pleasantville      IA     50225
   000006 111 11 0009  Hunn        Atilla     | Anamosa            IA     52205
   000007 111 11 0006  Kartblanch  Emil       | Swisher            IA     52338
   000008 111 11 0005  Rachanoffski Natasha   | Cedar Rapids       IA     52402
   000009 111 11 0001  Slick       Sam        | Mount Ayr          IA     50854
   000010 111 11 0004  Takahashi   Musashi    | Cedar Rapids       IA     52406
   000011 111 11 0011  Zanzibar    Tilly      |                           52755
   ****** ********  End of report   ********  |
                                                                    Bottom
   F3=Exit        F12=Cancel      F19=Left      F20=Right      F21=No split
```

Figure 8.24
Report of EMPZIPJLF2 (Outer Join) in Same Sort Sequence as Access Path

Joining More than Two Files

A join logical file often needs to include data from more than two files. To accomplish this, you must base the join operation on relationships among the files in a relational database. The relationships themselves are supported by the existence of common fields in the record formats of the different files. A database can consist of only two files, related by a one-to-many relationship (notated 1:n), but typically a larger number of files are involved. To illustrate, let's expand the structure of the employee/Zip code database described in Lesson 7. As we left it, the two related files were diagramed as follows:

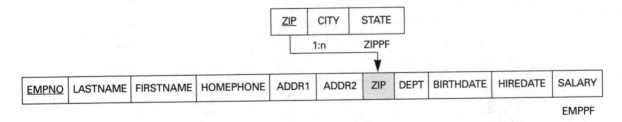

We would now like to add two new files to the database: one that identifies the different projects employees might be assigned to and another that keeps track of all current project assignments, or members of a project. Let's call the first file PRJPF; its source DDS is shown in Figure 8.25.

This file has a primary key of project code, PRJCD. The fields are all attributes of a project: the project's description, when the project started, when it's expected to finish, the project's leader, and so on. Using the column heading (COLHDG) keyword lets us use a more meaningful name as a field identifier on queries and 0 placing separate quotes around each word stacks the words of the column

Figure 8.25
DDS of Projects
Physical File

```
Columns . . . :    1  71              Browse             JAFINTRO/QDDSSRC
SEU==>_____          PRJPF
           *************** Beginning of data ********************************
0001.00    A******************************************************************
0002.00    A* Projects PF      Identifies a task having specific objectives,  *
0003.00    A*                   to which some number of employees will be as-  *
0004.00    A*                   signed for a total (estimated) number of hours.*
0005.00    A* Primary Key:      Project Code (PRJCD)                           *
0006.00    A* Compiled: 1998-06-01                          Programmer: J Fottral  *
0007.00    A******************************************************************
0008.00    A                                          UNIQUE
0009.00    A           R PRJPFR
0010.00    A             PRJCD        5A              COLHDG('Project' 'Code')
0011.00    A             PRJLDR       9S 0            COLHDG('Project' 'Leader')
0012.00    A             STRDAT       L               COLHDG('Start' 'Date')
0013.00    A             ENDDAT       L               TEXT('Need done by')
0014.00    A                                          COLHDG('Est' 'Finish' 'Date'
0015.00    A             DESC         40A             COLHDG('Description')
0016.00    A             ESTHRS       4S 0            COLHDG('Est' 'Hours')
0017.00    A           K PRJCD
           *************** End of data **********************************
```
(C) COPYRIGHT IBM CORP. 1981, 1995.

heading vertically instead of printing them side by side. Be sure to separate each quoted word by at least one space. The TEXT keyword allows for some explanation of field meaning or use. This keyword will not be printed on reports, but it is retained with the file object and can be seen, for example, by viewing the DSPFFD command output.

The second new file is the project-members physical file, PRJMBRPF. The source code for this file is shown in Figure 8.26.

Figure 8.26
DDS of Project-Member
Physical File

```
Columns . . . :    1  71              Browse             JAFINTRO/QDDSSRC
SEU==>_____         PRJMBRPF
           *************** Beginning of data ********************************
0001.00    A******************************************************************
0002.00    A* Project-Member PF    Identifies one employee's assignment to *
0003.00    A*                       one project.                           *
0004.00    A* Primary Key:          Composite of project code + employee no.*
0005.00    A* Compiled: 1998-06-01                       Programmer: J Fottral *
0006.00    A******************************************************************
0007.00    A                                          UNIQUE
0008.00    A           R PRJMBRPFR
0009.00    A             PRJCD        5A              COLHDG('Project' 'Code')
0010.00    A             EMPNO        9S 0            COLHDG('Employee' 'Number')
0011.00    A             ASDDAT       L               COLHDG('Date' 'Assigned')
0012.00    A             HRSTD        4S 0            COLHDG('Hours' 'To Date')
0013.00    A           K PRJCD
0014.00    A           K EMPNO
           *************** End of data **********************************
```
(C) COPYRIGHT IBM CORP. 1981, 1995.

The fields in file PRJMBRPF identify the participation of an employee in a project. If an employee were currently involved in five different projects, there would be five records in the file with the same employee number but different project numbers. The total number of records in this file should be the product of the number of projects multiplied by the average number of employees per project.

The project member file is keyed on two fields; project code is the high-order key, and employee number is the low-order key. Defining this composite key means an access path will be built that will allow quick lookup of employees within projects. By specifying the UNIQUE keyword, we are enforcing a primary key constraint, that only one record with a given project code and employee number can be present in the file. This prevents the error of assigning an employee to the same project twice.

If you add the new files to the diagram of the database (below), you can see how the common fields provide the connections for the relationships among files.

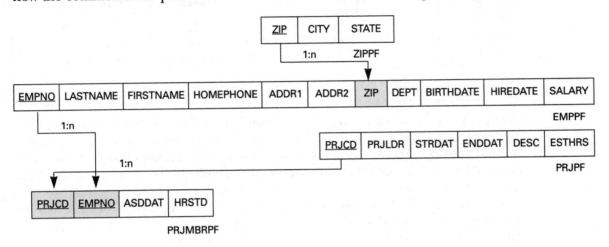

Both EMPPF and PRJPF have one-to-many relationships to the project-member file PRJMBRPF. When two parent files are both related in one-to-many relationships to the same child file, then a many-to-many (n:m) relationship must exist between the two parent files. A many-to-many relationship means that any one record of either file could be logically related to many records of the other file. In our example, one record of EMPPF, as defined by EMPNO, could be assigned to several projects, each defined by its PRJCD primary key. And likewise, one record of the project file could connect to many different employees, who are all members of that project. Notice that there are no common fields in the EMPPF and PRJPF files that can support this logical many-to-many relationship. This is, in fact, the nature of a n:m relationship; DB2/400 would be unable to extract project-member information from these two files if it were not for the presence of the PRJMBRPF file, which serves as the link between them. (Incidentally, there is a one-to-many relationship not shown in the Bachman diagram between EMPNO of EMPPF and PRJLDR of PRJPF, not to be confused with the n:m relationship described above.)

Figure 8.27 shows the DDS for a join logical file (JOINPME) that creates the linkage, through PRJMBRPF, between projects and employees.

Figure 8.27

DDS for Join File of
PRJPF, PRJMBRPF, and
EMPPF

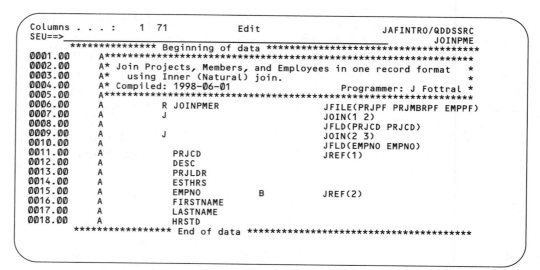

```
Columns . . . :   1  71              Edit              JAFINTRO/QDDSSRC
SEU==>_____ JOINPME
              *************** Beginning of data ********************************
0001.00    A*****************************************************************
0002.00    A* Join Projects, Members, and Employees in one record format   *
0003.00    A*   using Inner (Natural) join.                                 *
0004.00    A* Compiled: 1998-06-01                     Programmer: J Fottral *
0005.00    A*****************************************************************
0006.00    A          R JOINPMER              JFILE(PRJPF PRJMBRPF EMPPF)
0007.00    A          J                       JOIN(1 2)
0008.00    A                                  JFLD(PRJCD PRJCD)
0009.00    A          J                       JOIN(2 3)
0010.00    A                                  JFLD(EMPNO EMPNO)
0011.00    A            PRJCD                 JREF(1)
0012.00    A            DESC
0013.00    A            PRJLDR
0014.00    A            ESTHRS
0015.00    A            EMPNO       B         JREF(2)
0016.00    A            FIRSTNAME
0017.00    A            LASTNAME
0018.00    A            HRSTD
              *************** End of data ********************************
```

Because the main topic is projects, PRJPF is listed first in the JFILE values and so becomes the primary file. The JFLD keyword for the first join, between PRJPF and PRJMBRPF, establishes the project code fields of both files (PRJCD) as the relationship-supporting fields. Although it is certainly not necessary for these fields to have the same name, they "mean" the same thing in the two files, so using the same name would be appropriate. When two fields with the same name occur in the same context, they can be uniquely identified by qualification, as the JREF keyword does in line 11. The second join operation is specified on lines 9 and 10, between files PRJMBRPF and EMPPF. In this case, EMPNO is the relationship-supporting field.

The record format for logical file JOINPME includes eight fields: four from PRJPF, two from PRJMBRPF, and two from EMPPF. When no field-level attributes are provided in the logical file, all necessary information for the named fields is taken from the based-on physical files.

In the case of our join logical file, however, a slight problem exists. The second join specification uses the EMPNO fields from PRJMBRPF and EMPPF. While both fields are numeric, nine digit integers, the usage in EMPPF is binary (B) while in PRJMBRPF it is zoned decimal (S). To compare for equal values, they need to have the same usage, so in the logical file, the EMPNO from PRJMBRPF is redefined as binary. We could have redefined the EMPPF field as zoned decimal if we had been using it, but the JREF keyword tells us the join record format is using the EMPNO from PRJMBRPF, so that is the one whose usage must be redefined.

When no JDFTVAL keyword is used, the system returns a join record only when there are records in each file to satisfy the matching conditions defined by each JOIN and JFLD specification. This is an inner join or Query/400 type 1 join. For an inner join, if matching records must be present in each file, the only real significance of the primary file is that its records are read first and so become the starting point of matching to the other secondary files. In Figure 8.27, the project file, PRJPF, is not only the main topic of information, but has also been selected as the primary file because it is likely to contain the fewest records.

For an inner join, generally the file with fewest records should be made the primary file for purposes of efficiency. In our example, the process of returning join records proceeds like this:

a. The first record of the primary file is read, using arrival sequence (relative record number order) even if the physical file itself has a keyed-sequence access path. The first record is for project code Y2KCV. Data for file PRJPF, shown in arrival sequence, is shown in Figure 8.28.

```
Project     Project      Start       Est         Description                              Est
Code        Leader       Date        Finish                                               Hours
                                     Date

Y2KCV       111-11-0011  1997-03-23  1999-08-23  Make computer apps Year 2000 compliant   5,000
CLRSS       111-11-0002  1998-08-01  1998-11-15  Plan End-of-Year Clearance Sale Strategy   120
DSG99       111-11-0005  1998-08-01  1999-01-31  Develop Sales Goals for 1999                80
HDBA        111-11-0009  1998-10-01  1999-02-15  Hire a Database Administrator              120
EBUS        111-11-0013  1998-05-23  1999-05-22  Build E-Business Web site                3,600
NPADV       111-11-0010  1998-06-01  1999-02-15  New Products Advertising Campaign        1,280
RH400       111-11-0009  1998-04-15  1999-05-11  Recruit and hire AS/400 technical staff    740
URTUM       111-11-0013  1999-02-15  1999-07-04  Update, Revise Tutorials, User Manuals   1,250
VACT        111-11-0003  1999-01-01  2000-05-15  Develop Voice-activated CASE Tool        7,450

* * *  E N D   O F   R E P O R T  * * *
```

Figure 8.28

Data of the Project File PRJPF

b. Because project code is the join field, DB2/400 now attempts to find a matching project code in the related, secondary file, PRJMBRPF. Because it is searching for a specific matching value, Y2KCV, DB2/400 needs an index, a keyed-sequence access path on PRJCD. As it turns out, a suitable access path already exists because the file PRJMBRPF had a composite key of PRJCD and EMPNO. Because PRJCD is the high-order key, the existing access path works just fine. Using the access path, the first record is located with a matching project code, and that record is read from the PRJMBRPF file.

Part of PRJMBRPF, shown in sequence of its composite key, is illustrated by Figure 8.29.

Figure 8.29

Data of the Project-
Member File
PRJMBRPF

```
Project      Employee      Date          Hours
Code         Number        Assigned      To Date

CLRSS        111-11-0001   1998-09-05        20
CLRSS        111-11-0002   1998-09-01        12
CLRSS        111-11-0007   1998-08-15         6
CLRSS        111-11-0008   1998-08-05        24
DSG99        111-11-0004   1998-10-01        24
DSG99        111-11-0005   1998-10-01        20
DSG99        111-11-0006   1998-10-05        16
DSG99        111-11-0010   1998-10-12        12
EBUS         111-11-0012   1998-07-06       220
EBUS         111-11-0013   1998-05-23       445
NPADV        111-11-0002   1998-09-18         6
NPADV        111-11-0008   1998-08-01        22
NPADV        111-11-0010   1998-06-01       128
NPADV        111-11-0013   1998-07-01        55
RH400        111-11-0009   1998-04-15       118
RH400        111-11-0012   1998-07-04        36
RH400        111-11-0099   1998-09-02        46
VACT         111-11-0003   1999-01-01       388
VACT         111-11-0004   1999-03-01       244
VACT         111-11-0005   1999-01-29        12
VACT         111-11-0012   1999-02-01       245
Y2KCV        111-11-0011   1998-07-31       145
Y2KCV        111-11-0012   1998-06-01       240
Y2KCV        111-11-0013   1997-03-30       690

* * *  E N D  O F  R E P O R T  * * *
```

c. The employee number of the first matching project number record is 111-11-0011. Using that value, DB2/400 now tries to satisfy the second join condition, that employee number in the project member file equal an employee number of the employee file. Again, in matching specific values, an index is needed, and the keyed-sequence access path of EMPPF — keyed on EMPNO — is just what the system is looking for. An index search reveals a record with a key value matching the project member employee number and that record, for employee Tilly Zanzibar, is read from EMPPF. Assuming a keyed-sequence access path on employee number, the file would look like Figure 8.30 (not all fields are shown).

```
      EMPNO   LASTNAME     FIRSTNAME     DEPT          BIRTHDATE   HIREDATE

111-11-0001   Slick        Sam           Sales         1966-06-06  1992-10-01
111-11-0002   Fendor       Denton        Sales         1972-11-19  1997-03-29
111-11-0003   Einstein     Albert        Research      1909-04-25  1937-03-28
111-11-0004   Takahashi    Musashi       Research      1954-12-01  1992-03-30
111-11-0005   Rachanoffski Natasha       Sales         1960-04-16  1994-07-01
111-11-0006   Kartblanch   Emil          Sales         1947-05-15  1986-05-15
111-11-0007   Badman       Billy         Sales         1969-07-18  1997-04-15
111-11-0008   Gootch       Martha        Marketing     1935-02-21  1993-11-01
111-11-0009   Hunn         Atilla        Human Res     1940-06-17  1979-06-01
111-11-0010   Disney       Walter        Marketing     1912-10-10  1982-10-01
111-11-0011   Zanzibar     Tilly         MIS           1958-05-01  1997-01-01
111-11-0012   Stonehart    Rocky         MIS           1957-05-11  1998-06-01
111-11-0013   Deerfield    Cynthia       MIS           1966-08-02  1998-06-01

* * *  E N D  O F  R E P O R T  * * *
```

Figure 8.30
Select Data Fields of Employee File EMPPF Shown in Employee Number Key Sequence

d. Because both join conditions have been met, the first join record is assembled in the join logical file and made available to the program or utility requesting it, providing the field values from the three matched records as specified in the record format of Figure 8.27.

e. The system now returns to step b to see whether there is another Y2KCV record in the PRJMBRPF index. If so, steps c and d are repeated and another join record is assembled for the logical file. This continues until no more PRJMBRPF records with matching project codes are found. When that occurs, the system returns to step a above to read the next record of the primary file.

This loop-within-a-loop processing continues until all records of the primary file are read and all attempts to match the JFLD values are made. If there are not already keyed-sequence access paths to meet the system's need for indexes, it creates them on the fly, if the number of records in the file is large enough to warrant. Even if the employee file, EMPPF, had an arrival sequence access path, any related logical file keyed on EMPNO could supply the needed index as long as it didn't use select or omit (or, if so, specified the DYNSLT keyword).

Once the join logical file is compiled, running a query on the file is again a simple matter. Because the join operations have already been described in the file itself, and the fields have already been projected, you only need to identify the join logical file to Query/400. This is done for join logical file JOINPME in Figure 8.31, the Query/400 Specify File Selections screen.

Figure 8.31

Specify File Selections for JOINPME Query

```
                        Specify File Selections
Type choices, press Enter.  Press F9 to specify an additional
   file selection.

   File . . . . . . . . .   joinpme      Name, F4 for list
     Library  . . . . . .     JAFINTRO   Name, *LIBL, F4 for list
   Member . . . . . . . .   *FIRST       Name, *FIRST, F4 for list
   Format . . . . . . . .   *FIRST       Name, *FIRST, F4 for list




   F3=Exit              F4=Prompt         F5=Report           F9=Add file
   F12=Cancel           F13=Layout        F24=More keys
```

After the Specify Report Column Formatting feature is used to narrow column widths and edit employee numbers, the query output looks like the report shown in Figure 8.32.

Figure 8.32

Report Output of Query on JOINPME

Proj Code	Description	Project Leader	Est Hours	Employee Number	Employee Name	Hrs to Date
Y2KCV	Make computer apps Year 2000 compliant	111-11-0011	5,000	111-11-0011	T. Zanzibar	145
Y2KCV	Make computer apps Year 2000 compliant	111-11-0011	5,000	111-11-0012	R. Stonehart	240
Y2KCV	Make computer apps Year 2000 compliant	111-11-0011	5,000	111-11-0013	C. Deerfield	690
CLRSS	Plan End-of-Year Clearance Sale Strategy	111-11-0002	120	111-11-0001	S. Slick	20
CLRSS	Plan End-of-Year Clearance Sale Strategy	111-11-0002	120	111-11-0002	D. Fendor	12
CLRSS	Plan End-of-Year Clearance Sale Strategy	111-11-0002	120	111-11-0007	B. Badman	6
CLRSS	Plan End-of-Year Clearance Sale Strategy	111-11-0002	120	111-11-0008	M. Gootch	24
DSG99	Develop Sales Goals for 1999	111-11-0005	80	111-11-0004	M. Takahashi	24
DSG99	Develop Sales Goals for 1999	111-11-0005	80	111-11-0005	N. Rachanoffski	20
DSG99	Develop Sales Goals for 1999	111-11-0005	80	111-11-0006	E. Kartblanch	16
DSG99	Develop Sales Goals for 1999	111-11-0005	80	111-11-0010	W. Disney	12
EBUS	Build E-Business Web site	111-11-0013	3,600	111-11-0012	R. Stonehart	220
EBUS	Build E-Business Web site	111-11-0013	3,600	111-11-0013	C. Deerfield	445
NPADV	New Products Advertising Campaign	111-11-0010	1,280	111-11-0002	D. Fendor	6
NPADV	New Products Advertising Campaign	111-11-0010	1,280	111-11-0008	M. Gootch	22
NPADV	New Products Advertising Campaign	111-11-0010	1,280	111-11-0010	W. Disney	128
NPADV	New Products Advertising Campaign	111-11-0010	1,280	111-11-0013	C. Deerfield	55
RH400	Recruit and hire AS/400 technical staff	111-11-0009	740	111-11-0009	A. Hunn	118
RH400	Recruit and hire AS/400 technical staff	111-11-0009	740	111-11-0012	R. Stonehart	36
VACT	Develop Voice-activated CASE Tool	111-11-0003	7,450	111-11-0003	A. Einstein	388
VACT	Develop Voice-activated CASE Tool	111-11-0003	7,450	111-11-0004	M. Takahashi	244
VACT	Develop Voice-activated CASE Tool	111-11-0003	7,450	111-11-0005	N. Rachanoffski	12
VACT	Develop Voice-activated CASE Tool	111-11-0003	7,450	111-11-0012	R. Stonehart	245

```
* * *  E N D  O F  R E P O R T  * * *
```

The contents of the report show how the join logical file records have been assembled. You can see from the report that there are seven different projects, each with at least two employees assigned to it. Remember that for a record to be selected for this logical file, there must be a successful join of records from all three physical files. Records from the member file PRJMBRPF that have a project number not found in the primary file or that have an employee number not matched in the EMPPF file, would be omitted from the join logical file. But suppose there was a project with no members assigned. Because this is an inner join, a PRJPF record without a matching PRJMBRPF record would not be included in the join logical file.

Adding the JDFTVAL file-level keyword to the join logical file DDS, as shown in Figure 8.33, changes the way records are selected for the logical file.

```
Columns . . . :   1  71           Edit              JAFINTRO/QDDSSRC
SEU==>_____    JOINPMEO
          *************** Beginning of data ********************************
0001.00    A****************************************************************
0002.00    A* Join Projects, Members, and Employees in one record format   *
0003.00    A*   using Left Outer Join.                                      *
0004.00    A* Compiled: 1998-06-01                      Programmer: J Fottral *
0005.00    A****************************************************************
0006.00    A                                       JDFTVAL
0007.00    A           R JOINPMER                   JFILE(PRJPF PRJMBRPF EMPPF)
0008.00    A           J                            JOIN(1 2)
0009.00    A                                        JFLD(PRJCD PRJCD)
0010.00    A           J                            JOIN(2 3)
0011.00    A                                        JFLD(EMPNO EMPNO)
0012.00    A             PRJCD                      JREF(1)
0013.00    A             DESC
0014.00    A             PRJLDR
0015.00    A             ESTHRS
0016.00    A             EMPNO          B           JREF(2)
0017.00    A             FIRSTNAME
0018.00    A             LASTNAME
0019.00    A             HRSTD
          ***************** End of data ***************************************
                              (C) COPYRIGHT IBM CORP. 1981, 1995.
```

Figure 8.33
DDS for Outer Join,
Using JDFTVAL

By using this keyword, you are specifying a left outer join. In this case, when a primary file record is unmatched in the secondary file, it is still selected; but the missing fields are set to defaults. This lets you see any projects with no members yet assigned. Secondary file records unmatched in the primary file are still omitted.

When the same query specifications are used with the newly created logical file, the results would appear as shown in Figure 8.34.

Notice that the new report shows projects (codes HDBA and URTUM) that did not appear before. Because these project records did not match any project-member records, a join record was not selected using the inner join operation. With the left outer join, the fields from the two unmatched secondary files have been set to default values.

Also notice that the outer join report shows an additional record in the RH400 project. An employee was supposed to be a member of that project, but the incorrectly entered number (111-11-0099) of the project-member file did not match any employee file number, so the inner join did not select a join record for the missing employee. This is in accordance with the inner join rule that at least one matching record must be found in *all* secondary files. The outer join, on the other hand, selected the record but set the missing EMPPF fields (LASTNAME and FIRST-NAME) to blanks.

Figure 8.34
Query Report on
Left Outer Join
Logical File

```
Proj   Description                              Project Est      Employee  Employee            Hrs
Code                                            Leader  Hours    Number    Name                 to
                                                                                               Date

Y2KCV  Make computer apps Year 2000 compliant  111-11-0011 5,000  111-11-0011  T. Zanzibar     145
Y2KCV  Make computer apps Year 2000 compliant  111-11-0011 5,000  111-11-0012  R. Stonehart    240
Y2KCV  Make computer apps Year 2000 compliant  111-11-0011 5,000  111-11-0013  C. Deerfield    690
CLRSS  Plan End-of-Year Clearance Sale Strategy 111-11-0002   120  111-11-0001  S. Slick        20
CLRSS  Plan End-of-Year Clearance Sale Strategy 111-11-0002   120  111-11-0002  D. Fendor       12
CLRSS  Plan End-of-Year Clearance Sale Strategy 111-11-0002   120  111-11-0007  B. Badman        6
CLRSS  Plan End-of-Year Clearance Sale Strategy 111-11-0002   120  111-11-0008  M. Gootch       24
DSG99  Develop Sales Goals for 1999             111-11-0005    80  111-11-0004  M. Takahashi    24
DSG99  Develop Sales Goals for 1999             111-11-0005    80  111-11-0005  N. Rachanoffski 20
DSG99  Develop Sales Goals for 1999             111-11-0005    80  111-11-0006  E. Kartblanch   16
DSG99  Develop Sales Goals for 1999             111-11-0005    80  111-11-0010  W. Disney       12
HDBA   Hire a Database Administrator            111-11-0009   120                                0
EBUS   Build E-Business Web site                111-11-0013 3,600  111-11-0012  R. Stonehart   220
EBUS   Build E-Business Web site                111-11-0013 3,600  111-11-0013  C. Deerfield   445
NPADV  New Products Advertising Campaign        111-11-0010 1,280  111-11-0002  D. Fendor        6
NPADV  New Products Advertising Campaign        111-11-0010 1,280  111-11-0008  M. Gootch       22
NPADV  New Products Advertising Campaign        111-11-0010 1,280  111-11-0010  W. Disney      128
NPADV  New Products Advertising Campaign        111-11-0010 1,280  111-11-0013  C. Deerfield    55
RH400  Recruit and hire AS/400 technical staff  111-11-0009   740  111-11-0009  A. Hunn        118
RH400  Recruit and hire AS/400 technical staff  111-11-0009   740  111-11-0012  R. Stonehart    36
RH400  Recruit and hire AS/400 technical staff  111-11-0009   740  111-11-0099                  46
URTUM  Update, Revise Tutorials, User Manuals   111-11-0013 1,250                                0
VACT   Develop Voice-activated CASE Tool        111-11-0003 7,450  111-11-0003  A. Einstein    388
VACT   Develop Voice-activated CASE Tool        111-11-0003 7,450  111-11-0004  M. Takahashi   244
VACT   Develop Voice-activated CASE Tool        111-11-0003 7,450  111-11-0005  N. Rachanoffski 12
VACT   Develop Voice-activated CASE Tool        111-11-0003 7,450  111-11-0012  R. Stonehart   245

* * * E N D   O F   R E P O R T * * *
```

A more useful query of the join logical file might include a control break to separate projects, and perhaps a summary function to total the hours spent so far on each project by its members. Also, if the report break includes all four primary file fields together as break level 1 (Figure 8.35), **group indication** can be used in printing the report.

Figure 8.35
Query/400 Define
Report Breaks for Join

```
                              Define Report Breaks

Type break level (1-6) for up to 9 field names, press Enter.
  (Use as many fields as needed for each break level.)

Break    Sort
Level    Prty   Field        Text                          Len   Dec
  1             PRJCD        Project Code                    5
  1             DESC         Description                    40
  1             PRJLDR       Project Leader                  9     0
  1             ESTHRS       Est Hours                       4     0
  _             EMPNO        Employee Number                 9     0
  _             FIRSTNAME                                   10
  _             LASTNAME                                    12
  _             HRSTD        Hours To Date                   4     0




                                                                    Bottom
F3=Exit        F5=Report      F10=Process/previous   F11=Display names only
F12=Cancel     F13=Layout     F18=Files              F23=Long comment
```

When you use group indication, the control field values print on only the first line of a new report control group. On subsequent lines the values are replaced by spaces. This generally makes a report easier to read.

When the modified query is used to create a report of the outer join logical file, the appearance of the report is quite different. Figure 8.36 shows the modified report with page breaks and summary function.

```
                    Projects, Members, and Hours-to-Date

Project Description                      Project  Est    Employee    Employee           Hours
Code                                     Leader   Hours  Number      Name               to
                                                                                        Date

Y2KCV Make computer apps Year 2000 compliant   111-11-0011  5,000  111-11-0011  T. Zanzibar      145
                                                                   111-11-0012  R. Stonehart     240
                                                                   111-11-0013  C. Deerfield     690

                                                                           Hours for Y2KCV
                                                                                 TOTAL   1,075

CLRSS Plan End-of-Year Clearance Sale Strategy  111-11-0002   120  111-11-0001  S. Slick          20
                                                                   111-11-0002  D. Fendor         12
                                                                   111-11-0007  B. Badman          6
                                                                   111-11-0008  M. Gootch         24

                                                                           Hours for CLRSS
                                                                                 TOTAL      62

DSG99 Develop Sales Goals for 1999              111-11-0005    80  111-11-0004  M. Takahashi      24
                                                                   111-11-0005  N. Rachanoffski   20
                                                                   111-11-0006  E. Kartblanch     16
                                                                   111-11-0010  W. Disney         12

                                                                           Hours for DSG99
                                                                                 TOTAL      72

HDBA  Hire a Database Administrator             111-11-0009   120                             0

                                                                           Hours for HDBA
                                                                                 TOTAL       0

EBUS  Build E-Business Web site                 111-11-0013 3,600  111-11-0012  R. Stonehart     220
                                                                   111-11-0013  C. Deerfield     445

                                                                           Hours for EBUS
                                                                                 TOTAL     665
- - - - - - - - - - - - - - - - - - - - - - - - - - - - - - - - - - - - - - - - - - - - -
NPADV New Products Advertising Campaign         111-11-0010 1,280  111-11-0002  D. Fendor          6
                                                                   111-11-0008  M. Gootch         22
                                                                   111-11-0010  W. Disney        128
                                                                   111-11-0013  C. Deerfield      55

                                                                           Hours for NPADV
                                                                                 TOTAL     211

RH400 Recruit and hire AS/400 technical staff   111-11-0009   740  111-11-0009  A. Hunn          118
                                                                   111-11-0012  R. Stonehart      36
                                                                   111-11-0099                    46

                                                                           Hours for RH400
                                                                                 TOTAL     200

URTUM Update, Revise Tutorials, User Manuals    111-11-0013 1,250                             0
                                                                           Hours for URTUM
                                                                                 TOTAL       0

VACT  Develop Voice-activated CASE Tool         111-11-0003 7,450  111-11-0003  A. Einstein      388
                                                                   111-11-0004  M. Takahashi     244
                                                                   111-11-0005  N. Rachanoffski   12
                                                                   111-11-0012  R. Stonehart     245

                                                                           Hours for VACT
                                                                                 TOTAL     889

                                                                           FINAL TOTALS


  * * *   E N D   O F   R E P O R T   * * *
```

Figure 8.36

Query/400 Report of Left Outer Join Logical File, with Control Breaks

You can see how conveniently join logical files can present data from several related physical files; but as we mentioned earlier, join logical files do not let you update data records in the based-on physical files. However, it would be convenient to associate related records, such as projects and project members, when you add new records or update existing records. The third type of logical file, multiple-format logical files, provides this capability.

MULTIPLE-FORMAT LOGICAL FILES

Multiple-format logical files let you display or update related records from two or more physical files. These files specify a different record format for each of the based-on physical files — unlike join logical files, which combine the fields of related files into a single record format. Multiple-format logical files must specify key fields, and at least the higher order fields of composite keys must be common in each of the different record formats. DB2/400 merges records from the different physical files according to the values of these common key fields. This merging operation establishes the relationship between records of the different files and determines the access order of records. Records with matching key values are arranged first in the order in which the files are specified within the multiple-format logical file. If there are duplicate records within one record format, a file-level keyword telling how to process duplicate keys, such as FIFO (first in, first out), can be used.

Figure 8.37 shows DDS for a multiple-format logical file using the project (PRJPF) and project-members (PRJMBRPF) physical files.

Figure 8.37

Project/Project-Member Multiple-Format Logical File DDS

```
 Columns . . . :    1  71            Edit              JAFINTRO/QDDSSRC
 SEU==>_____     PRJMBRMFLF
        *************** Beginning of data ********************************
0001.00      A**********************************************************************
0002.00      A* Projects and Members multiple record format LF                    *
0003.00      A*    Combines project records and member records in one file.       *
0004.00      A* Compiled: 1998-06-01                      Programmer: J Fottral *
0005.00      A**********************************************************************
0006.00      A            R PRJPFR                 PFILE(PRJPF)
0007.00      A            K PRJCD
0008.00      A*
0009.00      A            R PRJMBRPFR              PFILE(PRJMBRPF)
0010.00      A            K PRJCD
0011.00      A            K EMPNO
        *************** End of data **************************************


                                    (C) COPYRIGHT IBM CORP. 1981, 1995.
```

Notice that both record-level entries (lines 6 and 9) use the same record format names as the physical files, and that no field-level entries are coded. This tells DB2/400 to include all fields with attributes unchanged. Each record format also names the physical file it is based on in the PFILE keyword value. The key field for the PRJPF record format is project code; for the PRJMBRPF record format, it is project code and, within project code, employee number. The important point here is that the project code key is common to both records and is in the same relative (high-order) position.

When the file is created, an access path that orders all records by their key field values is built. This access path is used to pull records from their based-on physical files as the multiple-format logical file is read by an application or utility. The first file serves as a primary file and is usually the parent file in a one-to-many relationship. In Figure 8.37, PRJPF is the primary file and its key field PRJCD is the primary key in the based-on physical file. The second file, PRJMBRPF is a child or dependent file of PRJPF and there may be zero, one, or many project-member records for each PRJCD value of the project file. **Referential integrity** dictates that all project member records have PRJCD values already existing in the parent file. So when the multiple-format logical file is read, the first record should be a project record (primary file) with the lowest key. The next record should be a project-member record with a matching project code. If there are several employees assigned to the project, all of their records with the same project code would be read from the project-member file before another record is read from the project file. The group of project-member records with the same project code appears in the logical file in order of employee number.

The following example should help illustrate this file merge operation. Assume records in the project (P) and project-member (PM) files are as shown and in key sequence.

PRJPF file (P)	PRJMBRPF file (PM)		Multiple-format logical file	
CLRSS...	CLRSS	002...	(P) CLRSS...	
DSG99...	CLRSS	011...	(PM) CLRSS	002...
EBUS...	EBUS	009...	(PM) CLRSS	011...
	EBUS	011...	(P) DSG99...	
	EBUS	012...	(P) EBUS...	
			(PM) EBUS	009...
			(PM) EBUS	011...
			(PM) EBUS	012...

Notice that the EBUS record from the (P) file immediately follows the DSG99 record also from the (P) file. This occurs because — in this example — no project members have been assigned to project DSG99. Unlike in join logical files, all records from both (or all) files are included in the multiple-format logical file, even if they have unmatched keys in another file.

When this multiple-format logical file is compiled, you can access the data through a temporary DFU using the logical file. Because data already exists in the underlying physical files, the DFU comes up in change mode, prompting for a project code of the PRJPFR record format. If we page down, the first record of that format is displayed in key sequence. Figure 8.38 shows the appearance of the DFU screen after you press the Page down key once. The record formats are identified in the upper left corner of the screen.

Figure 8.38
First Record Format
PRJPFR, Temporary
DFU on PRJMBRMFLF

```
WORK WITH DATA IN A FILE                    Mode . . . . :   CHANGE
Format . . . . :   PRJPFR                    File . . . . :   PRJMBRMFLF

Project Code:      CLRSS
Project Leader:    111110002
Start Date:        1998-08-01
Est Finish Date:   1998-11-15
Description:       Plan End-of-Year Clearance Sale Strategy
Est Hours:         120




F3=Exit                 F5=Refresh              F6=Select format
F9=Insert               F10=Entry               F11=Change
```

If you page down again (Figure 8.39), you see a record from the PRJMBRPFR format, with the same project code and the lowest employee number assigned to that project.

Figure 8.39
First Project-Member
Record, Format
PRJMBRPFR, for
Project CLRSS

```
WORK WITH DATA IN A FILE                    Mode . . . . :   CHANGE
Format . . . . :   PRJMBRPFR                 File . . . . :   PRJMBRMFLF

Project Code:      CLRSS
Employee Number:   111110002
Date Assigned:     1998-09-01
Hours To Date:     12




F3=Exit                 F5=Refresh              F6=Select format
F9=Insert               F10=Entry               F11=Change
```

Because the DFU is already in Change mode, you could update this record by tabbing to the Hours to Date field, changing it, and pressing Enter (or Page down) to save the change. You can also make changes to the PRJPFR records when they are displayed; and you don't need to rely only upon Page up/Page down to locate records. You can directly retrieve a project record by entering its key value in the Project Code entry field. Figure 8.40 shows a prompt screen with VACT entered as the project code.

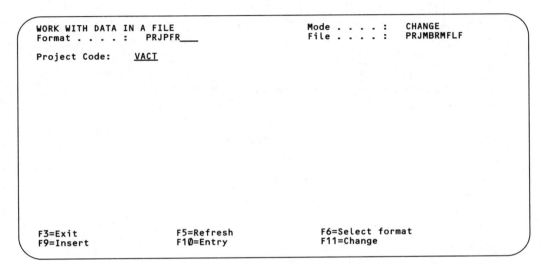

```
WORK WITH DATA IN A FILE            Mode . . . . :    CHANGE
Format . . . . :    PRJPFR___       File . . . . :    PRJMBRMFLF

   Project Code:    VACT




   F3=Exit            F5=Refresh          F6=Select format
   F9=Insert          F10=Entry           F11=Change
```

Figure 8.40

Prompt for Project Record with VACT Entered

When you press Enter, the project record of that code is displayed (Figure 8.41).

```
WORK WITH DATA IN A FILE            Mode . . . . :    CHANGE
Format . . . . :    PRJPFR          File . . . . :    PRJMBRMFLF

   Project Code:    VACT
   Project Leader:  111110003
   Start Date:      1999-01-01
   Est Finish Date: 2000-05-15
   Description:     Develop Voice-activated CASE Tool
   Est Hours:       7450




   F3=Exit            F5=Refresh          F6=Select format
   F9=Insert          F10=Entry           F11=Change
```

Figure 8.41

Project Record for VACT Displayed

From here, pressing Page down displays the project member records of that project in order by employee number, from low to high.

At any time, you can enter a new record of either format by pressing F9 when a current record of the desired format is displayed. The current record format is shown in the upper left corner of the DFU screen, and you can change it by pressing F6. When you use F10 to enter new records, the entry screen displayed is for the record format currently selected by the F6 function.

Because the multiple-format logical file uses a keyed-sequence access path, newly entered records are presented within the file by key sequence, regardless whether the insert or the entry function was used to add them to the file.

From this brief introduction you should have an idea of the power and flexibility of logical files for organizing and accessing data stored in the AS/400 database. There is much more to learn about logical files then we can possibly cover here; if you can't wait for your database management class, you can find about 1,000 pages of additional material in the IBM manuals *Database Guide* (SC41-9659) and *Data Description Specifications Reference* (SC41-9620).

Key Terms

access path

arrival sequence

compile listing

composite key

domain

duplicate key

group indication

join logical files

key field

keyed-sequence

logical file

physical file

primary key

referential integrity

response time

simple logical file

throughput

views

volatility

INTRODUCTION

In this lab, you begin by creating a simple logical file over the physical file STUPF, which you created in previous labs. Instead of keying in new DDS for this logical file, you copy the DDS source of the original physical file and modify it for the logical file. The new logical file will use a keyed-sequence access path, projection, and selection. It will also change field attributes of an existing field.

Lab 8

After completing this lab, you will be able to use PDM to copy a source file member, use SEU to edit the copied member creating DDS for a new logical file, use PDM to compile the new logical file description, and use DFU to browse through the file and add new records.

An error in the initial file description will cause the first compile to fail, providing an opportunity to examine the job log and compile listing to find the error. An additional lab exercise provides more practice in creating physical and logical files, and in setting up a query on a join logical file.

Part 1

Goals	Copy the DDS source code of STUPF Change the copied DDS to create a new logical file, STULF1 Save the changes
Start at	WRKOBJPDM, your library
Procedure	Work with object QDDSSRC Copy member STUPF to STULF1 Edit STULF1 Exit and save

1.1. Start PDM and Work with all objects in your library. From the Work with Objects Using PDM screen, take option 12 on your DDS source physical file.

1.2. From the Work with Members Using PDM screen, use the PDM option to copy member STUPF to a new member within QDDSSRC. Call the new member STULF1.

1.2a. After the copy option is executed, what message is displayed?

1.3. From the Work with Members Using PDM screen, you should now see member STULF1. What is its type? Using the Tab or Field advance key, move the cursor to the Type entry and change the type of STULF1 to LF, then press Enter. If the Type field is not an input-permitted field, press F18 from the Work with Members Using PDM screen to change PDM defaults. By typing Y in the Change type and text entry field, you should be able to change the member type of STULF1 from PF to LF. If you are not able to, the change can be made from within SEU.

1.4. Take the option to edit STULF1. From the SEU work screen, place the cursor anywhere on the Record format line and press F4.

1.4a. What happens?
1.4b. According to the prompter information above the entry fields, what is the prompt type?

If the prompt type is not LF, you need to use F13 to change session defaults, and from that screen change the source type to LF, then press Enter before continuing.

1.5. You should now see a screen like the one shown in Figure 8.42.

Figure 8.42
SEU Work Screen with
Prompted Line

```
Columns . . . :    1  71              Edit                      JSMITH/QDDSSRC
SEU==> _____
FMT LF  .....A..........T.Name++++++.Len++TDpB......Functions+++++++++++++++++++       STULF1
       *************** Beginning of data ******************************************
0001.00     A          R STUPFR
0002.00     A            SOCSEC       9S 0
0003.00     A            FNAME       15A
0004.00     A            LNAME       20A
0005.00     A            PHONE       10S 0
0006.00     A            ADDR1       25A
0007.00     A            ADDR2       25A
0008.00     A            ZIP          5S 0
       ***************** End of data ********************************************
Prompt type . . .  LF        Sequence number . . .  0001.00

Name
Type        Name          Length      Data     Decimal
  R         STUPFR____                 Type     Positions       Use
                          _____       _        ____            _
Functions

_____

F3=Exit    F4=Prompt    F5=Refresh          F11=Previous record
F12=Cancel              F23=Select prompt   F24=More keys
```

The cursor will be on the Name Type field, and the prompt type should be LF. Move the cursor to the Functions field using the New line key. Type in PFILE(STUPF) and press Enter. PFILE is a record-level keyword that identifies the physical file on which the logical file will be built.

1.6. Press the Refresh or Cancel function key to exit prompting. Position the cursor in the sequence number area of the **** Beginning of Data ***** line and type IP and Enter to insert a line with prompting just before line 1.00, the record format line.

1.7. The new first line will contain only a file-level keyword, UNIQUE. This specifies that the keys for this file must all be unique values; no duplicate keys will be permitted. Key UNIQUE in the function field and press Enter.

1.7a. What sequence number is given to the new line?

The COLHDG function lets you use a more descriptive identifier than the field name for fields appearing on DFU screens and Query/400 reports. If you don't provide a COLHDG value, the field name is used by the DDS compiler.

1.8. Press Refresh again. Move the cursor to the SOCSEC line and prompt again. Type in COLHDG('Social' 'Security') at the function field and press Enter. Remember that DDS keywords must be in uppercase. Be sure to leave at least one space between the two quoted words.

If you are unable to enter lowercase letters, find the function key for Change Session Defaults. The Change Session Defaults screen is shown as Figure 8.43.

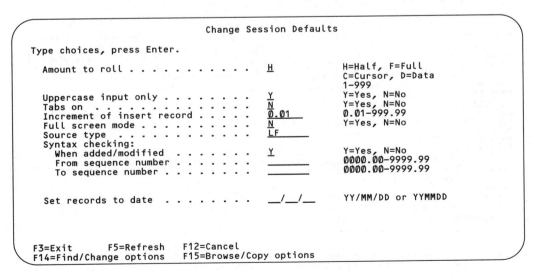

Figure 8.43
Change Session Defaults Screen

On this screen, change the Uppercase input only value to allow lowercase entry. Then press Enter. When you return to the editor, the display will show that the line you were working on is in error. (Errors are displayed in reverse image.) You can correct the error by prompting and finishing the column heading field.

Give appropriate column headings of First Name, Last Name, Address Line 1, and Address Line 2 to the respective fields, skipping the PHONE field.

Change the length of both the ADDR1 and ADDR2 fields to 20. Logical files can change certain field-level attributes of the based-on physical file fields. If, for example, the applications using the logical file placed tighter length restrictions on fields, those restrictions could be imposed once in the logical file description instead of in each application program. Of course, existing data in the physical file might be truncated if the field is shortened in the logical file; but the database administrator would anticipate this, and it should *not* result in mapping problems or a system-level error.

For fields whose length or type attribute you aren't changing, using only the field name would be enough to compile the DDS. The compiler uses the same attributes for each named field as defined in the physical file. Because we copied the physical file DDS to modify for the logical file, the length and type attributes are already there, and it's not necessary to erase them.

If you misspell key words, the SEU editor flags them and shows you the incorrect field in reverse image on the prompt line. If that happens, correct the error and press Enter. Remember that function keywords (e.g., COLHDG) must be capitalized.

1.9. Delete the PHONE field from the source DDS.

1.10. Insert with prompting after the ZIP field. At this point you will intentionally introduce an error into the DDS source code.

On the first inserted line, declare a Select operation (S for the Name Type field) for the ZIP field. (The previously defined Field name you are using for the Select goes in the S record's Name field.) In the functions field, enter an appropriate keyword to select records that have local Zip codes (e.g., all Zip codes with the same first two digits as those of your school or company). There is more than one way to do this, but for this lab, use the keyword that correctly specifies the select operation with only one line of DDS code.

1.10a. How could you code this selection using a different keyword (and two lines of code)?

Insert the select line, then on the next prompt declare a key field (Name type K) and name SOCSEC as the key (in the Name field). Press Enter.

1.11. Exit prompting (F5 or F12) and page up to the top of the screen. Check your work. The file-level keyword UNIQUE must be first, followed by the record format line, which now contains the PFILE keyword. The select and key fields should be last. Your source file should now look like Figure 8.44, except the Range values for the ZIP field will be different unless you live in eastern Iowa.

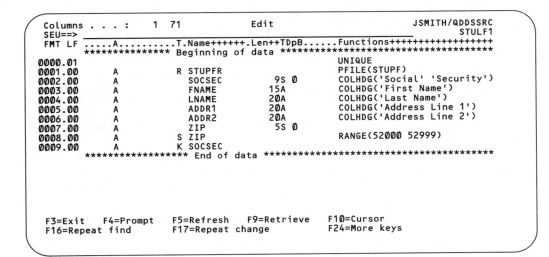

Figure 8.44
DDS for Logical File with Intentional Error

1.12. Exit SEU and save the updated member for STULF1.

    1.12a. What message displays on the bottom of the PDM screen to which you returned?

Part 2

Goals	Invoke the CRTLF command using the PDM option Find the Access Path Maintenance parameter Find and display the job log Find and display the spooled file of the compile listing Determine the cause of the compile failure
Start at	WRKMBRPDM, your library/QDDSSRC
Procedure	Prompt with option 14 on STULF1 Find the Access Path Maintenance parameter and read the context Help Compile STULF1 WRKSPLF to find the job log and compile listing Correct the DDS error and recompile

2.1. From the Work with Members Using PDM screen, compile the source logical file using option 14. Type 14 on the option line beside STULF1 and prompt.

    2.1a. What command did option 14 invoke?

Notice the current parameter values for File (the logical file to be created), Source file, and Source member. The values were supplied from the Work with Members Using PDM list processing screen for the option (14) taken for the particular source type (LF). You can change the new object name or library if you don't want the new logical file object to have the same name as the source member; you would simply overtype the file name.

    2.1b. Find the parameter for access path maintenance. To what value is it set?
    2.1c. What are the other two possible values for this parameter, and what is the difference between them?
    2.1d. Under what condition must the default value of this parameter be used?

2.2. Press Enter from the CRTLF command prompt screen and observe the message that appears after you run the command. Remember that option 14 submits (sends) the CRT*xxx* command to the batch subsystem, QBATCH. This lets you perform other requests and run commands interactively from your workstation while the compile (CRT*xxx*) runs in the background.
    When the compile completes, a message will be waiting in your message queue. Your terminal will beep at you when a message enters your message queue and no other message is already waiting. (If there are already unattended messages in your message queue, the torn form symbol or MW in reverse image appears on the status line.) Display the message.

    2.2a. What does the message say?

    Return to a command line.

2.3. When a submitted job, such as a program or DDS source compile, ends abnormally, two print files are created and sent to output queues. Enter the WRKSPLF command (or PDM option SP) to examine them. They should be the last two files listed: one named STULF1 in your output queue and the other named QPJOBLOG in the QEZJOBLOG output queue. The latter is a specially designated output queue for holding job logs — normally only of failed jobs.
    If you cannot find a QPJOBLOG file, it may be because you are using *BASIC assistance level. If so, use F21 to change the assistance level to intermediate. If you have more than one QPJOBLOG file in your list, use F11 to find the one most recently created by comparing the dates and times shown in View 2 (the one you are looking for should be the last spooled file in the queue).

2.4. Display the job log. On an 80-character display screen it is hard to read because it extends to 132 print positions. The F20 key shifts your view one screen to the right but often that doesn't make it easier to read the screen. Try it now to see how it looks. Use F19 to shift left again.

You can display one print line at a time, folded to two display lines, by using the F11 key and then paging down to display each next line. Try that now. If you looked far enough you might find the information you need, but the folded line is not very easy to read, either. Press F11 again to remove folding.

Another possibility is to shift the view a specified number of display/print positions to the right or left by using a Control command. If the cursor is not there, move it up to the Control field and press Help. Read the syntax summary for Control commands. You could use either absolute or relative windowing to shift the view to begin at column 36. When you are finished reading, exit Help and enter the command to window to column 36 on the Control input field. Page down to the error messages. Your screen should now look like Figure 8.45.

```
                          Print Key Output                          Page   1
      5716SS1 V3R6M0 950929              S1018A6G        05/30/98   17:47:32

      Display Device  . . . . . :  USERS1
      User  . . . . . . . . . . :  JSMITH

                            Display Spooled File
      File  . . . . . :  QPJOBLOG              Page/Line   1/21
      Control . . . . .   W36                  Columns     36 - 113
      Find  . . . . . :
      ....4....+....5....+....6....+....7....+....8....+....9....+....0....+....1...
          CCSID(65535) SRTSEQ(*N/*HEX) LANGID(ENU) CNTRYID(US).
           05/30/98   17:39:52   QWTSCSBJ              *N        QCMD        Q
        Message . . . . . :  -    CRTLF   FILE(JSMITH/STULF1)   SRCFILE(JSMITH/QDDSSRC
         SRCMRB(STULF1)
      30   05/30/98   17:39:53   QDDCLF       QSYS      126A      QCMD        Q
        Message . . . . :   Errors in DDS not allowed with specified GENLVL.
        Cause . . . . . :   Either the severity level of the errors found in DDS was
         greater than or equal to the error generation level (GENLVL parameter), or
         GENLVL(0) was specified. Recovery  . . . :   See the DDS source listing fo
         the GENLVL value and error messages. Either correct the errors or change
         the GENLVL value on the command, and then try the request again.
      40   05/30/98   17:39:54   QDDCLF       QSYS      12E6      QCMD        Q
        Message . . . . :   File STULF1 not created in library JSMITH.
        Cause . . . . . :   The file was not created because of errors.  Recovery .
         . :  See the error messages previously listed.  Correct the errors, and
         then try the request again.
                                                                    More...
      F3=Exit    F12=Cancel   F19=Left    F20=Right   F24=More keys
```

Figure 8.45

Job Log Display Windowed to Right (Second Page)

The error messages should be much easier to read now. If you scan through them, you will see a message to the effect that the file (STULF1) was not created because of severe errors that occurred during the create operation. In effect, the job log tells you the compile failed. Return to the WRKSPLF list when you are finished.

2.5. Because you are now finished with it, delete the QPJOBLOG print file. As a general rule, try to keep print files from "gathering dust" in output queues. If your job fails, find the job log, take any information you need from it, then get rid of it.

2.6. Display the compile listing for file STULF1. The first page of identification information is taken from the CRTLF command parameter values and current compiler options. Page down and the second page lists the DDS source. You should now see a screen like Figure 8.46.

Figure 8.46

Compile Listing of STULF1, Second Page

```
                         Print Key Output                                Page   1
      5716SS1 V3R6M0 950929                 S1018A6G           05/30/98  18:07:08

      Display Device  . . . . . :  USERS1
      User  . . . . . . . . . :  JSMITH


                                    Display Spooled File
      File  . . . . . :   STULF1                        Page/Line   1/19
      Control . . . . .                                 Columns     1 - 78
      Find  . . . . . .
      *...+....1....+....2....+....3....+....4....+....5....+....6....+....7....+...
                                        Data Description Source
        SEQNBR   *...+....1....+....2....+....3....+....4....+....5....+....6....+....
          100      A                                          UNIQUE
          200      A            R STUPFR                       PFILE(STUPF)
      *       CPD7956-**********
          300      A              SOCSEC         9S 0          COLHDG('Social' 'Security
          400      A              FNAME         15A            COLHDG('First' 'Name')
          500      A              LNAME         20A            COLHDG('Last' 'Name')
          600      A              ADDR1         20A            COLHDG('Address Line 1')
          700      A              ADDR2         20A            COLHDG('Address Line 2')
          800      A              ZIP            5S 0          COLHDG('Zip')
          900      A            S ZIP                          RANGE(52000 52999)
         1000      A            K SOCSEC
      *              CPD7913-*
                          * * * * *  E N D   O F   S O U R C E   * * * * *
      5716SS1 V3R6M0  950929             Data Description              JSMITH
                                                                      More...
      F3=Exit    F12=Cancel    F19=Left    F20=Right    F24=More keys
```

Notice the asterisk (*) on the far left of the listing, which indicates an error. The error code follows. You should see the error codes CPD7956 and CPD7913. Error codes have messages associated with them and you need to find these messages.

Page down until you can see the error messages under End of Expanded Source. Change the window through the Control field to view the complete error message text. You should be able to read the text as shown in Figure 8.47.

The error message for CPD7913 says, "Type of specification not valid…" and this error was really caused by the second error. The second error message, for CPD7956, tells us that the select or omit field was specified incorrectly. While a little more informative than the job log, this error message still doesn't really tell us *what* was incorrect about the select statement.

2.7. Return to the Work with Members Using PDM screen and edit the source for STULF1. From the SEU edit screen, find and press the function key for Browse/Copy options. Your screen should look like the one in Figure 8.48.

```
                   Print Key Output                        Page   1
      5716SS1 V3R6MØ 950929          S1Ø18A6G       Ø5/3Ø/98  18:Ø9:18

      Display Device . . . . . :  USERS1
      User . . . . . . . . . :  JSMITH

                         Display Spooled File
  File . . . . . :  STULF1              Page/Line   2/4
  Control . . . .  W33                  Columns     33 - 110
  Find . . . . .
  ..+....4....+....5....+....6....+....7....+....8....+....9...+....0....+....1
                                                   Field       Buffer p
  .+....3....+....4....+....5....+....6....+....7....+....8 length       Out
                     UNIQUE
  D   O F  E X P A N D E D  S O U R C E  * * * * *
           Data Description          JSMITH/STULF1         5/30/98  18:06
              Messages

  Message . . . . :   Type of specification not valid or out of sequence.
  Message . . . . :   Select or omit field specified incorrectly.
           Data Description          JSMITH/STULF1         5/30/98  18:06
           Message Summary
           Warning        Error        Severe
           (10-19)        (20-29)      (30-99)
              0              0             2
  Message . . . . :   File STULF1 not created in library JSMITH.
  *  E N D   O F   C O M P I L A T I O N  * * * * *
                                                          Bottom

  F3=Exit   F12=Cancel    F19=Left    F20=Right    F24=More keys
```

Figure 8.47
Compile Listing
Windowed to Show
Error Message Text

```
                   Print Key Output                        Page   1
      5716SS1 V3R6MØ 950929          S1Ø18A6G       Ø5/3Ø/98  18:27:33

      Display Device . . . . . :  USERS1
      User . . . . . . . . . :  JSMITH

                         Browse/Copy Options

  Type choices, press Enter.

     Selection . . . . . . . . . .   1          1=Member
                                                2=Spool file
                                                3=Output queue
     Copy all records . . . . . .   N          Y=Yes, N=No
     Browse/copy member . . . . .   STULF1     Name, F4 for list
        File . . . . . . . . . .   QDDSSRC     Name, F4 for list
        Library . . . . . . . .    JSMITH      Name, *CURLIB, *LIBL

     Browse/copy spool file . . . .  STULF1    Name, F4 for list
        Job . . . . . . . . . . .   STULF1     Name
        User . . . . . . . . . .    JSMITH     Name, F4 for list
        Job number . . . . . . .    *LAST      Number, *LAST
        Spool number . . . . . .    *LAST      Number, *LAST, *ONLY

     Display output queue . . . . .  QPRINT    Name, *ALL
        Library . . . . . . . . .   *LIBL       Name *CURLIB, *LIBL

  F3=Exit      F4=Prompt      F5=Refresh       F12=Cancel
  F13=Change session defaults   F14=Find/Change options
```

Figure 8.48
SEU Browse/Copy
Options Screen

Browse/Copy options provide a convenient way find compile errors and correct the offending source code at the same time. It uses a split screen format that lets you move easily from the source code to the compile listing. The options screen in Figure 8.48 gives you three choices: you can browse/copy another member of a source file, you can browse a spooled file, or you can get to a work with output queue screen. We want to examine the spooled file created by the attempted compile of STULF1, so we want option 2.

Notice that the input fields for each option have already been filled in with substitution values provided by SEU. Because you are editing STULF1, SEU assumes you want to examine the spooled file of the same name — the compile listing. A job name is also needed to identify a particular spooled file, and SEU assumes compiles are submitted to QBATCH (the PDM option 14 default) thereby causing the batch job name to be taken from the name of the program or file being compiled — in our example, once again STULF1. Jane Smith is the user who is signed on, so SEU takes the interactive job's user ID (JSMITH) for this value. Finally the job and spool file number are assumed to be most recent (*LAST).

Whenever you want to browse the spooled listing of a batch-submitted file or program compile, the only thing you should have to change on the Browse/Copy Options screen is the Selection. Change that to 2 now and press Enter.

2.8.   You should now see the SEU split screen similar to Figure 8.49.

Figure 8.49

SEU Split Screen with Spooled File for Failed Compile

```
                          Print Key Output                          Page   1
     5716SS1 V3R6M0 950929              S1018A6G         05/30/98  18:54:04

     Display Device . . . . . :  USERS1
     User . . . . . . . . . . :  JSMITH

     Columns . . . :   1  71          Edit                   JSMITH/QDDSSRC
     SEU==>_____
                                                                     STULF1
     FMT LF .....A...........T.Name++++++.Len++TDpB......Functions+++++++++++++++++++
            ************** Beginning of data *********************************
     0001.00    A                                     UNIQUE
     0002.00    A       R STUPFR                       PFILE(STUPF)
     0003.00    A         SOCSEC       9S 0            COLHDG('Social' 'Security')
     0004.00    A         FNAME        15A             COLHDG('First' 'Name')
     0005.00    A         LNAME        20A             COLHDG('Last' 'Name')
     0006.00    A         ADDR1        20A             COLHDG('Address Line 1')

     Columns . . . :   1  71          Browse       Spool file . . :     STULF1
     SEU==>_____
            ************** Beginning of data *********************************
     0000.01    5716SS1 V3R6M0  950929              Data Description
     0000.02    File name . . . . . . . . . . . . . . . . . . . . :  STULF1
     0000.03      Library name . . . . . . . . . . . . . . . . . :  JSMITH
     0000.04    File attribute . . . . . . . . . . . . . . . . . :  Logical
     0000.05    Source file containing DDS . . . . . . . . . . . :  QDDSSRC
     0000.06      Library name . . . . . . . . . . . . . . . . . :  JSMITH

     F3=Exit    F4=Prompt    F5=Refresh    F9=Retrieve   F11=Toggle   F12=Cancel
     F16=Repeat find        F17=Repeat change           F24=More keys
```

Notice that your source code is still in an Edit session in the upper screen while the beginning of the compile listing is in a Browse session in the lower screen. SEU Copy or Block Copy line commands can be used to copy single or blocks of lines from the Browse session to the Edit session, but that won't be necessary now.

The SEU command F *ERR can be used to locate compile errors. F is the abbreviated version of FIND and *ERR means any compile error. The cursor should be on the Browse session's SEU command line. If not, position it there and type F *ERR.

2.8a. What displays on the message line?

You should see the same message that you saw before when you displayed the compile listing in your output queue.

2.9. SEU lets you get more descriptive information about the message, the second-level message text.

Move the cursor down to the error message on the message line. (The message should display in white on color monitors). Now press F1 for Help.

You should now see the screen for Additional Message Information for message CPD7956. This screen should look like Figure 8.50.

```
                    Print Key Output                        Page   1
   5716SS1 V3R6MØ 950929            S1Ø18A6G        Ø5/3Ø/98  19:17:1Ø


   Display Device . . . . . :  USERS1
   User . . . . . . . . . :  JSMITH

                   Additional Message Information

   Message ID . . . . . . :  CPD7956       Severity . . . . . :    3Ø
   Message type . . . . . :  Diagnostic

   Message . . . . :    Select or omit field specified incorrectly.
   Cause . . . . . :    The select or omit fields must be specified after all of
     the key fields in the record format or the DYNSLT keyword must be specified.
   Recovery . . . :    Do one of the following, and then try the request again.
       Specify the key field before the select or omit fields.
       Specify *NONE as the key field.
       Specify the DYNSLT keyword.
       Omit the select or omit field.



                                                                  Bottom

   Press Enter to continue.

   F3=Exit    F6=Print    F9=Display message details
   F1Ø=Display messages in job log    F12=Cancel    F21=Select assistance level
```

Figure 8.50
Additional Message Information Screen for CPD7956

The first part of the Cause information should nail down our problem: Select fields must be specified *after* all of the key fields.

Press F12 to return to the split screen. Move the cursor up to the Edit screen and press Page down, then fix the problem by changing the order of the Select and Key entries, so that the K entry comes before the S entry.

If you needed to find additional compile errors, you could move the cursor back to the lower screen and repeat the find error command just by pressing F16.

2.10. Exit, save, and recompile. Check your messages (try DM from the option entry field) and make sure the CRTLF completed successfully.

2.11. If your compile was still unsuccessful, review the steps above, make the necessary changes to your source file, and try again! If the compile appears to be successful, but the logical file is not created, check your spooled files for a job log. Job logs are created when a batch job (e.g., running CRTLF from option 14) fails. Such a failure could occur if you attempt to create a logical file specifying a UNIQUE key-sequenced access path over a physical file already containing data. If the physical file data for the key field(s) were in violation of the UNIQUE key constraint (e.g. a logical file keyed on LAST-NAME and two Smith records are present), the system would not be able to create the access path and the job would fail.

    If your job has failed, read the job log and find the cause of the failure. If you are unable to determine the cause of the problem, ask your instructor/mentor for help.

Part 3

Goals	Examine the data member of your logical file Insert new records through the logical file Determine where the new records are added in the physical file
Start at	WRKOBJPDM, your library
Procedure	Take the PDM options to create a temporary DFU on your STULF1 Enter two new records Browse the logical file to see if you can find them Display the physical file member to find the inserted records

3.1. Use F12 to return to the Work with Objects Using PDM screen. Refresh the screen to make sure the logical database file you just created is in the list.
    Look at More options and select Change using DFU for your newly compiled logical file.

3.2. By taking the PDM option on a file object, you can avoid having to type the STRDFU command or select the file name for DFU.

    3.2a. When the Work with data ... DFU screen comes up, what does it prompt you for?

3.2b. What mode are you in? (Note: If you are in Entry mode, your logical file is empty. This would normally mean that no physical file records were selected for the logical file. Either you miscoded the Select entry, or there are no records with local Zip codes in your physical file. You need to add records to your physical file or fix your logical file Select so that at least three to four records are selected for the logical file.)

Type in a Social Security number of one of your physical file records and press Enter. (If you don't remember one, just page down).

3.3. Use the Page down and/or Page up keys to browse through the file.

3.3a. In what order are the records in the file presented?
3.3b. How many records are in this file compared to the based-on physical file STUPF?
3.3c. What is the reason for this difference?

3.4. Go into Entry mode and add two records, one with a local Zip code (within the RANGE of your Select) and one without.

3.5. Now return to change mode and browse through the file again.

3.5a. Are the records you added there?

Exit DFU and return to the Work with Objects Using PDM screen.

3.6. Select Work with for physical file STUPF. From the Work with screen, choose the display option.

3.6a. Are the new records there?
3.6b. Where in the physical file do they appear?
3.6c. From your observation of 3.5a and 3.6a, how would you say the selection operation of the logical file works regarding changes versus additions?

Print the display screen showing the records you just added and hand it in with your answer sheet.

ADDITIONAL LAB EXERCISE

You should attempt this exercise only after you have successfully completed the primary lab exercise above. This exercise assumes an understanding of the material presented in the previous lab steps, as well as in the text of this lesson and earlier lessons.

In this exercise you build three new physical files, populate them with test data, then create join and multiple-format logical files over them. You use a temporary DFU to add data through the multiple-format logical file, then you run a query to display the join logical file data.

1. Create a member in source file QDDSSRC named CATPF to describe a catalog file. This file will be a simplified version of the information contained in a college catalog, describing the various courses offered. Its record format name is CATPFR and it contains the following fields:

Field Name	Type	Length, Dec	COLHDG
CATNO	Char	6	'Catalog' 'Number'
CATNAM	Char	40	'Course' 'Title'
CATDES	Char	400	'Course' 'Description'
LECHRS	Zoned	1,0	'Lecture' 'Hours'
LABHRS	Zoned	1,0	'Lab' 'Hours'
PREREQ	Char	30	'Prerequisites'

Make CATPF a keyed file with unique keys. The key field is CATNO. Compile the file and check your message queue for successful completion. Use the DSPFFD command to ensure the fields of the compiled file exactly match those shown above. The DSPFFD command output should show that there are six fields and a record length of 478 bytes.

2. Use the CPYF command to copy the data from INTROCLASS/CATPF to your file. Change the MBROPT parameter to *ADD and make sure CRTFILE is set to *NO. This CPYF command will fail if there is any discrepancy between the INTROCLASS library's CATPF record format and that of the file you just created.

3. Create another QDDSSRC member to describe a file of section data. Name the file SECTPF. Section records document an occurrence at a certain place and time of one course of the catalog file being taught. For example, catalog number PC101T, General Psychology, may have several sections offered in a semester, each meeting in a specified room of a building at a specified time, and each taught by a certain professor. Our simplified version of the file will be keyed on field SECTNO, with unique key values. The record format name is SECTPFR and the record layout is

Field Name	Type	Length, Dec	COLHDG
SECTNO	Zoned	5,0	'Section' 'Number'
INSTID	Zoned	9,0	'Instructor'
CATNO	Char	6	'Catalog' 'Number'
DAYS	Char	5	'Days' 'Met'
STIME	Time		'Start' 'Time'
ETIME	Time		'End' 'Time'
BLDG	Char	2	'Building'
ROOM	Char	4	'Room'

For the fields STIME and ETIME, code the function TIMFMT (*USA) to get an 8-character date with a.m./p.m. format.

4. After entering and saving the DDS for this file, compile it and check for successful completion. The physical file should consist of eight fields with a total record length of 47 bytes.

5. A third file will describe a student's enrollment in a section. It will relate a record in your student file STUPF to a section of a course being taught. The file name is ENRLPF and it is also keyed, with a unique composite key of SECTNO (high order) and SOCSEC (low order). The unique key enforces the constraint that an individual student can enroll in a certain section only once. The record format name is ENRLPFR and it contains only two fields:

Field Name	Type	Length, Dec	COLHDG
SECTNO	Zoned	5,0	'Section' 'Number'
SOCSEC	Zoned	9,0	'Student' 'SSN'

Save the DDS for ENRLPF and compile it from the Work with Members Using PDM screen. Check for successful completion.

6. Run a temporary DFU on your SECTPF file, adding several sections. The section numbers should be easy to remember (e.g., 1, 2, 3). For the instructor ID, use all 9s except for the last 4 digits (e.g., 999990001, 999990002). Have at least one instructor teaching a couple of different sections. Use catalog numbers from the records copied to your CATPF, or add some new CATPF records to your file if you wish.

7. Create a multiple-format logical file that will let you conveniently display and update enrollment records through student records. The file could be called STUENRLMLF. The first record format is STUPFR, from the physical file STUPF. The record format should specify SOCSEC as the only key field. Use the same record format name as the physical file's, and include all fields. The second record format is ENRLPFR, from the physical file ENRLPF. The high-order key fields of all record formats must agree, so use SOCSEC as the first (high-order) key field and SECTNO as the second (low-order) key field.

8. Compile the file and use a temporary DFU on the new logical file to add from one to several sections for several students in your student file. Use section numbers that you have already added to the SECTPF file in step 6. Notice that keys cannot be changed when using DFU in change mode on a multiple-format logical file; so if you already created an ENRLPF record for a student using a wrong section number, you need to delete it and try again. On the other hand, nothing bad will happen if you just leave it there. If you are entering several sections for the same student, try typing

the SOCSEC value only the first time and then using the Dupe key (on micros use either the End key of numeric keypad when not in Num Lock, or Shift Insert). This will copy the previously entered record's value and store it in the current field. (But the copied value will not display in the field when you first press the Dupe key.)

9. Before creating a join logical file to pull all this data together in a report, it is important that you understand the file structure of your ever-expanding database. Using the examples in the text, create a Bachman diagram similar to the one on page 289. The diagram should show the relationships among the files, identifying their primary keys, the relationship-supporting fields (foreign keys) of each child file, and the type of relationship. Be sure to name each file. When you are satisfied with your diagram, hand in a copy of it to your instructor/mentor.

10. Now create a join logical file named SECTJLF1 that you can use to display or print all sections and the students enrolled in them. Include the section and catalog numbers from the SECTPF file; the course name, lecture hours, and lab hours from the CATPF file; the Social Security number from the ENRLPF file; and the first name, last name, and phone number from the STUPF file. ENRLPF supplies the Social Security number (SOCSEC) and functions as a link between the SECTPF and STUPF files. Because the SECTPF and STUPF files have a many-to-many relationship, there are no fields to directly relate records from these files. Therefore, joining records of SECTPF and STUPF requires going through the ENRLPF file.

The logical file should look like that shown in Figure 8.51.

Figure 8.51
DDS for Join Logical
File Using Four
Physical Files

```
     5738PW1 V2R1M0  910329                SEU SOURCE LISTING
 SOURCE FILE . . . . . . . JSMITH/QDDSSRC
 MEMBER . . . . . . . . . SECTJLF1
 SEQNBR*...+... 1 ...+... 2 ...+... 3 ...+... 4 ...+... 5 ...+... 6 ...+... 7 .
   100     A********************************************************************
   200     A* Logical file to join section, catalog, enrollment and student *
   300     A*  data to produce a listing of sections and all students        *
   400     A*  enrolled in each. Inner join excludes unmatched records.      *
   500     A*                                                                 *
   600     A* Compiled: 1998-06-01                                           *
   700     A********************************************************************
   800     A          R JREC1                    JFILE(SECTPF CATPF ENRLPF +
   900     A                                       STUPF)
  1000     A*
  1100     A          J                           JOIN(1 2)
  1200     A                                      JFLD(CATNO CATNO)
  1300     A          J                           JOIN(1 3)
  1400     A                                      JFLD(SECTNO SECTNO)
  1500     A          J                           JOIN(3 4)
  1600     A                                      JFLD(SOCSEC SOCSEC)
  1700     A*
  1800     A            SECTNO                    JREF(1)
  1900     A            CATNO                     JREF(1)
  2000     A            CATNAM
  2100     A            LECHRS
  2200     A            LABHRS
  2300     A            SOCSEC                    JREF(3)
  2400     A            FNAME
  2500     A            LNAME
  2600     A            PHONE
                       * * * * E N D   O F   S O U R C E * * * *
```

Four files are identified in the JFILE parameter list. File SECTPF is listed first, making it the primary file. It is joined to both CATPF (line 11) and ENRLPF (line 13). ENRLPF is then joined to STUPF to extract student name and phone number for each enrollment record. The fields to be included in the join record are listed beginning on line 18. Remember that if a field name is not unique, you must qualify it using a JREF keyword.

After entering the source DDS, compile your file and check to make sure it was a clean compile.

11. Finally, create a Query/400 report like the one shown in Figure 8.52.

```
                    Current Student Enrollment by Section

SECTNO  CATNO   CATNAM                 CHI LEC LAB    SOCSEC   LNAME       FNAME    PHONE
14050   DG138U  Introduction to AS/400  3   2   2  111-11-0001 Badman     Benny    319 234-3456
                                                   111-11-0003 Clapsaddle Karikool 707 683-4556
                                                   111-11-0004 Cool       Joe      319 365-9876
                                                   111-11-0006 Grubber    Norman   515 899-7890
                                                             Section 14050
                                                             COUNT  4

14051   DG132U  Database Management      4   3   2  111-11-0002 Baggins    Bilbo    319 988-8999
                                                   111-11-0003 Clapsaddle Karikool 707 683-4556
                                                   111-11-0005 Dowhopper  Jazmann  215 456-7654
                                                             Section 14051
                                                             COUNT  3

14052   PC230T  Abnormal Psychology      3   3   0  111-11-0001 Badman     Benny    319 234-3456
                                                   111-11-0002 Baggins    Bilbo    319 988-8999
                                                   111-11-0005 Dowhopper  Jazmann  215 456-7654
                                                   111-11-0006 Grubber    Norman   515 899-7890
                                                             Section 14052
                                                             COUNT  4

14053   AR220T  Advanced Wheel-throwing T 3  0   6  111-11-0006 Grubber    Norman   515 899-7890
                                                             Section 14053
                                                             COUNT  1

                                                             Total all sections
                                                             COUNT 12

* * *  E N D  O F  R E P O R T  * * *
```

Figure 8.52

Query/400 Report from SECTJQRY Inner Join Logical File, with Calculated Field and Control Breaks

Name the query SECTJQRY. This report lists all students enrolled in each section. The sort sequence is student last name within section. Because the join logical file to be used by the query is an inner join, to be listed, sections must have a valid catalog number and at least one valid student enrolled in the ENRLPF. The columns in Figure 8.52 have been narrowed to fit the report on the book page.

CHI is a calculated field. Select the Define result fields option of Define the Query and read the Help information. You must give the new field a name (CHI) and provide an arithmetic expression to define the calculation. CHI is equal to one-half lab hours plus lecture hours.

Don't forget to select the fields for output. Use all the fields from the SECTPF file together (SECTNO, CATNO, CATNAM, CHI, LECHRS, LABHRS) as break level 1 control fields. When all primary file fields are defined as the same (level 1) control field, group indication will be used automatically for printed reports.

When you are satisfied with your report, print a copy of it to hand in to your instructor/mentor.

Mastering the AS/400, Second Edition

Lab 8 Answer Sheet

Name: _____

Date Due: _____

Class Time: _____

1.2a. _____

_____

1.4a. _____

1.4b. _____

1.7a. _____

1.10a. _____

1.12a. _____

_____

2.1a. _____   2.1b. _____

2.1c. _____

_____

_____

2.1d. _____

2.2a. _____

2.8a. _____

3.2a. _____   3.2b. _____

3.3a. _____

3.3b. _____

3.3c. _____

3.5a. _____

3.6a. _____   3.6b. _____

3.6c. _____

_____

_____

In Summary

All database files have an access path. The access path defaults to arrival sequence or is specified as keyed sequence. When an arrival-sequenced database file is sequentially accessed, records are presented in the order in which they were added to the file. A keyed-sequence file presents records in order by the relative value of the key field data. Direct retrieval or random access requires a relative record number for arrival-sequenced files or a key value for keyed-sequence files.

Logical files can provide an alternate keyed-sequence access path over existing physical files. Such access paths require maintenance when the based-on physical file's records are changed or new records are added. Three options available for access path maintenance are immediate (*IMMED), delayed (*DLY), and rebuild (*REBLD). When duplicate key values are not permitted, the UNIQUE keyword is coded at the file level. Unique keyed-sequence access paths require immediate maintenance.

Besides providing alternate access paths, logical files are used to provide selection, projection, and join operations on physical file data. Selection creates a record subset of the physical file through the use of Select/Omit entries and the DDS keywords COMP, RANGE, and VALUES. Projection creates logical file record formats consisting of a field subset of the physical file record; projection is used to protect data elements from applications not requiring or not authorized to them. The join operation allows data from two or more separate but related physical files to be retrieved as a single record when relationship-supporting fields have matching values. An inner join returns a join record when at least one matching record is found in each of the related files. A left outer join returns a join record for each primary file record even if a matching record is not found in one or more of the secondary files.

The three types of logical files are simple, multiple-format, and join. Simple logical files are based on a single physical file and have one record format. Simple logical files can be used to provide selection, projection, and an alternate access path for the based-on physical file.

Multiple-format logical files provide a convenient way to display and update data in two or more physical files. Each record format in the multiple-format file is based on a record format of an underlying physical file and can include all or a subset of the fields of the physical file (projection). Multiple-format logical files must be keyed, and all record formats must specify at least the same high-order key. Records are arranged and presented by this merged key sequence, with the primary file (first record format) records being presented first within a key group.

Join logical files permit the join operation mentioned above to be specified within an actual file object, kept permanently, and used by queries or HLL applications. Join logical files cannot be updated, but they provide a powerful tool for pulling data together for reports and displays. When Query/400 is used to display or print records from a join logical file, the file selection needs to identify only the single logical file; specification of secondary files or type of join is not necessary.

When all primary file fields are defined as the same (level 1) control field, group indication is used automatically for printer reports.

In the lab, you have created a simple logical file and then expanded your database by creating three new physical files. You created a multiple-format logical file to add records to related files and a join logical file using four of the database physical files. You created a Query/400 report of students enrolled in sections of courses using your join logical file as input.

Additional Database Facilities

LESSON OVERVIEW

Despite the best planning and design methodology, record formats of existing database files may require modification at some point (i.e., fields may need to be changed or added). In this lesson we look at ways to accommodate these needs without destroying data already in the file to be changed. We use PDM options and CL commands to accomplish these tasks. We also introduce the idea of object authorization and see how library and object authorities can be used to limit access to database files. And we briefly discuss group profiles and authorization lists.

Objectives

Students will be able to

✓ Distinguish between the CRTDUPOBJ (Create Duplicate Object) and CPYF (Copy File) commands, and select the appropriate command for a specific situation

✓ Use the RNMOBJ (Rename Object) command to change the name of an object

✓ Modify and compile DDS for a database source physical file

✓ Use the necessary parameters of the CPYF (Copy File) command to accomplish field mapping in a copy operation

✓ Understand the capability of the CHGPF (Change Physical File) command and use it to modify an existing physical file

✓ Use the EDTOBJAUT (Edit Object Authority) command to observe and change individual and public authority to libraries and objects

CREATING A FILE (REVIEW)

As we begin this lesson, let's take a moment to review the process of creating a database file. Computer programs and file descriptions are written in a language, called a source language, that has its own syntax and vocabulary. Programming languages include Cobol, RPG, and C; data description languages on the AS/400 include DDS and SQL. DDS is always compiled from source statements, but SQL can be run directly from a command line — in which case it is more similar to an interpreted language such as Basic.

Usually, a separate source physical file is created to hold and organize source members for each language a programmer uses. A single source member may be all of the source code for a single Cobol or RPG program or all the DDS source statements to describe a single file.

For example, my library might contain several different source physical files: one named QDDSSRC for DDS source members, one named QLBLSRC for Cobol source members, and one named QRPGSRC for RPG source members. These source physical files are created using the CRTSRCPF (Create Source Physical File) command, and each one can hold any number of members. My DDS source physical file, QDDSSRC, might contain the members indicated in Figure 9.1.

Figure 9.1
Conceptual Content of JAFINTRO/QDDSSRC Source Physical File — Each Member is a "Recipe" for a Certain File

```
Library
    JAFINTRO

              +------------------------------------------+
              |       Source  Physical  File             |
              |              QDDSSRC                      |
              |                                          |
              | Member        Type                       |
              | ---------------------------------------- |
              | EMPPF         PF                          |
              | CUSPF         PF                          |
              | CUSLF1        LF                          |
              | EMPUPD        DSPF                        |
              | VENDPF        PF                          |
              |    .            .                         |
              |    .            .                         |
              |    .            .                         |
              +------------------------------------------+
```

Each of these members would contain the necessary DDS to externally describe a physical or logical database file, a printer file, or a display file, as indicated. You could think of a source physical file as a recipe box and each member as one or more recipe cards containing the list of ingredients and instructions for mixing and baking some delectable delight, such as banana bread, muffins, or rhubarb cream pie (Figure 9.2).

Figure 9.2
Like a Source Physical
File Contains
Instructions (Members)
for Creating File
Objects, a Recipe Box
Contains Instructions
(Recipe Cards) for
Creating Goodies

Like a source physical file, which may contain a few or many members, the recipe box may contain only a few or a large number of recipes. Also, just as we clearly realize the distinction between the recipe for the rhubarb cream pie and the pie itself, we understand that the source DDS for the employee master file, EMPPF, is not the actual file but merely instructions for creating the file.

And just as we keep the recipes in a box, we keep the source members in their source physical file even after the database or display file is created, although for slightly different reasons. The recipe lets us, for instance, create another pie after the current pie has disappeared. The source file member, on the other hand, undergoes a considerably more mundane transformation into a file object. But it's a transformation we may need to repeat, and keeping the source member in its source physical file makes that possible. The creation of the file object usually occurs via option 14 from the Work with Members Using PDM screen, as illustrated in Figure 9.3.

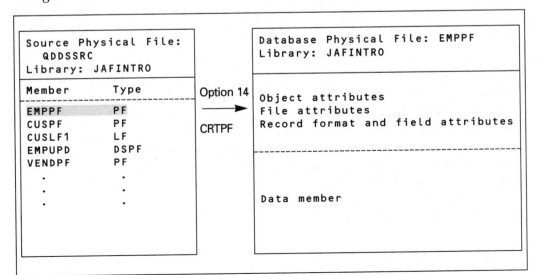

Figure 9.3
Results of Taking the
Defaults for Option 14
from Work with
Members Using PDM
on Source Member
EMPPF

Once the database physical file is created, the system maintains no physical link between it and its DDS source member description. But it is useful to keep the source member, whether it is a program or file description, so that we can correct errors or make modifications and recompile when necessary.

When changes are made to the source code of a program, we can normally recompile with little concern; but recompiling the source description of a database physical file is a different story. To recompile the modified DDS source for a physical file using the same name (i.e., executing the CRTPF command on the source member), we must first delete the previous file object and all its data. If data records have been added to the physical file's data member, we must save the data before recompiling the changed source description.

CHANGING THE SOURCE DDS

Let's use physical file EMPPF, which we created in an earlier lesson, to demonstrate how to modify DDS. Suppose we need to include a work phone number (WORKPHONE) field. Figure 9.4 shows the SEU Edit screen for the modified file EMPPF: field WORKPHONE has been inserted after DEPT. But this change made to the source member will have no effect on the existing *FILE object, EMPPF, until we recompile the DDS source.

Figure 9.4
SEU Edit Screen for
EMPPF, with Field
WORKPHONE Inserted

```
 Columns . . . :   1  71              Edit                    JAFINTRO/QDDSSRC
 SEU==>_                                                                 EMPPF
 FMT PF .....A..........T.Name++++++RLen++TDpB......Functions+++++++++++++++++++
        *************** Beginning of data *******************************************
0001.00     A         R EMPPFR
0002.00     A           EMPNO          9B 0
0003.00     A           LASTNAME      16A
0004.00     A           FIRSTNAME     12A
0005.00     A           HOMEPHONE      7S 0
0006.00     A           ADDR1         40A
0007.00     A           ADDR2         40A
0008.00     A           ZIP            5S 0
0009.00     A           DEPT          12A
0010.00     A           WORKPHONE      7S 0
0011.00     A           BIRTHDATE      L
0012.00     A           HIREDATE       L
0013.00     A           SALARY         7P 0
        ***************** End of data *******************************************




 F3=Exit     F4=Prompt    F5=Refresh   F9=Retrieve   F10=Cursor   F11=Toggle
 F16=Repeat find          F17=Repeat change          F24=More keys
```

After you exit SEU and save the changed member, the next step is to review the defaults assigned by PDM when the CRTPF (Create Physical File) command is invoked by option 14 from Work with Members Using PDM. Figure 9.5 shows the CRTPF command prompt screen. You reach this screen by typing 14 on the option field for physical file EMPPF and then prompting (F4).

```
/                    Create Physical File (CRTPF)
  Type choices, press Enter.
  File . . . . . . . . . . . . . . > EMPPF_____    Name
    Library . . . . . . . . . . . >    JAFINTRO__    Name, *CURLIB
  Source file . . . . . . . . . . > QDDSSRC          Name
    Library . . . . . . . . . . . >    JAFINTRO      Name, *LIBL, *CURLIB
  Source member . . . . . . . . . > EMPPF___         Name, *FILE
  Record length, if no DDS . . . .   _____         Number
  Generation severity level . . .    20_____         0-30
  Flagging severity level . . . .    0_____          0-30
  File type . . . . . . . . . . .    *DATA            *DATA, *SRC
  Member, if desired . . . . . . .   *FILE_____      Name, *FILE, *NONE
  Text 'description' . . . . . . .   *SRCMBRTXT


                                                                  Bottom
  F3=Exit    F4=Prompt    F5=Refresh   F10=Additional parameters   F12=Cancel
  F13=How to use this display          F24=More keys
\
```

Figure 9.5
CRTPF Command Prompt Screen, with Additional Parameters

PRESERVING THE EXISTING DATA

The File and Library parameters specify the name of the *new* file and the library in which it will be stored when the CRTPF command executes. Notice that, initially, the File name is the same as the Source member name. If we were to run the command as is, the Confirm Compile of Member screen would appear (Figure 9.6), unless the PDM session defaults had been changed from N to Y for the Replace object option.

```
/                    Confirm Compile of Member
  The following object already exists for the compile operation:

     Object which exists . . . . . . . . :    EMPPF
        Library . . . . . . . . . . . . :       JAFINTRO
     Object type . . . . . . . . . . . . :    *FILE

     Member to compile . . . . . . . . . :    EMPPF
     File . . . . . . . . . . . . . . . :    QDDSSRC
        Library . . . . . . . . . . . . :       JAFINTRO

  Type choice, press Enter.
  Press F12=Cancel to return and not perform the compile operation.

     Delete existing object . . . . . . . .   N   Y=Yes, N=No



  F12=Cancel
\
```

Figure 9.6
Confirm Compile of Member Screen

The Confirm Compile of Member screen should always serve as a warning — the system is telling us that if we override the default response (N) for Delete existing object, we will lose the existing object. If the object were a program still being tested and we simply needed to recompile the most recent version, we would not hesitate to type Y and press Enter. But in this case, the object that would be deleted is a data file, and we should proceed with caution! Because we already have data in physical file object EMPPF that we don't want to lose, we would cancel the CRTPF command for now by pressing F12.

We might consider returning to the CRTPF command prompt screen (Figure 9.5) and changing the File name parameter value to a different name than EMPPF so the existing file object would not be deleted when the CRTPF command is executed. But existing programs, queries, logical files, and display files expect to find their data in a file named EMPPF. If we changed the name of the modified physical file to something other than EMPPF, we would have to change all references in programs, queries, and logical files as well. And after performing significant maintenance on the source members, they would all have to be recompiled. Therefore, creating the file under a different file name is probably not a workable solution.

Let's analyze the problem (as illustrated in Figure 9.7) and consider an alternative:

Figure 9.7
A Solution for
Modifying an
Existing File

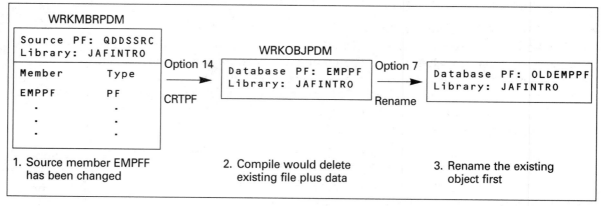

1. The changed DDS source member for file EMPPF needs to be recompiled, but
2. there is already a *FILE object, EMPPF, that contains data that would be destroyed.
3. So, let's *temporarily* rename the *FILE object containing the data to a different, unique name (e.g., OLDEMPPF), then recompile the modified DDS source for the new file object using the original name.

After the changed file has been recompiled, the data from the (old) renamed file can be copied back into the changed (new) file's record format.

RENAMING THE FILE

Renaming the file object is an efficient, fast way to get rid of the old file, EMPPF, without getting rid of the data. The data is still there under a different file name, OLDEMPPF, and we can recompile the changed source member and then copy the old data into the new recompiled file object.

The rename operation changes pointers — the pointer in the library containing the old object will be changed to recognize the different name, but it still points to the same object. Also, any logical files that reference the previous physical file name as the based-on file would automatically be changed to point to the new name; but programs, queries, DFUs, and so on, would not be changed automatically to reference the new file name. Because the file will only be renamed temporarily, it won't be necessary to change the file references in objects such as programs, queries, and DFUs. It will, however, be necessary to perform the rename operation and subsequent steps to change the physical file when the file is not being used by a program, query, or logical file.

Now let's step through the process for renaming our file. First, we look at any logical files built over physical file EMPPF. When you know the physical file name and want to find out which logical files, if any, are based on it, the DSPDBR (Display Data Base Relations) command is just what you need. The only required parameter is the name of the physical file you want to check on. If we ran the command `DSPDBR  EMPPF` from the command line, the information shown in Figure 9.8 would appear.

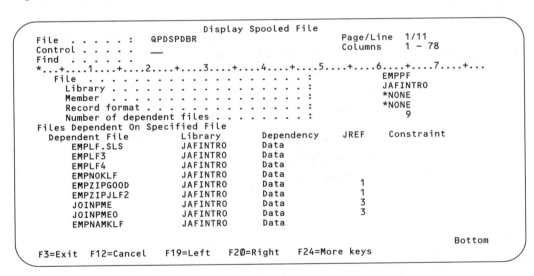

Figure 9.8
DSPDBR Output
for File EMPPF

In addition to telling you the number of dependent files, the command output also lists each of them. Before you decide to change a physical file record format, you should use this information to examine the logical files to determine what effect, if any, such changes might have on the logical files and their applications.

Looking at database relations from the other direction, you might need to determine which physical file a particular logical file is based on. An easy way to find out is to use the Display option (5) from Work with Objects Using PDM. Taken on a *FILE object, this option invokes the DSPFD (Display File Description) command. If you took option 5 on the simple logical file EMPNAMKLF (the keyed-sequence access path on last name and first name of file EMPPF), you would see the information shown in Figure 9.9 several screens down.

Figure 9.9

Display File Description:
Based-On File
Information for
EMPNAMKLF

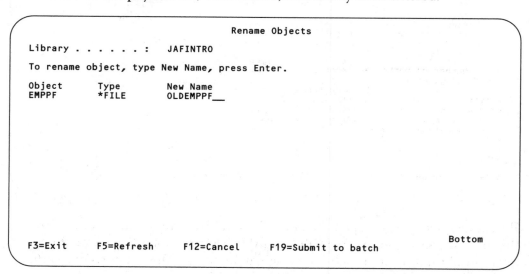

```
                              Display Spooled File
File . . . . . :    QPDSPFD                      Page/Line   2/46
Control . . . . .                                Columns     1 - 78
Find . . . . . :
*...+....1....+....2....+....3....+....4....+....5....+....6....+....7....+...
      Number of data members . . . . . . . . . :            1
      Based on file . . . . . . . . . . . . . . :       EMPPF
        Library . . . . . . . . . . . . . . . . :       JAFINTRO
        Member  . . . . . . . . . . . . . . . . :       EMPPF
        Logical file format . . . . . . . . . . :       EMPPFR
        Number of index entries . . . . . . . . :                  13
        Number of member accesses . . . . . . . :                   0
Record Format List
                         Record   Format Level
    Format      Fields   Length   Identifier
    EMPPFR        14       166     476E844C29B67
      Text . . . . . . . . . . . . . . . . . . . :
    Total number of formats . . . . . . . . . . :            1
    Total number of fields . . . . . . . . . . . :           14
    Total record length . . . . . . . . . . . . :          166
Member List

                                                             More...
  F3=Exit   F12=Cancel    F19=Left    F20=Right   F24=More keys
```

As Figure 9.9 shows, the based-on physical file is identified by the Based on file information. As you will see, this reference to the physical file changes when we rename the based-on physical file.

Let's do that now by using option 7 from the Work with Objects Using PDM screen. Option 7 takes us to the Rename Objects screen (Figure 9.10). Keep in mind that we are renaming the data file object itself, not the source member. The New Name for the physical file, OLDEMPPF, has already been entered.

Figure 9.10

Rename Objects Screen

```
                              Rename Objects
  Library . . . . . . :    JAFINTRO

  To rename object, type New Name, press Enter.

  Object      Type        New Name
  EMPPF       *FILE       OLDEMPPF__








                                                            Bottom
   F3=Exit     F5=Refresh     F12=Cancel     F19=Submit to batch
```

After you press Enter, the Work with Objects Using PDM screen will look like the one shown in Figure 9.11. A message at the bottom of the screen verifies that the rename operation worked.

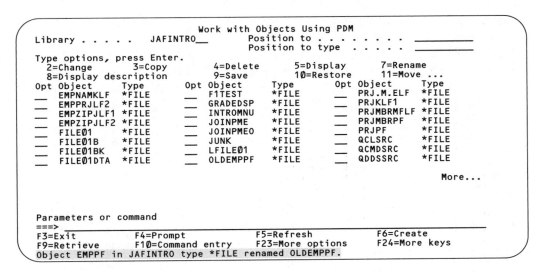

Figure 9.11
Work with Objects
Using PDM, JAFINTRO

By taking the Display option on logical file EMPNAMKLF again, we can see that the reference to the physical file has been changed. The logical file now points to the newly renamed file OLDEMPPF (Figure 9.12).

```
                        Display Spooled File
 File . . . . . :    QPDSPFD              Page/Line    2/46
 Control . . . . .   +5                   Columns      1 - 78
 Find . . . . . .
 *...+....1....+....2....+....3....+....4....+....5....+....6....+....7....+...
         Number of data members  . . . . . . . . :        1
         Based on file . . . . . . . . . . . . . :        OLDEMPPF
           Library . . . . . . . . . . . . . . . :        JAFINTRO
           Member  . . . . . . . . . . . . . . . :        EMPPF
         Logical file format . . . . . . . . . . :        EMPPFR
         Number of index entries . . . . . . . . :             13
         Number of member accesses . . . . . . . :              0
 Record Format List
                        Record   Format Level
         Format     Fields  Length   Identifier
         EMPPFR        14      166    476E844C29B67
           Text  . . . . . . . . . . . . . . . . :
         Total number of formats . . . . . . . . :           1
         Total number of fields  . . . . . . . . :          14
         Total record length . . . . . . . . . . :         166
 Member List
                                                       More...

 F3=Exit  F12=Cancel  F19=Left  F20=Right  F24=More keys
```

Figure 9.12
DSPFD Command
Output for Logical File
EMPNAMKLF, with
Based-On File Name
Changed

If we attempted to run a query built for file EMPPF, however, we would receive the error message "Input file EMPPF in JAFINTRO not found" because the query would still be pointing to the original file name. This supports our earlier observation: Logical file references to an underlying physical file are changed automatically when the physical file is renamed; other file references (e.g., for programs, queries, or DFUs) aren't changed.

Now that our physical file has been renamed, we can return to the Work with Members Using PDM screen and compile the changed DDS source for file EMPPF. When we enter option 14 to create file EMPPF this time, the Confirm

Compile of Member warning screen doesn't appear because we no longer have an EMPPF object in our library.

After successfully compiling, we can use the DSPFFD (Display File Field Description) command to display the field descriptions for the revised EMPPF physical file. The second page of the display (Figure 9.13) shows the changed record format with the addition of the new field, positioned several lines down in the Field Level Information.

Figure 9.13
DSPFFD Command Output Showing New WORKPHONE Field in Record

```
                          Display Spooled File
File  . . . . . :   QPDSPFFD                        Page/Line   1/26
Control . . . . .   +2                              Columns     1 - 78
Find  . . . . . .
*...+....1....+....2....+....3....+....4....+....5....+....6....+....7....+...
               Data       Field   Buffer  Buffer           Field    Column
   Field       Type       Length  Length Position          Usage    Heading
   EMPNO       BINARY       9  0     4       1              Both     EMPNO
   LASTNAME    CHAR          16    16       5              Both     LASTNAME
      Coded Character Set Identifier   . . . . . :    37
   FIRSTNAME   CHAR          12    12      21              Both     FIRSTNAME
      Coded Character Set Identifier   . . . . . :    37
   HOMEPHONE   ZONED        7  0     7      33              Both     HOMEPHONE
   ADDR1       CHAR          40    40      40              Both     ADDR1
      Coded Character Set Identifier   . . . . . :    37
   ADDR2       CHAR          40    40      80              Both     ADDR2
      Coded Character Set Identifier   . . . . . :    37
   ZIP         ZONED        5  0     5     120              Both     ZIP
   DEPT        CHAR          12    12     125              Both     DEPT
      Coded Character Set Identifier   . . . . . :    37
   WORKPHONE   ZONED        7  0     7     137              Both     WORKPHONE

                                                                  More...
 F3=Exit   F12=Cancel    F19=Left    F20=Right    F24=More keys
```

The file has been created successfully. The next step is to copy the existing data from the old file into the new file. Comparing the record format of the new file (Figure 9.13) with that of the old file verifies what we already know: The record formats are different and the field positions after the DEPT field are not aligned. Thus, we cannot simply move a whole data record left to right from the old record format into the new file because field boundaries would be violated; we would end up with zoned decimal data in date format fields and date data in packed decimal fields — in other words, our data would be corrupted. (In fact, unless you specifically overrode its warning, the system would prevent you from making such a mistake.)

THE COPY FILE COMMAND

The CPYF (Copy File) command, however, provides just what we need to get our existing data into the changed record format of the new file. The CPYF command is a powerful command that allows several significant variations on the copy process. These variations give the CPYF command flexibility that the CRTDUPOBJ (Create Duplicate Object) command, which simply creates a clone of an existing object, does not have. You can invoke the CRTDUPOBJ and CPYF commands by taking Work with Objects PDM options on the file to be copied (the From file). Option 3 invokes the CRTDUPOBJ command, and option 15 invokes the CPYF command.

For our example we will take PDM option 15 on the file containing the data, OLDEMPPF, and prompt. If you were not using Work with Objects PDM, you could simply type **CPYF** on any command line and prompt.

The first screen of the CPYF command prompt screen (with additional parameters) is shown in Figure 9.14.

```
                              Copy File (CPYF)
 Type choices, press Enter.
 From file  . . . . . . . . . . . . >  OLDEMPPF__    Name
    Library  . . . . . . . . . . . >   JAFINTRO__    Name, *LIBL, *CURLIB
 To file  . . . . . . . . . . . .      _____     Name, *PRINT
    Library  . . . . . . . . . . .      *LIBL_____    Name, *LIBL, *CURLIB
 From member  . . . . . . . . . . >    *ALL_____    Name, generic*, *FIRST, *ALL
 To member or label . . . . . . .      *FIRST____    Name, *FIRST, *FROMMBR
 Replace or add records . . . . .      *NONE___      *NONE, *ADD, *REPLACE
 Create file  . . . . . . . . . .      *NO_          *NO, *YES
 Print format . . . . . . . . . .      *CHAR         *CHAR, *HEX

                           Additional Parameters

 Which records to print . . . . .      *NONE__       *NONE, *EXCLD, *COPIED
 Record format of logical file  .      *ONLY_____    Name, *ONLY, *ALL
 Copy from record number  . . . .      *START_____   Number, *START
                                                                   More...



 F3=Exit    F4=Prompt    F5=Refresh    F12=Cancel    F13=How to use this display
 F24=More keys
```

Figure 9.14
CPYF Command Prompt Screen, First Screen

The required parameters are From file and To file. In our example the From file — which PDM has filled in for us — is OLDEMPPF (the original physical file holding the data). The To file should be EMPPF (the newly compiled file with an added field).

If we were simply creating an exact duplicate of an existing file, that is all we would need. In fact the new file (To file) would not even need to exist — the CPYF command creates the file for us if we change the Create file parameter value to *YES. In such a case, the CPYF command functions like the CRTDUPOBJ command. But we have already compiled the new file with an additional field so we don't want the CPYF command to create a clone of the From file for us. In this case, because the To file already exists, we need to tell the command whether copied records are to replace or be added to the existing file. Because we know that our newly compiled file doesn't contain data, we can specify *ADD to avoid the unnecessary clearing of the To file member. We would also use *ADD when we want to extend an existing file by adding data from another file. In a situation where bad data already exists in the To file, we could specify *REPLACE to clear the data so the member would be empty before the From file data is copied in.

Other features of the CPYF command include the capability to

- print the copied records in character or hexadecimal format
- specify a range of relative record numbers of the From file to be copied to the To file (or printed)
- specify which record format of a multiple-format logical file to copy
- specify, for a file ordered in key sequence, the beginning and ending key values to be included in the new file
- select records to be copied by specifying a relational test on one or more fields (e.g., DEPT *EQ 'Sales')
- tell the copy function to move data field-by-field from the From file record to the To file record with fields of the same name

It is this last feature we really need now, given the different formats of the From file and To file records of our original and modified files.

Record Format Field Mapping

Figure 9.15 shows the CPYF command prompt screen that includes the Record format field mapping parameter. (This is the fifth screen of parameters.)

Figure 9.15
CPYF Record Format
Field Mapping

```
                                    Copy File (CPYF)
        Type choices, press Enter.

        Include records by field test:   _
          Relationship . . . . . . . . .   *NONE        *NONE, *IF, *AND, *OR
          Field  . . . . . . . . . . . .   _____   Name
          Relational operator  . . . . .   ___          *EQ, *GT, *LT, *NE, *GE...
          Value  . . . . . . . . . . . .

                        + for more values _
        Record format field mapping  . .   *NONE__      *NONE, *NOCHK, *CVTSRC...

        Source update options  . . . . .   *SAME__      *SAME, *SEQNBR, *DATE

        Source sequence numbering:
          Starting sequence number . . .   1.00_____    0.01-9999.99
          Increment number . . . . . . .   1.00_____    0.01-9999.99
                                                                         More...

        F9=All parameters   F11=Keywords   F14=Command string   F24=More keys
```

The default value is *NONE, but this is valid for copying database files only when the From file and To file both have identical record formats. For two record formats to be identical, they both must have

- the same record length and number of fields
- corresponding fields with the same names and in the same order
- the same field length and data type of each pair of corresponding fields

In our case, the files don't have identical record formats, so we must provide a value — *MAP. *MAP tells the CPYF command that it should copy data in a From file field to a To file field of the same name. Any fields in the To file record format (e.g., our newly added field WORKPHONE) that don't exist in the From file record format will be set to default values (i.e., spaces for alphanumeric fields and zeros for numeric fields). In a separate step, and after the CPYF command completes, we need to replace the default values with actual data by using a temporary DFU data-entry program or by some other means.

Other Record format field mapping parameter values commonly used when copying database files include the following:

- *NOCHK (no check) for record formats whose field names are different but whose field boundaries align and whose data class is not in conflict. This value is also used when copying data from a program-described file with no defined fields to an externally described file whose named fields exactly coincide with the data contained in the From file.

- *DROP (to omit, or drop, certain fields) must be used with *MAP if not all fields in the From file will have corresponding named fields in the To file. For example, you might be copying data from an existing file but need only certain fields in the new file's record format. In such a case the unnecessary fields in the From file record format would have to be dropped.

The operation of a CPYF command with record format field mapping is illustrated in Figure 9.16.

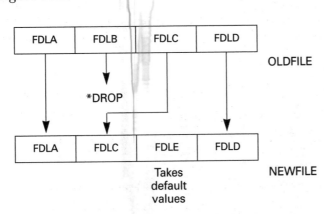

Figure 9.16
CPYF with Record
Format Field Mapping

```
CPYF  FROMFILE(OLDFILE) TOFILE(NEWFILE) +
      MBROPT(*REPLACE)  FMTOPT(*MAP  *DROP)
```

For each record in OLDFILE, a new record in NEWFILE is created by copying the data in FLDA to the new FLDA, FLDC to the new FLDC (in a different location in the record format), and FLDD to FLDD. The NEWFILE FLDE, which does not correspond to any OLDFILE field, is set to default values. The OLDFILE FLDB, which is not included in the new record format, is dropped.

For our example, we would run the CPYF command with the following parameter values:

From file	OLDEMPPF
To file	EMPPF
Replace or add records	*REPLACE
Record format field mapping	*MAP

When the CPYF command completes successfully, it tells us how many records were copied from the file.

Online Help information is available to explain these and other CPYF command parameters. And the multivolume IBM manual *CL Reference* (SC41-0030) is the exhaustive reference when you need detailed information about the CPYF command — or any other CL command for that matter.

Verifying the Copy Operation

We can see what the data looks like in the new version of physical file EMPPF by entering the DSPPFM (Display Physical File Member) command for physical file EMPPF on a command line. The output of the DSPPFM command for the new EMPPF, windowed to position 120, is shown in Figure 9.17.

Figure 9.17
Display Physical File Member — New EMPPF, Windowed to Position 120

```
                         Display Physical File Member
 File . . . . . . :    EMPPF          Library  . . . . :    JAFINTRO
 Member . . . . . :    EMPPF          Record . . . . . :    1
 Control  . . . . :    W120           Column . . . . . :    120
 Find . . . . . . :
 2....+....3....+....4....+....5....+....6....+..
 52854Sales        00000001966-06-061992-10-01
 50115Sales        00000001972-11-191997-03-29  &
 51632Research     00000001909-04-251937-03-28  rn
 52406Research     00000001954-12-011992-03-30  *
 52402Sales        00000001960-04-161994-07-01
 52338Sales        00000001947-05-151986-05-15  ç
 52345Sales        00000001969-07-181997-04-15  ?&
 50225Marketing    00000001935-02-211993-11-01  í
 52205Human Res    00000001940-06-171979-06-01
 52203Marketing    00000001912-10-101982-10-01  $
 52755MIS          00000001958-05-011997-01-01  ñ&
 52203MIS          00000001957-05-111998-06-01  $
 52203MIS          00000001966-08-021998-06-01  $
                      ****** END OF DATA ******

                                                              Bottom
 F3=Exit  F12=Cancel   F19=Left   F20=Right   F24=More keys
```

You can see the Zip code zoned decimal data in the leftmost column, followed by the alphanumeric department field data. Starting in position 137 is the new

WORKPHONE field, with all records set to default zeros because there was nothing to copy in from the From file.

You can get an easier-to-read version of the new EMPPF data by using the RUNQRY (Run Query) command on the file. This command lets you name an existing Query/400 query definition or a file. If you don't have an appropriate query definition and just want a default report to see the file data, you simply name the file and let Query/400 create the report.

To create a default report on any file, (we'll use EMPPF) you could enter

```
RUNQRY  QRY(*NONE) QRYFILE((EMPPF))
```

on any command line. The output is formatted and uses column headers. Also packed decimal and binary numbers are converted to display format making such data comprehensible as opposed to the DSPPFM command which performs no data conversion. The output of the above RUNQRY command, with split screen to show the new field, is shown in Figure 9.18.

```
                            Display Report
                                        Report width . . . . . :      211
    Position to line  . . . . .         Shift to column  . . . . . .     150
    Line    ....+....1....+....2....+.. ! 5....+...16....+...17....+...18....+...19.
              EMPNO    LASTNAME      !   DEPT         WORKPHONE   BIRTHDATE    HI
    000001 111,110,001  Slick        !   Sales             0     1966-06-06   19
    000002 111,110,002  Fendor       !   Sales             0     1972-11-19   19
    000003 111,110,003  Einstein     !   Research          0     1909-04-25   19
    000004 111,110,004  Takahashi    !   Research          0     1954-12-01   19
    000005 111,110,005  Rachanoffski !   Sales             0     1960-04-16   19
    000006 111,110,006  Kartblanch   !   Sales             0     1947-05-15   19
    000007 111,110,007  Badman       !   Sales             0     1969-07-18   19
    000008 111,110,008  Gootch       !   Marketing         0     1935-02-21   19
    000009 111,110,009  Hunn         !   Human Res         0     1940-06-17   19
    000010 111,110,010  Disney       !   Marketing         0     1912-10-10   19
    000011 111,110,011  Zanzibar     !   MIS               0     1958-05-01   19
    000012 111,110,012  Stonehart    !   MIS               0     1957-05-11   19
    000013 111,110,013  Deerfield    !   MIS               0     1966-08-02   19
    ****** ********  End of report  ********

                                                             Bottom
    F3=Exit  F12=Cancel   F19=Left   F20=Right   F21=No split
```

Figure 9.18
RUNQRY Command Output Using New Version of EMPPF

Now we could use the Change using DFU option (18) on the physical file to update each record with the proper information for work phone.

RECOMPILING PROGRAMS AND QUERIES THAT USE A CHANGED PHYSICAL FILE

Once you have created a new version of a physical file (in this case, EMPPF), you need to recompile any programs or query definitions that directly refer to the physical file. The system uses a safety feature called level checking to ensure that when a program or query opens a file, the file's current record format agrees with the version stored in the program or query when it was created. If the record format does not agree — and in the case of EMPPF it would not — the system issues a level-check error to call attention to the discrepancy. **Level checks** are generated at the time a program or query attempts to use the changed file and can be overridden by executing the OVRDBF (Override with Data Base File) command. To run the query EMPSALQ1 without recompiling and without a level check, for example, you would execute the command

```
OVRDBF FILE(EMPPF)  LVLCHK(*NO)
```

Although you can override level checks, it is best to recompile the query definition or program. When changes to a file have no effect on a related query or program, simply recompiling the query or program without change eliminates the level check. But if the new file was created because of a need to add fields to the old file, you might want the program or query to use those new fields. This would require some modification to the program or query and subsequent recompilation, thereby eliminating the level-check problem.

For example, in Lesson 7 we created a join query using the employee file EMPPF and the Zip code file ZIPPF. Now that we have changed EMPPF, the next time we attempt to run that query without using OVRDBF a level check will result. The message would say "Level for file EMPPF in JAFINTRO does not match query (I C)." The system would expect a reply of I to ignore the warning and try to continue or C to cancel the request (to run the query). In this case, because the fields used in the join were not deleted or changed in the new file, entering I and running the query would produce correct output. But if we did not want to include the new fields in the query and we wanted to avoid a level check in the future, we could simply take option 2 on that query from Work with Queries screen and immediately exit (with save definition Y). This would cause the query to be recompiled, eliminating the level check.

DEALING WITH BASED-ON LOGICAL FILES

You might imagine that existing logical files built over the original EMPPF will still function properly because none of their fields have been eliminated. To some extent you would be right. But because EMPFF was renamed to OLDEMPPF, those logical files' based-on pointers were changed to OLDEMPPF and are still pointing to OLDEMPPF. Remember that a logical file's based-on physical file is first identified in its PFILE or JFILE record-level keyword. When we renamed physical file EMPPF to OLDEMPPF, the pointers in all logical file objects based on EMPPF were changed so that they reference the same file by its new name, OLDEMPPF. Even though we re-created file EMPPF, the logical file references were not changed back again. Thus, if we wanted to delete file OLDEMPPF, even though we had all object authority to the file, we could not do so. The system will not let us delete any physical file that still has a logical file based on it. If the physical file were deleted, the logical file would be cut off from its data source, an unacceptable condition on the AS/400. So you must first change the logical file pointers so they reference the new file before the old file can be deleted. The source DDS for the logical files still names the original file (EMPPF) in the PFILE or JFILE keywords. So the easiest way to reconnect the logical files to the new EMPPF is to recompile them.

To be sure you understand the need to recompile the logical files, let's examine the DSPDBR command output for file OLDEMPPF. Figure 9.19 shows partial output from this command.

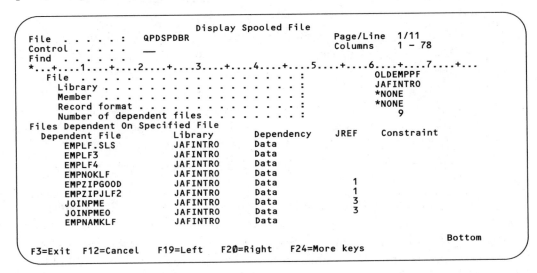

```
                         Display Spooled File
 File  . . . . . :    QPDSPDBR                    Page/Line  1/11
 Control  . . . . .   _                           Columns    1 - 78
 Find  . . . . . .
 *...+....1....+....2....+....3....+....4....+....5....+....6....+....7....+...
     File  . . . . . . . . . . . . . . . . . . :        OLDEMPPF
       Library . . . . . . . . . . . . . . . . :        JAFINTRO
       Member  . . . . . . . . . . . . . . . . :        *NONE
       Record format . . . . . . . . . . . . . :        *NONE
       Number of dependent files . . . . . . . :             9
 Files Dependent On Specified File
    Dependent File          Library      Dependency   JREF    Constraint
       EMPLF.SLS            JAFINTRO      Data
       EMPLF3              JAFINTRO      Data
       EMPLF4              JAFINTRO      Data
       EMPNOKLF            JAFINTRO      Data
       EMPZIPGOOD          JAFINTRO      Data          1
       EMPZIPJLF2          JAFINTRO      Data          1
       JOINPME             JAFINTRO      Data          3
       JOINPMEO            JAFINTRO      Data          3
       EMPNAMKLF           JAFINTRO      Data
                                                              Bottom
 F3=Exit  F12=Cancel   F19=Left   F20=Right   F24=More keys
```

Figure 9.19
DSPDBR Command Output for File OLDEMPPF Before Recompiling Logical Files

As you can see, all the logical files originally based on EMPPF are now dependent on OLDEMPPF so they all need to be recompiled to base them once again on EMPPF.

Those logical files naming the physical file record format (EMPPFR) and not naming individual fields will automatically pick up the new field WORKPHONE when they are recompiled. This would cause a problem for any non-SQL application using them, which we address shortly.

On the other hand, if the logical file projected only certain fields to its record format by naming them individually, any new physical file field would not be added to the logical file's record format automatically. If you wanted to include a new field, you would need to edit the logical file's source code, adding a field name entry identifying the new field to the DDS before recompiling.

Projected logical files not requiring the new field(s) should recompile without causing a problem to programs using them.

In summary, those logical files whose record format remains unchanged after recompiling do not require programs using them to be recompiled. But a logical file that, after recompiling, will include new or changed fields from its based-on physical file will have a different record format, thus causing programs using it to need recompilation to avoid level checks.

Once the logical files have been recompiled, the DSPDBR command output for OLDEMPPF should show no remaining dependent logical files. At that point, file OLDEMPPF can be deleted.

Let's summarize the steps we have described for changing the record format of a physical file without losing existing data:

1. Rename the existing physical file object. This changes file references in all based-on logical file objects. (EMPPF becomes OLDEMPPF.)

2. Add new fields, change existing field lengths, if necessary, in the source DDS of the original physical file. (Source member EMPPF in QDDSSRC is changed.)

3. Compile the modified source member, creating a new (empty) file object. (New EMPPF now exists, with no data.)

4. Use the CPYF command with record format field mapping (*MAP) to copy data from the renamed file (OLDEMPPF) to the new file (EMPPF).

5. Change DDS of based-on logical files where needed to recognize new fields; recompile logical files.

6. Recompile all programs and queries that use the physical file and any programs and queries that use changed logical files.

As you have seen, it is not difficult to modify an existing database file if you take proper precautions. (One such precaution for production files would be to create a duplicate object in a secure library before doing anything else.) Then by using PDM options and the powerful CPYF command, you can save data by renaming the physical file and then copying the data into a new, modified file with no danger.

As you work through the lab at the end of this lesson, you gain experience and confidence with PDM and various CL commands.

USING CHGPF TO MODIFY A PHYSICAL FILE

Current releases of OS/400 support an enhanced version of the CHGPF command that performs many of the functions discussed above for changing the record format of a file while keeping the data intact. Originally, the CHGPF command was used to change certain file information from how it was set at compile time. Values that could be changed (and still can) include maximum number of members, access path maintenance, file size, length of time a program waits for a record, whether deleted record space is reused, and whether record format level checking is done.

Some powerful new parameters have been added that now permit an existing file containing data to be rebuilt with new fields in only two steps. Renaming the current physical file is unnecessary, so the first step using the CHGPF command is to change the existing source DDS, adding the new fields or changing existing field attributes if necessary. The CHGPF command restores data by field mapping, just as the CPYF command with FMTOPT(*MAP) does, so of course one field attribute you would *not* want to change is field name.

After the source DDS has been changed, you are ready to run the CHGPF command. Figure 9.20 shows the first screen of the CHGPF command prompt with additional parameters.

```
                    Change Physical File (CHGPF)

Type choices, press Enter.

Physical file . . . . . . . . . > EMPPF        Name
  Library . . . . . . . . . .      *LIBL       Name, *LIBL, *CURLIB
System . . . . . . . . . . . .    *LCL        *LCL, *RMT, *FILETYPE
Source file . . . . . . . . . > QDDSSRC       Name, *NONE
  Library . . . . . . . . . . >    JAFINTRO    Name, *LIBL, *CURLIB
Source member . . . . . . . .    *FILE        Name, *FILE
Source listing options . . . .                *SRC, *NOSRC, *SOURCE...
                  + for more values
Generation severity level  . . .  20          0-30
Flagging severity level  . . . .  0           0-30
Delete dependent logical file  .  *NO         *NO, *YES
Remove constraint . . . . . . .   *RESTRICT   *RESTRICT, *REMOVE
Expiration date for member . . .  *NONE       Date, *SAME, *NONE
Maximum members . . . . . . . .   1           Number, *SAME, *NOMAX
Access path size . . . . . . . .  *SAME       *SAME, *MAX4GB, *MAX1TB
Access path maintenance . . . .   *SAME       *SAME, *IMMED, *REBLD, *DLY

                                                            More...
F3=Exit  F4=Prompt    F5=Refresh    F12=Cancel   F13=How to use this display
F24=More keys
```

Figure 9.20
Change Physical File Command Prompt Screen Showing Additional Parameters

The only required parameter is the Physical file name, but for our purposes, the Source file parameter must also be specified. The default value for this parameter is *NONE, and by giving it another value you are telling the CHGPF command not only that you are rebuilding the file but also where to find the modified DDS to use as a blueprint.

In Figure 9.20, we are telling the CHGPF command to use the DDS in source file QDDSSRC in library JAFINTRO. The Source member parameter defaults to *FILE, and as long as the member containing the source code has the same name as the physical file (this should normally be the case), there is no need to change it.

Using CHGPF has several advantages over the multistep process described in previous sections:

- No need to rename the old file
- No need to track down and recompile logical files just to redirect their based-on pointers
- No need to use the CPYF — the CHGPF command builds its own temporary file and maps data back into the changed file
- No need to remove physical file constraints from a renamed file and then add them back to the new file

Generally, the use of CHGPF makes modifying an existing physical file easier and less error prone, especially if a number of logical files or physical file constraints are based on the physical file. The system warns you if data could be lost in the process and gives you the option to cancel the command or ignore the warning and proceed. The default value of *NO on the Delete dependent logical file parameter automatically cancels the command if the new record format removes a field that is part of any based-on logical file's record format. Additionally, the Remove constraint parameter, with its default value of *RESTRICT, automatically cancels the command if the new record format attempts to eliminate a field that is the parent key for a foreign key field of a dependent physical file and the relationship is formalized by a database constraint. For example, if you wanted to make sure that all Zip codes entered or changed in the employee file were actually contained in the Zip code file, you would use the following ADDPFCST (Add Physical File Constraint) command:

```
ADDPFCST   FILE(EMPPF)   TYPE(*REFCST)    +
           KEY(ZIP)      PRNFILE(ZIPPF)   +
           PRNKEY(ZIP)
```

Once the command is executed, DB2/400 enforces the rule that all EMPPF Zip code values must exist in the ZIPPF.

Once the rule is established, DB2/400 doesn't let you remove the parent key field (ZIP) from the parent physical file's (ZIPPF) record format with the CHGPF command unless the Remove Constraint parameter of the CHGPF command is changed from its default value of *RESTRICT to *REMOVE. Doing so would permit removal of the referential constraint on file EMPPF that was established by the ADDPFCST command above, allowing the CHGPF command to complete.

As you can see, the pumped-up CHGPF command is a powerful and convenient way to change a physical file's structure, and its built-in safeguards protect you against making certain mistakes.

DATABASE FILE-LEVEL SECURITY

In earlier lessons you learned how logical files can be used to restrict access to groups of records in a physical file through the Select and Omit keywords. And you learned how, at the field level, projection can be used to limit access by building a logical file record format including only the fields a user needs to do his/her work. But what about the physical file itself — what authority do users have to it and how can access to it be controlled?

Every object has at least two explicitly authorized users: the owner of the object and everyone else not covered by another explicit authorization. "Everyone else" is given the special name *PUBLIC. The owner of an object has all authority to it — (s)he can display or change its description, save and restore it, rename it, copy it to another library, or delete it. If it is an object — such as a physical file — that has a data component, (s)he can read the data, delete or add new records, and change existing records. Although most object types (e.g., *PGM and *QRYDFN) don't have a data component, there are others besides physical files that do. For example, a library's data component is the objects in the library; for an output queue, it's the spooled files in the output queue.

Figure 9.21 shows the EDTOBJAUT (Edit Object Authority) command output for file EMPPF in library JAFINTRO. When you run this command, both the object name and type are required parameters.

Initially, the screen comes up with no detail displayed, but pressing F11 once displays object authority detail, as shown in Figure 9.21. Pressing F11 again displays data authority detail, as shown in Figure 9.22.

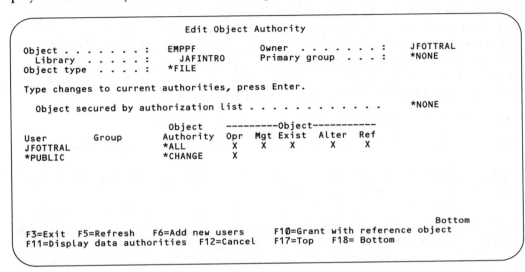

```
                         Edit Object Authority

Object . . . . . . . :   EMPPF            Owner . . . . . . . :    JFOTTRAL
  Library . . . . . :      JAFINTRO       Primary group . . . :    *NONE
Object type . . . . :    *FILE

Type changes to current authorities, press Enter.

  Object secured by authorization list . . . . . . . . . . .      *NONE


                           Object   ---------Object-----------
User         Group         Authority Opr Mgt Exist Alter  Ref
JFOTTRAL                   *ALL       X   X    X     X     X
*PUBLIC                    *CHANGE    X




                                                             Bottom
F3=Exit  F5=Refresh   F6=Add new users    F10=Grant with reference object
F11=Display data authorities  F12=Cancel   F17=Top   F18= Bottom
```

Figure 9.21
EDTOBJAUT for File EMPPF with Object Authorities Detail

```
                         Edit Object Authority

Object . . . . . . . :   EMPPF            Owner . . . . . . . :    JFOTTRAL
  Library . . . . . :      JAFINTRO       Primary group . . . :    *NONE
Object type . . . . :    *FILE

Type changes to current authorities, press  Enter.

  Object secured by authorization list . . . . . . . . . . .      *NONE



                           Object   -------------Data-------------
User         Group         Authority Read Add Update Delete Execute
JFOTTRAL                   *ALL       X    X    X     X      X
*PUBLIC                    *CHANGE    X    X    X     X      X




                                                             Bottom
F3=Exit     F5=Refresh   F6=Add new users   F10=Grant with reference object
F11=Nondisplay detail  F12=Cancel           F17=Top   F18=Bottom
```

Figure 9.22
EDTOBJAUT for File EMPPF with Data Authorities Detail

The detail object and data authority types and a brief statement of their usage is shown in Table 9.1.

Table 9.1

Object and Data Authority Types and Usage

Object Authorities	Usage
Opr — Operational	Look at the object's description; do whatever the data authority permits
Mgt — Management	Move, Rename, and Create Duplicate Object; grant authority
Exist — Existence	Delete the object; perform SAVE and RESTORE operations
Alter — Alter	Add, Clear, Reorganize database file members; change file structure (CHGPF)
Ref — Reference	Specify the object as parent file in adding a referential constraint (to a dependent file)

Data Authorities	Usage
Read	View the data (e.g., DSPFFD, RUNQRY) or read-only access from RPG, Cobol program
Add	Add records to a file, messages to a message queue
Update	Change records in a database file
Delete	Remove records from a file, spooled files from an output queue, objects from a library
Execute	Call a program

Because it is mildly irritating to toggle through several screens just to see or change the detail authorities for object and data, you should consider changing the User options (USROPT) parameter of the CHGPRF (Change Profile) command from *NONE to *EXPERT. This value condenses the detail authority information into a single screen (Figure 9.23). From this point on, in this text, all authority-related screens will be shown with the user profile option set to *EXPERT.

```
                    Edit Object Authority

Object . . . . . . . :   EMPPF          Owner  . . . . . . . :    JFOTTRAL
   Library . . . . . :     JAFINTRO     Primary group  . . . :    *NONE
Object type  . . . . :   *FILE

Type changes to current authorities,  press  Enter.

  Object secured by authorization list . . . . . . . . . . . .  *NONE


                        Object     -----Object------   ------Data-------
User          Group     Authority  O   M   E   A   R   R   A   U   D   E
JFOTTRAL                *ALL       X   X   X   X   X   X   X   X   X   X
*PUBLIC                 *CHANGE    X                   X   X   X   X   X




                                                            Bottom
F3=Exit      F5=Refresh    F6=Add new users   F10=Grant with reference object
F12=Cancel   F17=Top       F18=Bottom
(C) COPYRIGHT IBM CORP. 1980, 1995.
```

Figure 9.23
EDTOJBAUT Screen with User Profile USROPT Parameter Set to *EXPERT

As you can see, the owner, JFOTTRAL, of object EMPPF has all object authority; but why does *PUBLIC have *CHANGE authority? When an object is created, the authority parameter for the object, which determines public authority, is set to *LIBCRTAUT by default. This means that the system checks the create authority value of the library that the object will go into and uses the value found there. That value itself is normally set by default to the system value QCRTAUT. Because the QCRTAUT system value is shipped as *CHANGE, that is what appears as object public authority if no default values are changed. If you wanted to use a tighter public authority of *USE or even *EXCLUDE for all objects in a library, you could change the create authority parameter value when the library is created. After a library has been created, you can use the CHGLIB (Change Library) command to change the create authority (CRTAUT) parameter value. Of course, changing the CRTAUT value for an existing library has no effect on objects already created in it, but applies to newly created objects.

When an object is created, you can specify an authority class such as *USE or *EXCLUDE instead of the *LIBCRTAUT default for the object's authority parameter value. This overrides the create authority, and in this way you can choose a particular public authority class for each object at the time you create it.

If the object has already been created and you own it, you can change explicit authorities if you need to. Look again at Figure 9.23. Suppose you want to give user ASTUDENT change capability, BSIMPSON use capability, and exclude everyone else. Function key F6 lets you provide explicit authority to other user profiles not currently on the list. Pressing F6 from the Edit Object Authority screen for EMPPF takes you to the Add New Users screen shown in Figure 9.24 (two new users have already been entered in the figure).

Figure 9.24
Add New Users
Screen from
EDTOBJAUT

```
                                Add New Users
Object . . . . . . . . :    EMPPF              Owner  . . . . . . . . :    JFOTTRAL
   Library  . . . . . :       JAFINTRO         Primary group  . . . :    *NONE
Object type  . . . . :      *FILE

Type new users, press Enter.

                      Object     -----Object------   ------Data-------
User                  Authority   O  M  E  A  R    R  A  U  D  E
ASTUDENT__            *CHANGE__   _  _  _  _  _    _  _  _  _  _
BSIMPSON__            *USE_____   _  _  _  _  _    _  _  _  _  _

_____             _____   _  _  _  _  _    _  _  _  _  _
_____             _____   _  _  _  _  _    _  _  _  _  _
_____             _____   _  _  _  _  _    _  _  _  _  _
_____             _____   _  _  _  _  _    _  _  _  _  _
_____             _____   _  _  _  _  _    _  _  _  _  _
_____             _____   _  _  _  _  _    _  _  _  _  _

_____             _____   _  _  _  _  _    _  _  _  _  _
                                                                  More...
F3=Exit    F12=Cancel   F17=Top F18=Bottom
```

On this screen you can enter user profile names and specify authority levels either by typing an X for each object and data authority you want to provide or by using an authority class special value such as *CHANGE.

Now, let's return to the Edit Object Authority screen and change *PUBLIC authority to *EXCLUDE. We can do this simply by typing over the current value (*CHANGE) under Object Authority. When we press Enter to save the change, the screen will look like the one shown in Figure 9.25.

Figure 9.25
Object Authorities
Added and Changed
for Object EMPPF

```
                            Edit Object Authority
Object . . . . . . . . :    EMPPF              Owner  . . . . . . . . :    JFOTTRAL
   Library  . . . . . :       JAFINTRO         Primary group  . . . :    *NONE
Object type  . . . . :      *FILE

Type changes to current authorities,  press  Enter.

   Object secured by authorization list  . . . . . . . . . . . .       *NONE

                               Object     -----Object------   ------Data-------
User        Group              Authority   O  M  E  A  R    R  A  U  D  E
JFOTTRAL                       *ALL        X  X  X  X  X    X  X  X  X  X
ASTUDENT                       *CHANGE     X  _  _  _  _    X  X  X  X  X
BSIMPSON                       *USE        X  _  _  _  _    X  _  _  _  X
*PUBLIC                        *EXCLUDE    _  _  _  _  _    _  _  _  _  _

                                                                      Bottom
F3=Exit        F5=Refresh    F6=Add new users     F10=Grant with reference object
F12=Cancel     F17=Top       F18=Bottom
Object authorities changed.
```

Figure 9.25 clearly shows the different authority levels for the four classes: *ALL, *CHANGE, *USE, and *EXCLUDE. Considering this information, we can make a couple of observations. First, given the ultimate power of *ALL object authority, you would have to be very careful about who owned objects in a production environment to avoid possible harm to critical data, programs, and so on. For enterprise database files especially, it should go without saying that indiscriminately granting *ALL authority to casual users is asking for trouble. At the other extreme, for a user who has *EXCLUDE authority, an object's very existence would be unknown; any attempt to display the object's description or work with it in a PDM list would be thwarted. At the least, object operational authority is required to perform any action on an object. So you could assign a user who needs to view but not change, add, or delete records in a file the class *USE, which would provide the minimal object operational and data read authorities.

All levels of explicit authority provided to users of an object are still subordinate to that user's access to the library in which the object exists. For example, in Figure 9.25 users ASTUDENT and BSIMPSON are given some degree of access to object EMPPF in library JAFINTRO. But if object authority for library JAFINTRO were defined as shown in Figure 9.26, any attempt by either user to access EMPPF would fail.

```
                      Edit Object Authority
                                                                Figure 9.26
Object . . . . . . . :   JAFINTRO      Owner  . . . . . . . :   JFOTTRAL
   Library  . . . . . :   QSYS          Primary group  . . . :   *NONE
Object type  . . . . :   *LIB

Type changes to current authorities, press Enter.

   Object secured by authorization list . . . . . . . . . . .   *NONE

                        Object    -----Object------    ------Data-------
                        Authority  O  M  E  A  R    R  A  U  D  E
User        Group       *ALL       X  X  X  X  X    X  X  X  X  X
JFOTTRAL
*PUBLIC                 *EXCLUDE   _  _  _  _  _    _  _  _  _  _




                                                                Bottom
F3=Exit      F5=Refresh  F6=Add new users   F10=Grant with reference object
F12=Cancel   F17=Top     F18=Bottom
```

Figure 9.26
Edit Object Authority
for Library JAFINTRO,
Public is Excluded

This would be true as well for any other user not having the user profile special authority of *ALLOBJ. User profile *ALLOBJ (all object) special authority is extremely powerful (and dangerous); in a production environment it should be granted only to the security officer. It overrides any explicit or public revocation of authority.

Because neither ASTUDENT nor BSIMPSON have *ALLOBJ authority, an attempt by either to run the WRKOBJPDM command on library JAFINTRO, for example, would result in a message similar to that shown in Figure 9.27.

Figure 9.27

Main Menu Showing
Failed Command
Attempted by User
ASTUDENT or BSIMPSON
and Error Message

```
 MAIN                           AS/400 Main Menu
                                                     System:    S1018A6G
   Select one of the following:

        1. User tasks
        2. Office tasks
        3. General system tasks
        4. Files, libraries, and folders
        5. Programming
        6. Communications
        7. Define or change the system
        8. Problem handling
        9. Display a menu
       10. User support and education
       11. PC Support tasks

       90. Sign off

   Selection or command
   ===> wrkobjpdm jafintro_____

   F3=Exit    F4=Prompt    F9=Retrieve    F12=Cancel    F13=User support
   F23=Set initial menu
   You do not have the authority to display library JAFINTRO.              +
```

For ASTUDENT and BSIMPSON to use the data authority granted for object EMPPF, they would need at least object operational authority to library JAFINTRO, which contains the physical file. You can provide the proper level of object authority in three ways (short of giving *ALLOBJ special authority). You could use function key F6 from the Edit Object Authority screen for the library to grant explicit authority to each user (that would be done in the same fashion as adding new users for a file or program in a library). Or you could use an authorization list or group profiles. Let's look at these other two methods.

Authorization Lists

An **authorization list** is an AS/400 object that identifies a group of users and specifies individual authority levels for each user. Authorization lists are especially useful when a certain group of users needs authority to a number of different objects and/or libraries. Different users in the list can have different object and data authority levels. Then, instead of having to add individual **private authorities** for each of the needed objects, you can secure each object with the authorization list. (Private authorities are any other user profile names that appear under the User column of the Edit Object Authority screen. The object owner's authority and *PUBLIC authority aren't considered private.) If the group of users is subject to change (employees come and go), it is much easier to maintain one authorization list than the explicit private authorities for the tens or hundreds of objects secured by the authorization list.

To create an authorization list, you would use the CRTAUTL (Create Authorization List) command. The only required parameter is the name of the list. Once you create the authorization list, you can edit it using the EDTAUTL (Edit Authorization List) command. The Edit Authorization List screen is similar to the Edit Object Authority screen and lets you add users to the list using function key F6. If we use that function to add ASTUDENT and BSIMPSON to the list with minimal authority, the edited list would look like the one shown in Figure 9.28.

```
                      Edit Authorization List
Object . . . . . . . :  INTROAUTL      Owner . . . . . . . :     JFOTTRAL
  Library . . . . . :  QSYS           Primary group . . . :     *NONE

Type changes to current authorities, press Enter.

              Object    List    -----Object------  ------Data-------
User          Authority Mgt    O  M  E  A  R  R  A  U  D  E
JFOTTRAL      *ALL       X     X  X  X  X  X  X  X  X  X  X
ASTUDENT      *USE       _     X  _  _  _  _  X  _  _  _  X
BSIMPSON      *USE       _     X  _  _  _  _  X  _  _  _  X
*PUBLIC       *EXCLUDE   _     _  _  _  _  _  _  _  _  _  _




                                                            Bottom

F3=Exit   F5=Refresh   F6=Add new users    F12=Cancel
F15=Display authorization list objects     F17=Top   F18=Bottom
Object authorities changed.
```

Figure 9.28

Edit Authorization List for INTROAUTL Showing Two Users Added

Our two members have been given only *USE authority on this list. We intend to secure the library, and this authority level is adequate for them to gain access to the library.

Notice that *PUBLIC authority is still excluded. However, to use the *PUBLIC authority assigned through the authorization list and not the *PUBLIC authority granted for the object itself, the object's *PUBLIC authority would need to be changed to *AUTL.

Notice also that a new authority level, List Management, is shown. List management authority lets the owner of the list change the authority of list members or add new members to the list. The owner of the list may grant list management authority to other list members. A user with list management authority may add new members to the authorization list, granting them authority up to but not exceeding the manager's own authority.

Once an authorization list has been created and members have been added to it, you need to secure the necessary objects whose access will be controlled by the list. This is done by replacing the default (*NONE) with the name of the authorization list in the "Object secured by authorization list" entry field of the Edit Object Authority screen. Figure 9.29 shows that we have entered the authorization list name (INTROAUTL) for library JAFINTRO.

Figure 9.29

Edit Object Authority
Showing Library
JAFINTRO Secured by
Authorization List

```
                        Edit Object Authority
Object . . . . . . . :  JAFINTRO      Owner . . . . . . . :  JFOTTRAL
  Library . . . . . :    QSYS         Primary group . . . :  *NONE
Object type . . . . :  *LIB

Type changes to current authorities, press Enter.

  Object secured by authorization list . . . . . . . . . .   INTROAUTL

                          Object   -----Object------  ------Data-------
User          Group      Authority  O   M   E   A   R   R   A   U   D   E
JFOTTRAL                 *ALL       X   X   X   X   X   X   X   X   X   X
*PUBLIC                  *AUTL      _   _   _   _   _   _   _   _   _   _



                                                              Bottom
F3=Exit      F5=Refresh  F6=Add new users   F10=Grant with reference object
F12=Cancel   F14=Display authorization list F17=Top   F18=Bottom
(C) COPYRIGHT IBM CORP. 1980, 1995.
```

Now, when any authorization list member attempts to access the library through PDM, (s)he will be presented with a list of all objects in the library from which (s)he is not explicitly excluded.

Then the specific object authorities come into play. ASTUDENT, for example, will be able to run a change DFU on EMPPF because she has been given *CHANGE object authority; but BSIMPSON will not. He was given only *USE authority to EMPPF, which provides read-only access. He can display records using a temporary DFU (option 18), but any attempt to change records, add new records, or delete records will not be permitted. DFU will respond to such an attempt by displaying the End Data Entry screen (a not too subtle hint) and the message, "You are not authorized to perform the requested operation."

Group Profiles

The third way to provide access to a library, as well as to grant object authority to groups of users, is through the use of group profiles. A **group profile** is similar in certain respects to other user profiles. The security administrator creates it and gives it a user profile name. But because a group profile is not intended to be used for signing on to the system, it should be given a password of *NONE. You must also be careful about providing special authorities — such as spool control or job control — to a group profile because members of the group inherit any special authorities in addition to their own individual authorities. Once the group profile is created, you can assign individual users to it by changing the Group profile parameter of each group member's user profile. (The security administrator must perform this task.) Users with similar system needs can be assigned to the same group profile. There can be as many different group profiles as there are groups of users with distinct needs.

Once the membership of a group profile has been decided, the group profile can be given explicit private authority to objects and libraries like any other user profile. All members of the group are also implicitly granted the same level of authority to a given object as the group profile specifies.

Figure 9.30 shows the group profile INTROAS added to the private authorities for physical file EMPPF.

```
                        Edit Object Authority
Object . . . . . . . :   EMPPF          Owner  . . . . . . . :   JFOTTRAL
   Library . . . . . :      JAFINTRO    Primary group . . . :   *NONE
Object type . . . . :    *FILE

Type changes to current authorities, press Enter.

   Object secured by authorization list . . . . . . . . . .      *NONE

                         Object    -----Object------  ------Data------
User         Group       Authority  O   M   E   A   R   R   A   U   D   E
JFOTTRAL                 *ALL       X   X   X   X   X   X   X   X   X   X
ASTUDENT                 *CHANGE    X   _   _   _   _   X   X   X   X   X
BSIMPSON                 *USE       X   _   _   _   _   X   _   _   _   X
INTROAS                  *CHANGE    X   _   _   _   _   X   X   X   X   X
*PUBLIC                  *EXCLUDE   _   _   _   _   _   _   _   _   _   _

                                                                  Bottom
F3=Exit       F5=Refresh   F6=Add new users  F10=Grant with reference object
F12=Cancel    F17=Top      F18=Bottom
Object authorities changed.
```

Figure 9.30
Group Profile INTROAS Granted *CHANGE Authority

The *CHANGE authority for group INTROAS means that any user in that group could make changes to file EMPPF (with exceptions noted below). Of course, the group (or its individual members) also need at least object operational authority to the library.

To appreciate the pros and cons of these different approaches, you should know that the system uses a hierarchy of authorization checking. At the top is a user with all object (*ALLOBJ) special authority. This special authority overrides any attempted restriction through authorization lists, group profiles, or explicit private object authority.

If the requestor's user profile does not have *ALLOBJ special authority, the system next checks to see whether explicit object authority exists. If the user's name is in the list of private authorities shown by the EDTOBJAUT command, the user will have whatever level of authority is specified there. Explicit object authority takes precedence over both authorization lists and group profiles. And this is true whether the explicit authority limits or extends authority specified by the authorization list or group profile. For example, if BSIMPSON were a member of group profile INTROAS, he would normally share the *CHANGE authority to object EMPPF. But BSIMPSON's explicit authority limits his access to *USE or read-only, and the explicit authorization — even though limiting in this case — takes precedence over the group profile's authority.

If no explicit authorization has been specified for a user, the system checks the authorization list (if there is one) securing the object. If the user is found on the object's authorization list, the authority level granted there applies.

If the requesting user is not on the authorization list for the object (or if there is no authorization list), the system checks to see whether the user is part of a group profile given specific authority to the object. If the user is a member of such a group, the authority granted to the group applies to the user.

Finally, if none of the other cases has been true, the user receives the *PUBLIC authority (or lack of it) granted for that object.

Which object authorization method or combination of methods is most appropriate depends on the circumstances of use for each object. Nonsensitive objects to which most users require some degree of access can be handled by granting to *PUBLIC user *USE or *CHANGE authority for the object. When all users' access to an object (except the owner) can be handled by the *PUBLIC authority, so that no private authorities need to be granted, authority checking is the fastest and most efficiently performed.

Groups of users who generally need the same degree of authorization to groups of objects can probably best be handled by creating a group profile and granting explicit object authority of the necessary degree to the group profile. Group profiles, unlike authorization lists, do not permit the granting of variable levels of authority to different group members, but exceptions to the group-granted authority level can be handled by specifying private object authority for group members when necessary. As described above, such individual user authorization always overrides the group authority. Also, an object can have several different groups, with different levels of authority among its explicitly authorized users. When one group will be the only profile needing special authority beyond *PUBLIC (and the owner), a very efficient way to provide the authority is to make that group the **primary group** of the object. Each object can have one primary group associated with it. If the object already exists, this association can be made through the CHGPGP (Change Primary Group) command. The group profile so assigned must have a Group ID number. The security officer assigns this number when the group profile is created, or it can be added later using the GID parameter of the CHGUSRPRF (Change User Profile) command.

Once an object has been assigned a primary group, the primary group is granted authority to the object (using F6 from EDTOBJAUT). As long as no private authorizations are granted (that is, only owner, the primary group, and *PUBLIC appear under the EDTOBJAUT User heading), authority checking for group members is very fast because primary group information is kept with the object itself, and there is no need for private authority lookups in the requesting user profile.

Authorization lists are most useful when objects generally restricted to public use require different levels of authority among a group of users. Unlike members of a group profile, different users on an authorization list can be granted varying levels of authority (e.g., *ALL, *CHANGE, *USE) and the user-specific authority applies to all objects secured by the authorization list. However, each object can be secured by only one authorization list. So if different groups of users need different degrees of authority within groups, some combination of authorization list, group profiles, and individual private authorities may be required. The problem is that such complicated schemes are not only hard to manage, but also tend to be slower in granting (or refusing) the necessary authority to the requestor.

As discussed above, to override an individual's authorization list authority level for a particular object, you can grant private object authorization for that object to that individual. This type of override can either restrict the authority granted by the authorization list or group profile, or it can provide a higher level of authority.

Object-level security is one place where adherence to the old saw "keep it simple" really pays off. As mentioned above, the best case is to make public authority adequate for all requests. If that's not possible, a primary group or authorization list is still easy to manage and efficient, especially when no private authorities are used. Try to avoid long lists of private authorities, especially if any of them have less authority than *PUBLIC because this increases the number of private authority lookups. Combining long private authority lists with group profiles and authorization lists is almost sure to result in performance problems.

There is much more to learn about object-level security and authorization than we can possibly cover in this text. At best you now have a general idea of how individual users can be given certain levels of authority to different objects on the AS/400. Owners of objects can grant, change, or revoke authority to their objects. But for objects important to the enterprise, the system security officer and/or database administrator will decide which users will have what levels of authority, set up group profiles and authorization lists, and manage and maintain them. The security offered by library and object authorization together with selection and projection at the record and field levels should ensure that authorized users have adequate access to data in which they have legitimate business interests and no access to data they do not need.

For more information about AS/400 security issues, I highly recommend *Implementing AS/400 Security, Third Edition,* a readable and informative book by Wayne Madden and Carol Woodbury (Duke Press, 1998). The IBM manuals *Basic Security Guide* and *Security Concepts and Planning* also contain a lot of information, but they are not exactly easy reading.

Key Terms

authorization list

field mapping

group profile

level check

primary group

private authorities

Lab 9

INTRODUCTION

Upon completion of this lab, you will be able to use various PDM options, including 3=Copy to create a duplicate object and 7=Rename. You can use these options and the CPYF command to make changes to the record format of an existing database file without losing the data already in the file. You become aware of several important CPYF parameters and learn to move data from one file to another at the level of corresponding (mapped) same-named fields. You also examine logical file descriptions using the DSPFD command to see how renaming a physical file affects logical files over it.

You also use the CHGPF command to modify a physical file whose source member you have already changed. You will observe the record format of the changed file and its relationship to its logical files.

Part 1

Goals	Use the CRTDUPOBJ command to copy a file
	Use the DSPDBR command to identify logical files based on a physical file
	Rename objects using a PDM option
	Edit a DDS source member adding a new field
	Compile a DDS source member and check for successful completion
	Use the DSPFD command to identify the physical file that your logical file is based on
Start at	WRKOBJPDM, your library
Procedure	Take Work with Objects Using PDM option 3, and create a backup of STUPF
	Using the DSPDBR command, determine dependent logical files of STUPF
	Using the DSPFD command on STULF1, verify its based-on file
	Rename file STUPF to OLDSTUPF
	Add a field to the source DDS of STUPF; recompile

1.1. After signing on, run the WRKOBJPDM command. Make sure you are looking at the object list for your own current library.

When it becomes necessary to change the record format of an existing file, it is always a good idea to make a backup copy of the file in case the change doesn't go according to plan.

Although copying a large file can be quite time consuming and can require significant system resources, it is nonetheless a necessary precaution. Even the most careful programmer is not entirely immune to a careless mistake. In this lab you copy a file so that you have the experience of using the CRTDUPOBJ command.

You could use the CPYF command and prompt to copy your current physical file, STUPF, to a temporary backup file. But to simply clone an object without change, you can take the PDM Copy option on file STUPF and save some keystrokes.

Type the option number for Copy next to STUPF in the PDM list and press F4 to prompt.

1.1a. What command does this option invoke?

This command is similar in function to the CPYF command, but it has fewer options. However, it works for object types other than files. You can use it to duplicate an object in the same library under a different name, or to copy (and optionally rename) an object into another library. This command is especially useful for cloning multiple-member source physical files (e.g., copying all members of QDDSSRC to another library). Notice that the first three parameter values are supplied from the PDM list screen information.

Now press F12 to return to the Work with Objects Using PDM screen.

You should still see the option number on the input field for STUPF. Press Enter to run the option.———

1.2. The Copy Objects screen (Figure 9.31) has two input fields, To library and New Name.

Figure 9.31
Copy Objects Screen

```
                              Copy Objects

From library  . . . . . :    JSMITH

Type the library name to receive the copied objects.

  To library  . . . . . .    JSMITH

To rename copied object, type New Name, press Enter.

Object       Type        New Name
STUPF        *FILE       STUPF_____




                                                           Bottom
  F3=Exit      F5=Refresh      F12=Cancel      F19=Submit to batch
```

Notice that the current values provided for these fields are the original file's library and object names. Try running the option with those defaults (just press Enter).

1.2a. What message is displayed?

Usually when a file is copied, it is placed in a different library with the original name, or it is placed in the same library but given a different name. With the names already supplied, you can modify one or the other easily.

Move the cursor down and change the New Name to STUPFCPY, and press Enter.

1.2b. What message displays when the command finishes execution?

1.3. You have now made a copy of your original STUPF physical file. To verify that the data was copied to the new file, display the data in the file just created using the DSPPFM command. Prompt for parameters or enter the file name as a positional parameter value, then press Enter.

1.3a. Does the copied file appear to contain the same data as your original file? Press the function key to shift your view to the right and examine the rest of the data.

The copied file is a safeguard in case of an accident. We won't do anything more with it now, but it would be wise for you to keep it until you are sure you have successfully completed this lab.

1.4. We will now rename the original file object, STUPF, to OLDSTUPF. Renaming the file removes the entry for STUPF in your library; it will not be necessary to delete the original STUPF before creating a new file using the same name.

After changes are made to the DDS source code for the renamed member STUPF, it can be recompiled using its original name, in effect changing the record format of STUPF. Renaming STUPF to OLDSTUPF changes the pointers of any related logical files (e.g., STULF1) to reference the renamed physical file. This automatically eliminates the problem of unattached logical files mentioned in the text. If, for example, you chose to copy STUPF to STUPFCPY and then simply delete the original STUPF, you would first have to delete any logical files built over STUPF. Only then could the physical file, STUPF, be deleted.

First let's find out which logical files are dependent on STUPF by executing the command **DSPDBR STUPF**. Please do that now. The bottom of the first screen of Display Database Relations shows the number of dependent files, and they are listed on the second screen. You should have at least one dependent logical file, STULF1.

Before renaming physical file STUPF let's check the Files accessed by logical file value of STULF1, stored in the logical file's description.

Take option 5 on logical file STULF1 from your Work with Objects Using PDM list screen. This option creates a temporary spooled file of the DSPFD command output. You could see the same information by executing the DSPFD command, with a parameter value to name the file, from a command line. From PDM, the list item the option is taken on determines the parameter value.

Scan through the information. Check the Database File Attributes and the Access Path Descriptions values. Just before the Select/Omit Description is the list of Files accessed by logical file. For a simple logical file, we can expect this to be a short list of one. The screen should look like the one shown in Figure 9.32.

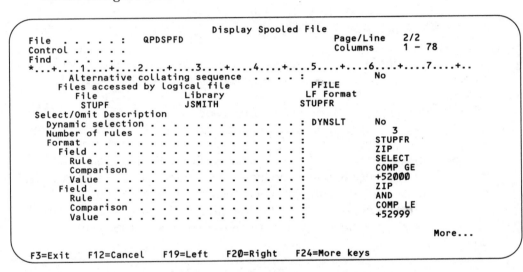

Figure 9.32

DSPFD Command Output for Logical File STULF1

1.4a. Write the name of the based-on physical file on the answer sheet.

When you are finished with the display, press F12 to return to the PDM screen.

1.5. You will now rename the physical file. From the Work with Objects Using PDM screen for your library, take the option to rename on file STUPF. This should take you to a Rename Objects screen like the one shown in Figure 9.33.

Give file STUPF a new name of OLDSTUPF and press Enter. You should now be back at the PDM screen. The message at the bottom of the screen should tell you the rename was successful.

Figure 9.33
Rename Objects Screen

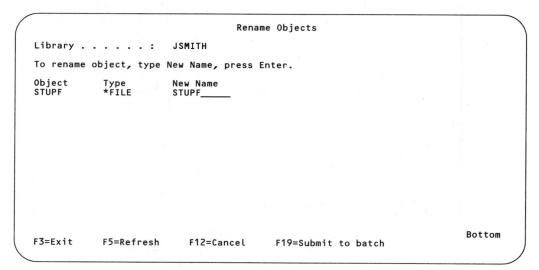

```
                                      Rename Objects
 Library . . . . . . :    JSMITH

 To rename object, type New Name, press Enter.

 Object        Type         New Name
 STUPF         *FILE        STUPF_____




                                                                         Bottom
 F3=Exit      F5=Refresh      F12=Cancel       F19=Submit to batch
```

Now use the Display option once again to check the description of logical file STULF1. Specifically, notice the file named under Files accessed by logical file. As you can see, the name has been changed to OLDSTUPF, the renamed physical file accessed through logical file STULF1.

Now press Enter or F12 to return to the Work with Objects Using PDM screen.

1.6. Choose the Work with option for your source physical file, QDDSSRC.

From the Work with Members Using PDM screen, edit physical file STUPF. Insert a field called ACTBAL right after the FNAME field. (We wouldn't normally put new fields in the middle of name fields, but doing so will help you easily see the data when we display the member.) Specify field ACTBAL as a signed numeric (zoned decimal) field with a length of 7 and 2 decimal places.

1.7. Exit SEU and save the changes. From the Work with Members Using PDM screen take the option to compile the source, creating a new physical file. At this point, if we had not already renamed the existing data file object, a Confirm Compile of Member screen would have appeared and we would have had to tell the system to delete the old STUPF, which it could do only if we had already deleted its based-on logical file(s).

Use the DSPMSG command (or the appropriate PDM option) to be sure the compile was successful. If it was not, edit the source member and use the Browse/Copy option to pull the spooled file into a split screen. Determine the error, make corrections to the source DDS, and recompile.

1.8. When the compile successfully completes, you will have a new version of file STUPF in your library, with field ACTBAL added.

Now return to the Work with Objects Using PDM screen by pressing F12 from the Work with Members Using PDM screen.

1.8a. Does the new file, STUPF, appear on the list screen? Why or why not?

Refresh the screen and make sure that file STUPF is listed.

Part 2

Goals	Verify the success of the Part 1 file change
	Use CPYF to move data from the old to the new file
	Verify the success of the CPYF command
	Delete the backup file
	Recompile the logical file(s)

Start at	WRKOBJPDM or any command line

Procedure	DSPFFD STUPF, check fields

```
CPYF FROMFILE(OLDSTUPF)   TOFILE(STUPF)          +
        MBROPT(*ADD)        FMTOPT(*MAP)
DLTF STUPFCPY
CRTLF on each logical file currently pointing to OLDSTUPF
DLTF OLDSTUPF
```

2.1. Run the DSPFFD command on STUPF from the command line (or take the appropriate PDM option) and verify the presence of the new field. The second page of the display should now look like the one shown in Figure 9.34.

```
                        Display Spooled File
File . . . . . :  QPDSPFFD                    Page/Line   1/22
Control . . . .                               Columns     1 - 78
Find . . . . .
*...+....1....+....2....+....3....+....4....+....5....+....6....+....7....+...
     Number of fields . . . . . . . . . . . . . :      8
     Record length . . . . . . . . . . . . . . :    116
Field Level Information
                  Data      Field  Buffer   Buffer        Field   Column
     Field        Type     Length  Length  Position       Usage   Heading
     SOCSEC       ZONED      9  0     9          1         Both    SOCSEC
     FNAME        CHAR      15       15         10         Both    FNAME
       Coded Character Set Identifier   . . . . :      37
     ACTBAL       ZONED      7  2     7         25         Both    ACTBAL
     LNAME        CHAR      20       20         32         Both    LNAME
       Coded Character Set Identifier   . . . . :      37
     PHONE        ZONED     10  0    10         52         Both    PHONE
     ADDR1        CHAR      25       25         62         Both    ADDR1
       Coded Character Set Identifier   . . . . :      37
     ADDR2        CHAR      25       25         87         Both    ADDR2
       Coded Character Set Identifier   . . . . :      37

                                                           More...

 F3=Exit   F12=Cancel   F19=Left   F20=Right   F24=More keys
```

Figure 9.34

DSPFFD Output for New STUPF, Page 2

2.1a. How many fields are now in physical file STUPF?

2.1b. What is the total record length?

Return to PDM and run the DSPPFM command on STUPF.

2.1c. What does the message say?

2.2. We can now copy the data from the original file, OLDSTUPF, to the new version of STUPF. Of course we could also use the copied file, STUPFCPY, as a data source in case anything happened to OLDSTUPF.

Because the record format of the new STUPF is different from OLDSTUPF, you need to copy corresponding fields of the From file to the To file for each copied record.

You could type the CPYF command on the command line and request command prompting. But using the Copy file PDM option on OLDSTUPF fills in some parameter values for you. Take option 15 on OLDSTUPF. Specify the newly compiled physical file, STUPF, as the To file. Although there is only one member to copy, leaving the From member default value of *ALL will be all right.

Type *ADD for the Replace or add records parameter. Leave the Create file parameter as *NO, because we have already created the physical file and only want to copy the data.

Do not run the command yet!

Press the function key for Additional parameters and Roll up (Page down) until you see the Record format field mapping parameter. Use Help to find out what this parameter does and the meaning of the possible parameter values.

2.2a. Define "Same record format" according to Help.

Find the parameter value that copies fields with the same name in the From file and the To file record formats.

2.2b. If you use this value, how will fields in the To file (the new STUPF) that do not exist in the From file (the old renamed file) be handled (e.g., the ACTBAL field)?

Did you choose the *MAP value? If not, check the Help information again and make sure you end up with *MAP entered for the Record format field mapping parameter value. The CPYF command prompt screen should look like the one shown in Figure 9.35.

```
                       Copy File (CPYF)

 Type choices, press Enter.

 Include records by field test:
   Relationship . . . . . . . . .   *NONE        *NONE, *IF, *AND, *OR
   Field  . . . . . . . . . . .     _____   Name
   Relational operator  . . . . .   ___          *EQ, *GT, *LT, *NE, *GE...
   Value . . . . . . . . . . . .    _____
                                    _____
               _____
                 + for more values
 Record format field mapping  . .   *map___      *NONE, *NOCHK, *CVTSRC...

 Source update options  . . . . .   *SAME__      *SAME, *SEQNBR, *DATE
 Source sequence numbering:
   Starting sequence number . . .   1.00___      0.01-9999.99
   Increment number . . . . . . .   1.00___      0.01-9999.99

                                                           More...


 F3=Exit    F4=Prompt    F5=Refresh   F12=Cancel   F13=How to use this display
 F24=More keys
```

Figure 9.35
CPYF Command
Prompt Screen
Showing Record
Format Field Mapping
Parameter

2.2c. If some fields in the old file (the From file) were not included in the new file and, thus, did not match any field names in the To file, which additional parameter value would you have to use?

When you are sure all values are correct, press Enter to run the CPYF command.

2.2d. What message displays on the Work with Objects Using PDM screen?

2.3. Display the physical file member of STUPF to examine the updated physical file.

2.3a. Locate the new field, ACTBAL. To what value has field ACTBAL been initialized?

Print a screen of the physical file data and clip it to your answer sheet.

2.4. Return to the Work with Objects Using PDM screen. If the data was copied properly into the new version of file STUPF, you can now prepare to delete the other copies of the old file, STUPFCPY and OLDSTUPF.

First take the PDM option to delete STUPFCPY. From the Delete screen, confirm by pressing Enter.

2.4a. What message is displayed on the PDM screen?

2.5. Now take the delete option for OLDSTUPF and confirm.

2.5a. What message is displayed this time?

To find out why this message was displayed, move the cursor down to the message line and press Help.

You are not able to delete physical file OLDSTUPF because logical files are still pointing to that physical file.

Leave Help, erase the delete option, and execute the CL command to display database relations on file OLDSTUPF.

2.6. The DSPDBR command lists all logical files currently dependent on a physical file. As mentioned in the text, the system will not let you delete a physical file that has dependent logical files. When the rename command changed the name of STUPF to OLDSTUPF, it also changed the dependent logical files to point to the renamed file.

   2.6a. Write on the answer sheet the names of logical files dependent on OLDSTUPF.

   You need to delete these files before the OLDSTUPF file can be eliminated, and you need to change the logical files so that they will once again be based on the new version of STUPF.

   Both goals can be accomplished by recompiling the logical files. The source DDS for the logical files will still refer to STUPF as the PFILE or JFILE parameter value. Even though the logical file objects were changed by renaming the original STUPF to OLDSTUPF, this had no effect on the source code used to originally create the logical files. Let's verify that by examining the source code of the first logical file in your list of dependent logical files (you developed the list in answer to question 2.6a).

   First, return to the Work with Objects Using PDM screen, then take the Work with option on source physical file QDDSSRC.

2.7. From the Work with Members Using PDM screen, display the DDS source for the first logical file you listed in 2.6a. Notice that its PFILE value is still STUPF even though, as we saw in Step 1.5, the rename operation changed the pointer in the logical file object. This emphasizes the fact that, once created, a file object is a separate entity from the source DDS member used to create it. Changing the file object has no direct bearing on the source member. To re-establish the based-on relationship between the logical file and the new, modified physical file with the original PFILE or JFILE name, you will simply recompile the logical file.

2.8. From the Work with Members Using PDM screen, take the Compile option on the logical file. You should now see the Confirm Compile of Member screen (Figure 9.36).

This is a very important screen, and whenever you see it you should pay close attention to it. Basically, the system is warning you that an object already exists in your library with the same name and type as the new object you are attempting to create. The implication is that if the existing object contains working code or data, the compile will, in effect, wipe out that code or data. For example, if you had a large data physical file and for some reason you compiled the DDS without saving the data, all the data in the file would be lost because the existing data member is deleted before the compile. It is important that you understand the implications for existing data files or programs when you create a new object.

Figure 9.36

Confirm Compile of Member Screen

```
                         Confirm Compile of Member

The following object already exists for the compile operation:

    Object which exists  . . . . . . . . :    STULF1
        Library  . . . . . . . . . . . . :       JSMITH
    Object type  . . . . . . . . . . . . :    *FILE

    Member to compile  . . . . . . . . . :    STULF1
    File . . . . . . . . . . . . . . . . :    QDDSSRC
        Library  . . . . . . . . . . . . :       JSMITH

Type choice, press Enter.
Press F12=Cancel to return and not perform the compile operation.

    Delete existing object . . . . . . . .    N     Y=Yes, N=No




F12=Cancel
```

In this case, the member you are compiling is a logical file. Because it contains no data and you are not changing the format of the logical file itself — you are only attempting to re-establish the based-on relationship to its physical file — it is safe to proceed.

From the Confirm Compile of Member screen, change the Delete existing object value to Y and press Enter.

The message on the message line should indicate that your old logical file has been deleted. Also notice that there is an additional message to be displayed (indicated by the plus sign on the right side of the message line). If you move the cursor down to the message line and press Page down, you can see the second line of the message. It indicates that the compile was submitted as a batch job to job queue QBATCH.

2.9. Display the message sent by the batch compile job to your message queue. Either take the user-defined PDM option, DM, or key in the DSPMSG command on a command line. Make sure the compile completed successfully, then press Enter or F12, and from the Work with Members Using PDM screen, take the compile option on any other file dependent on OLDSTUPF.

When you have successfully recompiled all the dependent files on your list, return to the Work with Objects Using PDM screen.

2.10. Use the Display option on the first logical file on your list again and check the Files accessed by logical file. The logical file should now point to physical file STUPF.

From the Work with Objects Using PDM screen, try again to delete file OLDSTUPF. You should be successful because OLDSTUPF should now have no logical files based on it. If the delete was not successful, use the DSPDBR command again to see which files are still based on file OLDSTUPF, and then recompile them. If all else fails, ask your instructor/mentor for help.

Part 3

Goals	Use DFU to update STUPF new field data Understand level check and how to respond
Start at	WRKOBJPDM, your library
Procedure	Take PDM option 18 on STUPF Change the ACTBAL field Take PDM option 16 to run a query

3.1. Now take the PDM option on file STUPF to Change using DFU and update the file using a temporary DFU program. Remember that Page down (Roll up) pages you through the file one record at a time. Also, when changes are made to a displayed record, temporary DFUs save the changes when you press Page up/down just as if you had pressed Enter on the updated record display.

Add values for field ACTBAL to each record using a range of different values. Press Field exit after typing numbers in field ACTBAL. Remember that the two low-order digits are cents, so if you enter 1234 it will be stored as 12.34.

3.2. Exit DFU and return to the Work with Objects Using PDM screen. Take the Run option on the query definition STUQRY1.

3.2a. What screen is displayed?

3.2b. What is the second line of the message that has displayed?

Move the cursor up to the message itself on either of the two lines under the screen header. Press the Help key.

You should now be looking at a display similar to the one shown in Figure 9.37.

Read the Cause and Recovery sections of the message. Now look at the header information for this screen; notice that the message displayed here has both an ID and a message type.

```
                    Additional Message Information

Message ID . . . . . . :  QRY1058       Severity . . . . . . . :  99
Message type . . . . . :  Inquiry
Date sent  . . . . . . :  06/10/98       Time sent  . . . . . . :  20:28:50

Message . . . . :  Level for file STUPF in JSMITH does not match query (I C).
Cause . . . . . :  The field, record format, or file definitions for this
input file have changed since query STUQRY1 in JSMITH was created or last
changed. This could be due to either a change to one of the files used in
the query definition, or an override of one of the files used in the query.
  Condition code 2 below indicates how input file definition information
saved with the query will be treated if you ignore this warning:
  1 No saved file information will be used.
  2 Some saved file information will be used.
  If the query can be run, the output may not be what you expect or want.
For condition code 2 for example, if input file definition information saved
with the query indicates that null values need not be expected in selected
                                                                  More...

Press Enter to continue.

F3=Exit    F6=Print    F9=Display message details
F10=Display messages in job log    F12=Cancel    F21=Select assistance level
```

Figure 9.37
Additional Message Information for QRY1058

Because this is an INQUIRY type message, a response is required. To continue, you need to enter either C or I as indicated under Recovery. But, first finish studying this screen, then press Enter to return to the Display program messages screen.

What has occurred is a level check. The system is telling you that the file on which the query is based has been changed so that its record format no longer agrees with that stored in the query itself. Therefore, the query either may not run or may not include changes made to the record format of the file. The system is warning you that you may need to modify and recompile the query for its results to be accurate, or for it even to run.

But let's see what happens if you attempt to run the query without change. Use the Tab key to return the cursor to the reply line and type I for Ignore. Press Enter.

3.3. A message should have appeared briefly at the bottom of the screen indicating that the query was running and that records were being selected. Because there was no error message, it seems that the query ran successfully; but let's check the report in your output queue.

Page up if necessary so that your output queue appears on your Work with Objects Using PDM list and take the Work with option on the output queue.

At this point, several spooled files may be in your output queue; the query report should be the last spooled file in the queue. If you're not sure, press F11 to show the date and time the spooled file was created.

3.3a. What is the file name of the query report?

Display that spooled file and make sure that it is your query. The date and time in the upper left corner of the header should indicate the current date and almost current time. Additionally, the report should include the records you added recently via the logical file.

The report should have run without error, but because you have not changed the query, the newly added account balance field is not included in the output. Essentially, that is what the level check was warning you about. If, however, you had deleted fields that the report needed, or had changed critical field attributes, you would not have been able to run the query without first changing and recompiling it.

Also, you should note that if a database file were accessed directly by high-level language (HLL) programs (e.g., Cobol or RPG) and changes were made to the file as you have done here, the programs using that file would have to be recompiled — unless the level check was specifically overridden — before the programs could be used again.

Return to your Work with Output queue screen and delete all spooled files not required for this lesson.

Part 4

Goals	Use CHGPF to modify an existing database file
	Use RUNQRY to verify new field and default data value
Start at	WRKOBJPDM, your library/QDDSSRC
Procedure	Edit source member STUPF in QDDSSRC
	Add GENDER with a default value
	Use CHGPF to cause the file to be modified
	Observe the database relations on the changed file
	RUNQRY on the changed file

4.1. From the Work with Objects Using PDM screen, take the Work with option on your DDS source physical file.

4.2 Edit member STUPF. Add a new field called GENDER after LNAME and before PHONE. Make it a 1-character alphanumeric field. Use the DDS keyword DFT (default), and specify either M or F as the default value, depending on whether you think there are more males or females at your school/office. The finished screen should look like Figure 9.38.

```
Columns . . . :  1  71          Edit                JSMITH/QDDSSRC
SEU==>_____  STUPF
FMT PF  .....A.........T.Name++++++RLen++TDpB......Functions++++++++++++++++++
         ************* Beginning of data ***********************************
0001.00     A          R STUPFR
0002.00     A            SOCSEC        9S 0
0003.00     A            FNAME        15A
0004.00     A            ACTBAL        7S 2
0005.00     A            LNAME        20A
0006.00     A            GENDER        1A         DFT('M')
0007.00     A            PHONE        10S 0
0008.00     A            ADDR1        25A
0009.00     A            ADDR2        25A
0010.00     A            ZIP           5S 0
         *************** End of data ****************************************



 F3=Exit   F4=Prompt    F5=Refresh   F9=Retrieve   F10=Cursor   F11=Toggle
 F16=Repeat find        F17=Repeat change          F24=More keys
                                      (C) COPYRIGHT IBM CORP. 1981, 1995.
```

Figure 9.38
Adding a New Field, GENDER, to File STUPF

4.3. Stay in your edit session and pull up the system command line by pressing F21. Type the command DSPDBR STUPF and verify that your logical file(s) are based on physical file STUPF. Then press F12 to remove the System command line, and exit SEU, saving your changed member.

4.4. From the command line on the Work with Members Using PDM screen, type the CHGPF command and prompt.

4.4a. How many required parameters does the CHGPF command have?

Type STUPF for the file parameter and QDDSSRC in your library for the Source file parameter. Then press Enter.

4.5. By providing a Source File value, you tell the command you are planning to change the record format, so it displays some additional parameters that you may need to consider.

Notice that the Source Member parameter defaults to *FILE, the assumption being the member will have the same name as the file being changed. Notice also that Delete dependent logical file value is set to *NO. This would stop the command if you were about to eliminate from the physical file any field needed by any based-on logical file.

Leaving all of the default parameter values as they are, run the command.

4.5a. What message appears on the message line of your screen?

4.6. Press F9 until you have retrieved the DSPDBR command, and execute it.

4.6a. Does STUPF still have the same logical files based on it?

4.7. Type the command DSPFFD STUPF on the command line and verify that the new field GENDER is indeed in the record format of STUPF.

As you can see, the CHGPF command has added a new field to the STUPF record format and kept the logical files still pointing at the newly changed file. So now the only question is, how about the data?

4.8. Type the RUNQRY command on the command line and prompt. Instead of naming an existing query, which — as we saw before — would not include newly added fields, we will ask Query/400 to create a report on the fly, using the current record format of STUPF. This is possible only because STUPF is an externally described file.

Tab down to the Query file: File parameter and type STUPF. Leave the other defaults alone and run command. You should see the newly added field GENDER in the report, as well as the ACTBAL field added earlier in the lab.

As you have no doubt realized from this exercise, the CHGPF command is a powerful and convenient way to modify an existing database file. It saves several steps compared to the rename/copy file/recompile method described in Parts 1 and 2, although it is important for you to understand what all is involved in a seemingly simple task like adding a new field to a file. As the number of based-on logical files and constraints on the physical file increases, the convenience of CHGPF becomes more apparent. Like the CPYF command, it is a good command to get to know well.

Return to a command line or the Main menu and sign off.

ADDITIONAL LAB EXERCISE

You should attempt this exercise only after you have successfully completed the primary lab exercises for this lesson.

In this exercise you change authorities of your library and an object in your library, and you sign on as another student to see the effect these changes have on another user's ability to access your library and object.

1. Sign on and work with objects using PDM for your library. From the command line, prompt for the EDTOBJAUT command. This command requires two parameters, object and object type. Enter your library name and *LIB for object and object type.

2. Initially, no detail authority displays on the screen, but authorized users and the system-defined authority level granted to each is displayed. To see detailed object authority, press F11 once. To see detailed data authority, press F11 again. Notice that you, the owner, have all object authority (*ALL) to your library.

   2a. What system-defined authority level is granted to the public?

For a library, data authority applies to the objects within the library. As you can see, *CHANGE authority to a library seems to allow any type of action to be taken on objects in the library that were not explicitly restricted. But let's examine that premise a little more carefully. (If your library is not *CHANGE public authority, make it *CHANGE for now.)

3.   Return to the Work with Objects Using PDM screen for your library. Use PDM option EA (supplied by IBM) to edit the object authority of your source physical file, QDDSSRC.

   3a.   What system-defined authority level is granted to the public for your source physical file?

   (If authority level is not *CHANGE, make it that for now.)

4.   Start an alternate session. To do so on a PC keyboard, hold down the Alt key and press SysRq (system request), the Alt-er ego of Print screen. Or if you are using 5250 emulation, try holding down the Shift key and pressing Esc.

   When the broken line appears at the bottom of the display screen (turquoise on color monitors), press Enter. This should take you to the System Request screen (Figure 9.39).

```
                          System Request
                                             System:    S1018A6G
    Select one of the following:

         1. Transfer to alternative job
         2. End previous request
         3. Display current job
         4. Display messages
         5. Send a message
         6. Display system operator messages
         7. Display work station user

        80. Disconnect job

        90. Sign off and transfer to alternative job

                                                       Bottom
    Selection ___


    F3=Exit    F12=Cancel
    COPYRIGHT IBM CORP. 1980, 1995.
```

Figure 9.39
System Request
Screen

The System Request screen allows several useful functions, including ending a program caught in a loop (option 2), sending a message to another user's message queue (option 5), or finding out who you currently are (option 7) — this need can arise when you frequently switch back and forth between active sessions. Option 1 lets you start an alternate job or switch to an alternate job if one is already started. Take option 1 now to start another job.

5. You can sign on as yourself for a second session if you need to alternate between different views of your empire. But this time, from the sign-on screen, type INTROSTU as both User and Password and press Enter.

   INTROSTU is a genuine student profile with the same class (*PGMR) and special authorities (*NONE) as yours. After signing on as INTROSTU, go to the Work with Objects Using PDM screen, specifying your own library (not INTROSTU's). If your library had *CHANGE authority, INTROSTU should have no trouble bringing up a PDM list.

   Take the Work with option on QDDSSRC. Take the edit option on the first member in the list.

   5a. What happened?
   5b. What message is displayed on the message line?

   Try making a syntactically vali) change to one of the records, then press F3 to exit. From the exit screen, with Change/create member set to Y, press Enter.

   5c. What happened?

   Change the Change/create member value to N and return to the Work with Members Using PDM screen.

   Based on your experience, complete the following sentence on the answer sheet:

   5d. "Just because I have *CHANGE authority to a source physical file…"

   To change a member of the source physical file you need more than *CHANGE authority; you also need object management authority to the object (QDDSSRC). Because the system-defined *CHANGE authority does not provide this, you — as INTROSTU — are not able to change a member of the file.

6. From the Work with Members Using PDM screen, take the option to copy the member you just tried to change. Remember you are INTROSTU, looking at another student's (your) source physical file. Copy the member using the same name to file QDDSSRC in library INTROSTU.

   6a. What happened?

   Change the library of your Work with Members Using PDM screen to INTROSTU. (Now you are INTROSTU looking at INTROSTU's own QDDSSRC member list.)

   6b. Is the copied member there?
   6c. Can you change the copied member?
   6d. Can you delete the copied member?

   If you have not done so, delete the copied member from INTROSTU/QDDSSRC.

6e.   On the answer sheet, write your conclusions about the limitations and capabilities of *CHANGE authority on source file members.

7.   Return to the Work with Objects Using PDM screen for your own library (not INTROSTU's). You should still be signed on as INTROSTU.

Take the PDM option to Change using DFU on the student physical file STUPF. Remember that you are INTROSTU trying to change another student's physical file.

7a.   What happened?

7b.   Are you able to change records in the physical file?

7c.   What conclusions do you draw regarding the power of *CHANGE authority for physical database files?

8.   Exit DFU and, without signing off as INTROSTU, switch sessions back to your own user profile's alternate job. (Shortcut: Press Alt and SysRq to bring up the broken turquoise line, then type 1 — transfer to alternate job — on the line and press Enter.)

9.   From your own job, use the EDTOBJAUT command (PDM option EA) on the STUPF physical file that INTROSTU just changed. Under Data authority for *PUBLIC users (use F11 to get to the Data authorities), erase the X for Update and press Enter to register the change.

9a.   What happened?

10.   Now switch back to the alternate session for INTROSTU and try the DFU on STUPF again.

10a.   Does the DFU come up?

Try changing a record and pressing Enter on the change.

10b.   What happened?

11.   Exit DFU and (remembering that you are INTROSTU) back out to the Main menu, but don't sign off. Switch sessions back to your own job again. This time, from the Edit Object Authority screen for the STUPF physical file, press F6. Add user INTROSTU and give him/her *EXCLUDE authority. Note that you are just excluding INTROSTU from one physical file object.

12.   Switch sessions back to INTROSTU's job. Retrieve the WRKOBJPDM command to bring up the list of objects in your own (not INTROSTU's) library.

12a.   What happened to STUPF?

12b.   What is your conclusion?

13. As INTROSTU, return to the Main menu. Switch sessions back to your own job. First change the authority on STUPF to *ALL for INTROSTU. After registering that change, return to a command line and retrieve the EDTOBJAUT command for your library. Run the command.

    Change public authority of your library to *EXCLUDE, and execute the command.

14. One last time, return to the alternate job for INTROSTU. From the Main menu, retrieve the command to Work with Objects Using PDM for your library and run it.

    14a. What happened?

    Keep in mind that you have given INTROSTU *ALL authority to your STUPF file. As INTROSTU, enter the following command to invoke a temporary update DFU on (your own) STUPF:

    ```
    UPDDTA (your lib)/STUPF
    ```

    14b. What happened?
    14c. What conclusion can you draw regarding the relationship of library and object authority?

    At this point you can sign off as INTROSTU and return to your own job.

    You can leave the public authority on your library set to *EXCLUDE. This prevents unauthorized users from accessing your source files, programs, data files, and so on.

    I hope you concluded above that if you are *EXCLUDED from a library, you can't do anything with any object in the library, even if you have *ALL authority to that object. For object authorities to be used, you must have at least object operational authority to the library containing the objects.

    In this lab you have seen how authority can be granted and revoked at different levels to give various users adequate access to data they need without endangering files that need to be protected. Group profiles and authorization lists extend this ability to tailor authorities to suit the needs of most applications.

    Although you need *SECADM (security administrator) special authority to create group profiles, you could create an authorization list and test its function by adding INTROSTU or one or two of your classmates to the list and then securing your library and/or objects in your library by the authorization list. To check out the various authorization list commands, try GO CMDAUTL.

Mastering the AS/400, Second Edition

Lab 9 Answer Sheet

Name: _____

Date Due: _____

Class Time: _____

1.1a. _____

1.2a _____

1.2b _____

1.3a. _____

1.4a. _____

1.8a. _____

2.1a. _____ 2.1b. _____

2.1c. _____

2.2a. _____

_____

2.2b. _____

_____

2.2c. _____

2.2d. _____

2.3a. _____

2.4a. _____

2.5a. _____

2.6a. _____

3.2a. _____

3.2b. _____

3.3a. _____

4.4a. _____

4.5a. _____

4.6a. _____

Mastering the AS/400, Second Edition

Additional Lab Exercise
Answer Sheet

Name: _____

Date Due: _____

Class Time: _____

2a. _____   3a. _____

5a. _____

5b. _____

5c. _____

5d. _____

6a. _____

6b. _____ 6c. _____ 6d. _____

6e. _____

_____

_____

_____

7a. _____ 7b. _____

7c. _____

_____

9a. _____

10a. _____ 10b. _____

_____

12a. _____

12b. _____

_____

14a. _____

14b. _____

14c. _____

_____

IN SUMMARY

A member of a source physical file functions as instructions or design specifications for creating an object — it is not the object itself. To change an existing file object, you must save the data first, then change the source member and recompile it. This creates a new file similar to the old file but which is a separate object that initially has an empty data member. The saved data from the old file can be copied into the new file using record-format field mapping. One way to save the data is by renaming the old file. This causes pointers in based-on logical files to be changed to the new name. Once the new file has been created, the based-on logical files need to be recompiled. The DSPDBR (Display Database Relations) command is useful for listing the logical files based on a physical file. The CPYF (Copy File) command is a powerful utility for copying existing data to a new record format. The CHGPF command is a convenient way to add new fields to an existing physical file. Using CHGPF, you don't need to rename, copy data into the new file, or recompile based-on logical files. Programs and queries using files that have been changed and re-created also usually need to be recompiled to avoid system level checks.

Objects can be secured by granting appropriate levels of authorization. After *ALLOBJ authority, explicit user authorization has highest priority, followed by authorization lists, then by group profiles. If a user is not among any of these, the public authority to the object applies. For a user to implement *USE or *CHANGE authority to an object, (s)he needs at least *USE authority to the library containing the object.

In the lab for this lesson, you used the CPYF command to restore the data component of a physical file whose record format had been changed. This is a very useful technique to solve a common problem that arises when you need to add fields or change field attributes in an existing file. You used the DSPDBR command to determine the dependent logical files of a physical file and recompiled logical files to re-establish PFILE and JFILE pointers. You examined the inquiry message resulting from a level check on a query whose compiled record format disagreed with the file object's current record format.

You also examined the effects of granting various levels of object and library authority to a user by signing on to an alternate session as that user. In the additional lab exercise, you demonstrated for yourself the relationship between library and object authorization.

Lesson 10

Using DFU and SQL

Lesson Overview

In this lesson we examine options available for creating permanent Data File Utility (DFU) programs — that is, those DFU programs that are tailored to update or display a particular file and that are stored as *PGM type objects. A brief introduction to Structured Query Language (SQL) provides you with another tool to query and update your files.

In the lab for this lesson, you create two different DFU programs: one over an indexed (keyed) file intended for display and one over a nonindexed file intended for update. You also create a new, more complex, query so that you can gain experience with additional Query/400 reporting options. You use command-line SQL to get information from and update records in your database.

Objectives

Students will be able to

✓ Explain several advantages of a permanent DFU program over a temporary DFU program

✓ Create a DFU program over a single record format file using display formatting and numeric editing

✓ Create a DFU program over a multiple-format logical file that allows updates on two different record formats

✓ Create a new, more complex, query so they gain additional experience with Query/400 reporting options

✓ Use command-line SQL to query the database, retrieving information to satisfy specific requests

✓ Use command-line SQL to add, change, and delete records in the database

WHY DFU?

The Data File Utility is a fast and convenient way to build an interactive file maintenance program over any physical or nonjoin logical database file. There are other such utilities available from third-party software vendors that many development shops will be using instead of DFU. These products generally offer features and capabilities not found in DFU, but DFU is available on any system that has the Application Development ToolSet/400 installed.

DFU is easy to use and doesn't require programming skills; the code for the DFU program is generated as you respond to a series of DFU entry screens. For programmers who need to build or change test data files, DFU is a handy tool. For end users with fairly straightforward data entry/file update needs, creating a DFU program could save a lot of time over conventional high-level language (HLL) application development.

DFU does have limitations, and if your application requires any of the following, you'll need to write an HLL program or use a more powerful utility:

- Creating derived (virtual) fields for display by performing calculations on other fields

- Field validation that requires testing the value of another field in the same record (e.g., HIREDATE > BIRTHDATE)

- Accessing field values from a different record of the same file or another record from a related file (e.g., showing new CITY and STATE for a change to ZIP)

- Formatting in subfile displays or other complex display formats

Despite these limitations, DFU is still a worthwhile utility with many useful features. Let's explore some of those features and see how to generate a working program.

ACCESSING DFU

Recall from Lesson 6 that you can access the DFU menu (Figure 10.1) by entering the STRDFU (Start DFU) command on any command line.

In Lesson 6, we used option 5 to create a temporary DFU. In this lesson, we use option 2 to create a permanent DFU. Other options available from the DFU menu include option 3, which is used to modify an existing DFU program; and option 4, which is used to delete a permanent DFU program (taking option 4 from the Work with Objects Using PDM screen on the DFU *PGM object accomplishes the same task).

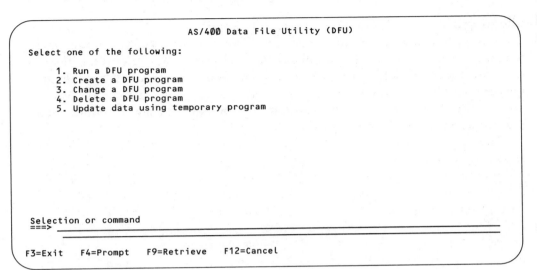

Figure 10.1
DFU Initial Menu

```
                          AS/400 Data File Utility (DFU)

     Select one of the following:

            1. Run a DFU program
            2. Create a DFU program
            3. Change a DFU program
            4. Delete a DFU program
            5. Update data using temporary program




     Selection or command
     ===> _____

     F3=Exit    F4=Prompt    F9=Retrieve    F12=Cancel
```

CREATING A DFU PROGRAM

When you take option 2 from the DFU menu, the Create a DFU Program screen
appears (Figure 10.2).

Figure 10.2
Create a DFU Program
Screen

```
                            Create a DFU Program
     Type choices, press Enter.

        Program . . . . . . . . . .   _____   Name, F4 for list
           Library . . . . . . . . .  *CURLIB___   Name, *CURLIB

        Data file . . . . . . . . .   _____   Name, F4 for list
           Library . . . . . . . . .  *LIBL_____   Name, *LIBL, *CURLIB








     F3=Exit     F4=Prompt     F12=Cancel
```

This screen asks you to name the program you will create, the data file the program
will use, and the libraries in which the program will reside. The first time you use
option 2, the Library value for the Program name parameter defaults to *CURLIB;
after that, DFU uses the value from the previously created program.

Likewise, the Data file value will either be blank (the first time), or it will display the previously used Data file name. If the Data file value is blank, the Library
value defaults to *LIBL.

With both the Program and Data file fields you can use function key F4 to
prompt for a list of existing programs or for a list of all physical and logical files in

the specified library. Prompting does require a specific library reference — you can use *CURLIB or a named library, but *LIBL won't work. For example, if we change the Library value of Data file to *CURLIB and press F4 with the cursor on the Data file input field, a Select File screen appears (Figure 10.3) that lists the physical and logical files in library JAFINTRO, my current library. (Instead of *CURLIB, you could name a library to which you have at least object operational and data read and add authority.)

Figure 10.3

Select File Screen that Results from Prompting for File Name

```
                                           Select File
  Library  . . . . :     *CURLIB

  Position to  . . . . . .

  Type option, press Enter.
    1=Select

  Opt     File        Type       Description
    _     EMPMSTPF    PF-DTA     Emp Mast PF Source
    _     EMPMSTPF1   PF-DTA     Alternate Employee PF
    _     EMPMSTPF1L  LF         Unkeyed version of EMPMSTPF1
    _     EMPNAMKLF   LF         Employee File keyed on Last, First Name
    1     EMPPF       PF-DTA     Employee File
    _     EMPPRJLF2   LF         EMPPF data w/proj, select, keyed on LNAM
    _     EMPZIPJLF1  LF         Natural join of EMPPF, ZIPPF data
    _     EMPZIPJLF2  LF         Outer join of EMPPF, ZIPPF data
    _     FILE01      PF-DTA     dds of PF file01
    _     FILE01B     PF-DTA     file 01 physical DB file
    _     FILE01BK    PF-DTA     RECFMT, 9 fields, 124 bytes
                                                              More...


  F5=Refresh     F12=Cancel
```

Notice in Figure 10.3 that we have already selected the data file the DFU program will use by typing a 1 in the option field next to physical file EMPPF. Note that although join logical files are also included in the list, attempting to select one would result in an error because DFU does not permit the use of join logical files. When you select a file from the prompted list, the list values — EMPPF for Data file and *CURLIB for Library — are filled in on the Create a DFU Program screen, as shown in Figure 10.4. As you can see, we also have given the DFU program a name, EMPPFUPD.

```
                         Create a DFU Program

  Type choices, press Enter.

      Program . . . . . . . . . .   emppfupd___   Name, F4 for list
        Library . . . . . . . . .     JAFINTRO__   Name, *CURLIB

      Data file . . . . . . . .     EMPPF_____   Name, F4 for list
        Library . . . . . . . . .     JAFINTRO__   Name, *LIBL, *CURLIB

  F3=Exit      F4=Prompt      F12=Cancel
```

Figure 10.4

Completed Create a DFU Program Screen

DEFINING GENERAL INFORMATION

When you press Enter from a completed Create a DFU Program screen, the next screen you see depends on the type of data file you named. If the specified file is **nonindexed** (i.e., the file can be accessed only in arrival sequence), such as file EMPPF, you see a Define General Information/Nonindexed File screen (as shown in Figure 10.5).

```
                 Define General Information/Nonindexed File

  Type choices, press Enter.

      Job title . . . . . . . . . . . . . .    EMPPFUPD_____
      Display format . . . . . . . . . .       2           1=Single,   2=Multiple
                                                            3=Maximum,  4=Row oriented

      Audit report . . . . . . . . . . . .     Y           Y=Yes, N=No
      S/36 style . . . . . . . . . . . . .     N           Y=Yes, N=No
      Suppress errors . . . . . . . . . .      N           Y=Yes, N=No
      Edit numerics . . . . . . . . . . .      N           Y=Yes, N=No
      Allow updates on roll . . . . . . .      Y           Y=Yes, N=No
      Record numbers:
        Generate . . . . . . . . . . . .       N           Y=Yes, N=No
        Store in a field . . . . . . . . .     N           Y=Yes, N=No
        Heading . . . . . . . . . . . . .     *RECNBR_____

      Processing . . . . . . . . . . . .       2           1=Direct
                                                            2=Sequential

  F3=Exit      F12=Cancel       F14=Display definition
```

Figure 10.5

Define General Information Screen for a Nonindexed File

For an **indexed** file (i.e., a file with a keyed-sequence access path), the display is slightly different; we examine the differences shortly. First, here's a brief description of the available options common to both file types:

Job title	This is the name (up to 36 characters) that appears in the upper left corner of the Change/Display screen, as well as on an optional audit report. Notice that the Job title defaults to the program name, which is limited to 10 characters. As you will see in our example, a more descriptive Job title can more clearly define the purpose of your DFU program.
Display format	This option tells how fields will be arranged on the display screen. 1=Single: DFU arranges fields in a single column down the screen. 2=Multiple: DFU arranges entry fields in two or more columns on the screen. 3=Maximum: DFU places as many fields as possible on a single screen, not necessarily in columns. 4=Row oriented: DFU arranges fields in rows across the screen, with column headers above each field.
Audit report	This option lets you turn on or off the generation of an audit report (audit log), which lists changes, additions, and deletions to a data file. You saw an example of an audit log when you used a temporary DFU. If you select Y, the next display you see is the Define Audit Control screen.
S/36 style	If this option is selected, function keys will not show on the bottom of the DFU Change/Display screen.
Suppress errors	This option tells DFU whether to attempt to suppress decimal data errors (invalid codes stored in numeric fields).
Edit numerics	If Y is chosen, edit codes and edit words specified for numeric fields will be used. For example, you could enter a decimal or a dollars and cents number with a decimal point. The edit codes could have been defined in the data file DDS, or they can be specified in the DFU itself.
Allow updates on roll	If N is used, the Enter key must be pressed to save changes. If Y is used, Page up/Page down will also save changes.

All the options described at left are available for both nonindexed and indexed files. The options specific to nonindexed files are

Generate (record numbers)	If Y is chosen, DFU assigns a relative record number. If N is chosen, you must provide a number when a record is added to a file.
Store in a field	If Y is chosen, a field must be named for storing the relative record number as part of the record format.
Heading	This option tells how the relative record number will be identified on the display — the default is *RECNBR.
Processing	This option indicates how new records will be added to the file. 1=Direct: Records can be added anywhere in the file. 2=Sequential: Records can be added only to the end of the file.

If we specified an indexed file for use by our DFU program, we would see a Define General Information/Indexed File screen like the one in Figure 10.6.

```
 _____
|           Define General Information/Indexed File            |
|                                                              |
|  Type choices, press Enter.                                  |
|                                                              |
|    Job title . . . . . . . . . . . . . .   EMPNAMKLF         |
|    Display format  . . . . . . . . . . .   2     1=Single,  2=Multiple    |
|                                                  3=Maximum, 4=Row oriented|
|    Audit report  . . . . . . . . . . . .   Y     Y=Yes, N=No |
|    S/36 style  . . . . . . . . . . . . .   N     Y=Yes, N=No |
|    Suppress errors . . . . . . . . . . .   N     Y=Yes, N=No |
|    Edit numerics . . . . . . . . . . . .   N     Y=Yes, N=No |
|    Allow updates on roll . . . . . . . .   Y     Y=Yes, N=No |
|    Keys:                                                      |
|      Generate  . . . . . . . . . . . . .   N     Y=Yes, N=No |
|      Changes allowed . . . . . . . . . .   Y     Y=Yes, N=No |
|                                                              |
|                                                              |
|                                                              |
|                                                              |
|  F3=Exit      F12=Cancel       F14=Display definition         |
|_____|
```

Figure 10.6
Define General Information Screen for an Indexed File

The only difference between this screen and the one you saw previously is that it offers options for the indexed file's keys. These two options are

Generate	Enter Y if you want DFU to generate numeric keys in multiples of 10 for records added to the file. If the key field is a data field, you would take the default, N.
Changes allowed	Y permits the value of a data key field to be changed when the DFU is in change mode. When keys should not be changed, use N.

Figure 10.7 shows the Define General Information/Nonindexed File screen properly filled out for our example.

Figure 10.7

Completed Define
General Information
Screen for EMPPF
Update

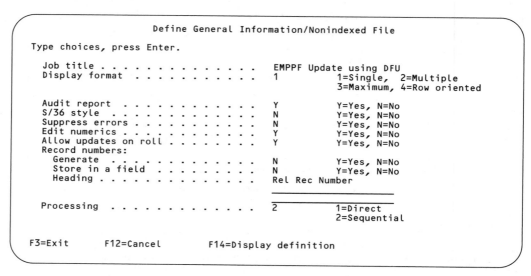

```
                    Define General Information/Nonindexed File

  Type choices, press Enter.

      Job title . . . . . . . . . . . . .   EMPPF Update using DFU
      Display format  . . . . . . . . . .   1        1=Single,  2=Multiple
                                                     3=Maximum, 4=Row oriented

      Audit report  . . . . . . . . . . .   Y        Y=Yes, N=No
      S/36 style  . . . . . . . . . . . .   N        Y=Yes, N=No
      Suppress errors . . . . . . . . . .   N        Y=Yes, N=No
      Edit numerics . . . . . . . . . . .   Y        Y=Yes, N=No
      Allow updates on roll . . . . . . .   Y        Y=Yes, N=No
      Record numbers:
        Generate  . . . . . . . . . . . .   N        Y=Yes, N=No
        Store in a field  . . . . . . . .   N        Y=Yes, N=No
        Heading . . . . . . . . . . . . .   Rel Rec Number
                                            _____

      Processing  . . . . . . . . . . . .   2        1=Direct
                                                     2=Sequential


  F3=Exit        F12=Cancel        F14=Display definition
```

Note that single-column display format has been requested; however, if all fields will fit in a single column, that's the way the screen will be formatted, even if you have chosen Multiple or Maximum for the display format.

Rather than retain the program name as the Job title, we have entered "EMPPF Update using DFU" to more clearly define the purpose of our DFU program. We also have chosen to print an audit report, selected edit numerics, allowed updates on a roll, and changed the record number heading to Rel Rec Number. The DFU program will process file EMPPF sequentially (new records will be added to the end of the file).

DEFINING AUDIT CONTROL AND CHOOSING RECORD FORMATS

After we press Enter on the completed Define General Information/Nonindexed File screen, we see the Define Audit Control screen, Figure 10.8. (This screen would not appear if we had chosen not to print an audit report — that is, if we had taken choice N, for Audit report.)

For our example, we will leave all the defaults as they are on the Define Audit Control screen. But, as you can see, you could change report width, spacing, and even the types of transactions to print.

```
                        Define Audit Control
    Type choices, press Enter.

        Print additions . . . . . . . .   Y        Y=Yes, N=No
        Print changes . . . . . . . . .   Y        Y=Yes, N=No
        Print deletions . . . . . . . .   Y        Y=Yes, N=No
        Printer:
          Line width  . . . . . . . . .   132      60-198
          Column spacing  . . . . . . .   1        0-9











    F3=Exit      F12=Cancel      F14=Display definition
```

Figure 10.8

Define Audit Control Screen

The next display is the Work with Record Formats screen. Our file, being a physical file, has a single record format and you would specify that format by typing option 2 next to the Format name (EMPPFR), as we have done in Figure 10.9. (If we were working with a multiple-format logical file, we would need to choose the record formats we wanted to use.)

```
                      Work with Record Formats
    File . . . :   EMPPF              Library  . . . . :    JAFINTRO

    Type options, press Enter.  Press F21 to select all.
      2=Specify    4=Delete


    Opt  Format      Defined  Description
     2   EMPPFR         N








                                                            Bottom
    F3=Exit                    F5=Refresh       F12=Cancel
    F14=Display definition     F21=Select all
```

Figure 10.9

Work with Record Formats Screen

SELECTING AND SEQUENCING FIELDS

After selecting the record format, we would see the Select and Sequence Fields screen shown in Figure 10.10.

Figure 10.10
Select and Sequence
Fields Screen

```
                      Select and Sequence Fields

 File . . . . . . . . . . . :    EMPPF         Library . . . . :    JAFINTRO
 Record format . . . . . . . :    EMPPFR

 Select fields and their sequence or press F21 to select all; press Enter.


 Sequence   Field          Attr     Length   Type      Description
 _____     EMPNO                     9,0     BIN
 _____     LASTNAME                   16     CHAR
 _____     FIRSTNAME                  12     CHAR
 _____     HOMEPHONE                 7,0     ZONE
 _____     ADDR1                      40     CHAR
 _____     ADDR2                      40     CHAR
 _____     ZIP                       5,0     ZONE
 _____     DEPT                       12     CHAR
 _____     WORKPHONE                 7,0     ZONE
 _____     BIRTHDATE                  10     DATE
 _____     HIREDATE                   10     DATE
                                                                    More...
 F3=Exit           F5=Refresh           F12=Cancel          F14=Display definition
 F20=Renumber      F21=Select all
```

From this screen, we can choose which fields to include on the DFU Update display by assigning them a sequence number. Those fields not given a number will not appear. The order of fields on the DFU Update display screen corresponds to the relative magnitude of the sequence number.

If we want all fields to appear, and we want them to appear in the existing record format order, we can press function key F21 to select them all. For our example, we will use function key F21; Figure 10.11 shows the Select and Sequence Fields screen with all fields selected.

Figure 10.11
Select and Sequence
Fields Screen with All
Fields Selected in
Default Sequence

```
                      Select and Sequence Fields

 File . . . . . . . . . . . :    EMPPF         Library . . . . :    JAFINTRO
 Record format . . . . . . . :    EMPPFR

 Select fields and their sequence or press F21 to select all; press Enter.


 Sequence   Field          Attr     Length   Type      Description
 _____1    EMPNO                     9,0     BIN
 _____2    LASTNAME                   16     CHAR
 _____3    FIRSTNAME                  12     CHAR
 _____4    HOMEPHONE                 7,0     ZONE
 _____5    ADDR1                      40     CHAR
 _____6    ADDR2                      40     CHAR
 _____7    ZIP                       5,0     ZONE
 _____8    DEPT                       12     CHAR
 _____9    WORKPHONE                 7,0     ZONE
 _____10   BIRTHDATE                  10     DATE
 _____11   HIREDATE                   10     DATE
                                                                    More...
 F3=Exit           F5=Refresh           F12=Cancel          F14=Display definition
 F17=Fast path     F20=Renumber         F21=Select all
 Press Enter to confirm or F17 to confirm with defaults.
```

At this point, we must decide whether to use extended field definitions or special features, such as autoduplicate for any fields. If we did not want to use any special features, we would press function key F17 (Fast path) to go directly to the DFU exit menu (this would create a DFU program using default field definitions, such as uppercase entry for alphanumeric fields). Otherwise, we would press Enter. Because we want to use the extended field definition feature, we will press Enter.

SPECIFYING EXTENDED FIELD DEFINITIONS

When we press Enter on the Select and Sequence Fields screen, the Work with Fields screen appears (Figure 10.12). This screen lists all the fields and lets you specify or delete extended definitions. The value (N or Y) under the Extended Definition column tells us whether there is currently an active extended definition for a field. Under Heading, we can change the field identification that will appear on the DFU Change/Display screen.

```
                           Work with Fields

  File . . . . . . . . . . . :   EMPPF        Library . . . . :   JAFINTRO
  Record format . . . . . . . :   EMPPFR

  Type options, press Enter.  Press F21 to select all.
    2=Specify extended definition
    4=Delete extended definition


                   Extended
  Opt   Field      Definition    Heading
  ____  EMPNO          N         EMPNO_____
  ____  LASTNAME       N         LASTNAME_____
  ____  FIRSTNAME      N         FIRSTNAME_____
  ____  HOMEPHONE      N         HOMEPHONE_____
  ____  ADDR1          N         ADDR1_____
  ____  ADDR2          N         ADDR2_____
  ____  ZIP            N         ZIP_____
  ____  DEPT           N         DEPT_____

                                                             More...
  F3=Exit                F5=Refresh      F12=Cancel
  F14=Display definition  F21=Select all
```

Figure 10.12
Work with Fields Screen

We will specify extended definitions for several fields. First we will take option 2 on field EMPNO and press Enter. This brings us to the Specify Extended Field Definition screen shown in Figure 10.13.

```
                    Specify Extended Field Definition

  Field . . . . . . . . :   EMPNO       Record format  . . . . :   EMPPFR

  Type choices, press Enter.

    Auto-duplicate . . . . . . . . . . .   N        Y=Yes, N=No
    Accumulate . . . . . . . . . . . . .   N        Y=Yes, N=No
    Extended field
      heading . . . . . . . . . . . . .   EMPNO_____
                                          _____
    Heading location . . . . . . . . . .   *BEFORE  *ABOVE, *BEFORE
    Initial value . . . . . . . . . . .   _____
    Auto-increment . . . . . . . . . . .
    Validity checks . . . . . . . . . .   _        2=Change, 4=Delete

                                                             More...



  F3=Exit    F12=Cancel    F14=Display definition
```

Figure 10.13
Specify Extended Field
Definition Screen
for EMPNO

Let's look at the options available on this screen.

If you select Auto-duplicate, you can use a Dupe key on the keyboard to copy the value of the previous record's field into the field where the cursor is positioned. When groups of records with a same field value are entered, this feature can save a lot of typing!

The Accumulate option is available for numeric fields. If you select this option, it provides running totals and final totals of changes, additions, and deletions to the field. You can display running totals during the DFU session; and if you request it, running totals and final totals are displayed at the end of the session and printed on the audit log. For a field such as employee number, accumulations would not be useful; but for dollar amount fields, they could be required as part of an audit trail.

Extended field heading lets you provide a more meaningful field description than the field name if the COLHDG keyword was not specified in the DDS. Because the employee file didn't use COLHDG, we will change the field name to "Employee Number". Heading location gives you the option of positioning the field heading above the field rather than to its left (*BEFORE).

If no value were entered for a certain field of a new record and you need its initial value to be something other than the defaults of spaces and zeros, you could specify that starting value in the Initial value field.

Auto-increment lets you set numeric fields to a value that is a certain fixed amount greater than the same field of the previously entered record. This feature works when entering new records in Entry or Insert mode, and it would be useful for serial number fields such as invoice numbers or order item line numbers. Using this feature could reduce the amount of data entry as well as the likelihood of keying errors.

If you specify validity checks, certain data validation will be performed on data entered into a field; for example, mandatory entry, mandatory fill, and testing against one or more valid values. If you select option 2, you will be presented with another screen to specify which validity checks to use. We will request changing validity checks for field EMPNO. (Even though we didn't specify DDS validity check keywords for any fields when the file was described, we can add them now by selecting option 2.)

Before we press Enter to process validity checks, we should examine the second page of the Specify Extended Field Definition Screen (Figure 10.14).

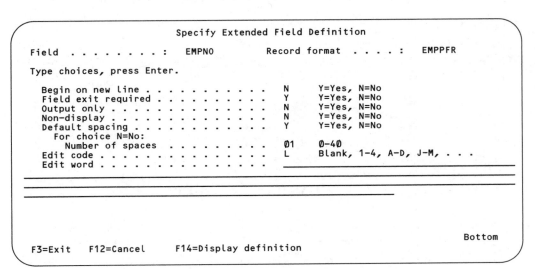

```
                    Specify Extended Field Definition

   Field  . . . . . . . . :   EMPNO          Record format  . . . . :    EMPPFR

   Type choices, press Enter.

        Begin on new line . . . . . . . . . . .    N       Y=Yes, N=No
        Field exit required . . . . . . . . . .    Y       Y=Yes, N=No
        Output only . . . . . . . . . . . . . .    N       Y=Yes, N=No
        Non-display . . . . . . . . . . . . . .    N       Y=Yes, N=No
        Default spacing . . . . . . . . . . . .    Y       Y=Yes, N=No
           For choice N=No:
              Number of spaces  . . . . . . . .    01      0-40
        Edit code . . . . . . . . . . . . . . .    L       Blank, 1-4, A-D, J-M, . . .
        Edit word . . . . . . . . . . . . . . .            _____

        _____
        _____

                                                                           Bottom
   F3=Exit    F12=Cancel      F14=Display definition
```

Figure 10.14

Specify Extended Field Definition Screen for EMPNO, Page 2

The first three options let you place the field at the beginning of a new line (useful for row-oriented formatting), require Field exit, and select a field that should be viewed only and not changed (Output only). The Non-display option lets you hide a sensitive field even though it is included in the file (e.g., a salary field in a general employee display DFU). You can specify spacing or use default spacing, and you can choose an edit code or edit word for numeric fields. When Edit numerics has been set to Y on the Define General Information screen, these edit codes work in Entry mode; otherwise, editing is not used. The edit codes, based on the RPG programming language, are used in DDS and in Query/400. A good RPG textbook or IBM's *RPG/400 Reference Manual* (SC09-1349) fully explain these codes. But from the limited perspective of DFU, you should note that the codes permit different combinations of four editing variables. These variables are

1. Whether commas are used to separate hundred thousands, thousands, and so on.

2. Whether decimal points are printed for noninteger numbers.

3. How a negative value is shown. In the Table 10.1, we distinguish the four possibilities as follows:
   NS — no sign
   R- — minus to the right
   CR — CR to the right
   -F — minus to the left (Floats to first digit)

4. Whether a zero value displays (0 for integers or .00 for decimals) or is replaced with all spaces.

The predefined edit codes and the values they take for the above variables are shown in Table 10.1.

Table 10.1

Predefined Edit Codes and Values

Code	Commas	Decimal point	Negative value	Zero value
(blank)	No	No	NS	0 all positions
1	Yes	Yes	NS	0
2	Yes	Yes	NS	
3	No	Yes	NS	0
4	No	Yes	NS	
A	Yes	Yes	CR	0
B	Yes	Yes	CR	
C	No	Yes	CR	0
D	No	Yes	CR	
J	Yes	Yes	R-	0
K	Yes	Yes	R-	
L	No	Yes	R-	0
M	No	Yes	R-	
N	Yes	Yes	-F	0
O	Yes	Yes	-F	
P	No	Yes	-F	0
Q	No	Yes	-F	
Y	No	No	NS	0/00/00

As you can see, the main difference between the groups of codes 1 – 4, A – D, J – M, and N – Q is in how they handle negative values; otherwise, comma insertion and print zero value patterns repeat from group to group. The Y code is used for editing date fields — it inserts slashes between month, day, and year values.

As you can see in Figure 10.14, edit code L is the DFU default. This code doesn't insert commas but displays a decimal point for a noninteger, a zero (or .00) for a zero balance, and a rightmost minus sign for a negative value. It is an acceptable code for an employee number that will always be a positive integer (so decimal point and negative sign are not significant).

Returning to our example, if we press Enter from the second page of the Specify Extended Field Definition screen for field EMPNO (Figure 10.14) we see the Specify Validity Checks screen (Figure 10.15).

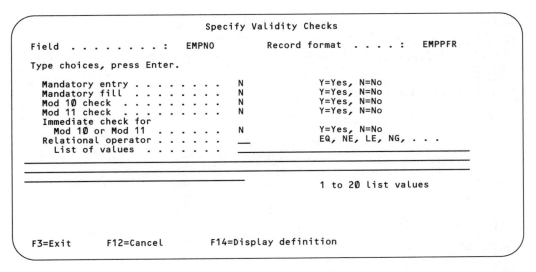

Figure 10.15
Specify Validity Checks
Screen for EMPNO

We reached this screen because we typed a 2 for the Validity checks field value of the first page of the Specify Extended Field Definition screen (Figure 10.13). If we had left that field blank, we would not have seen this screen. As you can see, this screen offers several ways to check the validity of numeric fields.

Mandatory entry means that a value must be entered when the DFU program is in Entry or Insert mode. You should select this option for any field that requires a value, specifically fields that will be used as primary keys or foreign keys in other files. Although EMPPF is not a keyed file, field EMPNO should be required because it is the identifying field for an employee and it serves as both a primary key and foreign key in other files. So on this screen, we would change the Mandatory entry value to Y.

Mandatory fill requires that all positions of a field be entered. Modulus 10 and 11 check for valid self-checking numbers using either of these two popular self-checking number algorithms.

Relational operator and List of values provide for comparing the contents of a field against a single value (using the EQ, NE, LT, LE, GT, GE, NG, or NL operator), a range of values (using the RG operator), or a list of up to 20 values (using the LS operator). When such validity checks are specified, any value entered in the field must test true for it to be accepted on input (e.g., if the LS operator is used, any value entered must be in the list). If an invalid value is entered, the system displays an error message and rejects the change or addition until a valid value is entered.

For field EMPNO, the only validity check we will use is Mandatory entry. Figure 10.16 shows the changed Work with Fields screen after finishing the extended definition for field EMPNO.

```
                              Work with Fields
File . . . . . . . . . . . :   EMPPF           Library . . . . :   JAFINTRO
Record format . . . . . . . :   EMPPFR

Type options, press Enter.  Press F21 to select all.
  2=Specify extended definition
  4=Delete extended definition


                       Extended
Opt  Field             Definition    Heading
___   EMPNO                Y          Employee Number_____
___   LASTNAME             N          LASTNAME_____
___   FIRSTNAME            N          FIRSTNAME_____
___   HOMEPHONE            N          HOMEPHONE_____
___   ADDR1                N          ADDR1_____
___   ADDR2                N          ADDR2_____
___   ZIP                  N          ZIP_____
___   DEPT                 N          DEPT_____

                                                              More...
F3=Exit                    F5=Refresh          F12=Cancel
F14=Display definition     F21=Select all
```

DFU reminds you that there is an extended definition for that field and shows how the column heading will appear. You can always take option 2 again if necessary to change a field's extended definition; but for now let's see what an extended definition for an alphanumeric (character) field would look like by taking option 2 on field LASTNAME.

Figure 10.17 shows the Specify Extended Field Definition for field LASTNAME.

```
                    Specify Extended Field Definition
Field . . . . . . . . :   LASTNAME        Record format . . . . :   EMPPFR

Type choices, press Enter.

    Auto-duplicate . . . . . . . . . . .   N          Y=Yes, N=No
    Allow lowercase . . . . . . . . . .    Y          Y=Yes, N=No
    Extended field
      heading . . . . . . . . . . . . .    Last Name
    Heading location . . . . . . . . . .   *BEFORE    *ABOVE, *BEFORE
    Initial value . . . . . . . . . . .    _____
    Validity checks . . . . . . . . . .               2=Change, 4=Delete


                                                                More...




F3=Exit    F12=Cancel    F14=Display definition
```

There are differences between a screen for a numeric field and a screen for a character field. First, notice the Allow lowercase option on this screen. The default value is N, but we have changed it to Y.

Allow lowercase must be set to Y if the data entered for a field will contain lowercase characters. For example, you should allow lowercase for fields that contain proper names and descriptions; you would not want to allow lowercase for coded fields such as a state code. We need to specify Y to allow lowercase for the last name field, unless we plan to store names entirely in uppercase. (When Allow lowercase is set to N, alphabetic characters typed in lowercase are displayed and stored in uppercase. The user doesn't need to shift or lock the keyboard in uppercase.) We have also changed the Extended field heading on this screen so that it appears as two words with only the first letter of each word capitalized.

Another difference between the two screens is that there is no Auto-increment field for a character field. This makes sense because we couldn't add to a non-numeric field. Validity checks are permitted for non-numeric fields, but with some differences from numeric fields. Figure 10.18 shows the display for specifying validity checks for a non-numeric field.

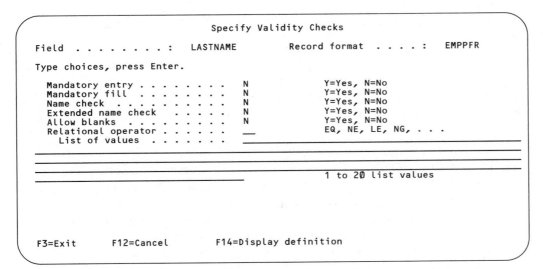

Figure 10.18
Specify Validity Checks Screen for Field LASTNAME

Notice that this screen has no options for self-checking numbers. Instead, you see options for Name check, Extended name check, and Allow blanks. If you choose Y for Name check, the field must contain a valid AS/400-style name (first character A – Z, @, #, $; remaining characters A – Z, 0 – 9, @, #, $, and _ — no embedded blanks). The Extended name check option also allows lowercase a – z, but converts the characters to uppercase in the record unless the entire name is enclosed with double quotation marks. These two options are mutually exclusive and neither can be used with range or list-of-values checks.

For field LASTNAME, no validity checks are necessary. But it is conceivable that last name should be a mandatory entry (every newly entered employee must have at least a number and a last name), so we will change the Mandatory entry value to Y before we press Enter.

After these extended field definitions have been taken for EMPPF, you could also select other fields from the Work with Fields screen for extended definitions. For example, FIRSTNAME, ADDR1, ADDR2, and DEPT would all need to allow lowercase entry, and you would probably want extended field headings as well.

Furthermore, DEPT could use a validity check to ensure that a valid department name is entered. The validity check to accomplish that is shown in Figure 10.19.

Figure 10.19
List of Values Check for
Field DEPT

```
                          Specify Validity Checks

   Field  . . . . . . . . :  DEPT          Record format  . . . . :    EMPPFR

   Type choices, press Enter.

       Mandatory entry . . . . . . . .   N          Y=Yes, N=No
       Mandatory fill  . . . . . . . .   N          Y=Yes, N=No
       Name check  . . . . . . . . . .   N          Y=Yes, N=No
       Extended name check   . . . . .   N          Y=Yes, N=No
       Allow blanks  . . . . . . . . .   N          Y=Yes, N=No
       Relational operator . . . . . .   LS         EQ, NE, LE, NG, . . .
         List of values  . . . . . . .   'Sales' 'Marketing' 'Research' 'Human Res'
   'MIS'_____

   _____
   _____          1 to 20 list values



   F3=Exit      F12=Cancel       F14=Display definition
```

Additional field definitions would be required for other fields as well. For example, HOMEPHONE and WORKPHONE could use an edit word (' - ') to make the telephone numbers easier to read. As in Query/400, edit words must contain a number of digit-replacement characters equal to the number of digits in the field. You can use spaces to represent digits, and you can use insertion characters, such as the hyphen in the HOMEPHONE edit word, where needed. When you specify an edit word, you must blank out the default edit code L.

Date and time fields do not provide for edit codes or words; they use the default format or that specified in the DATFMT or TIMFMT keywords of the DDS source code.

Field SALARY would be a good candidate for the Accumulate option so that at the end of a session the audit log would show total changes made to salaries. Also, an edit code that would show comma separators might be helpful. We will select edit code J for the salary field.

EXITING DFU

Once we have completed all Work with Fields specifications, we are ready to save the DFU. When we press Enter from the Work with Fields screen, the Exit DFU Program Definition screen appears (Figure 10.20).

```
                        Exit DFU Program Definition

    Type choices, press Enter.

        Save program  . . . . . . . . .    Y          Y=Yes, N=No
        Run program . . . . . . . . . .    Y          Y=Yes, N=No
           For choice Y=Yes:
              Type of run . . . . . . . .   1          1=Change, 2=Display
        Modify program  . . . . . . . .    N          Y=Yes, N=No
        Save DDS source . . . . . . . .    N          Y=Yes, N=No

        For Save program Y=Yes:
           Program . . . . . . . . . . .   EMPPFUPD      Name
              Library . . . . . . . . . .      JAFINTRO   Name, *CURLIB, . . .
           Authority . . . . . . . . . .   *CHANGE       Name, *LIBCRTAUT, . . .
           Text  . . . . . . . . . . . .   EMPPF Update using DFU _____

        For Save DDS source Y=Yes:
           Source file . . . . . . . . .   _____    Name
              Library . . . . . . . . . .     *CURLIB___  Name, *CURLIB, . . .
           Source member . . . . . . . .   EMPPFUPD__    Name


    F3=Exit      F14=Display definition      F17=Fast path
```

Figure 10.20

Exit DFU Program
Definition Screen

The values shown in Figure 10.20 are the defaults. Looking at the default values provided, we see that they are what we want for a new DFU program:

> Save program ... Y

If you changed this value, all your work would be lost.

> Run program ... Y

Normally, you need to test your program to make sure it is working as you planned; or you may need it to update a data file right away.

> Type of run ... 1

Type 1 allows updates, deletions, and additions to be made to the data file; type 2 allows display only, requiring only data read authority to the file.

> Modify program ... N

This DFU is brand new — if you had just changed an existing DFU, you would specify Y.

> Save DDS source ... N

If you planned to modify the DFU screen layouts directly through the DDS, you would need to select Y; otherwise, it is unnecessary.

The additional parameters use the information you supplied upon entry to name the new DFU program, including library name and specified text. If you were planning to save the DDS source code, you would need to name the source physical file (QDDSSRC) to contain the source member.

When we take the defaults and press Enter we see a message at the bottom of the screen telling us that the DFU program is being saved. After a moment the Change a Data File screen (Figure 10.21) appears because the DFU program is about to be run.

Figure 10.21
Change a Data File
Screen

```
                                    Change a Data File
   Type choices, press Enter.

      Program . . . . . . . . . .   EMPPFUPD       Name, F4 for list
         Library  . . . . . . . . .    JAFINTRO     Name, *LIBL, *CURLIB

      Data file . . . . . . . . .   EMPPF          Name, *SAME, F4 for list

         Library  . . . . . . . . .    JAFINTRO     Name, *LIBL, *CURLIB
      Member  . . . . . . . . . .   *FIRST         Name, *FIRST, F4 for list




   F3=Exit      F4=Prompt      F12=Cancel
   The DFU program was saved successfully.
```

A message at the bottom of the screen tells us the DFU program was saved successfully. The next screen we see after pressing Enter is the DFU work screen (Figure 10.22).

Figure 10.22
The DFU Update Screen
in Change Mode

```
   EMPPF Update using DFU                        Mode . . . . :    CHANGE
   Format . . . . :   EMPPFR                     File . . . . :    EMPPF

   Rel Rec Number:         0






   F3=Exit                F5=Refresh             F6=Select format
   F9=Insert              F10=Entry              F11=Change
```

Notice that the job title (EMPPF Update using DFU) appears in the upper left corner and that the field heading Rel Rec Number reflects the change we made earlier.

If we enter a relative record number, press Field exit, and then press Enter, the record will be displayed as shown in Figure 10.23.

Lesson 10 Using DFU and SQL **399**

Figure 10.23

Record 13 from File EMPPF

```
EMPPF Update using DFU                    Mode . . . . :   CHANGE
Format . . . . :    EMPPFR               File . . . . :   EMPPF

Rel Rec Number:          13
Employee Number: 111110013
Last Name:        Deerfield_____
First Name:       Cynthia_____
Homephone:        899-2323
Address Line 1:   1229 Oak Forest Rd._____
Address Line 2:   _____
Zip:              52203
Department:       MIS_____
Work phone:       _____
Birthdate:        1966-08-02
Hiredate:         1998-06-01
Salary:           ___65,000



F3=Exit              F5=Refresh          F6=Select format
F9=Insert            F10=Entry           F11=Change
```

Notice that the field we added in Lesson 9, work phone, appears to be blank. In fact, it contains the default value (zeros) placed there by the CPYF command; but with the edit word we chose for these fields, zero values are displayed as blanks.

The edit words and edit codes we selected when we created the DFU are used to format the data when it is displayed or printed. We do not need to type edit characters when we input or change data. For example, in Figure 10.24 you can see that the work phone for Ms. Deerfield was entered as a sequence of digits, although the home phone displays with the hyphen.

Figure 10.24

Change for Record 13 with Work Phone Typed Without Editing

```
EMPPF Update using DFU                    Mode . . . . :   CHANGE
Format . . . . :    EMPPFR               File . . . . :   EMPPF

Rel Rec Number:          13
Employee Number: 111110013
Last Name:        Deerfield_____
First Name:       Cynthia_____
Homephone:        899-2323
Address Line 1:   1229 Oak Forest Rd._____
Address Line 2:   _____
Zip:              52203
Department:       MIS_____
Work phone:       __3981253
Birthdate:        1966-08-02
Hiredate:         1998-06-01
Salary:           ___65,000



F3=Exit              F5=Refresh          F6=Select format
F9=Insert            F10=Entry           F11=Change
```

But after we press Enter or Page up/down to save the changes and then return to the same record, we see that both phone numbers are properly edited and displayed (as shown in Figure 10.25).

Figure 10.25

Record 13 Redisplayed — with Both Phone Numbers Edited

```
EMPPF Update using DFU                        Mode . . . . :   CHANGE
Format . . . . :   EMPPFR                     File . . . . :   EMPPF

Rel Rec Number:        13
Employee Number: 111110013
Last Name:       Deerfield_____
First Name:      Cynthia_____
Homephone:       899-2323
Address Line 1:  1229 Oak Forest Rd._____
Address Line 2:  _____
Zip:             52203
Department:      MIS_____
Work phone:      398-1253
Birthdate:       1966-08-02
Hiredate:        1998-06-01
Salary:          ___65,000



F3=Exit                  F5=Refresh               F6=Select format
F9=Insert                F10=Entry                F11=Change
```

Basically, the same thing is true of other numeric fields with numeric editing. You can enter data either using the edit symbols or as a sequence of digits; when displayed, the value will be properly edited. (If you are entering cents for an edited dollars and cents field, however, you do need to type the decimal point to assure proper alignment.)

Now let's enter a new record using our DFU program. If we press F9 on the screen in Figure 10.25, we see an an entry screen in Insert mode (Figure 10.26).

Figure 10.26

Blank Insert Screen

```
EMPPF Update using DFU                        Mode . . . . :   INSERT
Format . . . . :   EMPPFR                     File . . . . :   EMPPF

Employee Number: _____0
Last Name:       _____
First Name:      _____
Homephone:       _____
Address Line 1:  _____
Address Line 2:  _____
Zip:             ____0
Department:      _____
Work phone:      _____
Birthdate:       0001-01-01
Hiredate:        0001-01-01
Salary:          _____0_



F3=Exit                  F5=Refresh               F6=Select format
F9=Insert                F10=Entry                F11=Change
```

After we enter data for a new employee, the screen will look like the one shown in Figure 10.27.

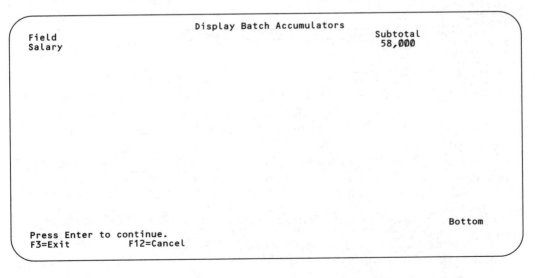

```
EMPPF Update using DFU                    Mode . . . . :    INSERT
Format . . . . :    EMPPFR               File . . . . :    EMPPF

Employee Number: 111110014
Last Name:       Stonehenge_____
First Name:      Rocky_____
Homephone:        8574131
Address Line 1:  2234 Falcon Rd_____
Address Line 2:  _____
Zip:             _52338
Department:      IMS_____
Work phone:      _3985899
Birthdate:       1947-09-23
Hiredate:        1998-07-04
Salary:          _____58000




F3=Exit                   F5=Refresh          F6=Select format
F9=Insert                 F10=Entry           F11=Change
```

Figure 10.27

New Employee Data

But when we press Enter to save the record, the Department field is displayed in reverse image and the message "Value entered for field is not valid…" appears at the bottom of the screen. As we hoped, DFU caught the incorrectly named department (IMS instead of MIS) and will not accept the new record until the error is fixed. Typing MIS instead of IMS allows the record to be saved.

When the change is saved successfully, DFU displays the message "The record was added to the end of the file" at the bottom of the screen.

Now that we have tested change and add functions, let's exit the program. Pressing F3 takes us to the normal DFU End Data Entry screen, which shows the number of records added, changed, and deleted. Pressing Enter again takes us to the Display Batch Accumulators screen shown in Figure 10.28.

```
                        Display Batch Accumulators
    Field                                           Subtotal
    Salary                                          58,000









                                                        Bottom

    Press Enter to continue.
    F3=Exit          F12=Cancel
```

Figure 10.28

Display Batch Accumulators Screen — Salary Subtotal

This screen shows the subtotals for each field selected to accumulate totals (in our case, only SALARY) since the last subtotal displayed. Although we reached this screen through the exit procedure, we could press function key F17 any time during the data entry procedure to view subtotals. Each time this is done, the previous subtotal is cleared. You could use this feature in order entry, for example, to calculate the order total immediately after entering the last line item of the order. Displaying the subtotal at that time would also clear the screen for the next order.

Pressing Enter once more takes us to the Display Total Accumulators screen, which is the accumulated total of all adds and changes to the selected field(s) since the program was started. No matter many times subtotals may have been displayed (and cleared), the Total accumulators will show the final totals added up during the entire DFU session.

Upon returning to the Work with Objects Using PDM screen, you would notice the new object in your list, as demonstrated in Figure 10.29.

Figure 10.29

Work with Objects Using PDM — New DFU Program Added to List

```
                              Work with Objects Using PDM              S1018A6G

     Library . . . . .  JAFINTRO          Position to . . . . . . .  _____
                                          Position to type . . . . .  _____

     Type options, press Enter.
       2=Change          3=Copy        4=Delete       5=Display      7=Rename
       8=Display description           9=Save        10=Restore     11=Move ...


     Opt   Object     Type       Attribute    Text
      __   CLPGM01    *PGM       CLP          CL driver for SDA MENU01
      __   CLPGM02    *PGM       CLP          Program to add up all object
      __   CLPGM03    *PGM       CLP          Submit to batch with delay
      __   EMPPFUPD   *PGM       DFU          EMPPF Update using DFU
      __   EMPPRJUPD  *PGM       DFU          Updates EMPPRJ MFLF
      __   EVALTST    *PGM       CBL          Tests EVALUATE statement
      __   GRADEPGM   *PGM       CLP          CL driver for SDA MENU01
      __   PRJMBRUPD  *PGM       DFU          Project-Member Update DFU
                                                                       More...

     Parameters or command
     ===>
     F3=Exit           F4=Prompt          F5=Refresh        F6=Create
     F9=Retrieve       F10=Command entry  F23=More options  F24=More keys
```

The object of type *PGM, attribute DFU, and name EMPPFUPD has been created. You can run this program directly from the PDM list using option 16. Doing so not only provides the custom formatting and validity checking defined in the program, but it also is much faster than waiting for a temporary DFU to be created and compiled.

Although DFU has its limitations, it is a quick and flexible utility for creating interactive update or file maintenance programs for physical or logical files. It generates its own program logic and creates display files using information supplied by the externally described file object and information you supply in extended field definitions. DFU is most useful for simple applications that don't require extensive data validation or special screen formatting.

In the lab exercise, you build two different DFU programs. We encourage you to try other options beyond the lab requirements to learn more about how DFU works.

IBM's, *Application Development Tools: Data File Utility Users Guide and Reference* (SC09-1381) is the ultimate source of DFU knowledge.

A BRIEF INTRODUCTION TO SQL

Structured Query Language is a complete database language with data definition, data manipulation, and control components. Whole books are written about it — some quite large. In this section, we provide just a taste of SQL to give you a hint of its capabilities. SQL is a powerful language, and you should learn it well before attempting to apply it to a production database. Our scope here is limited to part of the Data Manipulation Language (DML) that lets us retrieve information from the database and change (update, insert, delete) records in the database.

On the AS/400, SQL can be used on physical and logical files created by compiling DDS source code, as well as on SQL-created tables (physical files) and views (logical files). This is a very nice feature because on most AS/400s, the database will not have been created with SQL, yet we would still like to use SQL's powerful query and update capability to access the database.

SQL statements can exist in and be executed from several different environments on the AS/400. We limit our discussion to what IBM calls "dynamic SQL statements submitted to the interactive SQL facility," or what I call "command-line SQL." Besides command-line SQL, in which the statement is typed on an SQL command line (similar to a CL command), SQL can also be used from within a C, RPG, or Cobol program, either as static SQL — where the statements are hard-coded but typically use host program variables for comparison values, or as dynamic SQL — where the program prepares the SQL statement as a character string that is then passed to the AS/400 Database Manager for execution. When used from within a program, SQL typically takes over all or much of the traditional file I/O and data access responsibilities from the program logic. SQL is also used to create Query Management (QM) queries, which can be run from a CL command line or from within an HLL or CL program.

The basic form of an SQL statement to get information from a database file or files is

```
Select   field-list
  From   file-list
  Where  conditional-expression
```

Let's look at each of the values (in italics) more carefully.

SELECT field-list

In its simplest form, we can just replace *field-list* with an asterisk (*), which means all fields from the file(s). So if we coded

```
Select *
  From EMPPF
```

we would be instructing SQL to display data for all fields in the record format of file EMPPF. If we didn't want the entire record format, we could name the fields we did want, in any order, each separated from the next by a comma. SQL uses the comma as an item separator for any kind of list. We would need to know the field names as they are recorded in the record format of the externally described file. For field names and SQL keywords, case doesn't matter; "select *" is the same as "SELECT *". Only when dealing with quoted strings (e.g., 'Human Res') does case matter. If we misspell a field name, SQL displays the message, "Column (misspelled name) not in specified tables."

The words "column" and "tables" in the message give us an indication that SQL has its own way of naming things, and indeed it does, as you can see in Table 10.2.

Table 10.2

SQL Terminology

SQL calls it	We know it as a
Column	Field
Row	Record
Table	File
Collection	Library
Base table	Physical file
Result table	Output
View	Logical file
Index	Keyed-sequence access path
Token	Syntax element

In a field list, we can rename a field temporarily (just for the output of that statement) using an As clause: we can also perform arithmetic operations on numeric fields and string operations on alphanumeric field values to create new (virtual) fields. For example, the following statement creates a virtual column RAISE in the result table:

```
Select EMPNO, LASTNAME, SALARY,
   SALARY * .035 As RAISE
   From EMPPF
```

RAISE doesn't exist in the base table but is calculated for each row of the result table as 3.5 percent of that employee's salary by multiplying each record's current value of SALARY by the constant value .035. We can also use addition, subtraction, and division operators in this type of arithmetic expression.

Functions that work on the value of a field for each record selected are called **scalar functions.** Scalar functions as well as constants and arithmetic or string operators can be used to create virtual columns. For example, to create a field called NAME, consisting of the first initial plus the last name, and display it along with employee number we could code

```
Select Substring(FIRSTNAME,1,1) Concat '. ' Concat
  LASTNAME As NAME, EMPNO
  From EMPPF
```

The result would be displayed as shown in Figure 10.30.

```
                          Display Data
                                    Data width . . . . . . :      35
  Position to Line . . . . .        Shift to column  . . . . . .
  ....+....1....+....2....+....3....+
  NAME                    EMPNO
  S. Slick                111,110,001
  D. Fendor               111,110,002
  A. Einstein             111,110,003
  M. Takahashi            111,110,004
  N. Rachanoffski         111,110,005
  E. Kartblanch           111,110,006
  B. Badman               111,110,007
  M. Gootch               111,110,008
  A. Hunn                 111,110,009
  W. Disney               111,110,010
  T. Zanzibar             111,110,011
  R. Stonehart            111,110,012
  C. Deerfield            111,110,013
  ********  End of data   ********


                                                            Bottom
  F3=Exit      F12=Cancel     F19=Left      F20=Right     F21=Split
```

Figure 10.30

Display Output of Virtual Column NAME and EMPNO from file EMPPF

We could have specified the concatenation operation with two bar or pipe symbols (||) (Shift + Back slash on most keyboards) instead of spelling out Concat. The substring scalar function has three arguments as in Query/400 — Source String, Starting Position, and Length — but commas are used to separate the arguments.

SQL has many scalar functions for numeric and alphanumeric fields, data type conversion, date and time operations, and trigonometric operations. You can find explanations of these in IBM's *AS/400 SQL Reference* manual or in *Database Design and Programming for DB2/400* by Paul Conte (Duke Press, 1997).

FROM file-list

For a simple SQL query, *file-list* consists of one file name, and all fields named in *field-list* must be contained in that file's record format — or be derived from it if they are virtual fields. The examples above require that only EMPPF be named.

But if you need data from two or more files, each contributing file must be named in the file list, and the result will be a join select. Just as in a join logical file or a join query in Query/400, each pair of joined files must specify a join relationship to ensure that records are properly matched. For example, if I wanted name, address, city, state, and Zip code information for employees, I would need to join the EMPPF file to the ZIPPF file.

Because field names and relationships between files are so important in using SQL, the Bachman diagram illustrating the employee-project database used in earlier examples is re-created on page 406. Please refer to it to help understand the SQL examples that follow.

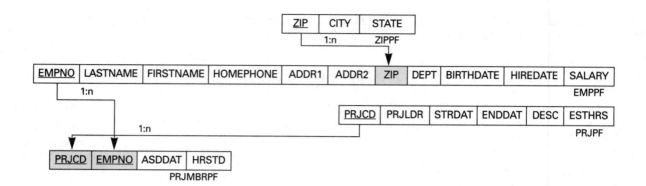

The From clause can be used to specify all three types of Query/400 join operations, inner join (type 1), left outer join (type 2), and exception join (type 3). The following three examples show the proper syntax for each of these join types.

Example 1

```
Select FIRSTNAME, LASTNAME, ADDR1, CITY, STATE, E.ZIP
  From EMPPF E Inner Join ZIPPF Z
  On   E.ZIP = Z.ZIP
```

All records from EMPPF that have a matching record (same Zip code) in ZIPPF will be displayed.

Example 2

```
Select FIRSTNAME, LASTNAME, ADDR1, CITY, STATE, E.ZIP
  From EMPPF E Left Outer Join ZIPPF Z
  On   E.ZIP = Z.ZIP
```

All records from EMPPF will be displayed. If a record is unmatched in ZIPPF, default values will be displayed for CITY and STATE.

Example 3

```
Select FIRSTNAME, LASTNAME, ADDR1, CITY, STATE, E.ZIP
  From EMPPF E Exception Join ZIPPF Z
  On   E.ZIP = Z.ZIP
```

Only EMPPF records that have no matching ZIPPF records will be displayed. Because CITY and STATE fields are included in the list, they will take default values.

Notice that as far as syntax is concerned, the only difference among the three statements is in the join specification keywords: Inner Join, Left Outer Join, and Exception Join.

Figure 10.31 shows the left outer join output.

Figure 10.31
Left Outer Join EMPPF
and ZIPPF on ZIP

```
                          Display Data
                                      Data width . . . . . . :     115
      Position to line  . . . . .          Shift to column  . . . . . .    75
      ....+....1....+....2....+.. !  +....8....+....9....+...10....+...11....+
      FIRSTNAME     LASTNAME     ! CITY                          STATE     ZIP
      Sam           Slick        ! -                               -     52,456
      Denton        Fendor       ! Guthrie Center                 IA     50,115
      Albert        Einstein     ! Clarinda                       IA     51,632
      Musashi       Takahashi    ! Cedar Rapids                   IA     52,406
      Natasha       Rachanoffski ! Cedar Rapids                   IA     52,402
      Emil          Kartblanch   ! Swisher                        IA     52,338
      Billy         Badman       ! -                               -     52,456
      Martha        Gootch       ! Pleasantville                  IA     50,225
      Atilla        Hunn         ! Anamosa                        IA     52,205
      Walter        Disney       ! Amana                          IA     52,203
      Tilly         Zanzibar     ! Swisher                        IA     52,338
      Rocky         Stonehart    ! Amana                          IA     52,203
      Cynthia       Deerfield    ! Amana                          IA     52,203
      ********  End of data  ********

                                                                  Bottom
      F3=Exit      F12=Cancel      F19=Left      F20=Right      F21=No split
```

The display output uses split screen and right windowing to hide ADDR1 and match up CITY, STATE, and ZIP with the name fields. All records of the primary file (the left side name in the From clause) are displayed, but Sam Slick and Billy Badman show no data for CITY and STATE because their Zip code, 52456, is not in the ZIPPF. The exception join output would show only those two.

The From clause of the examples above assigns abbreviated names, E and Z to the EMPPF and ZIPPF files, respectively. These abbreviated names are called **correlation names** and can be used for qualification when fields with the same name are referenced in two or more files. The intended purpose of a correlation name is to correlate or synchronize record pointers between records of two files (or copies of the same file) in something called a correlated subquery, which you will no doubt study in your database class. Although the full file name could have been used for qualification (e.g., EMPPF.ZIP), an abbreviated name is easier to deal with even if you're not using correlated subqueries.

If no qualification had been used, SQL would not have known which ZIP field was being referenced and would have displayed the message, "Column name ZIP is ambiguous." The qualifier serves the same purpose as the JREF keyword required for nonunique field names in a join logical file, and the file ID field of a Query/400 join.

More than two files can be joined in a single Select, and more than one type of join can be used. Suppose, for example, that we needed to list all employees with projects in the PRJMBRPF file, showing each project code to which an employee is assigned and that we also wanted to show the project leader and project description for each PRJMBRPF record. That information comes from the PRJPF file. You would want an inner join between EMPPF and PRJMBRPF to avoid listing employees with no projects. But if you suspected there might not yet be a PRJPF record created for a new project code already assigned in the PRJM-BRPF, you would want to specify a left outer join between PRJMBRPF and PRJPF. The Select statement to accomplish all that would be

```
Select E.EMPNO, LASTNAME, PM.PRJCD, PRJLDR, DESC
  from EMPPF E inner join PRJMBRPF PM
  on   E.EMPNO = PM.EMPNO
  left outer join PRJPF P
  on   PM.PRJCD = P.PRJCD
```

The output (first screen) from the above Select statement is shown in Figure 10.32.

Figure 10.32

Join of Three Files, EMPPF, PRJMBRPF, and PRJPF

```
                              Display Data
                                      Data width . . . . . . :      97
 Position to line  . . . . .          Shift to column  . . . . .
 ....+....1....+....2....+....3....+....4....+....5....+....6....+....7....+....
       EMPNO    LASTNAME          Project      Project     Description
                                  Code         Leader
    111,110,001  Slick            CLRSS      111,110,002   Plan End-of-Year Clear
    111,110,001  Slick            Junk           -         -
    111,110,002  Fendor           CLRSS      111,110,002   Plan End-of-Year Clear
    111,110,002  Fendor           NPADV      111,110,010   New Products Advertisi
    111,110,003  Einstein         VACT       111,110,003   Develop Voice-activate
    111,110,004  Takahashi        DSG99      111,110,005   Develop Sales Goals fo
    111,110,004  Takahashi        VACT       111,110,003   Develop Voice-activate
    111,110,005  Rachanoffski     DSG99      111,110,005   Develop Sales Goals fo
    111,110,005  Rachanoffski     VACT       111,110,003   Develop Voice-activate
    111,110,006  Kartblanch       DSG99      111,110,005   Develop Sales Goals fo
    111,110,007  Badman           CLRSS      111,110,002   Plan End-of-Year Clear
    111,110,008  Gootch           CLRSS      111,110,002   Plan End-of-Year Clear
    111,110,008  Gootch           NPADV      111,110,010   New Products Advertisi
    111,110,009  Hunn             RH400      111,110,009   Recruit and hire AS/40
    111,110,010  Disney           DSG99      111,110,005   Develop Sales Goals fo
                                                              More...

 F3=Exit       F12=Cancel      F19=Left        F20=Right       F21=Split
```

Notice output shows a project Junk for employee Slick. This invalid project code was inserted into PRJMBRPF using Slick's employee number to test the join operation. Project leader and description are empty for project Junk because no matching PRJPF record was found, and that is exactly as we would expect with the left outer join specified between those two files.

You can see that SQL supports the three types of Query/400 join and has the added advantage of letting you specify a different join operation for each pair of files.

Note that in earlier versions of DB2/400, the keywords Inner Join, Left Outer Join, and Exception Join were not recognized in SQL, and the only type of true join permitted was the inner join. A Where clause was used to specify the join relationship, and the output would not have shown the Junk project record because it was unmatched in the project file. The code to accomplish an inner join, without the Join keyword, would be

```
Select  E.EMPNO, LASTNAME, PM.PRJCD, PRJLDR, DESC
  From  EMPPF E, PRJMBRPF PM, PRJPF P
  Where E.EMPNO = PM.EMPNO
  And   PM.PRJCD = P.PRJCD
```

In this example, all of the files needed to get the desired information are listed in the From file-list, with their correlation names if used. Following the file list, one join relationship for each pair of files is coded as a Where condition. It is imperative that one equality relational expression (E.EMPNO = PM.EMPNO) is provided to define the equijoin relationship for each pair of files. This expression defines to SQL the relationship between two files documented in the Bachman diagram by the line connecting the relationship-supporting fields of the related files.

Where conditional-expression

The Where clause is used to limit the rows selected for the result table; it works in much the same manner as Select/Omit entries used for logical files. In fact, anything you can do with Select/Omit, you can certainly do with Where expressions, but the versatility and power of the SQL Where expression considerably exceeds DDS Select/Omit.

Probably the most common Where expression is some kind of relational expression, in the general form

operand1   relational-operator   operand2

Operands can be fields names, constants, string expressions, arithmetic expressions, scalar functions, and special registers such as CURRENT_DATE.

Relational operators include =, >, <, >=, <=, and <> (not equal). Multiple relational expressions can be combined into complex expressions by using the logical operators Not, And, and Or. Regardless how complex a set of expressions may become, SQL always evaluates it to a single true or false result, which determines whether a row is selected for the result table (true) or rejected (false).

Let's start with some simple examples of the Where clause. We'll assume all of the following eight examples begin with

```
Select   *
  From  EMPPF
```

Example 1 — List the employees who earn less than $25,000.

```
...Where SALARY < 25000
```

Notice no editing symbols are used in the numeric constant; both $25,000 and 25,000 would be errors.

Example 2 — List employees who earn less than $25,000 and are in the Sales Department.

```
...Where SALARY < 25000
     And DEPT = 'Sales'
```

The constant 'Sales' must be typed exactly as the value is stored in the database and in the same case. Neither 'sales' nor 'SALES' would produce any results. Alphanumeric constants must be enclosed in single quotation marks (apostrophes).

Example 3 — List all employees who have a Zip code in the range of 52400 to 52500 (inclusive).

```
...Where ZIP >= 52400
      And ZIP <= 52500
```

You cannot imply the subject (operand1) in the second expression – that is, ZIP >= 52400 And <= 52500 would be in error. However, there is a simpler syntax for a range test like the one above. It uses the SQL keyword Between and would be written as

```
...Where ZIP Between 52400 And 52500
```

Between Value1 And Value2 treats the range values as inclusive, so the statement above is exactly equivalent to the And complex expression of Example 3.

Example 4 — List all employees born between the months of January and March.

```
...Where Month(BIRTHDATE) Between 1 And 3
```

Here a date scalar function, Month, is used to extract the month value from the date field BIRTHDATE. Other date functions often used include Year and Day, which extract the 4-digit year and the 2-digit day of the month, respectively, from a date field or expression.

Example 5 — List all employees born in the months of November, December, January, or February.

```
...Where Month(BIRTHDATE) = 11
      Or Month(BIRTHDATE) = 12
      Or Month(BIRTHDATE) = 1
      Or Month(BIRTHDATE) = 2
```

Here, we use several relational expressions connected by Ors. But a far simpler approach is to use an In list. One way of using an In list works just the same as a VALUES keyword in DDS. You code the values you want to test against as constants, separated by commas, and enclose the whole list in parentheses. So for our example, we would code

```
...Where Month(BIRTHDATE) In (11,12,1,2)
```

Example 6 — List all employees who live in Cedar Rapids, Iowa.

You know there are several Zip codes for Cedar Rapids, but you're not sure what they are. Of course, you could look them up and code them in an In list as above, but SQL can also look them up. SQL will create a list of Cedar Rapids Zip codes for you from the data in the ZIPPF file, then compare each employee's Zip code against the list it created. To do this, we simply code another Select statement as the In list value:

```
...Where ZIP In
        (Select ZIP From ZIPPF
            Where CITY = 'Cedar Rapids')
```

When a Select statement is nested inside an outer Select statement's Where clause, it can be called a **subquery**.

If we wanted the results to include employees from several different cities, we could use an In list inside the subquery:

```
...Where ZIP In
        (Select ZIP From ZIPPF
            Where CITY In ('Cedar Rapids',
                        'Marion',
                        'Hiawatha'))
```

Note the need for two closing right parentheses to balance the expression.

Example 7 — List all employees who are not project leaders.

```
...Where EMPNO Not In
        (Select PRJLDR From PRJPF)
```

In this case, although EMPNO and PRJLDR are not the same field, they share the same domain — Social Security numbers of employees. We instruct SQL to create a list of project leaders using the subquery, then ask for employees who are not in that list. Using the Not logical operator with a subquery produces the same result as an exception join:

```
Select E.*
  From EMPPF E Exception Join PRJPF
    On EMPNO = PRJLDR
```

By qualifying * to the correlation name E for EMPPF, we can avoid including all of the fields from PRJPF in the output. If we had simply coded Select * , all fields from both files would have gone to the output, and all of the PRJPF fields would have had default values.

Example 8 — List all employees who have "Road" or "Rd" in their address.

```
...Where ADDR1 Like '%Road%'
      Or ADDR1 Like '%Rd%'
```

The Like operation provides a powerful technique for matching a search string against a substring of a field from each record. Two wildcard characters, the percent sign (%) and the underscore(_), can be used. The % is replaced in the target string by any number of unknown characters, while the _ is replaced by exactly one unknown character. For example, LIKE '%at' would return true results for "hat" or "Hat" or "cat" or "Rat" or "Frat" while LIKE '_at' would return true results for "hat" or "Hat" or "cat" or "Rat", but false results for "Frat". Neither would return true results for "Fraternity".

In Example 8, we checked the ADDR1 field but overlooked ADDR2. We could add ADDR2 checking to the Where clause with more Or operators:

```
...Where ADDR1 Like '%Road%'
     Or ADDR1 Like '%Rd%'
     Or ADDR2 Like '%Road%'
     Or ADDR2 Like '%Rd%'
```

or we could combine ADDR1 and ADDR2 by concatenation

```
...Where ADDR1 Concat ADDR2 Like '%Road%'
     Or ADDR1 Concat ADDR2 Like '%Rd%'
```

or we could try putting it all into a single simple expression

```
...Where ADDR1 Concat ADDR2 Like '%R%d%'
```

This seems like a clever way to do a fairly complex search with a single statement because the middle % could substitute for "oa" of "Road" or for the zero characters between the R and d of "Rd". And this expression would certainly pull out all addresses containing "Road" or "Rd", but it could also give us more than we bargained for. Suppose, for example, Mr. Hunn had moved to 2379 Redbud Boulevard?

SOME ADDITIONAL SQL CAPABILITIES

If you tell SQL to retrieve rows that have the same column values, it will do that, duplicating those rows in the result table. For example, if you wanted to list the employee numbers of any employees assigned to any project, you might simply type in

```
Select EMPNO
  From PRJMBRPF
```

But you would soon see that many numbers are repeated in the output — if an employee were assigned to four projects, his/her employee number would appear four times in the output list. You would also notice that employee numbers appeared in no particular order, making it difficult to analyze the list. In fact, because this request uses a single file and requires no index search, the output is ordered by the relative record numbers of the physical file or in arrival sequence, even if the file itself is keyed.

SQL provides a keyword for eliminating duplicate rows of the result table; it is Distinct. Another clause, Order By, can be used at the end of any Select statement to sort the output by one or more sort fields.

So to correct the statement above, we could type in

```
Select    Distinct EMPNO
  From    PRJMBRPF
  Order By EMPNO
```

Now we would have a sorted list of unique employee numbers. The Order By clause defaults to ascending, abbreviated Asc, but you can specify descending sequence by using the abbreviation Desc.

Using Order By we should be able to handle the following request:
List all employees by last name, showing department and salary. The output should be sorted by department and then within department from highest to lowest salary.

```
Select      DEPT, LASTNAME, SALARY
  From      EMPPF
  Order By DEPT, SALARY Desc
```

The output, shown in Figure 10.33, shows how the data has been sorted by descending salary within department.

```
                             Display Data
                                      Data width . . . . . . :      42
Position to Line . . . . .            Shift to column . . . . . .
....+....1....+....2....+....3....+....4..
DEPT          LASTNAME         SALARY
Human Res     Hunn            135,000
Marketing     Disney          165,000
Marketing     Gootch           55,000
MIS           Stonehart        65,000
MIS           Deerfield        65,000
MIS           Zanzibar         49,500
Research      Einstein        299,950
Research      Takahashi        75,000
Sales         Kartblanch       48,250
Sales         Fendor           32,500
Sales         Rachanoffski     32,000
Sales         Slick            28,000
Sales         Badman           22,500
********  End of data  ********

                                                           Bottom
 F3=Exit      F12=Cancel      F19=Left      F20=Right    F21=Split
```

Figure 10.33
EMPPF Data Ordered by DEPT, SALARY Descending

Notice that Stonehart and Deerfield are in the same department and have the same salary, but that Stonehart comes before Deerfield. That occurs because we didn't request sorting by last name, and in the physical file, the Stonehart record has a lower relative record number, and so comes first. You could easily fix that problem by adding a third Order By entry for LASTNAME.

A little warning about the use of the Order By clause: It causes a significant hit on performance, especially when you are dealing with large files that lack appropriate indexes. Therefore, use it with caution and only when required.

Besides the large number of scalar functions available, SQL also has a few useful **column functions**. These functions work on a set of field values as a whole, for example all SALARY values in the result table, as opposed to scalar functions that work on a field of each record. To show the difference consider the following examples. First, let's use a scalar function that returns a value for each row of the result table:

```
Select LASTNAME, Decimal(SALARY * 1.035,7,0)
    As NEW_SALARY
From EMPPF
```

The Decimal scalar function is useful to format a calculated value to a fixed precision (total digits) and scale (number of decimal digits). Its syntax is

`Decimal` (*expression, precision, scale*)

and if the result were stored in a data file, its type would be packed decimal. For display purposes, it is converted to readable numbers. This function works on the SALARY field of each record sent to the result table. Using the Decimal function, the results of the above Select statement appear in Figure 10.34.

Figures 10.34
Virtual Column
NEW_SALARY
Formatted to Integer
Using the Decimal
Function

```
                                     Display Data
                                           Data width . . . . . . :      29
    Position to line  . . . .            Shift to column  . . . . .
    ....+....1....+....2....+....
    LASTNAME            NEW_SALARY
    Slick                  28,980
    Fendor                 33,638
    Einstein              310,448
    Takahashi              77,625
    Rachanoffski           33,120
    Kartblanch             49,939
    Badman                 23,288
    Gootch                 56,925
    Hunn                  139,725
    Disney                170,775
    Zanzibar               51,233
    Stonehart              67,275
    Deerfield              67,275
    ********   End of data  ********



                                                                  Bottom
   F3=Exit      F12=Cancel      F19=Left      F20=Right    F21=Split
```

Without the Decimal function, the results look like those in Figure 10.35 – that is, NEW_SALARY would have three decimal places. SQL calculated the precision and scale of the NEW_SALARY field based on the arithmetic expression.

The Sum column function can be used to total all salaries:

```
Select Sum(SALARY)
    From EMPPF
```

Note that it is invalid (and nonsensical) to request

```
Select LASTNAME, Sum(SALARY)
    From EMPPF
```

Because LASTNAME has a value for each record, it can't be paired with Sum (SALARY), which derives a single value for the entire result table.

```
                              Display Data
                                       Data width . . . . . . :      34
 Position to line  . . . . .           Shift to column  . . . . .
 ....+....1....+....2....+....3....
 LASTNAME                 NEW_SALARY
 Slick                    28,980.500
 Fendor                   33,638.000
 Einstein                310,448.750
 Takahashi                77,625.500
 Rachanoffski             33,120.500
 Kartblanch               49,939.250
 Badman                   23,288.000
 Gootch                   56,925.500
 Hunn                    139,725.500
 Disney                  170,775.500
 Zanzibar                 51,233.000
 Stonehart                67,275.500
 Deerfield                67,275.500
 ********   End of data   ********


                                                             Bottom
  F3=Exit      F12=Cancel      F19=Left      F20=Right      F21=Split
```

Figure 10.35
Virtual Column
NEW_SALARY with
Decimal Precision
Calculated by SQL

But suppose we want the total salary for each department? SQL provides the Group By function to group records by a common value of a field, then perform the Sum operation on each group. The statement would be

```
Select     DEPT, Sum(SALARY)
  From     EMPPF
Group By DEPT
```

When you need a column function to act on a group of records, you must use the Group By clause, which must identify the grouping field or fields. The statement above instructs SQL to sort all EMPPF records by DEPT, then total the salary of the employees in each department, then write one record for each department to the result table. It is important to understand that only one record per group is sent to the result table. The output from the above statement appears in Figure 10.36.

```
                              Display Data
                                       Data width . . . . . . :      56
 Position to line  . . . . .           Shift to column  . . . . .
 ....+....1....+....2....+....3....+....4....+....5....+.
 DEPT                          SUM ( SALARY )
 Human Res                        135,000
 Marketing                        220,000
 MIS                              179,500
 Research                         374,950
 Sales                            163,250
 ********   End of data   ********





                                                             Bottom
  F3=Exit      F12=Cancel      F19=Left      F20=Right      F21=Split
```

Figure 10.36
Grouped Sum of
Salary Per Department

Let's say we want to list the last name, employee number, and the number of projects assigned and the total hours spent on all projects for any employee who is working on two or fewer projects or has less than 50 total project hours to date. We also want to sort by last name.

This request calls for grouping project member records by employee number, then selecting only those groups with no more than two projects or no more than 50 total hours. Also, to get the last name, we need to join each GROUP record with a matching record from the employee file, EMPPF, on employee number.

SQL provides a means for selecting or rejecting group records: The Having clause allows selection of group summary records in the same way that the Where clause allows selection of base table records. The syntax of the Having clause is

`Having` *conditional-expression*

but with some constraints on the expression. Field names used in the Having expression must be specified in the Select field-list. Function results can also be referenced in the Having expression and, except for Count(*), must also be identified in the Select field-list. Count(*) returns the number of rows in each group and can be referenced in a Having clause, even if it is not specified in the Select field-list. Subqueries can also be used in a Having clause.

We can produce the necessary Underutilized Employee Report with the following statement:

```
Select    LASTNAME, EMPNO,
            Count(*) As NUM_OF_PROJECTS,
            Decimal (Sum(HRSTD),4,0) As TOTAL_HRS
  From    PRJMBRPF PM Inner Join EMPPF E
    On    PM.EMPNO = E.EMPNO
Group By LASTNAME, EMPNO
  Having Count(*) <= 2
      Or TOTAL_HRS <= 50
Order By 1
```

Assuming a referential constraint on PRJMBRPF so that all employee number values of any of its records must already exist in the parent file EMPPF, either Inner Join or Left Outer Join produces the same results using PRJMBRPF as the primary (left) file.

Both LASTNAME and EMPNO must be used as the grouping fields, and it is important to understand that only fields that will always have the same value for all records of a group can be used as grouping fields.

The Having clause limits the output to those group summary records whose count of projects is less than or equal to two or whose sum of all project hours is less than or equal to 50.

The Order By clause must also refer only to list items from the Select field-list, but integer reference to the positional order of items of the Select field-list is permitted. In the example, Order By 1 is equivalent to Order By LASTNAME. This feature is especially useful when the ordering column needs to be a function

expression, to avoid having to rekey the expression. The output of the
Underutilized Employee Report is shown in Figure 10.37.

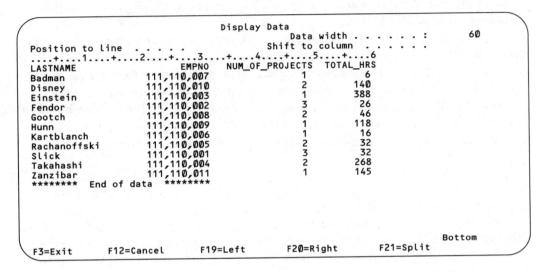

Figure 10.37
Underutilized Employee
Report

Another example might help clarify when to use the Group By clause. Let's
say we want to display the name and birth date of the oldest employee in the company.

Think of a date field as a numeric value with the high-order two digits being
century, then year, month, and day. Then the smaller the value of BIRTHDATE,
the older the person. The SQL Min function returns the smallest value in a table
or group. So you might be tempted to try

```
Select FIRSTNAME, LASTNAME, Min(BIRTHDATE)
   From EMPPF
```

But SQL would display the message, "Column FIRSTNAME or function specified
in SELECT list not valid" because you can't combine column (field) names with a
column function (Min) without using the Group By function. However, in this
case, using Group By would be inappropriate because there are no groups of
records in EMPPF with common values for the grouping columns, FIRSTNAME
and LASTNAME. So what would happen if you entered the following:

```
Select    FIRSTNAME, LASTNAME, Min(BIRTHDATE)
   From    EMPPF
   Group By FIRSTNAME, LASTNAME
```

SQL would create "groups" of records for each unique set of values for FIRST-NAME and LASTNAME, or, in our database, one group for each employee. And because the column function applies to each group, each employee's birth date would be the Min(BIRTHDATE) for the group (of one record). You would get a list of all employees' names and birth dates. Of course if you had two John Smith employees, you would get only one result row showing the elder Smith's birth date. So how can we attach a name to a birth date and be sure that it is the minimum birth date? Use a subquery! If you move the Min function to a subquery, you can compare each employee's birth date against the Min(BIRTHDATE) value of the whole file and select only the matching record.

```
Select  FIRSTNAME, LASTNAME, BIRTHDATE
  From   EMPPF
  Where BIRTHDATE = (Select Min(BIRTHDATE)
                          From EMPPF)
```

Instead of a list, this subquery returns a single value, the oldest person's birth date, against which we are comparing each employee's BIRTHDATE. The only way this would not retrieve a single result record is if your two oldest employees were born on the same day.

Now, let's list the birth date of the oldest employee in each department. To satisfy this request, you could use DEPT as the single grouping field and write the Select statement as

```
Select     DEPT, Min(BIRTHDATE)
  From      EMPPF
  Group By DEPT
```

This Select statement would show each department and the birth date of its oldest employee. However, it wouldn't tell us *who* the oldest employee is. When SQL requires that you name all Select list fields as grouping fields, there is no direct way to associate a department's oldest birth date with a name or number; the Select statement

```
Select     DEPT, LASTNAME, FIRSTNAME, Min(BIRTHDATE)
  From      EMPPF
  Group By DEPT, LASTNAME, FIRSTNAME
```

would take us right back to a list of all employees. And leaving the name fields out of the Group By clause but keeping them in the Select list, as in

```
Select     DEPT, LASTNAME, FIRSTNAME, Min(BIRTHDATE)
  From      EMPPF
  Group By DEPT
```

would be a syntax violation. There is a two step method to include the oldest employee's name as well as birth date, but let's come back to it momentarily. First let's see how we could use the Having clause in another related request.

Say we want to list the oldest employee of each department who is at least 50 years old. (So if the eldest employee of the Sales department were only 48, you wouldn't want a Sales department record in the output.)

You could easily satisfy this request with the Having clause to limit the group summary records to those that meet the age criteria as follows:

```
Select    DEPT, Min(BIRTHDATE)
  From    EMPPF
Group By DEPT
  Having  Year(Current_Date - Min(BIRTHDATE)) >= 50
```

In this example, we are extracting the year from the date arithmetic expression Current_date - Min(BIRTHDATE) and comparing it to 50. If you think of a date as a point on a time line, then in SQL, any two points can be compared and their difference expressed in years, months, weeks, or days.

Another way to write the Having clause above is to use a **labeled duration,** that is a date period expressed in one of the date units (e.g., years, months). Using labeled duration, our Having clause would be

```
Having Min(BIRTHDATE) + 50 years <= Current_Date
```

The "+ 50 years" is the labeled duration. A labeled duration is always used to add or subtract some period of time to a known point of time, such as BIRTHDATE, and so always starts with a plus or minus sign.

Now let's return to the question of how to include personal data with the birth date of each department's oldest employee. First visualize the output of the earlier statement

```
Select    DEPT, Min(BIRTHDATE)
  From    EMPPF
  Having Min(BIRTHDATE) + 50 years <= Current_Date
```

as the following:

DEPT	Min(BIRTHDATE)
Human Res	1909-04-25
Marketing	1912-10-10
MIS	1947-05-11
Research	1909-04-25

If we could find a way to store this data, we could join it to EMPPF records based on the values of DEPT and BIRTHDATE in EMPPF and extract any other employee data needed from the joined record. In fact, the data is already stored — in the EMPPF file itself; we just need to build a kind of logical file over EMPPF to get at it.

SQL's version of a logical file is a **view,** and while it is conceptually similar to a logical file, SQL's greater flexibility and ability to use functions and expressions make views far more powerful than logical files. For example, in a logical file there is no way to select group summary records based on the value returned by a column function, as we did in the previous example. But in SQL, creating such a view is easy; in fact, we already have most of the code for it. The only thing we need to do is prefix our earlier Select statement with a Create View statement and name the virtual column created by the Min function. Here is the statement to create the view of department elders:

```
Create View   JAFINTRO/DEPTELDER As
   Select     DEPT, Min(BIRTHDATE) As ELDERBDAY
     From     EMPPF
   Group By DEPT
     Having   Min(BIRTHDATE) + 50 Years <= Current_Date
```

The SQL Create statement is used to build base tables (physical files), views (logical files), indexes (access paths), and other SQL objects. The AS/400 object created by the Create View statement above will be a *FILE type object in library JAFINTRO. It will be an externally described logical file, attribute LF, SQL type VIEW. The Select statement used to define the record format and select the population of the view will be included in its file description so you will have a permanent record of the criteria used in creating the view.

The SQL Create command can be used instead of the native AS/400 CRTPF (Create Physical File) and CRTLF (Create Logical File) commands to build entire databases, but that is the topic of another class; our purpose here is limited to showing how a view could be used to access certain data already stored in a physical file.

Now that we have created a view of departments and elder employees' birth dates, we can complete the original task by getting the employee name data matched up with each row of the view. We can accomplish that by joining the view to its based-on physical file EMPPF using both department and birth date as join relationship-supporting fields; by doing so we can retrieve multiple same-age elders in the same department if such a condition were to exist.

```
Select DE.DEPT, FIRSTNAME, LASTNAME, ELDERBDAY
   From DEPTELDER DE Inner Join EMPPF E
     On DE.DEPT = E.DEPT
         And ELDERBDAY = BIRTHDATE
```

The display output of the above statement is shown as Figure 10.38.

```
                              Display Data
                                        Data width . . . . . . :        56
  Position to line  . . . . .           Shift to column  . . . . . .
  ....+....1....+....2....+....3....+....4....+....5....+.
  DEPT          LASTNAME      FIRSTNAME    ELDERBDAY
  Human Res     Hunn          Atilla       1909-04-25
  Marketing     Disney        Walter       1912-10-10
  MIS           Zanzibar      Tilly        1947-05-11
  MIS           Stonehart     Rocky        1947-05-11
  Research      Einstein      Albert       1909-04-25
  ********  End of data  ********



                                                              Bottom
  F3=Exit       F12=Cancel    F19=Left     F20=Right    F21=Split
```

Figure 10.38
The Eldest Members
of Each Department

Notice that the output includes the two eldest employees of MIS who have the same birth date, May 11, 1947.

Let's now take a brief look at updating the database using SQL Insert, Update, and Delete statements.

FILE MAINTENANCE USING SQL

The SQL Insert statement allows individual rows to be added to a table. The Update and Delete statements also work on individual rows, but they have the added ability to perform the operation on a set of rows, each of which tests True for a Where clause.

Each statement identifies a single file, which may be a physical file (base table) or an updatable logical file (updatable view). For a view or logical file to be updatable, it must *not*

- identify more than one file in its From clause (no join logical files or views)
- use the Distinct expression in its Select statement
- use either the Group By or Having clause in its outer Select statement
- use a column function in its outer Select statement
- use a correlated subquery on the same table identified in its From clause

The Insert Statement

The SQL Insert statement allows individual rows to be added to a table. Insert can act directly on the base table or indirectly by inserting through a view or logical file within the limitations described above. The syntax of the SQL Insert statement is

```
Insert Into file-name
             (field-list)
    Values   (value-list)
```

Here is an example using the ZIPPF file:

```
Insert Into ZIPPF
          (ZIP, CITY, STATE)
   Values   (50613, 'Cedar Falls', 'IA')
```

In this Insert statement, because values were provided for all fields and in the same order as the record format field order, the field-list itself is optional. Therefore,

```
Insert Into ZIPPF
   Values   (50613, 'Cedar Falls', 'IA')
```

works just as well. The field-list is required when you are not assigning values to all fields or when the values are not in the same order as the fields in the record format.

In either case, you need to specify which field a certain value is assigned to by putting it in the same relative position in the value list as its corresponding field name in the field list (e.g., the first named field takes the first value). Any field not listed is not assigned a value in the newly inserted record and takes the default value (zeros or spaces — unless a different default value was assigned in the physical file or base table definition).

Numeric values may have a leading minus sign and a decimal point if the field allows for decimal precision. Alphanumeric values and date and time values must be enclosed in single quotation marks (apostrophes). The Insert statement must not attempt to use values that are longer than the receiving field because doing so would cause significant digit truncation.

For example, the following statement would not work:

```
Insert Into ZIPPF
   Values   (506143, 'IA', 'Cedar Falls')
```

SQL would return the error message: "Value for column STATE too long." Given the actual order of fields in the record — ZIP, CITY, STATE — this error message indicates that SQL could insert IA into the CITY field, but assuming the third value, Cedar Falls, should be assigned to the third field, STATE, it refused to do so because only the Ce part of the value would fit in this 2-character field.

To add a new record to PRJMBRPF, you could use the following Insert statement:

```
Insert Into PRJMBRPF
          (EMPNO, ASDDAT, PRJCD)
   Values   (111110012, '1998-08-01', 'NPADV')
```

Proper values are assigned to each listed field even though the fields are not in the same order as in the record format. The values correspond positionally with the fields in the field-list. The date field is in *ISO format and enclosed in single quotation marks. The hours-to-date field, HRSTD, isn't listed and will be assigned the default value of zero in the new record.

The command-line Insert statement is a convenient way to add a record or two to a database file when you are working in a SQL session, but for industrial-strength data entry, it is a slow and error-prone method. DFU — with its labeled entry fields — is better, and for really heavy duty file maintenance, a custom program will normally be used.

The Update Statement

The SQL Update statement allows records within a file to be changed, using constants and expressions to change the values of named fields. The syntax for a Searched Update with a Where clause is

```
Update   file-name
   Set    field-name = expression
   Where  conditional-expression
```

It's important to remember that the Update statement can work on sets of records, not just single records. Whenever more than one record in the file tests True for the Where condition, all records testing True are updated according to the Set clause specification. For example,

```
Update   PRJMBRPF
   Set     HRSTD = HRSTD + 5
   Where   PRJCD = 'NPADV'
     And   EMPNO = 111110012
```

updates a single record in PRJMBRPF, incrementing the hours-to-date field by 5. How do we know only a single record is updated? Because the Where condition tests for specific values of the two fields that together constitute the composite primary key for this file. When primary key values are given to identify a record for update, only one record is updated. When the update is performed successfully, SQL displays the message, "1 rows updated in PRJMBRPF in JAFINTRO."

The real power of the SQL Update statement is its ability to change a set of records by executing one statement and selecting the set to be updated by evaluating the Where condition. All records in the table or view are tested by the Where condition, and all of those testing True will be updated. For example if you wanted to give a 6.5 percent raise to all MIS employees, you could do so easily by executing the following:

```
Update   EMPPF
   Set     SALARY = SALARY * 1.065
   Where   Dept = 'MIS'
```

This statement tests each record in the employee file for the condition DEPT = 'MIS' and applies the update salary increase to all records that test True.

The Update statement's Set expression must reference only field names of the Update table or view and cannot identify a virtual field derived from a scalar function, expression, or constant.

In an Update statement's Where clause, all listed column names must belong to the table or view being updated unless a subquery is used to create a value or list of values used as a comparison operand. Thus, an attempt to give a 2 percent raise to the employees assigned to the New Products Advertising project (project code NPADV) with the following code would fail:

```
Update   EMPPF
   Set   SALARY = SALARY * 1.02
   Where EMPPF.EMPNO = PRJMBRPF.EMPNO
     And PRJMBRPF.PRJCD = 'NPADV'
```

The Where expression references non-EMPPF field names, so the Update statement would fail with the message, "Column qualifier or table PRJMBRPF undefined."

The desired update can, however, be accomplished by using a subquery to create a list of employee numbers assigned to project NPADV. The modified update statement would be

```
Update   EMPPF
   Set   SALARY = SALARY * 1.02
   Where EMPNO In
         (Select  EMPNO From PRJMBRPF
            Where PRJCD = 'NPADV')
```

This statement has no ambiguous column references and violates no update rules.

When the same update rule can be applied to multiple records in a file, SQL offers a convenient way to get the job done using a single statement. But for updating one record at a time, it is not as easy to use as DFU or a custom-written file maintenance application. For programmers, it can be a quick way to change test data, but it is not a safe or efficient tool for nontechnical users.

The Delete Statement

The SQL Delete statement removes one or more records from a file either directly from the base table (physical file) or through an updatable view. The syntax of the Delete statement is similar to that of the Update statement but without a Set clause:

```
Delete
   From   file-name
   Where  conditional expression
```

As with the Update statement, multiple rows (or all rows) can be deleted with a single statement. For example,

```
Delete
   From EMPPF
```

clears all records from the physical file. Before doing so, command-line SQL displays the message, "You are about to alter (Delete or Update) all of the records in your file(s)" and gives you a chance to change your mind. The above Delete statement would have the same effect as the following CLRPFM (Clear Physical File Member) command:

```
CLRPFM    EMPPF
```

It removes all records from the member but doesn't actually delete the file. (The SQL counterpart to the DLTF (Delete File) command is the Drop statement.)

The rules for forming the Where clause of the Delete statement are basically the same as for the Update statement — any referenced field names must belong to the file named in the Delete From statement, with the exception of a field named in a subquery. For example, if you wanted to delete all employees who are older than 40 from the EMPPF file, you could do that using a labeled duration with the following statement:

```
Delete
  From  EMPPF
  Where Current_Date > BIRTHDATE + 40 years
```

Like the Update statement, the SQL Delete statement is useful when you need to delete a set of records having some common characteristic.

In this brief discussion of SQL, we have focused on some useful techniques for getting information out of a relational database and on the SQL file maintenance statements Insert, Update, and Delete. While not a comprehensive introduction to SQL, this brief tour should help you understand the potential usefulness of the language, particularly its code-efficient ability to query databases. Given the complexity and sheer number of end-user requests for information, there should be no doubt that SQL can help reduce backlogs and cut down on project completion times. When used within HLL programs, the power and ease of coding of SQL data access can be combined with the screen or report formatting flexibility of the HLL to create programs that are not only faster to design, code, and test, but whose maintenance costs will be far less over time.

Key Terms

audit report

column functions

correlation names

DFU

extended field definitions

indexed file

labeled duration

nonindexed file

scalar functions

subquery

view

Lab 10

INTRODUCTION

In this lab you create a logical file (keyed on the last name field) over your student file, STUPF. Then you create a DFU program that uses the logical file to update your student file. Part 3 of the lab introduces you to the SQL command line where you practice entering Select statements to query your database, and Update, Insert, and Delete statements to maintain your database files.

In Part 4, to gain more experience using Query/400, you produce a join query report that provides calculated results and control breaks. And in an additional lab exercise for this lesson, you create a DFU update program for a multiple-format logical file.

Part 1

Goals	Create a new logical file over your STUPF
Start at	Work with Objects Using PDM, your library
Procedure	Work with QDDSSRC
	Add a new member, source type LF
	Use SEU to insert the DDS source code
	Exit, save, and compile
	Check for successful completion
	Run Query/400 to view the data of the new logical file

1.1. Sign on as usual and go to the Work with Objects Using PDM screen for your library.

1.2. Take the Work with option on your DDS source physical file and, from Work with Members Using PDM, create a new logical file. Name the file STUNAMLF and make sure the member type is LF. An appropriate text description would be "STUPF data keyed on LNAME."

1.3. Enter the DDS for a logical file to include all fields from physical file STUPF, with the same field descriptions. (Use the same record format name as your physical file.) The file should be keyed on last name and duplicate key records should be processed in first-in, first-out sequence. Three lines of DDS source code should be adequate to describe the entire logical file.

1.4. Save and compile the logical file. Check your message queue to ensure successful compilation. If the file did not compile, find the errors in the spooled compile listing, fix the source file description, then recompile.

1.5. From the command line, type RUNQRY and prompt. Tab down to the Query file File parameter and enter the name of your new logical file, then run the command. You should see all of the records in your STUPF physical file, in arrival sequence. Remember that like SQL, Query/400 does not order records, even from a keyed logical file, unless sorting is requested. A default RUNQRY query does not provide the sort option.

Part 2

Goals	Create a permanent DFU program Be able to distinguish between CHGDTA (Change Data) and DSPDTA (Display Data) commands to select program mode
Start at	Any command line
Procedure	Enter STRDFU; create a DFU program Define the DFU program, using the Work with Fields screens to specify extended field definition Test the DFU program Run the CHGDTA and DSPDTA commands on your DFU program

2.1. From the command line, type STRDFU and press Enter. Select the option to Create a DFU program. The permanent DFU program you are about to create will store the code it generates as a *PGM type object in your library. A permanent DFU is much more efficient than a temporary DFU if you frequently need to add new records or make changes to a file. You will use the DFU program you create to update the logical file (STUNAMLF) you just compiled.

From the Create a DFU Program screen, name the program STUUPD (STUdent UPDate) in your own library, using logical file STUNAMLF. Press Enter.

2.2. From the Define General Information/Indexed File screen, change Job title to "Student File Update." Also, keep the default (2=Multiple) for Display format, select creation of an audit report, use edit numerics, allow updates on roll, and allow changes to keys. The completed screen should look like the one shown in Figure 10.39. Press Enter.

Figure 10.39

Define General Information Screen for an Indexed File

```
                    Define General Information/Indexed File
Type choices, press Enter.

    Job title . . . . . . . . . . . . . .   Student File Update_____
    Display format  . . . . . . . . . . .   2        1=Single,  2=Multiple
                                                      3=Maximum, 4=Row oriented

    Audit report  . . . . . . . . . . .     Y        Y=Yes, N=No
    S/36 style  . . . . . . . . . . . .     N        Y=Yes, N=No
    Suppress errors . . . . . . . . . .     N        Y=Yes, N=No
    Edit numerics . . . . . . . . . . .     Y        Y=Yes, N=No
    Allow updates on roll . . . . . . .     Y        Y=Yes, N=No
    Keys:
       Generate . . . . . . . . . . . .     N        Y=Yes, N=No
       Changes allowed . . . . . . . . .    Y        Y=Yes, N=No




F3=Exit        F12=Cancel        F14=Display definition
```

2.3. Use the default values for the Define Audit Report specifications.

2.4. Take the option to specify the record format shown (there should be only one) and press Enter.

2.5. From the Select and Sequence Fields screen, use function key F21 to select all; then change the ACTBAL sequence number so it will be placed last on the display. Press Enter. Your screen should now resemble the one shown in Figure 10.40.

Figure 10.40

Select and Sequence Fields Screen for Logical File STUNAMLF

```
                        Select and Sequence Fields
File  . . . . . . . . . . . . :    STUNAMLF      Library  . . . . :   JSMITH
Record format . . . . . . . :      STUPFR

Select fields and their sequence or press F21 to select all; press Enter.

Sequence   Field       Attr    Length   Type      Description
    1      SOCSEC               9,0     ZONE
    2      FNAME                 15     CHAR
    3      LNAME       KEY       20     CHAR
    4      GENDER                 1     CHAR
    5      PHONE               10,1     ZONE
    6      ADDR1                 25     CHAR
    7      ADDR2                 25     CHAR
    8      ZIP                  5,0     ZONE
    9      ACTBAL               7,2     ZONE




                                                                     Bottom
F3=Exit          F5=Refresh         F12=Cancel          F14=Display definition
F17=Fast path    F20=Renumber       F21=Select all
Press Enter to confirm or F17 to confirm with defaults.
```

When you are satisfied, confirm by pressing Enter again.

2.6.   At the Work with Fields screen, notice that headings have already been provided.

2.6a.   Where did these headings come from?

Change field headings (if necessary) so they all begin with a capital letter and continue with lowercase (as shown in Figure 10.41). Also, take option 2 on the Social Security number, name, phone, and address fields (as shown in Figure 10.41). Press Enter.

```
╭──────────────────────────────────────────────────────────────────────╮
│                         Work with Fields                               │
│                                                                        │
│  File . . . . . . . . . . :    STUNAMLF       Library . . . . :    JSMITH │
│  Record format . . . . . . :    STUPFR                                  │
│                                                                        │
│  Type options, press Enter.  Press F21 to select all.                  │
│     2=Specify extended definition                                      │
│     4=Delete extended definition                                       │
│                                                                        │
│                      Extended                                          │
│  Opt  Field          Definition   Heading                              │
│    2   SOCSEC            N         Social Security_____              │
│    2   FNAME             N         First Name_____              │
│    2   LNAME             N         Last Name_____              │
│    _   GENDER            N         Gender_____              │
│    2   PHONE             N         Phone_____              │
│    2   ADDR1             N         Address 1_____              │
│    2   ADDR2             N         Address 2_____              │
│    2   ZIP               N         Zip Code_____              │
│                                                                        │
│                                                        More...         │
│  F3=Exit                F5=Refresh          F12=Cancel                 │
│  F14=Display definition F21=Select al                                 │
╰──────────────────────────────────────────────────────────────────────╯
```

Figure 10.41

Work with Fields Screen with Extended Definition Selected for Several Fields

2.7.   The next screen you see will be the first page of the Specify Extended Field Definition display for field SOCSEC. Press Page down to see the second screen of Extended Field Definition options. Change the default Edit code (L) to space (i.e., blank it out). On the Edit word line, enter an edit word to insert hyphens in the Social Security number so that it will appear as *nnn-nn-nnnn*. Remember to enclose the edit word in single quotation marks (apostrophes). When you have finished, the screen should look like the one shown in Figure 10.42.

Lab 10

Figure 10.42

Specify Extended Field
Definition Screen
Showing Edit Word
Selected for Field
SOCSEC

```
                        Specify Extended Field Definition
Field . . . . . . . . :  SOCSEC        Record format . . . . :   STUPFR

Type choices, press Enter.

  Begin on new line . . . . . . . . . .  N      Y=Yes, N=No
  Field exit required . . . . . . . . .  Y      Y=Yes, N=No
  Output only . . . . . . . . . . . . .  N      Y=Yes, N=No
  Non-display . . . . . . . . . . . . .  N      Y=Yes, N=No
  Default spacing . . . . . . . . . . .  Y      Y=Yes, N=No
    For choice N=No:
      Number of spaces . . . . . . . . .  01     0-40
  Edit code . . . . . . . . . . . . . .  _      Blank, 1-4, A-D, J-M, . . .
  Edit word . . . . . . . . . . . . . .  '  -  - '   _____



                                                                  Bottom
F3=Exit    F12=Cancel     F14=Display definition
```

2.8. Each time you finish a Specify Extended Field Definition for a field and press Enter, you will see a similar screen for the next field. For example, after you press Enter from the Specify Extended Field Definition screen for field SOCSEC, you should see the Specify Extended Field Definition screen for field FNAME (as shown in Figure 10.43).

Figure 10.43

Specify Extended Field
Definition Screen for
Field FNAME

```
                        Specify Extended Field Definition
Field . . . . . . . . :  FNAME         Record format . . . . :   STUPFR

Type choices, press Enter.

  Auto-duplicate . . . . . . . . . . .  N          Y=Yes, N=No
  Allow lowercase . . . . . . . . . .  Y          Y=Yes, N=No
  Extended field
    heading . . . . . . . . . . . . .  First Name_____
    _____
  Heading location . . . . . . . . . .  *BEFORE     *ABOVE, *BEFORE
  Initial value . . . . . . . . . . .  _____
  Validity checks . . . . . . . . . .  __          2=Change, 4=Delete

                                                                  More...



F3=Exit    F12=Cancel     F14=Display definition
```

2.9. For all alphanumeric fields that permit use of lowercase alphabetic characters, you must change Allow lowercase to Y, as we have done in Figure 10.43. You need to make that change to each of the other alphanumeric fields as they come up.

2.10. When you get to the PHONE field, page down to the edit options and erase the default edit code. Use an edit word of

' & – '

The blanks (spaces) are digit replacements, the ampersand (&) inserts a space, and the hyphen will be inserted between the prefix and subscriber parts of the telephone number.

2.11. When you have finished with the last field, ADDR2, you should find yourself back at the Work with Fields screen. For those fields you have selected, the Extended Definition value should be changed to Y. When you press Enter on the Work with Fields screen, you will go to the DFU exit screen.

2.12. The Exit DFU Program Definition screen should look like the one shown in Figure 10.44.

```
                          Exit DFU Program Definition

   Type choices, press Enter.

        Save program . . . . . . . . .  Y          Y=Yes, N=No
        Run program . . . . . . . . . .  Y          Y=Yes, N=No
          For choice Y=Yes:
            Type of run . . . . . . . .  1          1=Change, 2=Display
        Modify program . . . . . . . .  N          Y=Yes, N=No
        Save DDS source . . . . . . . .  N          Y=Yes, N=No

        For Save program Y=Yes:
          Program . . . . . . . . . . .  STUUPD____   Name
            Library . . . . . . . . . .   JSMITH__   Name, *CURLIB, . . .
          Authority . . . . . . . . . .  *CHANGE___   Name, *LIBCRTAUT, . . .
          Text  . . . . . . . . . . . .  Student File Update_____
   ____
        For Save DDS source Y=Yes:
          Source file . . . . . . . . .   _____   Name
            Library . . . . . . . . . .   *CURLIB____   Name, *CURLIB, . . .
          Source member . . . . . . . .  STUUPD_____   Name


     F3=Exit      F14=Display definition      F17=Fast path
```

Figure 10.44
Exit DFU Program Definition Screen for Program STUUPD

From this screen, select both Save program and Run program (these should be defaults) and leave Type of run set to 1. Notice the information under For Save program Y=Yes: Using the program name, library, and text information you have already provided, DFU creates a program object of type *PGM that you can run from a CL command. Press Enter.

2.13. You should now be looking at the Change a Data File screen.

2.13a. What message appears at the bottom of the screen?

Press Enter to run the DFU program you just created.

2.14. The next display is your DFU work screen. Notice the text in the upper left corner and the mode. Because the DFU program is built on the logical file, it should use the LNAME field as a key to the file. Type a student's last name and press Enter. (Remember, DFU is case-sensitive.) Does the record display? Print the screen.

2.15. When you change one of the numeric fields, you must key all digits to the right of the changed digit(s), and then you must press Field exit.

2.15a. What happens if you move the cursor down and try to change the area code part of the phone number by typing over it, then pressing Enter?

After pressing Reset, you can key all digits of the phone number without edit characters, and then press Field exit. Or, if you don't want to change the field value, move the cursor outside the field and press function key 5.
Page down through your logical file. Are all records presented in last-name sequence?

2.16. Exit the DFU program and return to Work with Objects Using PDM. Now check your objects list. Is the DFU program present? If you didn't find it, try Refresh.

2.16a. Is there another object with the same name as your DFU program in the Work with Objects Using PDM list? (Check carefully — you may have to Page up/Page down.)
2.16b. Of what type and attribute is the object?

2.17. From the command line, type

```
CHGDTA DFUPGM(STUUPD)
```

and press Enter.

2.17a. What happens?
2.17b. If DFUPGM is the only required parameter, what is the short form (positional notation) of the previous command?

A DFU display or update program can be run from within a CL program or an HLL program such as Cobol or RPG. In fact, the CL command determines in which mode (CHANGE or DISPLAY) the DFU program runs. So the program we created for update could be run as a display-only program by using the command

```
DSPDTA STUUPD
```

instead of the CHGDTA command shown above.

2.18. Exit from the Change program and execute the DSPDTA command using your DFU program.

2.18a. What mode is the program in?

2.18b.What is different about the available function keys compared to other DFU screens (including temporary DFUs) you have used?

Retrieve a record.

2.18c.What happens when you move the cursor down to a field and try to change it?

2.19. Exit from the Display mode DFU and return to Work with Objects Using PDM. Find the PDM option to Run (a program). Type its number on the option field of your DFU program (STUUPD), but prompt instead of pressing Enter.

2.19a.What command does the Run option invoke when it is taken on a DFU program?

As you can see, the easiest way to use your update program is to select the Run option for it from Work with Objects Using PDM. Cancel the option for now.

2.20. Now type the option to Change using DFU on your program's option field. You have used this option before to run temporary DFUs on physical and logical files.

2.20a.Use the command prompt screen to find out which CL command is invoked when the Change using DFU option is taken on a DFU program object.

DFU option 3 passed from the command selects the Change a DFU program choice, so using this PDM option takes you immediately to the Define General Information screen of your program — a very convenient approach when you need to change an existing DFU program.

Part 3

Goals	Become familiar with the SQL command-line environment Use SQL to list all students living in local Zip codes Use SQL to insert ZIPPF records, update existing ZIPPF records Use SQL to find student records unmatched with the ZIPPF file
Start at	Work with Objects Using PDM, your library
Procedure	STRSQL Enter SQL statements; analyze results

This part of the lab is intended to provide you with initial exposure to the SQL command-line environment. To do the exercises in this part, you need to have your own copy of ZIPPF in your library. If you have not done the additional lab exercise for Lab 8, you need to use the PDM copy option to copy INTROCLASS/ZIPPF to your own library. Please do that now, if necessary, before continuing.

3.1. From the Work with Objects Using PDM screen, be sure that physical file ZIPPF is in your library. On the system command line, type STRSQL and press Enter.

　　　The interactive SQL command line initially appears as a screen full of empty lines. One SQL statement at a time is typed on as many lines as needed, then executed. If the statement executes properly, output is shown on an information screen. Pressing Enter or F12 from the information screen returns you to the SQL command line where the previously executed command is displayed just above a refreshed command line.

Figure 10.45
Specify SELECT
Statement Prompt
Screen

```
                        Specify SELECT Statement

  Type information for SELECT statement.  Press F4 for a list.

      FROM files . . . . . . . . .   _____
      SELECT fields . . . . . . .    _____
      WHERE conditions . . . . . .   _____
      GROUP BY fields . . . . . .    _____
      HAVING conditions . . . . .    _____
      ORDER BY fields . . . . . .    _____
      FOR UPDATE OF fields . . . .   _____
                                                               Bottom
  Type choices, press Enter.

      DISTINCT records in result file . . . . . . . .  N   Y=Yes, N=No
      UNION with another SELECT . . . . . . . . . . .  N   Y=Yes, N=No
      Specify additional options . . . . . . . . . .   N   Y=Yes, N=No



  F3=Exit        F4=Prompt    F5=Refresh    F6=Insert line  F9=Specify subquery
  F10=Copy line  F12=Cancel   F14=Delete line   F15=Split line  F24=More keys
```

3.2. On the SQL command line, type SELECT, then press F4. (All SQL commands can be typed in upper, lower, or mixed case.) You should see the SQL prompt screen for a Select statement, Figure 10.45.
This screen helps you fill in the necessary clauses of the statement for your request and provides lists of files and fields if you need them.
　　　To see how it works, lets code a SQL statement with a similar purpose to a logical file we created earlier — to list students from local Zip codes (those having the same two high-order digits as your company or school). Let's use only the first name, last name, address 1, and Zip code fields from STUPF.

3.3. Without pressing Enter, on the FROM files line, type STUPF. Tab to the SELECT fields line and enter FNAME, LNAME, ADDR1, ZIP. Be sure to separate each field name from another with a comma. Tab to the WHERE conditions line and enter ZIP Between 52000 and 52999. (Change the high-order digits (i.e., 52) to those of your own local Zip code. Your screen should now look similar to the one in Figure 10.46.

```
                        Specify SELECT Statement

Type information for SELECT statement.  Press F4 for a list.

    FROM files . . . . . . . . .   stupf _____
    SELECT fields . . . . . . .    fname, lname, addrl, zip _____
    WHERE conditions . . . . . .   Zip between 52000 and 52999 _____
    GROUP BY fields . . . . . .    _____
    HAVING conditions . . . . .    _____
    ORDER BY fields . . . . . .    _____
    FOR UPDATE OF fields . . . .   _____
                                                              Bottom
Type choices, press Enter.

    DISTINCT records in result file . . . . . . . .  N  Y=Yes, N=No
    UNION with another SELECT  . . . . . . . . . . .  N  Y=Yes, N=No
    Specify additional options . . . . . . . . . .   N  Y=Yes, N=No



F3=Exit        F4=Prompt    F5=Refresh   F6=Insert line  F9=Specify subquery
F10=Copy line  F12=Cancel   F14=Delete line  F15=Split line  F24=More keys
```

Figure 10.46
Specify SELECT
Statement Prompt
Screen to Retrieve
Students from
Local Zip Codes

Let me remind you again that case doesn't matter except in quoted strings. Because we don't need any other SQL clause for this request, let's press F21 to see what the command looks like. F21 constructs the SQL command from your entries so far. After pressing F21, you should see a screen similar to the one in Figure 10.47.

```
                        Specify SELECT Statement
SQL statement:

SELECT fname,lname,addr1,zip FROM stupf WHERE Zip between 52000 and
52999












                                                              Bottom
Press Enter to continue.

F3=Exit    F12=Cancel
```

Figure 10.47
F21 from the Specify
SELECT Statement
Prompt Screen

Notice how SQL keywords have been inserted into the command and appear in uppercase.

If you scan the command and notice an error, you can fix it after returning to the prompt screen. Press F12 to return to the prompt screen.

If the command looked all right, try to run it by pressing Enter from the specify SELECT Statement prompt screen.

If the statement is executable, the message "Query running..." appears at the bottom of your screen as the statement is being executed. You should now see output on your display screen showing the name fields, address 1, and Zip code of local students.

3.4. From the display, press Enter or F12 to return to the SQL command line. Press F9 to pull the previous command back onto the command line.

While using the prompt screen may be convenient, the statements it renders are not in good form. All syntax elements of the command follow each other with only a single space separating SQL words, lists, constants, field names, and so on. While the SQL command interpreter may have no trouble with this arrangement, it is not the best form for human use for at least three reasons:

• It is hard to read and understand.

• It is hard to modify when changing or adding clauses or new syntax elements.

• It is ugly.

Let's use function key F15, to make the statement more readable. Position the cursor on the F of FROM and press F15. Now position the cursor on the W of WHERE and press F15 again. Because there is no Join line function key, move the cursor to just after "and" and retype the high-range value Zip code that now appears on the next line by itself. After that, move the cursor down and use function key F14 to delete the line with the single Zip code value. (F14 deletes a line where the cursor is positioned.) Finally, use the Insert key to indent the two lines following the Select statement two positions each.

Now your Select statement should look like the neatly indented version, with each clause starting on a separate line, as shown in Figure 10.48.

Figure 10.48
SQL Statement Formatted for Readability and Maintenance

```
                         Enter SQL Statements
Type SQL statement, press Enter.
   > SELECT fname,lname,addr1,zip FROM stupf WHERE Zip between 52000 and
     52999
     SELECT statement run complete.
===> SELECT fname,lname,addr1,zip _____
       FROM stupf _____
       WHERE Zip between 52000 and 52999 _____
     _____
     _____
     _____
     _____
     _____
     _____
     _____

                                                            Bottom
 F14=Delete line    F15=Split line    F16=Select libraries
 F17=Select files                     F18=Select fields    F24=More keys
```

Run the reformatted command so that it will appear in your command log.

3.5. To see all fields and records of a file, you can use the syntax

```
Select *
  From filename
```

Enter that command now for your STUPF file and observe the data displayed. Probably the records are in order by the SOCSEC field if that's how you entered them. Unless you specify otherwise, SQL retrieves records using the arrival-sequence access path available for all physical files, even if the named file is a logical file or a physical file created with a key-sequenced access path.

Try to remember the order of records displayed, then return to the SQL command line and rerun the command (Press F9 to retrieve the previous command), this time using the logical file STUNAMLF, which is keyed on last name.

3.5a. What difference do you see in the displayed output from the previous STUPF output?

3.5b. Did SQL use the key-sequenced access path of STUNAMLF?

3.6. Now use the SQL Insert statement to add a record to STUPF. The syntax is

```
Insert Into filename
             (field-list)
  Values     (value-list)
```

Remember that all list items are separated by commas. Provide only the SOCSEC, LNAME, and FNAME fields. Use a SOCSEC value that you know already exists in STUPF, such as 111110001.

Your statement should look similar to the statement on the command line of Figure 10.49.

```
                    Enter SQL Statements
Type SQL statement, press Enter.
  > select *
      from stupf
    SELECT statement run complete.
  > select *
      from stunamlf
    SELECT statement run complete.
===> insert into stupf _____
        (socsec, lname, fname) _____
        values(111110001, 'Hammer', 'Sledge') _____
_____
_____
_____
_____
_____
_____
_____
                                                    Bottom
  F14=Delete Line    F15=Split Line    F16=Select libraries
  F17=Select files                     F18=Select fields    F24=More keys
```

Figure 10.49
SQL Insert Statement

Remember that non-numeric values must be enclosed by single quotation marks, as shown. Be sure your field names are spelled correctly, then run the statement.

3.6a. What message is returned above the SQL command line?

The message should have told you that one row was inserted into STUPF. If not, move the cursor to the error message and press F1 for extended message text and recovery advice, if the cause of the error is not obvious.

3.7. Now you will use the Order By clause to list all STUPF records, sorted by SOCSEC. You can use function key F9 to pull a statement at the cursor location in the command log back to the command line. Move the cursor up to the previous Select * statement and press F9. In case the statement has scrolled off the page, press Page up to see previously logged commands. Modify the command so it now reads

```
Select     *
   From      STUPF
   Order By SOCSEC
```

3.7a. Is the record you just inserted listed in the output?
3.7b. How do you explain that the record has been added to STUPF, yet STULF1 that you created in Lab 8 has a unique key-sequenced access path on SOCSEC? (Hint: you may need to go back and look at the file description of STULF1, especially at the Select/Omit rules.)

While you are looking at the output of the Select statement, note the first names of any females whose GENDER is still listed as M or any males whose GENDER is still listed as F. (Recall that in Lab 9, you selected a default value based on the predominance of males or females in your database.)

3.8. Retrieve the records from STUPF having SOCSEC equal to 111110001. One of them should be yours, and its Zip code should be local to your area. If you don't have a second record with a matching SOCSEC, insert one following the instructions in Step 3.6.

Retrieve the previous Select statement and change the file name to STULF1, then run it. Your record should still be there. If not, update STUPF changing your Zip code to a local one using the following SQL statement

```
Update     STUPF
   Set      ZIP=52338
   Where    SOCSEC = 111110001
     And    LNAME = 'Smith'
```

Use a local Zip code instead of 52338 and your last name instead of Smith.

3.9. Now try to update the record you just added to STUPF in Step 3.6 using the Update syntax shown above, but use the same last name as in Step 3.6 and change the Zip code to a local Zip code. The statement should look like that on the command line of Figure 10.50.

Figure 10.50
Updating a Record

```
                        Enter SQL Statements

Type SQL statement, press Enter.
    > insert into stupf
         (socsec,lname,fname)
         values(111110001, 'Hammer', 'Sledge')
      1 rows inserted in STUPF in JSMITH.
    > select *
         from stupf
         order by socsec
      SELECT statement run complete.
    > select *
         from stulfl
         order by socsec
      SELECT statement run complete.
===> update stupf _____
         set zip = 52338 _____
         where socsec = 111110001 _____
            and lname = 'Hammer' _____
_____
                                                             Bottom
  F14=Delete line    F15=Split line    F16=Select libraries
  F17=Select files                     F18=Select fields    F24=More keys
```

3.9a. Before running the statement, predict the outcome.

Now run the SQL Update statement.

3.9b. What message is returned?

Press the Help key on the message and Read the Cause information.

3.9c. State specifically why the update attempt failed.

3.10. Now delete the record added to STUPF in Step 3.6. *Caution:* when you use the SQL Delete statement, be sure to specify exactly which record(s) you want deleted.

3.10a.What is wrong with the following:

```
Delete
   From STUPF
```

3.10b. What is wrong with the following:

```
Delete
   From  STUPF
   Where SOCSEC = 111110001
```

To correctly identify the previously inserted record, we need another field value, such as last name. The following statement should work:

```
Delete
   From STUPF
 Where SOCSEC = 111110001
   And LNAME = 'Hammer'
```

Try that statement (using the inserted last name if different).

3.10c. What message is returned?

3.11. Now practice using the Update statement to set the STUPF GENDER field to appropriate values. You can update multiple records at once if you are able to tell SQL exactly which ones to update. The Update statement shown in Figure 10.51 should do the trick for the women whose first names are in the list.

Figure 10.51

SQL Update Statement to Correct GENDER Value from Default

```
                        Enter SQL Statements

Type SQL statement, press Enter.
   > update stupf
       set zip = 52338
       where socsec = 111110001
         and lname = 'Hammer'
     Duplicate key value specified.
   > delete
       from stupf
       where socsec = 111110001
         and lname = 'Hammer'
     1 rows deleted from STUPF in JSMITH.
 ===> update stupf _____
       set gender = 'F' _____
       where fname in ('Tillie', 'Millie', 'Jane') _____
     _____
     _____
     _____

                                                     Bottom
 F14=Delete line    F15=Split line    F16=Select libraries
 F17=Select files                     F18=Select fields    F24=More keys
```

3.12. Let's now turn our attention to join selects, but first let's find out how many records you have in your STUPF file, using the COUNT column function. Run the following command and note the results:

```
Select COUNT (*)
   From STUPF
```

Now let's create a simple name and address list using an inner join.

```
Select LNAME, FNAME, ADDR1, CITY, STATE, S.ZIP
   From STUPF S Inner Join ZIPPF Z
     On S.ZIP = Z.ZIP
```

This is an equijoin on relationship-supporting fields ZIP in the two files. Instead of using the shortened correlation names (S, Z), you could have qualified the ambiguous ZIP by using file names instead (e.g., STUPF.ZIP). Key in the statement and run it.

3.12a. How many records were selected for display?

3.13. If the join records were less than the count of STUPF, some STUPF records don't have matching values in ZIPPF. To find only those unmatched STUPF records, use the exception join. Key the statement as follows, and run it.

```
Select LNAME, FNAME, S.ZIP
  From STUPF S Exception Join ZIPPF Z
    On S.ZIP = Z.ZIP
```

Except for the shortened field list and the changed join, the syntax is very similar to that of the inner join.

3.13a. How many records were retrieved?

3.14. Using the information from the exception join, key in and execute the necessary SQL statements to eliminate all unmatched records in STUPF. Don't delete the STUPF records; either update them to matching ZIPPF values or insert new ZIPPF records to cover the unmatched student Zip codes.

3.14a. Write the SQL statement to add a new record to ZIPPF for Crested Butte, CO, 81224.

When you exit SQL, use F3 from the command entry screen. This takes you to the exit screen shown in Figure 10.52.

```
                        Exit Interactive SQL

  Type choice, press Enter.

    Option . . . . . . . .   1        1=Save and exit session
                                      2=Exit without saving session
                                      3=Resume session
                                      4=Save session in source file

  F12=Cancel
```

Figure 10.52

Exit Interactive SQL Screen with Default Option

You have four options, and the default should always be 1 = Save and exit session. Taking that option lets you return to your previous SQL session and all of its logged commands when you sign on to the same device using your same profile. You can also save the SQL session in a source file for later use. If you choose option 4, you must provide a source physical file name (SQL creates one if it doesn't already exist) and a member name. I recommend using QSQLSESS as the source physical file and a month+day+year name as the member name (e.g., AUG0298).

Saving the SQL session to source does not erase the session; instead it returns you to the SQL exit screen where you can then take option 1.

Part 4

Goals	Create a level-break report using Query/400
	Join files STUPF and ZIPPF for the report
	Define result fields
	Use report summary functions

Start at	Work with Objects Using PDM, your library

Procedure	Determine the existence of ZIPPF
	WRKQRY, create a query
	Define the query
	Exit, save, and run the query

Now you will create a level-break report using Query/400. This report joins files STUPF and ZIPPF. If you did not finish additional exercise for Lab 8 or Part 3 of this lab, you need to first copy the ZIPPF file from INTROCLASS into your own library and update it (or your STUPF file) so that most student records have matching Zip codes with ZIPPF records.

4.1. From a command line, type WRKQRY and press Enter. Create a new query called STUPAYQRY. This query will create a report similar to the one shown in Figure 10.53.

Lab 10

Figure 10.53
Sample Query of
Student Payment
Report

Student Payment Due Report
prepared by J Smith

10/30/98 22:15:47   PAGE 1

Name	Social Security Line 1	Address Line 1	Phone	Zip	City	State	Account Balance	Payment Due
S Owari	111-11-0011	9999 99TH St	999 999-9999	78915	Disney World	FL	99.99	20.00
B Badman	111-11-0001	#1 Nirvanah Ln.	319 234-3456	76484	Once Again		896.90	179.38
H Humpchucker	111-11-0008	1233 Shady Road	319 488-7865	78914	Toby Town		1,234.00	246.80
FL TOTAL							2,230.89	446.18
COUNT 3								
N Grubber	111-11-0006	RR 2	515 899-7890	52203	Amana	IA	890.99	178.20
M Muggins	111-11-0013	RR 2	555 234-4321	52205	Anamosa		1.12	.22
M Murkiwater	111-11-0044	Shady Lane	515 899-0923	51632	Clarinda		32.00	6.40
J Cool	111-11-0004	512 Belvedere Dr.	319 365-9876	50115	Guthrie Center		12.34	2.47
H Hopkins	111-11-0033	RR1	319 688-9234	52235	Hills		45,000.00	9,000.00
B Goodoboy	111-11-0015	12 E. Main	777 123-4567	52247	Kalona		45.00	9.00
B Baggins	111-11-0087	345 Hawthorne Ln.	319 988-8998	52302	Marion		98,425.00	19,685.00
D Dupekey	111-11-0009	319 Ditto Pl	319 555-1212	50854	Mount Ayr		222.22	44.44
E Engobber	111-11-0007	Clay Works	515 388-6543	50458	Nora Springs		5,432.10	1,086.42
C Mannaka	111-11-0012	55 Center St.	555 555-5555	50225	Pleasantville		55.55	11.11
J Fottral	111-11-0001	RR1	857-4101	52338	Swisher		350.00-	70.00-
IA TOTAL							149,766.32	29,953.26
COUNT 11								
I Tenkaichi	111-11-0010	111 Imperial Hwy.	111 111-1111	46614	South Bend	IN	.11	.02
IN TOTAL							.11	.02
COUNT 1								
S Slim	111-11-0016	10 W. Main	515 233-4566	44445	Dead Dog	UT	345.01	69.00
J Dowhopper	111-11-0005	12345 Clyde St.	215 456-7654	44446	Ghost Gulch		450.00	90.00
K Clapsaddle	111-11-0003	999 Sundown Rd.	707 683-4556	44444	Nowhere		865.96	173.19
UT TOTAL							1,660.97	332.19
COUNT 3								
FINAL TOTALS							153,658.29	30,731.65
COUNT 18								

*** END OF REPORT ***

4.2. When you define this query, you will use all options except Select records, Select collating sequence, and Specify processing options.

First, specify the proper files (your physical database files STUPF and ZIPPF). STUPF will be the primary file (use File ID S) and ZIPPF will be the secondary file (File ID Z). Specify a join for Matched records with primary file, so you will see student records that have unmatched Zip codes as well as all the matched records. Match the Zip code fields using an equal relationship.

4.2a. What is this type of join called in a relational database language like SQL?

4.3. Define a result field called NAME that concatenates a substring of FNAME to LNAME. The length of the FNAME substring should be 1 so that NAME will consist of first initial, one space, and last name. Use Help from Define a result field, and look down several pages under Character substrings and Character concatenation in extended Help for syntax and examples of use.

A space can be concatenated into a character expression by simply enclosing one hit of the space bar in single quotation marks. Use two bar (||) symbols for concatenation (on most keyboards, Shift + Back slash). Create another result field called PMTDUE that is 20 percent of the ACTBAL. It should be 7 digits long, with 2 decimal places. Give both fields meaningful column headings.

4.4. Select and sequence fields, placing the NAME field first, the other fields as shown in Figure 10.53, and the PMTDUE field last. Do not give a sequence number to FNAME, LNAME, GENDER, or ADDR2.

4.5. Select sort fields so that records will be sorted by city within state (lowest number is highest priority) in ascending sequence.

4.6. In report column formatting, adjust lengths of the alphanumeric fields so that the report will fit within 132 print positions. Specify column headings as shown in the sample report.

For fields that require special editing, such as embedded spaces or hyphens, create an edit word using choice 4 for the edit option of Define Numeric Field Editing. Review the instructions for Specify edit word.

Just as in DFU extended field description specifications, the edit word is enclosed in single quotation marks; within the edit word, each blank represents a digit. An embedded space is coded by an ampersand symbol (&). Other edit symbols (e.g., hyphens) can be inserted within the edit word where needed. Be sure that the number of blanks within the quotation marks equals the number of digits in the field.

Create edit words for phone and Social Security number fields so they print as shown in Figure 10.53. Remove commas from ZIP and other fields. Use the layout function to see the report format.

4.7. For Select Report Summary Functions, select the Count function on the name field and provide totals for fields ACTBAL and PMTDUE only.

4.8. Define a report break level 1 for STATE. Note that the Sort priorities are shown to remind you how the data will be sequenced. The relative order of fields selected for break levels and sort priorities should match, but you will not define a level break for CITY.

On the next screen, Format Report Break, level 0 is for final totals. Do not suppress summaries. For level 0, use the default FINAL TOTALS as Break text. Press Enter to continue.

For the STATE break (level 1), use the control field value itself, &STATE, as the Break text. The word TOTAL beneath the state code on the sample report prints automatically.

4.9. At this time, you should again check the report layout and try running the report (F5) to see whether it looks right.

4.10. For Select Output Type and Form, use Printer output. Make the form size wide enough to hold your entire detail line. You can use the layout function key at any time to check line width. If your report is wider than 132 characters, check with your instructor/mentor to make sure your printer will automatically change to condensed mode.

4.11. Specify Y for Define spooled output, leave Form type blank, and specify one copy. Because your report is spooled, you should not need to put it on hold. Don't print a cover page, but (from the next screen) print a page heading that includes your name and a title, so that your report will be similar to the sample shown in Figure 10.53. If you left align title data on the lines provided, it will automatically be centered on the report.

4.12. When the report is correct (you will not see the report headers when using the F5 function key), use F3 from the Define the Query screen to exit. Fill out the Exit screen. Save the definition. Run the query interactively. Make sure it is properly named in the proper library. Give it an appropriate text description (e.g., *Your Name* Payment Due of STUPF).

4.13. Exit Query/400 and return to Work with Objects Using PDM. Is the new query definition object in your library? Did you refresh your screen?

4.14. Now work with your output queue. If your report is correct, change it to go to PRT01 (or your designated class printer) for printing; otherwise, return to Query/400 and change your query definition to correct any errors.

4.15. Hand in a copy of the report and the DFU print screen.

Additional Lab Exercise

I highly recommend that you complete this exercise to gain additional experience in creating DFU update programs. You should have successfully completed the main parts of the lab exercise for this lesson before attempting this exercise.

In this exercise you create a DFU program that lets you update the multiple-format logical file STUENRLMLF, which you created in the additional exercise for Lab 8.

1. Start DFU and create a program similar to the one specified in Figure 10.54.

Figure 10.54

Create a DFU Program Screen for Multiple-Format Logical File STUENRLMLF

```
                                    Create a DFU Program
    Type choices, press Enter.

        Program . . . . . . . . . .   stuenrlupd    Name, F4 for list
          Library . . . . . . . . .     jsmith__    Name, *CURLIB

        Data file . . . . . . . . .   stuenrlmlf    Name, F4 for list
          Library . . . . . . . . .     jsmith__    Name, *LIBL, *CURLIB









    F3=Exit      F4=Prompt       F12=Cancel
```

2. Fill out the Define General Information/Indexed File screen with an appropriate job title. Also, choose Row-oriented display format, Audit report, Edit numerics, Allow updates on roll, and — to correct keying errors — allow changes to keys. The completed screen should look like the one shown in Figure 10.55.

3. Take the defaults for audit control.

4. Specify both record formats, but on the Multiple Records field for ENRLPFR, change the value to Y. This causes the program to display multiple enrollment records for a student on one screen.

5. Select all STUPFR fields, but in the order SOCSEC, LNAME, FNAME, ADDR1, ADDR2, ZIP, PHONE, ACTBAL.

6. From the Work with Fields screen for STUPFR, edit the Social Security number field with hyphen insertion, allow lowercase on the name and address fields, and edit the phone number field to appear as 123 456-7890.

```
                    Define General Information/Indexed File

 Type choices, press Enter.

     Job title . . . . . . . . . . . . . .   Student-Enrollment Update_____
     Display format  . . . . . . . . . . .   4        1=Single,  2=Multiple
                                                      3=Maximum, 4=Row oriented

     Audit report  . . . . . . . . . . . .   Y        Y=Yes, N=No
     S/36 style  . . . . . . . . . . . . .   N        Y=Yes, N=No
     Suppress errors . . . . . . . . . . .   N        Y=Yes, N=No
     Edit numerics . . . . . . . . . . . .   Y        Y=Yes, N=No
     Allow updates on roll . . . . . . . .   Y        Y=Yes, N=No
     Keys:
         Generate  . . . . . . . . . . . .   N        Y=Yes, N=No
         Changes allowed . . . . . . . . .   Y        Y=Yes, N=No




 F3=Exit      F12=Cancel       F14=Display definition
```

Figure 10.55

Define General Information/Indexed File Screen for New Program STUENRLUPD

7. Select both fields from ENRLPFR, but in the order SOCSEC, SECTNO.

8. Provide autoduplicate for field SOCSEC, and edit it so it appears the same as it does in the STUPFR record format.

9. The Exit DFU screen should be left to default values (Modify program and Save DDS source should both be set to N).

10. From the Change a Data File screen, press Enter to run the program. The program should come up in Change mode, and pressing Page down should display the student record having the correct Social Security number. Because all fields are input-enabled, changes to address, phone number, and so on could be made at this screen when a student registers for classes. The student record format, STUPFR, should look like the one shown in Figure 10.56.

Figure 10.56
Change Mode on the
Student Record Format

```
Student-Enrollment Update                      Mode . . . . :   CHANGE
Format . . . . :   STUPFR____                  File . . . . :   STUENRLMLF

        SOCSEC              LNAME                    FNAME
        111-11-0001         Smith_____         Jane_____

ADDR1                       ADDR2                    ZIP       PHONE
1308 L Rd NW_____     _____    52338     319 857-4101
                                     ACTBAL
                                     350.00-




F3=Exit                     F5=Refresh               F6=Select format
F9=Insert                   F10=Entry                F11=Change
```

Pressing Page down again should display all enrollment records (if any) for the current student. This screen should look like the one shown in Figure 10.57.

Figure 10.57
All Enrollment Records
for Student 111-11-0001

```
Student-Enrollment Update                      Mode . . . . :   CHANGE
Format . . . . :   ENRLPFR                     File . . . . :   STUENRLMLF

                    SOCSEC                          SECTNO
                    111-11-0001                     14050
                    111-11-0001                     14052







F3=Exit                     F5=Refresh               F6=Select format
F9=Insert                   F10=Entry                F11=Change
```

You can delete individual enrollment records from the list by pressing Field exit through both fields. You can delete the entire group of enrollment records by using the Delete function key (F23). You can add new enrollment records by pressing the Insert function key (F9) from the current ENRLPFR list. When you add multiple enrollment records, you can use the Dupe key to duplicate the Social Security number after the first one is typed in. Figure 10.58 shows an ENRLPFR screen in Insert mode.

```
Student-Enrollment Update              Mode . . . . :    INSERT
Format . . . . :  ENRLPFR              File . . . . :    STUENRLMLF
                  SOCSEC                   SECTNO
                  111110001                12345
                  LLLLLLLLLLL              12347
                  LLLLLLLLLLL              12350
                                              0
                                              0
                                              0
                                              0
                                              0
                                              0
                                              0
                                              0
                                              0
                                              0

                                              0
                                              0




 F3=Exit            F5=Refresh          F6=Select format
 F9=Insert          F10=Entry           F11=Change
```

Figure 10.58
A New Enrollment
Record

Several records have been added using the Dupe key to repeat Social Security number. Notice that when the Dupe key is used, the duplicated field value itself does not appear; rather, a special character appears to fill the duplicated field on the display. The proper value will be stored in the file, however.

To create enrollment records for a student who has none, you can use the Insert function key from another student's ENRLPFR display and key the new student's Social Security number and section number. Otherwise, use either the Insert or Entry function keys and then select the appropriate record format for data entry by using the Select format function. Remember, when keying the Social Security number (or other numeric edited fields), it is not necessary to key the edit characters — just key the digits and press Field exit.

12. Print screens of both record formats, showing multiple records for the ENRLPFR format, and hand these in to your instructor.

Mastering the AS/400, Second Edition

Lab 10 Answer Sheet

Name: _____

Date Due: _____

Class Time: _____

2.6a. _____

2.13a. _____

2.15a. _____

_____

2.16a. _____ 2.16b. _____

2.17a. _____

_____

2.17b._____

2.18a. _____

2.18b._____

2.18c._____

2.19a._____

2.20a._____

3.5a. _____ 3.5b. _____

3.6a. _____

3.7a. _____

3.7b._____

_____

3.9a._____

_____

3.9b._____

3.9c._____

(continued)

Lab 10 Answer Sheet, continued

3.10a. _____

3.10b. _____

_____

3.10c. _____

3.12a. _____   3.13a. _____

3.14a. _____

_____

4.2a. _____

In Summary

You can create temporary DFU programs by using PDM option 18 on a *FILE object, or by executing the UPDDTA command. Or you can create a permanent DFU program and store it in a user library. Permanent DFU programs have two advantages: They run faster because they are already compiled *PGM objects, and they provide useful functions such as customized display options and validity checking.

You create a permanent DFU program by taking option 2 from the DFU initial menu displayed when you execute the STRDFU command. The Define General Information Screen provides options to control field placement, audit reporting, numeric editing, updating on Page up/down, and changing key values or dealing with relative record numbers (nonindexed files).

You can select fields from the specified file for display and place them on the screen in a different order than in their record format. And you can easily change field headings.

By specifying extended field definitions, you can select features such as autoduplicate, uppercase lock, initial value, subtotal and total accumulation of numeric fields, and validity checks. You also can select fields for display only, change spacing between fields as they are displayed, and edit numeric fields.

Another nice feature of a permanent DFU, which was illustrated in the additional lab exercise for this lesson, is its ability to display, add, or change groups of related data file records on one display screen. This feature is particularly useful for grouping the secondary file records of a multiple-format logical file — for example, to display (and update) all projects to which an individual employee is assigned. Once a DFU program object exists, it can be run in change mode by using the CHGDTA command or in display mode by the using the DSPDTA command.

Permanent DFU programs lack some features necessary for thorough data validation, such as related file checking to enforce integrity constraints (e.g., you should not be able to enter an employee's Zip code if it doesn't exist in the Zip code file); nonetheless, permanent DFU programs provide a quick and convenient way to create fairly sophisticated file maintenance programs.

Command-line SQL is a convenient and powerful way to get information or update database files. The Select statement has many forms, allowing field projection, record selection, join operations, and column functions such as Count and Sum. The Group By clause allows column functions to be used on groups of records with common field values, and the Having clause allows conditional selection of group summary records.

The SQL Insert, Update, and Delete statements permit file maintenance. Both the Update and Delete statements work on sets of related records instead of one record at a time.

Lesson 11

Using SDA

Lesson Overview

Screen Design Aid (SDA) is a helpful utility that provides a quick and painless way to create menus and display screens. In this lesson we introduce SDA and explain how it works. Then we step through the design of a menu that could be used to select and run the queries and DFUs you have created in previous lessons. We also design a display screen that could be used to select customized work environments for different courses, such as Data Management or RPG Programming. As we work through the menu/screen design process, we examine the use of indicators and of some additional SDA functions (e.g., using display attributes and colors and testing the display screen for correctness).

In the lab you create a menu to select updates or queries of your files and run the necessary commands. You also create your own display file screen that you can use with a CL program (which you create in Lesson 12) to establish a tailored work environment when you sign on to the AS/400.

Objectives

Students will be able to

✓ Describe the general purpose and specific functions of SDA

✓ Describe the differences between a menu and a nonmenu display file

✓ Add constants, functions, and data fields to SDA work screens

✓ Use attribute commands to position fields and change their appearance

✓ Use SDA to create a simple menu that allows different actions to be taken on database files students have created

✓ Use SDA to create a display screen to be used by a program

✓ Test display screens to see how they would appear at runtime

✓ Identify the members and objects created by SDA menus and display screens and explain where they came from and how they work together

WHAT SDA DOES

On the AS/400, most end users work interactively by selecting choices from menus, filling in options from screens (e.g., list screens), or entering data into display-screen input fields to change or add database records (e.g., using DFU).

For the first type of activity, end users could work from a menu display — that is, any object whose type is *MENU and that looks and acts like a system-supplied menu. For the second and third types of activity, end users would work with a display screen created as a **display file** on the AS/400. Display files are objects whose type is *FILE and whose attribute is DSPF.

The main difference between a menu and a nonmenu display file is that a menu always has a numbered list of actions to be taken, and behind each action on the list is a single CL command to implement it. Of course, you don't see the command itself on the menu screen; but the actions and their associated commands are created together, most conveniently using **Screen Design Aid (SDA)**. Once a menu exists, you can make it work simply by using the GO command; you don't need a CL or high-level language (HLL) program.

A nonmenu display file, on the other hand, is only a screen image and pathway for moving data and indicators between the screen and the program that controls it. A nonmenu display file requires a CL or HLL program to make it appear on the display device and to control and monitor the movement of data between it and the program.

Both menus and display files are created by compiling the Data Description Specifications (DDS) source members that describe them. This process is similar to creating database files from physical and logical file DDS source members. However, the DDS syntax for DSPF type members is different and often more involved than for database physical file and logical file member types. Although certainly possible, it would be quite tedious for even an experienced programmer to code on coding forms or key in SEU the complete DDS for a display file of any complexity.

But because programmers frequently need to create and/or modify menus and display file screens to keep up with user application requirements, IBM provides SDA. SDA facilitates the creation of menus and display files by providing a combination of fill-in-the-prompt and blank screen work environments. By taking different combinations of options from the prompts and arranging constants and input/output fields on the blank screen, you define what the menu or display file screen will look like and how it will be used. With SDA you can create sophisticated screen designs and menus without dealing directly with DDS; SDA generates the DDS source code as you design the screen or menu.

Throughout this menu/screen design process, SDA constantly checks for, and discourages, entries that would result in DDS syntax errors. It is important to understand that whether you are using SDA to design a menu or a display file screen, the successful completion of the process results in DDS specifications that are stored as source physical file members. These source members are stored in a source physical file, by convention named QDDSSRC. Source members for menus and display file screens are similar to source members for physical and logical database file descriptions in the sense that all types are coded in DDS and stored in a source physical file (QDDSSRC).

GETTING STARTED WITH SDA

You invoke SDA when you enter the STRSDA (Start Screen Design Aid) command on any command line. If you need to modify an existing menu or non-menu display file using SDA, option 17 from the Work with Members Using PDM screen offers a convenient shortcut.

The initial SDA screen (Figure 11.1) shows the choices for designing screens, designing menus, and testing display files.

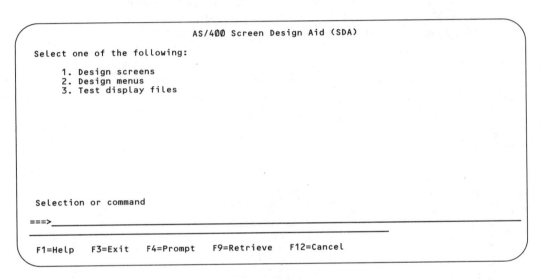

```
                    AS/400 Screen Design Aid (SDA)

    Select one of the following:

         1. Design screens
         2. Design menus
         3. Test display files




    Selection or command

    ===>_____


    F1=Help   F3=Exit   F4=Prompt   F9=Retrieve   F12=Cancel
```

Figure 11.1
SDA Initial Display
from STRSDA

The screens referred to under option 1 are nonmenu display files — those display screens that an application program will control.

SDA also lets you create online Help information for screens or menus. Because you create the online Help during the screen or menu design process, creating online Help is not provided as a separate menu option.

SDA, then, really has four distinct functions:

- Design screens
- Design menus
- Test display files
- Add online Help to screens/menus

We will work with the menu design function first, then with the screen design function.

MENUS

With SDA, you can quickly and easily create **menus** that look and act just like the system menus you have been using since the first lesson.

SDA provides a menu template that you can modify as needed. You associate a single CL command with each menu selection; the command is executed when the selection is made. But don't think that working with a single CL command is a limitation. That single command could be a CALL command to execute a program written in CL or an HLL, and that program could consist of hundreds or thousands of other commands.

When you use SDA to design a menu, five different entities are created automatically. Figure 11.2 illustrates the relationship among the members and objects created by SDA when a menu named M01 is designed. The numbers in parentheses refer to the five entities described below.

Figure 11.2

Representation of the Entities Created by SDA Design Menu Function

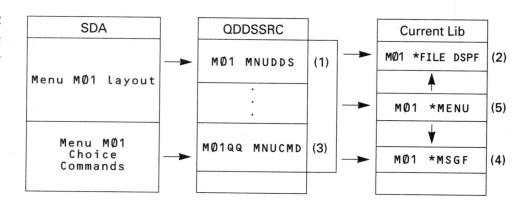

1. This entity is the DDS source code of the screen image of the menu, including the menu name, description, and information such as date and time. The constants used to describe the menu selections will be stored in a member whose type is MNUDDS in a source physical file (typically, source physical file QDDSSRC).

2. The source member of item 1 is compiled into an object of type *FILE with attribute DSPF (Display File). When you invoke the completed menu, using the GO command, this is the object that is written to the display device and that determines the menu's appearance.

3. The commands entered in SDA for each menu selection are stored together as a source member of the type MNUCMD in a source physical file (also, typically QDDSSRC).

4. The source commands are used to create a message file object whose type is *MSGF. These commands (messages) are retrieved from the message file and run when you make the corresponding menu selection.

5. Finally, an object whose type is *MENU is created. This is the object actually invoked by the GO command, and it contains the name of the display file that will be written to the display device and also the name of the message file that contains the commands to be run for each selection.

You must save the menu source members (1 and 3 in Figure 11.2) — SDA cannot create the objects without them. And if you ever want to change or expand the original menu design, the source members must be available for SDA to use.

Designing the Menu

The steps required to design a menu using SDA are straightforward. After taking option 2 (Design menus) from the initial SDA screen, the Design Menus screen appears. If you have not created a menu before, this screen will be mostly blank (Library name defaults to *LIBL). Otherwise, information from the most recently created menu will be filled in, as in Figure 11.3.

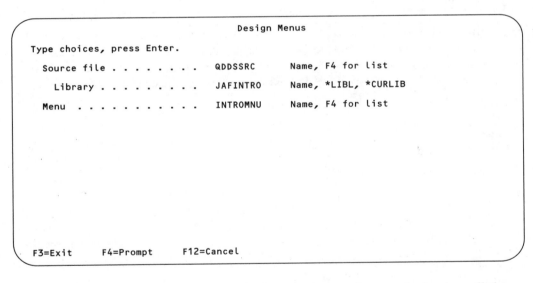

```
                                   Design Menus
    Type choices, press Enter.

        Source file . . . . . . . .    QDDSSRC      Name, F4 for list
           Library . . . . . . . . .   JAFINTRO     Name, *LIBL, *CURLIB
        Menu  . . . . . . . . . . .    INTROMNU     Name, F4 for list














     F3=Exit     F4=Prompt     F12=Cancel
```

Figure 11.3
SDA Design
Menus Screen

The screen asks you where to store the source members and what to call the new menu. Let's call our new menu STUMNU; we would type that name over the value that appears in the Menu prompt. (If we were modifying an existing menu, SDA would locate the source members using the Menu name we provide, and then retrieve them for us to work with. This is why it is necessary to save the source when you finish the design process.)

After we type the menu name and press Enter, we see the Specify Menu Functions screen (Figure 11.4).

Figure 11.4

Specify Menu
Functions Screen

```
                         Specify Menu Functions
File . . . . . . . :   QDDSSRC              Menu . . . . . . . :   STUMNU
  Library . . . . :     JAFINTRO

Type choices, press Enter.

  Work with menu image and commands  . . . . . .   Y   Y=Yes, N=No

  Work with menu help  . . . . . . . . . . . . .   N   Y=Yes, N=No




F3=Exit    F12=Cancel
Menu STUMNU is new.
```

From this screen we can choose to work with the menu image (screen layout) and commands or to work with online Help for the menu.

We will keep the defaults — Y for Work with menu image and commands and N for Work with menu help — and press Enter. This takes us to the SDA Menu template screen (Figure 11.5).

Figure 11.5

Work with Menu
Image Screen

```
STUMNU                            STUMNU Menu
Select one of the following:

     1.
     2.
     3.
     4.
     5.
     6.
     7.
     8.
     9.
    10.




Selection or command
F3=Exit                    F10=Work with commands      F12=Cancel
F13=Command area           F20=Reverse                 F24=More keys
Press Help for a list of valid operations.
```

This screen is a work screen — you can add descriptions for menu selections, change the header, and use function keys to access a screen to enter menu commands. SDA online Help (extended) provides a lot of information about how to customize the screen, but we summarize a few important points below.

- Lines 1 through 20, the body of the menu, identify the menu and also label and explain its selections. The words and numbers used to do so are called constants. **Constants** are one type of field SDA uses, and the main type used with menus. Each constant may consist of a single word or number or several words together (e.g., a menu selection title). Constants are typed on the screen enclosed in single quotation marks (apostrophes); but when you press Enter to save them, the single quotation marks disappear. On the starting menu template, the numbers for the selections are provided, but you need to enter the title of each selection as a constant. From this point on we refer to constants as fields. Another special type of field that can be used in menus is a system function that allows you to display system values. Of these special fields, the most commonly used are *DATE and *TIME. In addition, you can use the fields *USER and *SYSNAME to display user ID and system name, respectively.

- Once fields have been entered, they can be shifted right or left on a line, moved to a different line, or deleted. An attribute byte immediately precedes each field. The **attribute byte** is the single-character blank position to the left of a field's leftmost character. This byte is always reserved for controlling the field to which it is prefixed. You cannot see the attribute byte, but you can use it to perform operations on the field. These operations, or **attribute commands**, have several purposes. You can use them to change the appearance of a field, move a field on the work screen, call up a list of different attributes for a field, or delete a field. The attribute command is always entered starting on the attribute byte. If the command is longer than one character, you would type over the constant or data field — it will return as soon as the command is run. Attribute commands can be keyed for several different fields, then processed at the same time.

Specifying Attributes

The following are several commonly used attribute commands that control positioning.

AC	*centers* the field on the line
-	*moves* the field when you use the target =
-	*copies* the field when you use the target = =

When you reposition a field, be careful not to overlap another field or SDA will refuse to cooperate. You will receive an error message and have to press Enter to clear and continue.

Here are some attribute commands that determine appearance:

H	displays the field in *high intensity*
R	displays the field in *reverse image*
B	makes the field *blink*
U	*underlines* the field

and color:

CB	displays in *blue*
CT	displays in *turquoise*
CG	displays in *green*
CW	displays in *white*
CP	displays in *pink*
CY	displays in *yellow*
CR	displays in *red*

As for the existence of a field: D *deletes* the field. You can also delete a field by starting on the attribute byte and using the space bar to erase the field.

To turn off any of the appearance and color attributes, type a minus or hyphen (-) in the attribute byte followed by the same command used to turn on the attribute. For example, if you typed B in the attribute byte to make a field blink, you would type -B to turn off blinking. In every case, the leftmost character of the attribute command must start in the attribute byte of the constant or field. If part of the constant or field is erased by the rest of the command, it will be restored after the command is entered.

You can shift fields left or right by stringing together the < (shift left) or > (shift right) symbols. To shift a field left you would type the first < on the column where the leftmost character of the field is to be repositioned, and then type additional < characters up to and including the attribute byte. For example

```
<<<<<STUMNU Menu
```

would move the title five positions to the left.

To shift a field right, you would start in the first position immediately following the constant or field. For example

```
STUMU Menu>>>>>
```

would move the title five positions to the right.

Important: Do not use the Insert and/or Delete keys on the keyboard to change the contents of a constant, either while entering it or once it is entered. You can delete the constant and rekey it if it has already been entered. You can type over a constant to make changes before it is entered. If you forget and make a mistake, function key F5 undoes most errors.

Setting Field Attributes

You can access an entire screen of display options for a field by entering an asterisk (*) in the attribute byte. (The exact contents of the screen depends on the type of field and whether you are working with menus or display files.) For example, the Set Field Attributes screen shown in Figure 11.6 would appear if you entered an * in the attribute byte of the menu title. This screen allows modification of field attributes of constants from a menu design session.

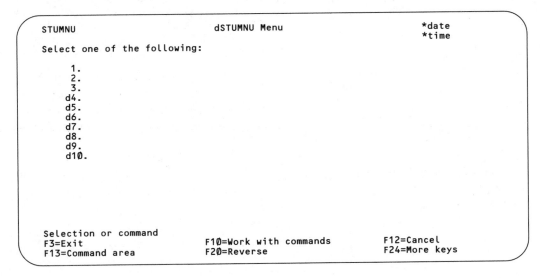

```
                          Set Field Attributes

     Field  . . . :    STUMNU Menu
     Length . . . :    11
     Row  . . . . :    1
     Column . . . :    33

     Type choices, press Enter.

        High intensity . . . . . . . . . . . . . .   Y    Y=Yes, N=No
        Reverse image  . . . . . . . . . . . . . .   N    Y=Yes, N=No
        Blink  . . . . . . . . . . . . . . . . . .   N    Y=Yes, N=No
        Underline  . . . . . . . . . . . . . . . .   N    Y=Yes, N=No

        Color of field . . . . . . . . . . . . . .   _    1=Blue
                                                          2=Green
                                                          3=Pink
                                                          4=Red
                                                          5=Turquoise
                                                          6=White
                                                          7=Yellow


     F3=Exit   F12=Cancel
```

Figure 11.6
Set Field
Attributes Screen

A menu title is automatically displayed in high intensity, which translates to the color white on a color monitor. Notice in Figure 11.6 that the color white is not selected from the Color of field list. Please refer to IBM's *Data Description Specification's Reference* manual (SC41-9620) under Display Files for a complete description of the translation of appearance attributes from monochrome to color monitors.

Using Attribute Commands

Now let's return to the SDA Menu screen template and continue designing our menu. In the template screen shown in Figure 11.7, we are using attribute commands to delete the menu title and options 4 through 10.

```
 STUMNU                      dSTUMNU Menu                    *date
                                                             *time
    Select one of the following:

            1.
            2.
            3.
          d4.
          d5.
          d6.
          d7.
          d8.
          d9.
          d10.








       Selection or command
       F3=Exit                 F10=Work with commands      F12=Cancel
       F13=Command area        F20=Reverse                 F24=More keys
```

Figure 11.7
STUMNU with
Initial Changes

In Figure 11.7, we also have indicated on the menu where we would like the system date and time display fields (*date, *time) to appear. Figure 11.8 shows the screen after we press Enter.

Figure 11.8
STUMNU with Initial
Changes Entered

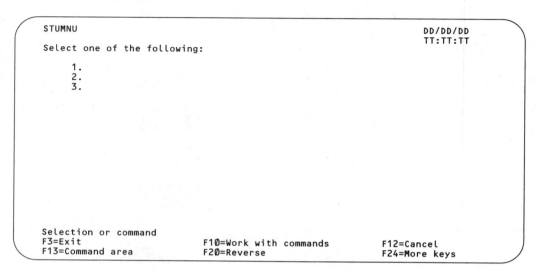

```
STUMNU                                                     DD/DD/DD
                                                           TT:TT:TT
Select one of the following:

     1.
     2.
     3.












Selection or command
F3=Exit                                                    F12=Cancel
F13=Command area       F10=Work with commands
                       F20=Reverse                         F24=More keys
```

Notice how (by default) the date and time fields have been formatted with editing characters added. When the completed menu is used (by a GO command), the current date and time system values will be displayed in the format indicated.

Figure 11.9 shows additional modifications to our menu template screen.

Figure 11.9
STUMNU with Second
Set of Changes

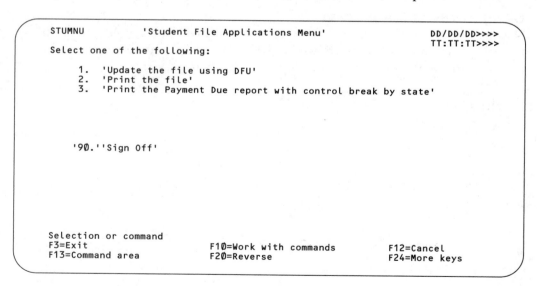

```
STUMNU              'Student File Applications Menu'       DD/DD/DD>>>>
                                                           TT:TT:TT>>>>
Select one of the following:

     1.   'Update the file using DFU'
     2.   'Print the file'
     3.   'Print the Payment Due report with control break by state'



     '90.''Sign Off'






Selection or command
F3=Exit                                                    F12=Cancel
F13=Command area       F10=Work with commands
                       F20=Reverse                         F24=More keys
```

We have entered a new menu title, we are shifting the date and time fields four positions to the right, we have entered constants to identify the menu choices, and we have entered an option (90) to allow sign-off.

When we press Enter, all our modifications will have been made, as shown in Figure 11.10.

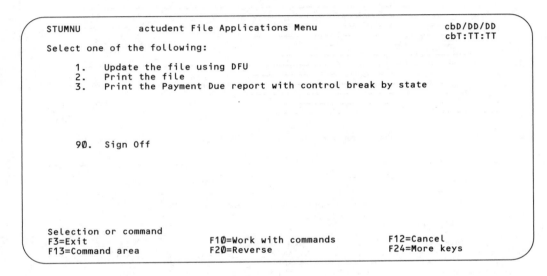

```
 STUMNU            actudent File Applications Menu              cbD/DD/DD
                                                               cbT:TT:TT
 Select one of the following:

     1.   Update the file using DFU
     2.   Print the file
     3.   Print the Payment Due report with control break by state




    90.   Sign Off







 Selection or command
 F3=Exit                    F10=Work with commands       F12=Cancel
 F13=Command area           F20=Reverse                  F24=More keys
```

Figure 11.10
STUMNU with Final Changes

In this figure we also have entered some new attribute commands to center the menu title (ac) and to color the date and time fields blue (cb). Note that even though the second character of the attribute command has been typed over the field, the field value will return after you press Enter.

Defining Menu Commands

Next, we need to enter the commands that will be executed for each menu selection. Function key F10, listed at the bottom of our menu template screen, provides an easy way to enter the commands we need.

When we press F10, the Define Menu Commands screen (Figure 11.11 page 464) appears. On this screen you can use the prompter (F4) for commands entered on the blank lines following the selection numbers, just as you can for commands entered on a command line.

Of course, it is not necessary to use prompting — you can type the full command, either in positional or keyword notation, just as you can on a command line. But if you need to enter several parameters, you will find that prompting is convenient and that you are less likely to introduce syntax errors.

The first selection on our menu is to Update the file using DFU. To provide the appropriate command for that selection, we would type the CHGDTA (Change Data) command on the Option 1 line of the Define Menu Commands screen. This is the command to run the update DFU that you created in Lab 10. If we prompt for the CHGDTA command, we see the screen shown in Figure 11.12.

Figure 11.11
Define Menu
Commands Screen

```
                            Define Menu Commands
Menu . . . . . . :    STUMNU              Position to menu option . . . . .

Type commands, press Enter.

Option   Command
  01     _____

  02     _____
         _____
  03     _____
         _____
  04     _____
         _____
  05     _____
         _____
  06     _____
         _____
  07     _____
         _____
                                                                More...

F3=Exit        F11=Defined only options      F12=Cancel       F24=More keys
```

Figure 11.12
CHGDTA Command
Prompt Screen

```
                           Change Data (CHGDTA)
Type choices, press Enter.

DFU program  . . . . . . . . . .   stuupd_____   Name
  Library  . . . . . . . . . . .   *LIBL_____   Name, *LIBL, *CURLIB
Data base file . . . . . . . . .   *SAME_____   Name, *SAME
  Library  . . . . . . . . . . .   *LIBL_____   Name, *LIBL, *CURLIB
Member . . . . . . . . . . . . .   *FIRST_____   Name, *FIRST




                                                                  Bottom
F3=Exit    F4=Prompt    F5=Refresh    F12=Cancel    F13=How to use this display
F24=More keys
```

Notice that we've already keyed the DFU program name (STUUPD) in the
prompt field.

When you press Enter from the CHGDTA command prompt screen, the
Define Menu Commands screen will look like the one in Figure 11.13.
Notice that the DFU program name, which was entered in lowercase, has been
changed to uppercase as a result of prompting.

```
                         Define Menu Commands
   Menu . . . . . . :    STUMNU            Position to menu option . . . . .

   Type commands, press Enter.

   Option    Command
     01      CHGDTA DFUPGM(STUUPD)_____
   _____
     02      _____
   _____
     03      _____
   _____
     04      _____
   _____
     05      _____
   _____
     06      _____
   _____
     07      _____
   _____
                                                                    More...
   F3=Exit      F11=Defined only options      F12=Cancel      F24=More keys
```

Figure 11.13
First Command Entered from Prompting

Initially, the Define Menu Commands display includes all options from 01 to 99, and entry fields for each command to be typed in. You can see the higher-numbered options by paging down; to immediately position a certain option at the top of the display, you can type its number (e.g., 90) in the Position to menu option field.

After we have entered the commands (with prompting) for options 2 and 3, the screen will look like the one in Figure 11.14.

```
                         Define Menu Commands
   Menu . . . . . . :    STUMNU            Position to menu option . . . . .   90

   Type commands, press Enter.

   Option    Command
     01      CHGDTA DFUPGM(STUUPD)_____
   _____
     02      RUNQRY QRY(STUQRY1)_____
   _____
     03      RUNQRY QRY(STUPAYQRY)_____
   _____
     04      _____
   _____
     05      _____
   _____
     06      _____
   _____
     07      _____
   _____
                                                                    More...
   F3=Exit      F11=Defined only options      F12=Cancel      F24=More keys
```

Figure 11.14
Three Commands Entered on the Define Menu Commands Screen

Notice (in the upper right corner of the screen) that we also have requested repositioning to option 90. Because we have chosen to use option 90 for sign-off, we can use this "position to" feature to conveniently get to the command entry field for that option.

After positioning the display to option 90 and typing in the SIGNOFF command, you could use function key F11 to display only those options for which a command has been entered. In our example, the resulting screen would look like Figure 11.15.

Figure 11.15

Define Menu
Commands "Defined
only options" Display

```
                              Define Menu Commands
   Menu . . . . . . :     STUMNU            Position to menu option . . . . .

   Type commands, press Enter.

   Option    Command
     01      CHGDTA DFUPGM(STUUPD)_____

     02      RUNQRY QRY(STUQRY1)_____

     03      RUNQRY QRY(STUPAYQRY)_____

     90      SIGNOFF_____

   _____




                                                                        Bottom
   F3=Exit        F11=Show all options      F12=Cancel      F24=More keys
```

This view eliminates option numbers that have no commands and makes it much easier to see — and change, if necessary — the commands for each of the options that will be allowed on the menu.

Notice that in Figure 11.15, F11 is now labeled Show all options. As on other displays you have used (e.g., Command prompt, Work with Spooled Files), F11 acts as a toggle switch from one view to another; so if you need to add commands for new options, pressing F11 from the display shown in Figure 11.15 would restore the entire list of options from 01 to 99, allowing you to enter new commands.

After typing in the necessary commands, we would press F3 to return to the Design Menu screen, and then press F3 again to exit. This takes us back to the Specify Menu Functions display; from there, we would press F3 again to go to the Exit SDA Menus screen (Figure 11.16).

```
                          Exit SDA Menus
  File . . . . . . :    QDDSSRC          DDS member . . . . . :    STUMNU
      Library . . . . :    JAFINTRO         Commands member . . . :    STUMNUQQ

  Type choices, press Enter.

      Save new or updated menu source  . . . .   Y        Y=Yes, N=No
         For choice Y=Yes:
            Source file  . . . . . . . . . . .   QDDSSRC____   Name,
                                                               F4 for list
            Library  . . . . . . . . . . . .    JAFINTRO__   Name, *LIBL, *CURLIB
            Text . . . . . . . . . . . . . . .
            Replace menu members . . . . . . .   Y        Y=Yes, N=No

      Create menu objects  . . . . . . . . . .   Y        Y=Yes, N=No
         For choice Y=Yes:
            Prompt for parameters  . . . . . .   N        Y=Yes, N=No
            Object library . . . . . . . . . .   JAFINTRO   Name, *CURLIB
            Replace menu objects . . . . . . .   Y        Y=Yes, N=No


  F3=Exit     F4=Prompt     F12=Cancel
```

Figure 11.16
Exit SDA Menus Screen

Exiting SDA Menus

The Exit SDA Menus screen first asks whether you want to keep the results of your work session (Save new or updated menu source). If you were not finished with the menu and planned to work on it more in a later session, or if you were done and wanted SDA to create (compile) an executable menu, you would choose Y here. You would choose N only if you did not want to keep any changes or new entries you had made. Notice (in the upper right corner of the screen shown in Figure 11.16) that two source members will be saved — the DDS member (STUMNU) and the Commands member (STUMNUQQ).

The values for Source file and Library name came from the entries we made on the Design Menus screen (Figure 11.3). For our example, we would take the rest of the defaults because we do want to save the source (in QDDSSRC) and we do want to create menu objects. If we wished, we could change the value of Object library and put the compiled objects in any library we were authorized to use.

After we press Enter from the Exit SDA Menus screen, the message "SDA is compiling menu STUMNU" appears briefly on the bottom of the display, and then we return to the Design Menus screen.

Now, when we return to the Work with Objects Using PDM screen, we would find three new objects in our current library list (as illustrated in Figure 11.2).

DISPLAY FILES

Although menus are easy to create, display files are more flexible and are needed more frequently by programmers. Let's compare the menu we just created with a display file screen that would be used with a start-up CL program (which you create in Lesson 12) to set up your work environment. The display file will look like a menu, but it will be controlled by the CL program. This technique allows several different actions (CL commands, in this case) to be taken for any option and provides a smooth transition to the work environment.

Creating a Nonmenu Display Screen

To begin designing your display file, take option 1 (Design screens) from the initial SDA screen (Figure 11.1).

On the Design Screens display, we would use QDDSSRC as the Source file and STRUPDSP as the Member name, as shown in Figure 11.17.

Figure 11.17
Design Screens Naming
New Member
STRUPDSP

```
                                  Design Screens
 Type choices, press Enter.

    Source file . . . . . . . .    QDDSSRC      Name, F4 for list

       Library . . . . . . . . .    JAFINTRO     Name, *LIBL, *CURLIB

    Member  . . . . . . . . . .    strupdsp     Name, F4 for list








 F3=Exit      F4=Prompt      F12=Cancel
```

As usual, it doesn't matter whether you use uppercase or lowercase (except for quoted strings) when filling in prompts. In Figure 11.17, QDDSSRC was already the default value, and it was entered in uppercase. We typed the Member name in lowercase, but SDA will change it to uppercase.

The next screen we see will be Work with Display Records. As you can tell by looking at Figure 11.18, it is of the normal list format, with options and function keys.

Figure 11.18
SDA Work with Display
Records Screen

```
                           Work with Display Records
 File  . . . . . . :    QDDSSRC              Member . . . . . . :   STRUPDSP
    Library . . . . :       JAFINTRO         Source type . . . :    DSPF

 Type options, press Enter.
   1=Add                2=Edit comments       3=Copy         4=Remove
   7=Rename             8=Select keywords    12=Design image

 Opt  Order      Record         Type      Related Subfile   Date        DDS Error
 1_              R1_____

    (No records in file)








                                                                      Bottom
 F3=Exit                       F12=Cancel        F14=File-level keywords
 F15=File-level comments       F17=Subset        F24=More keys
```

Initially, no list items are displayed because no records have been defined for the file. We have already selected option 1 to add a record, and we have named the record R1.

A record in a display file defines some part, or all, of the screen image that is controlled (i.e., made to appear or disappear) by the driving program. All display files have at least one record. A DFU screen, which you have worked with, illustrates the concept of records in a display file. When you begin a DFU file update or display, initially you see information about file and record format and about mode at the top of the display, followed by an input field for relative record number or key field (depending on the file's access path). The first record of the DFU display file could define all this information.

When you enter a valid relative record number or key field, a record appears in the middle of the screen with all fields identified. When this happens, the DFU program is writing a second record to the display device. A third record may exist to control the display of function keys, and a fourth record may control error or status messages.

A display file for a relatively simple application may have only one or two record formats while a complicated display may have many. As with physical or logical database files, each record of a display file is identified in DDS by an R name type entry. The fields that follow make up the record format of that record. Fortunately, SDA generates the DDS code for all file, record, and field-level entries for you, using information that you supply from work screens and entry screens.

In our example, which, except for an error message, is a simple display file, different parts of the screen image will not need to come and go, so we need only the single record, R1. But before continuing with the example, let me call your attention to two important options on the Work with Display Records screen whose purposes are not made entirely clear by their titles:

8=Select keywords	used to define record-level keywords
12=Design image	used to return to the work screen to change or add fields to an existing record

Returning to our example, we would press Enter on the Work with Display Records screen, which takes us to the Add New Record verification screen (Figure 11.19).

Figure 11.19
Add New Record
Verification Screen

```
                               Add New Record
File . . . . . . . :    QDDSSRC              Member . . . . . . :   STRUPDSP
   Library . . . . :       JAFINTRO          Source type . . . :    DSPF

Type choices, press Enter.

  New record . . . . . . . . . . . . . .   R1          Name

  Type  . . . . . . . . . . . . . . . . .   RECORD      RECORD,  USRDFN,
                                                        SFL,     SFLMSG,
                                                        WINDOW,  WDWSFL,
                                                        PULDWN,  PDNSFL,
                                                        MNUBAR




   F3=Exit      F5=Refresh      F12=Cancel
```

We could have named the record here; we also can change the record type, if necessary. In this course we use only RECORD types (the default), so we would make no changes to this screen before pressing Enter.

Using the Design Image Work Screen

Next, you would see a mostly blank screen displaying the message "Work screen for record R1: Press Help for function keys" near the bottom of the screen. (Figure 11.20).

Figure 11.20
Empty Work Screen for
Record R1

```




        Work screen for record R1: Press Help for function keys
```

It is a good idea to take the advice and browse through the Help text. You can also print the Help text, now that you are an expert at controlling spooled files. Much of the information covers topics we have already discussed, such as attribute bytes and positioning fields.

This screen is the work screen, or "blank slate," upon which you position the constants, system functions (e.g., *DATE, *TIME), and data fields that will make up your display image. Data fields are the third type of field that can be declared on an SDA screen. They are used to display variable data from a database file record, or to let the user type in a value to be sent to the program or menu, or both (e.g., when using an interactive update program). The rules for using a display file work screen are similar to those for menus. Constants are defined and manipulated in the same way, but a display file usually has more input and output fields to arrange. A user or system analyst may predetermine the screen layout and provide it to you in the program specification as a screen layout form, or you may compose it yourself as you go along.

On the SDA work screen only one record (i.e., R1, R2, and so on) is active at a time. The active record is the one you are currently working on (e.g., entering or moving fields and constants, or changing display attributes). However, by using function key F9, you can view other records while working on the active record to see how they fit together. You select the active record at the Work with Display Records screen by taking option 1 to add a new record or by taking option 12 to change an existing record. When you want to change active records, you return to the Display Records screen by pressing F3 or F12 from the work screen.

Useful Function Keys

The Help text includes a brief explanation of available function keys, but the list below includes the ones you need most at this point in your SDA experience.

F1	You can use the Help key for Design Image Work Screen help any time you get stuck in the middle of the design process.
F3	The Exit key lets you decide whether to keep the current Design Image session, then returns you to the Work with Display Records screen.
F4	This key prompts the Work with Fields screen, which provides a convenient way to select field-level attributes.
F9	You can work with only one record at a time, but this key lets you select additional records for display so you can ensure that the overall screen image is what you want.
F10	You can select database fields from one or more files and position them wherever you want them to appear. This function lets you use fields as described in the database file and copy their attributes so you don't need to repeat them.

F12   This function is similar to F3, but it automatically saves changes to the work screen.

F14   If your display device status line doesn't show cursor coordinates (line/column), the Ruler function can help you position fields and constants accurately. The function toggles on and off at the cursor location. Do not leave the ruler on the screen when you exit and save a record.

F17   This function lets you print the current contents of the work screen.

F18   This function lets you tab to the attribute byte of the next constant or field.

F19   With this function, you can back-tab to the attribute byte of the previous constant or field. Function keys F18 and F19 let you move quickly around the screen, as well as show you where fields really begin.

F20   This function displays constants in reverse image, which can help you determine the beginning and ending of multiword constants. The function toggles on and off and doesn't save in reverse image even if you exit with it on.

F21   When you press this key, additional records selected by using F9 appear and disappear.

Manipulating Constants and Fields

Constants for display screens work the same as they do for menus. Remember to enclose the entire constant in single quotation marks. Otherwise, a blank is considered a default delimiter, which causes a multiword constant to be stored as several different constants — one for each word — each generating a separate DDS field entry. When this happens, not only will the generated DDS be excessively lengthy, but moving constants or changing appearance attributes for the whole constant will be troublesome.

For example, in Figure 11.21 we have placed date and time functions and a screen header enclosed in quotation marks, on the first line. Selection 1, which we entered on line 5, has not been enclosed in quotation marks; but when we press Enter, the resulting screen (Figure 11.22) gives no indication of an error.

The error shows up when we attempt to manipulate Selection 1. Let's say we want to shift the first selection 11 positions to the right so that it lines up under the title (Figure 11.23).

```
*date                    'Select session work environment'              *time


              1)  Intro to AS/400












Work screen for record R1: Press Help for function keys.
```

Figure 11.21
Starting the Screen
Design — a Constant
(Selection 1) without
Quotation marks

```
DD/DD/DD                 Select session work environment            TT:TT:TT


              1)  Intro to AS/400
```

Figure 11.22
After Pressing Enter
from the Screen in
Figure 11.20

```
DD/DD/DD                 Select session work environment            TT:TT:TT


              1)  Intro to AS/400>>>>>>>>>>>
```

Figure 11.23
Attempting to Shift a
Constant 11 Positions
to the Right

As you can see in Figure 11.24, only the "AS/400" moves. This happens because, without the necessary quotation marks, SDA reads each word of the first selection as a separate constant. (If we pressed F20 to display constants in reverse image, we would see clearly that each word of the title for the first selection is a separate constant.

Figure 11.24
"AS/400" Shifted Right
as a Separate Constant

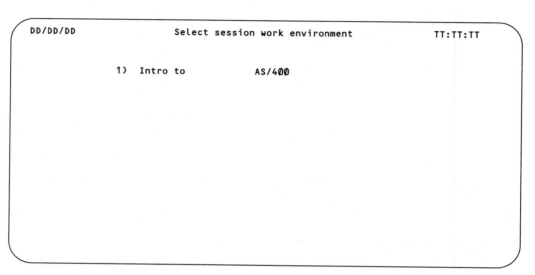

Even though the first selection consists of four separate constants, we can correct the mistake easily by placing single quotation marks around the entire text (just before 1 and just after AS/400) and then pressing Enter.

Figure 11.25 shows the work screen after we make the correction and add two more selections and another constant, "Enter selection:", which identifies an input field. We also have entered ac in the screen title's attribute byte to center the title.

Figure 11.25
Work Screen with
Additional Selections
Keyed but Not Entered

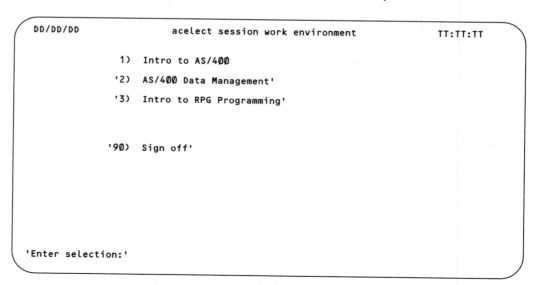

After we press Enter, the screen will look like the one shown in Figure 11.26.

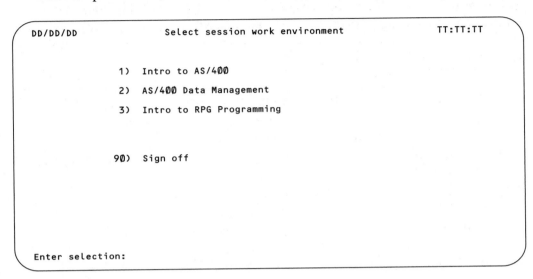

```
 DD/DD/DD                 Select session work environment              TT:TT:TT


                 1)  Intro to AS/400

                 2)  AS/400 Data Management

                 3)  Intro to RPG Programming



                90)  Sign off




 Enter selection:
```

Figure 11.26
Work Screen with
Constants, Date, and
Time Entered

Adding Input/Output Data Fields

Now we need to add a field where a user can enter his/her selection number. But first, let's discuss the use of **input/output fields** on display screens.

Data fields on an SDA work screen define locations where variable data can be keyed in by a user or displayed by the program. Unlike constants, fields are named because they must be referenced in the program(s) that work with the display file created by SDA.

The usage of a field (i.e., whether it is input, output, or both) is always determined from the program's perspective. If the program reads the data, the field is input; if the program writes the data to the display file, the field is output. If the program reads data and also writes to the display file, the field is both input and output. On our session selection screen, we need to let the user tell the program in which environment (s)he chooses to work. Because the selection will be read by the program, the field will be an input field.

Fields also must be declared as numeric or character. Numeric fields allow editing when displayed and accept only digits (and a decimal point if the number has a decimal point — e.g., a dollars and cents field). Character fields can be any combination of numbers, letters, and special characters.

On an SDA work screen, a new field is identified by a plus sign (+), followed by one or more symbols that determine the type and usage of the field. The following chart shows the symbols used for each possibility:

Usage	Character	Numeric
Input	I	3
Output	O	6
Both	B	9

The length of a field is determined by the number of symbols used or by a repetition factor. For example,

12-character output field	+OOOOOOOOOOOO or +O(12)
4-digit input field	+3333 or +3(4)
7-digit input/output field with 2 decimal positions	+99999.99 or +9(7,2)

For our session selection, with only a few options to choose from, we could define the field as a single-character input field. However, if we want to be consistent with the system's use of 90 as the sign-off option, we need to make it two characters. Because we do not need to do arithmetic or edit the field, we would use a character type rather than numeric. The field could be defined as +II.

But instead, we will define the field as input/output, which would be entered as +BB immediately to the right of the constant "Enter selection:". Note that when a field is declared, the + lines up on what will be the attribute byte of the field.

We chose to make the field input/output so that if the user enters characters other than 1, 2, 3, or 90, we can let him/her know an invalid character has been entered. We will do this by changing the color of the selection field and redisplaying it, with the message "Not a valid choice — press Enter and try again!"

To redisplay the choice in a different color, it must be written to the display file by our program; therefore, the Enter selection field must be declared so that it can be both read from and written to by the program.

On line 23, we will declare a constant for the message "Not a valid choice — press Enter and try again!" After we press Enter, the screen will look like the one in Figure 11.27. Notice that the + identifying the new field has disappeared.

We have finished designing our screen, but if we wanted to examine the attributes of our entries and perhaps make changes to some of them, we could press F4 to pull up the Work with Fields screen. This screen, shown in Figure 11.28, lists all the functions, constants, and data fields that we have declared so far, and shows their type, use (for data fields), length, and positions on the screen.

The options let you select keywords or delete an entry. We will select keywords for *DATE and *TIME so we can change their color (Figure 11.29).

```
DD/DD/DD                 Select session work environment              TT:TT:TT


          1)   Intro to AS/400

          2)   AS/400 Data Management

          3)   Intro to RPG Programming


          90)  Sign off




Enter selection: BB

Not a valid choice - press Enter and try again!
```

Figure 11.27
Work Screen with
Input/Output Field

```
                          Work with Fields

Record . . . :   R1

Type information, press Enter.
 Number of fields to roll . . . . . . . . . . . . . . . . . .    6

Type options, change values, press Enter.
  1=Select keywords    4=Delete field

Option   Order   Field      Type Use   Length   Row/Col   Ref Condition   Overlap
  _       10     *DATE       C           6,0     01 002
  _       20     Select ses  C            31     01 025
  _       30     *TIME       C           6,0     01 072
  _       40     1)  Intro   C            19     05 017
  _       50     2)  AS/400  C            26     07 017
  _       60     3)  Intro   C            28     09 017
                                                                   More...

Add     _____  _____     H  _____    Hidden
Add     _____  _____     M  _____    Message
Add     _____  _____     P  _____    Program-to-system

F3=Exit   F6=Sort by row/column    F12=Cancel
```

Figure 11.28
Work with
Fields Screen

```
                          Work with Fields

Record . . . :   R1

Type information, press Enter.
 Number of fields to roll . . . . . . . . . . . . . . . . .    6

Type options, change values, press Enter.
  1=Select keywords    4=Delete field

Option   Order   Field      Type Use   Length   Row/Col   Ref Condition   Overlap
  1       10     *DATE       C           6,0     01 002
          20     Select ses  C            31     01 025
  1       30     *TIME       C           6,0     01 072
  _       40     1)  Intro   C            19     05 017
          50     2)  AS/400  C            26     07 017
  _       60     3)  Intro   C            28     09 017
                                                                   More...

Add     _____  _____     H  _____    Hidden
Add     _____  _____     M  _____    Message
Add     _____  _____     P  _____    Program-to-system

F3=Exit   F6=Sort by row/column    F12=Cancel
```

Figure 11.29
Select Keywords for
*DATE and *TIME

When more than one selection is taken from the Work with Fields screen, the selections are processed one after another, just as on a PDM Work with screen. The Select Field Keywords screen for *DATE is shown in Figure 11.30, where we have typed in Y for colors.

Figure 11.30
Select Field Keywords
for *DATE,
Colors Selected

```
                            Select Field Keywords
  Constant . . . :    *DATE
  Length . . . . :    8,0                Row . . . : 1    Column . . . : 2

  Type choices, press Enter.
                                    Y=Yes    For Field Type
    Display attributes . . . . . . .  _      All except Hidden
    Colors . . . . . . . . . . . .    Y      All except Hidden


    General keywords . . . . . . . .  _      All types
    Editing keywords . . . . . . . .  _      Numeric Output or Both



    TEXT keyword . . . . . . . . .    _____



  F3=Exit   F12=Cancel
```

Pressing Enter takes us to the Select Colors display for *DATE, Figure 11.31, with the color blue given the first order of appearance (1).

Figure 11.31
Select Colors for
*DATE, Blue Selected
as First and Only Order

```
                            Select Colors
  Constant . . . :    *DATE
  Length . . . . :    8,0                Row . . . : 1    Column . . . : 2

  Type choices, press Enter.

                                  Keyword   Order    Indicators/+
                                            (1-7)
    Colors:                       COLOR
      Blue . . . . . . . . . . . . . . BLU    1      __ __ __
      Green . . . . . . . . . . . . .  GRN    _      __ __ __
      Pink . . . . . . . . . . . . . . PNK    _      __ __ __
      Red . . . . . . . . . . . . . .  RED    _      __ __ __
      Turquoise . . . . . . . . . . .  TRQ    _      __ __ __
      White . . . . . . . . . . . . .  WHT    _      __ __ __
      Yellow . . . . . . . . . . . . . YLW    _      __ __ __



  F3=Exit   F12=Cancel
```

SDA's default color for screen design is green for constants, functions such as *DATE, and data fields. To unconditionally change a color, we can go through the Work with Fields display as we have just done for *DATE; or more directly, we can type an attribute command (e.g., CB) on the field we need to change. But when multiple colors are selected, an indicator must be assigned to determine which color will be used when the field is displayed. This is where the need for the Select Colors screen becomes apparent.

When we finish selecting field keywords for *DATE, we will see the Select Field Keywords screen for *TIME.

Using Indicators

Indicators function as control switches between a program and a display file. They allow the user of the display file to signal the program. In the program, indicators are a special kind of variable, called a logical variable, whose value can be only 1 (on) or 0 (off).

The action of a display file signaling a program is often caused by a user pressing a key, typically a function key, which is associated in the display file with a **response indicator**. For example, if function key F3 were associated with indicator 03, when the user presses F3 and the program reads the display file, indicator 03 would be set on in the program.

Indicators are also used by the program when it writes a display file record — for example, to select which display attribute or color to use, or to determine whether a field will appear. These indicators, called **option indicators**, can be associated with display file records, fields, or individual (often mutually exclusive) field attributes. The program logic determines which option indicator(s) it needs to have on in a certain case and turns them on within the program, using the appropriate programming language statement. When the display file record is written and the indicator is on, the record, field, or attribute will appear on the screen.

Indicators are identified by 2-digit numbers in the range 01 – 99. When we specify indicators in SDA (e.g., on the Select Display Attributes screen), the 2-digit number identified for the attribute is associated with an on condition of the logical variable in the program, or the 2-digit number preceded by N for Not is associated with an off condition of the program variable. For example, if a display attribute of high intensity, DSPATR(HI), were specified with indicator 30, when logical variable IN30 was set on in the program and the record containing the field written, the field would appear in high intensity (or white on a color monitor).

In the case of colors, if a field that normally displayed as green needed to be red under certain conditions, we could choose an option indicator (e.g., 40) to associate with the color red for that field. Then green, the default color, would implicitly be conditioned by N40 (Not 40) and would display unless the program turned on indicator 40 before writing the display file record. When indicator 40 was on, the field would display as red.

In the case of the *DATE and *TIME functions, we want the date and time to appear in blue always, so we did not need to associate an indicator with them. As you can see in Figure 11.31, blue is given order 1, and no indicator is defined for it. When no indicator is specified, the color, display attribute, and so on is unconditional.

After processing these color changes for *DATE and *TIME, SDA returns us to the Work with Fields screen. The second page of the Work with Fields screen is shown in Figure 11.32.

Figure 11.32

**Work with Fields
Screen, Page 2**

```
                              Work with Fields
  Record . . . :    R1

  Type information, press Enter.
    Number of fields to roll . . . . . . . . . . . . . . . . .    6

  Type options, change values, press Enter.
    1=Select keywords    4=Delete field

  Option   Order   Field        Type Use  Length  Row/Col  Ref Condition  Overlap
    _        70    90) Sign o    C           12    13 017
    _        80    Enter sele    C           16    21 002
    _        90    FLD001        A   B         2    21 019
    _       100    Not a vali    C           38    23 002
                                                                          Bottom
  Add      _____   _____    H  _____   Hidden
  Add      _____   _____    M  _____   Message
  Add      _____   _____    P  _____   Program-to-system

  F3=Exit    F6=Sort by row/column    F12=Cancel
```

By paging down to row 21 (under the Row/Col heading), we can see the 2-character input/output field we declared. SDA has given it the default name FLD001. Whenever fields are added directly to a work screen without using F10 to select database file fields, SDA provides default names of FLD001, FLD002, and so on. These can be changed to more meaningful names when desired.

We can change the field name to something more meaningful by typing over the default field name that is displayed. We will change the name from FLD001 to CHOICE. Besides changing the field name, we will take the option to Select keywords for the Choice field.

We will also select keywords for the "Enter Selection:" constant so we can display it in high intensity, which will cause it to show up as white on a color display. The screen with the options entered and FLD001 changed to CHOICE is shown in Figure 11.33.

Figure 11.33

**Field Name Changed to
CHOICE and Option 1
Entered**

```
                              Work with Fields
  Record . . . :    R1

  Type information, press Enter.
    Number of fields to roll . . . . . . . . . . . . . . . . .    6

  Type options, change values, press Enter.
    1=Select keywords    4=Delete field

  Option   Order   Field        Type Use  Length  Row/Col  Ref Condition  Overlap
    _        70    90) Sign o    C           12    13 017
    1        80    Enter sele    C           16    21 002
    1        90    CHOICE        A   B         2    21 019
    _       100    Not a vali    C           38    23 002      Y
                                                                          Bottom
  Add      _____   _____    H  _____   Hidden
  Add      _____   _____    M  _____   Message
  Add      _____   _____    P  _____   Program-to-system

  F3=Exit    F6=Sort by row/column    F12=Cancel
```

When the Select Field Keywords screen for the constant "Enter Selection:" comes up, we will choose Y for display attributes. The next screen will be Select Display Attributes (Figure 11.34).

```
                    Select Display Attributes

Constant . . . :    Enter selection:
Length . . . . :    16              Row . . . : 21   Column . . . : 2

Type choices, press Enter.

                                   Keyword   Y=Yes   Indicators/+
                                                     ___ ___ ___
   Field conditioning . . . . . . . . . .
   Display attributes:             DSPATR
     High intensity . . . . . . . . . . . HI        Y     ___ ___ ___
     Reverse image  . . . . . . . . . . . RI        _     ___ ___ ___
     Column separators  . . . . . . . . . CS        _     ___ ___ ___
     Blink  . . . . . . . . . . . . . . . BL        _     ___ ___ ___
     Nondisplay . . . . . . . . . . . . . ND        _     ___ ___ ___
     Underline  . . . . . . . . . . . . . UL        _     ___ ___ ___
     Position cursor  . . . . . . . . . . PC        _     ___ ___ ___




F3=Exit    F12=Cancel
```

Figure 11.34
Select Display Attributes with High Intensity

This screen lets you select values for the DDS DSPATR keyword for the field or constant. Notice also that you can use indicators to control whether the field itself will appear (Field conditioning) and that you can select different indicators for individual display attributes. When a single display attribute is selected without an indicator, it will always be used whenever the field appears. Because we want the prompt "Enter Selection:" to always appear in high intensity, we have selected HI unconditionally (without an indicator) in Figure 11.34.

After we press Enter twice, the Select Field Keywords screen for input/output field CHOICE appears and we again ask for Colors, as shown in Figure 11.35.

```
                    Select Field Keywords

Field . . . . . :   CHOICE          Usage . . :  B
Length . . . . :    1               Row . . . :  21   Column . . . : 19

Type choices, press Enter.
                                 Y=Yes    For Field Type
   Display attributes . . . . . . .  _    All except Hidden
   Colors . . . . . . . . . . . . .  Y    All except Hidden
   Keying options . . . . . . . . .  _    Input or Both
   Validity check . . . . . . . . .  _    Input or Both, not float
   Input keywords . . . . . . . . .  _    Input or Both
   General keywords . . . . . . . .  _    All types

   Database reference . . . . . . .  _    Hidden, Input, Output, Both
   Error messages . . . . . . . . .  _    Input, Output, Both
   Message ID (MSGID) . . . . . . .  _    Output or Both


   TEXT keyword . . . . . . . . . . _____
   _____


F3=Exit    F12=Cancel
```

Figure 11.35
Select Field Keywords for CHOICE

This time, we want to choose red as the first-order color. Order refers to the relative position of the color keywords in the DDS. We will arbitrarily select option indicator 40, which the program will turn on when it wants to display field CHOICE in red. When 40 is not on, field CHOICE will appear in green, which is the default color and does not need indication. (In most installations, display screen designers follow standards that use a range of indicators for certain functions. By doing so, the use of indicators in programs is more consistent and easier to follow.)

Figure 11.36 shows the entries made on the Select Colors screen.

Figure 11.36
Select Colors for
CHOICE

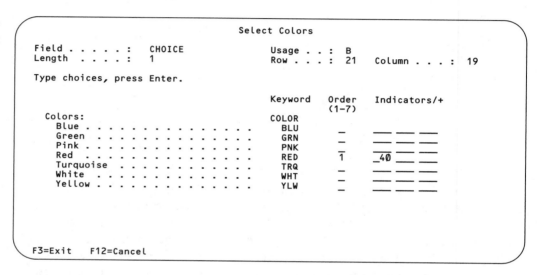

Note that if you were to select additional colors, you must give each color selected some indicator value; the value of indicators at the time of writing the record determines which color to use.

Finally, we need to select display attributes and color keywords for our error message, as we have indicated on the Select Field Keywords screen for the constant (Figure 11.37). On the Select Display Attributes screen (Figure 11.38), we will use the same indicator, 40, that we used for the color red for field CHOICE. This time the indicator applies to the field itself (Field conditioning) because we want the message to appear only after an invalid choice had been entered. When the program turns on option indicator 40 and redisplays the choice in red, the message constant on line 23 will also appear. Field conditioning, therefore, determines whether the entire field will appear on the display.

```
                        Select Field Keywords
 Constant  . . . :   Not a valid choice - Please try again!
 Length  . . . . :   38                 Row . . . :  23   Column . . . :  2

 Type choices, press Enter.
                                     Y=Yes    For Field Type
   Display attributes . . . . . . .    Y      All except Hidden
   Colors . . . . . . . . . . . . .    Y      All except Hidden


   General keywords . . . . . . . .    _      All types


   TEXT keyword . . . . . . . . .    _____
 _____



 F3=Exit    F12=Cancel
```

Figure 11.37
Select Field Keywords
for the Error Message
Constant

```
                      Select Display Attributes
 Constant  . . . :   Not a valid choice - Please try again!
 Length  . . . . :   38                 Row . . . :  23   Column . . . :  2

 Type choices, press Enter.
                                     Keyword   Y=Yes   Indicators/+
                                                               _40 ___ ___
   Field conditioning . . . . . . . . . . .
   Display attributes:                DSPATR
     High intensity . . . . . . . . . .    HI       _      ___ ___ ___
     Reverse image . . . . . . . . . .     RI       _      ___ ___ ___
     Column separators . . . . . . . . .   CS       _      ___ ___ ___
     Blink  . . . . . . . . . . . . . .    BL       _      ___ ___ ___
     Nondisplay . . . . . . . . . . . .    ND       _      ___ ___ ___
     Underline . . . . . . . . . . . .     UL       _      ___ ___ ___
     Position cursor . . . . . . . . . .   PC       _      ___ ___ ___




 F3=Exit    F12=Cancel
```

Figure 11.38
Select Display
Attributes for "Not a
Valid Choice" Message

Next, we will select red as the first-order (and only) color for the message. Because the field itself is conditioned by indicator 40, we don't need to further condition the color. Whenever the field appears, it will appear in red. This selection is shown in Figure 11.39.

Figure 11.39

Select Colors — Red
Chosen for "Not a Valid
Choice..." Message

```
                              Select Colors
Constant  . . . :    Not a valid choice - Please try again!
Length  . . . . :    38                   Row . . . :  23   Column . . . :  2

Type choices, press Enter.

                                    Keyword   Order   Indicators/+
                                              (1-7)
       Colors:                      COLOR
         Blue . . . . . . . . . . . . . .  BLU
         Green  . . . . . . . . . . . .    GRN      _      ___ ___ ___
         Pink . . . . . . . . . . . . .    PNK      _      ___ ___ ___
         Red  . . . . . . . . . . . . .    RED      1      ___ ___ ___
         Turquoise  . . . . . . . . . .    TRQ      _      ___ ___ ___
         White  . . . . . . . . . . . .    WHT      _      ___ ___ ___
         Yellow . . . . . . . . . . . .    YLW      _      ___ ___ ___




 F3=Exit    F12=Cancel
```

When we make these changes and we have returned to the Work with Fields screen, pressing Enter (or F3 or F12) returns us to the work screen for record R1. At this point, we can see on our color monitor that the date and time are in blue, the "Enter Selection:" constant is in white, and our message on line 23 is in red. But our screen title is still in green. We could press F4 to return to the Work with Fields screen, or enter an asterisk (*) in the attribute byte of the title constant to take us directly to the Select Field Keywords screen for that constant. But because we already know the attribute command is H for High Intensity, we will simply type H (in uppercase or lowercase) over the attribute byte. When we press Enter, the title will appear in high intensity (i.e., white).

A Brief Review

Before leaving the work screen, let's briefly summarize what we have learned.

1. SDA fields may be
   - constants (enclosed in single quotation marks)
   - data fields (input, output, both)
   - system functions (e.g., *DATE, *TIME)

2. These fields can be entered and moved around on the work screen using positioning attribute commands: << (shift left), >> (shift right), - (mark field) and then = (to move) or == (to copy) for the target.

3. Field attributes such as high intensity, colors, and others we have not explored can be changed by
   - using F4 to get to a Work with Fields screen of all fields for the record
   - typing an * in the attribute byte of a field to Select Field Keywords for that field
   - typing an attribute command (e.g., H for High intensity, CT for Color Turquoise) in a field's attribute byte

Try to visualize the completed work screen as it is shown in Figure 11.40, but with the date and time in blue, the screen title and "Enter selection:" in white, and the message "Not a valid choice…" in red.

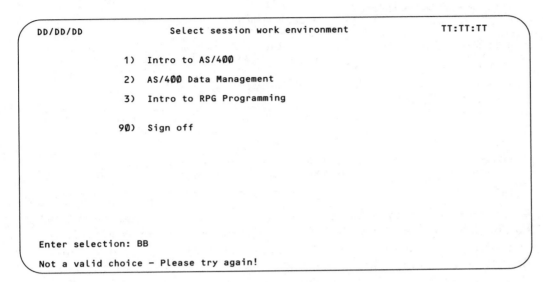

```
DD/DD/DD                 Select session work environment            TT:TT:TT

              1)  Intro to AS/400

              2)  AS/400 Data Management

              3)  Intro to RPG Programming

              90)  Sign off






Enter selection: BB
Not a valid choice - Please try again!
```

Figure 11.40
Completed Work Screen

When you are finished with a record's work screen (or have run out of time), F3 or F12 takes you back to the Work with Display Records screen. If you use F3, be sure to select option 1 to save work since last Enter, which is the default (Figure 11.41).

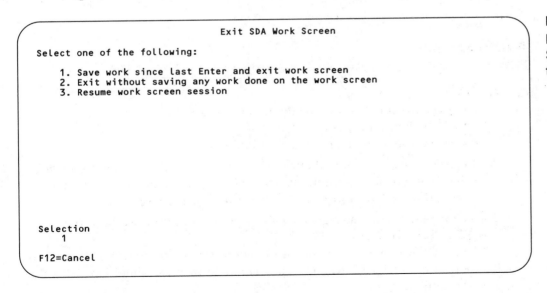

```
                         Exit SDA Work Screen
Select one of the following:

    1. Save work since last Enter and exit work screen
    2. Exit without saving any work done on the work screen
    3. Resume work screen session








Selection
    1

F12=Cancel
```

Figure 11.41
Exit SDA Work Session, Via F3 from the Work Screen

The Work with Display Records screen indicates changes made during your last session by displaying the message "Image updated for record R1" in the lower left of the screen, as shown in Figure 11.42.

Figure 11.42
Return to Work with
Display Records Screen

```
                         Work with Display Records
 File . . . . . . :    QDDSSRC              Member . . . . . . :   STRUPDSP
   Library . . . . :    JAFINTRO            Source type . . . :   DSPF

 Type options, press Enter.
   1=Add                2=Edit comments        3=Copy           4=Remove
   7=Rename             8=Select keywords      12=Design image

 Opt   Order    Record        Type     Related Subfile    Date        DDS Error
 ___    __10    R1            RECORD                       11/11/94

                                                                      Bottom
 F3=Exit                 F12=Cancel         F14=File-level keywords
 F15=File-level comments  F17=Subset        F24=More keys
 Image updated for record R1.
```

If, at any time, you need to return to a record's work screen to add to or change existing fields, option 12 (Design image) for that record takes you right back.

Saving the Display File

Now we are ready to save our display screen entries. Function key F3 from Work with Display Records takes us to the exit screen, Save DDS — Create Display File (Figure 11.43).

Figure 11.43
Save DDS — Create
Display File Screen

```
                       Save DDS - Create Display File
 Type choices, press Enter.

   Save DDS source . . . . . . . . . . . . .   Y          Y=Yes
     Source file . . . . . . . . . . . . . .   QDDSSRC    F4 for list
       Library . . . . . . . . . . . . . .     JAFINTRO   Name, *LIBL ...
     Member . . . . . . . . . . . . . . . .    STRUPDSP   F4 for list
     Text . . . . . . . . . . . . . . . . .    _____

   Create display file . . . . . . . . . .     Y          Y=Yes
     Prompt for parameters . . . . . . . .     _          Y=Yes
     Display file . . . . . . . . . . . . .    STRUPDSP   F4 for list
       Library . . . . . . . . . . . . . .     JAFINTRO   Name, *CURLIB
     Replace existing file . . . . . . . .     Y          Y=Yes

   Submit create job in batch . . . . . . .    Y          Y=Yes

   Specify additional
     save or create options . . . . . . . .    _          Y=Yes

 F3=Exit   F4=Prompt   F12=Cancel
 Member STRUPDSP and File STRUPDSP exist and will be replaced.
```

Usually, all the values displayed on this screen will be what we want, and that is true in this example. If you did not save DDS source (the default is to save) none of the work done during the previous session would be recoverable once you exited. Remember that SDA saves all of your screen design specifications as DDS, but if you tell it not to save, you will have nothing (or only an earlier version) to go back to when you need to modify your display file. If you leave the Create display file value set to Y, SDA attempts to create the display file by compiling the generated DDS right away. If you were not ready to compile yet, you could change this value to N. For this example, we will press Enter on this screen, using the defaults. A message will then appear at the bottom of the screen telling us that the member was saved and that the (batch) job (to compile the display file) was submitted. Pressing Enter returns us to the Design Screens screen, and then pressing F3 takes us to the initial SDA display (Figure 11.1).

The Test display files option on this screen, option 3, lets us see how the display file will appear at runtime with different records selected and different indicators in on or off states. This option is especially useful for more complicated display files that are not working correctly. Because a programmer may not be sure whether a problem lies in the display file or in the program, the test feature provides a good way to independently run the display file through all combinations of input, output, and indicators.

Testing the Display File

We will test our display file, but first it would be a good idea to make sure the compile we requested from the exit screen (Figure 11.43) was successful.

From the command line of the AS/400 Screen Design Aid (SDA) display, we can enter the command to display messages, DSPMSG. When the command executes, a message like the one shown in Figure 11.44 displays.

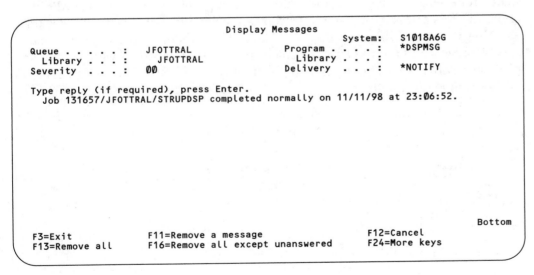

Figure 11.44
Display Messages Screen

It is always important when compiling or recompiling a program or display file to check the results. That way we know the test will be valid and that it will be working with the current version of the display file and not a previous version called up because of a compile error.

After we take option 3 from the main SDA screen, the Test Display File screen (Figure 11.45) asks for the name and library of the display file to be tested and the record to test. (It remembers the display file name from the previous test session, if there was one.)

Figure 11.45

Test Display File for
STRUPDSP in
JAFINTRO Record R1

```
                                  Test Display File
        Type choices, press Enter.

           Display file . . . . . . . . . . . . . .   STRUPDSP    Name, F4 for list
              Library  . . . . . . . . . . . . . . .   JAFINTRO    Name,
                                                                   *LIBL ...
           Record to be tested  . . . . . . . . .   R1          Name,
                                                                   F4 for list
           Additional records to display  . . . .               Name



        F3=Exit      F4=Prompt      F12=Cancel
```

We need to make sure the right values are provided by typing over previous values, if necessary. Notice that for multirecord display files, only one record's fields and indicators can be tested at a time; you can select other records for display only.

After we press Enter from the Test Display File screen, a screen appears that asks us to Set Test Output Data (the values that a program would write to the display file record). We will enter a valid selection number (3) in the CHOICE field, as shown in Figure 11.46.

Figure 11.46

Set Test Output
Data Screen

```
                                Set Test Output Data
        Record . . . :   R1

        Type indicators and output field values, press Enter.

        Field        Value
        *IN40        0:
        CHOICE       3 :




                                                                        Bottom

        F3=Exit    F12=Cancel
```

Because CHOICE is a 2-character field, a single digit would be stored as a 3 and a space; so we have typed a 3 followed by a space to see how the menu choice would actually be displayed. For now we will leave indicator 40 (*IN40) off (or 0). While it may seem a little strange to set an output value for the choice field, at this point we are only checking the formatting of screen constants and data fields.

When we press Enter from the Set Test Output Data screen, our display file, as it would appear with the values of 0 for indicator 40 and 3 for CHOICE, displays (Figure 11.47).

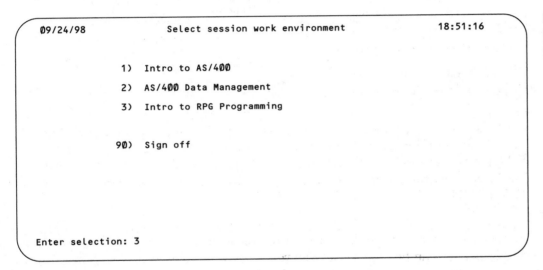

```
  09/24/98              Select session work environment          18:51:16



          1)  Intro to AS/400

          2)  AS/400 Data Management

          3)  Intro to RPG Programming


         90)  Sign off








  Enter selection: 3
```

Figure 11.47
Record R1 of the Display File

The test function shows the screen exactly as it would appear if a program had written record R1 to the display file with those values. The character 3 appears in green in the CHOICE field because indicator 40 is off, and the current system date and time have been substituted for the format image that appeared on the work screen.

Even though our intended startup program would not write the record back to the display file when the choice is valid (it would instead execute the program code to be used for choice 3), the test facility lets us see how the data is formatted on the screen and — if indicators are used — how turning them on and off affects the display. To illustrate, let's try testing with an invalid choice and the error indicators turned on.

First we press Enter from the test display. This takes us to the Display Test Input Data screen, Figure 11.48, which shows the value to be used as input for field CHOICE. For a simple display file such as this, there is not a lot of useful information here. This screen tells us only that if we enter 3 on the display file CHOICE field, the value 3 will be sent to the program as the input value for field CHOICE available to the program.

Figure 11.48
Display Test
Input Data Screen

```
                          Display Test Input Data

 Record . . . :    R1

 View indicators and input field values.

 Field         Value
 CHOICE        3 :







                                                                   Bottom

 Press Enter to continue

 F3=Exit    F12=Cancel        F14=Display input buffer
```

Pressing Enter again takes us back to the Set Test Output Data screen. This time we will test the display file with an invalid value (4) typed into the CHOICE field and written back to the display file, and with indicator 40 turned on, as it would be when the program realizes that an incorrect entry has been made (Figure 11.49).

Figure 11.49
Set Test Output Data,
Invalid CHOICE Entry
and *IN40 Turned On

```
                          Set Test Output Data

 Record . . . :    R1

 Type indicators and output field values, press Enter.

 Field         Value
 *IN40         1:
 CHOICE        4 :








                                                                   Bottom

 F3=Exit    F12=Cancel
```

Now when we press Enter, our display file appears quite different. The CHOICE value is in red and on line 23, in red, the error message "Not a valid choice — press Enter and try again!" stands out bright and clear. (Imagine Figure 11.50 with the cursor on the input field, and the 4 and the error message both displayed in red.)

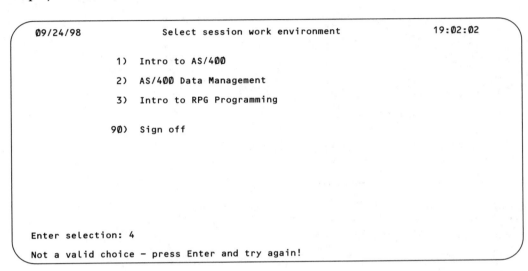

```
 09/24/98              Select session work environment        19:02:02


        1)   Intro to AS/400

        2)   AS/400 Data Management

        3)   Intro to RPG Programming

       90)   Sign off







 Enter selection: 4
 Not a valid choice - press Enter and try again!
```

Figure 11.50
Record R1 of the Display File with *IN40 Set On

This is what the display would look like if the program had read R1, found field CHOICE to contain an invalid value, turned on indicator 40, and written record R1 back to the display file.

When we test the display file in this way, we can be certain what it will look like under specific conditions. If it does not look like that when we run the program and type an incorrect value, we can be fairly certain the problem lies in the program logic — for example, the program doesn't recognize the CHOICE value as invalid, or it fails to turn on indicator 40, or it does not successfully rewrite the display file record.

Viewing the Members Created

At this point, we will leave SDA and return to the Work with Members Using PDM screen for source physical file QDDSSRC in our current library.

In Figure 11.51 we have selected option 5 (Display) for two menu members (STUMNU type MNUDDS and STUMNUQQ type MNUCMD) that we created earlier in this lesson. (Remember that when we exited from the Design Menus screen, we told SDA to save the source members.)

Now let's see what those members look like. The first one, the DDS for STUMNU, is shown in its entirety in Figure 11.52. We won't explain all the entries, but we will point out the similarities in structure to the DDS for physical or logical files.

Figure 11.51
WRKMBRPDM with
Menu Members
Selected for Display

```
                         Work with Members Using PDM            S1018A6G
 File . . . . . .   QDDSSRC
   Library . . . .    JAFINTRO           Position to . . . . .

 Type options, press Enter.
   2=Edit         3=Copy   4=Delete 5=Display      6=Print     7=Rename
   8=Display description  9=Save  13=Change text  14=Compile  15=Create module...

 Opt Member    Type      Opt Member    Type      Opt Member    Type
 ____ PRJ.M.ELF  LF       ____ SECTPF     PF       ____ STUMSTLF   LF
 ____ PRJKLF1    LF       ____ SECTPFI    PF       ____ STUMSTLF2  LF
 ____ PRJMBRLF1  LF       ____ STRUPDSP   DSPF     ____ STUMSTLF3  LF
 ____ PRJMBRMFLF LF       ____ STUENRLMLF LF       ____ STUMSTLF4  LF
 ____ PRJMBRPF   PF       ____ STULF1     PF       ____ STUMSTPF   PF
 ____ PRJPF      PF       ____ STULF1P    LF       ____ STUNAMLF   LF
 ____ RLUTEST1   PRTF      5__ STUMNU     MNUDDS   ____ STUPF      PF
 ____ SAMP01X    PF        5__ STUMNUQQ   MNUCMD   ____ STUPF.L5   PF
                                                                 More...
 Parameters or command
 ===>
 F3=Exit          F4=Prompt              F5=Refresh          F6=Create
 F9=Retrieve      F10=Command entry      F23=More options    F24=More keys
```

Figure 11.52
DDS for STUMNU

```
5716PW1 V3R6M0  950929              SEU SOURCE LISTING
SOURCE FILE . . . . . . .    JAFINTRO/QDDSSRC
MEMBER . . . . . . . . .       STUMNU
SEQNBR*...+... 1 ...+... 2 ...+... 3 ...+... 4 ...+... 5 ...+... 6 ...+... 7 ...
    1      A* Free Form Menu: STUMNU
   10      A*%%TS  SD 19980624  194624 JFOTTRAL    REL-V3R6M0  5716-PW1
   20      A*%%EC
   30      A                                       DSPSIZ(24 80 *DS3
   40      A                                             27 132 *DS4
   50      A                                       CHGINPDFT
   60      A                                       INDARA
   70      A                                       PRINT(*LIBL/QSYSPRT)
   80      A          R STUMNU
   90      A*%%TS  SD  19980624  194624 JFOTTRAL    REL-V3R6M0  5716-PW1
  100      A                                       DSPMOD(*DS3)
  110      A                                       LOCK
  120      A                                       SLNO(01)
  130      A                                       CLRL(*ALL)
  140      A                                       ALWROL
  150      A                                       CF03
  160      A                                       HELP
  170      A                                       HOME
  180      A                                       HLPRTN
  190      A                               1  2'STUMNU'
  200      A                                       COLOR(BLU)
  210      A                               3  2'Select one of the following:'
  220      A                                       COLOR(BLU)
  230      A                               5  7'1.'
  240      A                               6  7'2.'
  250      A                               7  7'3.'
  260      A* CMDPROMPT  Do not delete this DDS spec.
  261      A                              21  2'Selection or command
  270      A                                     '
  280      A                               1 72DATE
  290      A                                       EDTCDE(Y)
  300      A                                       COLOR(BLU)
  310      A                               2 72TIME
  320      A                                       COLOR(BLU)
  330      A                               1 26'Student File Applications Menu
  340      A                                       DSPATR(HI)
  350      A                               5 12'Update the file using DFU'
  360      A                               6 12'Print the file'
  370      A                               7 12'Print the Payment Due Report'
  380      A                              16  7'90.'
  390      A                              16 12'Signoff'
```

Notice the file-level keywords under the comments (A* ...) on lines 3–7. These attributes apply to the entire display file.

On line 8 the record format, R STUMNU, is defined. The keywords starting with DSPMOD(*DS3) on line 10 are all record-level keywords.

On line 19, the field-level descriptions begin with the constant STUMNU. Its location on the screen immediately precedes the constant: line 1, column 2. The constants we entered for menu title and menu choice descriptions follow, starting on line 33.

As you can see, the syntax for display file DDS is a little more complicated than for the physical and logical files we have created so far. There are a number of file and record-level keywords we'd have to study to know what they do or even whether we need them. Even a DDS expert would probably agree that using SDA is not only faster than coding the DDS yourself, but SDA also gives you a better chance of compiling a working menu on the first attempt!

The next member is the command source (Figure 11.53), which is simply a list of the menu selection numbers and the CL commands associated with each selection. It is used as the source for a CRTMSGF (Create Message File) command. When the message file is created together with the display file, it allows immediate execution of the command when the selection number is input through the display file. If we needed to change a command for a certain selection number, we could do so by editing this source member, then re-creating the message file and menu; but it is faster and less frustrating to work through SDA.

```
 Columns . . . :    1  71           Edit                 JAFINTRO/QDDSSRC
 SEU==>                                                            STUMNUQQ
 FMT **   ...+... 1 ...+... 2 ...+... 3 ...+... 4 ...+... 5 ...+... 6 ...+... 7
         ************* Beginning of data *********************************
0000.01 STUMNUQQ,1
0000.10 0001 CHGDTA DFUPGM(STUUPD)
0000.11 0002 RUNQRY QRY(STUQRY1)
0000.12 0003 RUNQRY QRY(STUPAYQRY)
0000.13 0090 SIGNOFF
         ***************** End of data ***********************************




 F3=Exit    F4=Prompt    F5=Refresh   F9=Retrieve   F10=Cursor   F11=Toggle
 F16=Repeat find         F17=Repeat change          F24=More keys
                                     (C) COPYRIGHT IBM CORP. 1981, 1995.
```

Figure 11.53
STUMNUQQ
Command Source

Finally, let's take a brief look at the source DDS created for our display file, STRUPDSP. Again using option 5 from Work with Members Using PDM, the DDS displays as in Figure 11.54.

Figure 11.54
DDS for STRUPDSP

```
5716PW1 V3R6MØ  950929                    SEU SOURCE LISTING
SOURCE FILE . . . . . . .  JAFINTRO/QDDSSRC
MEMBER  . . . . . . . . .  STRUPDSP
SEQNBR*...+... 1 ...+... 2 ...+... 3 ...+... 4 ...+... 5 ...+... 6 ...+... 7 ...+... 8
   100      A*%%TS  SD 19980624  184809  JFOTTRAL    REL-V3R6MØ  5716-PW1
   200      A*%%EC
   300      A                                     DSPSIZ(24 8Ø *DS3)
   400      A                                     PRINT
   500      A          R R1
   600      A*%%TS  SD 19980624  184809  JFOTTRAL    REL-V3R6MØ  5716-PW1
   700      A                              1  2DATE
   800      A                                     EDTCDE(Y)
   900      A                                     COLOR(BLU)
  1000      A                              1 25'Select session work environment'
  1100      A                                     DSPATR(HI)
  1200      A                              1 72TIME
  1300      A                                     COLOR(BLU)
  1400      A                              5 20'1)  Intro to AS/4ØØ'
  1500      A                              7 20'2)  AS/4ØØ Data Management'
  1600      A                              9 20'3)  Intro to RPG Programming'
  1700      A                             17 19'9Ø)  Sign off'
  1800      A                             21  2'Enter selection:'
  1900      A                                     DSPATR(HI)
  2000      A          CHOICE          2A  B 21 19
  2100      A  40                               COLOR(RED)
  2200      A  40                        23  2'Not a valid choice - press Enter t-
  2300      A                                     o clear and try again!'
  2400      A                                     COLOR(RED)
                        * * * *  E N D  O F  S O U R C E  * * * *
```

At the file level, the DSPSIZ keyword, automatically inserted by SDA, is shown on line 3.

On line 5 is the record format for R1, with constants and field-level descriptions for our color choices and display attributes following. On lines 21 and 22 you can see the indicator 40 for the CHOICE field and the message. Notice that the indicator for field CHOICE is only on the COLOR attribute (line 21); but for the message constant, the field itself, marked by its coordinates (line 23, column 2), is conditioned. As we saw in testing, when indicator 40 is not on, the field does not appear.

Although SDA generated this DDS source code, you can easily make changes directly to this code and recompile it. For example, if you wanted an invalid CHOICE value and its error message to appear in pink instead of red, you could simply change the color values on lines 21 and 24 to PNK, save the DDS source, and use the compile option, 14, from Work with Members Using PDM to recompile the display file.

For simple changes, this is probably faster and more efficient than going through SDA. You say you want to test those changes? Good idea, and here's a fast path: Option 5 of Work with Objects Using PDM, taken on a *FILE object of type DSPF, invokes the same Test Display File function as through SDA.

So you still don't need to return to SDA unless your changes are more extensive than your knowledge of DDS. Also, any changes made and saved in the DDS source will be included in the next SDA session. They have to be because SDA uses the same source file we are examining when it rebuilds its work screen images for the next session. If you decide to make changes to an existing display file or menu using SDA, remember that Work with Members Using PDM offers option 17=Change using SDA. On MNUDDS type members, this option takes you right into Specify Menu Functions; on DSPF members, this option takes you to the Work with Display Records screen.

There's much more to learn about SDA than we could possibly cover here, but hopefully this lesson will get you off to a good start.

Key Terms

attribute byte

attribute command

constants

display files

indicators

input/output fields

menus

option indicator

response indicator

SDA (Screen Design Aid)

Lab 11

INTRODUCTION

In this lab you first design a simple menu just like the one described in the text. From this menu, you will be able to update your student data file using the DFU program you created in Part 1 of the last lab, print the student data file, and print the Payment Due report created in Part 4 of Lab 10.

After you create and test the initial menu, you add an option to display student file records sorted by name.

You also create a display file that lets you select a work environment during sign-on. In Lab 12, you write a CL program to use the display file and process choices taken from it.

Instructions in this lab are less specific than in previous labs. We assume that you have read and studied the preceding text carefully. Refer back to the text and use online Help to answer specific "how to" questions.

Part 1

Goals	Use SDA to create a menu Test all menu options
Start at	WRKMBRPDM, your library/QDDSSRC
Procedure	STRSDA Design a menu Exit and save Go STUMNU; test all options

1.1. Starting from Work with Members Using PDM for your source physical file, QDDSSRC, run the STRSDA command.

1.2. Take the option to design menus. Name the menu STUMNU, with the source in QDDSSRC, in your library.

1.3. Work with menu image and commands.

1.4. Change the menu description to Student File Applications Menu and display it in high intensity. Display the system date and time in blue in the upper right corner of the screen. Provide text for three menu choices, as shown in Figure 11.55: Update the file using DFU, Print the file, and Print the Payment Due Report. Add an option 90, Signoff.

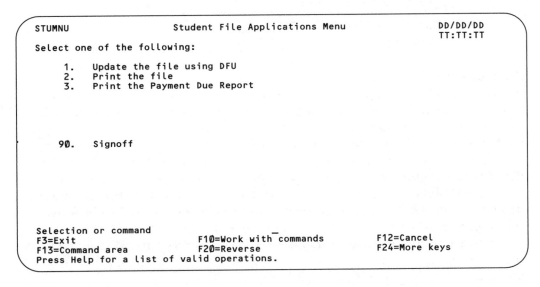

Figure 11.55
Work Screen for
Menu STUMNU

When your work screen looks like the one in Figure 11.55, press the function key to work with commands.

1.5. For the first option, type the correct CL command on the entry field next to the option number. To update a file using a DFU program, you need the CHGDTA command; then prompt for the command parameters. Use the name of the DFU program you created in the previous lab. For options 2 and 3, the command should be RUNQRY. The query that prints the entire file should be STUQRY1; the Payment Due report should be STUPAYQRY.

1.6   After entering the commands, page down or position to menu option 90 and enter the SIGNOFF command. When you press F11 to show only the options with commands, your screen should look like the one in Figure 11.56.

Lab 11

Figure 11.56

Options and Commands for STUMNU

```
                                    Define Menu Commands
   Menu . . . . . . . :    STUMNU              Position to menu option . . . . . . _

   Type commands, press Enter.

   Option    Command
     01      CHGDTA DFUPGM(STUUPD)_____

     02      RUNQRY QRY(STUQRY1)_____

     03      RUNQRY QRY(STUPAYQRY)_____

     90      SIGNOFF_____



                                                                             Bottom
   F3=Exit          F11=Show all options        F12=Cancel        F24=More keys
```

1.7. Exit the Define Menu Commands screen, Menu Image work screen, and Specify Menu Functions screen — you should be looking at the Exit SDA Menus screen. Make sure that the menu source will be saved and the menu objects will be created. Use "Menu of Student Applications" for the text. When you have completed the screen, press Enter to exit and save.

   1.7a. What message appears temporarily at the bottom of the Exit screen?
   1.7b. What message is displayed at the bottom of the Design Menus screen?

1.8. Exit to the AS/400 Screen Design Aid (SDA) screen and on the command line enter the command to go to your menu. Test all menu options and make sure they work. Although function keys are not listed, F3 or F12 still take you out of the menu.

Part 2

Goals	Copy an existing query definition Modify the copied query to create a different output Modify STUMNU to allow an option for the new query Identify the objects created by the new menu and query definition
Start at	Any command line
Procedure	Enter WRKQRY Copy query definition STUQRY3 to STUQRY4 Follow instructions to modify STUQRY4

2.1. From a command line use the WRKQRY command to copy STUQRY3, which you created during the additional lab for Lesson 7. Copy it to new query STUQRY4. If you don't have STUQRY3, you can just create STUQRY4 as a new query.

2.2. The new query should be an outer join (Query type 2) of STUPF and ZIPPF. You will keep the join as defined in STUQRY3 (equijoin on S.ZIP=Z.ZIP) but select, in the following order, fields LNAME, FNAME, PHONE, and ADDR1 (from STUPF); CITY and STATE (from ZIPPF); and ZIP (from STUPF). Sort the output by FNAME within LNAME. Send the output to the display device. Run the query before saving. The general display format should be similar to that shown in Figure 11.57.

```
Last Name      First Name      Phone    Address 1        City           State   ZIP

Badman         Benji       319 234-3456  #1 Nirvanah Ln.  Once Again     FL      76484
Baggins        Bilbo       319 988-8998  345 Hawthorne Ln. Marion        IA      52302
Clapsaddle     Karikool    707 683-4556  999 Sundown Rd.  Nowhere        UT      44444
Cool           Joe         319 365-9876  512 Belvedere Dr. Guthrie Center IA     50115
Dowhopper      Jazmann     215 456-7654  12345 Clyde St.  Ghost Gulch    UT      44446
Dupekey        Dingy       319 555-1212  319 Ditto Pl     Mount Ayr      IA      50854
Engobber       Emil        515 388-6543  Clay Works       Nora Springs   IA      50458
Fottral        Jerry       319 857-4101  1308 L Rd NW     Swisher        IA      52338
Goodoboy       Billybob    777 123-4567  12 E. Main       Kalona         IA      52247
Grubber        Norman      515 899-7890  RR 2             Amana          IA      52203
Hopkins        Harry       319 688-9234  RR1              Hills          IA      52235
Humpchucker    Harvy       319 488-7865  1233 Shady Road  Toby Town      FL      78914
Mannaka        Chuunan     555 555-5555  55 Center St.    Pleasantville  IA      50225
Muggins        Medford     555 234-4321  RR 2             Anamosa        IA      52205
Murkiwater     Millie      515 899-0923  Shady Lane       Clarinda       IA      51632
Owari          Saigo       999 999-9999  9999 99TH St     Disney World   FL      78915
Slim           Salamander  515 233-4566  10 W. Main       Dead Dog       UT      44445
Tenkaichi      Ichiro      111 111-1111  111 Imperial Hwy. South Bend    IN      46614

* * *   E N D   O F   R E P O R T   * * *
```

Figure 11.57

Display of STUQRY4 Join of STUPF and ZIPPF

Of course, you will have to shift your view to the right to see the entire display. (Fields of the report shown in Figure 11.57 have been narrowed to fit the entire display on the page.) If you are creating a new query instead of copying from STUQRY3, edit the PHONE and ZIP fields.

2.3. Modify your existing menu to include the new display as an option. You can either use the STRSDA command or option 17=Change using SDA on member STUMNU (type MNUDDS) from Work with Members Using PDM.

2.4. From Work with menu image and commands, add constants for an option 4: Display Student file by Last Name. Add the RUNQRY command to execute the STUQRY4 you just created.

2.5. Exit and save the menu, then test again to make sure the new option works. You may be requested to demonstrate your menu to your instructor/mentor in the computer lab.

2.6. Locate your menu source members in the Work with Members Using PDM list for QDDSSRC. There should be two.

    2.6a. What are the member names and types and what does each contain?

2.7. Search your Work with Objects Using PDM list for the three new objects created during this exercise.

    2.7a. List the three menu-related objects by name, type, and attribute.

Part 3

In this part of the lab you use SDA to design a simple screen. The screen will let you select a work environment (e.g., Intro to AS/400, Intro to RPG/400). The selection will be read and the environment set up by a program that you will write in Lab 12.

Goals	Use SDA to create a display file
	Test the created display file
Start at	STRSDA from any command line
Procedure	Identify the new display file as QDDSSRC/STRUPDSP
	Follow instructions to define constants, user-defined fields, date and time
	Exit and save; create the file
	Take the SDA option to test

3.1. From the SDA starting menu, take option 1, Design Screens.

    SDA creates DDS display file descriptions using information you provide through a series of work screens and entry displays. The result is a DDS source file stored as a member of source file QDDSSRC. SDA also compiles these source members, creating executable display file objects.

    From the Design Screens screen, the source file should be QDDSSRC in your library. Choose Member name STRUPDSP and press Enter.

3.2. The next screen is the Work with Display Records screen. Add a record named R1 by typing the option and the record name, then pressing Enter. Press Enter again from the Add New Record screen.

    You should now be at a mostly blank screen that has the message "Work screen for record R1" at the bottom.

3.3. This is the SDA display file work screen, used to design your display screen image. Press the Help key and scan through the Help information. Function keys do not display on a work screen, but they are available for use. Use the list in your text for reference during the exercise. Also, read about and make note of adding (user-defined) fields. You will need to define several constants on your screen, so read about adding constants. Now page down to the Help information about moving, copying, and shifting fields, and make note of the characters used to reposition fields on a screen. Note also how to remove fields and which characters are used to get into additional features.

3.3a. What do you type in the attribute byte of a field to rename the field?

When you are finished with Help, return to the work screen.

3.4. At what line and column is the cursor currently positioned? Coordinates are shown in the bottom right corner of most screens, in LL/CC (line/column) format. If your display does not show position coordinates, move to line 3, column 1 and display the ruler (function key F14). By pressing the same function key again, you can remove the ruler at any time. Do not exit the work screen session with the ruler still displayed.

Place system date at 1/3 and time at 1/72.

Starting at 1/12, enter the constant "Session Work Environment". Use the attribute command AC to center the screen title. Press F4 and select keywords on these fields to display date and time in blue and the title in display attribute high intensity.

3.5. Return to the work screen. Starting on line 5, column 20 (the left single quotation mark should be in column 19), enter constants describing two work environments:
  1) Intro to AS/400
  2) Intro to RPG Programming

Double-space these constants and don't forget to enclose each one with single quotation marks.

Then drop down to line 18 and enter another option:

   90) Sign off

Remember to use the repositioning attribute commands (-, =, <,>) — not the Insert and Delete keys — if you need to move these constants.

3.6. Drop down to 21/02 and type the constant "Enter selection:". Declare a 2-character input and output field so that the left character is positioned at 21/19. After you have entered this field it should display as BB. Move the cursor to the field's attribute byte, just before the leftmost B, and type a question mark (?). Then press Enter. The name, length, and text of the field display at the bottom of the screen. Rename the field CHOICE by typing over the SDA-supplied default field name, then press Enter.

3.7. Move the cursor to the last usable screen line — line 23, column 2 — and type the constant "F3=Exit" to allow use of the command attention key, CA03, which we will soon define; then press Enter. Color the function key

Lab 11

constant blue. Move the cursor over to 23/19 and enter the constant "Not a valid choice — press Enter to clear and try again!" so that the leftmost N is aligned with the leftmost B of the CHOICE field.

3.8. After you have entered all constants and the input/output field, press F4 to work with fields. The first screen of the Work with Fields display should look like the one in Figure 11.58.

Figure 11.58

Work with Fields Screen for Display File STRUPDSP, First Screen

```
                               Work with Fields

Record . . . :    R1

Type information, press Enter.
  Number of fields to roll . . . . . . . . . . . . . . . . .       6

Type options, change values, press Enter.
   1=Select keywords   4=Delete field

Option   Order   Field       Type Use  Length   Row/Col   Ref Condition  Overlap
  __       10    *DATE         C          6,0    01 003
  __       20    Session Wo    C           24    01 029
  __       30    *TIME         C          6,0    01 072
  __       40    1)  Intro     C           19    05 020
  __       50    2)  Intro     C           28    07 020
  __       60    90)  Signo    C           12    18 019
                                                                    More...
Add    _____  _____       H  _____  Hidden
Add    _____  _____       M  _____  Message
Add    _____  _____       P  _____  Program-to-system

F3=Exit  F6=Sort by row/column      F12=Cancel
```

Page down to the second screen of this display. It should look like the one in Figure 11.59.

Figure 11.59

Work with Fields Screen for Display File STRUPDSP, Second Screen

```
                               Work with Fields

Record . . . :    R1

Type information, press Enter.
  Number of fields to roll . . . . . . . . . . . . . . . . .       6

Type options, change values, press Enter.
   1=Select keywords     4=Delete field

Option   Order   Field       Type Use  Length   Row/Col   Ref Condition  Overlap
  __       70    Enter Sele    C           16    21 002
  __       80    CHOICE        A    B       2    21 019
  __       90    F3=Exit       C            7    23 002
  __      100    Not a vali    C           55    23 019           Y
                                                                    Bottom
Add    _____  _____       H  _____  Hidden
Add    _____  _____       M  _____  Message
Add    _____  _____       P  _____  Program-to-system

F3=Exit  F6=Sort by row/column      F12=Cancel
```

Compare the lengths and Row/Column values with your own display. They should be exactly, or very nearly, identical. If not, you need to return to your work screen and make the necessary modifications so that your screen is in agreement with the above specifications.

3.9. From the Work with Fields screen, take the option to select keywords on the last field, the constant "Not a valid choice . . .". From the next screen select both display attributes and colors. On the Select Display Attributes screen, type in indicator 40 for field conditioning, then press Enter. On the Select Colors screen, choose red as the first-order color (type 1 under Order next to Red).

3.10. From the Work with Fields screen, select keywords to make field CHOICE both input and output. From the Select Field Keywords screen, type Y on the Colors option. On the Select Colors screen, choose red as the first-order color, indicated by 40. When R1 is written with *IN40 on, CHOICE will appear in red — otherwise, it will appear in green, the default. Your screen should look like the one in Figure 11.60. (On color monitors, the color name abbreviations are colored.)

```
                           Select Colors

   Field . . . . . :   CHOICE        Usage . . :  B
   Length  . . . . :   2             Row . . . :  21   Column . . . :  19

   Type choices, press Enter.
                                     Keyword   Order   Indicators/+
                                               (1-7)
       Colors:                       COLOR
         Blue . . . . . . . . . . . . . .  BLU     _      ___ ___ ___
         Green  . . . . . . . . . . . . .  GRN     _      ___ ___ ___
         Pink . . . . . . . . . . . . . .  PNK     _      ___ ___ ___
         Red  . . . . . . . . . . . . . .  RED     1      _40 ___ ___
         Turquoise  . . . . . . . . . . .  TRQ     _      ___ ___ ___
         White  . . . . . . . . . . . . .  WHT     _      ___ ___ ___
         Yellow . . . . . . . . . . . . .  YLW     _      ___ ___ ___




   F3=Exit    F12=Cancel
```

Figure 11.60
Select Colors Screen for Field CHOICE

3.11. Return to your work screen and exit, being sure to save work since last Enter. From Work with Display Records, press F14 to select file-level keywords. These are keywords (e.g., UNIQUE, FIFO, and JDFTVAL for database files) that apply to the display file as a whole. Type Y for Indicator keywords and Print keywords.

3.12. You can use an Indicator keyword to set up a relationship between a certain key on the keyboard (e.g., a function key) and a special type of program variable called an indicator. In this way it is possible to communicate between display files and the programs running them. To illustrate, you will declare a Command Attention (CA*xx*) keyword to allow the function key F3 (Cmd 3) to be used to exit the program. Declaring the CA*xx* keyword creates the connection between the function key and the program indicator. The indicator then functions as a switch — it is turned on when a user working at the display presses the key (F3) and then the program reads the display file. On the program side, after a display file record is read, the indicator's status (on/off) is checked by the program logic so that appropriate actions can be taken as function keys are pressed.

You should now be looking at the Define Indicator Keywords screen. Type CA03 under Keyword, then tab or field-exit over and type 03 under Resp and suitable text, such as "F3 to Exit". (The text does not need quotation marks.) Do not enter anything in the three fields under Indicators.

This establishes a relationship between function key F3 (CA03) and a response indicator, 03, that can be tested in the program. When the user presses F3 and the program reads a display file record (R1), the indicator IN03 will be turned on in the program. When the program logic checks the indicator and finds it on, it ends the program by returning to the controlling program.

You can use any function key either as a CA*xx* or a CF*xx* key. A CA*xx* key signals the program by turning on the indicator (attention, program!) but does not send input field data to the program. A CF*xx* key signals the program, too; but it also transfers the current input field data of the record being read into the program buffer. In this case, because F3 will be used to exit the program, it would serve no useful purpose to transfer data; so CA03 is the proper choice.

When you have correctly entered the above values, press Enter.

3.13. Under Define Print Keywords, type a Y next to Enable keyword ... PRINT, and leave the rest of the screen as it is. (We will let the system handle printing.)

Selecting the PRINT keyword will enable (turn on) the PRINT key when the display file is active, allowing a user to print the screen. Press Enter to return to the Select File Keywords screen and then press Enter again to return to the Work with Display Records screen.

3.13a. What message displays on the Work with Display Records screen?

3.14. Now press F3 to exit to the Save DDS — Create Display File screen, which will save your description and attempt to compile the object. Note the defaults on the Save DDS — Create Display File screen. Especially note the name of your source member and that the display file will have the same name.

3.14a. Is the create job run interactively or in batch?

Provide suitable text for the member and then press Enter. Notice the message at the bottom of the screen. When you return to the Design Screens display, press F3 to return to the SDA menu.

3.15. From the AS/400 Screen Design Aid (SDA) menu, take option 3 to test your display file. The display file and library values should specify the display file you just created; the record to be tested is R1. From Set Test Output Data, keep IN40 off (0) and type a valid choice (digits 1 or 2, followed by a space) over the BB, then press Enter. The next screen shows how your display would appear when written to the display device with the values you assigned. (In this case, because you will not write the record back out when a valid choice is entered, the screen shows how the display will appear just after typing the selection and before pressing Enter.)

Press Enter twice to return to Set Test Output Data. This time turn on indicator 40 (value 1) and enter an invalid value.

3.15a. What happens when you press Enter this time?

You should now be looking at the screen as it would appear after an invalid choice has been entered. The program, detecting this, has turned on response indicator 40, and then has written the record back to the display file.

Any problems in formatting the display or using indicators should be detected by testing the display file. Then when the program is ready to test, you can be reasonably assured that the display file will work correctly and you can concentrate on testing the program logic.

When you are finished testing, press Enter and F3 until you have exited SDA.

3.16 Return to the Work with Objects Using PDM screen, refresh the screen, and look for a new object of type *FILE and attribute DSPF.

3.16a. Does the message in your message queue indicate normal or abnormal completion?

Look in your output queue. You should see a 4- to 5-page spooled print file with the same name as the object you just created.

3.16b. Where did this print file come from?

3.16c. Scan it for error messages. Are there any? Are they critical?

If your display file, STRUPDSP, did not compile, print the compiler diagnostics from your output queue and take them to your instructor/mentor for help. Otherwise, you may delete the spooled file.

Mastering the AS/400, Second Edition

Lab 11 Answer Sheet

Name: _____

Date Due: _____

Class Time: _____

1.7a. _____

1.7b. _____

2.6a. _____

_____

2.7a. _____

_____

_____

3.3a. _____

3.13a. _____

3.14a. _____

3.15a. _____

3.16a. _____

3.16b. _____

3.16c. _____

_____

In Summary

SDA gives you a way to create menus and display files without requiring extensive knowledge of DDS syntax. The SDA work screens and entry screens filled out in the design process are converted to DDS source code that is saved and also compiled, creating menu and display file objects. Fields can be of three types: constants (any word or text enclosed in quotation marks), data fields whose usage (input, output, both) is determined by the code used to define the field, or system functions such as *DATE. A program can use data fields for displaying information from a physical or logical file. Data entry operations or values for any prompt fields are also input to a program through data fields.

On work screens, you can position fields, move fields, and change the display attributes of fields. You can use an attribute byte that precedes each field for positioning, changing display attributes, and specifying colors. You can enter an attribute command, starting on the attribute byte, or you can enter an asterisk (*) on the attribute byte that will take you to a Select Field Keywords screen for that field. You can also use the prompt function key (F4) to go to the Work with Fields screen where you can select keywords for any field defined in the active record. You can use option indicators, which are turned on and off by a program, to determine whether — and how — a field will appear. And you can use Command Attention (Ca*xx*) and Command Function (CF*xx*) keywords to associate function keys with response indicators in a program. When the function key is pressed and the record is read by a program, the response indicator will be on. Then the program can check the indicator and respond accordingly.

When the screen is saved, a DDS source member is placed in your source physical file and a display file is compiled. For menus, a menu object and message file are also created.

You can test display files by taking SDA option 3 or by using Work with Objects Using PDM option 5 on the display file object. Testing lets you see how the display will appear when you use different combinations of input/output field values and indicators. If you have tested the display file beforehand, you can concentrate on the program testing phase, confident that your display file will perform properly.

Lesson 12

Getting Started with CL Programming

Lesson Overview

The Control Language of OS/400 is the programmers' and operators' tool for access to operating system functions. Although you have used individual CL statements in all the labs preceding this lesson, in this lesson you will see how a number of related statements can be combined to create a separate program object.

First we review CL use and syntax, then we present an overview of CL programs and their format. We then describe the function of several specific commands used in CL programs to handle variable declaration and manipulation, file I/O, selection, and iteration, and to send messages.

Some of these commands are used only within CL programs; they are provided to add structure, control, and flexibility to CL programs and are not used individually from a command line.

This lesson is intended only as a basic introduction to CL programming, to get you started on a couple of simple programs and give you an idea of the capabilities. Students with AS/400 programming aspirations will want to take a CL programming class, if available, and certainly obtain a copy of a good CL programming textbook, such as *Control Language Programming for the AS/400, Second Edition* (Duke Press, 1997), to work through.

Objectives

Students will be able to

✓ Describe common uses of CL programs

✓ Explain several advantages to using CL programs

✓ Specify the steps for creating a CL program

✓ Describe the parts of a CL program

✓ Explain what the DCLF and DCL commands are used for

✓ Use the IF command to code simple, combined, and nested IF operations

✓ Demonstrate selection and iteration control in a CL program

✓ Describe how a CL program can use an *OUTFILE for a display command

✓ Code, compile, and execute a CL program to use a display file

✓ Code, compile, and execute a CL program to create and access a data file

CL REVIEW

As you have seen through the use of various CL commands in previous lessons, OS/400 CL provides a single, consistent, and flexible interface to many different system functions. By assigning users to a user profile class and further restricting use through individual command object authority and authorization lists, CL commands can be provided to certain classes of users and restricted from others based on their needs. To summarize, CL

- uses a single, consistent syntax
- can be entered from the command line, placed in CL programs, or included as part of a batch job

You may remember from Lesson 2, or from your use of CL, that a CL command usually consists of a verb that identifies the action, a noun that specifies the object of the action, and optionally a modifier that limits or narrows the range of the command. Figure 12.1 summarizes command notation.

Figure 12.1
CL Syntax Notation

Command
D S P F D
Verb | Noun
Modifier

Parameter
F I L E (C A T P F)
Keyword   Value

Parameter Specification

Keyword Notation

```
DSPFD        FILE(CATPF)    TYPE(*ALL)    OUTPUT(*PRINT)
```
or, because the default value of TYPE is *ALL
```
DSPFD        FILE(CATPF)    OUTPUT(*PRINT)
```
or, because it is keyword notation, even
```
DSPFD        OUTPUT(*PRINT)    FILE(CATPF)
```

Positional Notation

```
DSPFD        CATPF    *ALL    *PRINT
```
or, because the second parameter value uses default,
```
DSPFD        CATPF    *N    *PRINT
```
but not
```
DSPFD        CATPF    *PRINT
```
and certainly not
```
DSPFD        *PRINT    CATPF
```

The operating system helps with the preparation and use of CL commands by providing

- prompting support for all commands
- default values for most parameters
- validity checking to ensure correct entry

- selective authorization by user, user class, and group profile
- extensive online Help for explanations of commands and parameters

CL Programs' Uses

There are many reasons for writing CL programs, but the majority of programs fall into one of the following three categories:

- User interface — CL programs can help provide nontechnical users with an interactive interface that is simple and easy to use. Such an interface lets users request application functions and control application flow, while insulating them from command line access. With such a user interface, users do not require knowledge of CL or operating-system functions, and they can work with greater efficiency and reduced likelihood of error.

- Operations — Although many system-maintenance and housekeeping functions are built into OS/400, specific operational procedures are always required on any system. When you can write these regularly needed operational procedures in CL programs, they can then be tested and stored in an efficient form that requires only a single command or menu choice for consistent, error-free execution. Applications might range from procedures that select records from database files to be input to batch report programs, to procedures that selectively save objects or libraries to backup media at a certain time every night. For example, at the beginning of each semester I use CL programs to create user profiles and class authorization lists and to clean up output queues; at the end of the semester, I use other CL programs to remove authorization list entries and to delete objects, libraries, and user profiles.

- Job attributes — Technical users and programmers may need to work in one of several different job environments, depending on immediate needs. These different environments may require changes to job attributes — for example, the composition or ordering of library list entries, selection of output queue and/or message queue, or change of run or print priorities. Also, a user might need a special work screen (e.g., Work with Objects Using PDM for a specified library) after signing on to the system. You can use a CL program as the initial program to automatically tailor the environment after sign-on. This initial program can execute appropriate CL commands based on the user's choice from a menu-like display screen. Along the same lines, CL programs often manage "flow control," the sequencing, setup procedures, and error handling of related high-level language (HLL) programs in a multi-job-step applicaton process.

Advantages of CL Programs

A CL program (an object of type *PGM) exists as an independent entity. Unlike a compiled RPG or Cobol program, a CL program is not in a "machine language" or a low-level form that can be immediately executed; but the CL program form is closer to being executable than the same sequence of commands entered from the command line. Additional advantages include the following:

- Some CL commands are available only from within a CL program. These include selection and iteration commands (IF-THEN and GOTO), error-testing commands (MONMSG), and file-processing commands (SNDRCVF). Also, CL programs let you declare and work with variables and retrieve values (e.g., system values, job attributes, object descriptions) that will be used as variables in a program.

- You can test and debug CL programs just as you can HLL programs. Once checked out, CL programs always provide consistent, error-free execution because the sequence of commands and the logic become part of the actual program. If factors outside the program require that the program be changed, you can modify and recompile the source CL program.

- CL programs can pass parameters to programs they call and they can receive parameters passed to them. The ability to pass and receive parameters makes CL programs very flexible and lets a single CL program meet the needs of different applications.

ENTERING CL SOURCE

You enter CL programs as source members of source physical file QCLSRC using SEU just as you have used it to enter and change physical and logical file DDS. As always, when creating a new member (F6 from WRKMBRPDM QCLSRC), it is important to correctly specify the source type from the Start Source Entry Utility (STRSEU) screen. The source type for CL programs that we will be looking at is CLP, the Original Program Model (OPM) source type that is commonly used to create a *PGM object from each source member. (For CL programs designed to function in the Integrated Language Environment (ILE), source type CLLE is used.) Figure 12.2 shows the STRSEU screen correctly filled out for a new member (STRUPPGM), which will be a program to control display file STRUPDSP, which you created in Lab 11.

Figure 12.2

Start Source Entry
Utility (STRSEU)
Screen to Create a
New CL Program

```
                        Start Source Entry Utility (STRSEU)
  Type choices, press Enter.

  Source file  . . . . . . . . . . >   QCLSRC        Name, *PRV
    Library  . . . . . . . . . . >   JAFINTRO      Name, *LIBL, *CURLIB, *PRV
  Source member  . . . . . . . .      struppgm      Name, *PRV, *SELECT
  Source type  . . . . . . . . .      clp           Name, *SAME, BAS, BASP, C...
  Text 'description' . . . . . . .      Program to process selections from STRUPDSP




                                                                        Bottom
  F3=Exit   F4=Prompt   F5=Refresh   F12=Cancel   F13=How to use this display
  F24=More keys
```

Once you are in SEU Edit mode, entering each command is a little different than describing a file in QDDSSRC. Because each CL command has its own unique prompt screen, the line command IP for a CLP type is meaningless; and if you enter it, SEU simply takes you to the Major Command Group menu, just as if you had pressed F4 on a blank command line.

So you just type I for insert, then the command name (e.g., PGM), and press F4 if you need prompting. Doing so takes you to the command prompt screen for that command. Then you can fill out the parameter values you need. Notice that all commands have a Label parameter as the first parameter on the list. This lets you attach a tag or label to any command so you can refer to it as the object of a GOTO command from another location in the program. (Using the GOTO command along with the IF command is the only way to accomplish iteration control, or looping, in a CL program.)

When you have finished with the command prompt screen, pressing Enter adds the command (in keyword notation) to your SEU work screen and inserts another line for you. Also, if the command and its parameters won't fit on a single line, the continuation character (+) is inserted after a parameter, and the command is continued on the next line.

We will soon see exactly how this facility works, but first let's examine the general structure of a CL program.

CL Program Structure

CL programs can take many different forms, depending on their function. Although the body of the program allows nearly limitless possibilities, there are a few general rules and guidelines. Figure 12.3 shows the general structure of a CL program.

```
/* Program ID */

PGM (optional)

DCLF (maximum of one)
DCL
DCL

IF  (cond) stmt1
ELSE   stmt2

AGAIN:     SNDRCVF
           MONMSG
           IF  (cond)
           DO  stmt1
                   stmt2          (Iteration)
             ENDDO
           ELSE
           GOTO AGAIN

           CHGVAR
           SNDPGMMSG
           SNDUSRMSG

ENDPGM (optional)
```

Figure 12.3
General Structure of a CL Program

The **program ID** is not formalized in a CL program and must be entered using comments. Comments are any text on a line bracketed by a beginning /*

and an ending */. The program ID should at least identify the program by name, briefly state the purpose or function of the program, and identify the author of the program.

The **PGM statement** must be the first statement in the CL program. It is required to list all CL variable names used to reference parameters passed to the program. When the program receives no parameters, the PGM statement is optional, but most often it is used anyway. When parameters are passed, the parameter-list variables in the called program must match the calling program's parameter list positionally. Each variable in the PGM parameter list of the called program must be identical to the calling program's corresponding parameter in size and type. For example, if a Cobol program called a CL program and passed it a 5-digit, packed-decimal section number, the CL program's PGM statement would look like this:

```
PGM     PARM(&SECTNO)
```

Variable &SECTNO would be defined as

```
DCL     &SECTNO *DEC (5,0)
```

The **DCLF statement**, if present, declares a file to be accessed by the CL program. Only one file, regardless of type, can be accessed by a single CL program. It can be a display file or a database file.

DCL statements are used to declare variables needed by the CL program. Variables serve the same purposes in a CL program as they do in an HLL program — counters, accumulators, indicators, or character strings. Any number of variables can be declared in a single CL program.

DCLF and DCL statements, when present, must immediately follow the PGM statement and precede any other statements in the program.

The body of the program follows. Sequence operations are implemented simply by one CL command following another. Practically any CL commands can be executed in any required order, but there are certain restrictions. For example, you cannot include commands that require an interactive environment in a program that will be run in batch. Selection is implemented using the IF-THEN-ELSE structure. When multiple statements must be executed for a certain selection result, the statements must be blocked within a DO-ENDDO group structure. Iteration (loop control) is limited to the branching statement GOTO, when it is executed from within an IF statement. You specify the command label of the statement to which control passes following the GOTO command.

The **ENDPGM statement**, which is optional, marks the end of the CL program. When the program encounters this command, control returns to the calling program (or interactive job). The best way to understand how the parts of a CL program work together is to design, code, and test one — and that is what we will do now.

DESIGNING THE START-UP PROGRAM

The function of our example program (which we will call STRUPPGM) is to set up a working environment based on a user's selection and take the user to a departure point within that environment. Upon exiting from one environment, the user should be able to enter another environment, sign off the system, or return to the calling program.

The program will display a screen that lists the possible work environments and that allows for a selection to be input. This screen already exists as your Lesson 11 display file, STRUPDSP, which lets you request and establish a certain work environment immediately upon signing on to the system. The display file allows the following choices:

1) Intro to AS/400

2) Intro to RPG Programming

90) Signoff

You could also use function key F3, which ends the program. Of course the display file and program could allow for many more choices, but for our purposes, these two choices plus signoff will suffice.

We make certain assumptions about each work environment:

- Each user will have a separate test library, which will be made the user's current library upon entry to the environment.

- Each user will have a separate output queue, which will contain the spooled files created while working in the environment.

- There will be a class library to which a user in that environment will have at least object operational authority.

An initial structure chart for such a program might look like this:

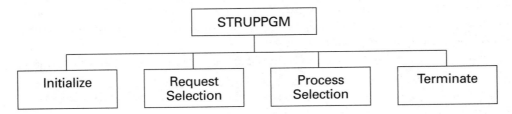

Examining the process steps for each of these modules might produce the following tentative list.

Initialize

- Declare the display file

- Declare a character variable for print message text

Request Selection

- Send (write) the display file to the display device

- Receive (read) the selection (CHOICE) entered by the user

Process Selection

- Evaluate CHOICE and if valid,
  — change the library list
  — change the job (output queue)
  — start Work with Objects Using PDM

  if invalid,
  — turn on an option indicator
  — send (write) the display file to show the error

Terminate

- End the program and transfer to the initial menu, or

- End the program (and the job) by signing off

An internal structure for modular programming (i.e., paragraphs/sections in Cobol, subroutines in RPG) doesn't exist in CL, so our division of the program structure into modules is more a logical than a physical division. But the concepts behind this approach are no less valid for relatively small CL programs than they are for large HLL applications.

ENTERING THE PROGRAM

Let's now examine the process for entering the CL program. As we go along, we explain statements in the program that have not been used in previous exercises, but only as needed for the task at hand. Keep in mind that we are limiting our objectives (and discussion) to what is required to compile and test a few very simple CL programs. The picture we must necessarily paint is far from complete, and a good CL textbook (and perhaps the IBM manuals) will be indispensable to a thorough understanding of this subject.

Figure 12.4 shows the program ID and PGM statement for program STRUPPGM.

Figure 12.4
Program ID as
Comments

```
 Columns . . . :    1  71              Edit                    JAFINTRO/QCLSRC
 SEU==>                                                                STRUPPGM
 FMT **  ...+... 1 ...+... 2 ...+... 3 ...+... 4 ...+... 5 ...+... 6 ...+... 7
 0001.00 /*****************************************************************/
 0002.00 /*    Display options list using display file STRUPDSP, input choice */
 0003.00 /*    and then process selection, setting up work environment.   */
 0004.00 /*    Signoff is allowed; F3 transfers to Initial Menu.          */
 0005.00 /*                                                               */
 0006.00 /*    Parameters: none                                           */
 0007.00 /*    DSPF variables: &CHOICE *CHAR 2  I/O  selection field      */
 0008.00 /*                    &IN40   *LGL   O   option ind for error    */
 0009.00 /*                    &IN03   *LGL   I   response ind for exit   */
 0010.00 /*                                                               */
 0011.00 /*    Author: J Fottral,                     Modified: 1998-08-02 */
 0012.00 /*****************************************************************/
 0013.00         PGM                 /* no parms */
 0014.00 /*****************************************************************/
 0015.00 /*    DECLARATIVES:                                              */
 0016.00 /*****************************************************************/
 '''''''         DCLF


 F3=Exit   F4=Prompt   F5=Refresh   F9=Retrieve   F10=Cursor
 F16=Repeat find         F17=Repeat change          F24=More keys
```

The program ID consists of comments — each line begins with /* and ends with */. Because no parameters are being passed to the program, there is no PARM list and, technically, a PGM statement is not required. The DCLF command lets a CL program interact with a file — either a display file or a database file. Only a single DCLF is permitted in a program. Notice in Figure 12.4 that a new line has been inserted after line 16 and that we have keyed in the DCLF command to declare the display file. Prompting after typing the DCLF command takes us to a command prompt screen for this command.

Declaring a File

The DCLF command prompt is shown in Figure 12.5 with the required File parameter name, STRUPDSP, typed in.

```
                        Declare File (DCLF)

 Type choices, press Enter.

 Label  . . . . . . . . . . . . . . .   _____
 File . . . . . . . . . . . . . . . : > STRUPDSP__    Name
   Library  . . . . . . . . . . .       *LIBL_____    Name, *LIBL, *CURLIB
 Record format  . . . . . . . . .       *ALL_____    Name, *ALL
                 + for more values      _____
 Comment  . . . . . . . . . . . . .   _____
                                      _____
                                      _____
                                      _____



                                                                   Bottom
 F3=Exit   F4=Prompt   F5=Refresh   F12=Cancel   F13=How to use this display
 F24=More keys
```

Figure 12.5
DCLF Command Prompt Screen

The first parameter, Label, which appears with all commands prompted from within a CL program, allows a programmer-defined name to be attached to any command in the program. The label functions as a marker or tag to a command so that the program can branch to the command from a GOTO command. We do not need a label on the DCLF command because it is a declarative and not part of the body of the program.

The Record format parameter, which defaults to *ALL, lets you specify a particular record format. Our file has only a single record format, R1, but the default value of *ALL will be fine.

When a program containing a declared file is compiled, all input and output fields — which are named in the file — become available to the CL program as variables. The CL program does not explicitly declare the variables, but it can reference them using the same name as that defined in the file (an ampersand (&) must be prefixed to the name). Indicators defined in the display file — both response indicators associated with command attention/function keys and option indicators used to condition display attributes, fields, and so on — are also available to the program. Each indicator will be referenced as a logical variable, whose name will start with &IN. For example, indicator 03, defined for CA03, will be referenced as &IN03. The file named in the DCLF statement must exist at the time the program is compiled so that its fields and indicators can be included in the compiled program.

When a file is declared in a program, the file can be accessed using other CL commands that allow input/output operations to the file. A display file can use the SNDF (Send File) command, which writes a record to the display file; the RCVF (Receive File) command, which reads input fields or indicators from the display; or the SNDRCVF (Send/Receive File) command, which writes a record and then waits until an indicator or input data is sent back to the program. When the declared file is a database file, you can use only the RCVF command. This means that updating or adding records to a database file is not an option for a CL program.

After you press Enter from the DCLF command prompt screen, the program looks like Figure 12.6.

Figure 12.6

Sample Program After Entering the DCLF Command

```
  Columns . . . :    1  71              Edit               JAFINTRO/QCLSRC
  SEU==>  _____ STRUPPGM
  FMT **  ...+... 1 ...+... 2 ...+... 3 ...+... 4 ...+... 5 ...+... 6 ...+... 7
  0002.00 /*   Display options list using display file STRUPDSP, input choice */
  0003.00 /*   and then process selection, setting up work environment.     */
  0004.00 /*      Signoff is allowed; F3 transfers to Initial Menu.         */
  0005.00 /*                                                                 */
  0006.00 /*      Parameters: none                                          */
  0007.00 /*      DSPF variables:  &CHOICE *CHAR 2  I/O  selection field     */
  0008.00 /*                       &IN40   *LGL   O    option ind for error  */
  0009.00 /*                       &IN03   *LGL   I    response ind for exit */
  0010.00 /*                                                                 */
  0011.00 /*   Author: J Fottral,                     Modified: 1998-08-02   */
  0012.00 /**********************************************************************/
  0013.00         PGM                      /* no parms */
  0014.00 /**********************************************************************/
  0015.00 /*   DECLARATIVES:                                                  */
  0016.00 /**********************************************************************/
  0017.00         DCLF       FILE(STRUPDSP)
  '''''''

  F3=Exit    F4=Prompt    F5=Refresh    F9=Retrieve    F10=Cursor
  F16=Repeat find         F17=Repeat change            F24=More keys
```

Notice the DCLF command has been shifted over to column 14 and the parameter, in keyword notation, has been entered in column 25. This is the standard indentation, but you can change it by inserting or deleting spaces on any line. Changing indentation may improve the readability of a nested IF statement, for example.

Declaring Variables

Variables are explicitly declared in a CL program by the DCL command. All variable names begin with the ampersand character (&). As mentioned earlier, it is not necessary to declare variables made available through a file.

As you can see from Figure 12.7, there are three types of CL variables: decimal (*DEC) for numeric packed-decimal variables, character (*CHAR) for character or string variables, and logical (*LGL) for indicators that function as switches (on

or off, true or false). Logical variables can have only the values 1 for on/true, or 0
for off/false.

Figure 12.7
CL Variable Types
and Attributes

DCL (Declare CL Variable)

```
DCL   VAR(&NAME)   TYPE(   )   LEN(   )   VALUE(   )
```

TYPE( )	LEN( )		VALUE( )
*DEC	default	(15 5)	default (0)
	maximum	(15 9)	
*CHAR	default	(32)	default ( )
	maximum	(9999)	
*LGL		1	default ('0')

Examples

```
1. DCL   &CODES   *CHAR 5       ABCD
2. DCL   &AMT     *DEC (5 2)    123.45
3. DCL   &ON      *LGL          VALUE('1')
```

When a variable is declared, only its name and type are required. Depending
on its type, the variable's length and value will default as shown in Figure 12.7.
Character variables default to a length of 32 and a value of spaces. Logical variables can have a length of only 1, so there's no need to declare a LEN attribute
for a logical variable.

Variables are used in CL programs much the same way they are used in HLL
programs — to reference data items, as indicators, counters, accumulators, and
working storage items used for data manipulation, intermediate arithmetic results,
type conversion, substring, or concatenation operations.

Changing the Value of a Variable

When a variable must be set to a value other than its initial value, or incremented
by some arithmetic expression, you need the **CHGVAR (Change Variable) command**. Figure 12.8 on page 520 summarizes the CHGVAR command and provides
examples of its use.

The CHGVAR command has two required parameters. The first is the VAR
parameter, which names the variable to be changed. The second is the VALUE
parameter, which specifies the new value the variable will assume. The VALUE can
be expressed as another variable, a constant, or a logical or arithmetic expression.
When expressions are used as the value, they must be enclosed in parentheses.

You can use the CHGVAR command to convert from decimal to character
types or, with caution, from character to decimal. A common reason for this type
of conversion is to be able to display as part of a message a decimal variable used
as a counter or accumulator. Suppose, for example, the variable &CNTR shown in
example 4 in Figure 12.8 had been used to count the objects deleted in a certain
library. If we wanted to display that information as a message to the interactive job

Figure 12.8
CHGVAR Summary

```
                          CHGVAR (Change Variable)

CHGVAR VAR(CL-variable) VALUE(expression)

Current value of CL-variable is replaced by expression

• Expression may be
    • constant
    • another variable
    • arithmetic or logical expression
• Data conversion between decimal and character variables

            Examples
            1. CHGVAR    &AMT     200.2
            2. CHGVAR    &NAME    'ZZ TOP'
            3. CHGVAR    &CODE    Z
            4. CHGVAR    &CNTR    (&CNTR +1)
            5. CHGVAR    &IN05    (&A > &B *OR &IN10)
            6. CHGVAR    &IN03    (&CHOICE = QUIT)
            7. CHGVAR    &AMT     ((&PRICE * &QTY) - &DISCOUNT)
```

calling the program, we would first need to convert it to character type. If &CNTR were declared as a 4-digit integer, we could declare a new variable

```
DCL    &ACNTR *CHAR 4
```

and after the count was completed, we could convert the numeric &CNTR to a character variable by coding

```
CHGVAR &ACNTR &CNTR
```

This command would place the character equivalent of the packed-decimal value in &CNTR into the character variable &ACNTR. Then it could be concatenated to a message and sent to a message queue or job by using a command such as

```
SNDPGMMSG MSG(&ACNTR *BCAT 'objects have been deleted')
```

Selection and Iteration

You use the IF statement to implement selection in CL programs. The syntax of a simple IF statement is

```
IF (condition) THEN(command)
```

The *condition* may be a simple relational or logical expression, a negated expression using the logical operator *NOT, or a combined expression using the logical operators *AND and *OR.

The keyword THEN is optional; but if it is used, you must enclose the command in parentheses. Although the syntax allows for execution of only a single command for true or false results, any number of commands can be grouped within a DO ... ENDDO block structure, and because DO is counted as a single command, this arrangement satisfies the syntax. The relational operators used with a CL IF command are

<	or	*LT	less than
>	or	*GT	greater than
=	or	*EQ	equal to
>=	or	*GE	greater than or equal to
<=	or	*LE	less than or equal to
¬<	or	*NL	not less than
¬>	or	*NG	not greater than
¬=	or	*NE	not equal to

The alphanumeric versions of the relational operators (*EQ, *NL, and so on), as well as the logical operators *NOT, *AND, and *OR, must be separated from their operands by one or more spaces. For example, (&A *EQ &B) is all right, but not (&A*EQ&B). However, (&A=&B) is fine.

Testing logical variables does not require a relational operator, although you may use a relational expression if you wish. For example,

```
        IF (&IN40 = '1') is equivalent to IF &IN40
also,   IF (&IN40 = '0') is equivalent to IF (*NOT &IN40)
```

In the above examples, it is important to remember that a single logical variable (e.g., &IN40) is implicitly either true or false (1 or 0) at any time — it does not require evaluation. Any other type of conditional expression, even *NOT &IN40, requires evaluation and must be enclosed in parentheses.

You would use the ELSE command in an IF statement to code a command to be executed for true results and a different command to be executed for false results. The ELSE command must always be paired with a preceding IF. CL has no END-IF command, but because the IF command only executes a single command (and a DO group is terminated by ENDDO), determination of scope should not be a problem.

A linear nested IF takes the general form

```
IF              (condition1)    command1
ELSE IF         (condition2)    command2
    .
    .
    .

ELSE                            commandn
```

A nonlinear nested IF takes the form

```
IF              (condition1) +
     IF         (condition2) +
          IF    (condition3) command1
          ELSE  command2
     ELSE        command3
ELSE            command4
```

and is justified by the fact that there are commands to be executed for false results of conditions 1 and 2. Without commands for false results of conditions 1 and 2, a simpler alternative could be written:

```
IF     (condition1 *AND condition2 *AND condition3) command1
ELSE   command2
```

The + symbols in the above example are continuation characters. When one command does not fit on a single line (or if you choose to break a command across lines) you must indicate that the command is continued on the next line. The + character causes the command to be continued from the first nonspace character on the next line. If you break the command at the end of one parameter, be sure to leave at least one space between the rightmost character of the parameter and the + symbol or a syntax error will result.

For a nonlinear nested IF, the second IF command is actually the THEN (command) parameter value of the first IF command and syntactically part of it. Therefore, if you code it on a separate line, as we have shown above, a continuation character is required at the end of the preceding line.

Instead of using continuation characters, as in the example above, the nested IF could have been written as

```
IF (condition1) IF (condition2) IF (condition3) command1
ELSE command2
ELSE command3
ELSE command4
```

assuming the first IF statement could ever fit on one line.

Generally, the earlier example is regarded as being easier to read and interpret. Figure 12.9 summarizes the different forms of IF commands.

When you use command prompting, the prompter automatically inserts + continuation characters when it needs to continue a command that has several parameters on a following line. For example, in program STRUPPGM, we might want the loop for the Request Selection and Process modules to simulate a PERFORM loop. A PERFORM loop tests the condition at the top and terminates when the condition evaluates true. The IF command to test the condition would be

```
IF            (&CHOICE = '90' *OR &IN03) +
     GOTO     TERMINATE
```

IF command variations

Figure 12.9

Different Forms of
IF Commands

```
    Simple:
        IF          (&A = &B)           CALL  PGMX

    Negated:
        IF          (*NOT(&A = &B))     CALL  PGMX

    Combined:
        IF          (&A = &B *AND &C = &D)  CALL  PGMX

    Nested linear:
        IF          (&A = &B)           CALL  PGMX
        ELSE IF     (&C = &D)           CALL  PGMY
        ELSE                            CALL  PGMZ

    Nested nonlinear:
        IF          (&A = &B)           +
            IF      (&C = &D)           CALL  PGMX
            ELSE                        CALL  PGMY
        ELSE                            CALL  PGMZ
```

But if we enter the command with prompting, it comes out

```
IF                  COND(&CHOICE = '90' *OR &IN03) THEN(GOTO +
                        CMDLBL(TERMINATE))
```

This keyword notation becomes even harder to follow as the complexity of the command increases (e.g., with nested IF statements). Personally, I usually avoid prompting for IF commands. Because the IF syntax is simple, keywords don't really add anything — they just get in the way of meaningful indentation.

Figure 12.10 shows several different forms of the same code. The code is extracted from a working program and is not complete; it is intended only to illustrate different ways to code the same linear nested IF.

Figure 12.10

Different Versions
of the Same Linear
Nested IF

```
5738PW1 V3R6M0  910329                  SEU SOURCE LISTING
SOURCE FILE . . . . . . .  JAFINTRO/QCLSRC
MEMBER  . . . . . . . . .  IFXMPL1
SEQNBR*...+... 1 ...+... 2 ...+... 3 ...+... 4 ...+... 5 ...+... 6 ...+... 7 .
  100 /* Prompted Version:                                 */
  200              IF          COND(&ATTR *EQ 'RPG') THEN(DO)
  300              RUNQRY      QRY(JAFCL/OBJLST)
  400              ENDDO
  500              ELSE        CMD(IF COND(&ATTR *EQ 'CLP') THEN(DO))
  600              RUNQRY      QRY(JAFCL/CLPLST)
  700              ENDDO
  800              ELSE        CMD(SNDPGMMSG MSG('valid parameters are "RPG" +
  900                              or "CLP" only.'))
 1000
 1100 /* Unprompted, indented Version:                     */
 1200              IF              (&ATTR *EQ 'RPG')                    +
 1300              DO
 1400                 RUNQRY      QRY(JAFCL/OBJLST)
 1500                 ENDDO
 1600              ELSE IF         (&ATTR *EQ 'CLP')                    +
 1700              DO
 1800                 RUNQRY      QRY(JAFCL/CLPLST)
 1900                 ENDDO
 2000              ELSE            SNDPGMMSG MSG('valid parameters are "RPG" +
 2100                                  or "CLP" only.')
 2200
 2300 /* Acceptable, indented for Readability:             */
 2400              IF              (&ATTR *EQ 'RPG')                    +
 2500                 RUNQRY      JAFCL/OBJLST
 2600              ELSE IF         (&ATTR *EQ 'CLP')                    +
 2700                 RUNQRY      JAFCL/CLPLST
 2800              ELSE            SNDPGMMSG 'valid parameters are "RPG" +
 2900                                  or "CLP" only.'
 3000                                                              continued
```

Figure 12.10
continued

```
SEQNBR*...+... 1 ...+... 2 ...+... 3 ...+... 4 ...+... 5 ...+... 6 ...+... 7 .
3100 /* Bare bones, poor style:                        */
3200          IF       (&ATTR *EQ 'RPG') RUNQRY JAFCL/OBJLST
3300          ELSE IF (&ATTR *EQ 'CLP') RUNQRY JAFCL/CLPLST
3400          ELSE     SNDPGMMSG 'valid parameters are "RPG" +
3500                   or "CLP" only.'
                      * * * *  E N D   O F   S O U R C E  * * * *
```

The first version of the code, lines 2–9, appears just as it would when each command was prompted, showing default indentation and keyword notation.

The second version, lines 12–21, has been indented for readability, and the keywords from the IF and ELSE commands have been eliminated. Also notice the DO ... ENDDO commands on lines 13 and 15 and on lines 17 and 19. Although these are technically not necessary (each IF command executes only a single command, RUNQRY), many programmers argue in favor of their use. The rationale is that not only do they enhance the immediate comprehension of the structure, but they also make future maintenance of the program easier — you can simply insert new statements between the DO and ENDDO statements as required.

The third version, lines 24–29, has eliminated the DO ... ENDDO structures and the remaining keywords. This example still places the command to be executed from each IF statement on a separate line for readability and for easier maintenance.

The last version, (lines 32–35) while most compact, is not particularly easy to comprehend; and if it became necessary to execute more commands for true results, their addition would be troublesome.

File I/O in CL Programs

CL programs can access two types of files: display files (e.g., STRUPDSP, which you created in Lesson 11) and database files, both physical and logical. However, a single CL program can declare only one file, and that file must exist at the time the CL program is compiled. When the program compiles, data fields from the file are made available to the program as variables.

Besides the DCLF statement that identifies the file to the CL program, three other commands are commonly used to process files. You can use two of these commands — SNDF (Send File) and SNDRCVF (Send/Receive File) — only with display files. These commands write records to the display file, causing the display to appear on the workstation display screen. CL programs cannot directly write to a database file, so these commands are restricted to files of attribute DSPF. You can use the third command, RCVF (Receive File), with display files and database files. The actions of the SNDF and RCVF (or SNDRCVF) commands are illustrated in Figure 12.11, and a brief description of each follows.

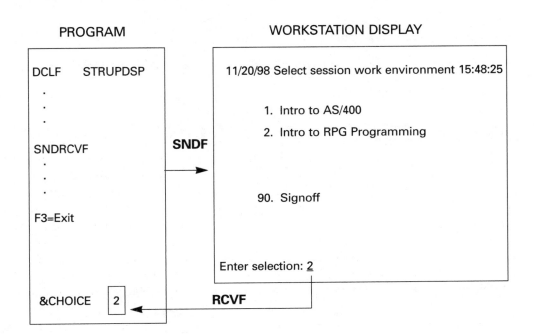

Figure 12.11

An Illustration of SNDF and RCVF Command Functions

SNDF

The SNDF command writes a record to a display device. The display device parameter defaults to the value associated with the display file. The record format parameter defaults to the record format named in the display file, if there is only one. If the display file has more than one record format, the RCDFMT parameter must name the record to be sent. In many cases, including our example program, it is not necessary to change any parameters and the command can simply be coded as SNDF.

When this command is executed, all constants defined for the record, as well as the current values of all output data fields, will be written to the workstation display. If option indicators are defined for the record, they will also be output, using their current values. By setting these indicators before executing the SNDF command, the programmer controls the appearance of the display.

Although CL has no command to write a record to a database file in a manner similar to the SNDF command, CL programs can execute commands that add to or replace data records in existing files. These are typically some form of DSP*xxx* commands (e.g., DSPOBJD — Display Object Description), and they allow the output they generate to be sent to an output file.

We use such a command in the lab for this lesson, and at that time we provide more detail about how these commands work.

RCVF

The RCVF command is the opposite of SNDF; when used with a display file, it reads any input fields defined in the record into the program variables. Also, if RCVF was triggered by a user pressing a function key, then the result indicator (e.g., &IN03 for CA03) defined for that function key will be set on in the program. A command prompt screen for a RCVF command is shown in Figure 12.12.

Figure 12.12
Command Prompt
Screen for a RCVF

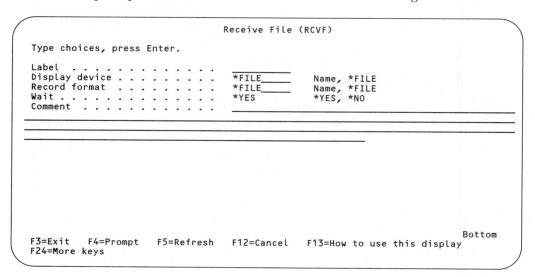

```
                                Receive File (RCVF)

Type choices, press Enter.

Label  . . . . . . . . . . . . .     _____
Display device . . . . . . . . .     *FILE_____     Name, *FILE
Record format  . . . . . . . . .     *FILE_____     Name, *FILE
Wait . . . . . . . . . . . . . .     *YES           *YES, *NO
Comment  . . . . . . . . . . . .     _____

     _____

     _____




                                                                    Bottom
F3=Exit    F4=Prompt    F5=Refresh    F12=Cancel    F13=How to use this display
F24=More keys
```

The RCVF command has the same display device and record format parameters as the SNDF command. These have the same default values and are used in a similar way. If the display file had more than one record format, you would need to name the record to be read. An additional parameter, WAIT, tells the program what to do when it gets to the RCVF command. Usually, the program goes into a wait state until the request to receive the record can be fulfilled. This happens when a user replies to a prompt or finishes typing in a data field and presses the Enter key (or an enabled function key, such as F3 or F12). Pressing the key triggers the input operation to the program, which lets the program logic continue. The default value for the WAIT parameter is *YES, and unless you want the program to continue with some process not dependent on the data coming from the screen, you would use the default.

You can use the RCVF command with a database file. When the file named in the DCLF is a physical or logical file, the RCVF command reads the next record sequentially from the file. As mentioned earlier, CL has no command to write a record to a database file, and the RCVF command is limited to sequential access. This limitation means that if the physical or logical file uses a keyed-sequence access path, the records will be retrieved in order of their key field values; otherwise, they will be retrieved in arrival sequence.

SNDRCVF

The SNDRCVF command combines the functions of the two previously described commands. It sends (writes) a record to the workstation display with all output fields and option indicators set to current values. Then it waits for the user's action (e.g., pressing Enter or F3) and receives (reads) the record from the display file, passing all input fields and response indicators into the program variables. The parameters, defaults, and usage are the same as for the RCVF command. This command is more commonly used in CL programs because usually there is nothing for the program to do but wait for the response once it has sent the display file record.

Sending Messages

A message is simply a communication sent from a program or a user to a message queue. A message queue functions as a mail box to hold the incoming message until it can be handled. Every user on the system has a message queue identified by the same name as the user ID, and when you sign on and start an interactive job, your workstation message queue also becomes available. These are permanent message queues that continue to exist after the user is signed off or the terminal is not in use; if you return to examine these message queues from a later session, they will still be there and the old messages will still be available (unless they were deleted). In addition to these message queues, every running program has a program message queue that is created when the program begins and deleted when the program ends. Furthermore, every job has an external message queue that is created when the job starts and is available during the life of the job.

An external message queue is often used to display an inquiry message (one requiring a reply) when a CL or HLL program experiences a severe run-time error during testing.

There are several types of messages, but we mention only two here: informational and inquiry. Informational messages are just that — they inform the recipient of some condition or convey the results of a process. They are not usually used for error messages and do not require a response. Inquiry messages request a response and are often used to display error messages that require a reply.

You can use a number of commands to send messages; we mention three of them:

- SNDMSG (Send Message) — You can use the SNDMSG command interactively or from within a CL program. It works only with messages whose text is included within the MSG (Message text) parameter of the command. It can deliver the message to a named message queue or a user.

- SNDBRKMSG (Send Break Message) — The SNDBRKMSG command delivers messages only to a workstation message queue. If the workstation is active at the time of delivery, the command interrupts the job and displays the message. If the message type is an inquiry message, you can specify a message queue for the response. As with the SNDMSG command, you can use the SNDBRKMSG command interactively or from a CL program, and the message text is part of the command.

- SNDPGMMSG (Send Program Message) — You can use the SNDPGMMSG command only from within a CL program. You can define the message text within the MSG parameter, or you can use a predefined message that exists in a message file and that has a unique message identifier. The command can deliver its message to any type of message queue, including program and external message queues. For messages requiring a response, you can designate a reply message queue. This command is especially useful when a running program needs to send a message back to the program that called it.

Message handling is a very rich feature of OS/400, and it involves a degree of complexity entirely beyond this course. But you can refer to Figure 12.13 to see some common uses of these commands.

Figure 12.13

Sample Program to Illustrate Different Ways to Send Messages

```
Columns . . . :    1  71              Edit                    JAFINTRO/QCLSRC
SEU==> _____    MSGTEST
FMT **  ...+... 1 ...+... 2 ...+... 3 ...+... 4 ...+... 5 ...+... 6 ...+... 7
*************** Beginning of data ****************************************1
0001.00        PGM
0002.00             SNDMSG      MSG('Hello from SNDMSG to user JFOTTRAL') +
0003.00                           TOUSR(JFOTTRAL)
0004.00
0005.00             SNDMSG      MSG('Hello from SNDMSG to msgq PCSTAFFS1') +
0006.00                           TOMSGQ(PCSTAFFS1)
0007.00
0008.00             SNDBRKMSG   MSG('Hello from SNDBRKMSG to PCSTAFFS1') +
0009.00                           TOMSGQ(PCSTAFFS1)
0010.00
0011.00             SNDPGMMSG   MSG('Hello to *PRV program from SNDPGMMSG')
0012.00
0013.00             SNDPGMMSG   MSG('Hello to EXTernal msgq from SNDPGMMSG') +
0014.00                           TOPGMQ(*EXT)
0015.00
0016.00        ENDPGM


F3=Exit    F4=Prompt    F5=Refresh    F9=Retrieve    F10=Cursor
F16=Repeat find         F17=Repeat change            F24=More keys
```

The first command, line 2, sends a message to the message queue for user profile JFOTTRAL. Other possibilities for the TOUSR parameter are *SYSOPR, the system operator's message queue; *ALLACT, all currently active (signed-on) user profiles' message queues; and *REQUESTER, the user profile currently running this interactive job.

The second command, on line 5, shows the alternative parameter to TOUSR, namely, TOMSGQ. With this parameter, you identify by name the exact message queue to which you want the message delivered. We have chosen the message queue of the workstation we are currently signed on to. But we could specify any other permanent message queue to which we had access.

The SNDBRKMSG command, line 8, delivers the message to the workstation message queue PCSTAFFS1 and interrupts the interactive job. If an operator needed to notify all users of an impending shutdown or of some emergency situation, the special value *ALLWS (instead of PCSTAFFS1) would broadcast the message to all workstations.

The first SNDPGMMSG command, line 11, sends the message text to the previous program's message queue by default — i.e., the TOPGMQ (send to program message queue) parameter is using the default value of *PRV. The previous program is the one calling this program; but if this program were run from a command line, the message would display at that screen when the program finished.

The last SNDPGMMSG command, line 13, has specified *EXT, the external job message queue, as the recipient of the message.

If we ran this compiled program, after first clearing both the JFOTTRAL and PCSTAFFS1 message queues, the sequence of events would be as follows.

First, you would hear two beeps as the message from the first two SNDMSG commands are delivered to the two empty message queues. This really sounds like one long beep because the commands are executed one after another. After an instant, you would hear another beep as the break message is delivered and the job is interrupted. Break messages always beep as they interrupt an active job. Figure 12.14 shows the first display after the program is called.

```
                          Display Messages
                                          System:    S1018A6G
   Queue  . . . . . :    PCSTAFFS1        Program . . . . :   *DSPMSG
     Library . . . :      QSYS              Library . . . :
   Severity  . . . :    00                 Delivery  . . . :   *NOTIFY

   Type reply (if required), press Enter.
      From  . . . :    JFOTTRAL        11/27/98   16:54:17
      Hello from SNDBRKMSG to PCSTAFFS1




                                                         Bottom
   F3=Exit            F11=Remove a message            F12=Cancel
   F13=Remove all     F16=Remove all except unanswered  F24=More keys
```

Figure 12.14
Break Message Display

The screen displays the message and the program is interrupted, waiting for us to acknowledge the message. We don't need to reply; we simply press F12 or Enter.

But, knowing that an earlier message was sent to the same workstation message queue, we can first Page up to see whether it was delivered. Pressing Page up changes the display to that shown in Figure 12.15. Now we can see that the earlier message from the SNDMSG command did make it to the queue.

```
                          Display Messages
                                          System:    S1018A6G
   Queue  . . . . . :    PCSTAFFS1        Program . . . . :   *DSPMSG
     Library . . . :      QSYS              Library . . . :
   Severity  . . . :    00                 Delivery  . . . :   *NOTIFY

   Type reply (if required), press Enter.
      From  . . . :    JFOTTRAL        11/27/98   16:54:17
      Hello from SNDMSG to msgq PCSTAFFS1
      From  . . . :    JFOTTRAL        11/27/98   16:54:17
      Hello from SNDBRKMSG to PCSTAFFS1




                                                         Bottom
   F3=Exit            F11=Remove a message            F12=Cancel
   F13=Remove all     F16=Remove all except unanswered  F24=More keys
```

Figure 12.15
Showing Previously Sent Message as well as Break Message

When we press Enter from this display, the PDM screen appears for an instant, but then we move on to the message delivered to the external job message queue. That display is shown in Figure 12.16.

Figure 12.16
Display Program
Messages Sent to *EXT

```
                           Display Program Messages

Job 150762/JFOTTRAL/PCSTAFFS1 started on 11/27/98 at 16:19:27 in subsystem Q
 Hello to EXTernal msgq from SNDPGMMSG




 Press Enter to continue.






 F3=Exit    F12=Cancel
```

When we press Enter from the external message display, we return to the Work with Members Using PDM screen from which the program was called. Because this is the previous level to the called program, the defaulted SNDPGMMSG command message appears here. You can see the message displayed on the message line of the screen shown in Figure 12.17.

Figure 12.17
Message Delivered
to *PRV Program

```
                           Work with Members Using PDM

 File . . . . . .    QCLSRC____
    Library . . . .    JAFINTRO__          Position to . . . . .  _____

 Type options, press Enter.
    2=Edit         3=Copy  4=Delete 5=Display       6=Print    7=Rename
    8=Display description 9=Save 13=Change text   14=Compile  15=Create module

 Opt  Member      Type       Text
 __   MSGTEST     CLP        Message commands_____
 __   RCVFTEST    CLP        I/O commands_____
 __   SNDLPRT     CLP        CL driver for dspf LPRINT_____
 __   STRUPPGM    CLP        Select work environment using STRUPDSP_____
 __   STRUPPGMA   CLP        Select work environment using STRUPDSP_____
 __   STRUPPGMB   CLP        _____
 __   TEST        CLP        _____
 __   TEST2       CLP        _____

                                                                     Bottom
 Parameters or command
 ===>_____
 F3=Exit           F4=Prompt         F5=Refresh        F6=Create
 F9=Retrieve       F10=Command entry F23=More options  F24=More keys
 Hello to *PRV program from SNDPGMMSG
```

At this point, we can see that the message waiting indicator is turned on, so running the DSPMSG command (or taking PDM option DM) will show us the waiting message. Because the messages sent to the workstation have not been cleared, we will first see them again, just as we did in Figure 12.15. Whenever messages are still on your workstation message queue, execution of the DSPMSG command with no parameters takes you to that queue. Pressing Enter from the workstation message queue display will bring up the message sent to user JFOTTRAL's message queue. That display is shown in Figure 12.18.

```
                          Display Messages
                                         System:    S1018A6G
   Queue  . . . . . :    JFOTTRAL         Program . . . . :    *DSPMSG
     Library . . . :      JFOTTRAL          Library . . . :
   Severity  . . . :    00               Delivery  . . . :    *NOTIFY

   Type reply (if required), press Enter.
     From  . . . :    JFOTTRAL      11/27/98    16:54:17
     Hello from SNDMSG to user JFOTTRAL




                                                          Bottom
   F3=Exit              F11=Remove a message             F12=Cancel
   F13=Remove all       F16=Remove all except unanswered F24=More keys
```

Figure 12.18
Display Messages
for User JFOTTRAL

   As you can see from this example, there are several ways a program can send a message to a user or another program. In fact, there are many more possibilities that we have not mentioned here because their discussion belongs in a CL programming class. But hopefully, this discussion provides enough information to help you start sending messages from your CL programs.

Using Concatenation
Concatenation is the joining of two character variables or constants. In CL programs, programmers often use concatenation to form messages by combining several character variables and string constants to be assigned to a single variable or to be used as a single message text value. In fact, concatenation is very often used when a CL program needs to communicate with its user or to send a message to a message queue; for that reason we briefly introduce concatenation here.

   Three different concatenation operations are available in CL programs: *CAT, *TCAT, and *BCAT. The following example illustrates their differences. First, assume two character variables declared as follows:

```
DCL    &VAR1 *CHAR(10) 'WATER'
DCL    &VAR2 *CHAR(10) 'MELON'
```

   When an explicit length is included in the declaration of a character variable, the string constant value is left aligned and the remaining bytes are replaced with spaces. So the actual contents of &VAR1, for example, would be the five characters

WATER followed by five spaces. Note that, because the values WATER and MELON consist solely of alphabetic characters, it is technically not necessary to enclose them in single quotation marks (apostrophes); but using apostrophes to delimit quoted strings is a good habit to acquire.

- *CAT — The *CAT operation joins the full length of the first variable or string to the second variable or string, so the command

```
SNDPGMMSG  MSG(&VAR1 *CAT &VAR2 *CAT 'IS KING')
```

would produce the message

```
WATER     MELON     IS KING
```

- *TCAT — This operation truncates any spaces to the right of the rightmost, nonspace character in the first variable. Then it joins what is left of the first variable to the second variable or string. In our example, this means that the five rightmost spaces of &VAR1 and &VAR2 would be truncated. The command

```
SNDPGMMSG  MSG(&VAR1 *TCAT &VAR2 *TCAT 'IS KING')
```

would produce the message

```
WATERMELONIS KING
```

- *BCAT — The *BCAT operation is similar to *TCAT except that it leaves (or inserts) a single space after the last (rightmost) character of the first variable. In effect, this inserts a single space between the nonspace characters of the first variable and the variable or string to which it is joined. The command

```
SNDPGMMSG  MSG(&VAR1 *BCAT &VAR2 *BCAT 'IS KING')
```

would produce the message

```
WATER MELON IS KING
```

with one space between each word.

Combining *TCAT and *BCAT produces proper formatting of our example message. The command

```
SNDPGMMSG  MSG(&VAR1 *TCAT &VAR2 *BCAT 'IS KING')
```

would produce the message

```
WATERMELON IS KING
```

FINISHING THE START-UP PROGRAM

We have now introduced some CL commands that you haven't used before but that are needed to make our example program work. Before we can finish the program, we need to decide exactly what we want the program to do when we have made a certain choice. For example, if choice 1 to set up the Intro to

AS/400 environment is entered, which CL commands must be executed? For any class environment, we would want to

1. Change the library list to make the user's library for that class current and to place the class library first on the user part of the library list. Other libraries owned by the user should probably follow the class library in the library list.

2. Change the current job so the user's output queue for the selected class will be used, and so a message (30 or fewer characters) identifying the user and the class will be printed at the bottom of each page of printed output.

3. Send the user directly to the Work with Objects Using PDM screen showing all objects in the user's current library (selected above).

Having decided the specific actions to be taken for any selection made, we can complete the source code for the start-up program. Figure 12.19 shows the complete source code for the program, using display file STRUPDSP created in Lesson 11.

Figure 12.19
CL Source Code for
Program STRUPPGM

```
5716PW1 V3R6M0   950929                SEU SOURCE LISTING
SOURCE FILE . . . . . . .  JAFINTRO/QCLSRC
MEMBER  . . . . . . . . .  STRUPPGM
SEQNBR*...+... 1 ...+... 2 ...+... 3 ...+... 4 ...+... 5 ...+... 6 ...+... 7 ...
  100 /*****************************************************************/
  200 /*   Display options list using display file STRUPDSP, input choice */
  300 /*     and then process selection, setting up work environment.     */
  400 /*     Signoff is allowed; F3 transfers to Initial Menu.            */
  500 /*                                                                  */
  600 /*     Parameters: none                                            */
  700 /*   DSPF variables: &CHOICE *CHAR 2  I/O  selection field          */
  800 /*                   &IN40   *LGL   O    option ind for error      */
  900 /*                   &IN03   *LGL   I    response ind for exit      */
 1000 /*                                                                  */
 1100 /*   Author: J Fottral                      Modified: 1998-08-02 */
 1200 /*****************************************************************/
 1300        PGM                    /* no parms */
 1400 /*****************************************************************/
 1500 /*   DECLARATIVES:                                              */
 1600 /*****************************************************************/
 1700        DCLF   FILE(STRUPDSP)
 1800        DCL    &MYNAME *CHAR 15 'Jerry Fottral -'
 1900 /*****************************************************************/
 2000 /*   PROCEDURE:                                                 */
 2100 /*****************************************************************/
 2200
 2300 REQUEST:   CHGVAR        &CHOICE ' '
 2400            SNDRCVF
 2500
 2600            IF            (&CHOICE = '90' *OR  &IN03)         +
 2700              GOTO        TERMINATE
 2800
 2900            IF            (&CHOICE = '1')                     +
 3000              DO
 3100                CHGLIBL   (INTROCLASS JAFRPG ALLUSER          +
 3200                          QTEMP QGPL) JAFINTRO
 3300                CHGJOB    OUTQ(JAFINTRO/JAFINTRO)             +
 3400                          PRTTXT(&MYNAME *BCAT 'INTRO AS/400')
 3500                WRKOBJPDM LIB(*CURLIB)
 3600              ENDDO
 3700
 3800            ELSE IF       (&CHOICE = '2')                     +
 3900              DO
 4000                CHGLIBL   (RPGCLASS JAFINTRO ALLUSER          +
 4100                          QTEMP QGPL) JAFRPG
 4200                CHGJOB    OUTQ(JAFRPG/JAFRPG)                 +
 4300                          PRTTXT(&MYNAME *BCAT 'RPG/400')
```

continued

Figure 12.19
continued

```
4400                    WRKOBJPDM LIB(*CURLIB)
4500           ENDDO
4600
4700           ELSE           /* This would be an error */        +
4800           DO
4900             CHGVAR     &IN40 '1'
5000             SNDRCVF
5100             CHGVAR     &IN40 '0'
5200           ENDDO
5300
5400           GOTO       REQUEST
5500
5600  TERMINATE: IF        (&CHOICE = '90') SIGNOFF
5700           ELSE        RETURN
5800
5900           ENDPGM
```

* * * E N D   O F   R E P O R T * * *

Let's step through the lines of the source program to see how it corresponds to the structure chart we presented earlier and how the commands discussed in this lesson have been used.

1–12	These lines are all comment lines, intended to provide program identification and documentation.
13	The PGM statement is optional here, but it is usually included.
14–16	This section of comment lines is "window-dressing" used to highlight the declarative section of the program.
17	This line declares the display file. The DCLF statement causes all variables and indicators of display file STRUPDSP to be available as program variables at compile time.
18	This line includes a character variable to use as part of the print text for printed output. Lines 17 and 18 correspond to the Initialize module of the structure chart.
19–21	These comment lines are more window-dressing.
23	This line initializes &CHOICE to spaces before sending it out with the display file. Because we need to do this each time a new selection is made, this line is tagged with the command label REQUEST:.
24	This line writes the display file record and waits for the user's response. Lines 23 and 24 together initialize the workstation display and correspond to the Request Selection module of the structure chart.
26–27	These lines check to see whether the user has requested signoff or transfer to an initial menu. If so, the CL program exits the Request Selection–Process Selection loop by branching to command label TERMINATE:. If the user did not enter a terminal value, the program evaluates &CHOICE and takes the appropriate action.
29–36	If the user entered 1 for &CHOICE, these lines change the library list (line 31) to make INTROCLASS the first user library and JAFINTRO the current library. A common user library, ALLUSER, is also added to

the library list. The CHGJOB command (line 33) makes output queue JAFINTRO in library JAFINTRO the job's output queue, and the print text for the job is changed to identify both the user of the menu and the class. In line 35, Work with Objects Using PDM is started, using all objects of the current library previously set by the CHGLIBL command.

29–52   This block of code is one linear nested IF structure. The ELSE IF on line 38 provides a second condition (&CHOICE = '2') to be evaluated if the first condition tested on line 29 proves false. If the choice had been 1, so that the condition on line 29 would evaluate as true, then after returning from the WRKOBJPDM entered on line 35, the logic path would immediately leave the IF structure and execute the GOTO command on line 54.

38–45   The set of statements for choice 1 has been copied (using line command CC) from lines 29–36 and modified for the RPG environment. The order of libraries in the library list, the specification of current library and output queue, and the print text message have all been changed.

47–52   If an improper value has been entered for &CHOICE, processing falls through the preceding conditions and into the error trap set with the ELSE command at line 47. The option indicator &IN40 is turned on, causing the choice to turn red and the error message to appear when the display file record is written — as it will be by the SNDF part of the SNDRCVF command at line 50. When the user has pressed Enter, as requested by the message, the RCVF is satisfied and the indicator is turned off by the CHGVAR command at line 51. This prepares the program to reinitialize the display to try again, as we shall do by executing the GOTO statement at line 54.

56–57   These commands terminate the program, either by executing the SIGNOFF command if choice 90 has been entered, or by executing the RETURN command. If a program is called by another program, RETURN passes control back up to the calling program. In our case, if the program were being run as the initial program from the user profile, RETURN would take us to the menu designated as the initial menu in the user profile — the MAIN menu, by default.

59   The ENDPGM statement tells the compiler that nothing follows and marks the physical end of the CL program.

CREATING A CL PROGRAM

Generally, the source code for each CL program is maintained as a member of a source physical file (QCLSRC). Before you can begin coding a source CL program, you need to have created QCLSRC in your library using the CRTSRCPF (Create Source Physical File) command. When you have completed the CL source code, you use the CRTCLPGM (Create CL Program) command to create the *PGM type object. You can key this command on the command line and prompt or, more conveniently, invoke the command from Work with Members Using PDM by taking option 14 on the CLP source member.

The screen shown in Figure 12.20 appears when we prompt for option 14 taken on list item STRUPPGM (Figure 12.21 illustrates the process).

Figure 12.20
Command Prompt
for CRTCLPGM,
Prompted from PDM

```
                         Create CL Program (CRTCLPGM)
 Type choices, press Enter.

 Program  . . . . . . . . . . . . . > STRUPPGM__    Name
   Library  . . . . . . . . . . . >   JAFINTRO__   Name, *CURLIB
 Source file  . . . . . . . . . . > QCLSRC         Name
   Library  . . . . . . . . . . . >   JAFINTRO     Name, *LIBL, *CURLIB
 Source member  . . . . . . . . . > STRUPPGM       Name, *PGM
 Text `description'  . . . . . . .   *SRCMBRTXT


                         Additional Parameters

 Replace program  . . . . . . . . > *NO_           *YES, *NO




 Bottom
 F3=Exit   F4=Prompt   F5=Refresh   F10=Additional parameters   F12=Cancel
 F13=How to use this display        F24=More keys
```

Figure 12.21
Using PDM Option 14
to Create a CL Program
from a Source Member

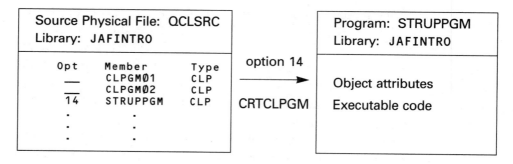

PDM supplies all necessary parameter values. Otherwise, the CRTCLPGM command requires us to name the program to be created. The command assumes source file QCLSRC and uses that as the default value if prompted from a command line. PDM fills in the Source member parameter for us, but command prompting assumes the default (*PGM) — that the source member we use will have the same name as the program we create.

When the CRTCLPGM command executes successfully, a new object of type *PGM is created in your library.

Key Terms

CHGVAR command

concatenation

DCL statement

DCLF statement

ENDPGM statement

PGM statement

program ID

variables

INTRODUCTION

In this lab exercise you enter the CL source code for program STRUPPGM, which we covered in the lesson. After a clean compile, you test the program to see how it works with display file STRUPDSP and to make sure it is responding properly to any choice value entered. To demonstrate the ease of modifying display files, you then make a minor change to your STRUPDSP file and recompile it. Because the change you make will not affect the record format of the display file, you can test the modified display file without changing and recompiling the program.

The additional lab exercise will prove a little more challenging. You design and enter the source code for a program to calculate the sum of storage space used by all objects in your library. In the process you encounter — and fix — a compile error caused by a type mismatch. Then you experience a runtime error that causes the program to end abnormally. You use diagnostic information supplied by the error message to change the program, recompile the program, and then successfully execute the program.

Finally, you write a short program and demonstrate the difference between a program running interactively and the same program submitted as a batch job.

Part 1

Goals	Enter source code for CL program STRUPPGM
	Compile the program
	Change and recompile the display file source using SEU
	Change your user profile's initial program parameter

Start at	WRKOBJPDM, your library

Procedure	CRTSRCPF QCLSRC (if it doesn't already exist)
	WRKMBRPDM QCLSRC
	F6 to create new member, STRUPPGM
	Enter source code with SEU
	Compile, test program
	WRKMBRPDM QDDSSRC to change STRUPDSP
	Compile changed display file, test
	CHGUSRPRF initial program parameter to STRUPPGM

1.1. Starting from the Work with Objects Using PDM screen, if you have not already done so, you should now create a source physical file for CL programs. Enter the CRTSRCPF command on the command line, then prompt. The source file name will be QCLSRC. Use the other defaults and give the source file an appropriate description.

1.2. Work with source file QCLSRC and create a member called STRUPPGM, of type CLP, with text such as "Start-Up Program for display file STRUPDSP."

1.3. From the SEU Edit screen, press Enter to clear the work space. Then type I and press Enter again to get into line-by-line Insert mode. To enter the program, it is usually easier to type only the command itself, then press F4 to prompt for parameters when necessary. Remember that when you use command prompting, the parameters you type will be entered in keyword notation.

Enter the entire program shown in Figure 12.19. Whenever a name reference is used (e.g., Author: J. Fottral), change it to your own name. In the body of the program, all library and output queue references (e.g., JAFINTRO, JAFRPG) must be changed to name your own libraries and output queues. These must exist before you attempt to test the program. Check with your instructor/mentor for names of common user libraries (e.g., ALLUSER) that need to be added to your user library list. Use the SEU copy line command to duplicate lines or blocks of code, then make necessary changes using typeover, delete, and insert.

After you have entered the program, exit (and save).

To compile the program, the referenced file, STRUPDSP, must exist. If you were unable to successfully complete Part 3 of Lab 11, during which you would have created the display file, and if a copy of the display file is not available to you, you cannot continue with this lab.

1.4. From the Work with Members Using PDM screen, compile the source program. Check your message queue to determine whether the compile was successful. If not, return to edit mode for the source program, use SEU Browse/Copy option (F15) to browse the compile listing and the SEU command F *ERR to locate the errors. Make necessary changes to the source member, and recompile.

1.5. At this point, assuming that you have clean compiles of the display file and the CL program, you should be ready to test the program. Remember, the libraries and output queues referred to in the program must exist before you can test the program. Create any libraries and output queues referred to in the CHGLIBL and CHGJOB commands in your program, if you have not done so already. If the class libraries do not exist or if you are not authorized to use them, remove them from the CHGLIBL library lists in your program or ask your instructor to grant you authority to them.

1.6. From the command line, type CALL STRUPPGM. When your display appears, enter the various options to test all functions.

1.7. When you have tested the program successfully, you should notice that the function key message "F3=Exit" displays even when the red error message has been written. Because F3=Exit is not really enabled at that time, you should either change the program logic to support its use (so that F3 could be used to exit the program as an alternative to the Enter key that clears the error message), or you should erase the F3=Exit message when the error message is displayed.

We'll take the second option. To erase the function key message when the error message is displayed, you could use an option indicator at the field level. Because indicator 40 is turned on when the error message is sent, you could condition the function key message by using the opposite indicator, N40. That would cause the function key message to be erased any time the error message appears.

Although you could make a simple change like this through SDA, it is often faster to make the change directly to the DDS — and that is what you will do now.

1.8. From the Work with Members Using PDM screen, change the Source file to QDDSSRC, then locate and edit the source member for the STRUPDSP display file.

The line that defines the constant F3=Exit should have the coordinates 23 2. Move the cursor to that line and prompt. Type in N40 as the leftmost entry of the indicator field, as shown in Figure 12.22.

```
 Columns . . . :   1  71          Edit              JSMITH/QDDSSRC
 SEU==> _____  STRUPDSP
 FMT DP  .....AAN01N02N03T.Name++++++RLen++TDpBLinPosFunctions++++++++++++++++++
 0024.00    A                                  23  2'F3=Exit'
 0025.00    A                                      COLOR(BLU)
 0026.00    A   40                             23 19'Not a valid choice - Press
 0027.00    A                                      o clear and try again!'
 0028.00    A                                      COLOR(RED)
           **************** End of data *****************************************

 Prompt type . . .  DP       Sequence number . . .  0024.00
 And/Or/                     Name
 Comment     N01N02N03       Type     Name         Ref      Length
             N40 ____
 Data        Decimal                  --- Location ---
 Type        Positions       Use      Line    Position
             ____            _         _23        ____2
 Functions
 'F3=Exit'_____


 F3=Exit   F4=Prompt    F5=Refresh       F11=Previous record
 F12=Cancel             F23=Select prompt  F24=More keys
```

Figure 12.22
Edit of STRUPDSP Showing Prompt and Option Indicator N40 for Constant F3=Exit

After making this change, exit SEU and save the source, and immediately recompile. Because a file object for STRUPDSP already exists, you need to give permission to delete the existing object.

1.9. Check your message queue to ensure that the display file compiled successfully. Although the display file was changed and recompiled, the change does not affect program STRUPPGM. When this is the case, it is not necessary to recompile the program.

Test the program again. This time the F3=Exit message should disappear when an invalid code is entered and the error message appears.

1.10. If your program is working successfully now, use the CHGPRF command with prompting to change your user profile so that it will execute your STRUPPGM as the initial program to call. After making this change, sign off, then sign on again. Your program should run and you should see your display file. If the program is not found or abnormally terminates, you can bypass the user profile initial program by entering *NONE for Program/procedure from the sign-on screen. This lets you get on the system to locate and repair the error.

Additional Lab Exercise

In this lab, you gain familiarity with additional CL commands by first writing a CL program to accumulate the storage used by all objects in the student library, then displaying the total at the workstation as a program message.

The program uses the following CL commands:

- DCL — Declare (defines a program variable)
- DCLF — Declare File (defines a file to be accessed by the program)
- DSPOBJD — Display Object Description
- RCVF — Receive File (reads records from the file)
- MONMSG — Monitor for a Message
- CHGVAR — Change Variable (changes the value assigned to a variable)
- GOTO — Go To a specified label
- SNDPGMMSG — Send Program Message (sends a message to another program, message queue, or user)

1. Sign on to your Intro AS/400 work environment.

2. Many display type (DSP*xxx*) commands allow the option of directing the output to a file instead of a display device or printer.

You will first create the file that the CL program will work with by running the DSPOBJD (Display Object Description) command interactively. Enter the command on the command line and prompt for parameters.

3. Display *ALL objects in your own library. Use object type *ALL. Be sure to specify only your own library by name and not the default, *LIBL.

The Output parameter will be *OUTFILE. Press Enter.

4. Because you have indicated your intention to send the output to a file, the command prompter requires that you name the output file. Name the file DSPODOUTF. Notice the output member options. The output will be placed in the first member, and it will replace any existing output if the DSPOBJD command is rerun specifying the same file to receive output. In other words, each time the command is run with the output file specified, the results of each run will replace the results of the previous run, when the default parameter values are used. After typing the file name, be sure the prompt screen looks like the one in Figure 12.23 (using your own library name, of course); then press Enter.

```
                    Display Object Description (DSPOBJD)

Type choices, press Enter.
Object . . . . . . . . . . . . . . > *ALL           Name, generic*, *ALL
    Library . . . . . . . . . . . > JAFINTRO       Name, *LIBL, *USRLIBL...
Object type . . . . . . . . . . . > *ALL           *ALL, *ALRTBL, *AUTL...
                + for more values
Detail . . . . . . . . . . . . .    *BASIC         *BASIC, *FULL, *SERVICE
Output . . . . . . . . . . . . . > *OUTFILE        *, *PRINT, *OUTFILE
File to receive output . . . . .    dspodoutf      Name
    Library . . . . . . . . . . .    *LIBL          Name, *LIBL, *CURLIB
Output member options:
    Member to receive output . . .   *FIRST         Name, *FIRST
    Replace or add records . . . .   *REPLACE       *REPLACE, *ADD




                                                                    Bottom
F3=Exit    F4=Prompt    F5=Refresh    F12=Cancel    F13=How to use this display
F24=More keys
```

Figure 12.23
DSPOBJD Command
Prompt Screen

4a. After the command runs, what displays on the message line at the bottom of your screen?

5. Refresh the PDM screen and find the file you just created.

5a. What is its type and attribute?

5b. What text has been provided for this file?

6. When an output file is created from a DSPOBJD command, the system creates an externally described file to assign field names to each of the object description attributes that the command references. For example, there will be a named field for the object name, another for the object type, and another for the text description. Each object that is accessed by the DSPOBJD command will create one record in the output file. Each record will describe one object and store field values that are attributes of that object in the corresponding record format fields.

   To find out what the field names are, run the DSPFFD (Display File Field Description) command on DSPODOUTF. As you examine the field-level information of the DSPFFD output, keep in mind that the field text that describes the field applies to the name and data type and length attributes listed above it, not below it.

Find the field name, data type, and field length of the Object size field; write in below, as well as on the answer sheet.

6a. Name of field _____

6b. Type (character or packed) _____

6c. Size of field _____

7. Return to PDM and work with QCLSRC.

8. From the Work with Members Using PDM screen for QCLSRC, create a new CLP source member named ADDERPGM. Be sure to make the member type CLP. Use "Calculate sum of object size" for text.

9. Keep in mind the order of statements in a CL program:

   • Program identification /*programmer ID and program function*/

   • PGM statement

   • Declare statements

   • Selection, flow control, and executable CL commands

   • ENDPGM statement

10. Use SEU's prompting facility to enter your source CL program. Clear the work space and insert one statement. Enter a comment block to identify the program and its author. After that, for each statement enter only the command, then prompt for parameters. The order of entry should be as follows:

    a. Enter the PGM statement.

    b. Declare the output file you created in Steps 3 and 4.

    c. Declare a variable to accumulate the sum of storage used by the objects in your library. Remember that all CL program variables (including field names from files) begin with the ampersand (&) character. Make the accumulator variable one byte longer than (with 0 decimal positions) and of a type compatible with the field from Step 6.

    d. Code a DSPOBJD command using the same parameters you used in Steps 3 and 4. Be sure to specify objects in your library only!

    e. Code a RCVF command. It needs no parameter, but give the statement a label such as READNXT.

    f. Code a CHGVAR command to add the size of each object into the accumulator variable. The form of this statement will be

    ```
    CHGVAR VAR(&ACCUM) VAL(&ACCUM + &SIZE)
    ```

    but you must substitute for &ACCUM the name of the accumulator variable declared in your program, and for &SIZE the Object size field name from the DSPODOUTF file! (See 6a above.)

g. Code a GOTO command. Make the Command label parameter the label name given to the RCVF command in Item e above.

h. Code a SNDPGMMSG command. The message text will consist of a character-string literal (enclosed in single quotation marks) concatenated to the accumulator. You can perform the concatenation by using the *BCAT function:

```
'Total storage used is' *BCAT &ACCUM
```

You want the function to include the value of the total storage accumulator in the message sent to your terminal:

```
SNDPGMMSG MSG('Total storage used is' *BCAT &ACCUM)
```

i. Code an ENDPGM statement.

HINT: If at this point the program seems a little fishy to you, that's a good sign! We have again intentionally allowed a couple of errors into our program to provide some debugging practice. They will soon be apparent.

11. Save the program and compile it. Check the message returned.

11a. What does the message say?

When a compile ends abnormally, take the PDM edit option on the member. Then use SEU Browse/Copy option and select the Spooled file option (2). When compiled in batch, you should not have to change any other parameters from Browse/Copy Options.

11b. Was it a clean compile?

12. Locate the compile errors in the spooled file. (Remember the SEU command F *ERR.) After running the F *ERR command, you should see the error message ID, CPD0712, and its text in the lower helf of the screen (Figure 12.24).

```
Columns . . . :    1  71            Edit              JSMITH/QCLSRC
SEU==>                                                 ADDERPGM
FMT **   ...+... 1 ...+... 2 ...+... 3 ...+... 4 ...+... 5 ...+... 6 ...+... 7
0004.00            DCLF      FILE(JSMITH/DSPODOUTF)
0005.00            DSPOBJD   OBJ(JSMITH/*ALL) OBJTYPE(*ALL) +
0006.00                        OUTPUT(*OUTFILE) OUTFILE(JSMITH/SDPODOUTF)
0007.00  BEGIN:    RCVF
0008.00            CHGVAR    VAR(&TOTSTG) VALUE(&TOTSTG + &ODOBSZ)
0009.00            SNDPGMMSG MSG('Total storage used is ' *BCAT +
0010.00                        &TOTSTG)

Columns . . . :    1  71            Browse         Spool file . . :  ADDERPGM
SEU==>
0001.25    1000                          &TOTSTG)
0001.26 * CPD0712 30  Operand  does not have valid type for operator.
0001.27 * CPD0711 30  Operands in expression not same type.
0001.28    1100-              GOTO      BEGIN
0001.29    1200-
0001.30    1300-              ENDPGM
0001.31                          * * * * *  E N D  O F  S O U R C E

 F3=Exit   F4=Prompt   F5=Refresh   F9=Retrieve    F11=Toggle  F12=Cancel
 F16=Repeat find       F17=Repeat change           F24=More keys
 Operand  does not have  valid type for operator.                    +
```

Figure 12.24
Display Spooled File Screen

Diagnostic messages appear in the compile listing just below the offending lines of source code. The errors indicate that there is a type incompatibility in the SNDPGMMSG message text expression. In fact, the *BCAT function works only on character-type operands and the accumulator variable is numeric.

13. To correct the error, move the cursor up to the active edit session and declare another variable similar to the accumulator but with a different name and character type. Then insert a CHGVAR command just before the SNDPGMMSG command to convert the numeric accumulator to character data type. The CHGVAR command should resemble

```
CHGVAR VAR(&CHARVAR) VAL(&DECVAR)
```

where &CHARVAR is the variable to be changed (to receive the converted value) and &DECVAR is the accumulator variable whose packed decimal value will be converted. Remember the CHGVAR command works from right to left; in other words, the value of the right-side parameter replaces the previous value of the receiver variable (the left-side parameter).

Change the SNDPGMMSG command to use the character variable.

14. Exit and save. Recompile the program. Verify normal completion from your message queue.

15. Execute the CL program using the CALL command.

16. The Display Program Messages screen should indicate an abnormal end to the CL program. Copy the second line of the error message below and on the answer sheet (starting with CPF):

Move the cursor to the second line of the message and press Help. You should see the Additional Message Information, with cause and recovery information (Figure 12.25).

Figure 12.25
Additional Message
Information Screen

```
                    Additional Message Information
Message ID  . . . . . . :   CPA0701      Severity . . . . . . . :   99
Message type . . . . . :   Inquiry
Date sent  . . . . . . :   07/01/98      Time sent  . . . . . . :   09:32:52

Message . . . . :   CPF0864 received by ADDERPGM at 700. (C D I R)
Cause . . . . . :   Control language (CL) program ADDERPGM in library JSMITH
  detected an error at statement number 700. Message text for CPF0864 is: End
  of file detected for file DSPODOUTF in JSMITH.
Recovery  . . . :   This inquiry message can be avoided by changing the
  program. Monitor for the error (MONMSG command) and perform error recovery
  within the program. To continue, choose a reply value.
Possible choices for replying to message . . . . . . . . . . . . . . . :
  C   Cancel the CL program.
  D   Dump the CL program variables and cancel the CL program.
  I   Ignore the failing command.
  R   Try the failing command again.
                                                                   Bottom
Press Enter to continue.

F3=Exit   F6=Print   F9=Display message details
F10=Display messages in job log   F12=Cancel   F21=Select assistance level
```

16a. What is the message text for CPF0864? (Look under Cause of Additional Message Information.)

16b. What advice is given for recovery?

Press Enter and then type C to cancel the program on the reply line. When an end-of-file condition is not handled by the program, it is an error. To avoid the error, take the Help advice and add a MONMSG command to your program to monitor (test) for the EOF condition.

17. Return to the CL source and insert a MONMSG command immediately after the RCVF command. For Message identifier, enter the CPF message number you copied from the Display Program Messages screen. The MONMSG command is used within a CL program to check for certain types of messages sent to the program message queue. When used in the body of a program, the MONMSG command is associated with the preceeding statement. When the execution of that statement causes the message to be sent, the MONMSG command intercepts the message and allows a command to be executed.

For the EXEC parameter value, use

```
GOTO CMDLBL(ENDIT)
```

Enter the command.

Then add the label ENDIT to the CHGVAR statement just before the SNDPGMMSG command.

18. Review your program logic:
- Declare variables and file
- Execute the DSPOBJD command to place current data in the file
- Read a record (one object description) from the file
- Check for end-of-file; if so, branch to ENDIT
- Add the object size to the accumulator variable
- Branch to read another record
- At end-of-file, change the numeric accumulator to character
- Send a program message
- End the program

Exit and save, then recompile. Check for normal completion.

19. Now run the program (CALL). Your message should print on the bottom of the screen. If not, determine the reason the program failed, correct the error, and try again!

20. Print the Work with Members Using PDM screen showing the message at the bottom. Also, use the print option from PDM to print a copy of your CL source program.

Hand in the two print listings together with the answer sheet from this lab. Next, we will enter and run a program to demonstrate how submitting a job to the batch subsystem affects the interactive job.

Lab 12

21. From Work with Members Using PDM, create a new member called MARKTIME and key in the CL program shown in Figure 12.26; be sure to make appropriate changes to the comments.

Figure 12.26

Source Code for Program MARKTIME

```
5716PW1 V3R6M0  950929                    SEU SOURCE LISTING
SOURCE FILE . . . . . . .  JSMITH/QCLSRC
MEMBER . . . . . . . . .   MARKTIME
SEQNBR*...+... 1 ...+... 2 ...+... 3 ...+... 4 ...+... 5 ...+... 6 ...+... 7 ...
   100 /**********************************************************************/
   200 /* Program to test batch submit job.                                 */
   300 /* Author: J Fottral                          Modified: 1998-08-02 */
   400 /**********************************************************************/
   500
   600          PGM
   700
   800          DCL       VAR(&SYSDATE) TYPE(*CHAR) LEN(6)
   900          DCL       VAR(&SYSTIME) TYPE(*CHAR) LEN(6)
  1000
  1100          RTVSYSVAL SYSVAL(QDATE) RTNVAR(&SYSDATE)
  1200          RTVSYSVAL SYSVAL(QTIME) RTNVAR(&SYSTIME)
  1300          SNDMSG    MSG('the program started on' *BCAT +
  1400                      *SYSDATE *BCAT 'at' *BCAT &SYSTIME) +
  1500                      TOUSR(JSMITH)
  1600          RCVMSG    WAIT(30)
  1700
  1800          RETURN
  1900          ENDPGM

* * *  E N D   O F   R E P O R T  * * *
```

After keying in the CL program, save and compile it.

For the SNDMSG command, remember that the whole message must be enclosed in parentheses, and the constant parts must be enclosed in single quotation marks (apostrophes). Be sure to specify your own user ID for the TOUSR parameter value.

The RCVMSG command on line 14 of the source code is usually used to retrieve the text and attributes of a message being sent to a specified message queue, allowing a CL program to intercept and respond to messages. In that case, variables are included as parameter values to store message fields. When no message queue is specified, the current program's message queue becomes the default. When the WAIT parameter is used, the program will wait the specified number of seconds until a message becomes available. Because the previous SNDMSG command went to a user message queue, no message is expected in the program message queue; the program will wait the full 30 seconds and then go on. In effect, the RCVMSG command, as it's used here, halts processing for the specified time.

22. After the program has compiled successfully, clear the messages in your message queue. Do this either by using the DSPMSG command or PDM option DM and the appropriate command key to remove all messages, or by using the CLRMSGQ (Clear Message Queue) command. If you use the CLRMSGQ command, key it on the command line, prompt for parameters, and give it your message queue name (user ID). Let the library parameter default to *LIBL.

23. Run the program interactively using the CALL command.

   23a. Why does your terminal beep right away, but your keyboard remains locked (II in reverse image at the bottom right of the screen or X at the bottom left of the screen)?

24. When the program completes, look at your message queue. The program should have sent a message to it. Using the print key, print the message in your message queue.

25. Clear your message queue again.

26. From the command line, key in the WRKACTJOB (Work with Active Jobs) command and press Enter. First, find your own job under subsystem QINTER.

   26a. What is the Function of your job currently?

      Now look at subsystem QBATCH, which should be at the top of the list.

   26b. How many jobs are running in QBATCH at this time?

27. Key in the SBMJOB (Submit Job) command on the command line and prompt for parameters. For the "Command to run" parameter value, type CALL MARKTIME. Do not put quotation marks or apostrophes around the command. Leave the other parameters at their default values and execute the command.

28. From the Work with Active Jobs screen, press the Refresh function key and watch for your job to appear in the QBATCH subsystem.

   28a. Why does your terminal free up right away although the job is still in the subsystem?

29. Continue refreshing the screen until your job disappears from the QBATCH subsystem.

30. Now examine your message queue again. There should be two messages associated with the submitted job.

   30a. Where did each message come from?

      Print the screen showing the two messages and hand it in together with your answer sheet and the other print output created in this lab.

Mastering the AS/400, Second Edition

Lab 12 Answer Sheet
Additional Lab Exercise

Name: _____

Date Due: _____

Class Time: _____

4a. message: _____

5a. type: _____

    attribute: _____

5b. text: _____

6a. name: _____

6b. type: _____

6c. size: _____

11a. _____

11b. _____

16. _____

16a. text: _____

_____

16b. recovery: _____

_____

23a. _____

_____

26a. _____

26b. _____

28a. _____

_____

30a. _____

_____

IN SUMMARY

A CL program is an object compiled from a number of related CL commands, which together perform some specific function. You can use CL programs to provide an interface between users and programs or to provide a communications and control switch among a number of HLL programs. You also can use CL programs to standardize common operational procedures and to set up and manage different work environments.

Normally, you use SEU to enter source CL programs as members of source physical file QCLSRC. CL programs usually have a program ID section, declaratives, and a body. The declaratives begin with a PGM statement, and the body ends with an ENDPGM statement. A single program may declare only one file but any number of variables. The three types of variables allowed are character (*CHAR), packed decimal (*DEC), and logical (*LGL). When a file is delcared, all fields and indicators defined in it become available to the program as variables, without explicit declaration.

A number of CL commands are allowed only within a program. Some of these have to do with the provision of selection and iteration operations IF...ELSE, DO...ENDDO, and the branching command GOTO. Others require the availability of variables to store returned values (e.g., RTVSYSVAL), provide for the manipulation of variables (e.g., CHGVAR), or require the program environment for their operation (e.g., MONMSG and SNDPGMMSG). CL programs can write (SNDF) to display files, read (RCVF) from display files, or do both (SNDRCVF). But they can only read sequentially from database files, using the RCVF command.

Concatenation is often used to compose messages that include values of variables. You can use Send Message commands to send such messages to users, workstations, or program or job message queues.

You use the CRTCLPGM command to compile a source CL program into an object of type *PGM. This command is most conveniently invoked from Work with Members Using PDM, option 14.

In the lab, you first created a start-up program to permit selection of a work environment and execution of the appropriate commands to change the library list and job attributes. An additional lab assignment created a program to calculate the total storage used by objects within a specified library. Finally, to help you understand the distinction between interactive and batch jobs, you created a program to send a message, then time out. As part of this exercise, we demonstrated the difference between running this program as an interactive job and in batch mode.

CL Command Cross-Reference

The CL commands listed here were discussed in the text or used in the labs.

Command	Page(s)	Description
ADDLIBLE	79–80	Add Library List Entry — Required parameter is the name of a library that will be added to the top of the user library list (by default). Additional parameter allows a different position in the user library list.
CALL	75, 81, 544	Call — Causes the named program to be loaded and control passed to it. Allows a parameter list for parameter values to be passed to the program.
CHGCURLIB	78–79, 100	Change Current Library — The single parameter value is the name of a library that will become the new current library.
CHGDTA	432, 450, 497	Change Data — Calls an existing DFU program that is named in the required parameter. The DFU program runs in change mode to allow file maintenance.
CHGJOB	534, 535, 538	Change Job — Changes certain runtime attributes of a job. When * is specified for Job name, CHGJOB changes current job attributes, such as output queue and print text.
CHGLIBL	71, 80–81, 538	Change Library List — Changes user library list entries by deleting, typing over, or typing new library names. Also allows changing current library.
CHGPRF	57, 59, 101, 129, 346	Change Profile — Changes the value of user profile attributes specified as parameters. Best to type the command and prompt.
CHGPRTF	106	Change Printer File — Changes attributes of an existing printer file (e.g., page size, characters per inch).
CHGSPLFA	109, 116, 120	Change Spooled File Attributes — "Sends" a spooled file to a different output queue, changes number of copies, sends a spooled file to a printer, and so on. If not invoked by option 2 of WRKOUTQ or WRKSPLF list screens, requires

		detailed field-level attributes, including field name, data type, length, and buffer position.
DSPJOBD	97	Display Job Description — Shows settings of various job attributes of specified job description (e.g., job priority, job queue, output queue). Job description name is required.
DSPLIBL	64, 77–78	Display Library List — Shows the current content of the job's library list. No parameter is required.
DSPMSG	179, 194, 360, 487	Display Message — Displays messages in a named message queue or in the workstation message queue and/or user message queue if no name is provided for a parameter.
DSPOBJD	42, 181, 199, 525, 540–542	Display Object Description — Displays information the system maintains for all objects, including owner, when and by whom created, when last changed, and when last saved and restored. If not invoked from option 8 of Work with Objects Using PDM, requires object name and type parameters.
DSPPFM	155, 241, 338	Display Physical File Member — Displays unformatted records of a named physical file in arrival sequence. No data type conversion is performed. The physical file name is the only required parameter.
DSPSYSVAL	53–54	Display System Value — Displays the current setting of the named system value, which is the only required parameter.
DSPUSRPRF	52, 74, 98	Display User Profile — Displays current values of user profile named as required parameter. Except for security administrator, the only valid profile name is your own.
EDTAUTL	350	Edit Authorization List — Allows new users to be added or authorities changed on an existing authorization list. Authorization list name is the only required parameter.
EDTLIBL	71, 81–83	Edit Library List — Allows adding or deleting one or more libraries and changing the order of existing user library list entries by assigning different sequence numbers.
EDTOBJAUT	325, 344–345, 347, 350, 370	Edit Object Authority — Displays and allows changes and additions to list of authorized users of specified object. Also allows assignment of authorization list. Required parameters are object name and type.

ELSE	521, 535	Else (alternate selection) — When paired with preceding IF, specifies command to be executed for false results of the IF condition evaluation. Used only within a CL program and only following an IF command.
ENDDO	514, 520, 524	End Do — Marks the end of a DO group. Must be paired with a DO command. Used only within a CL program.
ENDPGM	514, 535, 543	End Program — Marks the physical end of a CL program. If executed (CL flow passes to ENDPGM), ends the program and returns control to the calling program.
GO	50–53, 57, 59	Go (to a menu) — Takes you directly to a named menu, the only required parameter. May be a system menu or a user-created *MENU object.
GOTO	512–514, 517, 535, 540	Go To — Allows you to branch to a different command in a CL program. The command to branch to must be identified with a command label, the only parameter on the GOTO command. Valid only in a CL program.
IF	520–525, 535, 549	If (selection operation) — Tests a first parameter condition and, if true, executes the second parameter command. Valid only within a CL program.
MONMSG	512, 540, 545	Monitor for Message — When used at the command level (for an individual command), checks for a message having a certain message identifier (first parameter) resulting from the previous command's execution. If the message is received, a specified command is executed as the second parameter. Used only in a CL program.
PGM	514, 517–518	Program — Marks the beginning of a CL program. Required only when parameters are passed to the program. Used only within a CL program.
RCVF	518, 524–526, 540, 549	Receive File Command — Reads input fields and indicators from a display file or database file. Used only within a CL program.
RCVMSG	546	Receive Message — Allows the CL program to read a message from a specified message queue. Optionally waits for a message to be received by the message queue. Valid only within a CL program.
RETURN	535	Return — Used in a CL program to end the program by passing control to the program or command environment that issued the call.

RMVLIBLE	80	Remove Library List Entry — Single parameter is the name of a library to be removed from the user library list.
RNMOBJ	142–143, 325, 332	Rename Object — Changes the name of an existing object. If not invoked from option 7 of PDM, requires specification of object name, object type, and new name.
RUNQRY	203, 251, 258, 339, 499	Run Query — Executes an existing query definition (object type *QRYDFN) whose name is supplied as the only required parameter.
SBMJOB	547	Submit Job — Allows the current job to submit another job to a job queue to run as a batch job. The "Command to run" parameter specifies the command, often a CALL command, to be submitted.
SIGNOFF	101	Sign Off — Immediately ends the current interactive job and takes you to the AS/400 sign-on screen.
SNDBRKMSG	527	Send Break Message — Sends the message contained within the message text parameter to a specified workstation message queue. If the workstation is active, the system interrupts the interactive job and displays the message.
SNDF	518, 524, 525, 535, 549	Send File — Writes a display file record to a workstation, along with current values of output fields and indicators. Used only within a CL program.
SNDMSG	527–529, 546	Send Message — Sends a message contained within the message text parameter to a named message queue.
SNDPGMMSG	527, 540	Send Program Message — Sends a message defined in the message text or from a message file to any type of message queue, including program and external message queues. Used only within a CL program.
SNDRCVF	512, 518, 526–527	Send/Receive File — Writes a display file record and then reads the display file record's input fields and indicators when they become available. Used only within a CL program.
STRDFU	183, 380, 427	Start DFU — Takes you to the Data File Utility menu, which provides options to run, create, change, or delete a DFU program or to create a temporary DFU. No parameter is required.
STRPDM	140	Start Programming Development Manager — Takes you to the PDM menu from which you

WRKOUTQ 105, 110–114, 132, 188, 240 — Work with Output Queue — Lists all spooled files, regardless of user, in the named output queue. If the command is run without naming the output queue, a list of all output queues is displayed.

WRKQRY 203–204 — Work with Queries — Takes you to an entry screen that allows you to choose an option such as create, change, or copy for a query identified on the Work with Queries screen. Also invoked by Work with Objects Using PDM option 12 for any *QRYDFN type object.

WRKSPLF 105, 115–116, 132, 308 — Work with Spooled Files — Lists all spooled files belonging to one user, regardless of output queue. The default parameter specifies the current user.

WRKSYSVAL 29, 30 — Work with System Values — Provides a list screen for all system values and allows display of current value and change if authorized.

WRKUSRJOB 91, 92, 96 — Work with User Jobs — Default parameter values show all jobs of any status belonging to the user and that are currently on the system. The status can be limited by assigning a STATUS parameter value such as *ACTIVE. All jobs, regardless of user, can be displayed if USER is changed to *ALL.

Glossary

access path — information that describes the way in which records can be read or retrieved from files. The two types are keyed sequence and arrival sequence.

activity level — the number of jobs that can run concurrently (i.e., that contend for the system processor) in a subsystem.

advanced assistance level — allows all system functions and shows the same information as intermediate assistance level, but increases the usable screen size by not displaying options and enabled function keys.

audit report — a listing of adds, deletes, and changes made to a database file. Also called audit log by DFU.

arrival sequence — the order in which records were added to a file. Unless otherwise specified, the records in a physical file are both stored and retrieved in arrival sequence.

AS/400 — a multiuser, multitasking computer system designed for the efficient execution of business database applications.

assistance level — determines the amount of information displayed on certain screens and how the information is formatted. May also limit the range of functions available. The assistance levels are basic, intermediate, and advanced. The initial assistance level is set by a system value, but it can be changed for individual users by a user profile parameter. Also, you can change it as you view certain screens by using function key F21 (Select assistance level). When this method is used, the system returns you to the same assistance level the next time you use the same display. See also **advanced**, **basic**, and **intermediate assistance level**.

attribute — a property or characteristic of one or more entities. For files and programs, describes the usage (e.g., PF, LF, DSPF) or source language (e.g., RPG, CBL, CLP).

attribute byte — on a display screen or menu, the single-character position to the left of a field's leftmost character. This byte is always reserved for controlling the field to which it is prefixed. You cannot see the attribute byte, but you can use it to perform operations on the field. See also **attribute command**.

attribute command — used to perform operations on a field that appears on an SDA display screen or menu. For example, you can change the appearance of a field, move a field, call up a list of different attributes for a field, or delete a field.

authorization list — an AS/400 object that identifies a group of users and specifies authority levels for each user. Authorization lists are especially useful when a certain group of users needs authority to a number of different objects and/or libraries. Different users in the list can have different object and data authority levels.

auxiliary storage — on the AS/400, a storage device that is not main storage.

basic assistance level — provides the most assistance using nontechnical terms, but limits the system functions and options available. See also **advanced** and **intermediate assistance level**.

batch job — a job that requires little or no interaction with the user and usually involves printing multiple reports or processing complex transactions. Batch jobs are sent to a job queue until they can begin execution. Usually, several batch jobs can run concurrently in a subsystem.

binary — in DB2/400, a numeric data type that stores numbers using a representation of the number in base 2.

CL program — an executable AS/400 object (*PGM) consisting of Control Language (CL) commands that together perform specific procedures or operations on the AS/400. CL programs can be used to control an application's workflow.

column function — in SQL, a function that calculates a value from a set of records. Contrast with **scalar function**.

command line — a line beginning with the symbol ===> that appears near the bottom of certain types of display screens. Individual commands can be entered on a command line.

command parameter — a value, specified along with a command, that controls and limits the operation of the command and names the files, programs, or other objects it will work on. Such values add to a command's flexibility.

command prompt screen — a type of entry screen listing command parameter choices that the system provides to help enter CL commands correctly. The title of the screen is the name of the command. On the AS/400, function key F4 invokes the system's prompting facilities. When you press F4 from a screen containing a command line on which you have entered a command, the AS/400 displays a formatted prompt screen for the command's parameters. See also **entry screen**.

compile listing — a printed report of a program's or data file's source code, expanded source code, diagnostics (error messages), and other optional information.

composite key — a key, specified in the DDS source code of a file description, that consists of several fields used together. Each (subkey) field is specified in major to minor order by a K coded for the Name type field in the DDS.

concatenation — joining two string expressions or non-numeric fields together, creating a single string to be used as a parameter value or to be assigned to a named variable.

constants — one type of field used by SDA, and the main type used with menus. Each constant may consist of a single word or number, or several words together (e.g., a menu selection title), in which case it should be enclosed by single quotation marks (apostrophes).

context-sensitive Help — one of two types of AS/400 Help displays for commands. Context-sensitive Help is cursor-sensitive; that is, the information displayed is specific for a certain section of the display. Context-sensitive Help is also referred to as field Help. See also **extended Help**.

control break — a query feature that lets you print or display groups of records sorted by the values of designated sort control fields. Using Query/400, you can select control fields to be used on up to six levels of report breaks (e.g., department within section within division). When a control field changes, you can print subtotals of the previous control group and use special line spacing.

Control Language (CL) — a programming language that provides a single, consistent user interface to various OS/400 functions. More than 1,000 individual CL commands are available. Each individual command is an object on the AS/400. Most CL commands consist of a command name and one or more command parameters.

correlation name — in SQL, an identifier that designates a table, a view, or an individual row of a table or view within a single SQL statement.

current library — the default library into which newly created objects are placed. When a current library is specified, it follows the product library in the job's library list. The current library is significant because it is searched before other user libraries when an object is requested using a simple name.

data authority — specific authorities granted to a user for the data in an object (e.g., a physical file or library), including Read, Add, Update, and Delete authorities.

database management system (DBMS) — any software product used to define, manipulate, and control a collection of related files.

Data Description Specifications (DDS) — a fixed-format language used to describe database and display files on the AS/400. Entries are made at the file, record, and field levels; also supports key and select/omit entries for certain member types.

Data File Utility (DFU) — an AS/400 utility that provides a convenient and easy way to change records in and add to or delete records from a physical (or logical) database file without the need to write an HLL data-entry or file-maintenance program.

declaratives — the section of a program used to identify files and to define program variables and constants. In a CL program, this section immediately follows the PGM statement and consists of zero or one DCLF commands and any number of DCL commands.

default values — AS/400-supplied command parameter values for optional parameters that will be used during execution of a command unless you specifically tell the command to use some other value.

difference — a query operation that lists or displays only the records that do not have matches in all files designated for the query (e.g., students not registered in any class or customers not having any outstanding invoices). Think of the operation as "subtracting" from the primary file all records with matching records in the secondary file(s). What is left, the difference, is the unmatched primary file records.

direct access — a class of storage device allowing random retrieval of individual records. Of a data file, the ability to retrieve individual records by key field value or relative record number.

display device — the workstation hardware (monitor and keyboard) you use to communicate with the system.

display file — files that define the screens that a program presents as it runs. Display files allow values keyed by a user in response to screen prompts to be input as data to the program; therefore, display files serve as the mechanism that allows the user and the program to interact. Display files are objects whose type is *FILE and whose attribute is DSPF. See also **menu**.

domain — the entire list of possible values that are valid for a certain field in any record.

duplicate key — a record whose key field value is the same as that of an already existing record. When a primary key is declared by specifying the UNIQUE keyword, the system does not permit duplicate keys.

EBCDIC (Extended Binary Coded Decimal Interchange Code) — the 8-bit per character encoding used for most DB2/400 character data.

edit code — special symbols used in DDS and RPG that indicate how numeric data is to be formatted regarding thousands separator, negative value indicator, and display of zero values.

edit word — specifies how numeric values are to be formatted to make them more readable upon output; an edit word supplies a template into which a numeric value is inserted and may include instructions for zero-suppression and insertion of special characters. The digit replacement character is the space. An edit word is delimited by single quotation marks (apostrophes).

entry screen — a type of AS/400 display screen used to request information from a user. This type of screen is considered an entry screen because the system is waiting for you to enter the value or values it needs to process your request. See also **command prompt screen**.

equijoin — a join that selects records based on equal values in specified fields of the joined files.

exception join — a join that includes only those records whose primary file record is not matched to any records in at least one secondary file.

extended field definitions — in DFU, specifications that allow selection of features such as auto-duplicate, uppercase lock, initial value, and validity checks for selected fields.

extended Help — one of two types of AS/400 Help displays for menus, list screens, command prompts, and other entry screens. Extended Help includes a general description of the topic, all the context-sensitive Help, and all other available Help information about the topic. See also **context-sensitive Help**.

externally described file — an AS/400 database file whose layout is described within the *FILE object itself. The detailed record format thus exists outside of and is available to any program that uses the file. Externally described files are usually created using DDS.

field exit — special key that causes any input field positions to the right of the cursor to be erased and the cursor to be positioned on the next input field. The right control key on a PC keyboard.

field Help — see **context-sensitive Help**.

field-level specifications — DDS coded on the same line as a field name or on lines immediately following a field name. Describes type, length, and use attributes, at least.

field mapping — the capability (of the CPYF command) to change the order of fields in a "to file" record format from that specified in the "from file" record format by copying the data from each individual named field to its new location. Requires the same field names and compatible types and lengths.

floating point — in DB2/400, a numeric data type that stores real numbers using a representation of the number as a mantissa and exponent.

foreign key — a nonkey or subkey field in a dependent (child) file that shares the same domain as the primary key in the parent file. It relates the child file record to a parent file record through its primary key. The relationship-supporting field of a child file in a 1:n relationship.

function keys — special keys on the keyboard that activate predetermined actions when pressed. Depending on your keyboard, these keys are labeled F1 through F12 or F1 through F24. On the AS/400 command line, for example, F3 is the Exit function key; pressing F12 returns you to the previous screen; pressing F9 returns previously entered commands to the command line; and pressing F24 displays any additional function key options.

GO command — the CL command that takes you directly to any menu, including menus of command groups. This command always has one required parameter, a menu name. For example, if you want to go directly to the menu of Clear commands, you would enter the command GO CMDCLR on any command line and the CMDCLR menu would be displayed.

group indication — a report feature that causes control field values to print on only the first line of a new report control group. On subsequent lines the values are replaced by spaces.

group profile — a user profile that lets you grant object authority to groups of users. Individual users are added to a group when a security administrator changes their user profile group profile parameter value to the group profile name. You must be careful about providing special authorities to group profiles — members of the group inherit the special authorities in addition to their own individual authorities.

Help key — the function key that accesses AS/400 Help. Always F1, or the Help key if available.

high-level language (HLL) — a programming language such as Cobol or RPG that may perform a number of machine language instructions for each HLL command.

high-level machine interface (MI) — the instruction set that translates operating system and compiled application code into microcode. Separates the logical machine (application programs and operating system) from the physical machine (hardware). Also called **technology-independent machine interface (TIMI)**.

index — an internal structure, part of a keyed-sequence access path, relating a key value of a database record to its storage address.

index search — a feature of AS/400 Help that lets you enter a search word that the system tries to find in its large internal index of topics. If the system finds topics in the index related to the search word, it returns a list of those topics. For each topic listed, you can choose to display or print the stored text.

indexed file — a file using a keyed-sequence access path. Each record in the file is identified by a key field. Also called indexed-sequential.

indicator — an internal switch, or variable, with only two states or values — off or on (or 0 or 1) — used by a program to signal or determine whether a particular event has occurred and to control, or condition, subsequent processing. Used to communicate between a display file and a program.

informational message — a message sent to a message queue to inform the user of some event or to convey the results of some process; typically, not requiring a reply and not used for error messages.

information screen — a screen type that displays information you request and gives you a way back to where you were when you asked for the information. A common type of information screen is a Help screen.

Initial Program Load (IPL) — the AS/400 version of a "boot" process. The IPL loads the system programs, performs hardware diagnostics, and starts the operating system.

input/output fields — fields of a data or display file that may be read only (input); written only (output); or read, changed, and rewritten (both input and output).

inquiry message — a message requiring a reply. Typically, sent to inform the user of an error condition that requires a decision (reply) to continue, cancel the job, and so on.

interactive job — a job that requires constant interaction between the user and the computer. An interactive job begins when a user signs on to an AS/400 at a workstation and terminates when the user signs off (or is disconnected). The name of an interactive job is the same as the name of the workstation at which it starts.

interface — a common boundary between two different entities that serves to translate and forward communications between them. A connecting layer between two different hardware or software products.

intermediate assistance level — one of three assistance levels supported by the AS/400; provides all system functions and shows all command options. See also **advanced** and **basic assistance level**.

job — on the AS/400, the term that refers generally to a unit of work, including all programs, files, and instructions necessary to perform that work. Examples of jobs running on an AS/400 would be an interactive user session for updating a customer master file or a program compilation running in a batch subsystem.

job description — an AS/400 object type (*JOBD) containing a set of attributes that can be used by one or more jobs. Such attributes include the job's execution priority, the name of the printer upon which reports will be printed, the name of the job queue upon which the job will be placed, and the library list associated with the job.

job log — a record of the actions taken, system requests made, and critical errors encountered as a job is processed on the system. Usually saved only for jobs ending abnormally in output queue QEZJOBLOG.

job queue — an AS/400 object type (*JOBQ) that acts as a staging area, managed by the subsystem in which the job will run, where batch jobs wait in line (queue) for their turn at batch processing.

join field — the relationship-supporting field of one of two or more related files. Usually, the primary key of one file and the foreign key of the other. The fields describe or define the same entity and share the same domain.

join logical file — combines data elements from two or more physical files in a single record format. Projection and selection are permitted. If a keyed-sequenced access path is specified, the key field(s) must be from the primary file.

join operation — allows data elements from records with matching join field values from two or more files to be included in a single result record.

key field — a field in a record used to identify the record and whose contents are used to build an access path or index for the file allowing keyed-sequence or direct access to records of the file.

keyed-sequence — an access path for a physical file created by defining one or more fields in the record format as keys. A program can then process a file's records in key field order, instead of in arrival sequence, or it can directly access an individual record by supplying its key value.

keyword notation — the presentation of each of a command's specified parameters preceded by its corresponding keyword. The keyword itself identifies the parameter to the command processor. When you use parameter keywords, the parameter value must immediately follow the keyword and the value must be enclosed in parentheses.

labeled duration — in SQL, a number and keyword (e.g., 2 Days) that represents a duration of years, months, days, hours, minutes, seconds, or microseconds.

left outer join — a query operation that selects all records in the primary file regardless whether there are matching records in the secondary file(s). Result fields from unmatched secondary files are set to default values. Sometimes called an **outer join**.

level check — a warning issued by the system when a program or utility attempts to access a file whose current record format does not agree with that known to the program at the time it was compiled.

library — a directory of related objects on an AS/400. A logical grouping of objects by application or owner, or for security or backup purposes. All objects are associated with a library; this association serves in part to identify an object.

library list — the definition of the path of libraries a job will search when trying to find programs, files, or other AS/400 objects named in a command. An initial library list exists for each job and can be changed during the job. The library list is searched from top to bottom and includes system libraries, a product library (optional), one current library (optional), and user libraries.

licensed internal code (LIC) — the low-level (machine) microcode that drives the hardware. On the AS/400, the proprietary code below the high-level machine interface licensed by IBM.

line command — see **SEU line command**.

linear nested IF — an IF structure where the statement or command for each condition's false result tests the next condition (except the last false result, which may execute unconditionally).

list screen — a screen type that displays a list of topics. A list screen is also referred to as a "list processing screen," or as a "work with list screen" because it so commonly results from a Work with CL command being run.

logical files — files that describe how data appears to be stored in the database. Logical files do not actually contain data records but rather rules for selecting physical file records and fields and usually access paths to records in physical files. Logical files may be simple, join, or multiple format.

logical machine — the software above the MI; application programs and utilities, and operating system commands and functions.

logical operator — a symbol specifying how the results of relational expressions are to be combined or negated, including *NOT, *AND, and *OR.

logical variable — a variable of type *LGL that can have only one of two values: on (1) or off (0). In CL programs, used to define indicators.

member — the component of a physical or logical file that contains records.

menu interface — the AS/400 user interface that provides easy access to most OS/400 functions. Menus are connected in a hierarchical fashion starting with the Main menu. As you choose a series of menu selections, the system determines the CL commands to be run to satisfy your request.

menu — a screen display of a numbered list of items from which a user can make a selection. See also **display file**.

message — a communication sent from a program or a user to a message queue. See also **informational message** and **inquiry message**.

message queue — a storage area for holding incoming messages until they can be acknowledged and acted upon. A permanent message queue is created for each user and each workstation on the system.

multiple-format logical file — a logical file having two or more record formats, each based on a single underlying physical file record format. Allows update, change, and delete. Must specify a keyed-sequence access path.

multitasking — a system able to perform multiple, nonrelated units of work in a period of time.

multiuser — a characteristic of a system whereby two or more people are able to interact with the system and share processor and storage resources concurrently.

natural join — a query operation that selects join records when at least one matching record is found in every file. In other words, every primary file record must have at least one matching record in each of the secondary files. But if a record in the primary file has no match in one or more of the secondary files, that primary file record is ignored and nothing is added to the result table or query output. See also **primary file** and **secondary file**.

nonindexed file — a file having only an arrival-sequenced access path.

object — anything on the AS/400 that has a name and takes up space in storage. The system can locate an object by its name, and once located, the object can further identify itself to the system by functional attributes that are a part of the object. Objects are grouped into types. See also **object type**.

object authority — specific authorities granted to a user for a particular object, including operational (i.e., the use of the object as permitted through data authority), management (i.e., move, rename, and so on), and existence (i.e., control of an object's existence and ownership).

object name — the identification of an object, either by the 10-character (maximum) simple name or by including a library name (explicit object name) or reference. See also **simple object name** and **qualified object name**.

object type — determines how an object is used on the AS/400 (i.e., what actions can be taken when using the object). Common object types include programs (*PGM) and data files (*FILE). Object types also include user profile objects, which contain information about a user; and subsystem description objects, which define the characteristics of a subsystem. Object type is determined by the system depending on the command used to create the object.

one-to-many relationship — describes a common relationship between files in a database. This common type of relationship (abbreviated 1:n) is the foundation of relational database systems, including DB2/400. It occurs when a field is a primary key in one file and a nonkey or subkey field in the related file. For example, a single record with a Zip code primary key in a Zip code file may be related to many records in an employee file sharing the same value for Zip code (e.g., whenever two or more employees live in the same Zip code area). Another name for this type of relationship is parent–child relationship.

option indicator — an indicator used by a program when it writes a display file record; for example, to select which display attribute or color to use or to determine whether a field will appear. These indicators can be associated with display file records, fields, or individual (often mutually exclusive) field attributes. See also **indicator** and **response indicator**.

OS/400 — the object-based AS/400 proprietary operating system. A complex and rich operating system performing not only traditional functions such as storage and task and data management, but also incorporating features that would normally require separate software components such as database management, communications support, security, and interactive support.

outer join — a query operation that selects all records in the primary file, regardless whether there are matching records in the secondary file(s). Result fields from unmatched secondary files are set to default values. More correctly called a left outer join. See also **primary file** and **secondary file**.

output queue — an object containing a list of spooled files that you can display on a workstation or write to a printer device.

packed decimal — in DB2/400, a numeric data type that stores numbers using a representation of the number with one digit per half-byte.

parameter — a value supplied to a program or a command that is used to control or limit the actions of the program or command. See also **command parameter**.

parameter keyword — a significant word that identifies a command parameter, placed at the beginning of the parameter in keyword notation, that exemplifies the primary meaning of the parameter. In the command DSPTAP DEV(TAP01), the parameter keyword is DEV.

parent–child relationship — see **one-to-many relationship**.

physical files — database files that actually store data records.

physical machine — proprietary firmware below the machine interface specific to a particular make and model of computer and the hardware upon which translated microcode instructions are implemented.

positional notation — the specification of command parameters in the predetermined order set in the command syntax. To be correctly interpreted, the relative position of each parameter value is significant. Keywords are not used.

predefined value — a word starting with an asterisk (*) whose meaning is already decided by the operating system. These words are reserved words and are often used to assign default values to command parameters. Examples include *LIBL for library list, *OUTFILE for output to a file.

primary file — a file that contains the critical data you want to include in a query report (i.e., the main topic or focus of the query). In a join logical file, the first file specified for the JFILE keyword. In Query/400, the first file identified in Specify file selections.

primary key — a field whose value uniquely distinguishes one record from any other record in a file. No two records in a file would have the same primary key value.

printer device — a hardware device that writes output data from a printer writer to paper or other media. Known to the system through a device description object, type *DEVD.

printer file — determines the attributes printed output will have. A printer file defines the formatting, page size, and special printing features, and may specify an output queue. Numerous IBM-supplied printer files are available for use by general-purpose printing and system utilities. Also, users can use the CRTPRTF (Create Printer File) command to create new printer files for special reports or printing conditions.

printer writer — the software connection between an output queue and a physical printer device. A printer writer is generated automatically when a printer device (a physical printer) is described to the system. The creation of this device description generates not only a printer writer but also an output queue, both of which have the same name as the printer device.

product library — an optional entry in a job's library list, automatically managed by the system when using certain commands or IBM-supplied program products. For example, if a user requests compilation of an RPG program, the library containing the necessary translator programs, QRPG, will be inserted as a product library during the compile process and then removed when the compile is finished.

program ID — the initial comments of a CL program that identify the program, its function, author, date written, and so on.

program-described files — AS/400 files that are created without field-level specifications and that have a record length only. Having no external data definition, a program-described file's record layout must be defined within each program that uses the file.

Programming Development Manager (PDM) — a workbench environment that lets programmers and system operators navigate through the three levels of the AS/400 object-based architecture: the library level, the object level, and the member level. PDM, which provides access to AS/400 functions through a standard list interface, lets you move easily from one level to the next and provides various options for taking actions on list items at each level.

projection — the operation of specifying the fields of the based-on physical file's record format to be included in the logical file's record format (or in the result table).

qualified object name — an object name, specified together with the name of the library containing the object, or a reference to part of a library list. A qualified name is specified in the form *libref/objname*, with the slash (/) being the qualifier character.

Query/400 — an IBM-licensed program product that serves as a report generator or query utility.

record format — a named part of an OS/400 file that identifies records with a specific layout.

record-format specification — in DDS, the naming of a record format using an R Name type entry. For logical files, a PFILE or JFILE keyword will also be included as a function entry. Follows file-level specifications (if any) and precedes all field-level specifications.

record number — a number that specifies the location of a record in relation to the beginning of a database file member. For example, the fifth record entered in a database file member would be record number 5, the hundredth record number 100, and so on.

referential integrity — in the relational database model, the requirement that records that exist in separate relations, but that are interrelated, be unambiguously interrelated by corresponding field values.

relational operator — a symbol specifying how two expressions are to be evaluated in relation to each other. Common symbols include "equal to" (*EQ or =) and "greater than" (*GT or >).

relative record number — see **record number**.

report break — see **control break**.

report generator — a utility program allowing fast and efficient file selection and formatting to create standard reports. See also **Query/400**.

required parameter — a value that must be specified for the AS/400 to execute a CL command.

response indicator — an indicator used in a display file that signals to the program that a user has pressed a function key. For example, if function key F3 were associated with indicator 03, when the user presses F3 and the program reads the display file, indicator 03 would be set to an "on" state in the program. See also **indicator** and **option indicator**.

response time — the time that elapses between a user's request for an action (e.g., rewrite a certain record whose fields you have changed) and the system's completion of the action (e.g., the record is rewritten and the system is waiting for the next request).

scalar function — in SQL, a function that calculates a value from an expression that involves no more than one record. Contrast with **column function**.

Screen Design Aid (SDA) — a utility provided by IBM that lets you design a screen interactively without being familiar with all the DDS conventions. SDA creates the DDS source statements for you automatically.

secondary file — a file whose records are matched, on the join field, to the primary file records. In Query/400, all files identified after the first in the Specify file selections.

selection — the relational operation of choosing records for a logical file by applying a criterion or test to the based-on physical file records.

SEU line commands — commands used within SEU that let you change the edit work area and manipulate source member lines; for example, you can move, copy, delete, add, or insert new lines. Line commands are typed over sequence numbers.

sign-on screen — initial screen to identify a user. With proper values entered, the system proceeds to collect attributes to define the interactive job.

simple logical file — a logical file with a single record format created over a single physical file, which must already exist as a *FILE type object.

simple object name — on the AS/400, up to a 10-character name without a library reference; synonymous with **object name**.

single-level storage — the technique of addressing multiple levels of storage (both main and hard disk) through a single addressing structure as if they were homogeneous storage.

Source Entry Utility (SEU) — a full-screen editor used to enter all kinds of source code on the AS/400. SEU is a "smart editor" that not only knows the line formats of different languages' source statements, but also can check for syntax errors in the source statements of the various languages, including RPG, Cobol, CL, and DDS.

source physical file — a special type of physical file whose members, instead of storing user data, store the source descriptions of other files and source programs. Source physical file names usually begin with Q and end with SRC (e.g., QDDSSRC, QRPGSRC); they are distinguished by PDM as having attribute PF-SRC.

spool control special authority — a special authority over files spooled to a printer output queue, granted through the user profile, that lets the system operator take necessary actions (e.g., hold, change, release, delete) on spooled files in the output queue.

spooled file — a file that contains output data formatted for printing that has been saved for later processing (e.g., a report, query, or compile listing).

spooling — performing a peripheral operation such as printing while the AS/400 is busy with other work.

Structured Query Language (SQL) — an ANSI-standard, nonprocedural language developed by IBM to define, manipulate, and control access to relational databases. Used widely by relational DBMS products on a variety of platforms. On the AS/400, SQL is available as a licensed program product and can be used to create externally described files.

subkey field — a named field of a record format that is part of a composite key.

subquery — a subselect that's part of a predicate.

substring — part of a non-numeric field that can be used in a larger expression or assigned to a named variable.

subsystem — an operating environment, defined by a subsystem description, through which OS/400 coordinates work flow and resource usage. Can be tailored to efficiently process different types of jobs.

subsystem description — an object that contains information defining a subsystem and that OS/400 uses to control the subsystem.

syntax — the rules governing the structure of a language. The selection and ordering of language elements to form valid expressions.

system library list — a list of up to 15 libraries needed by the system to operate; you usually won't modify the system library list. You can determine which libraries will be placed in the system portion of your library list by looking at the system value QSYSLIBL.

System Licensed Internal Code (SLIC) — internal code for the RISC-based AS/400 systems. See also **licensed internal code**.

system spooler — a subsystem that controls and coordinates printed output, holding it in an output queue or sending it to a printer writer to create hard copy.

system values — the set of AS/400 configuration attributes common to the entire system. System values contain systemwide control information you will need to control and customize certain day-to-day operating system functions. System values are grouped into the broad categories of date/time, editing, system control, library list, allocation/storage, message/logging, and security. System values are supplied by IBM within the system and can be displayed and often can be changed, but cannot be created or deleted.

technology-independent machine interface (TIMI) — usually just called MI (machine interface). See **high-level machine interface**.

throughput — the amount of work a system can perform within a certain period of time.

user — any person who is signed on to the system; this may include students, programmers, data entry personnel, operators, or administrators.

user library list — names the libraries that organize the programs, screens, data files, and applications users need to do business on the system; the user library list can contain up to 25 library names.

user profile — an object that identifies a user and describes the user's authority and some operational characteristics of his or her job.

validity checks — error-testing logic to ensure that values entered into a field conform to specific requirements (e.g., within a range of values, belonging to a list of values, not less than a certain value).

variable — a named storage location serving as a counter, accumulator, intermediate result field, program switch or indicator, subscript, message string work field, and so on. Used in a CL program of type *CHAR (character), *DEC (packed decimal), or *LGL (logical). CL variable names must always begin with an ampersand (&).

view — when speaking of relational databases systems, term that corresponds to nonkeyed logical files.

volatility — term used to describe the relative frequency of change (adds and deletes) to the record population of a file.

work management — term used to identify how the AS/400 organizes, manages, and processes work (i.e., how jobs enter, run, and leave the system). Key work management concepts include interactive jobs, batch jobs, job descriptions, job queues, and library lists.

zoned decimal — in DB2/400, a numeric data type that stores numbers using a representation of the number with one byte per digit.

Index

VISIT OUR WEB SITE AT WWW.29THSTREETPRESS.COM FOR A MORE DETAILED LISTING OF ALL
29TH STREET PRESS BOOKS

New Books in the 29th Street Press Library

1001 SECRETS FOR WINDOWS NT REGISTRY

By Tim Daniels

For the accomplished user, *1001 Secrets for Windows NT Registry* is the definitive reference for system customization and optimization. Organized into sections that cover networking, applications, system management, hardware, and performance, the book also has an accompanying CD that is packed with innovative registry monitoring and performance utilities, plus an Internet link to our Registry Secrets home page (www.registrysecrets.com). 321 pages.

THE A TO Z OF EDI, SECOND EDITION

By Nahid M. Jilovec

The A to Z of EDI, Second Edition, gives you the practical details of EDI implementation. Not only does it show you how to cost justify EDI, but it gives you job descriptions for EDI team members, detailed criteria and forms for evaluating EDI vendors, considerations for trading-partner agreements, an EDI glossary, and lists of EDI organizations and publications. And this edition includes all-new information about EDI and the Internet, system security, and auditing. 221 pages.

THE ACCOUNTING SOFTWARE HANDBOOK
Your Guide to Evaluating Vendor Applications

By Stewart McKie

This second edition of *The Technology Guide to Accounting Software* will help you understand how you can apply technologies such as client/server (or browser/server), workflow, imaging, and the Internet to deliver effective accounting systems. The accompanying CD contains more than 50 profiles of selected vendors and products. Also included is a step-by-step selection process to help you efficiently arrive at a vendor shortlist for your evaluation. 265 pages.

ESSENTIALS OF SUBFILE PROGRAMMING
and Advanced Topics in RPG

By Phil Levinson

Essentials of Subfile Programming teaches you to design and program subfiles, offering step-by-step instructions and real-world programming exercises. You learn to design and create subfile records; load, clear, and display subfiles; and create pop-up windows. In addition, the advanced topics help you mine the rich store of data in the file-information and program-status data structures, handle errors, improve data integrity, and manage program-to-program communication. An instructor's manual is available. 260 pages.

IMPLEMENTING AS/400 SECURITY, THIRD EDITION

By Wayne Madden and Carol Woodbury

This third edition of *Implementing AS/400 Security* not only brings together in one place the fundamental AS/400 security tools and experience-based recommendations that you need, but also includes specifics on the latest security enhancements available in OS/400 V4R1 and V4R2. In addition, you will find completely new chapters that include discussions about Internet security and business contingency planning. 424 pages.

INTERNET SECURITY WITH WINDOWS NT

By Mark Joseph Edwards

Security expert and *Windows NT Magazine* news editor Mark Edwards provides the quintessential guide to Internet and intranet security from the Windows NT platform that covers network security basics as well as IIS and MPS, and includes specific advice about selecting NT tools and security devices. The accompanying CD-ROM includes security-related utilities, tools, and software packages that, combined with the tips and techniques in the book, are powerful weapons in your security efforts. 520 pages.

RAPID REVIEW STUDY GUIDES

Series Editor: Mike Pastore

You know that becoming a Microsoft Certified Systems Engineer can be lucrative. Still, seeking the certification isn't a goal for the faint of heart. Our *Rapid Review Study Guides* give you pre- and post-assessments to measure your progress, exam preparation tips, an overview of exam material, vocabulary drills, hands-on activities, and sample quiz questions on CD and in the book. Current titles include

NETWORKING ESSENTIALS	WINDOWS 95
SYSTEM MANAGEMENT SERVER 1.2	WINDOWS NT 4.0 SERVER
TCP/IP FOR MICROSOFT WINDOWS NT 4.0	WINDOWS NT 4.0 WORKSTATION
INTERNET INFORMATION SERVER 4.0	WINDOWS NT 4.0 SERVER IN THE ENTERPRISE

VISUALAGE FOR RPG BY EXAMPLE

By Bryan Meyers and Jef Sutherland

VisualAge for RPG by Example brings the RPG language to the GUI world and lets you use your existing knowledge to develop Windows applications. Using a tutorial approach, *VisualAge for RPG by Example* lets you learn as you go and create simple yet functional programs start to finish. The accompanying CD-ROM offers a scaled down version of VARPG and complete source code for the sample project. 236 pages.

WINDOWS NT MAGAZINE ADMINISTRATOR'S SURVIVAL GUIDE: SYSTEM MANAGEMENT AND SECURITY

Edited by John Enck

In this first book in our Survival Guide™ series, head "Lab Guy" John Enck has assembled the best articles and authors from *Windows NT Magazine* to share their experience with mission-critical system management and security issues. Topics include optimization, tuning, troubleshooting, programming, installation, securing the Internet connection, testing, encryption, firewalls, data access, system policies, file servers, passwords, and more. 359 pages.

WINDOWS NT MAGAZINE ADMINISTRATOR'S SURVIVAL GUIDE: NETWORKING AND BACKOFFICE

Edited by John Enck

In this second book in our Survival Guide™ series, John Enck has assembled the best *Windows NT Magazine* articles about networking and BackOffice issues. Topics include Remote Access Service; PPTP; assigning IP addresses and IP routing; name resolution with WINS, NetBIOS, and DNS; using NT with the Internet; telephony; NT Services for Macintosh; connectivity; performance tuning; clusters; enhancing SQL Server performance; implementing MS Exchange; Systems Management Server; and more. 469 pages.

FOR A COMPLETE CATALOG OR TO PLACE AN ORDER, CONTACT

29th Street Press

Duke Communications International
221 E. 29th Street • Loveland, CO 80538-2727
(800) 621-1544 • (970) 663-4700 • Fax: (970) 203-2756

OR SHOP OUR WEB SITE: **www.29thStreetPress.com**